THE RETURN

Russia's Journey from Gorbachev to Medvedev

Daniel Treisman

Free Press

NEW YORK · LONDON · TORONTO · SYDNEY

FREE PRESS
A Division of Simon & Schuster, Inc.
Avenue of the Americas
New York, NY 10020

First Free Press hardcover edition January 2011

FREE PRESS and colophon are trademarks of Simon & Schuster, Inc.

For information about special discounts for bulk purchases, please contact
Simon & Schuster Special Sales at 1-866-506-1949
or business@simonandschuster.com

The Simon & Schuster Speakers Bureau can bring authors to your
live event. For more information or to book an event contact the
Simon & Schuster Speakers Bureau at 1-866-248-3049
or visit our website at *www.simonspeakers.com*.

Designed by Paul Dippolito

Manufactured in the United States of America

1   3   5   7   9   10   8   6   4   2

Library of Congress Cataloging-in-Publication Data
Treisman, Daniel.
The return : Russia's journey from Gorbachev to Medvedev / by Daniel Treisman.
p.   cm.
1. Russia (Federation)—Politics and government—1991–   I. Title.
JN6695.T74 2010
947.086—dc22
2010011520
ISBN-13: 978-1-4165-6071-5
ISBN 978-1-4516-0574-5 (ebook)

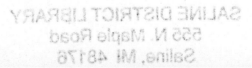

To Susi, Alex, and Lara

CONTENTS

PREFACE

R ussia has returned. Not to the West, of which it was never truly a part. But to the world. Twenty years after the iron curtain was drawn back, Russians vacation in Turkey and on the Côte d'Azur, place international calls on Finnish cell phones, and debate the hairstyles of Hollywood celebrities on internet forums. Their leaders no longer dream of infiltrating Marxist revolutionaries into the capitalist democracies. They are too busy planning G20 summits or conducting war games with China. Russian businessmen, now regulars at Davos, own American steel mills, African gold mines, French chateaus, and British sports teams. In London, Rome, and New York, it is no longer rare to overhear conversation in the language of Pushkin.

This is not the first time Russia has come out of isolation. In the twelfth century, the princes of Kievan Rus were integrated into the West through trade and marriage with the royal families of Europe. Then the Mongols penetrated the forests. Conquered and colonized, Russians lost touch with the outside world for more than two centuries. Reintegration was slow. It took the Europeanizing demon of Peter the Great to shave the beards off his country's upper classes, dress them in German clothes, and turn them into cosmopolitans again. If Peter's revolution was Russia's first return to the world, the journey back after communism has been its second.

This book is about that journey. It has been a complicated one, part obstacle course, part voyage of discovery. The transition started with an economic crisis that lasted a decade. In politics, two steps forward toward democracy were often followed by one, two, or three steps back. Early hopes for a partnership with the United States and Europe gave way in time to mutual recrimination. But Russia is here to stay. With

one elbow on Germany, the other on China, as the philosopher Chaadaev put it, the country is itself of global proportions. Its leaders have no
plans to retreat into a third period of isolation. Most of the international
problems that concern the West will be hard to solve without Russia's
cooperation—from climate change and Islamic terrorism to nuclear proliferation and energy security. It is important to understand the Russia
that has returned.

I first visited the country in 1988 and have gone back almost every
year since then, first as a doctoral student, later as a professor. To make
sense of Russia's recent history, I draw on the memoirs of those who
shaped it, the analyses of other scholars, statistical data and public opinion surveys, as well as my own observation, interviews, and research. Of
course, much is still not known and much is debated. I have tried to indicate when questions have no generally accepted answer and to justify the
interpretive paths I have taken.

Along the way, I have done my best to avoid two familiar styles of
writing about the country. Common among both Western and Russian
authors, these seem to me to obscure more than they reveal. The first
approach is to focus on the country's dark side, to present Russia as a
land of deformity. This genre has a long history. From sixteenth century
European travelogues, one learns that Russian peasants at that time were
drunks, idolaters, and sodomites. Seventeenth century travelers report
that the country's northern forests were a breeding ground for witches.
Then come the famous denunciations of the Marquis de Custine, along
with the jeremiads of Chaadaev—a homegrown convert to the idiom—
who, just as Pushkin was publishing *Eugene Onegin*, chastised Russia for
failing to contribute anything to human civilization. Russia, he charged,
was a "blank page in the intellectual order," which existed only to "teach
the world some great lesson." Much journalism and historical writing
shares this preoccupation with the country's dismal side.

The second approach is to turn mystical when Russia is mentioned,
to exult in paradoxes and wallow in the exotic. Russia, it is said, is unique
and unknowable. It hides its secrets from social scientists and statisti-
cians. Russia, writes the novelist Tatyana Tolstaya, "possesses certain
peculiarities that verge on the fantastic, and its inner geometry is decid-
edly non-Euclidean." Its roads are Möbius strips; its parallel lines cross

many times. Such talk usually progresses to speculation about the Russian soul, itself conceived as a jumble of contradictions. Russians, wrote the philosopher Nikolay Berdyaev, are Dionysian yet ascetic, violent yet gentle, ritualistic yet hungry for truth: "In the Russian soul there is a sort of immensity, a vagueness, a predilection for the infinite, such as is suggested by the great plain of Russia." In short, an easy place to get lost.

As a literary trope, such word spinning—a kind of orientalism practiced by the orientals—is harmless enough. As a business proposition, it has a certain logic. Today's Russians surely have a right to market their onion domes and spiritual intensity, just as a century ago Diaghilev, with his *Ballets Russes*, sold the "mysterium of Russia" to pre–World War I Parisian audiences. But as a pathway to understanding, neither the mystification nor the vilification of Russia gets us very far. A generation of work by social scientists from both Russia and the West has shown that the country's economics and politics are perfectly susceptible to careful observation, measurement, and reasoned interpretation. The apparently chaotic surfaces of political and economic life often turn out to conceal quite intelligible patterns that are in many ways similar to those found elsewhere. Most of the sinister features that upset the critics are, sadly, typical of countries at similar levels of economic development. Russia is unique, but in the way that Belgium, Argentina, and Malaysia are unique—no more, no less.

THE RETURN

CHAPTER 1

The Captain

Mikhail Gorbachev steered the Soviet ship of state for six years and nine months. An idealistic socialist, he set out to revitalize the communist order he had inherited, to inject open discussion, creativity, and common sense into an ossified Leninist party. He ended forty years of nuclear confrontation with the West and introduced the beginnings of democracy and economic freedom. Yet, to his dismay and despite his energetic maneuvering, the course he charted led into a hurricane. By the time he left office, the economy was in ruins, the ruling communist parties in his country and its European satellites had been swept from office, and the Soviet multinational state had fractured into fifteen pieces.

Why did Gorbachev's attempts to revive the Soviet political and economic order end in its overthrow? To some observers, the fall of Soviet communism seemed—in retrospect, at least—inevitable. The inefficiency of centralized control and state ownership could not help but erode economic performance, while a political system based on repression could not last forever. "Communism," wrote the historian Martin Malia, "cannot be reformed or given a human face; it can only be dismantled and replaced." To others, the system's demise seemed a "highly contingent process . . . frequently spurred on by chance occurrences and twists of fate." In this view, the Soviet order could have survived but fell apart because of Gorbachev's mistakes or failures of leadership. To orthodox communists, he was incompetent or treacherous; to liberals, he was indecisive and inflexible. Gorbachev, in his writings, mostly blames the destructive ambitions of the radical democrats who came to oppose him toward the end.

Twenty years later, one can begin to distinguish what might have been from what could never have occurred. The weight of evidence suggests that although a major crisis had become unavoidable by 1989, this was not the case in 1985 when Gorbachev assumed the leadership. The system could have persisted for several decades. Its collapse cannot be blamed simply on the actions of Boris Yeltsin or other advocates of radical change. In criticizing Gorbachev and urging faster reform, they were not merely indulging personal ambition: they were articulating what the Russian public said it wanted at that time. Similarly, Gorbachev's mistakes towards the end—although almost as striking as his achievements—explain only how the end came, not why it did. Had he acted with greater political skill in 1990–91, or even with more determined force, this would not have saved the Soviet system. By that point, it was too late. The seeds of the crisis that swept Gorbachev from power were sown in his first three years in office, when his improvisational attempts at economic reform created budgetary and financial imbalances that would, a few years later, destroy the consumer market and purge the last remnants of popular support for Soviet rule.

The Southerner

Mikhail Gorbachev was born into a peasant family in Russia's agricultural South in 1931, the first of two children. His father repaired tractors on a recently formed collective farm. Gorbachev was ten when the Nazis invaded. A year later, as the fighting approached, he recalls watching the "fiery arrows" of Katyusha rockets explode across the night sky. German motorcyclists burst into his village, followed by infantry, which stayed through the winter months, uprooting orchards, commandeering food, and terrorizing the population. Just eleven, Gorbachev witnessed prisoners of war being executed in the street. He remembers, as a teenager, after the war, driving combine harvesters twenty hours a day in the grime and sweat of southern summers, sleeping under haystacks with his father and the other farmhands. He emerged from this with a Red Banner of Labor medal, enormous self-confidence, and an ear for diagnosing trouble in the internal organs of farm machinery.

The medal helped propel him to the Law Faculty of Moscow State

University, where he studied among children of the communist elite. Despite the tense climate of the late Stalin years, Gorbachev's professors introduced students not just to Soviet criminal procedure but also to logic, Roman law, Latin, German, and the history of ideas. With a young wife in tow, Gorbachev returned to his home region of Stavropol after graduating, where he worked his way up through the party ranks, first in the Communist Youth League (the Komsomol) and then the party itself. At thirty-nine, he became first secretary of this outpost of 2 million people and 10 million sheep. Some eight years later, in 1978, he was promoted to Moscow to serve as party secretary in charge of agriculture.

The Soviet state machine was a pyramid with three faces. The Communist Party held ultimate power. At its peak in Moscow were two governing bodies. The Politburo, a committee of fifteen or so political heavyweights, set policy. (A few "candidate members" could join in discussions, but not vote.) Politburo meetings were chaired by the general secretary, who was chosen by the other members and served for life or until his colleagues contrived to oust him, as happened to Nikita Khrushchev in 1964. Each Thursday morning, to the wail of police sirens, a stream of ZIL limousines would pour down Kuybyshev Street from the party's head office on Staraya Ploshchad ("Old Square") to the Kremlin, home of the Soviet government. After chatting in the wood-paneled "walnut room," the Politburo members would take their assigned places along an enormous conference table covered in green cloth. The second body, the Secretariat, consisted of ten or twelve party secretaries, who headed the administrative departments that implemented the Politburo's decisions and managed party membership and property. The Secretariat met on Tuesday afternoons on the fifth floor of the grey stone building on Staraya Ploshchad.

A hierarchy of command connected these communist bosses to every corner of the country. A Central Committee, with three hundred full members in 1986, ratified the Politburo's decisions at its plenary sessions held every few months. It was elected by a Party Congress of several thousand that met every five years or so. All fourteen Union republics except Russia had their own central committees, and below these were party committees at the regional, town, and village levels. At the base of the pyramid, primary party organizations existed in all enterprises, collective farms, schools, army units, police stations, and other bodies. Although members were indirectly elected, from the grass roots to the Politburo, the leadership provided lists that usually named just one candidate per slot.

The Communist Party was the pyramid's first face. The other two were the hierarchies of legislative and executive bodies. Both of these were tightly controlled by the party. Legislative councils or "soviets," based at all levels from the rural settlement to the Union, passed laws and ordinances. Members were elected, again from party-approved lists without alternatives. At the top of the executive branch, councils of ministers (of the Union and of the fifteen republics) administered public services and branches of the planned economy. The ministries, and the regional associations they directed, coordinated the activity of the country's 46,000 industrial companies, 50,000 state and collective farms, and several hundred thousand smaller enterprises and organizations.

A political career meant rising through the party, perhaps holding executive or legislative posts along the way, perhaps heading an industrial enterprise. This required fitting into the spider's web of factional ties that linked party and economic managers at different levels. These ties came in many forms—from bonds of mutual trust between idealistic fellow communists to the murkiest pacts between partners in corruption.

Operating within this system was a complicated, high-stakes poker game, in which one always had to guess what cards the other players held and how each would play. A wrong guess and one might land in jail, a psychiatric ward, or, in the best case, a dead-end job in some provincial outpost. Suppose, for instance, a journalist is assigned to investigate claims that the captain of a whaling ship has been selling souvenirs carved from ivory for profit during layovers at foreign ports. He finds the allegations are true. What to do? File the story, expose the corrupt captain, and advance the interests of the journalist's editor and his official backers, who presumably provided the lead? Or cover up for the captain in case his protectors turn out to be even more highly placed? In the latter case, if the reporter writes the truth he may be dragged into court and punished for making "slanderous" accusations. In this incident, which actually occurred in the 1970s, even Brezhnev, the general secretary, turned out to have received gifts from the captain. After a tense meeting, the Soviet leader regretfully decided to sacrifice the nautical entrepreneur. "Just don't whistle!" he reportedly barked at the journalist's protectors.

Profiteering was a crime within the Soviet centrally administered economy. All property, except for some personal possessions and houses in the countryside, belonged to the state. Enterprises took orders from the central planners, who were based in an imposing building near the Kremlin. Five-year plans set strategic goals; these were then broken down annually, with production targets, prices, and supplies calculated on enormous input-output tables. Although the plans listed up to 750,000 items, this still represented only 2–3 percent of the 24 million goods produced in the early 1980s. The planners told enterprises what to make, what materials they would receive, and where to ship their output. Managers and workers won bonuses if they met their targets. Money flowed among the enterprises' bank accounts, mostly just for accounting convenience. When companies needed cash to pay workers, the state banks simply transfered the funds.

In principle, this system was hypercentralized. The Politburo was once asked to rule on the size of servings fed to police horses and dogs. Gorbachev later joked that under Brezhnev "you had to ask the permission of the Council of Ministers to install a toilet." In practice, to get things done managers improvised, lobbied the ministers in Moscow for special breaks, and sent agents around the country to strike illegal bargains for supplies. The planners themselves gave up on optimizing and just raised targets a little each year. Of course, this meant managers took pains to avoid overfulfilling their plans so future targets would remain low. In the late 1960s, the prime minister Aleksey Kosygin tried to give enterprises a little more autonomy, but his reforms, opposed by the planners, never got off the ground.

Two other elements were key to the system's operation. The first was fear. Although prison camps and political executions were scaled back after Stalin's death, dissent was suppressed by force and intimidation. State terror was somewhat decentralized under Brezhnev, who permitted regional leaders considerable discretion in return for loyalty. One Uzbek party boss operated a private prison and underground torture chamber. Security agents worked hard to keep citizens on edge, tapping phones, and recruiting informers. Under Stalin, Politburo member Anastas Mikoyan had said that: "Every citizen of the USSR is a collaborator of the NKVD," the acronym then used for the secret police. Under Brezhnev, the secret services remained large and mostly unsupervised.

The second key ingredient was a preoccupation with controlling information. No independent media were allowed, and all photocopiers had to be registered with the police. Under Stalin even owning a typewriter had required police permission. Most statistical reports were marked "secret," "top secret," or "for official use only." Quite often, efforts to deceive the population ended up blinding the policymakers. Not even top leaders received briefings on military expenditures. As a Politburo member in the early 1980s, Gorbachev asked to see the state budget, but he writes that: "[General Secretary] Andropov simply laughed that off: 'Nothing doing! You're asking too much.'" In the 1960s, party leaders ordered the Ministry of Communications to jam foreign radio broadcasts, a technically challenging and costly task in a country covering eleven time zones. But the party bosses insisted, so the ministry found a solution. According to Aleksandr Yakovlev, then a Central Committee secretary, it built two powerful jamming stations in central Moscow—one across the street from the Central Committee office, the other on Kutuzovsky Prospekt, where most party leaders lived. Presumably, officials who heard static when they tried to tune to the Voice of America did not know that a few dozen miles outside major cities the broadcasts came through loud and clear. The main victims were the party leaders themselves. By 1980, half the Soviet population had access to shortwave radios. The other main sources of information were the spinners of rumors, who, as Boris Yeltsin put it, became "the main telegraph agency of the Soviet Union."

By the late 1970s when Gorbachev arrived in Moscow, the absurdities and waste this system generated were obvious to all who cared to look. Many, of course, did not. An army of time-servers in the party's higher and middle ranks wanted only to expand their privileges. But a number of mostly younger, better educated officials were becoming disillusioned with the empty speech making, decrepit health, and blatant cynicism of Brezhnev and his cronies. These covert free thinkers were by no means all democrats or believers in capitalism; in fact, they ranged from adamant Leninists to Western-style liberals. But most had two things in common:

impatience with the stagnant atmosphere of Brezhnev's last years and respect for—and sometimes the support of—the most enigmatic Politburo member, Yury Andropov.

A hard-line ideologue, Andropov had helped suppress popular uprisings in Hungary in 1956 and Prague in 1968. As KGB chief, he trained foreign terrorists, and committed dissidents to psychiatric hospitals, where they were diagnosed with "sluggish schizophrenia" and shot up with drugs. He authorized the murder by ricin pellet of the Bulgarian exile Georgy Markov. At the same time, he stood out for an "indifference to luxury" amid the crassness of Brezhnev's circle. He read the literary journals and could write passable verse in the style of Pushkin's *Eugene Onegin*. Genuinely concerned about the country's problems, he encouraged his advisors to speak frankly, and sought practical solutions, although he did not find many. According to one aide, he was looking for a way out of Afghanistan as early as 1980. Many of the communist reformers of the Gorbachev era grew up in his shadow.

Gorbachev was his greatest discovery. The two had become close while vacationing in the Stavropol resort of Kislovodsk. Gorbachev's *Memoirs* contains an intriguing photograph of the two future party leaders playing dominoes outdoors. The secret police chief looks relaxed, in short sleeves and a white fedora. His protégé, in what looks like a nautical cap, is leaning back to laugh, while two other companions focus on the game. With Andropov, Gorbachev allowed himself to express doubts about the party leaders quite openly, complaining about their advanced age on one occasion, and reminding Andropov, himself no spring chicken, of the saying "There are no trees without saplings." "Congratulations, sapling," Andropov joked when, in 1978, Gorbachev arrived in Moscow to join the Secretariat.

Although assigned to agriculture, Gorbachev was soon "poking his nose into political affairs," as one fellow secretary put it. What distinguished him at this time was a kind of ingenuous gutsiness. The morning after his appointment, Gorbachev stopped by the general secretary's office unannounced because he felt it impossible to get down to work without having first "shared his ideas" with Brezhnev. To Gorbachev's surprise, Brezhnev did not appear particularly interested in his ideas. He stared into space and seemed to be thinking only about Gorbachev's predecessor, who had died of a heart attack after an evening of heavy drinking. "It's a pity about Kulakov," was all Brezhnev said. "He was a good man." Gorbachev soon found much to dislike about the tawdry mores of the Brezhnev court. He writes of Brezhnev that: "Whenever abuses and mismanagement were mentioned to him, tears would well up in his eyes and he would ask, bewilderment in his voice: 'Is it really that bad?'"

A couple of months earlier, Gorbachev had met Brezhnev on a railway platform in the southern resort of Mineralnye Vody, where the general secretary was stopping en route to Azerbaijan. Andropov and Gorbachev were there to pay their respects. Andropov had told his young colleague to keep the conversation flowing, so Gorbachev held forth about the spring lambing season, the record grain harvest, his work on a long-planned irrigation canal. In his memoirs, Gorbachev gives this incident a nostalgic, almost lyrical flavor, recalling the warm night, the mountains, the dark sky studded by enormous stars. Then Brezhnev, heaving himself back into the carriage, asked Andropov for an update on his speech. "Good, good, Leonid Ilich," Andropov reassured him. Only later did Gorbachev realize it was not a draft address to a party meeting that Brezhnev had in mind but whether his pronunciation, slurred by the aftereffects of a stroke and his addiction to tranquilizers, was intelligible.

Four years after Gorbachev arrived in Moscow, Brezhnev died, the first in a chain of dominoes. Andropov, who succeeded him, set out to tighten labor discipline, sending police to hair salons, saunas, and beer halls to round up those skipping work. He jailed mafia bosses, and purged some of the most corrupt bureaucrats. But Andropov was dying of kidney disease, and Konstantin Chernenko, the Brezhnev acolyte who followed, was himself stricken with emphysema. With Chernenko clearly on his last legs, the struggle for succession pitted Gorbachev against older Brehznev intimates such as the Moscow party leader, Viktor Grishin. Andrey Gromyko, the dour traditionalist who had served as foreign minister since Khrushchev's time, played a pivotal role. Through his son, Gromyko opened a channel of secret negotiations with Gorbachev's associate Aleksandr Yakovlev. In return for promising to let him move sometime later to head the Supreme Soviet, Gromyko offered to nominate Gorbachev—which he did, leaping to his feet at the Politburo meeting after Chernenko's death on March 10, 1985, before anyone had time to propose someone else. Afraid of ending up in the minority and being blamed for splitting the party, allies of other possible candidates all lined up behind Gorbachev.

Changing the World

As of 1985, a zone of barbed wire and minefields bisected Europe, dividing the Western industrialized democracies of NATO from the communist Warsaw Pact. Deterred from direct attacks by fear of mutual nuclear annihilation, the two sides competed by expanding their alliances and fighting proxy wars in the third world. In the 1970s, détente had eased tensions for a while, but the 1979 Soviet invasion of Afghanistan and the 1981 crackdown on striking Polish miners had set off a "new cold war." President Reagan increased military spending, labeled the Soviet Union an "evil empire," and began deploying Pershing II and Cruise missiles in Western Europe to counter the threat of Soviet SS-20s (see Chapter 9).

Gorbachev came to office determined to change this. During his first three years, traditional Soviet positions and Marxist rhetoric were progressively displaced by a different approach to international affairs that Gorbachev called the "new thinking." Impressed by the horror that a nuclear war would unleash, Gorbachev decided that the fabric of international politics must change. In the future, states would treat each other with mutual respect and resolve conflicts through peaceful negotiations. As he told the United Nations General Assembly in 1988: "the use or threat of force no longer can or must be an instrument of foreign policy." Security could only be mutual, not at others' expense, and peace required creating trust between the leaders and peoples of the world. Each state had the right to choose its own course without interference. Ideologies should no longer drive international behavior. Rather than pursuing the interests of class or nation, Soviet foreign policy would seek to further the "universal interests of humanity." With Rajiv Gandhi in Delhi in November 1986, Gorbachev insisted that: "human life must be acknowledged as the supreme value" and "non-violence must become the basis of human co-existence."

The "new thinking" was not just about changing Soviet policy. Gorbachev hoped for a global revolution, and pursued it with what one aide called a "messianic enthusiasm." In 1987, he took time away from governing to write a book titled *Perestroika: New Thinking for Our Country and the World*, which was published in almost 100 countries and sold five million copies worldwide. The message of nuclear disarmament and universal respect was understandably popular, and the excitement in the faces of ordinary people Gorbachev met in his travels abroad indulged him in the belief that he had started an international reconceptualization of politics between states.

On the face of it, all this appears disconcertingly naïve. Could Gorbachev really have believed his homilies would persuade world statesmen to abandon the use of force? Among Soviet professionals, the "new thinking" aroused skepticism, if not alarm, and in the West it was initially viewed as a propaganda ploy. As Gorbachev's head of foreign intelligence, General Leonid Shebarshin, saw it: "Any reasonable person hearing a government talking about values common to the whole of humanity must conclude that this government either intends to cheat the whole of humanity or else consists of bloody fools." Nor was the "new thinking" particularly original. Many others had looked into the nuclear abyss and concluded, as Gorbachev did, that "violence . . . must be renounced." What made this different was that Gorbachev was the leader of the superpower with the most nuclear warheads, and that he was willing to make concessions—big ones—to get the ball rolling.

He started by announcing a unilateral moratorium on nuclear testing. Then, after ten months in office, Gorbachev declared the goal of a nuclear-free world by the year 2000. At a summit with Reagan in Reykjavik, Iceland, in October 1986, he agreed to a bilateral reduction in strategic forces of 50 percent over five years and the complete elimination of ballistic missiles within ten, although he also insisted that Reagan restrict research on space defenses, something the latter was unwilling to do. In December 1987 in Washington, Gorbachev signed the Intermediate Range Nuclear Forces Treaty (INF) which committed both the United States and the Soviet Union to destroying all their ground-launched, intermediate-range nuclear and conventional missiles. Then, at the United Nations in New York in December 1988, Gorbachev announced a unilateral reduction of Soviet military forces by 500,000 troops and 10,000 tanks.

Besides disarming, Gorbachev ended the policy of external expansion that had characterized Soviet policy since Stalin. He signaled to the East European satellites that he would not use force to keep them in the alliance. "They're sick of us," he told his aide Anatoly Chernyaev, "and we're sick of them. Let's live in a new way, that's fine." This led to the crumbling of the Eastern Bloc, and, in November 1989, the dismantling of the Berlin Wall. The prospect of a reunited Germany posed a particular challenge, given the historical resonance for the Soviet people, who had lost more than 20 million citizens in the fight against Nazism. But Gorbachev realized it was inevitable and accepted it, while nevertheless trying unsuccessfully to persuade Chancellor Kohl to keep the reunited Germany outside NATO. In 1988, he began withdrawing Soviet troops from Afghanistan, where they had been bogged down fighting Muslim guerrillas.

Was Gorbachev as starry-eyed as his speeches suggest? Other interpretations are possible. Some have seen in the "new thinking" a clever strategy to win over world public opinion while making the best of the Soviet Union's weakness in the development of new weapons. Gorbachev may have felt the need to break out of the stagnant routine into which arms control negotiations had fallen—the painstaking search for reciprocal concessions, frequently disrupted by diplomatic flaps, while the American technological lead grew ever wider. The appeal to grand goals and transformative politics was actually well targeted to catch the expansive if sometimes trite imagination of President Reagan, who also saw world affairs in moral terms and dreamed of making nuclear weapons "impotent and obsolete." And engaging Reagan personally was the only way to make progress with an administration in Washington that was unusually stacked with hawks. At the same time, international prestige could be leveraged to advance domestic reform. Reducing military spending and the sense of external threat was important to weaken hardliners at home and buy space for economic experiments. At times, utopian gestures can serve the goals of realpolitik.

Such calculations may have played a role at times. Gorbachev was not naïve in an unworldly way. He resented rebuffs from Washington, and, alone with his aides, cursed his adversaries using the rich vocabulary of an agricultural mechanic. But in public he continued to focus on common interests and exploit his skill in forging personal relationships.

Even if he did not always embody such ideals in practice, his belief that international relations could be attuned to universal human interests appears sincere. Similar new age rhetoric infuses his post-retirement writings. And he failed to extract enforceable commitments from the West in return for his own concessions, even when such possibilities existed.

The naïve sincerity was most evident in February 1991 as Gorbachev worked the phones trying to persuade President Bush that he could convince Saddam Hussein to leave Kuwait, rendering a U.S.-led ground invasion unnecessary. This was a moment of truth for Gorbachev's vision of a world in which diplomacy replaced force. As his aide Chernyaev looked on with a mixture of admiration and embarrassment, Gorbachev talked to Bush, Major, Andreotti, Mubarak, Assad, Mitterand, Kohl, Kaifu, Rafsanjani, and other world leaders. In fact, the order to invade had already been given.

In retrospect, what is most remarkable is how effectively Gorbachev neutered opposition from the military and the foreign policy establishment, for whom his unilateral concessions looked like capitulation. Some compared him to Chamberlain at Munich, and saw his globalism as a fig leaf to conceal surrender. Although the Soviet Union was no longer the overt target of U.S. and NATO hostility, it seemed to be giving up more than it got in return. Under the INF treaty, the Soviets agreed to destroy more than thirteen times as many medium-range missiles as the United States did, and five times as many short-range ones. Even Gorbachev's sympathizers had doubts.

The results of Gorbachev's foreign policy did not match his declared aims. Despite his entreaties, world leaders did not give up the use of force. Nuclear weapons were reduced, but not abolished, and they continued to proliferate to new countries. Statesmen did not abandon realpolitik to pursue universal interests. In fact, the weakening of the Soviet military initiated an era of U.S. unilateralism, in which the one remaining superpower was increasingly determined to use its muscle worldwide. Russians could only watch as a Washington-led military alliance spread eastward across Europe, an alliance that, privately if not publicly, treated Russia as the main potential enemy. Gorbachev had ended the division of Europe, but at the cost of pushing Russia to the margins. By agreeing to give up more than his adversary, he had changed the world. The question for the leaders who succeeded him in Russia was whether the changes justified Gorbachev's concessions.

The Home Front

In between efforts to denuclearize the globe, Gorbachev set out to repair the Soviet economy. In its first sixty years, the Soviet Union had recorded some impressive economic achievements. Within two generations, a country of peasants had become one of the most literate in the world: by the late 1950s, 98.5 percent of Russians aged ten to forty-nine could read. Soviet mathematicians had pioneered modern probability theory and topology. Soviet workers had built the world's largest steel plant and aluminum smelter. The country's scientists had launched the first artificial satellite, put the first man in space, and engineered the world's largest arsenal of nuclear warheads.

By the early 1980s, however, this sprint to modernity had slowed to a crawl. Objective observers of the Soviet economy found it had two defects. It produced the wrong things. And it produced them badly.

Consumers had always been the lowest priority. In 1990, the Soviet Union produced almost twice as many lathes as the United States and four times as many bulldozers, but only one-fiftieth as many pairs of women's underwear. By then, hunger was not widespread, but most Soviet children "grew up without ever seeing a steak, a piece of unprocessed cheese, an orange, or a banana." In 1989, one-quarter of Russians had homes with no indoor toilet, and a third had no hot running water. Fewer than one family in three had access to a telephone. Russia had more doctors per capita than almost any other country, but two out of five graduates from Soviet medical schools did not know how to read an electrocardiogram, and for lack of scalpels some surgeons were known to perform appendectomies using safety razors. In 1991, the country had one-third as many personal computers per capita as the Czech Republic, one-tenth as many as South Korea, and one fiftieth as many as the United States.

With no market competition to discipline enterprises, no "creative destruction" to sort the wheat from the chaff, industrial productivity had become a joke. It took Soviet factories 60 percent more steel to manufacture 75 to 80 percent as much machinery as the United States. Even Soviet cows gave less than half as much milk as their American counterparts. Two-thirds of Russian industrial equipment was obsolete in 1991, by one estimate. In the United States, the average service life of physical capital was about seventeen years; in the Soviet Union it was forty-seven. The quality of goods was so low that many could be sold only under duress. In 1986, Russian collective and state farms had to be ordered to buy 12,000 combine harvesters they did not want. In Armenia in the late 1980s, "mountains of defective shoes were simply destroyed."

Vast numbers of Soviet enterprises were dangerous polluters, far too large to be efficient, or located in remote spots with forbidding climates. Based on economics alone, it would have made sense to empty much of Siberia. According to the former head of the national electric company, it would have been cheaper to relocate the entire populations of most Siberian and Far Eastern cities than to restructure their energy and electricity systems. In short, a large share of enterprises were producing goods that few consumers would freely choose to buy, and were doing so inefficiently, in inappropriate locations, using energy-wasting and ecologically harmful technologies. It would save the country money if these unsalvageable enterprises were closed, the materials they used exported, and the profits used to import consumer goods.

In economics, Gorbachev's first steps were modest. To "accelerate social and economic development," he set about squeezing waste out of the system, firing corrupt and ineffective officials, disciplining workers, and intensifying propaganda. In his first two years, Gorbachev replaced 60 percent of regional and local party secretaries. At the same time, "acceleration" meant increasing industrial investment to hasten technological progress. Officials announced that investment in civilian machine building would increase 80 percent by 1990. Plants were run around the clock.

One cause of low productivity was drinking on the job, so Gorbachev quite logically took aim at alcohol abuse. Production of vodka, wine, and beer was slashed, and sales were restricted to certain hours of the day. Between 1980 and 1987, the volume of vodka sold fell by almost 60 percent. The policy did not win him many friends. It prompted an epidemic of home brewing, cost the government large sums in foregone tax revenues—alcohol had made up 20 percent of retail sales—and is still widely considered a major blunder. One vineyard owner committed suicide after his rare vines, grafted in the nineteenth century to make wine for the Imperial court, were ripped out of the ground. However, as I discuss in Chapter 10, the campaign probably saved more than 1.2 million lives, at least temporarily. The death rate dropped sharply, and rose even more sharply when the alcohol restrictions were repealed a few years later.

A second campaign, launched in May 1986, targeted "unearned incomes" and "speculation." It was billed as a struggle against organized crime. In fact, the "shadow economy" of the late Soviet Union had provided a safety valve, offsetting the failures of the planners. An estimated 20 million people—about 12 percent of the working age population—provided underground services that ranged from shoe repairs and video sales to house construction and abortions. The victims of Gorbachev's campaign often turned out to be grandmothers who grew cucumbers and sold them outside metro stations, or farmers whose private plots were alleviating consumer shortages. In the Volgograd region, prosecutors enlisted thugs to smash hundreds of greenhouses where tomatoes were growing. Prices at farmers' markets soared.

To improve the apalling quality of consumer goods, 70,000 state inspectors were dispatched to the country's industrial plants. Among Moscow enterprises, during the experiment's first month only one-fifth of output was found to be "acceptable." Not one automatic lathe produced at the Red Proletarian machine tool plant made the grade. The standards were gradually softened, but still 15 percent of output was being rejected in early 1988. The results were bottlenecks along supply chains, falling production, missed plan targets, canceled bonuses for workers, and bitterness on the factory floor. This campaign also became "polluted by bribery," to quote Gorbachev's aide Vadim Medvedev. It was quietly abandoned.

At the same time, in a policy known as *glasnost*—literally "giving voice"—Gorbachev began loosening restrictions on the press and public association. The aim was to mobilize the party's propaganda machine behind reform. Gorbachev hoped to win over the intelligentsia, channel the idealism of the young, and expose corrupt and inept apparatchiks. "We have no opposition party," he told a gathering of writers in June 1986. "How then can we control ourselves? Only through criticism and self-criticism." However, the policy did not mean license for advocates of "bourgeois ideology." Glasnost notwithstanding, the editor of one leading magazine was told to fire a young reporter who had made the mistake of citing polls that said 60 percent of Siberians supported Gorbachev's reforms. Gorbachev had just said the reforms had the backing of *all* Soviet citizens.

Over time, however, the policy grew beyond initial expectations into something close to freedom of speech, press, and association. Newspapers and magazines began covering ecological disasters, organized crime, Stalin's terror, and social problems such as poverty, homelessness, and prostitution. Informal clubs, civic groups, professional associations, and embryonic political parties appeared. The dissident physicist Andrey Sakharov was allowed to return to Moscow from exile in the city of Gorky and to speak out about the mistreatment of other dissidents. By 1989, the liberal media had progressed from explorations of social problems and Soviet history to analysis of current politics and biting personal attacks on the country's leaders. Conservative media, meanwhile, were preaching Russian nationalism and defending Stalin.

In a new phase of economic reform christened *perestroika*, or "restructuring," efforts to force the pace of growth were combined with minor steps to redesign the administrative system. Some measures sought to decentralize decision making to those with local information. Others purported to strengthen incentives for workers and managers to behave efficiently. The goal, said the liberal economist Yevgeny Yasin, was "to implement the Chinese model in Russia" or to introduce "socialism with a human face" as in Hungary or Yugoslavia.

Already in 1986, several dozen organizations had been allowed to export and import directly, bypassing the Ministry of Foreign Trade. From January 1988, the "Law on State Enterprises" permitted companies to decide for themselves what to produce, after filling state orders, and to keep part of the profits thus earned for investment or workers' bonuses. Managers, from the directors down to the foremen, were to be elected by the workers rather than appointed by the ministries. Enterprises were supposed to become financially independent, but prices remained controlled. In May 1988, it became legal to set up small, essentially private cooperatives to sell consumer goods and services at market prices.

By early 1988, Gorbachev had concluded that these reforms would not work unless combined with major political changes to democratize the country. In March 1989, the first competitive elections were held in a 2,250-person Congress of People's Deputies, which during its first two-week session elected a two-house permanent parliament, the Supreme Soviet, from among its members. Gorbachev, while retaining his position as general secretary of the party, was chosen by the Congress to serve as the new parliament's chairman. Although independent candidates could run, these elections were still dominated by the party apparatus. One-third of the seats were reserved for "public organizations," almost all party controlled, including one hundred seats for the Communist Party itself. Among new deputies, 88 percent were party members, and 72 percent had been members of the previous Supreme Soviet. Still, the Congress included several hundred supporters of radical political and economic reform, including Sakharov, independence seekers from the Baltic Republics, and the former Moscow city party boss, Boris Yeltsin.

Yeltsin, whose contribution to Russian politics is the subject of Chapter 2, had been plucked from the Urals region of Sverdlovsk, and seconded to clean up the Moscow party organization. A blunt-spoken former construction foreman, he had turned out to have acute antennae for changes in public sentiment and an impatience with hypocrisy. At first, Gorbachev's most liberal associates saw in Yeltsin an energetic ally. "It turns out there's even someone to the left of us," Gorbachev's aide Medvedev scribbled enthusiastically to Aleksandr Yakovlev during one Politburo meeting. But Yeltsin became disaffected when he concluded that conservatives in Staraya Ploshchad were sabotaging him in his battles with the Moscow bureaucracy. He also sensed that ordinary people were losing faith in perestroika, with its endless speeches and slogans, ill-planned campaigns, and disappointing economic results.

When Yeltsin, breaking party protocol, voiced his criticisms at a Central Committee plenary session in October 1987, Gorbachev pounced with poorly concealed fury. His face, according to one witness, turned "purple with rage." What followed was an unintended validation of Yeltsin's charge that the General Secretary was surrounded by sycophants. Rising to Gorbachev's defense, twenty-six speakers queued at the microphone to hurl insults at Yeltsin—so many, in fact, that a coffee break had to be called in the middle: "Political immaturity," "a weakling," "delusions of grandeur," "political nihilism," "disproportionate ambitions," "slander," "vanity," "personal caprice," "primitivism," "defeatism." Then, as Yeltsin tried to respond, Gorbachev let his own bile pour out, interrupting to lecture him about his "political illiteracy."

> It's not enough for you that only Moscow revolves around you. The Central Committee has to occupy itself with you as well? . . . What egotism, what self-importance it must take to place your own ambitions above the interests of the party and our business.

Several weeks later, after Yeltsin had apparently tried to commit suicide, Gorbachev had him dragged from a hospital bed to repeat the flagellation in front of the Moscow City Party Committee—another four hours of denunciations by former colleagues and assistants—before throwing him the bone of an appointment as deputy minister for construction. At that meeting, Yeltsin recalls that Gorbachev told him: "I will not let you back into politics!"

The intensity of Gorbachev's anger was striking. It was as though for a second he glimpsed deep into the future and saw the chain of mistakes Yeltsin would goad him into making, the humiliations that lay ahead. George Shultz, the U.S. secretary of state, who visited Gorbachev the next day, found him despondent, like a prize fighter who had just been knocked down. To his Politburo colleagues, Gorbachev explained that Yeltsin suffered from the " 'infantile' disease of leftism." There was, perhaps, legitimate reason to fear that Yeltsin's flat-footed intervention would energize the opponents of reform. Aleksandr Yakovlev, the master of "two steps forward, one step back," had been congratulating himself on having slipped some choice new phrases into Gorbachev's speech when he saw Yeltsin's bull stride into the china shop. Even he found cutting words for the Sverdlovsk ingenue. In any case, Gorbachev's overreaction was a tactical mistake. As word of Yeltsin's flaying by the old guard filtered out, his popularity surged. In 1989, he was elected to the Congress of People's Deputies and the USSR Supreme Soviet, where he forged an alliance with the democratic intelligentsia. In 1990, Yeltsin was elected to the Supreme Soviet of the Russian Republic in elections even more competitive than those in 1989, and was narrowly chosen as its chairman, making him the chief executive of Russia.

From this position, Yeltsin championed radical opposition to Gorbachev. He accused the Soviet leader of wavering and equivocating, permitting hard-liners to obstruct his reforms. Gorbachev, attacked from both right and left, began to weave between the two, tilting the tiller first left, then right. In March, he had the USSR Supreme Soviet elect him to a new position, president of the Soviet Union. A turning point came in the summer of 1990 when, with both Yeltsin's and Gorbachev's support, a team of economists under Grigory Yavlinsky and Stanislav Shatalin drew up an ambitious plan to create a market economy in "500 Days." During the first three months, the authorities would privatize small firms and break up monopolies. Then prices would be gradually deregulated. By the end of the five hundred days, most enterprises would have been either sold or leased, and most prices would be free. Yeltsin and the Russian parliament embraced the plan. At first Gorbachev was enthusiastic, calling Shatalin with questions "five times a day," and telling Yeltsin that he would support the plan "to the end." But he changed his mind and instead endorsed a program devised by his prime minister, Nikolay Ryzhkov, to rescue the collapsing planned economy.

Having rejected radical market reform, Gorbachev turned for support to conservatives within the party and state. Orthodox communists were horrified by the party's weakening position and by the demands for independence advanced by various republics. Gorbachev appointed Boris Pugo, a hard-line former secret police chief from Latvia, as interior minister, and grew more attentive to the alarmist prognoses of his KGB chief, Vladimir Kryuchkov. Proud as ever of his tacking to the wind, Gorbachev denied he had given up on reform. Was he moving to the right, a journalist asked around this time. No, said Gorbachev, with a pained expression: "I'm going around in circles."

With that, he began a characteristic dance. He flirted with the idea of forceful solutions, as best we know never quite ordering one but directing the security services to prepare options, dropping hints, thinking out loud. In December 1990, Kryuchkov told two aides to plan for a state of emergency—on Gorbachev's instructions, so he said. Then in January 1991, the armed forces struck, apparently trying to overthrow the elected republic governments of Lithuania and Latvia and replace them with KGB-created "Committees of National Salvation." A blueprint for such an intervention, prepared by the reactionary general Valentin Varennikov, had been discussed at a Politburo meeting as early as March 1990. On January 8, Soviet troops started occupying buildings in Vilnius, the Lithuanian capital. Two days later, as soldiers stormed the telephone exchange and railway station, Gorbachev issued an ultimatum to the Lithuanian parliament threatening to impose direct rule from Moscow if it did not stop trying to restore the "bourgeois system." Then on January 13, troops attacked the city's television and radio stations, killing at least fourteen unarmed civilians and injuring more than one hundred.

Gorbachev denies having ordered the crackdown, and no document has been found with his signature on it. But he knew about the ongoing operations and did not call them off. On January 8, when he met the Lithuanian prime minister, Kazimiera Prunskiene, he told her to restore order back home, adding: "Otherwise I will be obliged to do the job myself." Gorbachev conducted no investigation, and no one was punished. He did not condemn the military action until nine days later, and he actually blamed the Lithuanians for provoking the bloodshed. By this point Yeltsin had flown to Tallin to express solidarity with the Balts, and militia commandos had spread the violence to Latvia, attacking a government building in the capital, Riga.

In late January, Gorbachev authorized the army to patrol cities in Russia and other republics to combat crime. Troops fanned out across Moscow and other towns armed with pistols and bayonets. When Gorbachev's close aide Anatoly Chernyaev complained to him about this, Gorbachev told him: "Mind your own business! . . . It's a normal practice. And in general, you fuss too much, you're always panicking together with your intellectuals." The leaders of most republics rejected the armed patrols, so they had to be canceled.

At times, Gorbachev's mood, manipulated by his KGB informants, came close to paranoia. One Saturday morning, his liberal aide Aleksandr Yakovlev was in the woods picking mushrooms with his grandchildren. An urgent call came through on the car phone from Gorbachev, who wanted to know what he was doing outside Moscow conspiring with the interior minister and the head of the General Staff. In March 1991, Yeltsin led supporters of radical reform in a march through central Moscow, defying the thousands of troops deployed to intimidate them. Yakovlev says Gorbachev phoned him in a panic with news that the democrats had hooks and ropes to scale the walls and storm the Kremlin. No, the mayor of Moscow laughed when, at Gorbachev's request, Yakovlev called to inquire—as with everything else, there was a shortage of ropes in the city.

But while Gorbachev seemed to believe almost any disinformation about supporters of reform, he waved off repeated warnings that his hard-line allies were planning to overthrow him. Already in December 1990, Eduard Shevardnadze had resigned as foreign minister, predicting the imposition of dictatorship. In June 1991, advocates of military rule tried to stage a constitutional coup. Prime minister Valentin Pavlov asked the Supreme Soviet to transfer powers to him—"I can't run to the President for decisions on every question," he explained—and Kryuchkov and defense minister Dmitry Yazov demanded a state of emergency. The parliament, controlled at this point by anti-Gorbachev communists, might have acquiesced had Gorbachev not appeared unexpectedly to scotch the plan and joke to reporters that: "The coup is over."

Of course, it was not. By July, alarming signs were appearing daily. Aleksandr Yakovlev had been getting reports that the top military generals were meeting suspiciously often. He resigned that month, warning that a coup was imminent. Others sent word of odd movements of military divisions outside Moscow. Even the American ambassador, Jack Matlock, was asked to relay to Gorbachev a message from Moscow mayor Popov that a takeover was planned. Yevgeny Primakov, another advisor, with close KGB ties, called to tell Gorbachev he should not trust the security services so much. To such warnings, Gorbachev replied with anything from suppressed irony to open derision. "You exaggerate!" he told Yakovlev. "What a chicken!" he said of Primakov, recounting the latter's phone call to his aide Chernyaev. "I told him: 'Zhenya, calm down. You of all people shouldn't yield to panic.'"

In the spring of 1991, Gorbachev had persuaded the leaders of nine of the republics to negotiate a new Union treaty that would redefine the USSR as a confederation of sovereign states. This was to be signed on August 20. Gorbachev told Yeltsin—and presumably the KGB agents bugging his offices—that he planned to fire Kryuchkov and Yazov and call elections for the position of president of this new confederal Union. These arrangements made, Gorbachev departed for a two-week vacation in Foros on the Black Sea.

The coup that followed, in which Gorbachev's hard-line ministers—Kryuchkov, Yazov, Pugo, and others—confined him to his villa and announced the rule of a State Committee for the State of Emergency, has been picked over by scholars. I will return to the details below. Yeltsin, surrounded by supporters, coordinated resistance from the Russian parliament, or "White House." Within three days, the rebellion had crumbled, and Gorbachev flew back to Moscow. Although the communist leadership had discredited itself completely, Gorbachev held an embarrassing press conference in which he rose to the party's defense. Leaders of the republics, suddenly aware of the fragility of their new freedoms, were racing to secede. But Gorbachev still hoped to negotiate a new Union treaty. As he told the Egyptian president, Hosni Mubarak, he thought the nationalist grandstanding in the republic legislatures was just a "temporary phenomenon."

At first Gorbachev had the support of Yeltsin, who appeared happy to preserve the Union so long as it was no more than a very loose confederation and Russia could take over most Soviet property. But as the months went by, all but two of the remaining republics declared independence. Ukraine demanded to keep parts of the armed forces based on its territory. Then in December, the Ukrainians held a referendum on the country's future; 84 percent of registered voters participated and 90 percent of them voted for independence. A week later, Yeltsin met with the presidents of Ukraine and Belarus in a hunting lodge near Minsk and the three signed the Belovezha Agreement, dissolving the Soviet Union and creating a new Commonwealth of Independent States (CIS).

To Gorbachev, this was a treacherous conspiracy. But he had little leverage to resist. In mid-November, according to the Soviet defense minister, Marshal Yevgeny Shaposhnikov, Gorbachev called him to his Kremlin office, offered him coffee, lamented the Union's disintegration, and then apparently invited him to stage another coup: "You, the military, take power into your hands, install a government that suits you, stabilize the situation and then step aside." Shaposhnikov pointed out that he would end up in prison with the August putschists, who had tried something similar. "What do you think, Zhenya," he says Gorbachev replied. "I am not proposing anything to you. I'm just laying out possibilities, thinking out loud." On December 10, Gorbachev met with five hundred army officers to discuss the state of the country. But by the next day he had resolved against any attempt to mobilize the military and spoke out in an interview against those who would "play the army card" and would "use tanks to achieve political goals."

Having decided force was not an option, Gorbachev agreed to leave office. On December 23, Yeltsin met him in the Kremlin to discuss logistics, with Aleksandr Yakovlev as a witness. The two talked for several hours, and then Gorbachev said he did not feel well and retreated to a side room. Yakovlev records in his memoirs that he found Gorbachev there, lying on a couch.

> "*Vot vidish, Sash, vot tak*,"—said a man in perhaps the most difficult minutes of his life, as if complaining of his fate and simultaneously embarrassed by his weakness. "You see, Sasha. That's how it is."

On December 26, he left his Kremlin office for the last time.

Why Reform?

Why did he do it? What led Gorbachev, after working his way to the pinnacle of the pyramid, to start redesigning its foundations? Why did he feel such an urgent need to reshape the economic and political order that had endured through seven turbulent decades?

One possibility that can be rejected is that the reforms he chose were forced on him by a looming economic crisis. Growth was slowing, and there was a sense among the elite that the system's batteries were running down. In the West, the personal computer revolution was taking off. Not only could the Soviet system not innovate, it could not even borrow technology successfully. Still, gradual decline, even stagnation, is not crisis. The planners viewed the economy as "inefficient but stable," and forecast growth rates averaging 1.5 percent a year till the end of the century. Only in 1990, after four years of perestroika, did output begin to decline.

As I will argue later, a serious crisis *was* brewing related to hard currency earnings, monetary policy, and the budget. But this was not widely recognized, and although Gorbachev was occasionally warned of monetary and fiscal imbalances, his policies only made them worse.

Nor was there any sense in 1985 that public discontent was about to get out of control. There was widespread grumbling, which Gorbachev heard in his travels. Many goods were in short supply, and consumers had to wait years or decades for an apartment or a car. The low quality of Soviet manufactures was an embarrassment. In Moscow alone, by one economist's count, more than two thousand Soviet-made color televisions spontaneously combusted every year. The level of waste was shocking. Up to one-third of potatoes and vegetables rotted in the fields or were lost during transportation. Still, personal consumption appeared to have increased during the previous decade. Per capita consumption of meat, milk, eggs, vegetables, and fruits all rose between 1980 and 1985, as did the proportions of families with radios, televisions, tape recorders, refrigerators, electric vacuum cleaners, and cars.

Some have argued that the Soviet leadership was driven to perestroika and the "new thinking" by military competition from the United States. President Reagan increased defense spending to combat the "evil empire," and set out to build high-technology missile defenses that could shoot down Soviet nuclear missiles in space. Memoirs suggest the Soviet leaders were anxious about their technological backwardness and alarmed by the rhetoric emanating from Washington in the early 1980s. Oleg Gordievsky, a KGB officer in the Soviet Embassy in London, reports that Andropov and others were so concerned about a possible preemptive nuclear strike that they had their spies count how many windows were lit at night in British government buildings.

However, by Gorbachev's time, the scare had receded. By 1986, the brunt of the Reagan military buildup was over and U.S. defense spending had stabilized in real terms. Soviet experts were confident the USSR could outwit any missile defense system the Americans built at a fraction of the cost. Had the sense of military vulnerability been as intense as in earlier years, this would most likely have pushed Gorbachev in exactly the opposite direction. According to his advisor, Georgy Arbatov, hawkish moves in the West tended to strengthen the communist old guard and military-industrial complex, making it harder for reformers in the Kremlin to cut military spending. When Andropov broached the U.S. military threat in the Politburo in 1983, he did not infer the need for liberalization. On the contrary, he proposed increasing armaments, intensifying diplomacy with China, and tightening control over the East European satellites.

To a degree, Gorbachev's reforms were the outgrowth of generational change. A new cohort of leaders was breaking into the Kremlin, made up of idealists with a belief in the system's perfectibility and a nagging sense that things could not go on as before. Many had come of age during the Khrushchev cultural "thaw" of the early 1960s. "It would have been possible to renovate, patch things up, and continue to sit in the General Secretary's chair," Gorbachev said when asked in 2006 why he had started perestroika. "But to live as before was unacceptable [*nelzya*]." Major reform could be seen as the result of what historian Stephen Kotkin calls the "inescapable generational change in the party leadership." However, although the generational shift was inescapable—the old guard was rapidly dying off—the turn to reform was not. Many in Gorbachev's generation would have been quite happy to "patch things up . . . and continue to sit in the General Secretary's chair."

Economic stagnation, the competition with the West, and the maturity of the post-Stalin generation together created the setting in which Gorbachev *could* emerge. Yet it is hard to imagine any of his 1985 Politburo colleagues trying anything quite as bold and destabilizing. Ultimately, Gorbachev's personal characteristics explain the course he chose. Enormous confidence in his own abilities merged with a liberating ignorance of the details of the challenges he faced. Ultimately, says Chernyaev, his closest, most loyal aide but also his most perceptive critic, it came down to "just *hope*, which the people had long entertained, irrational and confused. Hope that—suddenly—something would change for the better."

Why Perestroika Failed

So what went wrong? Of course, for those who value democracy, civic freedoms, and nuclear disarmament, much went right. Still, Gorbachev aimed to reform communism, not to bury it. Until close to the end, the Soviet political and economic order had appeared stable—*too* stable. The challenge had seemed to be to shake things up, to awaken the spirit of innovation, to let in some fresh air. And then, under the gentle prodding of the country's most educated leader since Lenin, the whole structure had crumbled like a sand castle, burying the ideology of communism for good and scaring even advocates of the democratic left into global retreat.

After the fact, some argued that reforms failed because the system was unreformable. Communism, wrote the historian Martin Malia, was "an intrinsically nonviable, indeed impossible, project from the beginning." The Soviet order "collapsed like a house of cards . . . because it had always been a house of cards." However, if the Soviet system was so fragile, it is hard to understand how it lasted seventy-four years, through famines, war, nuclear confrontation, and leadership crises, as the country developed from an agricultural backwater into an industrialized superpower. The Soviet economy was inefficient. But many inefficient states and empires last a long time. Scholars have been criticized for failing to predict the collapse of the Soviet Union before 1985, but they were right not to predict its collapse. Before Gorbachev came to power, it was not collapsing.

Others attributed the Soviet demise to particular mistakes and character defects of its last leader. Gorbachev's orthodox communist critics held him personally responsible. In his memoir, Yegor Ligachev casts Gorbachev as the pawn of radical advisors such as Yakovlev, who kept Gorbachev rushing forward like an overloaded freight train, so concentrated on avoiding immediate crashes that he could not see where the rails were leading. Some put the point in even harsher terms. Nikolay Ryzhkov, the former prime minister, titled his memoirs *Perestroika—The Story of a Betrayal*. In Ryzhkov's view, Gorbachev led his country not to socialism with a human face, as he had promised, but to a savage form of capitalism.

From a different angle, many of Gorbachev's liberal critics also attribute his failure to personal weaknesses. Instead of his recklessness or treachery, they point to his indecisiveness, his love of political games, his romantic socialism, and his reluctance to see that the party he continued to praise would happily have confined him to a lunatic asylum. In Shevardnadze's view, Gorbachev simply "enjoyed maneuvering too much." From early on, Chernyaev, Yakovlev, even Medvedev and Georgy Shakhnazarov were pressing Gorbachev to coopt Yeltsin rather than attack him, to abandon the party and form an independent base of support in the state, to side with the democrats against bloodthirsty hard-liners, and to offer the Baltic separatists some civilized, realistic path to greater autonomy. They seem tortured in recollection by their inability to persuade him and by the thought of what might have been. "In the end," writes Chernyaev, "it was emotions, fear of risk, and an unwillingness to break with the old ways of ruling that won out."

What if, instead of punishing Yeltsin after his outburst at the 1987 plenum, Gorbachev had picked up the muddy gauntlet flung at his feet and promoted him? (Chernyaev counseled him at the time to keep Yeltsin on as Moscow party chief.) What if Gorbachev had out-Yeltsined Yeltsin, appealing to the public for support against the party bureaucrats, and had run for popular election as president in 1989? What if he had abandoned the old guard to found a party of democratic reform along with Sakharov, Yeltsin, and others? What if in 1987 or 1988 he had begun negotiating with the Balts and other republics on a new constitution for a decentralized federation? And what if he had appointed democrats rather than reactionaries to the key ministries in 1990 and introduced a program of radical economic reform?

Gorbachev would not hear of such things. Chernyaev says that in the later years he used to surreptitiously erase the phrase "the socialist choice" from Gorbachev's speeches, but Gorbachev would sneak it back in. He remained loyal not just to the ideas but to the party. By late 1989, it was clear to all that the communist elite could not stand him. At a plenum in December 1989, when Gorbachev threatened to resign, a stage whisper came from the audience: "It's high time!" At another plenum that month, when Gorbachev rejected demands to use force against the Lithuanians for fear of civilian casualties, a whisperer chimed in: "Enough blackmail! We're soooo scared! It's just the right time for you to leave!"

Gorbachev explained his stubborn attachment by saying that the party still had the power to reverse perestroika. In July 1990, after an afternoon of being crudely abused by provincial party hacks, Gorbachev exploded in front of Chernyaev.

"Self-interested scum, they don't want anything except a feeding-trough and power . . ." He swore at them in the foulest language. I replied: "To hell with them, Mikhail Sergeyevich. You're the president. You see what kind of Party this is. And [so long as you remain at its head] you'll be its hostage, its permanent whipping boy." He replied: "You know, Tolya, you think I don't see . . . But you must understand me, I can't let this lousy, rabid dog off the leash. If I do that, all this huge structure will be turned against me."

For his part, Gorbachev accepts some share of blame for the failure of perestroika, and also implicates the reactionary party bosses. But most insistently he blames the "excessive revolutionism" of the radical democrats and their leader. From October 1987, the Moscow intelligentsia's attacks on Gorbachev's foot-dragging always seemed to him to be spoken in Yeltsin's stentorian bass. His critics, he complained, were "muddying people's minds," "sowing confusion," and engaging in "Yeltsin-style babbling." In March 1990, when Gorbachev's interior minister, Vadim Bakatin, suggested that he set up a round table discussion with the leading democrats, Gorbachev reacted with scorn:

It seems that the minister is in a panic. . . . The idea of a "round table" is nonsense. . . . They don't represent anyone or anything. . . . All of them are political scoundrels . . . there's no trusting them and certainly no sitting down to a "round table"!

Twenty years later, Gorbachev was still bitter enough to say that his greatest mistake was not to have sent Yeltsin off "to gather citrus fruits in some banana republic." He apparently meant as an ambassador.

There are elements of truth in all these mutually conflicting accounts. Reading of Gorbachev's flirtations with those who would later betray him, the reader, knowing the ending, sometimes feels the urge to shake him awake. Still, he is right that, at least until 1990, the "lousy, rabid dog" could have turned on him and probably reversed his reforms. Nor is it fair to say he was a prisoner of ideology. While remaining loyal to the "idea of socialism," he stretched the meaning of the term like a piece of chewing gum until it had no clear content. Gorbachev is also right that Yeltsin and the democrats placed other goals ahead of preserving the Union. Even the communist critics have a point. Gorbachev and his aides did deliberately misrepresent their aims in order to get the assent of Politburo conservatives. Yakovlev later boasted of his deceptions: "The conditions required guile. . . . Someone had to walk in fire and wash in dung. Without this, reforms would not have advanced in Russia." And Gorbachev was proud of his maneuvering.

However, all these analyses overemphasize the details of how things went wrong and miss the importance of the context. Treachery, indecision, hypocrisy, and ambition are all quite common in politics, but they rarely cause regimes to collapse. Reviewing the economic, political, and sociological evidence twenty years later suggests a different focus.

Simply stated, the Soviet political and economic order died in 1991 because the vast majority of citizens had lost faith in it, and because those commanding the armed forces were not prepared to order a bloody crackdown and an at least temporary return to Stalinist repression. It was a close call, as we shall see. Some generals would happily have pulled the trigger, but they were not in charge. Yeltsin's criticisms of Gorbachev and demands for deeper reform were not—as Gorbachev thought—just the grandstanding of a vengeful egotist; they reflected public opinion. Support for communist rule evaporated during 1990, not because of the system's chronic inefficiency or inhumanity, but because of an extreme crisis in the consumer market that sparked fears of mass hunger. As they gave up on Gorbachev, citizens transferred their hopes and loyalties to new leaders—most notably, the elected Russian president—who felt that the people's trust and the Soviet government's abject failures gave them the right to determine policy. After this sea change in opinion, the Soviet leaders could only implement their decisions by force. Yet the depth of disaffection meant that even the military and security service generals could not be sure their orders would be obeyed.

A variety of evidence supports this account. In 1988, new, sociologically trained polling organizations began taking nationally representative surveys of the Soviet—and more often Russian—population. The most professional and widely respected was the All-Union Center for Public Opinion Research (VCIOM) headed by the sociologists Tatyana Zaslavskaya and later Yury Levada. Although some are skeptical about the quality of polls conducted in the Soviet Union, at least from 1989 the imperfections do not seem greater than those in other countries (see Chapter 7 for more on this point).

What do these polls show? First, that until late 1989 the Communist Party and Gorbachev personally still retained a great deal of support. That summer, two-thirds of respondents believed the party had the public's trust, in whole or in part, and 56 percent thought the influence of its Central Committee should increase or stay the same—more than twice as many as thought it should decrease. Gorbachev's personal rating was extremely high. In December 1989, 52 percent of Russians fully approved of his actions, and another 30 percent partly approved. The next month, 59 percent said they were completely or partly sure that perestroika would succeed. Popular backing for the communist order was not—as sometimes thought—undermined by decades of Stalinist repression and economic efficiency. As late as 1989, most Russians still seemed to blame the country's problems on corrupt individuals and a bureaucratic mentality rather than on the party itself.

But then during 1990 support for Gorbachev and communism crumbled. From 52 percent, the proportion of Russian respondents fully approving of Gorbachev's actions fell to just 15 percent in February 1991. Faith in the party crashed in parallel. The proportion who thought the party deserved to be trusted, either wholly or in part, plunged in the same period from 51 to 26 percent. Misgivings infected even the membership. In 1988, 18,000 party members left; in 1989, 137,000 turned in their cards. During 1990 and the first half of 1991, no fewer than 4.2 million members—almost one quarter of the total—reportedly quit.

What happened? Why did the public's confidence in the party and its leaders suddenly collapse in 1990, after surviving reasonably unscathed through the first revelatory years of glasnost? Several factors may have mattered, but one was crucial.

In 1990, for the first time since the start of perestroika, Russians' living standards fell sharply. In late 1989, about as many Russians said their family's material situation had improved in the previous two to three years as said it had worsened. But by December 1990, more than four times as many saw deterioration as saw improvement. Ninety-three percent said food supplies had worsened during the previous year, and 92 percent said the same about manufactured goods. Already by the summer, consumer riots were breaking out around the country. In Chelyabinsk, frustrated shoppers outside a wine store smashed bus windows and stormed a district council building. From Moscow to Sverdlovsk, smokers rioted and ransacked tobacco kiosks. Rationing, by then, had reached a "scale unprecedented in peacetime."

Frightened by the empty store shelves, Russians gravitated toward radical economic reform, leaving Gorbachev, with his ideological hairsplitting, far behind. By the fall of 1990, 73 percent favored privatizing small workshops, service firms, and stores and 87 percent supported privatizing farmland. By late 1991, as the crisis deepened, 74 percent of Russian respondents favored transition to a market economy—33 percent for rapid, 41 percent for gradual—while only 11 percent opposed it. Deserting Gorbachev, Russians transferred their hopes to his most vocal critic. In December 1989, only 27 percent of Russians fully supported Yeltsin. But as he stepped up attacks on Gorbachev, endorsed more radical economic reform, and championed the cause of striking coal miners, the total rose, hitting 70 percent in December. Asked in spring 1991 whether Gorbachev or Yeltsin was "closer to the people," 59 percent of Russians picked Yeltsin, compared to 16 percent for Gorbachev. By this time, Yeltsin was so close to the people he was standing on their toes.

If it was economic crisis—manifested in severe consumer shortages—that discredited Gorbachev and the party in 1990, what caused the consumer crisis? The chronic inefficiency of Soviet central planning did not help. However, while this can explain the slow decline in output, it does not account for the crisis that broke out in the late 1980s. There were four main causes. First, shifts in world commodity prices hit the Soviet economy hard. As agriculture stagnated, Moscow had taken to importing grain to feed the population, paying for it with dollars earned from oil and natural gas exports. However, between 1980 and 1989 the price of oil fell by more than 50 percent. Making matters worse, grain prices soared, rising by 56 percent between just 1987 and 1989. Desperate for dollars to import food, Gorbachev borrowed from Western banks, increasing Soviet foreign debt from $29 billion in 1985 to $97 billion in late 1991, and ruining the country's credit rating. By 1990, German banks would lend to Moscow only with a full guarantee from the German government.

Second, as Gorbachev let the East European satellites go free, the framework of coercive trade among the communist countries broke down. While Russia ultimately stood to benefit—it had been providing energy at a fraction of the world price to Eastern Europe, and being paid in overpriced machinery—the immediate effect was a drastic collapse in trade.

Within Russia, perestroika destroyed the machinery of central coordination before markets could fill the gap. Once enterprises were free to choose what to produce, none could rely upon their previous suppliers. Partial reforms left million-dollar loopholes for quick thinkers to exploit. The cooperatives, free to set their own prices, could earn enormous margins buying materials cheaply from state enterprises and auctioning them on the market. Decentralizing power to local governments set off a "bacchanalia of local protection," in the words of Yeltsin's economic adviser Yegor Gaidar, as regional populists responded to shortages by blocking shipments of goods outside their borders.

Fourth, even more damaging was the authorities' mismanagement of fiscal and monetary policy. Letting workers elect their managers produced a wage explosion which the state then had to fund. In 1989, the budget deficit reached 12 percent of GDP. By 1991, it was estimated at 30 percent. To finance this, the government simply spent the public's accumulated savings with no means of repaying them. It borrowed from the banks, and in 1991 simply appropriated $6 billion from the hard currency accounts of citizens and firms in Vneshekonombank, including Gorbachev's own book royalties, apparently without his knowledge. And, increasingly, it turned to the printing press. The amount of cash in circulation doubled between the end of 1985 and the end of 1990, and then doubled again in the first nine months of 1991.

With prices fixed, this flood of rubles exacerbated consumer shortages. As too much money chased too few goods, store shelves were picked clean. In April 1991, only 12 percent of Russians said they had seen meat in the stores, 6 percent had seen flour or vegetable oil, and 3 percent had seen adults' clothes. Even the ubiquitous ration coupons were rarely honored: only 14 percent said they could freely exchange their coupons for goods. Queues were atrocious. The average urban family spent almost twelve hours a week shopping. In 1991, republic governments—led by Yeltsin's Russia—started cutting remittances of tax revenue to the center. By mid-1991, the Soviet state was essentially bankrupt.

In short, it was not the inherent inefficiency of central planning that caused the Soviet economic system to implode and the public to give up on communism. It was the combination of difficult external conditions—the drop in oil prices and collapse in trade—with misguided reforms that undermined coordination, destroyed the value of the ruble, and emptied the stores of vital goods. Could this have been avoided? Between 1985 and 1987, a determined stabilization would probably have succeeded. If in response to the plummeting oil price Soviet leaders had cut investment and spending on imported machinery, increased revenues, and raised prices to absorb the much smaller monetary overhang that then existed, they could have bought some breathing space. Such measures would have been unpopular, but at that time the authorities had the means to control protest. After stabilization, they could have streamlined the planning mechanism, or even transitioned to free markets in more auspicious macroeconomic circumstances similar to those faced by most of the East European countries.

Gorbachev was warned many times about the looming macroeconomic explosion. His aides repeatedly urged him to introduce price and monetary reforms—Ryzhkov in April 1987, Medvedev in August 1987, Ligachev in January 1990. Ryzhkov considered it his greatest mistake not to have insisted. Gorbachev typically replied that it was "too early." Then, when in spring 1989 the U.S. secretary of state, James Baker, raised the subject, Gorbachev told him his country was "about twenty years late with price reform" so "two or three more years won't make any difference." It was left to Gorbachev's successor to restore macroeconomic stability in the worst possible conditions.

By 1988–89, it was too late to stabilize without major disruption. Had Gorbachev joined forces with Yeltsin behind the "500 Day" plan in late 1990, the shock that accompanied liberalization might have been slightly less painful. If prices had been freed then, their initial jump would have been smaller. But the political consequences would have been similar. Gorbachev and Yeltsin would together have confronted the eruption of discontent that Yeltsin later faced alone. Or the putschists of August 1991 might have struck earlier, with similarly polarizing effects, provoking the Union's disintegration.

Consumer shortages and public unhappiness do not always lead regimes to collapse. This depends on people's expectations, the ability of protesters to organize, and, especially, on the capacity and readiness of the leadership to use force. Perhaps the strangest aspect of the Soviet demise is the failure of the men in epaulettes to prevent it. In 1985, the Soviet military was the largest in the world, almost six million strong including the KGB and Interior Ministry forces as well as the army, navy, and air force. It boasted more than seven thousand generals and admirals. Gorbachev's reforms attacked the prestige and corporate interests of those in uniform and were deeply unpopular with many of them. From 1989, Gorbachev cut defense procurement by 30 percent a year. He gave up the East European satellites without a fight. He refused to strike hard against the Baltic separatists. "The army is no longer with you," the hardline colonel, Viktor Alksnis, yelled at Gorbachev during a meeting in November 1990. But the generals never intervened to remove him until August 1991, and then only in a putsch so disorganized and ambivalent it struck some as a parody.

Why was there no counterattack? The Soviet military's strong tradition of subordination to civilian leadership created an initial hurdle. Concern that the army could lose prestige and cohesion by stepping into politics may have outweighed the fear of losing corporate and geopolitical interests. Then, in a mostly unintended manner, Gorbachev's flirtations and hesitations—encouraging plans for force, then drawing back at the last minute to provide deniability—may have so confused and enervated the armed forces that they lost the ability to act. At moments, such as late 1990, the hard-liners may have genuinely believed Gorbachev was leaning towards imposing martial law. Even on August 18, the plotters thought it possible Gorbachev would join their coup. In an odd way, the halfhearted, demoralizing, aborted operations in Vilnius and elsewhere may have inoculated the system against successful praetorian intervention. Officers lower down the command chain watched as their peers became scapegoats each time force was used against civilians.

Then, there were the personal divisions among the hard-liners, who lacked a charismatic leader. As became clear during the coup, the reactionaries Gorbachev had promoted—Kryuchkov, Pugo, Pavlov, Yanayev, even Yazov—were not well respected within their own organizations, let alone the country. They could not even stand each other. Yazov had laughed at his fellow conspirators, or so his wife tearfully reminded him after he joined their ranks. Yanayev and Pavlov—whom Yazov once called a "drunk prostitute"—were viewed as buffoons. The level of mutual distrust was staggering. During the coup, the KGB even bugged the conversations of its "own" vice president, Yanayev. An attempt to impose military rule threatened to split the armed forces. Had the putsch not ended when it did, it could have developed into civil war. Shaposhnikov, the Air Force commander, says he considered sending planes to bomb the Kremlin if the conspirators ordered troops to storm the White House. Whether or not Shaposhnikov would have done this, Yazov knew by the third day that high- and mid-level officers were resisting and even disobeying orders.

Another reason for the armed forces' caution was the bleak situation they would inherit after a military coup. They had no idea how to halt the economic free fall. Even if they managed to restore order, grain shipments and credits from the West would no doubt stop, and then what? In August 1991, the putschists wanted to fill the stores with food to buy the public's support, but the army strategic reserve would only feed the army itself for a few days. William Odom asked Soviet lieutenant general Leonid Ivashov why he and his colleagues had not intervened before August 1991 to overthrow Gorbachev. "We tried," Ivashov replied, "but we had no leader. We begged Yazov to lead a coup, but he always asked, 'What will we do with the power if we take it?'" It was not an easy question to answer.

From 1990 on, the armed forces had to contend with the likelihood of resistance from Yeltsin and the Russian government. Especially in 1991, the difficulties were increased by Yeltsin's astute efforts to build his own base of support within the armed forces. He got permission to install a twenty-person staff within the Lubyanka building as the kernel of a Russian KGB. Just months before the coup, Yeltsin had visited the Tula airborne troops division for a vodka-fueled lunch with the commander, Pavel Grachev, who would later play a crucial role in the August days.

The coup itself has puzzled many observers. General Aleksandr Lebed, who was sent with a batallion to "defend the Supreme Soviet," was so shocked by the chaos and improvisation that he thought it some kind of farcical provocation. To the former Polish leader, General Jaruzelski, who knew a thing or two about coups, the action showed "extraordinary amateurism." From a military standpoint, the operations necessary to impose order posed no great challenge. The battle-hardened Afghan veterans of the KGB and army special forces had studied and practiced similar actions many times. Viktor Karpukhin, the leader of the KGB's A7 or "Alfa" unit, later said his men had infiltrated the White House and could have shot Yeltsin at any moment. The barricades outside, said Karpukhin, were "like toys" that could have been crushed in "fifteen minutes at the most." Two years later in the crisis of October 1993, it took only a few tank shells to flush a straggle of defiant Supreme Soviet deputies out of the White House.

The coup's actual execution was another story. The conspirators deployed KGB troops in the woods around Yeltsin's dacha, but apparently did not order his arrest. Later, they did not cut water, power, or telephone lines to the White House or even cordon it off effectively. Reporters could wander in and out. Even Diane Sawyer, the American television journalist, turned up in Yeltsin's office to record a corny interview. The putschists' use of television was almost comically inept. Their press conference on the first day projected the image of a clique of indecisive bureaucrats, unable to intimidate even a hall of journalists, who asked probing questions and laughed out loud at their lies. On the evening news, the main Soviet television channel broadcast footage of Yeltsin standing on a tank and denouncing the coup. The tanks sent into Moscow stopped politely at traffic lights. General Lebed found that no one at the Defense Ministry had even drawn up a plan for the proposed storming of the White House. The Deputy Minister asked if Lebed could sketch one on a piece of paper, but was irritated when Lebed asked to know what troops could be used.

When coffee tastes bad, that may be because it is actually tea. The best explanation for this apparent bungling is that the military coup was not initially meant to be a military coup. The conspirators hoped for Gorbachev's support or at least tacit complicity. They thought the public, weary of chaos and disillusioned with Gorbachev, would rally behind them. They did not arrest Yeltsin, anticipating that he would discredit himself through his speeches; they could arrest him later quite legally after he had broken the law on states of emergency. They may also have hoped that Yeltsin's dislike of Gorbachev would prove stronger than his distaste for the putschists. The plotters meant to legalize their action by getting the USSR Supreme Soviet to ratify the transfer of presidential powers to Vice President Yanayev. Only on the second day did they realize they probably could not get the two-thirds of votes necessary for this. The plan was to intimidate opponents by putting tanks in the street, while gradually weeding radical democrats out of positions of power. Something similar had worked in Prague in 1968, and it was not crazy to imagine it might work in the USSR. Most of the country did not rise up in support of Gorbachev or Yeltsin. One promise of the putschists—to provide all urban residents with plots of land to grow vegetables—was genuinely popular. On the first day, no significant demonstrations or strikes occurred around the country. The coup's leaders thought they were winning.

When a few days later Marshal Yazov, in his isolation cell, got a chance to listen to the radio, he was shocked by how badly he had misread public opinion:

> I understood how far I was from the people. The view I had formed about the collapse of the state, about poverty—I supposed that the people shared it. No, the people did not accept the Appeal [from the Emergency Committee]. The people are politicized, felt freedom, and we supposed the exact opposite. I became a toy in the hands of political schemers [*politikanov*]!

By the middle of the second day, the soft option no longer seemed viable. The coup leaders were losing the initiative. They now had to arrest Yeltsin to convince the public they were in control. But the White House defenses made this impossible without significant bloodshed. At this point, the coup ran into resistance, or more often delaying tactics, from some in the second and third echelons of the military.

General Pavel Grachev, commander of Airborne Forces, had been "tacking between the army leadership and the Russian government," as he put it, ever since Yeltsin phoned him from his dacha on the first morn-

ing. On the afternoon of the second day, he and Shaposhnikov decided
they would not obey orders to storm the White House if such orders
came, and General Boris Gromov, Pugo's deputy in the Ministry of Internal Affairs, agreed to do the same. In the KGB's "Alfa" unit, Karpukhin
was prepared to order an attack. But his men were uneasy, perhaps anticipating major civilian casualties, perhaps because they expected to suffer heavy losses themselves from the armed defenders. When Karpukhin
asked his commander to come and brief the troops in person, he was
relieved of his command.

Why did the second echelon resist? In a sense, the coup was just
another round in the high-stakes poker game. Each officer had to guess,
minute by minute, who would come out on top, and position himself to be on the winning side. The leaders' disorganization and apparent incompetence made them look like losers. At the press conference,
Yanayev's shaking hands betrayed his nervousness, and the chaos that
officers such as Lebed glimpsed in the Defense Ministry raised doubts.
The mid-level generals feared that yet again their leaders would scape-
goat them if the operation proved unpopular.

The putschists could still have found a unit to do the dirty work. Had
General Varennikov, the mastermind of the Vilnius operation, been in
Yazov's place, he would not have flinched. "They were too naïve," he said
later of the coup's leaders, "not firm enough." But Yazov, realizing the
extent of potential bloodshed and the likelihood of splitting the army,
ordered his troops to withdraw. He must also have wondered why he had
not heeded his own question to Ivashov. What a hopeless mess would
confront them the day after Yeltsin's resistance was crushed. Blood in
the streets, total collapse of the economy, a cupboard bare of reserves,
the hatred of most of the population—and to face all this with this junta
of nonentities—the quivering Yanayev, the raving Pavlov, the devious
Kryuchkov, and the bloodthirsty Varennikov! "I am an old fool," he said.

Columbus

Since Gorbachev's departure, a flood of memoirs by his associates and
rivals have told and retold the minutiae of his almost seven years in
power. From this torrent of words, an all too human figure emerges,

alternately inspiring and aggravating, articulate and prickly, gregarious yet not good at friendship, a workaholic with a tenacious memory, gifted at tactical maneuvers, prone to petty jealousy, yet, despite all his faults, sincerely well intentioned. He could be perversely obtuse, as when an old man in Norilsk complained about dangerous waste left for years in the street where children played, and Gorbachev told him he should "give the authorities a harder shake." But he wanted the best for his country.

And, though he flirted with the hard-liners, he drew back repeatedly from the use of force. It just did not come naturally to him. "They say we need to thump our fists," he once told associates, clenching his hand to demonstrate. "Generally speaking, we could do that. But I don't feel like it [*ne khochetsya*]." "I was never afraid of him, even when he shouted," wrote Vitaly Korotich, the editor of the glasnost flagship magazine *Ogonyok*, "because his shout was never the shout of a cruel and all-powerful person. I always tried to understand, what does the shout mean, why does the scenario call on him at exactly this moment to shout." Korotich viewed most of the public scoldings as acts, brilliantly performed, to placate the cultural conservatives on the Politburo. Glancing at the leading Politburo liberal, Aleksandr Yakovlev, during one such outburst, he saw the latter's eyes were calm, as though he were watching "the televised replay of a game, the result of which he already knew."

Like a good captain, Gorbachev stayed with his ship until the end. Steering between right and left, proud of his skill at avoiding the sandbars, he did not notice where the current was taking him until too late. He thought the destination was a humane form of socialism. But as he drifted further and further, he found himself destroying the system he had meant to save, opening the way for a market economy and multiparty democracy. Had he abandoned the communist ship earlier, he could not have wrecked it so thoroughly. To the economist Nikolay Petrakov, Gorbachev was like Christopher Columbus "who discovered America but to the end of his days believed it was India. Like Columbus, Gorbachev did something marvelous but only found out afterwards what it was."

In the process, he aged. To quote Korotich again:

Not so much every year but every month that he was in power, the young Komsomol plushness, the deliberate exaltation, went out of

him, but pain was rising inside him, gradually rendering Gorbachev
ever tougher and more selfless. It seems to me he experienced the
satisfaction of a major sportsman, thinking how to go as far as possible. Thus, an American football player tears along, knowing that
he will be stopped and that it will be painful: a powerful defender
is already on his way. But the next skirmish will already be closer
to the opposite line; on the way to it, he will probably be knocked
down again more than once.

The game had to end. The future mayor of Moscow, Yury Luzhkov, visited Gorbachev in the Kremlin shortly after the August coup, and noticed
that he had lost the old charm—"that latent, demonic cheerfulness that
previously hid behind every phrase and served as subtext to every conversation, suppressing his interlocutor's ability to object."

Finally, no longer welcome in the Kremlin, Gorbachev became less a
man than a trademark. The familiar *naevus flammeus* front right of the
scalp flickered in ads for Pizza Hut and Louis Vuitton. He settled into the
usual pastimes of celebrities—cameo appearances in a film or two, char-
ity work, directing a personal foundation, memoirs, opinion columns.
Against his wife Raisa's advice—against everyone's advice—he ran for
Russian president in 1996, endured the hecklers, and won 0.5 percent of
the vote. And in the lengthening gaps between the interviews and travels,
there was time to replay repeatedly the tapes of history.

In a lucid moment of despair, Gorbachev told his faithful aide
Chernyaev: "All revolutions end in failure, although they change the
country, and some—the whole world." Gorbachev may come to be seen
as history's most successful failure.

CHAPTER 2

The Natural

W ith slow, deliberate steps, Boris Yeltsin, Russia's first democratic politician, makes for the crowd. Stamped on his face is a smile that manages to be both confident and opaque, expansive and reserved. It is 1996—or is it 1991, or 1990, or 1989? The country's fate depends on whether this man can connect to the mass of ordinary Russians in front of him, the grandmothers in headscarves, the men with missing teeth, their children on their shoulders. They love him or they hate him. But they are here for him. They have come to yell something out, to reach for his hand. He is focused, in his element, doing this thing he does the best, practicing the art he has introduced into Russia, more subversive than Western jazz or pornographic movies—the art of the electoral campaign.

From such meetings with the people, he will write, he draws a vital strength. This is his communion, his wine and holy wafer. He listens, jokes, promises, stretches out to shake and touch, conjuring their smiles, their faith that something will be better tomorrow, a sad faith because they know at the same time that nothing will be better tomorrow, but the faith connects them to this man, this hulk of battered flesh, six foot two and 227 pounds, his shock of white hair ruffled by the breeze. For an hour they will bask in his belief that he can make things happen.

The Siberian

One night in 1934, uniformed men appeared in the Yeltsins' drafty barracks room. Boris, aged three, was woken by the commotion. He fell back to sleep in his mother's arms, echoing her sobs without knowing why. It would be three years before he saw his father again. Nikolay Yeltsin, a carpenter, had helped the local branch of Stalin's secret police fulfill its monthly quota for arresting anti-Soviet agitators.

Many decades later, his son, now president, would hold the yellowing case file in his hand, inspect its fading purple ink, its crumbling onionskin pages with their misspelled denunciations, and remember that spring night. Repression had already scattered the Yeltsin clan across the Urals. Before the 1917 Revolution, one of Boris's grandfathers had owned a watermill and a blacksmith's forge. The other, a house builder, had been successful enough to hire assistants. Under Stalin, such enterprise was punished. Both grandfathers were run out of the village and exiled to a desolate northern settlement.

The Yeltsins were descended from Old Believers, a sect of religious purists who split from the Orthodox Church after Patriarch Nikon reformed the liturgy in the 1650s. To escape persecution, many had fled into Siberia, much as, a little later, Huguenot communities had disappeared into the mountains of southern France. Ascetic and fiercely self-reliant, the Old Believers had an almost Puritan ethos that emphasized hard work, individual strength, and social conservatism. They crossed themselves with two fingers instead of three and did not shave their beards. Smoking was considered a sin and swearing was not tolerated.

By the late 1930s, Nikolay Yeltsin, back from the labor camps, had moved the family to the town of Berezniki, near Perm on the Urals' western foothills. Unlike Gorbachev, the young Yeltsin did not experience German occupation during World War II. But food was scarce. His mother later recalled how the ten-year-old Boris would sit in the corner of the family's room after school, moaning inconsolably: "I'm hu-u-u-u-ngry, I ca-a-a-an't take it." The family goat served as Yeltsin's radiator.

In the first installment of his memoirs, published in 1990 as he ran for parliament, the young Yeltsin appears as a mischievous prankster. In fact, his account consists mostly of tricks and escapades—inciting his class to jump out of a window before the teacher arrived, placing sharp objects on her chair, leading treks through the woods, joining gang rumbles, in one of which his nose was broken. During the War, he stole into an ammunition dump and tried to discover how a hand grenade worked by striking its fuse with a hammer. He lost the thumb and index finger on his left hand.

After high school, Yeltsin studied civil engineering in the industrial city of Sverdlovsk (now Yekaterinburg). Between classes, he captained the volleyball team and courted his future wife Naina. He stayed in Sverdlovsk after graduation, working his way up from foreman to boss of the city construction trust. Surprising his subordinates, Yeltsin insisted on learning all aspects of the job, from bricklaying and carpentry to concrete mixing and crane operation: his first year passed in a series of apprenticeships. At thirty, he joined the party, a prerequisite for further promotion, and was recruited into its local organization. Yeltsin threw himself into party work, he wrote, as he had once thrown himself into striking a volleyball. Seven years later, he was picked to head the regional party committee's construction department, supervising all builders in the province. Having impressed his superiors with his ability to get jobs done, he was promoted in 1976 to first secretary of Sverdlovsk Oblast—the regional party boss.

Although respecting the taboos of the time, Yeltsin proved quite an unusual provincial leader. Zealous, exacting, hungry for recognition, he was a workaholic who relished pushing himself and his subordinates to the limits of physical endurance. Resolving to visit all the province's sixty-three towns once every two years, he wore his helicopter pilot out with endless trips into the sticks. Like any good Communist, he could grovel on demand. Brezhnev's "brilliant and deep" speech at the 1976 party plenum earned Yeltsin's adulation, and he commended the general secretary on his seventieth birthday for his "wisdom, giant talent for organization, human charm and bubbling energy." Were such exaggerated bootlicking not common practice, one might have thought this an ironic joke. The old man was not yet quite the walking corpse he would become, but the "bubbling energy" was hard for most to detect.

However, while genuflecting to the Moscow gerontocracy, Yeltsin brought a new tone to administration in Sverdlovsk—one of more open communication and well-publicized responsiveness to local concerns. He used television adeptly and appeared for unscripted question-and-answer sessions with the public, revealing a respect for ordinary people that was completely foreign at the time. In small ways, he expanded the

limits of freedom. As one Sverdlovsk native put it, he "loosened the cor-
set a bit."

By 1985, when Gorbachev became general secretary, Yeltsin had a
reputation as a hard-driving but popular provincial party boss. Ignoring some colleagues who cautioned him about Yeltsin's personality, Gorbachev brought him to Moscow to serve first in the party secretariat, and
then from December 1985 as the Moscow city party chief, replacing a
corrupt Brezhnev crony. With this position, Yeltsin became a candidate
member of the Politburo.

Moscow consisted of two parallel worlds. It was home to the Communist aristocracy, the families of top party and state officials, who
existed in a cocoon of privilege, with their chauffeured cars, special
stores and clinics, elite schools, country dachas, Black Sea vacation
resorts, superior housing, and nepotistic networks to haul up the next
generation. Meanwhile, around them the metropolis was crumbling.
Dingy apartment blocks stretched for miles on the outskirts, their
plumbing corroding, their vandalized entryways reeking of urine. The
public transit system was overloaded and dangerous, the retail trade
network rife with corruption, waste, and shortages. The city's future
mayor, Yury Luzhkov, got his first look at Moscow's vegetable warehouses around this time. "Permanent filth, stench, mold, rats, flies,
cockroaches," he recalled, "it seemed there was no vermin that could
not find a haven there."

Yeltsin turned to the techniques tested in Sverdlovsk. He held public
meetings, visited all corners of the city. To hear what ordinary Muscovites had to say, he took trips on the subway or waited outside factory
gates to meet the morning shift. He implored his subordinates to break
out of "the paper prison of bureaucracy, the spider's web of directives."
Throughout, he paid attention to his popularity, taking a television crew
with him on his jaunts. At the same time, he pushed glasnost as far as
Gorbachev's elastic would stretch. Insisting that "two half-truths do not
make the truth," he encouraged hard-hitting investigative reporting and
permitted grassroots groups to organize.

As in Sverdlovsk, Yeltsin worked punishing hours himself and
demanded similar exertion from subordinates, scolding and firing
officials to energize the others. But facing an entrenched and haughty

bureaucratic class, he went much further. He replaced the city's long-serving mayor, and 40 percent of the party committee. Not only did he fire twenty-three of the city's thirty-three ward chiefs, he humiliated them: the newspaper *Moskovskaya Pravda* published details of their shortcomings. He ordered closed many of the redundant research institutes that had sprung up around the city to provide jobs for the intelligentsia, and even told the scientists to take requalification exams, threatening them with factory jobs if they failed.

Amid the tedium of Soviet life, Yeltsin was an incandescent figure, indefatigable, peremptory, in love with theatrical gestures, and often funny. "We hear that Yeltsin travels by Metro, but we haven't seen you," a questioner complained in one of his public jaw sessions. "Well, I haven't seen you either," he shot back. Social justice became his trademark theme. In a country that had "abolished class distinctions," he found four cafeterias in one Moscow enterprise catering to different categories of workers, each with a different quality of food. Corruption was everywhere. "We are scooping and scooping and scooping the mud," he said in April 1986, "but we still do not see the bottom of this dirty well." At his behest, eight hundred store directors were arrested.

Yet, despite his exertion, Yeltsin's campaigns had almost no effect on the city's management. Life did not improve for most Muscovites. In part, the bureaucrats sabotaged his efforts; in part, they were overwhelmed by the nationwide economic slump. In any case, it was naïve to think that replacing the most incompetent and venal officeholders or humiliating them into trying harder would cure the system's deep dysfunctions. It was a mistake he would make repeatedly.

To his Politburo colleagues, Yeltsin seemed uncouth. Alternately sulky and abrasive, he appeared to have no concept of teamwork, no sense of appropriate time and place. Gorbachev wavered between a kind of patronizing mentorship—if only the yokel could learn to behave, he might become an asset to perestroika—and fury at the uninvited interruptions. The bureaucrats Yeltsin targeted found a defender in Yegor Ligachev, the party's personnel chief, who thought the Moscow purges excessive. As pressures on Yeltsin mounted, as other Politburo members poked sticks in his wheels, and as Gorbachev found ways to snub him, he came to feel isolated and irritated by the deferential atmosphere of Gorbachev's circle. The fuse was lit to the bomb that would explode in the October 1987 confrontation described in Chapter 1.

After his challenge to Gorbachev and public whipping, Yeltsin sank into months of depression. His heart felt like a "burned-out cinder." In his office at the Construction Ministry, where Gorbachev had found him a job, he spent afternoons staring at the silent phone. But then letters started coming, at first a trickle, then a flood, from Sverdlovsk and elsewhere, urging him to keep his spirits up, not to give in. The family piled them into a wooden crate. Soon the Sverdlovsk post offices had to put up signs: "Letters to Boris Yeltsin will not be forwarded."

By the summer of 1988 when Gorbachev called a party conference, Yeltsin felt confident enough to demand to speak, practically storming the podium when Gorbachev tried to trick him into leaving the hall. He lambasted the "hungry nomenklatura," with its "millionaire bribe takers," and, in a clever gambit, asked to be rehabilitated "in his lifetime." Gorbachev—who had just rehabilitated several famous Communists from the 1930s—could either take him back and be eclipsed or refuse and show the party meant to accord its members freedom of speech only posthumously. Gorbachev chose hypocrisy over danger. Loyalists were given the floor to attack the troublemaker. This time, parts of the proceedings were televised, and Yeltsin's popularity soared.

Then, as Gorbachev unlocked the door to competitive elections, Yeltsin was ready to barge through. Nominated by more than fifty districts, Yeltsin ran for the new Soviet parliament—the Congress of People's Deputies—from Moscow, and won with almost 90 percent of the vote. There followed the electrifying, nationally broadcast first session of the Congress—ten days in which Russians hardly left their television sets. By its end, the reformist Interregional Deputies Group had emerged, led by Yeltsin, the dissident physicist Andrey Sakharov, and three others. The next year, Yeltsin ran for the new 1,068–member *Russian* Congress of People's Deputies, and won by a landslide. After some intrigue, he was elected by the deputies to the smaller, regularly meeting Supreme Soviet, and, by just four votes, chosen as its chairman. (Together, the Congress and the Supreme Soviet constituted Russia's parliament.) That summer, Yeltsin made his final break with communism, returning his party card at the party congress, and striding out of the hall to shouts of "Shame!"

"Only Yeltsin, with his animal instinct, heard the distant thunder of history," Gorbachev's aide Anatoly Chernyaev noted with sneaking admiration. "He's decisive if nothing else."

As the store shelves emptied and Gorbachev dithered, Yeltsin demanded radical economic reform. Gorbachev approved but then rejected the ambitious "500 Days" program that leading economists had drafted. Yeltsin embraced it. As chairman of the Russian parliament, Yeltsin pushed for and won constitutional amendments to create a Russian presidency. In the summer of 1991, running on a platform of radical economic measures against four Communists and a demagogic ultra-nationalist, Yeltsin won with 57 percent of the vote.

Riven by internal conflicts, the Soviet state was drifting towards dissolution. In a mansion at Novo-Ogaryovo, the six republic leaders who still accepted Gorbachev's invitations patched together a treaty for a loose federal union (see Chapter 5). On August 19, the junta of grey-faced reactionaries struck. For three glorious and terrible days, Yeltsin became the personification of Russia, standing with grim resolve against those who threatened to plunge the country into an "eternal night" of "terror and dictatorship." Then, as the Soviet state crumpled in the autumn months, Yeltsin's lieutenants scrambled to take possession of the key ministries and grab the levers of administration.

To lead the government, he chose a thirty-five-year-old economist, Yegor Gaidar, who, together with a team of young scholars, had been developing a blueprint for radical reform (see Chapter 6). The planned economy was disintegrating, and both Yeltsin and Gaidar were sure only a rapid move to market exchange would motivate producers to supply food and other goods. Hunger threatened as the state's grain stocks dwindled. On October 28, in a speech to the Russian Congress, Yeltsin outlined his plans for a complete transformation of the economy, including the freeing of prices, tough monetary policy to stabilize the ruble, and the privatization of enterprises. Change would be painful, he warned, but, in words that would haunt him, he promised some improvement by the end of 1992.

Given subsequent events it is hard to believe but the Congress supported Yeltsin's program almost unanimously. Its new chairman, Ruslan Khasbulatov, told his colleagues: "We should create for the president a free legal field of activity, constrain neither the president nor the government, and adopt the necessary laws so that the executive power can decisively advance the deepest economic reform." The deputies voted for Yeltsin's proposal by 876 to 16, and authorized Yeltsin for a year to issue decrees that would supercede laws, to appoint and suspend regional governors (who were supposed to be elected), and to serve himself as both president and prime minister, investing his authority in the reforms. The parliament accepted the entire package of Yeltsin's economic decrees in November. Even Gorbachev, who had shrunk from such reforms himself and who would soon turn caustic critic, approved. "The main thing is that he found the courage to speed up reform," he told his press secretary Andrey Grachev. "That's not easy, and it's important that he has decided on this."

In December, Yeltsin met the leaders of Belarus and Ukraine in the Belovezha Forest in Belarus (see Chapter 5). Together, they signed an agreement dissolving the Soviet Union and creating a loose Commonwealth of Independent States. By the end of the year, Yeltsin had lowered the red flag from the Kremlin's flagpole, sent Gorbachev packing, and occupied his Kremlin office.

In Command

Yeltsin had barely dispatched Gorbachev to think tank purgatory when a new conflict split the Russian elite. The next two years would see relentless feuding between president and parliament. Khasbulatov, the Congress's chairman, was an economics professor of Chechen descent who had served as Yeltsin's deputy. An undistinguished academic, whose articles Gaidar, as editor of the journal *Kommunist*, had rejected as banal, Khasbulatov had risen to the top only with Yeltsin's vigorous backing. As chairman, he revealed a Florentine grasp of political intrigue. Offended at not being made prime minister himself and sensing the points to be scored channeling economic discontent, he set out to lead opposition to his former patron.

Ten days after reforms began, Khasbulatov demanded the government's replacement. He found a kindred spirit in Yeltsin's own vice president, the Afghan War hero Aleksandr Rutskoy, whose dashing mustaches

Yeltsin had hoped would woo the female vote. On a tour of Siberia, Rutskoy mocked Gaidar's "scholarly boys in pink shorts" and promised to resign if price reform was not abandoned. It was not the last promise he would break.

The ostensible reason for the rift was disagreement over economic policy. From January 1992, Gaidar began implementing the program Yeltsin had presented in October. Prices were unfrozen; private trade became legal; restrictions on foreign trade were reduced. State stores and other small firms were auctioned to private bidders, and in late 1992 the government began privatizing the country's 14,000 large enterprises, under a program organized by Gaidar's colleague Anatoly Chubais.

Despite initially supporting these measures, Khasbulatov and the other parliament leaders now struck a populist pose. Representing the lobbies of the old Soviet economy—the collective farm managers, enterprise directors, and state bureaucrats—they called for cheap credit and industrial subsidies, along with generous social spending—in short, the policies that, under Gorbachev, had undermined the budget, emptied consumer markets, and lit the fuse to hyperinflation. Gaidar resisted, knowing a further collapse of the ruble would harm the very groups the parliament claimed to protect (see Chapter 6).

Behind the disputes over economic policy lay a bare-knuckled fight for power. Little by little, Khasbulatov consolidated control within the parliament and used its extensive prerogatives to sap Yeltsin's authority. He built a pyramid of patronage, distributing Moscow apartments, desirable committee assignments, places on foreign delegations, and other perks among the deputies. A network of informers updated him on who was and who was not loyal. To isolate the executive, he forged informal alliances with the heads of regional legislatures as well as the chief justice of the Constitutional Court, Valery Zorkin.

In April 1992 when the Congress convened, Khasbulatov was ready to strike. Sensing public anger at falling wages and the erosion of savings (which plunged in value as the flood of money printed in Gorbachev's last years sent prices soaring), he sought to repeal Yeltsin's emergency powers and reverse the reforms. The whole government threatened to resign, and, afraid to take responsibility, Khasbulatov retreated. Still, conscious of his falling rating, Yeltsin began compromising. In May, he replaced some of Gaidar's reformers with industrial managers. Bowing to the oil lobby, he postponed freeing energy prices, allowing insiders to continue exploiting the huge gap between domestic and world prices. In December, when the Congress refused to confirm Gaidar as prime minister, Yeltsin chose Viktor Chernomyrdin, a canny veteran of the Soviet gas industry, to lead the government.

With reforms blocked by the parliament, Yeltsin tried to reach over its head to the Russian people. In return for his surrender of Gaidar, the Congress had promised to hold a referendum the following April on a new draft constitution. By January 1993, Khasbulatov had changed his mind. The existing constitution, which gave supreme power to the parliament, was, in his view, already "truly democratic." At its next session in March 1993, the Congress reneged.

A week later, on March 20, Yeltsin went on television to announce he had introduced a "special form of rule" and that a referendum would be held on April 25. The Constitutional Court immediately ruled this unconstitutional. Under the patched and darned 1978 Russian charter, the president had no right to call referenda or impose undefined "special" regimes. The Congress quickly voted on a motion to impeach Yeltsin, but fell seventy-two votes short of the required two-thirds majority. The next day, Khasbulatov agreed to compromise and hold a referendum, but with new questions drafted by the parliament: on confidence in the president, confidence in his social and economic policies, and whether to hold early presidential or parliamentary elections.

Yeltsin's democratic supporters campaigned tirelessly. The referendum's results shocked Khasbulatov and his allies. Of the 65 percent of eligible voters who participated, 59 percent expressed confidence in Yeltsin and 53 percent even supported his social and economic policies. Fifty percent approved an early presidential election and 67 percent an early legislative one (these questions were not binding because a majority of the electorate, not just of those voting, was required). The opposition's revenge came a few days later when, during a May Day demonstration, thugs in the crowd brutally attacked the police. About sixty people were injured, twenty-five policemen were hospitalized, and one died.

Many of Yeltsin's supporters thought he should exploit the referendum victory to dissolve the Congress and call new elections. His aide

Georgy Satarov would later say that not doing so was "a colossal omission." But Yeltsin still sought a compromise. That summer, he invited regional leaders, legal experts, heads of parties, and representatives of social organizations to the Kremlin to draft a new basic law, combining alternate versions prepared by the president's aides and the Supreme Soviet's Constitutional Commission. Khasbulatov, whose speech was heckled, walked out angrily and would not return, but many parliamentary deputies remained. Still, at the end of the summer the Kremlin's and Supreme Soviet's drafts remained far apart.

Khasbulatov's confidence and ambitions were growing. He had taken personal control of the Supreme Soviet Guard, and, assisted by a former KGB deputy chairman, Filipp Bobkov, and one of the 1991 coup organizers, General Vladislav Achalov, he turned it into a five-thousand-man force. He sent this Guard to take over the liberal newspaper *Izvestia*, which was nominally subordinate to the Supreme Soviet but had adopted an independent editorial line. The guards almost came to blows with the Moscow police and KGB troops sent to defend the paper. Eventually Khasbulatov's praetorians retreated.

That summer, many in Moscow assumed Khasbulatov was planning another bid to impeach Yeltsin. In early August, the Supreme Soviet's Committee on Constitutional Legislation proposed constitutional amendments that would reduce the president to a figurehead, no longer commanding the armed forces or appointing ministers. These changes were to be adopted in November. Convinced now that there was no chance of an acceptable compromise, Yeltsin decided on a risky gambit. On September 21, he signed Decree No. 1400 abolishing the Congress and Supreme Soviet and calling elections in December to a new bicameral parliament. He had agonized, he wrote. He was stepping outside the Constitution, but he did so in the paradoxical belief that only this could protect democracy and strengthen the rule of law. There was simply no other way to end the "fruitless and senseless fight to the death" between the branches of government.

To many observers, the demoralizing struggle seemed all about personalities. Yeltsin's imperiousness and self-regard crashed into the oversized ambitions and instinctive belligerence of Khasbulatov and Rutskoy. But beneath the clash of egos, there were powerful objective reasons why conflict emerged. A basic incongruity existed between a president with a mission and a mandate to lead but minimal powers and a parliament that, under the inherited Constitution, had virtually unchecked authority.

"All power to the soviets!" Lenin had insisted in 1917, and the 1978 Russian Constitution faithfully embodied this principle. Tacking on a presidency, the deputies had made sure to define its powers narrowly. The parliament could void presidential decrees and override presidential vetoes with a simple majority in both chambers, the same margin required to initially pass the vetoed bill. Most importantly, it could amend the Constitution by a two-thirds vote of its members, changing any rule it did not like and expanding its authority without limit. Between 1990 and 1993, the Congress passed more than four hundred amendments—more than twice the number of articles in the charter. The president, although directly elected by the people and held responsible by them for the country's condition, could make almost no policy decisions without parliament's consent and had no powers that parliament could not take away.

This unbalanced constitution virtually guaranteed conflict. As economic conditions worsened, Khasbulatov and Rutskoy saw political gain in opposing the Kremlin's initiatives. With its obstruction and populism, the parliament exacerbated the crisis, but the decline discredited Yeltsin, and Khasbulatov believed support was rallying to his side. A parliamentary speaker of wisdom and restraint might have acted differently. But the conflict was not merely personal. Any ambitious politician would have been tempted to exploit the rising economic discontent to bolster his own presidential prospects.

Defying Yeltsin's decree, the Supreme Soviet refused to disband. Khasbulatov and his supporters hunkered down in the battleship-like, marble and granite White House on the banks of the Moskva River. Within hours, the deputies had impeached Yeltsin and sworn in Rutskoy as "acting president." Rutskoy appointed "ministers" to head the military and security agencies—General Achalov, who would now experience a siege from inside the building he had sent forces to surround in 1991; Andrey Dunayev, a former Soviet interior minister; and Viktor Barannikov, Yeltsin's own ex-minister of state security. All three worked their contacts in the armed forces, as Rutskoy appealed to soldiers to defy Yeltsin's "criminal orders." The deputies approved a law prescribing the death penalty for Yeltsin's "particularly dangerous accomplices."

Paramilitary volunteers were soon streaming to the White House from assorted trouble spots and arming themselves from Khasbulatov's cache of weapons. (When the building was stormed, 163 submachine guns, five machine guns, two snipers' rifles, one grenade launcher, 420 pistols, 248 gas pistols, one explosive device, and twenty-three other weapons were found.) Commanding the defenders was the Stalinist general Albert Makashov, an enthusiastic supporter of the 1991 coup known for his invective about the "Yids," who now promised to make traitors "wash their faces in their own blood." He was backed by the neo-Nazi Aleksandr Barkashov, whose militiamen wore uniforms with a swastika-like insignia on their sleeves and studied *Mein Kampf.* Cossacks, veterans, and assorted thugs milled around the building, beating up journalists and others they suspected of being Jewish. Hoping to avoid violence, Yeltsin sent police to surround the White House armed only with rubber truncheons and plastic shields.

On September 23, gunmen supporting the White House attacked the CIS Armed Forces building, shooting one policemen; an elderly woman was also killed by a bullet while looking out of her apartment window. Under the auspices of the Orthodox Church, the Kremlin tried to negotiate with Khasbulatov, offering to restore light and heat to the parliament building, withdraw the police, and discuss "legal and political guarantees" if the White House agreed to turn in its weapons. Khasbulatov refused. On October 2, radical communists led by the far left agitator Viktor Anpilov rioted on Smolensk Square, attacking police with Molotov cocktails and sharpened metal rods; they killed one policeman and injured twenty-four. The next day, Anpilov's mob, some 10,000–15,000 strong, broke through the police cordon to the White House. Khasbulatov and Rutskoy, elated, urged them to march across the street together with Makashov's troops and occupy the mayor's office, which they did, smashing military trucks through the glass walls, shooting, and leading out disarmed policemen. "It is time to finish off the fascist dictator Yeltsin," Khasbulatov enthused to the remaining deputies. "This very minute a seizure of the Kremlin is being planned under the command of the acting president. The Kremlin will be taken today!" Makashov's gunmen commandeered buses and drove to the Ostankino television center in northern Moscow, followed by crowds of supporters armed with Molotov cocktails. They rammed a truck through the doors and shot a hand grenade at the building. To prevent the rebels broadcasting, the defenders pulled programming off the air.

Yeltsin, attentive to his relations with the army, had visited local divisions on August 31, watching parachute jumps and dining with the officers. Led by Defense Minister Pavel Grachev, they had toasted his health, shouted "Hurrah," and promised their full support. Now when Yeltsin confronted the generals, he was told that some soldiers "were picking potatoes and others didn't feel like fighting." He persuaded Grachev to send a few tanks to the parliament. Next, Yeltsin visited the KGB Alfa troops. "Will you fulfill my orders?" he asked—to be met by silence. Reluctantly, the commandos deployed near the White House; they only agreed to storm it after one left his armored vehicle to help a wounded civilian and was killed by a sniper.

Four T-80 tanks fired twelve shells—ten dummies, two containing explosives—at the parliament building, shattering windows, sending chunks of marble flying, and setting the top floors on fire. Within hours, the Alfa troops had occupied the building. They led out Khasbulatov, pasty faced, into the sunlight, looking as though he had spent two weeks inside a cave. A bus transported him and Rutskoy to prison. Makashov's snipers disappeared into the city, shooting civilians in a cowardly spree of violence. Of the 187 killed on October 3 and 4, according to the official count, none were deputies or parliamentary staffers: the dead consisted of police, ordinary Muscovites caught in the crossfire, and Khasbulatov's armed defenders.

That December, as promised, elections were held for the new two-chamber parliament, composed of a State Duma and Federation Council. For the Duma, voters cast one ballot for a party—which won seats proportional to its share of the vote—and one for a representative from their local district. To the reformers' horror, the winner in the party-list voting was not the party of Gaidar's reformers but that of the ultra-nationalist firebrand Vladimir Zhirinovsky, whose program included reconquering the lost Soviet territories. One of the Duma's first acts was to grant amnesty to Khasbulatov and the other White House rebels, along with the 1991 putschists. Yeltsin, although furious, abided by the decision and the individuals were released.

Simultaneously with the election, Russians got to vote on a proposed constitution. Yeltsin's aides had revised a draft from the convention that summer and circulated it to the regional leaders for comment. It guaranteed citizens a comprehensive list of rights and freedoms—from freedom of speech, the press, and association, to the right to a free higher education—and established a division of powers between branches and levels of government.

More controversially, it strengthened the Kremlin's authority. The Communist leader, Gennady Zyuganov, thought this constitution "gave the president more powers than the tsar, the Egyptian pharaoh, and a sheikh of Araby put together." This was nonsense. In fact, the Russian president became slightly stronger than his French or American counterpart. He commanded the armed forces, could dissolve the Duma under certain conditions, and could issue decrees that did not contradict laws or the Constitution. But parliament could overturn his decrees, override his vetoes, and impeach him. It had to pass the annual budget law and tax legislation and so retained the power of the purse. The president's choice of prime minister had to be confirmed by the Duma, and his choices of procurator general and high court judges had to be ratified by the upper house. The upper house also had to approve the imposition of a state of emergency or the use of the armed forces outside Russia.

According to the official results, 55 percent of the electorate voted, and 57 percent of them supported the constitution. It was declared enacted. A commission that examined the results concluded that turnout had been inflated and had, in fact, not reached the 50 percent required for passage. An odd drop of more than one million registered voters between April and December 1993, along with some statistical oddities, supported this assertion. However, the evidence was circumstantial, and other explanations were possible for the statistical anomalies. Yeltsin's press secretary Vyacheslav Kostikov, later claimed in his memoirs that turnout had originally been 53 percent, with 52 percent favoring the constitutional draft, but that the figures had been "corrected" during a private meeting between Yeltsin and the head of the electoral commission. (Although shocking if true, the "original" figures would also have been enough for the constitution to pass.) In the event, there was little pressure for a recount, even from the opposition, and all accepted the new constitutional rules of the game.

As he battled the parliament, Yeltsin also had to wrestle another set of adversaries. Gorbachev's glasnost had prompted a flood of demands for autonomy not just from the non-Russian republics of the Soviet Union, but also from many small minority ethnicities within Russia itself. Since 1990, ethnically distinct Russian provinces from Karelia to Tyva had been declaring themselves sovereign states; adopting constitutions, flags, and national anthems; asserting the supremacy of their local laws; and claiming natural resources on their territory. To extract concessions from Moscow, regional leaders threatened to call general strikes, to impose tariffs at their borders, to confiscate federal property, or to declare local states of emergency.

Not to be outdone, even ethnically Russian regions soon followed. Woody Vologda, north of Moscow, metamorphosed into the Vologda Republic. Yeltsin's home province of Sverdlovsk rechristened itself the "Urals Republic." The conflict was not just about names. Many regions also cut the tax they were remitting to the federal budget, much as the Soviet republics had starved Gorbachev's central government in 1991. At one point in 1993, about one-third of the country's provinces were withholding some or all of their assessed taxes, threatening Russia with what Finance Minister Boris Fyodorov called "financial asphyxiation."

In Chapter 8, I discuss the controversial but ultimately successful way Yeltsin and his ministers defused the crisis. Against the advice of most economists, the government made concessions to those regions that posed the greatest risk of outright rebellion. Provinces that declared sovereignty, staged strikes, and voted against Yeltsin in elections and referenda won tax breaks and subsidies. Then, from 1994, Yeltsin signed a series of "power-sharing agreements" with individual regions, starting with the most troublesome ones, granting some of the rights they demanded. Although costly, these concessions calmed the local mood, and by the end of 1994 the threat of Russia's disintegration had passed.

The one exception was Chechnya, a Muslim republic on the northern slopes of the Caucasus Mountains, which had only been incorporated into Russia in 1859. Accused of disloyalty by Stalin, the whole population had been exiled to Kazakhstan in 1944, and only allowed to return in the late 1950s. Now the republic demanded full independence. Under its authoritarian leader, General Dzhokhar Dudayev, Chechnya had become a center of lawlessness, the home base of arms traders, bank fraudsters, and other varieties of criminal. In this case, negotiations got nowhere. And as tensions between Moscow and the other ethnic republics abated, this left Chechnya more isolated, vulnerable, and irritating to the federal authorities.

In mid-1994, Yeltsin authorized the security service to covertly assist opponents of Dudayev who were preparing to storm the capital, Grozny. The plan went disastrously wrong, and Russian tank drivers were captured and paraded in front of the press by Dudayev's officers. Humiliated, Yeltsin ordered the army to invade. The poorly trained, ill-equipped Russian troops met strong resistance, and it took more than two months of brutal fighting to occupy Grozny, which was badly damaged. Dudayev and his forces retreated to the mountains, from where they ambushed the Russian troops. Chechen guerrillas staged bloody raids across the borders in Stavropol and Dagestan. At Budyonnovsk, the former plane hijacker Shamil Basayev took an entire hospital hostage. Prime Minister Chernomyrdin, speaking to Basayev by phone, managed to negotiate a deal that saved the lives of many hostages but also allowed the terrorists to escape. Then, in January 1996, a band led by the field commander Salman Raduyev, crossed into Dagestan, took more than two thousand hostages, and hunkered down in the village of Pervomayskoe. Despite a brutal bombardment, the guerrillas managed to slip back across the border, taking many of their hostages, who were later exchanged for Chechen prisoners.

In 1996, Yeltsin would call Chechnya "the most botched war in the history of Russia." According to the authorities, 5,500 Russian troops died, although other estimates run as high as 14,000. Some 35,000 Chechen civilians were killed, by one credible estimate. Even those with little sympathy for Yeltsin report that he took his blunder hard. At one Security Council meeting, according to Yevgeny Primakov, then head of foreign intelligence, Yeltsin announced he was resigning, but was persuaded to change his mind. "I don't think this was a game Yeltsin was playing. Everything connected with Chechnya was painful to him," Primakov recalled. Andrey Kozyrev, the foreign minister, whom Yeltsin abruptly fired in 1996, says Yeltsin "suffered terribly, seeing the civilian population dying, the destruction." Yeltsin would later deplore the army's "monstrous lack of preparation" and the "disarray in the actions of the power ministries." Of course, no one was more responsible than he for that lack of preparation and coordination.

In 1994 and 1995, Yeltsin became more isolated from his democratic supporters, most of whom were shocked by the Chechen misadventure. To relieve the tension, he turned increasingly to alcohol and the companionship of the military types with whom he felt most at ease—first and foremost, his bodyguard, Aleksandr Korzhakov. Korzhakov had adopted a broad interpretation of his job that included lobbying for particular economic policies, bugging the phones of Kremlin officials, and intervening in personnel decisions. In August 1994, Yeltsin, in Berlin to mark the withdrawal of Russian troops from Germany, drank too many glasses of champagne, and on a whim grabbed the baton and jerkily conducted a police band before breaking into a chorus of the folk song "Kalinka." It was an embarrassing spectacle, replayed repeatedly on television. As his drinking increased, Yeltsin's health deteriorated, and in July and October 1995 he suffered heart attacks.

Since 1992, inflation had been surging, defying repeated attempts to control it. Despite inauspicious political conditions, Chubais, whom Yeltsin made vice premier in late 1994, achieved a breakthrough, bringing the rate below 40 percent a year in the first half of 1996. Desperate to raise money for the budget, Chubais permitted some of the country's leading bankers to privatize potentially valuable enterprises, transferring them to themselves under a scheme known as "loans for shares" (see Chapter 6). The bankers lent about $800 million to the government, with stock in the enterprises as collateral. When—as anticipated—the government failed to repay the loans in 1996, the bankers were allowed to auction off the shares—which they did, at low prices, to themselves.

The presidential election of 1996 was the second time—after October 1993—that a reversion to Soviet-style communism looked possible. By September 1995, only 14 percent of Russians said they approved of Yeltsin's performance. In the Duma election that December, the Communists led the party list ballot with 22 percent of the vote, and the party's leader, Gennady Zyuganov, was the clear favorite to win the presidency. Renominating Yeltsin, said Gaidar, would be the "best present to the Communists." He tried to persuade the young, reformist governor of Nizhny Novgorod, Boris Nemtsov, to run—but Nemtsov convinced him the only option was for the democrats to rally behind Yeltsin.

By that point, Yeltsin had already thrown his hat into the ring. He had hesitated. "Sometimes I have a feeling which says: step down, step down, step down, step down," he had told an interviewer in November 1993. Why didn't he? "Then I think: who else, who else, who else, who else?" In the summer of 1995, he seemed to have pinned his hopes on Chernomyrdin, who, as prime minister, had proved loyal, reasonable, and mostly committed to free markets and democracy. But his party's dismal 10 percent in the the Duma election made him look like a loser. Despite his own mortifying poll ratings and his wife Naina's attempts to dissuade him, Yeltsin made his decision. The sense of impossible odds awoke the battler in him. He could not bear to think of the Communists returning to power. And so one morning in February 1996, hoarse and coughing, weakened by his heart attacks, Yeltsin stood in Yekaterinburg, the former Sverdlovsk, where he had begun his career, and announced his candidacy.

From the start, his strategy was to turn the election into a referendum not on Yeltsin but on communism, to remind people that, no matter how bad current conditions were, a return to bread lines and labor camps, censorship and political executions would be worse. At the same time, he promised to solve the most aggravating public problems. As many industrial enterprises approached bankruptcy, rather than firing workers they had delayed paying wages. The government was also behind in payments to doctors, teachers, and pensioners. Yeltsin pledged to clear the wage and pension arrears. He also promised to end the deeply unpopular Chechen war.

To run the campaign, he picked one of his vice premiers, Oleg Soskovets, a metals industry lobbyist and intimate of the bodyguard Korzhakov. Soskovets ran the campaign in traditional Soviet style, so badly in fact that some suspected deliberate sabotage. The team almost failed to collect the required one million nomination signatures. After one visit to Stavropol, during which a thick cordon of guards shielded the candidate from the public, twice as many local voters said their view of

Yeltsin had worsened as said it had improved. Korzhakov, convinced Yeltsin would lose, tried to persuade him to postpone the election for two years, illegally, while another candidate—preferably Soskovets—could be groomed to run. In secret negotiations with the Communist leaders, Korzhakov offered them cabinet posts in return for condoning such a postponement.

Zyuganov looked hard to beat. With a nationwide network of twenty thousand party cells, containing 530,000 members—the remains of the once dominant Soviet Communist Party—he had a formidable machine for canvassing door-to-door. More than 150 pro-Communist local and national newspapers relayed his appeals to their tens of millions of readers. For the true believers, he offered a message of paranoid populism, endorsing an anticapitalist, anti-Western, anti-Semitic crusade against Yeltsin's backers, the "insatiable carnivores" of the "comprador bourgeoisie." Privately, he had cordial relations with some of the "compradors," and was delighted by the attention he got when he showed up in February at the Davos World Economic Forum. Observers were left to guess which Zyuganov—the fire-breathing Marxist or the temperate champion of social justice—would move into the Kremlin if he won.

In March, Korzhakov persuaded Yeltsin to cancel the elections. Yeltsin ordered his aides to draft a decree dissolving the Duma, banning the Communist Party, and postponing the vote. Gaidar, alerted by a call from Chubais, cut himself shaving and raced across town, dripping blood, to urge the American ambassador to get President Clinton to reason with his friend Boris. Three individuals were key to talking Yeltsin out of his decision. Chernomyrdin opposed it. Anatoly Kulikov, the interior minister, warned that the police might split, some of them supporting Communist protesters, making civil war possible. Most critically, Chubais—whom Yeltsin had recently said was "guilty for everything"—convinced Yeltsin that he would lose his legacy as a democrat. Yeltsin tore up the decree.

He also gave Chubais a central role in the campaign. A group of businessmen donated several million dollars to finance Chubais's headquarters. Two of these, Boris Berezovsky and Vladimir Gusinsky, controlled respectively the ORT and NTV television networks, and they ordered their journalists to slant coverage in favor of Yeltsin. The journalists, aware that freedom of the press would suffer under Zyuganov, were happy to oblige. Singers who had been harassed or banned under Brezhnev held concerts to rally the youth vote.

The sixty-five-year-old candidate threw himself into campaigning as if he were an athlete in his prime, visiting twenty-three regions, mingling with the crowds, dancing with rock musicians, doling out largesse, promising and promising. "Russians have already forgotten what empty shelves are," he told the government newspaper *Rossiyskaya Gazeta*. "Now what's needed is for people to forget about empty wallets." He did his best to help them. In the first half of 1996, Yeltsin signed more than seventy-five decrees conferring benefits on particular geographic, social, or economic groups—from students, medical workers, and pensioners to war invalids, Cossacks, and diabetics. In Arkhangelsk, he announced he had come "with full pockets." In a coal mine in Vorkuta, a woman asked for a car; he gave her one. Television cameras relayed such acts of generosity nightly on the news. To reduce the almost $5 billion of wage arrears that had accumulated by February, he sent tax police to investigate delinquent enterprises and fired regional officials where delays were worst. His poll ratings rose. He started negotiations to end the Chechnya war—a process that led to the signing in August 1996 of the Khasavyurt Accords, which established an armistice and deferred agreement on the republic's final status for five years. In the end, Yeltsin slipped past Zyuganov to win the first round by 35 percent to 32 percent.

Between the rounds, Korzhakov sent the Chubais team into a panic when his men detained two staffers who had been leaving campaign headquarters carrying more than $500,000 in cash. Permitted spending per candidate was $3 million, but everyone assumed all the main candidates were exceeding this. Korzhakov, who had helped organize the overspending, seemed determined to discredit the Chubais team, even if it risked his boss's reelection. After a tense night, Chubais persuaded Yeltsin to make the agonizing decision to fire his bodyguard of almost ten years. Almost immediately, Yeltsin suffered yet another heart attack, which was concealed from the voters until after the runoff election. Yeltsin beat Zyuganov by 54 percent to 40 percent.

The secret of Yeltsin's political rise from the dead in 1996 is still debated. Some think he won by scaring the population with the specter of communism, broadcasting newsreel footage of labor camps and food shortages. However, polls suggest most Russians looked back on Soviet times nostalgically. One taken right after the election found that 71 percent evaluated the pre-perestroika economic system positively while 60 percent were positive about the Soviet political order. Yeltsin prevailed despite this—in my view, because he gave undecided voters hope with his efforts to cut wage arrears, his economic promises, and his steps towards ending the Chechen war. He also benefited from the increase in real wages that followed the defeat of inflation in 1995. These developments did not make most Russians enthusiastic about Yeltsin. But they persuaded enough of the waverers to give him another chance. Most would be disappointed. Few promises were kept, and Yeltsin's rating dove almost immediately after July 1996 as economic indicators deteriorated again.

The rest of 1996 was devoted to rescuing Yeltsin's heart. That November, he underwent a quintuple bypass operation. Chubais, as his new head of administration, handled business during Yeltsin's convalescence, but no major policies could be introduced. The tycoons who had helped in the election campaign—now christened "oligarchs"—felt entitled to meddle in politics, and two were given government jobs for a while, exacerbating the appearance of corruption. Only in early 1997 was Yeltsin well enough to plan a new round of reforms. He moved Chubais back to the government and brought Nemtsov from Nizhny Novgorod to join him. Chernomyrdin stayed as prime minister. The reformers' key goal now was to establish clear and fair rules of interaction between business and the state—in Nemtsov's words, to end the era of "bandit capitalism" and throw the businessmen out of the Kremlin.

This meant war. In 1997, Gusinsky, who had not participated in loans for shares, decided it was his turn to profit. That year, the government sold a stake in the national communications company, Svyazinvest. Although Chubais insisted that whoever made the highest bid would win, Gusinsky exploded when another oligarch, backed by the financier George Soros, offered more than he did. Gusinsky and Berezovsky, who joined him out of solidarity, unleashed a public relations jihad against Chubais and Nemtsov. Yeltsin, by this point annoyed with both the oligarchs and his ministers, demoted Nemtsov and Chubais, and accepted the resignation of some members of Chubais's team who had accepted large honoraria for writing chapters in a book on privatization.

Having soured on Chernomyrdin, Yeltsin decided to shake things up in March 1998. He fired the loyal retainer and replaced him with another young reformer, this time a protégé of Nemtsov from Nizhny Novgorod called Sergey Kirienko. Since late 1997, the financial crisis in Asia had been threatening Russia as well, and the new government spent the summer desperately trying to force major businesses to pay more tax. With the Communist-led Duma in resolute opposition, and the oligarchs feuding with the Kremlin, the reformers had few options. In August, the market crashed and the government let the ruble's value slide, announcing a forced restructuring of its short-term bonds and a moratorium on foreign debt payments by domestic banks. Prices jumped 38 percent in a month. Yeltsin, rattled by the return of economic instability, fired Kirienko. After the Duma refused to confirm Chernomyrdin again, he reluctantly accepted as prime minister his former intelligence chief and foreign minister, Yevgeny Primakov. Despite his good relations with the Communists, Primakov did not order the lavish spending that many of them wanted, and inflation quickly subsided.

From early in his second term, Yeltsin had been searching for an "heir" whom he could trust to continue reforms. In the spring of 1999, or so he writes, he became convinced that Vladimir Putin, a deferential former spy whom he had appointed to head the Federal Security Service, was the man. Nevertheless, when he fired Primakov in April 1999, Yeltsin chose another loyal security service veteran, Sergey Stepashin, to succeed him. Primakov, whose popularity was soaring, joined with Moscow's mayor, Yury Luzhkov, to prepare a bid for the presidency. Yeltsin's circle feared both and was determined to prevent either from coming to power. When Stepashin seemed too diffident in fighting them, Yeltsin fired him and as his sixth prime minister—this time one "with prospects," as he put it— he appointed Putin.

In Chapter 3, I describe how Putin, responding forcefully to an invasion of Dagestan by Chechen guerrillas and the bombing of a series of apartment buildings, captured the public's attention. To compete with Primakov and Luzhkov, the Kremlin formed a new political party which, with Putin's endorsement, shot to second place in the December Duma election. Yeltsin, now confident Putin could win if the presidential election came soon enough, decided to step down, and on New Year's Eve he delivered a moist-eyed farewell address to the Russian people. After transferring the nuclear suitcase to Putin and dining with the security ministers, Yeltsin told his successor to "take care of Russia," and left the Kremlin in his hands.

The Destroyer?

"This man," wrote Gorbachev in his memoirs, "was by nature a destroyer." General Aleksandr Lebed agreed: "He could not remain in people's memories as a great builder. He would go down in history as a destroyer." It became a cliché to say that in politics Yeltsin knew how to wreck but not to recreate. He was a construction engineer who only did demolition, a human bulldozer who razed the Soviet state to its foundations just as in Sverdlovsk, on Andropov's orders, he had demolished the historic mansion where the last Tsar and his family had been murdered.

In fact, ten years after he left office, the troubling question is why Yeltsin did not do more to dismantle the apparatus of tyranny left by Soviet rule. There were no lustrations, no truth commissions, no opening of the secret police files. The KGB underwent splits and recombinations, repeated acronym changes, but little genuine reform. In 1992, recruits were still studying the work of Feliks Dzerzhinsky and training with manuals written in the 1970s and 1980s. The police avoided even cosmetic remodeling. Not even reports that police units were moonlighting as guards for organized crime figures shook the official torpor. As for the military, its thousands of generals were allowed to continue planning to repulse a massive NATO land invasion, as their weapons rusted, their combat readiness dwindled, and their demoralized officers, unpaid for months and stuck in temporary housing, took sadistic revenge upon the teenage conscripts.

Instead of reorganizing and retraining them, Yeltsin seemed to think he could control the security agencies personally and turn them to democratic purposes. He would visit the army top brass for long lunches, jovial affairs with vodka toasts and backslapping, and hand out medals and promotions, the main criterion for which appeared to be not achievement but loyalty. He appointed trusted friends to top positions, an approach undercut by his often wretched judgment of his close associates.

Was more possible? Some informed observers thought so. The journalist Yevgeniya Albats, who spent time in the Lubyanka as a member of one parliamentary commission, found the old guard in disarray, grasping at individual lifelines: "If either Gorbachev or Yeltsin had been bold enough to dismantle the KGB during the autumn of 1991, he'd have met little resistance." In her view, parliamentary oversight could have been imposed, and the former KGB strictly subordinated to other government agencies, with its operations subjected to judicial review. A group of Yeltsin's aides agree that in late 1991 the KGB was "demoralized" and "preparing for self-liquidation." Instead, Yeltsin appointed a drinking companion to lead it and soon restored some of its old powers.

He was clearly conflicted. His own father had been sentenced to hard labor by Stalin's OGPU. Visiting Warsaw, he would kneel before a Polish priest and lay a wreath at the memorial to the twenty thousand Polish officers and others murdered by Stalin's NKVD near Katyn in 1940. He established a committee that exonerated 4.5 million Russian victims of political repression. Yet when a parliamentary commission proposed to liquidate the security service, this "provoked a tirade" from Yeltsin that "intimidated" the commission's chairman. When, meeting with him in 1992, his advisor Galina Starovoytova brought up the KGB's resurgence, it was the end of their friendship. He subsequently froze her out.

Why the reluctance to contemplate serious reform? Initially, Yeltsin— like most of his democratic colleagues—was keen to avoid a spirit of vengeance. Sergey Kovalyov, the human rights campaigner, said the democrats should be ready "to perish defending the Communists when the crowd demands that they be hung from the lampposts." Then there was the treacherous political context. Locked in battle with Khasbulatov, he could not risk driving the security services into the parliament's camp. Forcing the military to accept one massive change—the withdrawal of troops from Eastern Europe and the Baltics—he may have felt that further reform would push the generals over the edge. Finally, there was the difficult question *who* could clean out the Augean stables. The soapbox orators and courageous dissidents of the democratic movement had little administrative experience. Albats thought demobilized army troops could replace most of the KGB officers. But the army was by this point even more corrupt than the KGB. Moreover, the hundreds of thousands of fired KGB operatives could have taken their networks, blackmail materials, secret poisons, and assassination skills underground and used them to subvert the democratic order.

The obstacles were formidable. Still, even if reforms would have been risky and imperfect, more could have been done. Instead, Yeltsin enlarged the security service's powers in ways that invited abuse: authorizing it to define and protect state secrets, conduct searches without a warrant, and—in blatant violation of his own constitution—detain suspects for thirty days without charge. For one who relied on personal management, his personnel choices were dubious at best—appointing Barannikov in 1992, failing to rein in Korzhakov and his cronies until 1996, and, most significantly, endorsing a KGB colonel to succeed him. He felt comfortable among such men, and was too ready to trust those in epaulettes. Forced to fire Barannikov for corruption, his aides write that Yeltsin "even shed a few tears." After his retirement, he admitted to Aleksandr Yakovlev that he had "not thought through everything" and had relied too much on changing the KGB's leadership rather than reforming the organization. He was right.

A Tool of the Oligarchs?

According to many accounts of Russia in the late 1990s, real power lay not in the Kremlin but with the cabal of billionaires known as the oligarchs. Led by the hyperactive Boris Berezovsky, it is said, these tycoons ran the ailing Yeltsin from behind a curtain, guiding him towards measures that enriched them at the expense of ordinary citizens. Yeltsin, grateful to the billionaires for having financed his 1996 reelection, allowed them to pillage state assets and set policy. In later years, Berezovsky supposedly exercised control via Yeltsin's impressionable daughter, Tatyana Dyachenko, and the president's longtime advisor Valentin Yumashev.

It is easy to understand how the myth of the all-powerful oligarchs took root. For different reasons, this image appealed to almost everyone. For the oligarchs themselves, it paid off richly when investors, attracted by their connections, sought to partner with them; it also gratified their vanity. Among the Russian public, it resonated with the distrust of wealth and enterprise left by decades of communist socialization. For the Communists, the image of a clique of supercapitalists—many of them Jewish!—dangling the president on golden strings was almost too good to be true. For Western journalists, the oligarch saga made for a simple story that could explain the corruption and chaos of Russian politics to readers in terms of a few vivid personalities. For reformers in the government such as Boris Nemtsov, the oligarchs became a convenient excuse for failure and a target against whom public anger could be deflected.

Berezovksy worked night and day to create the impression that he was on intimate terms with Yeltsin and calling the shots. Having learned from his far-flung sources about some measure the Kremlin was about to announce, he would race onto the airwaves, hint at the forthcoming decision, and intimate that he had recommended it. After watching Berezovsky perform this trick repeatedly, Kirienko concluded that tales the tycoon told about his ability to influence the president were "pure fiction."

Like most myths, this one grew from something quite real, which was later stretched and misinterpreted in fanciful ways. One of the oligarchs, Vladimir Potanin, invented the "loans for shares" scheme of 1995, and he and two others used it to obtain stakes in valuable companies. Several of them profited from handling government money in their banks until 1999, when such accounts were transferred to the Federal Treasury. Potanin and Berezovsky both served for a while in Yeltsin's government. Until 2000, Berezovsky and Gusinsky controlled two national television stations, which were obviously important in shaping public opinion. That appears to be about the extent of it.

That the oligarchs "bought" Yeltsin his victory in 1996 is often asserted but rarely scrutinized. They were a conduit for money and instructed their media companies to help—redundantly, in fact, since the journalists had no desire to return to writing *Pravda* editorials. Did they pay for the campaign? According to David Hoffman of the *Washington Post*, they actually profited from their participation. He reports that the government sold them bonds at a discount, the proceeds from which were split between the campaign kitty and the oligarchs' pockets. The effectiveness of the advertising campaign was, in any case, far from obvious. Asked about criticism of Zyuganov in the media, 40 percent of poll respondents said it aroused in them mostly "irritation at the criticism;" only 16 percent said it aroused their "indignation at Zyuganov's actions." The oligarchs did make one clear contribution—persuading Yeltsin to involve Chubais—and the $800 million they paid in "loans for shares" helped the government reduce wage and pension arrears. Beyond that, their role remains to be proven.

The one person who gained least from the association with the tycoons—and who was greatly irritated by it—was Yeltsin himself. Although recognizing that capitalism implied capitalists and viewing the magnates as basically on his team, Yeltsin did not enjoy their company and met with them rarely, almost always in groups. They struck him as alien, built out of some kind of "cosmic metal," shortsightedly unwilling to compromise even in their own interest. "I never liked Boris Berezovsky, and I still don't like him," he wrote. "I don't like him because of his arrogant tone, his scandalous reputation, and because people believe that he has special influence on the Kremlin. He doesn't." By both Yeltsin's and Berezovsky's own accounts, which have not been challenged, Yeltsin never had dinner with the businessman, never invited him to his house, never even talked to him on the telephone.

> There were a few fleeting meetings, a few brief conversations, always official. Even so, people considered Berezovsky my constant shadow. . . . No matter what I did, no matter whom I appointed or dismissed, people always said the same thing. "Berezovsky!" And who was creating this mysterious aura, this reputation of an eminence grise? Berezovsky himself.

When in 1997 Nemtsov proposed that Yeltsin throw the tycoons out of the Kremlin, Nemtsov records that he replied: "It's past time. They have already annoyed me so much, walking around here from office to office. And what do they want? What are they—my colleagues (*sotrudniki*)?" To underline Berezovsky's insignificance, Yeltsin made a point of firing him with a minor executive order rather than a regular decree. Even Berezovsky got the hint: "I felt that Yeltsin was not fond of me personally."

As for Tatyana Dyachenko, Berezovsky reports that she "also kept her distance." They met only once every two or three months. The story that

Berezovsky gave Dyachenko a Russian jeep, or Niva, turns out to be, in Timothy Colton's evaluation, "claptrap." Dyachenko told Yeltsin's biographer that she respected Berezovsky's intellect and drive but was suspicious of his motives and so treated him with caution. Both she and Yumashev opposed Berezovsky's appointment as executive secretary of the CIS in 1998 and favored his removal in 1999.

It is hard to find examples of government policies that served the businessmen's interests after 1996, the year in which the "oligarch" label first caught on. On the contrary, the period of their supposed dominance was precisely that in which the government frontally attacked their interests. The main new economic policy after 1996—that further privatizations of state enterprises should be for high cash prices—was one they angrily opposed. Svyazinvest was auctioned transparently, for an impressive price, to a consortium involving foreign money. The starting price for the June 1998 auction of the oil company Rosneft was so high that the government received no bids. Berezovksy had "lobbied furiously to shape the conditions to his advantage," but got nowhere. After 1998, the government began withdrawing its accounts from the oligarch banks and running all money through the Treasury. Berezovsky intrigued to be made chief executive of Gazprom. He never got through the door. As Chubais campaigned to force Russian companies to pay their taxes, the first two delinquent enterprises he threatened to seize belonged to the oligarchs Berezovsky and Potanin.

The most likely example of the oligarchs benefiting came in August 1998 when the government softened the blow of devaluation by adding a moratorium on foreign debt payments by Russian banks. But this was much more plausibly an attempt to save the depositors. Despite the moratorium, almost all the oligarchs' banks failed. Even in their lobbying on personnel decisions, the oligarchs often ran into a wall. In early 1998, Berezovsky agitated against the appointment of Kirienko as prime minister. He lost. Berezovsky opposed hiring Chubais to head the national electricity company. He lost again. After Yeltsin fired Kirienko, Berezovsky lobbied to get Chernomyrdin reappointed, which Yeltsin would also have preferred. In fact, the new prime minister was Berezovsky's nemesis Primakov, whose procurator general raided Berezovsky's offices and issued a warrant for his arrest.

The oligarchs did not often get their way; but they did get *in* the way. They became an irritating presence, wasting officials' time, squabbling among themselves, recommending their protégés for state jobs, corrupting officials, obtaining advance information, slandering their opponents in their newspapers, and tirelessly promoting themselves. They made it hard to collect taxes, though no harder than did the managers of large majority state-owned enterprises like Gazprom. As obstacles to reform, the Communists in the Duma—who blocked the passage of most of the tax code, the free sale of land, and the emergency economic program of July 1998—were much more significant. In access to Yeltsin, all the oligarchs together did not come close to equaling that of Korzhakov in 1994–95. The oligarchs were an annoyance, a focus of public resentment, a source of corruption, and a symbol of increasing economic inequality. But their political influence was greatly exaggerated.

The Successor

They sat together in the president's Kremlin office, the clock's ticks punctuating the silence. It was early one morning in August 1999. "I don't like election campaigns. I really don't," Putin said. "I don't know how to run them, and I don't like them." Yeltsin reassured him. There would be others to manage organizational details. Seeing the president was not about to back off, Putin replied with "military terseness" that he would work wherever Yeltsin assigned him.

At this point, one wishes there were some way to leap into the historical vignette and shake the president to his senses. The one thing Yeltsin cared most about at this point was his legacy. He was the president who brought freedom to Russia. When, at difficult moments, Yeltsin had been tempted to dispense with democratic procedures, what saved him—and Russia—was precisely that he *did* like election campaigns and believed he could win them. Yet here he was, about to hand the country to a KGB colonel who "didn't like election campaigns," who spoke with "military terseness," whose character would each day nudge him in the other direction. What could he have been thinking?

Yeltsin would never publicly admit that backing Putin had been a mistake. He did, in retirement, express deep disappointment with some of his policies. After Putin abolished the direct election of regional governors, Yeltsin warned in an interview against "the stifling of freedoms and the rolling back of democratic rights." In early 2005, when a group of former aides asked if there was anything he was unhappy about, Yeltsin replied glumly: "Yes, the state of the country."

Succession had always been a sore point. Perhaps because of what he had done to Gorbachev, Yeltsin was deeply suspicious of subordinates who showed personal ambition. He underestimated the abilities and prospects of those around him. In 1995–96, the improving economic mood that followed the defeat of inflation might well have carried a younger Kremlin-backed candidate—Nemtsov or even Chernomyrdin—to an even more decisive victory than Yeltsin's in the presidential election. By that point, Yeltsin's negatives were weighing him down. I believe he would genuinely have preferred not to run. But he thought no one but he could defeat the Communists.

Almost immediately after 1996, he began to think about 2000. He sensed the growing hunger for order, the appeal of a candidate close to law enforcement or the armed forces—a *silovik*—and knew that if he did not find such a candidate first, the Russian people and the political elite would. So he focused his gaze on those in the younger generation who spoke with "military terseness," looking for one who could strengthen the state but would also continue his reforms.

And there was Putin. Not just a silovik, but, so it seemed, a democrat, a former law student and loyal aide of the liberal reformer Anatoly Sobchak, exactly the man who, in Sobchak's view, could reintegrate the security services into the new democratic Russia. He was young, cautious, modern in outlook, with no hang-ups about business. He had good relations with many of the St. Petersburg liberals, the economic technocrats that Chubais had brought into the Moscow ministries. He had been loyal to Yeltsin at difficult moments. But he "did not like elections."

Was there a more suitable silovik? Since 1998, Yeltsin had conducted what his legal advisor Mikhail Krasnov called a series of "bridal inspections." General Lebed's impetuous actions, bizarre statements, and penchant for picking fights ruled him out. Nikolay Bordyuzha, the head of the border guards, Primakov, and then Stepashin were all considered and rejected. Putin was certainly not the least liberal and democratic of

these. Primakov was just as ambivalent about press freedom and more
hostile towards free markets. Chubais and Gaidar both lobbied for Stepashin, who got along well with the reformers and would later run for
parliament for the social democratic Yabloko party. Yet Stepashin had
strongly supported the first Chechen war and had, in various roles, eased
the rebirth of the former KGB. Putin later praised him for behaving in a
very "adult" way as head of the St. Petersburg Security Ministry branch
in 1992: "He shielded the Leningrad security service with his democratic
authority" at a time when people wanted "to wreck, to break, to tear up."
His leadership might have brought a softer, gentler version of Putinism,
but probably not a radically different approach.

Yeltsin could not know what we know now—that the economic
recovery that began in 1999 would be strong enough to carry many possible Kremlin candidates to victory in 2000, and that it would give the
winner unusual latitude to change Russia's course (see Chapter 7). It is
likely that by June 2000 even a young reformer like Nemtsov, if endorsed
and supported by the Kremlin, could have beaten Luzhkov or Primakov.
And yet Yeltsin chose to back a KGB colonel with at most a pragmatic
commitment to democracy. His intuition, which so often guided him
correctly, failed on this occasion.

The Character Question

Sooner or later—but usually sooner—all writers get to the question
of Yeltsin's character. Few find it to their liking. Yeltsin was "stubborn,
awkward," "prickly," "tough, demanding," "closed," "reserved with new
acquaintances," "dependent on his ego," and liable to "fly off the handle
in a stupid way, like a child." That, at least, is how he described himself.
Others were less complimentary.

His faults could fill a phone book. He could be vain, sentimental,
self-pitying, petty. He might take offense at well-intentioned advice and
sulk for months, refusing to talk to those who had wounded his amour
propre. He was a sore loser in sports, childishly so. He could be mean
spirited. His closest assistants, former friends, sometimes waited by the
phone for years for a call that never came, their only sin to no longer be
useful. Georgy Khizha, an economics minister in 1992, tried to call in on

his car phone to check a radio report that he had been fired, only to find the phone already disconnected. He was jealous and distrustful of protégés who became popular, who appeared too often in the press, or who revealed their own political ambitions. His judgment of people could be execrable.

Then there was his susceptibility to the "Russian vice." Yeltsin was, as Joseph Brodsky wrote of Peter the Great, a "man of sober mind, though of frightful drinking habits." Ground down by the stress of office, he threw himself into the abuse of alcohol with the verve of a lapsed Puritan. His favorite drink, after 1993, was Tarkhun grass-infused vodka. "Do you have the green stuff?" he would bark at the Kremlin waiters. Before that, it was cognac. Once, after a press conference, his chief of staff Sergey Filatov found him in a back room in an undershirt with five shot glasses containing different brands of the liquor on a table in front of him. He selected the worst drinking partners he could find—the meaty men with jowly faces, sportsmen, jokesters, policemen on the make. One by one, he promoted them, and later had to fire them all. Barannikov, whose wife shopped in Zurich at a foreign businessman's expense. Korzhakov, the loyal bodyguard who bugged the phones of Kremlin aides to incriminate his colleagues. Mikhail Barsukov, who cooperated in Korzhakov's conspiracies.

For all the sanctimony and rumors that surround Yeltsin's problem drinking, it seems to have occupied a shorter period than most people believe. Sources from Yeltsin's Sverdlovsk and Moscow days confirm that he drank normally but not excessively before 1991. After 1996, on doctor's orders, he cut out heavy drinking almost entirely. His weakness, occasional distraction, and unsteadiness on his feet in that period had more to do with his heart problem, blood pressure, stress, insomnia, and the many medications he took to alleviate them.

Still, to age in public was embarrassment enough. And how public it was! The press corps, accustomed to his lapses, his tendency on trips outside Moscow to mistake journalists for local residents, his bizarre misstatements, and his wobbly steps, referred to him as *Dyedushka*, "Grandfather." He sensed the snickering around him. To Nemtsov, he once said: "You and Chubais laugh at me, you think I'm drunk and foolish, I understand. . . . But bear in mind that I'm the president and you are just boyars." The exhaustion was such that Naina placed an armchair in the hallway of the family home so he could collapse into it as soon as he came through the door.

Sometimes the echoes of the dying Brezhnev were mortifying. In his resignation speech, he seemed to pull each word out with effort, punctuating the long gaps. "Saying goodbye . . . I want . . . to say . . . to each . . . of you: . . . Be happy . . . You have earned . . . happiness. . . . You have earned . . . happiness and calm." In his second term, he seemed to visit the hospital almost as often as the Kremlin. When his aides said Yeltsin was at his dacha "working with documents," journalists took this as a euphemism. In fact, Yeltsin took fewer vacation days per year than either Ronald Reagan or George W. Bush. "Working with documents" often meant just that.

Even when in good health, he would disappear at key moments for weeks at a time. After the August 1991 coup collapsed, he took a six-week holiday on the Baltic and Black Sea coasts. After the April 1993 referendum victory, he vanished again. Quick witted, courageous, and charismatic in a crisis, he descended into depression and lethargy when the tasks before him were mundane. He composed his life, as Leon Aron put it, "not in long, elaborate blocks but in short, energetic and bold paragraphs followed by empty spaces." Some of this was artfulness—lying low to tempt others to expose their hands—or rational caution—waiting for his intuition to fit the pieces together. But to supporters he sometimes seemed incapable of grasping an opportunity.

Was he personally corrupt? The press tried and convicted him many times. However, the claim that he personally enriched himself in office was backed by little solid evidence. In 1998, Swiss and Russian prosecutors investigated allegations that an Albanian businessman whose company obtained contracts to renovate the Kremlin had given Yeltsin's daughters credit cards from his Swiss bank and paid their bills. The businessman admitted obtaining the credit cards for the Yeltsins as a courtesy—no Russian banks were issuing them at the time—but he denied having paid any bills. No evidence contradicting this has been made public, and no charges were filed by either the Swiss or Russian prosecutors. On the other hand, accusations against some in Yeltsin's entourage were much more credible. The head of the Kremlin property management department, Pavel Borodin, was indeed convicted in a Swiss court of laundering money paid to him in bribes by the same Albanian businessman. Even if Yeltsin was not personally enriched by office, he bears responsibility for doing so little to stop blatant corruption among his associates.

Flawed as a human being, flawed as a president—and yet, a mere list of the defects only scratches the surface of his extraordinary personality. Within the same body as the clownish egotist was the other Yeltsin, the Urals self-made man, to whom Margaret Thatcher instantly warmed. There was the Yeltsin whose courage was taken for granted even by his enemies. Gorbachev assured his aide Chernyaev that, "when imprisoned by the putschists at Foros, Yeltsin won't give up and nothing would break him." There was the Yeltsin who, although cavalier with his friends, could be merciful towards his enemies. When he heard that Khasbulatov, who had come down in the world, was asking for a pass to the presidential medical clinic, he immediately approved the request. There was the Yeltsin who was not afraid to take responsibility upon himself, who would unfreeze prices and let the neighboring republics go free, knowing he would always be blamed, even hated, but knowing also that it was the right thing to do.

His close acquaintances were often stunned by the contradictions. The boisterous carouser was, in business hours, a person of almost painful discipline, a human stopwatch, who refused to receive aides who arrived five minutes late for a meeting; who took pleasure in his neatly arranged, color-coded folders; who could not abide smoking or—unlike most in Kremlin politics—bad language (Marshal Shaposhnikov was amazed at his fastidiousness; hadn't he been a builder, after all?). The flouter of protocol, who at a royal reception in Stockholm sought to engage the Swedish crown princess to the already married Boris Nemtsov, was in his office unusually formal, insisting on jackets and ties, addressing even close aides with the respectful *vy*, rather than the intimate or patronizing *ty*. He was, says his aide Satarov, an introvert—but an introvert who felt most alive in front of a crowd. A leader with a powerful ego, a "greed for self-realization," as another aide, Lev Sukhanov, put it, he nevertheless hated the pronoun "I" and cut it out of his speeches. A politician of sometimes astounding intuition, he could make embarrassing blunders, as when he walked out of the Congress in December 1992, calling on his supporters to follow him—but without warning them in advance, so that many were confused and missed the moment.

Intelligent, with an impressive memory, he would speed-read down the page, filing away information for later use. Afflicted by a horror of boredom, he could not stand "stupid monotony," the torrents of empty words that were the lingua franca of Soviet administration. To exorcise his irritation, he would pull out a pencil and snap it in three on the desk in front of him. (If no pencil were at hand, he would send an aide to fetch one.) He respected strength of convictions, lost all faith in ministers who changed their minds when challenged, and fired such weak individuals quickly. Hating to be contradicted, hating bad news, he did nevertheless listen. And at some critical junctures, he changed his mind.

The Natural

Yeltsin is often blamed for things over which he had little control. A painful economic crisis was inevitable in the early 1990s for reasons that had little to do with him—the macroeconomic bomb left behind by Gorbachev's profligate money printing, the nonviability of much of Russian industry, and the plunging world oil price (see Chapter 6). Yeltsin's decision to appoint Gaidar and support rapid liberalization was courageous and responsible. He made mistakes, but for the most part the economic disaster of the 1990s was not caused by Yeltsin and could not have been avoided by him. That did not prevent it from demolishing his public support.

Likewise, Yeltsin is often condemned for failing to compromise with Khasbulatov's parliament and using force to storm the White House in October 1993. This criticism assumes the parliament was willing to compromise. But with a constitution that gave it absolute power, and an economic crisis that was sapping Yeltsin's support, the parliament had no incentive to come to terms and no intention of doing so. Khasbulatov and colleagues would soon be able to neuter or abolish the presidency, concentrating authority in their own hands. One might argue that Yeltsin should have accepted this outcome and left quietly. After all, under the existing Constitution, the parliament had the right to remove all checks on its power. But given Khasbulatov's willingness to collaborate with Stalinists and neo-Nazis—the Anpilovs, Makashovs, and Barkashovs—

democrats should be grateful that Yeltsin chose another course. Once armed mobs were terrorizing the center of Moscow, Yeltsin was right to use force to stop them.

Some thought Yeltsin had erred by not enacting a new constitution and calling elections for a new parliament after his triumph in August 1991. Yeltsin himself wondered about this. But even in late 1991, the Congress would not have peacefully surrendered its power. When, that November, Yeltsin sent over a draft constitution for a presidential republic, the deputies buried it in committee; when he tried to switch control of the Central Bank to the president, they unanimously overturned his decree. As in 1993, he would have had to suspend the constitution and illegally disband the parliament. Legal niceties aside, to do this in late 1991 would have struck most Russians as insane. Having just fought the putschists to defend democracy and constitutionality, for Yeltsin to violate the constitution and dissolve an elected parliament—one that was enthusiastically supporting his initiatives—would have seemed a bizarre act of Bonapartism. Even supposing Yeltsin had managed to call new elections in late 1991, it is unlikely they would have returned a staunchly pro-reform legislature. At the time, Kremlin aides estimated that pro-Yeltsin candidates would win in only about one quarter of the regions.

Yeltsin's genuine failures were significant enough. He started an avoidable war in Chechnya in which tens of thousands died and hundreds of thousands became refugees. He failed to dismantle the Soviet security apparatus and reform the army, and he appointed incompetent officers to lead them because he thought them loyal. He paid too little attention to the corruption around him. He chose to support a successor who would roll back some of the freedoms he had introduced. At times, he embarrassed his countrymen with his public drinking, erratic behavior, and physical deterioration.

But his successes transformed both his country and the world. None of these was foreordained; all resulted from statecraft in difficult times. Following Gorbachev's lead, he brought home most remaining troops from Eastern Europe and the former Soviet republics. He drastically reduced Russia's armaments, cutting strategic nuclear warheads from 10,271 in 1990 to 6,758 in 1997. He negotiated a peaceful end to the Soviet Union, establishing good relations with Russia's neighbors, including those with large ethnic Russian communities. Facing down nationalist critics, he signed a friendship treaty with Ukraine, and agreed on a peaceful division of the Black Sea Fleet. He helped to negotiate the denuclearization of Ukraine, Belarus, and Kazakhstan.

At home, he prevented Russia's territorial disintegration. He defused the threat of communism, both as an ideology and as a party. He helped a market economy develop based on private property, free prices, and market exchange. Expanding on what Gorbachev had begun, he introduced the foundations of democracy to Russia—relatively free, competitive elections; a democratic constitution, including protections for human rights and a division of powers; freedom of the press. Never before—nor since—have Russians had so much freedom. He was both "the first leader in Russia's 1,000 years of history to be popularly elected in a free and fair election" and "the first Russian leader ever to voluntarily step down from office."

So, in the end, the image that rises to the surface is not that of Yeltsin the drinker, or even Yeltsin the Communist anti-Communist, but that of Yeltsin the candidate, stepping into the crowd, braced against recriminations, just as he would dive into the icy water of a Siberian river, suddenly alive and breathing deeply. Some found it strange that this *muzhik* from the Urals, this construction foreman, would be the one to bring democracy to Russia. He had not read the books, had not sat up nights in dimly lit kitchens debating political philosophy. The intelligentsia condescended to him. "I'm afraid Yeltsin is a know-nothing, a crude demagogue of low culture," said Dmitry Likhachev, a great cultural historian, in 1990. Starovoytova hoped he would "listen to the wiser voices around him." But Yeltsin had two things: a loathing for the smug cynicism of the Communist placeholders and a natural talent for connecting with the ordinary people whom his colleagues feared and the intelligentsia patronized. Elections were a game he knew he could win. He was a campaigner long before he was a democrat.

It went back to Sverdlovsk. There, one thousand miles from Moscow, in a Russia still cut off from the West, he had invented the elements of the electoral campaign from scratch, long before the ballot box became anything more than a wastepaper receptacle. He had made it all up—the public meetings, visits to distant villages, populist promises ("Each pillowcase must be justly distributed!" he told miners angry at the linen shortage), the use of television. With the excitement of an Edison or an Amundsen, he reported to colleagues that: "microphone and camera allow [one to] crisply and quickly respond to the problems people are concerned about, pre-empt uninformed questions and, sometimes, unnecessary speculation around difficulties and shortcomings." From the start, he understood the theater of politics. He would turn up unannounced at colleges, wander into a classroom, and, apologizing for distracting the students, invite them to tell him their concerns.

Running, running, running—the "permanent campaign" was nothing new to him—driving his exhausted body into the ground, finding words for each audience, stumbling, getting up. And suddenly, a miracle—the Russians in front of him had become not just the long-suffering, continually victimized people, the *narod*, as under tsars and Soviets, but *voters*, players together in the new game that meant Russia had grown up, had joined the modern world.

He did not just hold his finger to the wind, he thrust his whole body into it. Even before his first real election in March 1989, he says he knew the results of "all the official and unofficial public opinion polls (including those of the Americans)." Two years later, his campaign headquarters was full of "sociologists, economists, scholars in other areas, journalists, people from Tatyana Zaslavskaya's institute, who were constantly 'measuring' the pulse of public opinion." But the best information came from his walkabouts. "I see the eyes of many people. I feel their emotions, their condition, their pain, their hope. One does not get this from any memos, coded intelligence reports, or news digests."

He could craft the perfect rejoinder. The Communist insiders called him a populist. "As for popularity," he wrote in reply, "for some reason, no one apart from me wanted to win it." On the campaign trail in 1991, his opponents accused him of planning to reestablish capitalism. "When I am constantly asked during my trips—are you for socialism or for capitalism?—I say: I am in favor of Russians living better—materially, spiritually, culturally," he replied. "As for a name, people will think one up." He had a feel for improvisation, for the gestures that would congeal into history—climbing out on a rootop to address a crowd, clambering up on a tank. And then history grabbed him. It is still considering just where to put him.

CHAPTER 3

Unreasonable Doubt

The movie would begin with a wide-angled shot of the bombed-out building. Shards of glass, rubble, bricks, smoke, and dust. Voices. Confusion. A woman repeating a meaningless phrase over and over. Ambulances stuck in the morning traffic as policemen carry the wounded on stretchers, stumbling over the debris.

Cut to the manicured lawn of an elegant dacha off the Rublyovskoe Highway, outside Moscow. The prime minister is drinking coffee with his daughter, intermittently tossing a ball to his labrador. As the camera lingers on his face, we see a tough but devoted father. He will not let her go shopping with her friend. The secret service says it is too dangerous at the moment. A telephone rings. The aide whom we have not noticed until now steps forward and hands a phone to the prime minister. We watch his expressionless face.

And then, throughout the movie, as the young lead, a rookie newspaper reporter, pieces together the clues, we are brought back over and over to the same impossible question. Could this statesman, father, dog lover, national hero, somehow be responsible for the devastation witnessed in the first scene? The official story is that Chechen terrorists have planted bombs in cities around the country. But something does not add up. Did the prime minister have some kind of advance notice? Did he ignore warnings he should have heeded? Was he himself set up? Implicated in some way? Or is he entirely blameless?

If it were a movie, the director would quarrel with the script writer over the ending. The director would want a resolution—something inspirational, life affirming. The prime minister must be innocent. One cannot betray the audience, who will have come to like him. The writer would argue for something more artful and realistic, preserving ambiguity. In life, after all, not everything gets resolved. At least, not by the end of the film. Or the hero's term in office.

Vladimir Putin's eight years as president passed to the whir of cranes, the mixing of cement, the sight of skyscrapers rising on every horizon. Stability was the name the Kremlin grandees gave it. Most Russians seemed content to call it that. They worried less, earned more, even began to have more babies. When pollsters called, they gave the president enthusiastic reviews. Yet, to the attentive, these years brought something else as well. Not fear, in its hard Stalinist or soft Brezhnev era varieties. Not even a feeling of significant freedoms departing. Just a kind of background music of uncertainty, a sense that things could suddenly change, that not all was as it seemed.

Critics of the men in the Kremlin accused them of terrible things. Most Russians did not take their complaints seriously. They were irresponsible accusations, the fantasies of conspiracy theorists and tabloid scribblers. And yet, beyond the reasonable doubts, there are the unreasonable ones, the questions that arrive uninvited and refuse to leave. Ignored or repressed, such questions lingered for years in the margins of consciousness until in the end doubt became so familiar it was hardly noticed—a vague taste in the mouth, a smell in the air, as characteristic of Russia under Putin as the Mercedes luxury models clogging urban intersections.

The Agent

Leningrad in the early 1950s was a wounded city. Ten years earlier, Wehrmacht troops had surrounded the Imperial capital, crushing it with artillery shells. Hitler's plan to erase the city from the face of the earth and hand the land over to his Finnish allies almost succeeded. Families burned their books to keep warm; ate stray dogs, cats, rats, and crows; and boiled a kind of soup out of the carpenter's glue they leached from their wallpaper. With the spring, corpses that had lain buried in the snow came out of hibernation.

On the bank of the River Neva just outside the city, one of its defenders, Vladimir Spiridonovich Putin, had been wounded in the winter of 1942. His legs were shot through with shrapnel and he was losing blood and sure to die. But a comrade dragged him across the ice to safety, dodging the bullets of enemy snipers. His young wife survived the blockade only by sharing her husband's hospital rations. Their infant son died of diphtheria.

The Putins' third and only surviving child, Vladimir Vladimirovich—Volodya or Vova, in the Russian diminutives—was born on October 7, 1952. His father, who limped from his war wounds, worked at a factory making railway cars. Volodya grew up in a single, twenty-square-meter room within a fifth-floor communal apartment a couple of miles from the Winter Palace. There was no bathroom or hot water, only a toilet off the dark hallway. Rats ran in the building's foyer and steps were missing on the stairs.

Putin was too fidgety to be a good student—average abilities, said his eighth grade teacher, except for a remarkable memory—and he was accepted into the Pioneers youth group late on account of his unruly behavior and mediocre grades. His free time passed in the yard with the other street toughs. *Shpana*, he called himself later—a hoodlum. One friend remembers him on the rooftops, jumping between balconies. Physically small, he took up sambo—a kind of Russian self-defense—and then judo, which he practiced assiduously, winning the Leningrad city championship at twenty-four.

As the war was spun from recent trauma into popular culture, a genre of spy fiction and adventure films came into vogue in the late 1960s. The typical hero was a Soviet secret agent behind Nazi lines. Disciplined, psychologically penetrating, with nerves of steel and an inchoate patriotism, such heroes were always just one false step away from an SS firing squad. When Putin was fifteen, the film *Shchit i mech* [Sword and Shield], came out to a rapturous reception; 134 million people saw it in its first few days.

A short walk from Putin's apartment, in a building known as the "Big House," the KGB had its Leningrad headquarters. One day, as a teenager, Putin says, he dropped in at the reception area to offer his services. "We don't take volunteers," the desk officer told him. When Putin asked what was the best preparation, the man suggested law school. Against the advice of his parents and judo coach, who thought he should take a guaranteed spot at the local aviation institute, Putin applied to and was accepted by the law department of Leningrad State University (in its Russian acronym, LGU). Four years later, after he had already given up on spying and was seeking assignment to the prosecutor's office, a man appeared one afternoon to offer Putin a job in state security.

Did he not think of Stalin's terror, an interviewer asked him much later. "My ideas about the KGB were formed from romantic spy stories," he said. "I went to work in the organs with romantic ideas." Little is known of what he did from day to day during the next ten years. He says he performed various desk jobs and then underwent training in foreign intelligence. In 1983, Putin married an airline stewardess, Lyudmila Shkrebneva, who gave up flying to return to the university and write a dissertation on Spanish grammar.

Putin's first and only foreign assignment came in 1985, when he was sent to the KGB station in the East German town of Dresden, near the Czech border. The German Democratic Republic was on the frontline of the cold war, hosting 380,000 Soviet troops. It was also a museum of communist orthodoxy. As the new Soviet leader, Mikhail Gorbachev, began relaxing political controls in his country, East Germany's aging dictator, Erich Honecker, refused to follow suit. "We have done our perestroika," Honecker told Gorbachev, "we have nothing to restructure."

Putin arrived in Dresden at the age of thirty-two. What little we know of his time there comes from his own interviews and from the sympathetic recollections of some of his fellow spies. One later published a memoir under the pseudonym Vladimir Usoltsev. For almost five years, the Putins lived with their colleagues in a nondescript, two-story villa at No. 4 Angelikastrasse, near the Elbe River. The neighbors worked for the Stasi, the East German intelligence service, notorious for its ruthless control over citizens' lives. Some became good friends of the Putins.

Putin's main assignment, he says, was to recruit East Germans who had some cover story for traveling to the West. How well he succeeded is hard to determine, although at least one of his informers was later arrested by West German security. Moscow busied its agents with a variety of other tasks. A key one was keeping the home front supplied with catalogs from West German mail order outlets containing pictures of the latest fashions for Russian seamstresses to copy. The Lubyanka—headquarters of the KGB—also had a voracious appetite for written reports. Putin's colleague Usoltsev joked that a Soviet spy's sharpest weapon was the awl used to punch holes through the corners of stacks of paper in order to fasten them together.

From this Saxon backwater, between trips to the Radeberger Brewery and long hours reading the Russian classics—Gogol and Saltykov-Shchedrin were favorites, Usoltsev says—Putin watched the Soviet empire fall apart. Usoltsev portrays him as an ambivalent ironist—modern in outlook, aware of the corrosion within the Soviet system, a little pedantically legalistic, even, at times, democratic in outlook, but careful to hide any incorrect attitudes in public and skilled at ingratiating himself with his superiors. He was taken aback by the haste with which Moscow raced from Eastern Europe. As protesters mobbed the Stasi headquarters across the street in 1989, a crowd appeared outside the KGB office. Colonel Putin, brandishing a pistol, went out to warn them off. Without orders from Moscow, the local Soviet troops refused to come to the KGB staff's defense, and, writes Putin, "Moscow was silent." The agents were burning so many confidential papers that they broke the stove.

Sobchak's Shadow

A few months later, Putin was back in Leningrad. The KGB leadership, preoccupied with the crumbling of Soviet power structures, had no exciting plans for the young agent. He had to settle for a position as assistant rector at LGU, spying on foreign students for his bosses in the Big House.

By this point, Gorbachev's reforms had thrown Leningrad's political life into a state of exhilarating vibration. In the City Council, the newly elected deputies could not agree on a leader. Anatoly Sobchak, an LGU law professor who had become a telegenic democrat, was invited to head the city government. To staff his office, Sobchak looked to his old university. A colleague put Putin in touch.

As Putin tells it, the two sat in Sobchak's office getting acquainted one afternoon, and Sobchak impulsively announced he would hire Putin as his assistant. He promised to phone the university rector and have him transferred. Putin, with a touch of melodrama, took the opportunity to impart his secret:

I could not not say: "Anatoly Aleksandrovich, I will be very happy to do this. It's interesting for me. I even want to do it. But there's one circumstance that, apparently, will be an obstacle to this transfer."

He asks: "Which?"

I answer: "I must tell you that I am not just an assistant to the rector, I'm a staff officer of the KGB."

To which Sobchak responded with an unprintable expression that conveyed a certain lack of concern about what the organs of state security might think. This, to Putin, was new and, apparently, refreshing. He accepted.

Why would Sobchak, a leading liberal known to loathe the secret police, turn to a KGB colonel to run his administration? The short answer is that he was out of his depth.

St. Petersburg—Leningrad's historic name which Sobchak promptly restored—was the country's artistic capital. With its neoclassical and Baroque facades, its colonnades and embankments, its Bronze Horseman always about to come to life as in Pushkin's poem, it resembled the enormous stage for some Olympian ballet. The city's windswept squares and frozen canals were haunted by the ghosts of countless writers. Had Putin as a child wandered a few minutes from the yard of his tenement, he might have glimpsed the poet Joseph Brodsky sailing past on the Liteyny Prospekt streetcar to his job at the main armaments factory.

But, over the years, the Imperial capital had been hammered into Leningrad, a proletarian metropolis of defense factories and shipyards. Giant blocks of barracks-like apartments accumulated on the outskirts. As the Baltic republics seceded in the early 1990s, Leningrad's port became one of the country's main export hubs. In the harbor, ships were loaded with oil and other valuables. Later, as central planning collapsed, the military plants, their storerooms stocked with rare metals, lost their subsidies and state orders. The depressed economy was a perfect breeding ground for organized crime.

Besides the mobsters, the other force in the city with guns and money was the KGB. As the security organs infiltrated undercover agents into the criminal gangs, it became hard to say where one ended and the other began. Throughout Russia, criminals and law enforcers were locked in a

peculiar embrace in which antagonism and commerce were hardly dis-
tinguishable. They alternated in the roles of predator and prey. The crime
reporter Oleg Utitsyn told me in 1993 of a conversation he had had with
one of the lead detectives of the police's organized crime squad. "If the
mafia did not pay me," the detective explained, "I would not fight them."
It hardly seemed to matter to the two sides whether they were exchang-
ing bullets or banknotes.

At the time Putin met Sobchak, one of the latter's aides was Yury
Shutov, a reputed criminal authority who was in between jail spells. In the
early 1980s, Shutov had served five years for setting the city's Communist
headquarters on fire in an attempt to destroy documents incriminating
him. Years later, he would be sentenced to life for a series of murders, kidnappings, robberies, and acts of embezzlement. But in the early fever of
democratic reform, when a jail term was considered a badge of honor by
the anti-Soviet dissidents, Shutov had managed to score complete reha-
bilitation and talk his way onto Sobchak's staff. "I'm afraid to go out into
my reception room," Sobchak said, according to Putin.

They made an odd—but complementary—couple. Sobchak, something of a dandy, whose trademark checkered jacket soon gave way to a
wardrobe of expensive suits, was most comfortable mingling with opera
singers and novelists, pop stars and television anchors. He was so often
away on trips that Leningraders joked about his rare visits to the city.
When in town, he devoted as much time to entertaining celebrities as to
the details of administration. Putin, the deferential manager, hovered just
outside the frame of every photograph. After Sobchak was elected mayor
and moved the government into the elegant Smolny Institute, a former
academy for noble women that the Communists had used as their city
headquarters, Putin would not at first even take an office on the same
floor as his boss. During Sobchak's trips, it was Putin who attended to
city business. While Sobchak's oratory painted the new Russian landscape in black and white, Putin operated in a world of dirty grey. One
could not run the city without dealing with its powerful and often dangerous inhabitants.

Putin was personally devoted and intensely loyal to Sobchak, despite
their somewhat different views of the world. At the same time, in the
book of autobiographical interviews Putin published in 2000, he does

not explicitly deny that he was spying on his boss. In 1991, Putin's request to resign from the KGB was—he says—granted. Still, his superiors kept in touch. Once, Putin writes, his KGB bosses asked him to obtain a blank sheet of paper with Sobchak's signature that could be used for incrimination or blackmail. Putin whipped out a set of such blanks. "You see, this person trusts me," he told his superviser. "What do you want from me?" In the Big House, they apparently decided Putin's closeness to Sobchak was worth more than a forgeable signature.

And Sobchak did trust him. His wife, Lyudmila Narusova, said that one of the few times she heard her husband swear was when she mentioned the rumors that the KGB had sent Putin to watch over him. Sobchak responded with the same unprintable expression he had used when Putin confessed his KGB affiliation. In fact, the organs had many other sources in City Hall. Although most city governments employed law enforcement professionals, Sobchak's team contained a surprising number for such a scourge of the KGB. In addition to Putin, the staff included at least five intelligence or KGB veterans, and probably more. Almost all were appointed to prominent national positions after Putin became president.

Putin's main responsibility was to attract investment to the city and revive its depressed economy. He set up St. Petersburg's first currency exchange and approved the privatization of many hotels, enterprises, and city apartments. With his backing and his German contacts, several Western banks opened affiliates. The first was Dresdner Bank, whose office was headed by a former Stasi officer, Matthias Warnig, who had reportedly worked with Putin during his Dresden days.

Some initiatives were more controversial. In the winter of 1991–92, the city faced the prospect of hunger. With the financial system seizing up, the only way to obtain food was with barter deals. Putin won permission for certain local companies to export more than $90 million worth of raw materials and use the proceeds to import food. The exports were delayed, and almost no food arrived. Critics claimed the prices for the exported goods were set artificially low, creating large profits that then disappeared into the intermediaries' Western bank accounts. The City Council investigated and recommended that Sobchak fire Putin. The mayor declined.

In another initiative, Putin and his law enforcement allies sought to take over the city's mafia-infiltrated gambling business. He set up a municipal enterprise, with representatives of the Federal Security Service (FSB), Tax Service, and Tax Police, and gave it 51 percent of the shares in all casinos. The idea, he wrote later, was to use the dividends to finance city programs. But, as he admitted, the gaming firms hid their profits, so the city received little for its efforts.

As a promoter of economic development, Putin's results were mixed. The city lagged behind Moscow, where commerce was bustling under Sobchak's rival, Yury Luzhkov. Despite the extensive presence of law enforcement officers, St. Petersburg remained one of the more criminalized cities. Through the late 1990s, as gangster-style killings were subsiding in most places, they continued in St. Petersburg. During his last year working for Sobchak, Putin carried a gun.

Can one swim in the ocean without getting wet? Putin's work could not fail to bring him into contact with some of the city's most notorious businessmen. Journalists have scoured the St. Petersburg registry of business licenses. Among the hundreds of documents authorizing privatizations and property deals and bearing Putin's signature, some have attracted scrutiny.

On a trip to Frankfurt in the early 1990s, Putin met a Russian businessman, Vladimir Smirnov, who was setting up a joint venture with German investors to develop real estate in St. Petersburg. Smirnov's firm, the St. Petersburg Real Estate Holding Company, became known by its German acronym SPAG. According to several publications, quoting company documents and the firm's German chairman, Putin himself served on SPAG's unpaid advisory board, representing the St. Petersburg government. In 2003, German prosecutors accused SPAG and some associated firms of laundering "tens of millions of Euros" for the St. Petersburg–based Tambov organized crime group. One of SPAG's founders, Rudolf Ritter, was indicted in Liechtenstein in 2001, accused of laundering money for the Cali cocaine cartel. Despite the numerous reports to the contrary, the Kremlin has denied that Putin had any connection with SPAG.

From 1997, Smirnov served on the board of the Petersburg Fuel Company (PFC), which under Putin had received contracts to supply the city's ambulances, police cars, and buses. From 1998, the vice president of PFC was a widely feared, one-handed St. Petersburg businessman, Vladimir Kumarin, who changed his name in the mid-1990s to Barsukov. Barsukov was later arrested and charged with extortion, fraud, and attempted murder. After Putin became president, he brought Smirnov to Moscow to serve in the Kremlin's property department and then in the state nuclear fuels exporter. In the mid-1990s, Smirnov, Putin, and some friends set up a cooperative to build dachas for its members beside a lake near St. Petersburg. By 2008, one member, a physicist turned banker, Yury Kovalchuk, was featured on *Forbes*'s list of the world's billionaires. Another, Vladimir Yakunin, who helped Kovalchuk build his banking business, was director of Russian Railroads, and a third, Andrey Fursenko, was Putin's minister of education.

By 1996, Sobchak had fallen out with Yeltsin, who had been fed malicious gossip about him. The procurator general in Moscow started an investigation into claims that Sobchak had handed out city apartments at low prices, including one to himself. Whether or not these accusations were true, the alleged offenses were relatively minor; far worse could be found in most city governments. Sobchak, whose jet-setting had finally caught up with him, lost his reelection bid and was left to face the prosecutors with few friends by his side. Putin, ever loyal, helped arrange an evacuation to France on medical grounds before he could be arrested, and Sobchak lived there in self-imposed exile for three years until the charges were dropped. He died in 2000, shortly after returning to Russia.

Under the Radar

After Sobchak's defeat, Putin found himself out of work. A network of former Sobchak staffers based in Moscow now pulled in its latest member. Putin climbed rapidly—from helping to manage the Kremlin's enormous, corruption-ridden property holdings, to serving as chief inspector of the federal bureaucracy, then first deputy head of the presidential administration. One day in 1998, Putin was sent to the airport to meet the prime minister, Sergey Kirienko, who congratulated him on his appointment as head of the security service, the FSB. The next March, he added the chairmanship of the Security Council, which coordinated the law enforcement and defense ministries. Then, as Yeltsin scanned the horizon for a dependable "heir," his glance fell on the deferential Putin. On August 9, 1999, Yeltsin announced that he had found a man who could "unite around himself those who will renew Great Russia in the new 21st Century." A week later, the Duma confirmed Putin as Yeltsin's sixth prime minister.

Most observers were perplexed by Putin's rapid rise. In Moscow, as in St. Petersburg, he had seemed a mediocrity without ambition, content to fill in the blanks in the plans of others. To the journalist Yelena Tregubova, Putin was an almost translucent figure, so intent on not standing out that he "blended masterfully with the colors of his own office." Anatoly Chubais, himself from St. Petersburg and usually a Putin backer, is said to have tried to talk Yeltsin out of appointing Putin, only to be outmaneuvered by the head of the presidential administration, Aleksandr Voloshin.

The St. Petersburg clique pulled Putin up the first steps of the administrative ladder. Aleksey Kudrin, a colleague from Sobchak's office, who served later as finance minister, was a strong backer. The high burnout rate at the top created openings. Putin's reputation for unwavering loyalty, evident in his relations with Sobchak, no doubt helped. Along the way, he showed himself willing to fight dirty on the Kremlin's behalf. When the procurator general, Yury Skuratov, insisted on investigating corruption in Yeltsin's inner circle, a grainy video surfaced showing a man who looked like Skuratov frolicking naked with two young women said to be prostitutes. Putin, as FSB chief, vouched for the video's authenticity and helped press Skuratov to resign.

At some point during this period, Putin was adopted by the group of insiders known as "the Family" (which included Yeltsin's daughter Tatyana, his aide and ghostwriter Valentin Yumashev, and the oligarchs Boris Berezovsky and Roman Abramovich). Berezovsky later claimed to have engineered Putin's rise. His account is hard to confirm—there were few witnesses, still fewer who might be considered reliable, and his penchant for self-promotion is well known. But it is clear that sometime in early 1999 Berezovsky came to view Putin as someone who would defend his assets and personal security.

Putin's path from prime minister to president led through two elections and the outbreak of one war, all compressed into a few months. Few would have given him any odds of success. He seemed to the press corps a charmless bureaucrat, compromised by his links to the deeply unpopular Yeltsin. The previous week the Chechen warlord Shamil Basayev had invaded the republic of Dagestan in an attempt to create an Islamic caliphate (see Chapter 8). Chechen terror seemed to be spreading across the North Caucasus and maybe beyond. Putin sent Russian troops to fight the insurgents, whom they managed to drive out after about a month. Then, following a plan worked out that spring under Putin's predecessor, troops advanced into Chechnya.

As Russians were recoiling from the shock of Basayev's incursion, a series of apartment buildings in Dagestan, Moscow, and the Rostov region exploded, one after another, killing about three hundred people. The central authorities immediately announced a Chechen connection, although the evidence for this was never clear. Many Russians were close to hysteria, as families went to bed wondering whether they would wake up. A week later, in the city of Ryazan, inhabitants of one apartment block found sacks of white powder in their basement attached to a timing device. Initial tests found the sacks contained the explosive hexogen, which had been used in the other bombings. However, FSB headquarters in Moscow quickly announced that the sacks contained sugar and were part of a training exercise to test local vigilance. These oddly contradictory reports caused some to suspect that the bombings had been organized by the secret services to justify the war in Chechnya and rally support for Putin. Putin responded to the explosions with calm fury, insisting as television cameras rolled that the authorities would pursue the terrorists without mercy and would "kill them even in the toilets," if that was where they found them.

Against this backdrop of trauma, Putin's popularity rose sharply. The December Duma election was widely seen as a primary for the presidential contest scheduled for June. As of September 1999, the favorite was Yevgeny Primakov, the old Soviet journalist and Middle East expert with long-standing secret service ties whom Yeltsin had been forced to accept as prime minister by the Communist-led parliament. Primakov had joined Moscow mayor Yury Luzhkov to lead a new party of regional governors called Fatherland–All Russia. In mid-September, 16 percent supported Primakov for president, while about 5 percent favored Putin, fewer than planned to vote "against all."

As prime minister, Primakov had said he was freeing up jail cells for the economic criminals he planned to arrest. To Berezovsky and other members of the Family, a Primakov or Luzhkov presidency was an alarming prospect. Kremlin political operatives quickly patched together a new pro-Putin party, called Unity, and recruited an Olympic wrestling champion, a police official, and the popular minister of emergency situations to lead it. Meanwhile, Berezovsky's key anchorman at the ORT channel, Sergey Dorenko, slung mud at Putin's opponents. To draw attention to Primakov's age, Dorenko played footage of a grisly operation he said the candidate had undergone. He accused Primakov of participating in an attempt to assassinate Georgian president, Eduard Shevardnadze, and insinuated that Luzhkov was implicated in the 1996 murder of an American hotel developer. Luzhkov, Dorenko claimed, owned real estate in Spain and was somehow linked to the Japanese doomsday cult Aum Shinrikyo. Vladimir Gusinsky's NTV station was almost as brazen—but less effective—in its support of Luzkhov and Primakov.

In the December election, Unity came from nowhere to place second, just behind the Communists, and far ahead of Luzhkov and Primakov's bloc. Putin's approval rating had reached 79 percent, and 42 percent said they planned to vote for him as president, compared to 6 percent for Primakov, who dropped out the following month. To lock in Putin's advantage, Yeltsin resigned early, making Putin the acting president for three months until an election could be held.

As Putin sailed toward victory in the March election, Berezovsky, giddy with excitement, was eager to claim credit. One week before the vote, a journalist asked him whether capital supported Putin. "Of course. What do you think—am I not capital?" he replied. Putin had promised to end the oligarchs' political influence. "This is normal, absolutely right," Berezovsky conceded. "Only, it's infeasible. But the words are right. For the voters." When, the next morning, I visited Mikhail Margelov, one of Putin's campaign organizers, he was fuming. Not only was Berezovsky trying to weaken Putin by implying he was in bed with odious oligarchs like himself, he was doing this when it was already too late for the campaign to repair the damage. "Berezovsky knows how to pick his moment!" he exploded. "He farts when the door and windows are closed." Putin won anyway with 53 percent of the vote.

Accidental President

In the Kremlin, Putin found himself, in Chubais's words, "fantastically free" to pursue whatever agenda he liked. His approval rating was above 70 percent. In the Duma, the Unity party occupied the pivotal center, from where it could forge majorities on almost any issue by allying with Left or Right. The regional governors, still digesting their gains of the previous eight years, had little desire to challenge a wartime leader with astronomic popularity. The only parallel was the brief period in 1991 when Yeltsin, fresh from his triumph over the August putschists, had seemed to have all Russia on his side. But while Yeltsin's rating peaked just as the economy was collapsing, Putin had better luck: although few realized it yet, a rapid recovery had begun that would last through his second term.

Besides his relentless prosecution of the Chechen war, Putin advanced policies on three fronts. First, he turned out to be an enthusiast for free market ideas—such an enthusiast it made some of the liberal scholars who counseled him nervous. He hired Andrey Illarionov, a libertarian economist, to advise him, and told aides to draw up plans to cut taxes and reduce the regulatory burden on business. Mikhail Leontyev, an economics commentator who had become a nationalist Putin fan, did an interview with him that March, in which Putin praised the much maligned privatizer-in-chief, and said that what Russia needed was six or seven more Chubaises. "I asked him respectfully not to say this again in public, at least until after the election," Leontyev told me.

Suddenly in demand, frustrated liberals in the ministries pulled from their back drawers legislation that had long been blocked. Within a few years, they replaced the progressive income tax, which almost no one paid, with a flat rate of 13 percent; reduced the profit tax from 35 to 24 percent; eliminated turnover taxes and the sales tax; reduced the payroll tax from 36 to 26 percent and the value added tax from 20 to 18 percent. Expenditures were also cut as a share of GDP. In 2000, the federal budget deficit turned into a surplus. Currency reserves grew from $8 billion in December 1999 to $44 billion in 2003, and $460 billion in 2007. A new land code which, for the first time, clearly legalized sales of urban land was passed in 2001; agricultural land was added in 2002.

Other reforms sought to reduce regulation and improve the business climate. Officials were required to register firms within five days and charge no more than 2,000 rubles (then about $69). Other legislation limited the activities regional governments could license and how often agencies could inspect a given firm. Police and sanitary inspectors lost the right to close firms without a court order, a power sometimes used to blackmail entrepreneurs. Although enforcement was imperfect and corruption remained, the reforms did lighten the burden on small business. Surveys found that the proportion of new firms registered within five days rose from 17 percent in early 2001 to more than half in 2006. (More than two-thirds still had to pay more than the maximum fee, however, and the average cost was rising.) The average company was inspected about seven times in 2001, but only four times in 2006. A favorite bureaucratic ploy was to require licenses to be renewed frequently, increasing opportunities for bribery. Between 2001 and 2006, the proportion of licenses that remained valid for at least five years jumped from 13 to 84 percent. Putin also passed legislation to combat money laundering in 2001.

Next came an ambitious plan for judicial reform. New criminal and civil procedural codes were enacted in 2002–3. The criminal code entrenched the adversarial principle, introduced the presumption of innocence, increased the rights of defense lawyers (for instance, they were allowed to conduct their own investigations), and extended the use of jury trials—previously implemented in only nine regions—to all regions except Chechnya. The right to approve searches and detention of suspects for more than forty-eight hours was transferred from prosecutors to judges. The number of arrests initially fell by a third. The government quadrupled judges' salaries in the hope that this would reduce corruption and provided more funding for bailiffs and court websites where judges' decisions were to be posted.

Putin's second main initiative was in international affairs. He set out to improve relations with the West, which had cooled after the bombing of Serbia and NATO's eastward expansion. Overruling his military advisers, he closed bases in Cam Ranh Bay, Vietnam, and Lourdes, Cuba. When asked about NATO, he wondered aloud whether Russia might not also join. And, in a widely noted act of solidarity, he was the first world leader to phone President Bush after Al Qaeda struck on September 11, 2001, reaching the latter while still airborne for security reasons.

However, the project that came to define Putin's presidency, overshadowing and eventually undermining the others, was the centralization of power. Even as he sought to liberalize the economy and the courts, he set about concentrating authority in the hands of top executive officials, first and foremost his own. Under Yeltsin, political power had leaked from the Kremlin to a number of other actors—the governors, opposition parties, the media, big business—each of which found ways to lobby for its interests and impede central policies. On one hand, this had hamstrung economic reform and caused disastrous deadlocks when crises loomed. On the other, competition among the various interests had produced a kind of pluralism, albeit unruly and often corrupt. During his election campaign, Putin had promised to reimpose order, by which he meant cutting each of these actors down to size and enforcing loyalty to the Kremlin.

First in line were the oligarchs. Under his administration, Putin had told voters, the "class of oligarchs will cease to exist." In his view, the tycoons had won Russia's most valuable firms in the 1990s by bribing officials, intimidating or murdering rivals, and exploiting legal loopholes. At a Kremlin meeting with twenty-one leading businessmen two months after his inauguration, Putin set new rules. The FSB had files detailing the laws each magnate had broken on the way from rags to riches. Henceforth, they should stay out of politics and consult the Kremlin on major deals. Otherwise, the prosecutors would be set on their trail.

Three of the oligarchs, and several lesser tycoons, failed to heed the warning. Each lost the battle and either fled into self-imposed exile or, as in the case of oil billionaire Mikhail Khodorkovsky, ended up in jail. Other heavyweights, such as Gazprom chief Rem Vyakhirev, were persuaded to retire quietly. Berezovsky, who had complained of boredom after Putin's victory, soon found himself packing for London. In supporting Putin against Primakov, he had jumped out of the fire into the frying pan.

Khodorkovsky, who hoped to finance the growth of an independent civil society in Russia, chose not to leave. On October 25, 2003, a team of FSB agents in flak vests and masks stormed onto the tycoon's plane as it refueled outside Novosibirsk in Western Siberia and arrested him. Over the next two years, he and his colleague, Platon Lebedev, were tried, found guilty of tax evasion and fraud, and sentenced to nine years, later reduced to eight, in a Siberian labor camp. Meanwhile, Khodorkovsky's oil company, Yukos, which despite a reputation for having bent the law in the 1990s had become a model of corporate transparency, was dismembered and the main assets sold off quickly and cheaply via a shell company to the state-owned Rosneft, which by 2007 had jumped from the country's sixth largest oil producer to first place. In the summer of 2004, Putin's longtime aide Igor Sechin was appointed chairman of the Rosneft board. The court proceedings, both to convict Khodorkovsky and to bankrupt Yukos for tax debts, were marred by so many irregularities and procedural violations—including the harassment and prosecution of Khodorkovsky's lawyers—that the state of Russia's judicial system became an international scandal.

Saying a strict "vertical of power" was needed to stop Russia from disintegrating, Putin also set about taming the regional governors. In the 1990s, Russia had become less federal than feudal. Many governors ruled their fiefdoms with a heavy hand, pressuring voters to reelect them, while playing the Kremlin, Duma, and oligarchs against each other. By 2005, Putin had restructured relations between Moscow and the regions. Instead of being directly elected, governors were now nominated by Putin and confirmed by the regional legislature. They had lost their seats in the parliament's upper house and the associated legal immunity. Regional budgets now received just 35 percent of government revenues, down from 54 percent in 1999. Seven presidential prefects, with staffs recruited from the security services, monitored the governors' financial activities. No governors were overtly fighting the Kremlin, and some seemed positively enthusiastic about the new setup.

Taking office, Putin already had a jaundiced view of the Russian media. The average Russian newsroom, in his judgment, differed from a brothel mainly in its décor. The press was "for sale down to its hair roots." Regrettably, he had a point. Planting untrue stories for a fee had become widespread. Putin began reimposing control. The campaign started with the takeovers of ORT (from Berezovsky) and NTV (from Gusinsky). Both were threatened with jail if they did not hand over their shares, and chose exile over prison. Gazprom, through a subsidiary, began buying leading newspapers and magazines, as did certain individual tycoons loyal to the Kremlin. Newspapers nevertheless remained more independent than television, presumably because of Putin's disdain for the print media—"But who reads it, your press?" he teased the journalist Vladimir Solovyov. Open political discussion, from the mild to the scabrous, flourished on the Internet. This may have reflected Putin's scorn for the medium. Why should officials pay attention to the Internet, he asked in January 2010. "On the Internet, 50 percent is porn material." Russia had freedom of speech, as one opposition politician put it in 2002, just "not in prime time."

Many smaller changes kept journalists censoring themselves. Editors grew accustomed to angry phone calls from the Kremlin. To save reporters the trouble of thinking up their own questions, Putin's press secretary, Aleksey Gromov, took to handing them out in advance. "How dare you!" he exploded when one Western journalist asked something that had not been vetted. "Don't you know the rules?! Unapproved questions are not to be asked! Do it one more time and you'll be flying out of here!" The heads of the three main television channels were summoned to the Kremlin every Friday to hear how the week's events were to be covered. A number of journalists, some of whom had been investigating corruption in the armed forces or the Kremlin, were murdered. Few such crimes were solved.

Elections became less free and fair as officials at every level sought to shape the outcome—pressuring citizens to vote for particular candidates, or even falsifying the results. Circumstantial evidence suggests that in the 1990s it was actually opposition parties—first the Communists, and, in 1999, Luzhkov's party of governors—that benefited from such electoral manipulation. Fraud thus served to weaken the Kremlin. Under Putin, the pattern reversed. The irony was that in each presidential election from 2000 to 2008 the Kremlin candidate could have won easily without any funny business: Putin was genuinely popular. Why the Kremlin would support such redundant fraud remains a puzzle.

Especially after 2003, when the pro-Putin party (now renamed United Russia) had an absolute majority, parliament no longer functioned as a check on presidential power. In all countries, legislative oversight weakens when president and parliamentary majority are of the same party. But under Putin, informal disincentives to such oversight were particularly pronounced. The Duma refused to investigate the 1999 apartment bombings, and voted to seal all materials concerning the Ryazan incident for seventy-five years. Nevertheless, several deputies tried to investigate independently. One died after apparently being poisoned. A second was shot in the street.

To centralize the party system, Putin got the Duma to change the voting rule for its elections to pure proportional representation. Previously, half the deputies had been elected proportionally from party lists while the other half ran in individual districts. Some of the deputies representing individual districts had shown an unwelcome independence. Confident it could always coopt the leaders of the opposition parties, the Kremlin preferred a system—such as closed list proportional representation—run by the party bosses. To keep small parties out, the threshold for seats was raised from 5 to 7 percent of the national vote.

Nervous about opposition, the authorities tightened regulations for street rallies, and made it harder to call national referenda. Under Putin, demonstrators were often clubbed and arrested by riot police. Parties out of favor with the Kremlin were denied registration, and newspapers were warned not to report on them. "If there is no party," a government spokesman explained, "it's impossible to write about it." Within United Russia, discipline came from the top. The party's freshman legislators were called to the Kremlin, according to one of them, scolded by one of Putin's political aides for "behaving like they were elected representatives," and instructed to "just vote like you're told." More onerous registration procedures were introduced for nongovernmental organizations, and an official "Public Chamber" was formed and filled with moderates to debate social issues and represent "civil society."

Even the judiciary, which Putin, the lawyer, had seemed so eager to reform, became increasingly subordinated to the Kremlin. Launching criminal cases against judges was made easier. Although they were appointed for life terms by a collegium, composed mostly of other judges, the president still got to choose the chairman of each court, who assigned cases among the other judges, awarded promotions, and could initiate proceedings to fire them for cause. Such appointments were vetted by Putin's old St. Petersburg colleague, FSB General Viktor Ivanov. In 2005, two judges accused Moscow's chief judge of having them fired because they resisted pressures to rule for the authorities. In 2008, the first deputy chairperson of the Supreme Arbitration Court testified that a Kremlin official had made her reappointment conditional on reversing an anti-government ruling. In one regard, judges did continue to follow predictable rules: they still acquitted only 1 percent of criminal defendants.

Critics saw in this concentration of power the forging of an authoritarian state. Yet what was authoritarian was more Putin's style of government than the state itself. He changed formal political institutions relatively little. When, later on, he had the votes to amend the constitution, he almost pedantically refused to do so. Significant rule changes that did occur, such as in the appointment of governors and the introduction of proportional representation in Duma elections, hardly added up to tyranny, and many of the innovations that were harshly criticized in Russia mirrored features found in many respectable democracies (see Chapter 10). More sinister laws established penalties for loosely defined acts of "extremism" and authorized secret service agents to kill terrorists abroad. But for the most part, rather than crafting authoritarian institutions, Putin's team exploited and abused powers they enjoyed within the prevailing democratic framework. Confident of the public's support, they showed little patience for the opposition and no sentimental attachment to fair play.

Putin's rationale for this centralization of power was simple: it was vital to provide order and restore the effectiveness of the state after the turmoil of the 1990s. Only a strong central state could protect the population and bring about economic modernization.

But did the bureaucracy become more effective and the population safer? The state certainly grew. In Putin's eight years as president, about 363,000 additional bureaucrats were hired, mostly federal agents stationed in the regions. Law enforcement mushroomed. In the United States, there are two judges and prosecutorial employees per 10,000 residents. When Putin took over, Russia had eight; when he left, it had fourteen. Federal spending on law enforcement and national security rose from $4 billion in 1998 to $26 billion in 2007.

Despite this influx of resources, most indicators suggest the state became less, not more, effective. It built less housing, paved fewer roads, and laid fewer water mains and gas lines per year than under Yeltsin. The number of public schools and buses in service fell faster than before. Reforms of the education and health systems were repeatedly postponed.

Only 22 percent of Russians thought that there was less corruption and stealing among the country's leadership under Putin than under Yeltsin; 71 percent thought there was the same amount or more. The head of the Interior Ministry's Investigations Committee said that the number of crimes related to corruption had doubled between 1997 and 2007.

As for keeping citizens safe, few saw any improvement. Each year under Putin, far more poll respondents reported that law enforcement had deteriorated than said it was working better, and more said their personal security had declined than said it had improved. Although official crime statistics need to be treated with extreme caution (see Chapter 10), they paint a similar picture. The number of crimes registered under Putin—3.1 million per year—exceeded the 2.6 million a year under Yeltsin. Meanwhile, the number of convictions per registered crime fell from .36 under Yeltsin to .31 under his successor.

Putin had burst onto the political scene amid a wave of panic about terrorism, promising to provide security. In fact, it was under Putin that the country suffered its bloodiest incidents. In October 2002, a band of mostly Chechen gunmen seized the Dubrovka Theater in central Moscow during a performance of the musical "Nord-Ost" and threatened to blow it up. Then in September 2004, another group took over a school packed with children in the North Ossetian city of Beslan. At least 129 people died in the first incident, and at least 334, many of them children, in the second. Both times, federal troops stormed the location and were later accused of causing many of the deaths. After Dubrovka, the chairman of the Moscow City Health Committee said almost all victims had been killed not by the terrorists but by the gas the authorities piped in to disable the gunmen. After Beslan, local residents said many had been killed by the special forces that stormed the school. In a 2006 survey, 52 percent of respondents agreed at least in part that the "inaction and negligence" of the authorities had contributed to the high fatalities at Dubrovka and Beslan.

According to Interior Ministry statistics, terrorist attacks were much more frequent under Putin (251 per year) than during Yeltsin's last three years (24 per year). The number of incidents peaked at 561 in 2003, and then declined, but even in 2007 there were more than in any of Yeltsin's last three years. The public evidently did not feel safer. In October 1999, right after the apartment bombings, only 38 percent of Russians believed the authorities could protect them against terrorist attacks. Seven years later in 2006, even fewer—just 31 percent—believed this. As for external security, the military continued to molder without significant reform, its pilots unable to fly more than a few dozen hours a year because of fuel shortages, its sailors at sea only one or two days a month, its conscripts terrorized by horrific hazing. In 2006 and 2007, 423 soldiers killed themselves.

One bright spot was the growing use of commercial (*arbitrazh*) courts by businesses to settle their disputes—the number of their cases rose from 497,000 in 1999 to 905,000 in 2007. Firms that contested decisions of the tax authorities in court won an impressive 89 percent of the time. So long as no well-connected figures were involved, the courts sometimes worked quite well. This was overshadowed, however, by the scandalous cases in which judges caved into pressure from highly placed officials. Crudely politicized proceedings in cases like that over Yukos's tax debt discredited the judiciary.

In short, the "cumbersome, slow-moving, ineffective state apparatus" that Putin criticized early in his presidency grew even more cumbersome and ineffective on his watch. Rather than modernizing and imposing order, Putin used his country's oil revenues to paper over the state's decline.

Yet, year after year, despite the creaking bureaucracy and the appearance of worsening corruption, Putin's popularity remained astronomically high. His approval never fell below 60 percent of respondents, and sometimes reached into the 80s. Many factors may have played a role, but one was crucial. As I discuss in Chapter 7, much evidence suggests Putin's popularity stayed high because of the economy's exceptional performance. Between 2000 and 2007, disposable income, adjusted for inflation, increased by 12 percent a year. Most Russians credited this in large part to the country's leaders, and were grateful.

Reelected in 2004 in a landslide tainted by irregularities, Putin seemed less concerned in his second term with reforming the state than with expanding the business empires of his friends. By 2007, nine members of Putin's inner circle, each with a security service background or close relationships with high-ranking siloviki (as law enforcement or security professionals were known), headed companies the combined revenues of which totaled around 18 percent of GDP. Little remained of his early liberalism except strict fiscal and monetary policy. At the same time, Putin seemed to grow increasingly tired of lectures from the West about Chechnya, democracy, and the imprisoned oligarch Khodorkovsky. His rhetoric hardened. He seemed to believe the reports the FSB, under his old St. Petersburg friend Nikolay Patrushev, was feeding him. Russia was encircled by enemies. The West was funding terrorists in Chechnya. Foreign-financed nongovernmental organizations were fomenting revolution. Kremlin guidance of television became even more heavy-handed. Certain topics and people—such as former prime minister Mikhail Kasyanov and the extreme opposition National Bolshevik party—were not to be shown on the air. Call-in programs in which Putin answered supposedly spontaneous questions from ordinary Russians were scripted and staged in excruciating detail.

In an embarrassing miscalculation, Putin injected himself into the 2004 Ukrainian presidential election, openly supporting the pro-Russian candidate, Viktor Yanukovich, against the former prime minister, Viktor Yushchenko, and sending a team of Kremlin spin doctors to help his campaign. When Yanukovich was declared the winner, thousands of Yushchenko's supporters, claiming electoral fraud, camped out in Kiev's main square in a series of protests dubbed the "Orange Revolution," until the election was annulled and a new one held, which Yushchenko won. Putin's angry comments suggest he took this reversal quite personally.

Like Yeltsin, Putin became preoccupied in his last years with choosing a successor who would be both popularly accepted and reliable. As the 2008 vote approached, conflict broke out between two factions of siloviki, which started arresting each other's agents. Some observers believed administration hard-liners were trying to destabilize politics and inflame relations with the West in the hope of persuading Putin to stay for an unconstitutional third term. During 2006, two vocal critics of the Kremlin were murdered. The journalist Anna Politkovskaya was shot in what looked like a contract hit. Then, Aleksandr Litvinenko, a former KGB officer granted political asylum in Britain, was poisoned with radioactive polonium in a London hotel when he drank tea with two other former KGB agents. In both cases, Putin's critics pointed the finger at him. Relations with the West turned frosty.

It seemed as though Putin was being backed into a corner by his security service partners. In response, he deftly changed direction. Surprising even close aides, he thrust himself into the campaign for United Russia in the December 2007 Duma election, heading its national list, appearing on its billboards (some hardly mentioned the party's name), and giving an unusually vituperative preelection speech, in which he attacked unpatriotic opposition groups who "feed off foreign embassies like jackals and count on support of foreign funds and governments." United Russia won with 64 percent of the vote.

Putin then announced he would back Dmitry Medvedev, a former law professor who had been his loyal aide since St. Petersburg, for president. Medvedev, perceived as the softest and most modern of the contenders, was at odds with the main silovik factions. In turn, Medvedev asked Putin to serve as prime minister if he were elected. With the United Russia Party behind him and the premiership in his sights, Putin would clearly be able to protect his allies and manage the factions after leaving the Kremlin. On March 2, Medvedev won the presidency with 70 percent of the vote, just one percent less than Putin in 2004.

Putin's Motivation

What accounts for the choices he made? Why did he, who could have swept every election with a landslide, instead choose to jerry-rig his country's democratic institutions, engineering victories when he could have won fair and square? Why did he protect an ineffective and corrupt bureaucracy rather than build the modern state he talked so much about? And why did the tone of his administration change over the years? In the early days, the concentration of political power was leavened by an enthusiasm for economic liberalism, legal reform, and integration with the West. By his final year, his rhetoric hit notes of extreme anti-Americanism, and his entourage hardly bothered any more to conceal its expanding wealth.

Here we push up against Putin's often-noted opaqueness. His public speech always served more as a shield or mirror than as a window. The newspaper *Kommersant*'s Andrey Kolesnikov followed him around for years. But already after the first twenty-four hours, he knew Putin was a "completely closed person." To get any further, we need at this point to mix analysis with speculation. Although we cannot know what happened inside Putin's head, we can replace uninformed guesses with those that fit better with available information.

The Chekist

One interpretation popular in the West rooted Putin's behavior in his identity as a former KGB agent. He was, some said, the prototypical Chekist, the name given to true believers in the mission of the Soviet security service, after the Cheka, the Bolsheviks' first secret police. Initially, so the argument went, Putin thought it prudent to conceal his true objectives. But his goals were always to roll back the freedoms established by his predecessor, to restore the power of the security services, and to expand Russia's geopolitical influence throughout the former Soviet region.

Those who cast Putin in this light have plenty of material on which to draw. On his first day as FSB chief in 1998, Putin told the generals assembled to greet him: "I have come home." The next year, he laid flowers at the grave of Yury Andropov, the longtime KGB head and Soviet leader, and mounted a plaque outside the Lubyanka to honor him. With the Communist leader, Gennady Zyuganov, he drank a toast to Stalin. Speaking to a group of FSB brass four months after becoming prime minister, he deadpanned: "I want to report that the group of FSB operatives sent to work undercover within the government is succeeding in the first stage of its assignment." During his presidency, bursts of cold war invective—about enemies and traitors, external and internal—would sometimes break through his confident speeches about modernization and the rule of law.

Under Putin, siloviki flooded into all branches of the state. By 2002, according to Olga Kryshtanovskaya, a sociologist who studied Russia's elite, 33 percent of government ministers had a security or military background, up from 22 percent in 1999, and there were many more lower down. The parliament and corps of governors also had increases, although less dramatic.

There is no question Putin relied on the security services, considered himself a Chekist, and had at most a formal commitment to democracy. At the same time, he was quite a peculiar Chekist. He had gone over to the other side, resigning from the security organs in 1991 to work for Anatoly Sobchak, one of the KGB's harshest critics, and had shown respect and personal sympathy for this odious democrat. Then, in Moscow, he had become mixed up with the Family and its intrigues. He associated with Berezovsky, a character the KGB veterans viewed as evil incarnate (the tycoon even said that he had taken Putin on skiing trips). The generals had been shocked when in 1998 Yeltsin sent this lieutenant-colonel, still wet behind the ears, to command them. Putin had promptly cut the KGB's central apparatus by a third, pushing hundreds into retirement, while promoting his St. Petersburg colleagues over the heads of those who remained. The old guard had lobbied Primakov to get him fired, even telling the prime minister that Putin was having him tailed. Then, in the midst of all this, Putin's friend Berezovsky had staged a press conference in which a renegade officer called Aleksandr Litvinenko had accused his superiors of planning murders and other crimes. To say relations between Putin and the KGB brass started out cool would be an understatement.

Even the details that seem at first to confirm Putin as a KGB insider suggest, on examination, the opposite. Why was he tripping over himself to nail up plaques, place wreaths, drink toasts to Stalin, and so on? A true insider would not need to make such gestures. The charm offensive shows precisely that he was unsure of his reception among the KGB barons. The "I have come home" with which he entered the Lubyanka in 1998 is what the prodigal son says, not his dependable brother. Like Kennedy's "Ich bin ein Berliner," it is a line that resonates only if not literally true. As for the joke about KGB agents infiltrating the government, again, this only works if the listeners know it is not actually the case. It is hard to imagine, say, Kryuchkov making such a remark to his deputies. It would have perplexed them; why would the chief reveal his secrets so publicly?

Two traditional preoccupations defined the Chekist mind-set—anti-Semitism and anti-Americanism. Putin lacked both of these. He made a point of cultivating the Russian Chief Rabbi, Berel Lazar, who became one of his strongest supporters, and, for the first time since the Revolution, the Russian army was given its own chief rabbi. He sought from the start to improve relations with Washington (although later he grew frustrated at the lack of reciprocation). To the alarm of former KGB and army generals, he closed the listening station at Lourdes, Cuba, which had collected 40 percent of Russia's intelligence on the United States. His enthusiasm for liberal economics and legal reforms earned him the admiration of *New York Times* columnist Tom Friedman—"keep rootin' for Putin," he advised his readers—but it cannot have won him friends in the Lubyanka. Adversarial trials, the expanded use of juries, limits on holding suspects, and the weakening of prosecutors relative to judges must all have aggravated the FSB and their law enforcement allies. Law enforcers found ways around the new restrictions. But they must have resented having to.

Putin's profile and priorities were not those of the average Chekist. Conversely, one did not need to be a Chekist in 1999 to want to strengthen the executive, to rein in the governors and oligarchs, even to transform the media from an instrument for corporate mudslinging. Politicians of all stripes agreed on these points. Putin's rivals' plans were, if anything, more extreme in these regards. Even liberals saw the political order of the late Yeltsin years as pathological.

Putin did not dream up the idea of replacing elections of regional governors with presidential appointment, subject to confirmation by the regional legislatures. As prime minister, Primakov had proposed exactly this. His plan differed from Putin's only in that he announced it five years earlier. Primakov called for constitutional changes to "reestablish a rigid vertical power structure" before Putin even thought of the phrase. The other possible presidential contenders, Moscow mayor Luzhkov and Communist leader Gennady Zyuganov, were expected to impose even tighter control over the governors. Even many pro-Western democrats thought the president should be able to fire governors, even if not to appoint them.

As for disempowering the oligarchs, both Primakov and Luzhkov favored reexamining the privatization deals of the 1990s, and under Primakov's government arrest warrants were issued for Berezovsky and for Aleksandr Smolensky, another tycoon. Even the liberal Boris Nemtsov favored pressuring businessmen with threats of arrest to compel them to invest more in Russia. In the summer of 1999, he took a list of oligarchs that he thought should be targeted to the prime minister Sergey Stepashin, but Stepashin was fired too soon to do anything with it. It was Nemtsov who organized the meeting between Putin and the leading businessmen at which Putin announced the new rules.

Primakov showed his regard for freedom of the press by trying to pack the Russian state-owned media with former intelligence agents. On taking office as prime minister, one of his first acts was to place a gag order on his cabinet. Nemtsov writes that whenever he discussed Putin's backsliding with Chubais, the latter always replied that: "Primakov and Luzhkov would have been worse." From the point of view of economic policies, and maybe also civic and political freedoms, he was right.

The contrast with the Yeltsin era can also be overdrawn. Yeltsin, after all, had himself replaced the election of governors with presidential appointment during the first years of his rule. In words that, again, foreshadowed Putin's, he had said this was necessary to "build a tough, strong system of administration along vertical lines." Where Putin was labeled a dictator, Yeltsin's move drew almost no criticism in the West. As early as 1996, Yeltsin's aides had drafted a law similar to the one Putin later passed that would have allowed the president to fire governors who broke federal laws. They were unable to get it through the Duma.

In 2001, the parliament passed a Kremlin-supported Law on Political Parties that made registering new parties harder. This was seen as part of Putin's centralization project. But many observers had been advocating measures to stimulate consolidation of the party system. Yeltsin had called for such a law as early as 1997, and the chairman of the Central Electoral Commission had pushed for one in 1999. A 2002 Law on Combating Extremist Activity was rightly attacked for its broad and vague definition of "extremism," which included such things as "humiliation of national dignity." Again, the impulse predated Putin. An early draft of the law had been introduced in the Duma in the summer of 1999 amid concern over attacks by racist skinheads against ethnic minorities.

Nor was Putin doing anything new in recruiting siloviki to high office. Yeltsin had done the same throughout his presidency. According to Kryshtanovskaya, the share of security and military veterans in government doubled between 1988 and 1993, and then doubled again by 1999. Yeltsin's last three prime ministers all had FSB or intelligence backgrounds. By the late 1990s, almost the entire political class had come to favor bringing security professionals into the leadership to strengthen the state. "It was not just Putin who brought in the siloviki," writes Kryshtanovskaya. "The political elite invited them to impose order in the country, admitting by this their own powerlessness."

In short, Putin was far from a traditional Chekist. Although he showed respect and loyalty towards the FSB, his views were much more modern (pro-market, pro-Western, not anti-Semitic) than those associated with the Lubyanka, and the old guard initially eyed him with suspicion. He believed he needed the siloviki as a support base and an instrument to get things done, and he overestimated their effectiveness. But he saw them as a tool rather than a fount of wisdom. Nor did his courting of siloviki drag Russia in a radically new direction; it continued a trend begun under Yeltsin, which had support across the political spectrum. In confronting the oligarchs and governors, he did what almost all political leaders thought necessary. Finding himself in unusually auspicious conditions, he centralized power more than some would have, although his main rivals for the presidency would likely have done more to revisit privatization. Simultaneously, Putin pursued other policies that an old school silovik would have vigorously opposed.

Were such policies just window dressing to conceal his true intentions? A real KGB insider would have seen no *need* for such window dressing. "Order" could have been imposed more quickly if done with less circumspection. Putin might have lost some parliamentary support from the dwindling liberal fringe, but he would have more than made up for it on the nationalist and Communist side. At the same time, Putin's liberal initiatives went beyond what might be expected in even a sophisticated public relations campaign. From the perspective of most siloviki, there were real costs to unilaterally closing down important intelligence assets in Cuba and Vietnam, weakening prosecutors, limiting detention of suspects, and reducing the military draft from two years to one. Even had an old KGB hand wanted to reassure the markets, he would probably not have gone as far as to cut the income tax rate to 13 percent, legalize the sale of land, ease registration for businesses, scrap currency controls, and hire Andrey Illarionov as his adviser. And if concealing his true intentions was a good idea in 2000, why was it not in 2005? Seeing Putin as a simple KGB loyalist leaves the evolution of his policies mysterious.

Hungry for power?

Some assumed Putin's motivating impulse was simply hunger for power. If so, he did an excellent job of hiding it. The day Yeltsin presented him as his favored successor, a journalist asked Putin if he was ready to run for president. His reply made the race for the Kremlin sound about as appealing as a colonoscopy: "It would be awkward if I said I wasn't ready if the President said I was." This was after Yeltsin's public backing removed the need to be coy. The footage of Yeltsin introducing Putin as his favorite is almost painful to watch. The young bureaucrat stands, looking queasy, in a dark suit. Yeltsin clings to Putin's arm above the elbow as though afraid that he will run away. Once president, Putin very often looked as if he would rather be somewhere else. Watching him on television, one commentator wrote, the burden of power seemed to have turned Putin's face "literally grey-green, like the coastal waters near the malodorous region of industrial Odessa."

He never ran for office until 2000, when he had to be talked into it. And then, he chose to leave after two terms. Had he wanted to stay in the Kremlin after 2008, Putin clearly had the votes to amend the constitution to permit a third term. He would have won with a landslide. His supporters implored him to stay on, but he refused. I have never seen Putin look as happy as he did on election night 2008, when, in gently falling snow, he appeared on a stage outside the Kremlin to congratulate Medvedev on his victory.

Of course, Putin did remain as prime minister, and during the first two years he still seemed to be making the key decisions. In this role, he looked simultaneously bored and anxious not to be upstaged, as when he almost elbowed Medvedev out of the picture at the latter's inauguration. He studiously reserved the right to run for president again in 2012. When Medvedev introduced legislation in November 2008 to lengthen the president's term from four to six years, it was seen as preparation for a return of Putin to the Kremlin for an even longer spell.

Still, if hunger for power were the true motive, why settle for second best when he could have kept the top position? What leader with a true vocation for autocracy would choose instead this delicate constitutional two-step? Whatever hunger he had seemed well checked by his desire for respectability. Most of the time, the pundit Stanislav Belkovsky seemed more believable when he speculated that what Putin loved was not power itself but the attributes of power—"palaces, airplanes, limousines, yachts, honor guards, Charles Lafitte 1815 vintage . . ." His true ambition, it often seemed, was to be not president, but an ex-president, a member of the elder statesmen's club of retired leaders and multinational CEOs who met in Davos and at conferences of the Trilateral Commission. He had bonded once with Kissinger in a limousine. They kept in touch.

The Chechnya obsession

The brutal and uncontrolled pacification policies Putin authorized in the Chechen war zone seemed to undercut his statements about—and commitment to—legal order and modern administration in the rest of Russia. For Putin, Chechnya was a fixation. It was personal, so personal a satirist could joke that he kept a letter knife carved out of Shamil Basayev's shinbone on his desk. When challenged, he could erupt, as when he bizarrely invited a French journalist whom he judged too sympathetic to the Chechens to convert to Islam and obtain a circumcision such that "nothing would grow back." At moments he seemed genuinely to fear an army of terrorists might ferry Islamic fundamentalism up the Volga. The war pushed him towards harsher approaches and drove him closer to the military and security forces. Each terrorist attack prompted a further tightening of control over the press or centralization of political power.

Chechnya also seemed to him to demonstrate the hypocrisy and cynicism of the West. It infuriated him that the United States and Britain would give asylum to Chechen leaders and tolerate pro-Chechen groups conducting propaganda on their territories. He appeared to believe that elements in the West—presumably in the security agencies of the United States and Britain—were assisting the Chechen separatists in the hope of keeping Russia weak. Shortly after the Beslan attack, a Moscow-based newspaper published a list of organizations, mostly in the United States, that it said were "providing aid to the Chechen separatists under the cover of charitable activities." According to the newspaper, the list had been leaked to it by one of the Russian security services. One of the groups on the list, which had offices in both the UK and the United States, was reported to be "controlled and financed by the special services of Britain." One can assume that Putin was receiving similar reports on FSB stationery. Whether or not they were true, he seemed to believe them.

Clearly, Chechnya was a background influence on his style of rule. It may have accelerated his disenchantment with the West. Yet Putin's most intense involvement in the Chechen horrors—during 1999–2001—coincided with his liberal period. Conversely, stabilization in Chechnya after 2006 brought no revival of civil liberties elsewhere. The war's frustrations, thus, seem more a catalyst for other trends than a major determinant of Putin's policy direction.

Disappointment with Washington

The increasingly strident notes of hostility towards Washington in Putin's speeches suggested personal disappointment, even a sense of betrayal. He had gone out on a limb. While still new in the Kremlin, he had reoriented policy from the sulky resentment that lingered after NATO's bombing of Serbia to an open-armed embrace of the West. He had agreed with the United States to cut nuclear arsenals by two-thirds; raised no objection to the stationing of U.S. troops in Central Asia; offered overfly rights and intelligence cooperation during the war in Afghanistan; closed down the main Russian listening station in Cuba; and even wondered out loud if Russia should join NATO.

What did he get in return? The United States withdrew from the Anti-Ballistic Missile Treaty, which Moscow considered a cornerstone of its nuclear security. Washington pushed for the rapid expansion of NATO, not just into the Baltic states, from where NATO spy planes peered into Russia's interior, but even into Ukraine—the heartland of historic Rus—and Georgia, right up to Russia's sensitive borders. Showing it cared about international law only when convenient, the United States invaded Iraq without a UN mandate, based on distorted intelligence, and then had the temerity to lecture Moscow about throwing its geopolitical weight around in its own neighborhood. Congress refused even to stop applying the Jackson-Vanik amendment, a relic of the cold war that denied most favored nation status to countries that restricted emigration. Russia had been permitting free emigration since the early 1990s.

By his second term, Putin clearly felt he had been played for a fool, shown up as naïve in hoping for a real partnership with the United States.

This doubtless left him vulnerable to the arguments of the conservative generals who had warned against trusting the Americans all along.

Hostage of the security services?

When Putin decided to leave the KGB in 1991, his friend Sergey Roldugin reminded him of the saying, "There are no former spies." He could have had no illusions. The KGB was an organization that never forgot or forgave anything. Someone who became powerful after learning the organization's secrets could use his knowledge to harm it. The organization would want to defend itself.

We do not know—may never know—what mutual obligations connected Putin to the generals in the Lubyanka. Given how much each could damage the other, it seems fair to assume that their relationship was complicated. In September 2006, reviving a corruption case that had been frozen for years, Putin fired a number of high level FSB officials. But reporters soon found that some of these continued to work in the same jobs. No one would explain how this had come about. The journalist Yuliya Latynina described a session at FSB headquarters in which a young major, concerned about the line of command, asked Putin if he should continue to obey the officers that Putin had supposedly fired. Latynina writes that Putin's face darkened and he did not reply.

Was Putin afraid to pick fights with the Lubyanka? Some, most notably the dissident FSB officer Aleksandr Litvinenko, claimed that the security services had blown up the apartment buildings in 1999 in order to incriminate Putin and acquire leverage over him. If he investigated and exposed FSB complicity, he would make both the FSB and himself—a former spy—hateful to the country. If he did not, he would always be vulnerable to leaks showing that he had covered this up. Mutually vulnerable, he and the FSB would be tied together forever.

The notion that Putin was being held hostage by FSB inner circles struck veterans as implausible. Yevgeniya Albats, the journalist and expert on the KGB and its successors, had little doubt based on her conversations with insiders that Putin was in full control and retained freedom of maneuver. For all the rumors loose-lipped generals were spreading in 2007 about conflicts among silovik factions, almost none cast Putin as less than a powerful commander. In itself, the idea that operatives, acting in a centralized or decentralized way, would seek to ease Putin's path to power by blowing up apartment buildings does not make much sense. First, in 1999, the KGB insiders were still suspicious of him. Primakov, with his long connections to foreign intelligence, would have been at least as attractive to them as a presidential candidate. Second, it could have backfired: the Russian public might easily have reacted with rage against those—first and foremost, Putin—who failed to protect them. The evidence presented by Berezovsky's associates such as Litvinenko, hardly impartial analysts, is at best suggestive, at worst farfetched. If false, the allegation was, as Putin said, "immoral."

And yet, one after another, those who sought to investigate the apartment bombings ended up dead. When the Duma refused to hold hearings, the former dissident and human rights activist Sergey Kovalyov set up an independent commission to examine the evidence. One member, the Duma deputy Sergey Yushenkov, was shot in April 2003. Another, the investigative reporter Yury Shchekochikhin, died three months later, apparently killed by a rare poison. A third, the prominent journalist Otto Latsis, was beaten severely in the street in November 2003, but survived; he died after a car accident two years later. As of mid-2010, Kovalyov, who had publicly expressed skepticism about the theory that FSB agents blew up the apartment buildings, was himself unharmed. Aleksandr Litvinenko, who had promoted this theory and provided documents to the commission, was poisoned with polonium in London in 2006. There was no clear evidence linking any of these deaths to the apartment bombings inquiry, but the pattern was unsettling. Then there was the odd announcement made by the Duma's Communist Speaker, Gennady Seleznyov, during the session on September 13, 1999. After being passed a note, Seleznyov informed the deputies that a residential building had just been blown up in the city of Volgodonsk. The information was accurate in all but one respect—the explosion occurred three days *after* Seleznyov's announcement. If for no other reason than the cursoriness of the official investigation, questions persisted.

The politician

In part, Putin's shortchanging of democracy might reflect an inferiority complex about the kind of open competition it entailed. He had been more than honest when Yeltsin first raised the question of succession. "I don't like election campaigns. I really don't," Putin had said. "I don't know how to run them, and I don't like them" (Chapter 2). He thought it unseemly to hand out promises like Snickers bars. He felt out of his depth in the arena of public politics, in the uncontrolled settings that Yeltsin so relished. He had no confidence in his ability to connect to people.

And yet, in spite of everything, at moments one could not help seeing Putin as a public politician—even a gifted one. One such moment occurred in Vidyaevo, an arctic naval base on the Barents Sea. On August 12, 2000, the Kursk nuclear submarine had sunk after an explosion. The families of the lost sailors had gathered on a hospital boat in the port for a sleepless watch. Naval officers plied them with false and muddled information. And on the tenth day after the submarine went down, Putin entered the lion's den. The Kremlin press pool had been left in Moscow. But Kolesnikov had arrived two days earlier, mixed with the families, and witnessed Putin's visit.

Tragedy is rarely pure, clean, virginal. Everything gets mixed up together—the bone-chilling pain, exhaustion, anger, denial, thoughts of money, greed, fear, boredom, loneliness, always circling back to the pain, exhaustion, anger. The president's task was to feel his way through the waves of emotion, talking to the families late into the night. If he brought up money when the focus was on mourning, that would not be forgiven. If he did not mention compensation or if the money was not enough, that would be equally bad.

At first Putin stumbled, as the mutinous family members interrupted, shouting him down. He lashed out strangely at the oligarchs, as though they had let the fleet fall into disrepair. But then, as Kolesnikov tells it, Putin found a path across the minefield. Gradually, he found the right tone, felt the mood changes as they rippled across the hall, edged his way into the heart of the volatile crowd, until he had won them over. It took two hours and forty minutes. But by the end they were his. He left, in Kolesnikov's words, "the president of all these people who, before the meeting, had been ready to tear him apart."

Perhaps this, in part, is why he was so angry with Berezovsky, whose ORT had shown grieving relatives screaming at the camera. He had faced the families, listened to their anguish in person, while the oligarch sat in Moscow, using the tragedy to undermine Putin's authority. He had never been more exposed. And he had risen to the occasion. Then, what to make of that unsettling grin on Putin's face when the American interviewer Larry King asked what had happened to the Kursk—as if he didn't know!—and Putin replied simply: "*Ona utonula*. [It sank.]"? Could there be any explanation for that eerie smile except that Putin was imagining in delicious detail the pleasure of drowning the obnoxious questioner, suspenders and all, three hundred feet beneath the Arctic Ocean?

The CEO

The conjecture that makes most sense of Putin's behavior—perhaps too much—is that his main motive was not power but profit, his true vocation not politics but business. Putin's goal, in this view, was to build an empire of international companies, controlled by close associates, many from the security services. On his watch, a network of new oligarchs emerged, often with security backgrounds. Combining the words "oligarch" and "silovik," one might call these new magnates *silovarchs.*

At the heart of this empire was Gazprom, the gigantic, majority state-owned gas company. For Putin, Gazprom was a personal obsession. He memorized the details of the company's accounts, its pricing rules and pipeline routes. He personally approved all appointments down to the deputy level, sometimes forgetting to tell the company's actual CEO, Aleksey Miller, as when he tapped former German Chancellor Gerhard Schroeder to serve on a Gazprom pipeline subsidiary along with his old acquaintance, Matthias Warnig. In the 1990s, various Gazprom assets had disappeared into companies owned by friends and relatives of the managers. Putin spent the first few years recovering these. But then, during his second term, control over valuable Gazprom assets began to pass into the hands of one of Putin's old friends, the banker Yury Kovalchuk, whose business empire grew at a phenomenal rate. After Gazprom bought the oil company Sibneft from the oligarch Roman Abramovich, much of its oil was sold by another old Putin acquaintance, Gennady Timchenko. By 2008, both Kovalchuk and Timchenko appeared on *Forbes*'s billionaire list.

Of course, Putin was not a narrow profit-maximizer, and there was no evidence that he personally owned a stake in any of these companies. But seeing his actions from a business angle resolves some of the apparent contradictions in his policies. His early liberalism and careful macroeconomic management surprised those who had expected an unreconstructed Chekist. On his trips abroad, Putin actively lobbied on behalf of the interests of Russian business. "Under Yeltsin, Russian companies lost the Libyan market to France," observed Pavel Teplukhin, president of Troika Dialog Asset Management, the country's largest investment bank, in 2002. "Under Putin, this is different." Friendly relations with the West also made business sense. Foreign investment was key to boosting the capitalization of Kremlin-connected companies and opening the doors to major bank loans.

But then those who had come to see Putin as an economic liberal were taken aback by the crude expropriation of Yukos and renationalization of profitable private firms. It seemed perverse for a regime determined to cut red tape and lower business taxes to itself use tax collectors and environmental inspectors to pressure Russian and foreign companies. For a silovarch, however, this too makes sense: the goal of accumulating assets must sometimes take priority over improving the investment climate. Even restrictions on the media—not necessary politically given Putin's sky-high popularity—may have been meant primarily to limit unwelcome reporting on the network's business operations. The topic on which journalists remained most intimidated was that of corrupt profit making in the security services.

In 2007, the Kremlin began creating massive "state corporations," to achieve certain important social goals—development of nanotechnology, stimulating high-tech exports, and so on. Putin cronies were assigned to top jobs in each. The corporations were given billions of dollars in state cash as well as the state-owned shares in hundreds of companies. All these needed to be bundled together under state control, it was said, in order to achieve economies of scale and compete internationally. But apparently not for long. As Putin explained in February 2008: "In general, we will be seeking to encourage state corporations to launch IPOs, up to their full privatization several years later, after the state makes significant investment in them." One corporation head, Putin's friend from Dresden spying days, Sergey Chemezov, seemed quite eager to get rid of some of the assets his company had been given. "Of course, I do not consider it necessary to hold on to everything that has been transferred to us," he was quoted as saying. "Some parts might be sold." Why he had lobbied so hard to get them in this case was a bit of a puzzle.

Or consider the "gas war" that broke out when in 2005 Gazprom, on Putin's orders, raised the price of gas for Ukraine to the world price, and then cut gas supplies when Kiev refused to pay. Many in the West saw this as an attempt to expand Russia's geopolitical influence and intimidate the Orange revolutionaries. This was probably what it was, in part. But it was also a straightforward business decision, aimed at increasing Gazprom's profits and pressuring neighboring countries to sell Gazprom their pipelines and distribution networks. Despite Belarus's political fealty to Moscow, its gas price was also doubled the following year.

Even the choice of the mild-mannered Medvedev as Putin's successor makes sense from a business angle. During the Putin presidency, the priority had been capital accumulation—capturing major companies and their cash flows. By 2007, this was far along. The group's next task would be to legalize its wealth through reprivatization and share offerings, and to diversify through Western asset purchases. To do this successfully, the Kremlin magnates—even Medvedev's security force rivals—knew they needed to keep foreign investors optimistic and share prices buoyant. Medvedev was the West-friendly, business candidate par excellence, a former corporate lawyer who felt comfortable at Davos. He could send the right signals internationally, while Putin as prime minister managed the transformation of assets.

Some journalists claimed Putin was fabulously rich. But, although he took to wearing a Patek Philippe watch worth $60,000, there is no proof Putin had more than a few hundred thousand dollars in personal wealth. In any case, the question whether Putin personally owned shares or had a trust in Liechtenstein containing billions of dollars was really a red herring. Much as top Washington insiders know that wealth awaits them on the other side of the revolving door, Putin and his aides could be sure that their favors would be reciprocated, that friendships would pay off in the future. The difference was just in the scale of the returns, which were many times greater in oil-rich Moscow. With their security service networks, Putin and his allies would remain dangerous men to cross.

The business motive clarifies why Putin's policies changed during his time in power. Early on, the Kremlin's empire builders moved cautiously, concerned not to alarm foreign investors. However, the Yukos affair, in 2003, was a revelation. Not only did markets not panic, stocks almost doubled during the following two years. The reason could be spelled in three letters. One morning in April 2004, Vladimir Milov, a former deputy energy minister and expert on oil markets, was woken by a call from the economics minister, German Gref, in a state of nervous excitement. Alan Greenspan, chairman of the Federal Reserve, had just been quoted on the newswires saying high oil prices were "here to stay." Was it true, Gref wanted to know. As oil revenues soared, Putin's business associates threw caution to the wind. Foreign investors would come to Russia for its mineral reserves, almost regardless of the political risk. In January 2005, Andrey Illarionov, the libertarian economist whose provocative criticisms of economic policy Putin had initially heeded, was demoted. That December, he resigned. Reassured that their hostile takeovers would not scare the markets, the Kremlin tycoons set about building their empires faster and more openly.

For Putin, business prowess was not just about money. Rather, he recognized that—for both individuals and states—in the modern world there could be no power without large amounts of cash. Wealth was needed to provide security for his personal network of associates, whom the vicissitudes of Russian politics might threaten in the future. Precisely because the "vertical of power" did not work, because law enforcement was so corrupt, one needed the truly gigantic sums it took to buy vast networks of officials. One had to be able to spend more than one's enemies. At the same time, given Russia's military decline, projecting power abroad could only be done by muscular business conglomerates, supported by a thriving economy. "There can be no superpower where weakness and poverty reign," he told the Russian voters even before his first election. Geopolitics had become geoeconomics.

Both Sobchak and Yeltsin had hoped that Putin would be the man to reconcile the security services to democracy, integrating them into the new political order. Shortly before his death, Sobchak told an interviewer:

> We're not threatened by dictatorship if Putin becomes president. There will be something else ... an organic integration into the state

of the law enforcement structures, which until now have been like foreign bodies. . . . What is our tragedy? That we received courts, the procuracy, police, army, and FSB that are completely communist in mentality, structure, methods of work, and personnel. And they have been estranged, and to this day still feel their foreignness. Even, you know, a kind of alienation (*neprikayannost*). They have not found their organic place in the system of Russian democratic statehood.

In fact, however, it was not democracy that Putin integrated the law enforcement bodies and secret services into, but the capitalist marketplace.

Between Freedom and Fear

Disappointed with the aggressive hypocrisy of Bush-era Washington, frustrated by the carnage in Chechnya, doubting his own skills as a democratic politician, and buoyed up by the economic boom, Putin seemed to coast along in his second term, animated mostly by cynicism. He had always seen the world through the dark glasses of an intelligence agent. He had been attuned to the conspiracies and mercenary motives that hid behind the surfaces of politics. But now he seemed to see little else.

He had not started out this way. Some four decades back, he had been the kind of wide-eyed teenager who thought one could volunteer for the KGB, who had believed the cloak-and-dagger stories, only to find in the organs he had romanticized an atavistic bureaucracy staffed by anti-Semites, paper pushers, careerists, and more than a few sadists. Sensibly, he had given up before he started. He became a cog in the machine. His ethics had been compressed into a fierce loyalty to friends and a mercilessness towards those who betrayed him. Besides ethics, he had aesthetics. He kept the elegant notions he had learned from Sobchak about the rule of law, the sovereignty of constitutions. He took them out to admire every now and then, used them in speeches. Early on in the Kremlin, he had seemed to think they could make a difference. Such concepts were part of the veneer of modernity that he admired in the West. But when push came to shove, the survivalist ethics were what mattered. Over the years, he had lost touch with the idealistic teenager. He had become a dif-

ferent person, his character no longer made up of intentions and principles but of a history of decisions that had brought other decisions in
their wake, driving him down a path that at the start perhaps he would
not have chosen.

He was a cog that became a switch. Some urged him to smash the
machine. But he lacked the hubris of a Yeltsin, the self-importance that
allowed one to change late in life, to take irrational risks. Lacking any
strong political convictions, he let the machine drive where it wanted to
go. He had not had to invent anything, after all. The staffers Yeltsin hired
toward the end—shrewd operators such as Voloshin and his deputy,
Vladislav Surkov—had prepared everything: the inducements to Duma
leaders, the double-crossing of political opponents, the twisting of governors' arms, the vote managing.

And, year by year, his cynicism grew. Communication outside his circle of friends had always been an act of distancing. He seemed to relish
his ability not just to say with conviction what he knew to be untrue,
but to say what he knew everyone in the room knew to be untrue—
and to seem to believe it. It came down to self-control and training. He
was a professional. Corruption in the Kremlin? How absurd! Yanukovich
elected by fraud in Ukraine? Nonsense. A businessman being harassed
by officials? He should sue! Both times I met him, in a group of scholars
and journalists, the event had the atmosphere of a celebrity tennis match.
A handshake before, a handshake after, a group picture. In between, the
champion volleyed the balls we served, darting from one corner of the
court to the other, lobbing them back gently or smashing them at our
feet, scarcely blinking or pausing for breath.

At times, it was even too easy. He seemed almost disappointed by how
readily the opportunists and sycophants of the political class fell into
line. We must not stoop to populist measures, he told a roomful of governors. "The people sitting at the table, as one, wrote down this sentence
exactly," reported Kolesnikov. "Moreover, some of them were writing for
such a long time that it seemed to me they were doing it several times
in a row, like schoolboys at their lessons, writing out lines." Out of boredom, he liked to tease those who professed higher principles, much as his
Chechen protégé Ramzan Kadyrov liked to taunt his pet lion, riling it up
to see if it would growl back.

Once, flying from Barnaul to Moscow in the summer of 2005, the president invited Kolesnikov to dine with him. Kolesnikov, probing for a scoop, asked if Putin had already picked a successor. Suppose I have, Putin answered. "If it were a person who is decent in all respects, honest, competent, would you personally help him become president?" Kolesnikov demurred. It was not his role as a journalist to help a candidate get elected. But Putin would not let him off so easily. "You're also a citizen," he insisted. "Why wouldn't you help an honest person become president?" Under his host's persistent badgering Kolesnikov eventually slipped and said he would help an "honest candidate." Putin, writes Kolesnikov, seemed delighted with this victory, having convinced himself once again how easily Russian journalists could be talked out of their pretense of objectivity.

Later, on the same flight, Kolesnikov took the opportunity to complain to Putin about the lack of press freedom. What exactly did he not like, Putin asked.

"I don't like that some time after you arrested Khodorkovsky, I lost the feeling that I live in a free country. I have not yet started to feel fear . . ." I wanted to add: "But, evidently, it will soon appear," but he interrupted.

"That is, the feeling of absolute freedom is gone, but the feeling of fear has not yet appeared?"

"Yes, the feeling that existed under your predecessor is gone," I said.

"But the feeling of fear has not appeared?" he clarified once again, as if reflecting on what I was saying.

"Not yet," I answered.

"And did you not think that perhaps this was what I was aiming for: that one feeling disappeared, but the other did not appear?"

"I didn't think that," I answered. "I did not expect it."

He shrugged his shoulders and his expression became once again indifferent.

Was he being sincere, or still just playing with Kolesnikov to make the time pass? Did he imagine himself a Grand Inquisitor, rescuing Russians from the burden of too much freedom? Hard to say. It was true that most Russians felt neither completely free nor afraid. What I think they felt, for the most part, was a kind of dullness—a not unpleasant dullness, as incomes rose and apartments were remodeled. The winds of history seemed to have died down for a while.

But, for a large minority, the dullness was tinged with doubt, a lingering uncertainty that gave political life an edge of cinematic suspense. Most people had only the foggiest notion who the men in the Kremlin really were. The apartment bombings had been declared the work of Chechen and Wahhabi terrorists. Six suspects were eventually tried and convicted. And yet, a poll in February 2000 found that 28 percent of Russians thought it at least possible the authorities had been involved; 8 percent thought this the *most* likely scenario. The simple certainties of life in rich democracies still seemed far away. For politically attentive Russians, as for many in the West, Putin would remain the president of unreasonable doubt.

CHAPTER 4

The Understudy

Like his predecessor, Dmitry Medvedev had never imagined he would end up Russia's head of state. He had none of that slow-burning fire in the belly that convinced a Nemtsov or a Yeltsin that the desk in the main Kremlin office had been fitted to his dimensions. The presidency was something that happened to him—not destiny but an unexpected invitation, an opportunity the consummate professional could not turn down, the ultimate entry under "employment history" on any curriculum vitae. As was said of Nicholas II's minister Count Sergey Witte, Medvedev "fell upstairs," promoted rapidly to the highest positions.

Whereas a favorable economic environment gave Putin broad leeway to reshape Russia's political and economic systems, Medvedev's challenge was far greater and his freedom of maneuver, initially, almost nonexistent. When he took office, the Putin model of economic growth was faltering as mineral prices gyrated and the accumulating costs of corruption made themselves felt. Then came the global financial meltdown. However, the liberal path to revive and modernize the economy that Medvedev might, otherwise, have chosen was blocked to him, if not by his personal deference to his longtime mentor then by the political harness that the Putin system imposed.

The comparison to Witte might seem fanciful. On the face of it, few people could have been more different than the blunt-spoken, gum-chewing bear of a man who built the Trans-Siberian Railway and the diminutive law professor, polished and reserved, who reminded one journalist of an "Englishman from a good family." But in important ways the two were similar. Both aimed at the same goal: modernizing Russia through eco-

123

nomic development in cooperation with the West. Both had faith in free markets, but also saw a major role for government in attracting investment. Both recognized the faults of the democracies of their time, yet declared freedom to be the ultimate value—a value that both believed could only be secured by a strong state. Each served a suspicious superior who was primarily concerned about political order, and each was distrusted by that leader's militaristic courtiers. For all their words about freedom, both were deeply loyal to the regime under which they governed.

Witte, as finance minister, presided over a decade of robust growth. He balanced Russia's budget and doubled state revenues. But then he was called to serve as prime minister in 1905 as all hell was breaking loose. Across the country, workers' strikes, peasant jacqueries, anti-Jewish pogroms, radical students' sit-ins, and campaigns by the gentry for political reform were linking up into a legendary "Russian revolt, senseless and merciless," punctuated by the bombs of revolutionary terrorists. In the Far East, Russia had lost its entire Baltic Fleet to the Japanese, undercutting the confidence of Russian elites in their rulers. As the upheavals climaxed, Witte persuaded the tsar to sign the "Manifesto of October 17," in effect replacing absolutism with constitutional monarchy. Nicholas never forgave him. When, ten years later, Witte died, the tsar remarked that the news gave him great "peace of mind." In the few months before Nicholas replaced him as prime minister, Witte floundered, attacked by right and left. Unwilling to abjure the use of force—"Withdraw the troops? No, better to be without newspapers and electricity," he told a meeting of newspaper editors—yet sincerely seeking to give the new parliament real powers, he satisfied no one, and soon lost his job to a tougher reformer, Pyotr Stolypin, who favored the hangman's noose. Witte spent most of his last years abroad, depressed and bitter, predicting doom.

Medvedev's history, as of early 2010, was still his to make. If the economy deteriorated, stimulating protests across the country, he might at some point face a dilemma similar to Witte's in 1905. Would he try to persuade Putin to liberalize politics, reversing the antidemocratic legislation of the previous years? Might he even try to bypass his mentor and lead a movement for greater openness and freedom by himself? If so, would he manage to channel the pressures for change and build a bridge to forces in society? Would he lose control to Putin and end up, like Witte, abandoned and hated by his former patron? Or would he remain always the faithful subordinate, watching quietly as the Putin system either righted itself or headed toward collapse?

The Lawyer

A subway ride south of St. Petersburg's historic center, Kupchino is a nondescript suburb of identical five- and nine-story, grey and brown concrete apartment blocks. Built in the early 1960s, between the Hungarian Uprising of 1956 and the Prague Spring of 1968, its streets bear the names of Eastern European capitals and of the region's native Communist luminaries. There is one for the Bulgarian leader Georgy Dimitrov, and further south one for the Croat commander, Aleksa Dundić, who fought with Budyonny's Red Cavalry in the Russian Civil War. Bisecting Budapest and Belgrade Streets, a wide boulevard lined by bedraggled trees commemorates Béla Kun, the Hungarian revolutionary who in 1919 founded the short-lived Hungarian Soviet Republic and was later executed by Stalin for his pains.

On this street, in a forty-square-meter apartment at No. 6, Dmitry— or Dima—Medvedev grew up, an only child in a family that was, by all accounts, quite typical of the Soviet intelligentsia of that time. His father, Anatoly Afanasyevich, an expert on the technology of chemical processing, taught at a scientific institute. The young Dima was struck by how his father could work late into the night, surrounded by books, papers piling up on his desk beside him under the lamplight. Dima's mother, Yuliya Venyaminovna, had studied the Russian language at graduate school in Leningrad, and, in between raising Dima, taught intermittently at the Herzen Teachers' College.

He was a "purposeful child," according to his first grade teacher, Vera Smirnova, studious and mature for his age, a "dreadful why-asker," who tortured her with questions. Years later, she remembered having to rifle through reference books to find for him the water displacement of the Aurora, the famous battleship whose crew had mutinied and joined the Bolsheviks in 1917 and which remained moored in Leningrad's harbor. After school, Dima would play with friends in the yard for only ten minutes before racing off to do his homework. In the third grade, he set out to study his father's ten-volume *Small Soviet Encyclopedia*, poring over its maps, biographical sketches, and pictures of animals.

In summer, the three Medvedevs would flee the dusty city, travelling first to Pavlovsk, nineteen miles south of Leningrad, where they would rent a small wooden cabin by the estate that Catherine the Great had built for her son, the Grand Prince Pavel, in the late eighteenth century. Yuliya Venyaminovna, who had qualified as a tour guide, escorted visitors around the grounds. Dima would run wild in the park, or else tag along, watching proudly as his mother rattled off facts about Russian history. Next they would bundle into a train and head south to the relatives—first the maternal grandparents in Belgorod Oblast, on the border with Ukraine, then on to Anatoly Afanasyevich's parents in Krasnodar, on the Black Sea, an exotic world where a boy from the North could find trees laden with plums and apples and see locals bringing home buckets of green crabs, still wriggling, to boil up for dinner. Afanasy Fyodorovich, the southern patriarch, was an idealistic communist who had worked his way up to secretary of the rural district committee, and received a golden watch on his fiftieth birthday as a present from Khrushchev—to be berated ever after by his wife for modestly choosing this reward rather than the other option, a car.

At fourteen, on a winter school trip—the teacher recalls much throwing of snowballs—Dima got to know a blonde-haired girl called Sveta Linnik, who was studying in the parallel seventh grade class. This was, as he describes it, an epochal event, both natural and shocking.

> In the second and third grades, I was very interested in dinosaurs. We studied them, drew them, discussed them. I learned all the periods of the Earth's development, starting with the Archaean and ending with the Cenozoic era . . . In the fourth and fifth grades, I was taken by chemistry. . . . I did experiments. Then it was sports. We would practice three or four times a week. And then all of that ended in a single moment. A new life began.

Ten years later, the two were married. Their son, Ilya, was born in 1996.

Thirteen years and nine subway stops separated the young Medvedev from the somewhat older Vladimir Putin. By the time Dima was in high school, the latter was already at work in the "Big House," the Leningrad KGB headquarters. In their accounts of their early experiences, the two project quite different images. Putin's autobiographical interviews present him as something of a teenage hooligan, practicing boxing and judo to protect himself in street brawls, and stowing away with friends in the lifeboat of a Black Sea liner. Medvedev sees no need to accentuate the macho element. He describes himself in the Kupchino apartment listening with his mother to the music of Engelbert Humperdinck, and says things like: "One must give reasonable attention to one's clothes." He drank and smoked, he says, "without fanaticism." By his teenage years, the craze for patriotic spy movies and war fiction was yielding to fascination with the popular culture of the West, which had been seeping into Soviet society through the interstices of détente. The young Medvedev dreamed of owning a pair of genuine Levi's jeans or Pink Floyd's 1982 album *The Wall*, either of which cost on the street about the equivalent of the average Russian worker's monthly wage.

In the fall of 1982, as he was turning seventeen, Medvedev enrolled at Leningrad State University (LGU) to study law. Putin had graduated from the same department seven years earlier, having written an undergraduate thesis on international law. At first, Medvedev could only get into the night school, but he worked so hard that he was allowed to transfer into the regular program after the first year. What was it that one learned in such establishments? Given Medvedev's strong self-identification with the law and with his alma mater, the question is worth examining.

In Marxist thought, law was quite simply a means by which the economically dominant class in a given era repressed other classes. There was no place in this conception for the notion of law as the embodiment of transcendent values or as an autonomous system that checked the power of rulers. Marx derided the "ideological nonsense about law (*Recht*) and other trash" that one could find in the writings of "democrats and French socialists." Lenin, faithful to the master, saw the legal codes that the Bolsheviks inherited as just the operating manuals of capitalist domination. Under the dictatorship of the proletariat, they would be replaced by laws that served the working class. New statutes—even if they could not at first be reliably enforced—would serve to educate the masses about social justice, and the courts would be used as an instrument of compulsion, along with terror, to expropriate the bourgeoisie and defend the revolution.

Under Stalin, the "political elasticity" of the law, as one theorist of the 1930s described it, served to spread vulnerability, to create something akin to original sin, from which no citizen could escape. Laws were written in ways so out of tune with Soviet reality that everyone was forced to violate some statute. "*Byl by chelovek, a statya naydyotsya*," the prosecutors joked. "If you have the man, you'll find the article [in the criminal code]." The show trial, used with aplomb by Stalin's gifted prosecutor Andrey Vishinsky, incorporated the props of law into the new theater of terror. With an almost pedantic legalism, Vishinsky sought to hijack the positive connotations of court procedures and cloak violent coercion in the rituals of order.

After Stalin's death, a gradual and fluctuating process of rationalization and deradicalization began. Scholars placed greater emphasis than before on procedural formality, precision, and consistency. This did not result from a sudden upswell of liberalism among the country's leaders. On the one hand, it was part of the general reaction against the stresses of Stalinism and reflected the recognition of the need for predictability as the economy grew more complex. On the other, the new emphasis on procedures appealed to the guild interests of the legal professionals, whose status was tied to the requirement that the courts follow the complicated codes that only they had memorized. A truly lawless society, after all, would hardly need lawyers.

Soviet law remained profoundly illiberal. Although "personal property" had been recognized in the 1936 Constitution, "private property" was not. (One could own clothes, furniture, cars, even some housing for personal use, but the means of production and land were off limits.) There was no adversarial system, no separation of powers. The courts, like all other state bodies, were subordinate in practice to the party, and judges were simply state employees. Rights of individuals against the state were guaranteed only "in accordance with the interests of the people and in order to strengthen and develop the socialist system" (Article 50 of the Brezhnev 1977 Constitution). "Telephone law"—the instructing of judges by party officials over the telephone—was common.

The law faculty at LGU, housed in a classical, grey building on

Vasilievsky Island, was probably the most prestigious in the country. Founded in 1724 by Peter the Great, it had educated both sides of the October Revolution—Kerensky and Lenin—as well as numerous writers and artists, including the poets Gumilyov and Blok, the composer Stravinsky, and the ballet director and impresario Diaghilev. The school's professors prided themselves on having preserved a tradition of open discussion and fiercely independent questioning, inherited from the pre-revolutionary generation of legal scholars, some of whom had survived and continued teaching even into the Stalin era. It was a bastion of that particular brand of legalism—*zakonnost*—that had developed in the postwar period, a legalism that highlighted the intellectual content of legal debate and the professional qualities of the lawyerly caste, but that remained very much the legalism of the prosecutor rather than that of the defense lawyer.

There were some genuine free spirits. Olimpiad Solomonovich Ioffe, who chaired the civil law department in the 1970s, lectured in shirt-sleeves, smoking and joking with his listeners, deliberately ignoring the usual protocol. One student later recalled how Ioffe had opened his lecture series in February 1953, while Stalin was still alive and in his final paranoid, anti-Semitic phase. "I could tell you about the influence that Stalin's work *Marxism and Problems of Linguistics* has had on Roman law," Professor Ioffe began, staring up at the dirty snow falling beyond the classroom's unwashed skylights, "but I will not say this and will get right down to business." In the 1970s, Ioffe's daughter joined the wave of Jewish emigration permitted under détente, and Ioffe was harassed into also leaving for the United States, where he taught at Harvard and then the University of Connecticut. "Soviet law proclaims democracy, freedom, and legality," he wrote, in the early 1980s, "while Soviet reality proves its inseparability from dictatorship, suppression, and arbitrariness." Back in St. Petersburg, his works were kept under strict lock and key, available to faculty but not students.

One of Ioffe's graduate students and then junior colleagues, Anatoly Sobchak, also pushed the boundaries at times, introducing subtle praise for market mechanisms into his lectures, rendering himself—at least, to those who listened carefully—something of a dissident. But, for the most part, for all the talk of free debate, Soviet law schools taught conformism. Their role was to train recruits for the police, the KGB, and the procuracy—a distinctive Russian institution that combines the roles of prosecutor and overseer of the entire justice system—and the matriculants came mostly from privileged families with law enforcement backgrounds. It was an environment in which, as one of Medvedev's contemporaries put it, "political conversations and jokes were not popular" because "everyone understood where they could lead."

In this setting, Medvedev flourished. Teachers and fellow students remember him as correct, diplomatic in argument, making his points firmly yet without offending his opponent. After graduating, he stayed on to write a dissertation, which he completed in three years, to the envy of some of his less productive colleagues. He was the type, one friend complained, that other people's mothers would hold up as a positive example. Medvedev's dissertation examined the legal status of state-owned enterprises in a market economy, a topic that would remain relevant to him throughout his career.

In Moscow, at this time, Gorbachev, the former Moscow State University law student, was calling for the creation of a "law-based state" and edging towards allowing competitive elections. In his quiet way, Medvedev absorbed the new spirit. His colleague Ilya Yeliseyev remembers one department party in the late 1980s at which a recent doctoral recipient was being honored. Eventually Medvedev's turn arrived to offer congratulations, and he stood and delivered a toast to: "The rebirth of private law in Russia!" Private law—the ensemble of mostly civil and labor laws that defended the interests of the individual against the state—had been abolished by the Bolsheviks. "We do not recognize anything 'private,' and regard *everything* in the economic sphere as falling under *public* and not private law," Lenin had declared. It was a slightly shocking outburst, a breach of taste that, given the mores of the time, might have slowed down Medvedev's graduate career. But Dima was well liked. People quickly drank and restarted conversations, pretending not to have noticed anything untoward.

Then in 1989, Sobchak, the closet liberal, who had sat on Medvedev's dissertation committee, decided to run for Gorbachev's new Congress of People's Deputies. "No one wins an election singlehandedly," Sobchak would later write. Medvedev and a couple of friends were among those who walked the streets for him, pasting up posters and giving speeches through a metal bullhorn. Dmitry "was drunk with the air of freedom that, as it seemed to us, then reigned," recalled his more politically conservative teacher Yury Tolstoy. Unlike Putin, who felt ill at ease in a political campaign, Medvedev clearly enjoyed the adrenalin and exertion. At one point, the authorities confiscated some of Sobchak's leaflets that they judged inappropriate. Medvedev spent the evening running off a new set on an old mimeograph machine. On election night, he stayed up until dawn in the campaign headquarters as the results came in.

Sobchak, victorious, disappeared to Moscow, where he helped found the Interregional Group in the new Soviet parliament. Medvedev, his dissertation defended, got a job in 1990 as an assistant professor teaching civil and Roman law at LGU. He would remain on the faculty until 1999. During this time, he co-authored a three volume textbook on civil law that went through multiple editions and sold more than one million copies. One student recalled him as a popular teacher, "strict, but not harsh," and "very well-dressed." He could throw students into confusion by returning papers to them covered with comments in Latin.

On the side, to supplement his modest academic salary, Medvedev offered legal services to some of the city's new private businessmen. Previously, while still in graduate school, he and two friends—Yeliseyev and Anton Ivanov—had formed a small consulting firm. They rented a room in a nearby nautical institute, stretching their savings to equip it with one black-and-white computer, a table, and three chairs. From the institute's staff, they cadged a dark green, dilapidated couch for clients to sit on. As Yeliseyev describes it, this piece of furniture got little use. The three did not advertise and relied on clients referred by word of mouth. In some months, there was no business at all and the three would dig into their own pockets to pay the secretary's salary.

In 1990, democrats in the Leningrad City Council invited Sobchak back home to lead the body. The law professor, now a national celebrity, persuaded Medvedev to come and help him part-time. There, in the corridors of the neoclassical Mariinsky Palace, mediating between the deputies and their colorful new leader, the twenty-four-year-old Medvedev got a taste of the quarrels and improvisations that characterized Russia's early democratic politics. A month later, another of Sobchak's former students, Vladimir Putin, arrived to join the team, at first as just one of the advisers. But soon, "having seen the Putin style," as Medvedev put it, Sobchak appointed the former intelligence agent leader of the group. The next summer, Sobchak ran for mayor of the northern capital and won, and soon afterwards the team moved into the Smolny Institute, the orange and white former academy where the daughters of the St. Petersburg nobility had once been educated, evicting the Communist Party leaders who had occupied it since the Revolution.

Over the next few years, Medvedev used to stop in at Smolny once or twice a week to help Putin, who was chairing the city's Committee on Foreign Relations. He would sit at a tiny desk in the anteroom, where visitors sometimes mistook him for the receptionist. The two became friends. Sometimes on weekends, Medvedev would join Putin at his family's dacha next to Lake Komsomolskoe, about sixty miles north of St. Petersburg, where neighbors included the businessmen Vladimir Yakunin and Yury Kovalchuk. Putin also took him along on some of his foreign trips. "It was very interesting for me," Medvedev recalled much later. "It was then that I first visited a number of major, developed states, and got some experience resolving practical legal issues." Which exactly, he did not say.

One day in the early 1990s, as Medvedev tells it, he was passing the time in the office of Putin's committee when some entrepreneurs from a newly founded wood and paper company turned up, looking for assistance preparing a document. "I was free and helped them." The company—Ilim Pulp Enterprise (IPE)—was registered by the Committee on Foreign Relations in April 1992. By 1993, Medvedev had become the head of its legal department. It was quite a step up from the lonely reception room at the nautical institute. Within seven years, IPE would have grown into Russia's largest lumber company, with annual revenues of half a billion dollars. By 2009, it would boast the sixth largest timber reserves and logging volume in the world.

Medvedev did not just provide legal counsel to the firm. By September 1994, he had come to own 20 percent of it. The value of this stake at that time is hard to estimate precisely. In the 1990s, the Russian lumber industry was in a slump. In 2000, as the economy picked up, the company was assessed by auditors at $400 million, according to IPE's head of public relations, implying a value of $80 million for a 20 percent stake. By 2007, according to the magazine *SmartMoney*, a 20 percent stake in IPE would have been worth $300 million. Medvedev has said that he sold all his shares before he left to join the government in 1999, adding that: "attempts to count up how many hundreds of millions of dollars my share came to are, unfortunately, groundless." Whatever Medvedev's actual returns from the company, it remains a puzzle what prevailed upon the other partners in IPE—by all accounts, some hard-nosed individuals—to give this unknown assistant professor of law, who a few years earlier had not been able to afford decent office furniture, a large chunk of their business, potentially worth millions of dollars, rather than simply to buy his legal services at the market rate.

Throughout the 1990s, Medvedev helped devise the firm's legal strategy as it expanded, swallowing lumber, cellulose, and wood-processing plants from across Russia's Northwest and Siberia, in ways that sometimes attracted the scrutiny of regulators. In 1994, IPE purchased 20 percent of the shares in the Kotlassky Cellulose and Paper Combine in an investment auction. Under the terms of the deal, IPE was required to invest about $77 million in fixed capital for the paper mill. According to an investigation by the state auditing agency, by the 1997 deadline less than one percent of the required investment had been made.

Medvedev has not spoken in detail about his role in IPE, nor have his partners. One can surmise that his experiences in the lumber industry helped shape his dark view of Russian capitalism in the 1990s. "These days one can get mad that the government periodically runs after you, squeezes taxes out of you," he said in 2008.

> But in the 1990s, businessmen had to think about their lives. Some kind of criminal elements might come, and that would be it—no one would help you: not the court, nor the FSB [Federal Security Service], nor the MVD [Ministry of the Interior].
>
> During my trips around the country back then I also saw examples of the way people did business the "wise guy" way (*chisto konkretno*). In each region there were certain criminal groups that were in charge. Often people viewed them as an alternative—and even as a more effective—system of power. . . . Nowadays I can say for

certain, if one goes to the provinces they no longer take you to meet the regional boss (*smotryashchy*) of the criminal gangs. They will say that there's the mayor, the governor; if you want to start a business in the region, meet with them, negotiate about investment and so on.

In 1997, IPE bought a large stake in the Bratsk Lumber Combine, and Medvedev was seconded to serve on its board. The Siberian city of Bratsk was, at the time, infamous for its mafia. In the early 1990s, local Russian bandits had fought a gang war to drive out a number of Georgian professional criminals—*vory v zakone*—who had set up shop there. One general director of the Bratsk Lumber Combine had been shot in Moscow in 1993. In 1999, a Bratsk deputy prosecutor who had been looking into cases involving the Bratsk organized crime group was assassinated.

By that time, Medvedev had left to take up a job in the central government, by his account cutting his ties with the business. Journalists have speculated about why he would have sold out at this point. One motive might have been to avoid conflicts of interest, although this would make him quite exceptional in Russia. Some referred to rumors that local law enforcement in Bratsk had been working up a case against him on behalf of a rival businessman. Others saw in Medvedev's hasty departure an attempt to avoid being implicated in the Kotlassky paper mill scandal, which the Auditing Chamber had recently begun investigating.

In the Wings

In August 1999, President Yeltsin had appointed Vladimir Putin prime minister and endorsed him for president. One day in October, Medvedev got a call from Igor Sechin, an acquaintance from the St. Petersburg government, who was in Moscow as Putin's aide. The boss wanted to talk, Sechin said. When Medvedev made it to the Kremlin, Putin asked him to head the securities and exchange commission. To Medvedev, who had seen firsthand how Russian capitalists were drilling holes in the securities legislation, the job seemed an exciting challenge. Along with Sveta and his three-year-old son Ilya, he moved to Moscow.

But it turned out he was needed in another position. After a few months as deputy head of the government staff, Medvedev—who had mimeographed flyers for Sobchak—was appointed to run Putin's election campaign. The candidate, already far ahead in the polls, could indulge his aversion to stumping for votes and run as the dedicated statesman, too busy saving the country to perform in the electoral circus. He refused to appear in televised debates or advertisements, scorning those who sold themselves—like Snickers or Tampax—between segments of the evening news. But there was still plenty for Medvedev to do in this non-campaign campaign. "I got enormous satisfaction from this work," he recalled. "From involvement in the main political process, from the fact that much depended on me personally. It was a test of strength." He passed.

After Putin's election, Medvedev retreated to the Kremlin's ornate corridors, serving as deputy head of the presidential administration. Yeltsin's chief of staff, Aleksandr Voloshin, a formidable behind-the-scenes operator, stayed on to head Putin's team. According to Voloshin, Medvedev proved "a quick learner, very rapidly mastering the bureaucratic technology." To outsiders, he appeared a self-effacing technocrat, seldom speaking to the press, and, when he did, rarely making headlines. "He is capable of smooth talking for an hour and a half and yet you won't remember what he has said and might not remember what he looks like," said one commentator. Putin's economic advisor Andrey Illarionov, who served in the Kremlin between 2000 and 2005 alongside Medvedev, could not recall in late 2007 "anything that could be considered his personal [view] on any idea, any project, any movement, any action."

Until one of the insiders breaks *omertà*, what role Medvedev played in the development of Putin's policies will remain obscure. But, he is sure to have been deeply involved in many of the key initiatives. As one of the administration's leading lawyers, he is known to have participated in discussions of the early legal reforms, and he took credit for increasing judges' salaries to make bribe taking less attractive. He also publicly promoted the Kremlin's 2003 attempt at administrative reform, which reorganized the executive branch and catalogued the different agencies' functions, but evidently did not improve government performance.

Throughout the 2000s, Medvedev also went along with the Kremlin's more undemocratic and economically illiberal initiatives, even spearheading some of them. Yet, with the skill of an accomplished law-

yer, he managed, even as he defended such measures, to subtly disasso-
ciate himself from them—no easy task, given his boss's preoccupation
with loyalty. He would start by justifying the action—be it the abolition
of elections for regional governors or the destruction of Yukos—yet, in
defending it, he would assert the most respectable rationale, while reassuring listeners that the intervention was limited to the issue or case at
hand. He was the Kremlin's resident "good cop." Plenty of others aspired
to play the opposite role.

Characteristically, when Khodorkovsky's arrest prompted Voloshin's
resignation and Medvedev took over as chief of staff in November 2003,
his immediate concern was to calm the markets. While not criticizing
the arrest itself, and insisting that "all people, irrespective of their posts
and material status, must observe the law," he nevertheless wondered out
loud about the wisdom of freezing Yukos's shares, and urged his colleagues to "think out all the economic consequences of the decisions they
are taking." Encouraging as this may have sounded to investors, it is hard
to think of a case in which Medvedev's nuanced doubts ever led to a per-
ceptible change in the policy in question.

In late 2004, as the pro-Russian Viktor Yanukovich squared off
against the pro-Western Viktor Yushchenko in the Ukrainian presidential election campaign, Medvedev organized the Kremlin's ultimately
counterproductive efforts to influence the outcome, dispatching Kremlin-connected political consultants to Kiev. Putin quickly congratulated
Yanukovich on his victory. The result was a humiliation for Putin and the
Kremlin when the election was annulled as fraudulent and Yushchenko
won the revote. Medvedev reportedly took this failure hard.

For much of the decade, Medvedev combined his Kremlin jobs with
that of chairman of the Gazprom board. Although insiders said Putin
was making all the key decisions, Medvedev must nevertheless have been
closely involved and signing off on most projects. During Medvedev's
chairmanship, restrictions on nonresidents owning Gazprom shares
were removed and the company's capitalization grew from $7 billion to
$244 billion. Assets that had disappeared under the previous manage-
ment were recovered. But then some of these assets, along with others
that had never left the fold, were either sold or transferred to the management of businessmen close to Putin (see Chapter 3). Besides natural gas,

Gazprom branched out into the media business, buying various publications and taking over Gusinsky's NTV television station, which muted its criticism of the Kremlin. Gazprom also bought the oil company Sibneft from its private owners, renaming it Gazprom Neft. Rather than sell gas directly to Eastern Europe, Gazprom engaged a mysterious trading firm, RosUkrEnergo, owned half by Gazprom itself and half by two Ukrainian businessmen. In 2006, RosUkrEnergo was being investigated by the U.S. Justice Department's Organized Crime Unit. On Medvedev's watch, Gazprom abruptly halted gas supplies to the Ukraine several times to protest unpaid bills and force agreement on higher prices, interrupting supplies to countries further West.

Over time, a number of Medvedev's old friends and colleagues appeared in management posts in Gazprom and its subsidiaries. His college classmate, Konstantin Chuychenko, served as head of Gazprom's legal department, as executive director of RosUkrEnergo, and on the boards of Gazprom Neft, Gazprom-Media, and NTV. In 2008, according to his income declaration, Chuychenko earned $12.5 million. Another classmate, Valeriya Adamova, served as vice president of Sibur, a previously Gazprom-controlled petrochemicals company that Gazprom worked to recover, only to transfer it to the indirect management of Bank Rossiya, whose largest shareholder was Putin's friend Kovalchuk. Medvedev's first legal partners also turned up. Ilya Yeliseyev served as deputy CEO of Gazprombank and member of the board of Gazprom-Media and NTV. Anton Ivanov became first deputy general director of Gazprom-Media, before being named chairman of the Supreme Arbitrazh Court—at which point Mikhail Krotov, one of Medvedev's LGU colleagues and co-authors, took Ivanov's place in Gazprom-Media. When Valery Musin, Medvedev's LGU colleague and Putin's teacher, joined the Gazprom board in June 2009, it almost seemed that time spent in the LGU law department had become a prerequisite for work in the gas monopoly.

Medvedev's reputation as a relative liberal did not depend entirely on rhetorical nuance. On several occasions, at the behest of human rights activists, he pushed for minor legal reforms. Ruslan Linkov, an old acquaintance who chaired the St. Petersburg division of Democratic Russia, says that when he approached Medvedev in the early 2000s about problems in the penal system, Medvedev was responsive. At Linkov's request, for instance, he pressed behind the scenes to improve medical provision for convicts.

In November 2005, Putin moved Medvedev from the presidential administration to the government to serve as a first deputy prime minister. Observers concluded that Putin was grooming him—along with Sergey Ivanov, an old KGB colleague whom Putin also promoted at this time—as a possible successor. Putin gave Medvedev responsibility for four newly announced "national projects," aimed at improving housing, health care, education, and agriculture. Given some of the country's oil windfall to spend, Medvedev increased wages for medical personnel and funded the construction of some additional apartments. However, the financing—equal to about 4 percent of the federal budget—was too low to fuel a breakthrough. The projects amounted to "little islands of support in a sea of dilapidated infrastructure," in the words of the economist Ruslan Grinberg. As of March 2008, 53 percent of Russians thought the money had been spent ineffectively, and another 15 percent thought it had simply been stolen. A year later, the cabinet department responsible for the projects was quietly disbanded.

As 2008 approached, Medvedev was widely considered too soft, too pro-Western, too liberal to be a plausible candidate for the presidency. Commentators expected Putin to endorse one of his silovik associates, most likely Sergey Ivanov. So it came as a surprise when in December 2007, in Putin's office, the leaders of four pro-Kremlin parties—United Russia, A Just Russia, the Agrarian Party, and Civil Force—having invited in the press, informed the president, with all the spontaneity of a show trial, that they had decided to propose Medvedev's candidacy. "Dmitry Anatolyevich, have you been consulted on this?" Putin asked Medvedev gravely, injecting a note of unintended comedy into the proceedings. Satisfied that the scheme had not been concocted behind his protégé's back, Putin graciously approved the deputies' choice. The next day, Medvedev announced that, if elected, he would ask Putin to serve as his prime minister.

Why had Putin chosen his old colleague? "I am confident that he will be a good president and an effective manager," the president explained. "But besides other things, there is this personal chemistry: I trust him. I just trust him."

Two months later, after a desultory campaign permeated by super-fluous electoral manipulation, the two men stood together on a stage outside the Kremlin in the light snow to thank the voters. Medvedev promised to continue the course Putin had begun. After his inaugura-tion in May, he moved into the oak-paneled presidential office in the Kremlin's Senate Building. Putin repaired to the fifth floor of the White House on the embankment above the Moskva River, where a large suite had been renovated for the new prime minister, with a swimming pool and two banquet halls newly added.

Riding Tandem

How this new system would work in practice, no one quite knew. In the confusing transition after Putin's endorsement of Medvedev, the reporter Andrey Kolesnikov caught one young professional who had been called to brief Putin and Medvedev glancing back and forth between the two with a look of embarrassment "as if by mistake she had set up a meeting with both of them at the same time in the same place." Journalists took to referring to the arrangement—with Medvedev as president, Putin as prime minister—as government by tandem.

It had seemed that the goal of the next few years would be to reassure foreign investors and reengage with the West so that the silovarch net-work could continue to cash out through IPOs and diversify into inter-national profit streams. Putin's choice of Medvedev suggested a decision to placate the liberal critics with subtle nods towards democracy, to fine-tune the administrative mechanism and give hope to the rising genera-tion of modern, young professionals who might be coopted to invigorate the system. With Putin watching his back, Medvedev would be able to grow into his new office, allowing his predecessor to withdraw into the background for some well-earned rest and recreation.

Medvedev seemed eager to encourage expectations of a shift toward more liberal policies. In February 2008, addressing business leaders in Krasnoyarsk, he declared that: "Freedom is better than non-freedom." By this, he meant "freedom in all its manifestations—personal freedom, economic freedom, and, finally, freedom of expression." In his inaugu-ration speech, he challenged the country "to achieve true respect for the law, to overcome legal nihilism." The phrase would become a kind of Medvedev mantra. To the journalist Nikolay Svanidze, he lamented: "We are all legal nihilists to our bone marrow." To work out the details of modernizing initiatives, Medvedev backed the formation of a new think tank, the Institute of Contemporary Development, and agreed to serve as chairman of its board of trustees.

By the end of his first year, however, Medvedev's liberal support- ers were frustrated. Optimists could point to a handful of pocket-sized reforms, humanitarian gestures, eloquent speeches, and thoughtful meetings. One Yukos lawyer, a mother with young children, had been released from prison early; another, dying of HIV-related illnesses, had been let out on bail. One much-criticized judge had been removed. Med- vedev had met with the editor of the opposition *Novaya Gazeta*, dis- cussed Hume and Rousseau, and praised the paper for refusing "to suck up to anyone." A campaign of technocratic tinkering had nibbled away at some of the Putin era antidemocratic changes. Battling corruption, Medvedev had required all high-level officials, starting with himself, to submit annual declarations of their income and wealth.

But these gestures and tweaks were offset by others that rendered the state even less open and responsive. In December, with no explana- tion to speak of, the Constitution was amended to lengthen the presi- dent's term from four to six years and the Duma's from four to five. The president was given the right to nominate the chair of the Constitu- tional Court, subject to confirmation by the Federation Council; previ- ously, the judges had elected their own chair. A new law eliminated the use of juries in trials related to terrorism or political matters. Special police units responsible for fighting organized crime—which, although less pervasive than in the 1990s, certainly remained a problem—were abolished and replaced by divisions to fight "extremism." Although Russia *was* suffering from an alarming spread of racist violence, the fight against "extremism" under Putin had focused on monitoring and harassing the political opposition.

In early 2008, Medvedev had said that history text books "should be maximally depoliticized." A year later, he set up a commission, includ- ing military and intelligence officials, to combat "falsified" interpreta- tions of Russia's past, which he said were becoming increasingly "harsh, depraved, and aggressive." As a presidential candidate, Medvedev had called the unlawful "raiding" of companies—forcible takeovers using blackmail and corrupt law enforcement agents—"shameful." Raiding continued, sometimes with the apparent support of government members. Finally, as the end of Khodorkovsky's prison term approached, the prosecutors filed new charges against him and his colleague Platon Lebedev. The most Medvedev appeared willing or able to do was to have the trial moved from a distant Siberian city to Moscow.

The income declarations might have a positive effect in time. In the short run, they generated mostly cynicism. As wits noted, Russia turned out to be governed by the poor husbands of rich wives. "Russia's bureaucrats just laugh," said the Duma deputy and former KGB general Gennady Gudkov. "There is no one to check these Potemkin declarations." Medvedev, a successful businessman who had owned a large stake in what would become one of the world's largest lumber companies, declared ownership of one Moscow apartment (with his wife) and about $84,000 in savings. His wife Svetlana, who often appeared in designer clothes, had about $4,000 in savings and drove a ten-year-old Volkswagen Golf. While there was no evidence that this was not accurate and complete, the family's modest circumstances raised many eyebrows.

So great was the gap between Medvedev's rhetoric and the government's record that he often seemed to be running against himself. Addressing parliament in November 2008, he lambasted the administrative machinery he headed.

> The state bureaucracy is guided by the same distrust of free people, of free activity, as 20 years ago. . . . The bureaucracy periodically creates nightmares for businesses—to make sure that they don't do something wrong. It takes control of the mass media—to make sure it doesn't say something wrong. It intervenes in the electoral process—to make sure they don't elect someone wrong. It pressures the courts—to make sure they don't give the wrong sentences. . . .
>
> As a result our state is the biggest employer, the most active publisher, the best producer, its own judge, its own party, and, in the end, its own public. Such a system is absolutely inefficient and creates only one thing—corruption. It generates widespread legal

nihilism, contradicts the Constitution, and delays the development of the institutions of an innovative economy and democracy.

It was a powerful speech . . . for a leader of the opposition. The president's penetrating diagnosis of Russia's problems contrasted with the timid steps he proposed by way of reform. Bureaucrats—first and foremost, those in Medvedev's press office—were stifling media freedom, instructing television stations about what they could not show. Not to worry—technology would come to the rescue.

> Experience has shown that to persuade bureaucrats to "leave the media alone" is practically useless. Instead of persuading, we need as actively as possible to broaden the free space of the internet and digital television. No official can obstruct discussion on the internet or simultaneously censor a thousand channels.

Officials were bullying judges into ruling in their interests. The solution? Medvedev would "recommend to judges at all levels that they minimize their contacts with businessmen and even representatives of state services." Why not, instead, recommend to officials that they minimize their contacts with judges? The president did not say.

Why had hopes for a thaw in the chill of late Putinism proved deceptive? There were two interpretations. Some thought Medvedev had genuinely wanted to move faster but had been blocked by Putin. Others saw his verbal attacks on the bureaucracy as mere rhetoric and his aims as essentially conservative: the bows to freedom and the rule of law had been merely lines in the old "good cop, bad cop" routine.

The skeptics could make a creditable case. Putin too had regularly extolled the virtues of freedom and honest government, while overseeing the expansion of an intrusive and venal bureaucracy. His goal, Putin had said in 2004, was to create "a free society of free people." He had called for a law enforcement system that would "inspire pride in respectable citizens rather than prompting them to cross the street at the sight of someone in epaulettes." Medvedev, for his part, had often dismissed the need for reform. "What needs to be done urgently?" he had asked rhetorically in 2006. "Nothing. There is no Problem No. 1 that the government isn't handling." Taking office, he seemed to think the main challenge was not to cure the patient but to avoid doing harm. Most Russians, he insisted, were thinking: "I just hope he doesn't spoil anything!"

Still, Medvedev's people had tried to push some more ambitious changes in the early days. In the summer of 2008, a plan had surfaced to gradually reduce political pressure on television and privatize the state-owned, second national channel, VGTRK. A concrete proposal was being drafted in one of the Duma's committees. In the Kremlin, a major restructuring of the law enforcement system was seriously discussed. Under a plan debated off-and-on since the early 1990s, the various separate criminal investigators—from the procuracy, the Interior Ministry, the Federal Security Service (FSB), and other bodies—would be united in a single investigatory agency, analogous to the American FBI. Later, the procuracy would merge with the Ministry of Justice. Municipal police forces would become independent of the federal police.

These initiatives went nowhere. The idea of privatizing VGTRK was frozen, and Kremlin guidance of television news continued much as before, with the added complication that coverage of Putin and Medvedev had to be kept in rough parity. Reforms of law enforcement never happened (although in 2010 new proposals were suddenly again on the agenda). To understand why the impulse failed, one must consider first the constraints Medvedev faced, and then two external events that in 2008 changed the landscape of Russia's politics.

From the way experts discussed the Russian presidency under Putin and Yeltsin, one might have assumed that Medvedev could enact his reforms with the stroke of a pen. Commentators had called the Russian presidency close to dictatorial. Yet, the experience of Medvedev's early tenure illustrates, once again, how little one can conclude about the power of Russia's president from merely reading the Constitution. Depending on the context, the "super-presidency" that critics accused Yeltsin of designing for himself could be either extremely strong or very weak.

Under Medvedev in 2008–2010, it was the latter. The president could not hope to make major—or even minor—policy changes without the prime minister's agreement. Why not? To begin with, Medvedev had no reliable base of support, either in society or within the state. In 2000, Putin had won a personal mandate from the voters. By contrast, Medvedev's 2008 victory was both universally attributed to Putin's support and tarnished by blatant electoral irregularities. Medvedev's approval rating moved in lockstep with Putin's, some 5 to 10 points below the latter. Within the corridors of power, Medvedev had no "team" of his own beyond a few law school friends and former colleagues who were seconded to Gazprom or scattered across a number of second-rank positions. Even his chief of staff, Sergey Naryshkin, was a Putin loyalist, whom Medvedev was not allowed to replace. Indeed, Medvedev had been selected by Putin in part because his lack of political or administrative resources made him the least threatening of potential successors. "His main strength," the sociologist Olga Kryshtanovskaya had quipped, "is his weakness."

Then there were the institutional realities. The way Putin had arranged the political scenery, his successor was effectively boxed in, surrounded by tripwires. Should Medvedev desire to introduce a policy Putin disliked, he would need the government to implement it—a government chaired by Putin as prime minister. Should he decide to pass a law, the United Russia party, which dominated parliament, would need to vote for it—the party, that is, that Putin commanded, having led it to victory at the polls. Constitutionally, Medvedev could deal directly with the heads of the law enforcement and security ministries. Informally, the ministers still viewed Putin as the center of power. In the regions, all the governors were initially Putin appointees.

In extremis, Medvedev had the authority to fire Putin as prime minister. But he would have to get his replacement approved by the Duma, which would almost certainly rally behind the United Russia leader. If the Duma refused three times, Medvedev could then dissolve it and call new elections, appointing his chosen candidate in the interim. Thus, *if* the public supported Medvedev against Putin—and Medvedev could get a more sympathetic Duma elected after dissolving the old one—his constitutional powers might count for something. But without such strong public support against Putin, he had little chance of prevailing.

Additionally, the president could not dissolve the Duma if it was trying to impeach him (Article 109 of the Constitution). To impeach a president, the Duma and Federation Council would each have to approve a motion to impeach on grounds of "high treason or some other grave crime" by a vote of two-thirds of the body's members. The Supreme Court would then have to confirm that a crime had been committed, and the Constitutional Court that the correct procedures had been followed (Article 93). As of 2010, United Russia held 70 percent of the seats in the Duma. The Federation Council consisted of representatives of the regional legislatures (dominated in the late 2000s by United Russia) and of the governors. Eventually, perhaps, Medvedev could replace enough Putin-appointed governors with his own to create a faction loyal to him in the Federation Council, which might block impeachment. But this would take time. Meanwhile, a motion to impeach Medvedev supported by Putin would probably have passed, throwing the battle into the Supreme and Constitutional Courts, whose decisions are harder to predict.

Finally, besides the political and institutional constraints, Medvedev was probably bound to Putin in less visible ways. Their business involvements—from the St. Petersburg Foreign Relations Committee in the early 1990s to Gazprom in the 2000s—had overlapped. If the two had skeletons in their closets, they were most likely the same skeletons. More cynical observers suspected that some kind of mutual incrimination might have been necessary for Putin's siloviki to accept Medvedev's leadership. At Gazprom, Medvedev had signed documents on numerous deals that critics delicately characterized as "nontransparent." "That has engendered confidence among his senior comrades that he will obey them," said Vladimir Milov, a former deputy energy minister and liberal Putin opponent. If this was true, any major attempt to investigate Putin's cronies for corruption could quickly ensnare the president himself.

In short, even if he disagreed with Putin's approach on certain issues, Medvedev would need—and want—Putin's consent for any reform. He could not redirect the tandem from the back seat, and to try to grab the handlebars as they raced along was a sure way to crash the vehicle.

Medvedev may well have thought he had his mentor's backing for significant changes. Putin himself often declared the need to modernize the state and clean up the judiciary. Perhaps he had led Medvedev to believe he was ready to restore the kind of technocratic, market-friendly government of his first three years, even to rein in the silovarchy, gradually easing the security magnates into private life. Perhaps, in his own cautious way, that is what Putin initially thought he was doing. As Medvedev took over, the former president was maneuvering his KGB henchmen—Sechin, Patrushev, the two Ivanovs—into jobs that although important had less operational power than their previous positions, making room for younger professionals such as Igor Shuvalov or Arkady Dvorkovich, who became Medvedev's economic adviser.

Having secured the transition, Putin at first seemed ready to disengage. Initially, he struck reporters as tired and bored by his new job. He would turn up fifteen minutes before cabinet meetings and leave right after them. Sometimes, key decisions had to be delayed because Putin's personal bodyguard said he could not be reached. The phrase "working with documents," familiar from Yeltsin's day, was coming back into vogue.

Putin might have continued to withdraw into the background had history not intervened with characteristic abruptness. Two events, originating outside Russia's borders, transformed the dynamic and tone of politics, and apparently changed Putin's plans. By the end of 2008, he looked determined to stay at the center of the action.

Financial Mayhem

Two weeks after Medvedev's election victory, the Wall Street investment bank Bear Stearns collapsed. Its share price fell in one week from $62 to $5, as the Federal Reserve scrambled to arrange a bailout. Markets quaked. "One thing is for certain," President Bush announced. "We're in challenging times."

Like the financial shock that had struck the country ten years earlier, Russia's economic emergency of 2008–2009 started far away. In 1998, a virulent case of the so-called Asian flu had infected Moscow's markets. A decade later, the virus came from America.

The story of the global financial crisis of 2008–2009 is already well known. Rising U.S. interest rates starting in 2004 depressed American house prices, prompting an increase in defaults on mortgages, especially among high risk subprime borrowers. Wall Street financiers had bundled these subprime mortgages into complicated securities and sold them to the world's banks, insurance companies, and other financial institutions, which bought them with only a vague notion of how much risk each bundle contained. As mortgage defaults spread, the prices of these securities crashed. Credit markets dried up because lenders had no way to assess the risks on borrowers' balance sheets. Starved of liquidity, the U.S. stock market plunged, along with business confidence and then activity in the real economy.

From Moscow, all this seemed, at first, like a distant sideshow. The Russian authorities followed events on Wall Street with nonchalance, even a little superiority. Russian banks had not been issuing subprime mortgages. Nor did they have much direct exposure to the "toxic assets" poisoning Western markets. Russia continued to receive record inflows of foreign investment. In January 2008, Finance Minister Aleksey Kudrin, speaking at the annual Davos economic meeting, boasted that his country remained an "island of stability" in the global tempest.

Russia's macroeconomic policy had been among the most responsible in the world (see Chapter 6). For eight years the government had run a budget surplus. It had paid down its foreign debt to just three percent of GDP. The Central Bank had amassed almost $600 billion in currency reserves—the third largest in the world, after China and Japan. Since 1999, Russia's current account surpluses had averaged more than 10 percent of GDP. While keeping inflation low, the authorities had done their best to avoid too rapid an appreciation of the ruble. Rather than spending the country's windfall oil profits, they had saved these in a stabilization fund, which by February 2008 contained $157 billion.

So one can understand the frustration in Moscow when later that year the country found itself again in a humiliating meltdown. Prime Minister Putin—who had pinched and saved to put Russia's financial house in order, working "like a slave in the galleys," as he put it—could not conceal his anger at the injustice. "Everything happening now in the economic and financial sphere began in the United States," he lamented in October. "The authorities in that country mishandled their power and infected the world with the crisis," he complained in December.

Russia's trouble began in the spring of 2008, as some of its large banks and corporations, which had been borrowing heavily abroad via bond issues and bank loans, felt credit tightening. Some were forced to pay higher interest rates to turn over their bonds. Hedge funds that had been investing in Russia started liquidating their positions. As world stock prices followed the American markets down in the early summer, Russian shares joined the slide. Their decline accelerated when oil prices, having peaked in July, began falling even faster than they had risen. As investors anticipated a worldwide recession, demand for all Russia's export commodities shrank. Then, in a terrifying week in mid-September, the U.S. investment bank Lehman Brothers filed for bankruptcy, and global markets seized up.

Investors simply panicked, fleeing emerging markets regardless of how good or bad their policies had been. As late as August 2008, according to the investment bank Renaissance Capital, Moscow had been "flooded with international bankers competing to provide funding to Russian entitities." By October, "the only financiers visiting were those trying to get their money back." The interbank loan market virtually froze. Russia's authorities had to close the stock exchanges for two days to prevent hysterical selling. On September 16, Moscow's MICEX stock index fell 17.5 percent. Between May 16 and October 24, the RTS share index fell by 78 percent, erasing more than $1 trillion worth of value. Despite the country's huge currency reserves, as the oil price sank some began to bet against the ruble, and the Central Bank sold billions of dollars to prevent a rapid devaluation. Between August 2008 and March 2009, the currency reserves shrank by about $220 billion, and the ruble fell from 23 to the dollar in July 2008 to 36 to the dollar in February 2009.

Some saw in the stock market's slide the effects of unwise government actions that scared away investors. In July, Prime Minister Putin accused the steel company Mechel of manipulating the price of its coking coal to reduce its taxes. Apparently irritated that Mechel's main shareholder, Igor Zyuzin, had called in sick rather than attend a government meeting, Putin threatened to send Zyuzin a "doctor" to "clean up all the problems." Mechel's share price promptly plunged, wiping out $5 billion of its capitalization, as investors wondered whether the company was about to suffer Yukos's fate. It was not; Zyuzin and the Kremlin made up in subsequent weeks. Then, in August, came Russia's war in Georgia (see below), which also appeared to alarm investors. These events did not cause the markets' collapse—stocks were already plummeting, driven lower by the credit squeeze, investors' new risk aversion, and the sinking price of oil. The price of Urals crude oil fell from around $140 a barrel in early July to about $34 a barrel in early January 2009. Still, the attack on Mechel and the Georgian war cannot have helped. Among emerging markets, including those dominated by oil, Russia's stock slide was particularly large.

By winter, the disease was spreading from the financial sector to the real economy. Tight credit, plunging business confidence, and the cutback in consumption as wealth evaporated combined to produce a decline in output. Industrial production fell by almost three percent in the last quarter of 2008 and by 15 percent in the first quarter of 2009. Real disposable incomes were down six percent in the last quarter of 2008 (compared to the last quarter of 2007), and about one percent in the first quarter of 2009 (compared to a year before). By early 2009, more than half the enterprises in mineral extraction were making losses.

In September, the government sprang into action. To boost liquidity and prevent bank failures, it extended more than a trillion rubles (about $40 billion) in credit to the banks and reduced their reserve requirement. At the same time, the authorities provided $50 billion to lend to companies. Some of the leading oligarchs had pledged shares in their industrial holdings as collateral for foreign loans. Fearing foreigners might ensnare the country's largest corporations, the Kremlin put up money for bailouts. The automobile producer AvtoVAZ received a loan of about $806 million, and Oleg Deripaska's RusAl got one of $4.5 billion. The government cut export tariffs on oil in line with the drop in world prices, and hiked tariffs on imported cars to protect domestic producers. To prevent bank runs, it increased the maximum sum insured by the state in individual savings accounts to about $28,000. As stocks fell, the government also spent about $5.3 billion in a vain attempt to prop up the market by buying shares. In all, the government's various stimulus measures came to about 7 percent of GDP in 2009, larger proportionately than the U.S. stimulus, which constituted about 5.5 percent of GDP.

The emergency measures achieved their main aims. Only a few minor banks failed completely. Although at huge cost, the ruble devaluation was kept moderate. By the spring of 2009, most of the oligarchs were breathing more easily. At least temporarily, the markets had stabilized, with the oil price recovering from its low of $34 a barrel to around $70 a barrel in

June. The ruble was appreciating again, and stocks had bounced back, by June recouping about one quarter of the previous year's losses.

Yet uncertainties remained. First, no one knew if the global crisis was over or if the calm of late 2009 and early 2010 was just the eye of the storm. Second, even if the world economy was gradually stabilizing, it was not clear what would drive Russia's future growth. From 2005 through 2007, growth had depended on rising oil prices; higher export revenues had boosted domestic demand, financing a boom in services— retailing, real estate, transport, and financial services (see Chapter 6). Were oil prices to rise again, Russia might repeat this experience for a while. But even if commodity prices recovered, tight international credit would limit the impact on demand. The age of cheap money appeared to be over. Could Russia grow by expanding mineral output? To develop new oil and gas fields would require major investments, and it would take time for these to come on line. For years, the government had been talking about stimulating innovation. Yet it shrank from the most effective means—enhancing market competition, restraining venal bureaucrats, and protecting property rights, including those to intellectual property.

The August War

The second development that complicated the Kremlin's plans was the outbreak of war. On the night of August 7, 2008, around 11:35 p.m. according to observers from the Organization for Security and Cooperation in Europe (OSCE), Georgian forces began bombarding the city of Tskhinvali with heavy artillery. Tskhinvali was the capital of South Ossetia, a separatist region on the border between Georgia and Russia. Early the next morning, Georgian infantry moved in and began fighting for control of the city.

The Ossetians, a mountain people, speak a language related to Farsi and are traditionally Orthodox Christians. The region's parliament had first demanded to separate from Georgia in 1989, voting to unite with the North Ossetian republic, which lies inside Russia on the other side of the Caucasus mountain range. In 1991, Georgia's nationalist leader, Zviad Gamsakhurdia, sent police troops to drive the Ossetian population across the border, ethnically cleansing the region for Georgians. As

Gamsakhurdia put it, subversive minorities "should be chopped up" and "burned out with a red-hot iron from the Georgian nation."

Some five-hundred or six-hundred people died in that conflict, and tens of thousands of refugees—both Ossetians and Georgians—fled the war zone. The Ossetians, assisted by some Russian army troops and irregulars, managed to repel the Georgian attackers. An agreement was negotiated, under which South Ossetia achieved de facto autonomy, and peacekeepers commanded by a Joint Control Commission, made up of Georgian, Russian, and South Ossetian representatives, were stationed in the region, along with OSCE monitors. For twelve years, no military confrontation occurred, and Ossetians and Georgians traveled back and forth and traded freely with each other.

In January 2004, a pro-Western Georgian nationalist, Mikheil Saakashvili, had come to power in Georgia in the "Rose Revolution" that overthrew the previous president, Eduard Shevardnadze. Saakashvili had two declared goals: to bring Georgia into NATO, and to restore Tbilisi's control over the country's three separatist regions—South Ossetia, Adjara, and Abkhazia. Kneeling at the grave of King David the Builder, the twelfth century Georgian ruler who had united the country, he pledged on the eve of his inauguration that: "Georgia . . . will restore its wholeness and become a single, strong state." The next day, as helicopters dropped rose petals on the crowd, he promised to dedicate his presidency "to the unification and strengthening of Georgia."

Over the next few years, Saakashvili retrained and reequipped the Georgian army, increasing military spending to one quarter of the government budget and buying weapons from the United States, Israel, Ukraine, and Eastern Europe. He quickly succeeded in forcing Adjara into submission with an economic blockade. But attempts to intimidate the Abkhazians and South Ossetians failed. In August 2004, he sent three hundred special forces troops to South Ossetia, but they were repelled by the local militia after heavy fighting. Two years later, the South Ossetians held a referendum, in which 95 percent of the province's voters participated, of whom almost 100 percent voted for independence. That same year, Tbilisi sent security forces and police into the Kodori Gorge in Eastern Abkhazia, where they established a base for a Tbilisi-backed Abkhaz "government in exile."

What prompted Saakashvili to escalate the conflict in 2008 remains unclear. Five hundred Russian peacekeepers were posted in South Ossetia under the Joint Control Commission, and some reports suggest more Russian soldiers had been infiltrated into the region. Russian leaders had repeatedly promised to defend the South Ossetians should Georgia attack them again. Moscow had also issued Russian citizenship and passports to some 70,000 of South Ossetia's 80,000 inhabitants, and had provided generous aid to the separatist regions. Following joint exercises with American troops in July 2008, Georgia's military began to deploy troops near South Ossetia. By the evening of August 7, about 12,000 were massed on the border. There were exchanges of fire between the Georgian villages inside South Ossetia and the Ossetian zone.

Then, during the night of August 7, several hours after declaring a unilateral ceasefire, Saakashvili ordered his troops to attack South Ossetia in an operation codenamed "Clear Field." In bombing the region, the Georgian authorities said they were responding to shelling of Georgian villages from Tskhinvali. However, OSCE peacekeepers posted in the city later said they did not hear outgoing missiles. The Georgians shot Grad BM-21 rockets, a weapon that military experts say should never be used in civilian areas because of its vast destructive power and indiscriminate effects. Later, Georgian tanks fought their way into the city, shooting at the Ossetian militia men who resisted. Two of the Russian peacekeepers in Tskhinvali were killed, five were wounded, and their building was set on fire.

The next morning, a column of Russian troops pushed south to reinforce the Russian peacekeepers, through the Roki Tunnel that connects North and South Ossetia. Russian aircraft bombed military bases and infrastructure further south inside Georgia proper, and naval forces blockaded Georgia's ports. Some Russian shells landed in civilian areas of the city of Gori, causing casualties. The next day, Russian paratroopers and marines landed in Abkhazia to open a second front.

After three days of intense combat, the Russian troops, fighting alongside South Ossetian militias, pushed the Georgians back, clearing Tskhinvali by the end of August 10, and controlling the whole of South Ossetia by late August 11. The Russian troops continued south, occupying Gori as the Georgian army fled to Tbilisi. The Russian advance halted thirty-four miles from the capital. The occupation lasted until August 22. South Ossetian militias marauded within the Russian controlled areas, looting and burning Georgian villages and terrorizing the local population. At the same time, Russian troops from Abkhazia moved south, destroying the Georgian military base at Senaki, and sinking Georgian naval vessels in the port of Poti. Russian soldiers also drove the Georgian forces out of the Kodori Gorge.

On August 12, Medvedev announced that he had ordered an end to military operations, but fighting continued. Over the next couple of days, all parties agreed to a peace plan, negotiated by the European Union's president, Nicolas Sarkozy. Russia gradually withdrew from Georgia proper, handing over buffer zones on the borders of South Ossetia and Abkhazia to European Union monitors. Then on August 26, after a unanimous vote by the Russian parliament, President Medvedev recognized the two regions as independent states—a move that was not widely imitated. By early 2010, only Nicaragua, Venezuela, and the Micronesian island of Nauru had followed Russia's example.

As usual, precise assessments of the costs of the war—both human and financial—are hard to reach. A Russian investigating committee published a list of 365 Ossetians who were confirmed dead, presumably including both civilians and militia men. The Georgian authorities said 228 Georgian civilians had been killed. The Russian military said it lost forty-eight soldiers, including ten peacekeepers. The Georgians reported the loss of 170 servicemen and 14 policemen. Around 200,000 people were reportedly forced to flee the conflict, and 35,000 were still displaced more than a year later. Human rights organizations accused both sides of violating humanitarian law, in part by using cluster bombs. The destruction of infrastructure in South Ossetia and Georgia proper was extensive, and the Georgian defense minister assessed damage to bases and equipment at $250 million.

In the West, many commentators and officials cast the August events as a case of Russian imperialism, and some warned that Ukraine would be next in line, with the Crimea a likely flashpoint. One neoconservative pundit, Robert Kagan, compared Russia's intervention to the 1938 Nazi invasion of the Czech Sudetenland. Britain's foreign secretary, David Miliband, invoked the Soviet crushing of the 1968 Prague Spring and said the war showed that Russia remained "unreconciled to the new map of Europe." The U.S. presidential candidate John McCain accused the Russians of invading "a small, democratic neighbor to gain more control over the world's oil supply, intimidate other neighbors, and further their ambitions of reassembling the Russian empire." President Bush chimed in, informing his friend Vladimir that: "Bullying and intimidation are not acceptable ways to conduct foreign policy in the twenty-first century."

To many Russians this reaction seemed so biased that it reinforced their cynicism about the West's intentions. Not just the usual Putin supporters and nationalists, but Russians from across the political spectrum considered the intervention justified. As former Soviet president Gorbachev put it, given the Georgian shelling of Tskhinvali: "Russia had to respond. To accuse it of aggression against 'small, defenseless Georgia' is not just hypocritical but shows a lack of humanity." Russians found it hard to imagine that if U.S. peacekeepers had been attacked—and several of them killed—in a country where they were monitoring a ceasefire, Washington would not send troops to reinforce them. It also seemed to many Russians that intervening to protect the Ossetian minority from repeated attempts by Georgian troops to forcibly reincorporate them was similar to what NATO had done in the 1990s to protect Kosovars in Kosovo from Serb aggression. During that war, NATO planes had bombed civilian infrastructure and inhabited areas of Serbia, flying more than 38,000 missions over the course of seventy-eight days, and dropping almost twenty thousand bombs. The American media proved so ready to take the Georgian side that it too lost credibility with Russians. Even as reputable a paper as the *New York Times* had to retreat from its early reporting, which had credited Georgian claims that later turned out to be unreliable.

To Russian eyes, the Ossetian war showed how U.S. assistance could embolden states on Russia's perimeter to attack Russia or its allies. Although Washington insisted it had warned Saakashvili against aggression, Russians found it hard to believe that Bush had not secretly given the go-ahead. The United States had been training Georgia's army, and about 160 American military advisers remained in Georgia during the war. Visiting Tbilisi a month before the outbreak, the U.S. secretary of state, Condoleezza Rice, had promised Saakashvili she would push for Georgia's quick admission to NATO, and had chatted with the head of Saakashvili's "provisional" South Ossetian government. Vice President Richard Cheney's top aide appeared in Tbilisi days before the war began. During the hostilities, the U.S. airlifted a Georgian infantry brigade back from Iraq.

All these circumstances probably help explain why 74 percent of Russians, surveyed on August 15–18, said they thought the Georgian people "had become hostages of the geopolitical aspirations of the U.S. leadership." Seventy percent believed that "the Russian leadership did everything possible to avoid escalation of the conflict and bloodshed." Approval of both Putin and Medvedev jumped that September.

New Realities

Even had the financial crisis passed Russia by and Georgian guns not fired on Tskhinvali, it is not clear that Putin would have permitted a redirection of domestic policy. He had resisted the privatization of VGTRK. Reorganization of law enforcement was stalling even before the summer's events. Any intention to move his band of siloviki out of the spotlight was weakened by Putin's almost pathological loyalty to his friends. In May 2009, in a magazine edited by his shadow of eight years, Kremlin reporter Andrey Kolesnikov, Putin published an intriguing meditation entitled "Why It's Hard to Fire Someone." "I am deeply convinced," he wrote, "that constant reorganizations improve nothing . . . the new ones who replace those who have been fired will be just like their predecessors."

Nevertheless, the war and financial upheaval changed things. At least for a while, rapprochement with the West and a softening at home seemed out of the question. Medvedev's liberal program had been overwhelmed by a burst of nationalism and economic anxiety. And as GDP contracted and unemployment rose, Putin apparently abandoned the idea of retreating to the sidelines. Once again, he was saddling up to ride to the rescue.

Paradoxically, Medvedev was viewed as having proved his mettle in the Georgian events. He had staked out a position as tough as Putin's, and reportedly won the generals' respect and their acquiescence in dramatic military reforms. Far from a lightning response, post-mortems suggested the Russian action had begun as a familiar mess, with a traffic jam of tanks blocking the Roki Tunnel. The commander, General Anatoly Khrulev, had been injured, and needed to borrow a satellite phone from a journalist since army communications were not working. Russia had prevailed not because of modern tactics and warcraft but because of its overwhelming numerical and material superiority. In the aftermath, Medvedev got quick consent to restructure the army's unwieldy divisions of up to 12,000 troops into compact brigades of 4,000 men, and to give field commanders authority to call in air strikes themselves rather than having to relay them through the command hierarchy.

Yet, although Medvedev had passed this test, Putin had upstaged him. It was Putin who rushed back from the Beijing Olympics to hear the refugees' gruesome tales and confer with the generals, while Medvedev remained cloistered in the Kremlin. It was Putin who, once again, became not just the country's political focus but its "emotional center," expressing the outrage of his compatriots at the attacks on Russian peacekeepers.

This was no time to be caught holding an olive branch. On the day the new U.S. president, Barack Obama, was elected, Medvedev threatened to deploy Iskander missiles in Kaliningrad to target the missile defense system Washington proposed to station in Poland. In his first annual address to the parliament he castigated Washington's "selfish" and "unilateral" approach to international affairs.

Behind the scenes, the economic crisis prompted a fierce debate about policy responses. Macroeconomic hawks like Finance Minister Aleksey Kudrin insisted on limiting government spending. Statists demanded bailouts for the Kremlin's favorite businessmen and the nationalization of distressed companies. Although some got bailouts, for the most part the inflation hawks won. First, the Kremlin did not want to relieve the pressure on foreign creditors to restructure the oligarchs' debt. Second, Putin worried that the government's reserves would quickly run out. When the government did try to fight the market, its failure strengthened the liberals' case. "We should admit, in all honesty, that direct government support of the stock market achieved nothing," Medvedev acknowledged in May 2009, after the authorities had spent $5.3 billion bidding up share prices. "The stock market develops according to its own laws." Banks that received government credits quickly converted them into dollars, putting even greater pressure on the ruble and forcing the Central Bank to spend more of its reserves.

On nationalizations, the story was not so clear. The silovarchs' plans for IPOs had to be postponed. In the meantime, plummeting stock prices created juicy targets for raiding. Chemezov, of Rostekhnologii, seemed eager to capitalize. When the jet engine producer NPO Saturn approached the state-owned Vneshekonombank for a loan, the bank demanded that in return Saturn sell a 13 percent stake to Chemezov's company. Initially, at least, the scope of such state takeovers appeared relatively narrow and focused on enterprises that were essentially bankrupt, such as the Amur Shipbuilding Plant, renationalized in May 2009. But as time passed, appetites grew. By July 2009, Russian Railways chief Vladimir Yakunin was champing at the bit: "We see in the anti-crisis measures of other countries that they are not little girls," he complained. "If they need to save private banks, they nationalize them. If they have to support some industrial sector, they don't just throw money at it, they nationalize it."

Meanwhile, the crisis had galvanized Putin into action. Not content to leave things to the market, he was personally banging heads together and browbeating entrepreneurs into producing more or lowering their prices. Commentators christened the new style "manual control." After unpaid workers blocked highways in the town of Pikalyovo near St. Petersburg in June 2009, Putin dragged the oligarch Oleg Deripaska, who owned one of the town's main factories, out to be cross-examined and ordered to sign a new production contract, with a pen Putin imperiously tossed across the table. It later turned out that the document did not actually require Deripaska's signature—indeed, the whole event had been staged. It also transpired that the state bank VTB was to lend Deripaska an extra $8.1 million and that the plant supplying raw materials had been persuaded to give Deripaska a good price. But the spectacle for television viewers was impressive. The messages of Pikalyovo echoed around the country. Workers learned that if they blocked highways, the prime minister would fly to their aid. Businessmen saw that if they invested in troubled enterprises they might be publicly humiliated and bullied into producing unprofitably.

Putin also developed a personal approach to fighting inflation. On

June 24, he leapt up from the table at a meeting with executives of the country's main retail chains and took them off to the nearest supermarket to discuss exorbitant markups. An opinion poll had just shown that 75 percent of Russians were concerned about high food prices.

"Why do your sausages cost 240 rubles (about $7.70)?" Putin scolded the chain's head of corporate relations. "Is that normal?"

"But those are high quality sausages," the cornered executive pleaded, trying to interest the prime minister in a more affordable packet. "Look, these are just 49 rubles (about $1.60)."

His adversary had come prepared. Pulling a printout from his pocket and brandishing it before the television cameras, Putin recited the store's markups on delicatessen with an expression of suppressed triumph. "We'll lower it tomorrow," the crestfallen executive promised.

There was something oddly familiar about the whole performance. It was classic Yeltsin, circa 1992. That year Boris Nemtsov, then governor of Nizhny Novgorod, had tried to explain to Russia's first president that in a free market system he could not simply order the heads of his region's private dairies to lower their milk prices. It appeared that Putin could. Such interventions, whether or not they raised the prime minister's still soaring ratings, seemed likely to accelerate the increase in bankruptcies. The Sedmoy Kontinent chain, a major rival of the Perekryostok supermarket Putin was inspecting, had just gone into technical default after bondholders refused to restructure its debt.

Indeed, Putin was coming to be seen as a problem for economic recovery. Almost everything he did reduced the desire of private businessmen to risk their money investing in Russia. One might be forced to sell out below the market price to one of the prime minister's friends, or to appoint an ex-FSB officer to the board to help fend off attacks. Or the prime minister himself might turn up on one's doorstep to complain about markups or insist that one restart an unprofitable line of production. Such inconveniences might be worth it if minerals prices and consumer demand were rising steadily. But if one had to compete by raising productivity, Russia looked less attractive.

Putin could be quite unpredictable. Out of the blue, in June 2009, after lobbying for years to get Russia admitted to the World Trade Organization (WTO), the government suddenly announced it was no longer so interested and would join only in a trade bloc with Belarus and Kazakh-stan. There were arguments for and against Russia's entering the WTO. But the unexpected reversal reminded investors how vulnerable policy was to the prime minister's whims. (The government later backtracked.) Then, in a vice-fighting initiative, the authorities abruptly closed down the country's casinos, permitting gambling only in four remote regions. In the midst of a devastating economic crisis, this move was expected to throw tens of thousands of people out of work.

By mid-2009, one thing was clear—for better or worse, Putin was back. He would not be withdrawing to the sidelines, leaving his younger protégé in charge. Quite the opposite—he was evidently considering a quick return to the presidency if things threatened to slip out of control. After he proposed extending the presidential term to six years, Medve-dev claimed to have been considering this change for a long time. To his aides, it came as a flash out of the blue. The idea suddenly appeared in Medvedev's speech without their knowledge the day after Medvedev had had a long private talk with Putin. The most plausible explanation was that Putin planned, should his popularity ever plummet, to have Med-vedev resign and call a quick election while he could still win. Given the severity of the economic crisis, a longer term would increase the odds that he would be able to ride it out.

Moment of Truth

Although he did not say so, the political model Putin appeared to favor was that of postwar Italy. There, for thirty-five years after World War II, the Christian Democratic Party had dominated all governing coali-tions, always providing the prime minister. Governments might come and go—indeed, the turnover rate became something of a joke, with twenty-one changes of prime minister in thirty-five years—but familiar faces tended to reappear, and the same leader might return as many as five times to head cabinet meetings at the Palazzo Chigi. The Commu-nist Party, permanently in opposition, retained a sizeable parliamentary faction and even won some executive power in the cities and regions. But it never had a serious prospect of controlling the government. Thus, the model—also found in Japan—came to be known as a "one-and-a-half party system."

If this was Putin's plan—a long period of dominance by United Russia and its leaders, with the Communists, picturesque but powerless, in opposition—there was one problem. As they were building their one-and-a-half party systems, both postwar Italy and Japan had been lucky enough to enjoy three decades of uninterrupted economic growth. Every year from 1945 to 1975 in Italy, and 1945 to 1974 in Japan, GDP per capita rose. Such steady improvement allowed the incumbent party to consolidate itself, benefiting from both the voters' gratitude for rising incomes and the elaborate pyramids of patronage that the party constructed. Only the oil shock of 1973 and the recessions it generated interrupted the growth, eventually eroding the ruling party's control.

Could Putin's one-and-a-half party system survive a period of stagnation or contraction? Or would the model he had built so painstakingly, which had seemed so stable while growth continued, come crashing down around his ears?

The economic downturn in 2008 triggered rumblings of discontent. Riot police had to be flown to Vladivostok that December to club and arrest dozens of protesters angry that Putin had raised tariffs on imported automobiles. Vladivostok was the main entry point for used Japanese cars, and the trade in these was important to the local economy. A year later in Kaliningrad, a similar demonstration attracted ten thousand protesters who waved signs demanding Putin's resignation. Some governors seemed restive. In a scathing interview, Bashkortostan's longtime president Murtaza Rakhimov assailed the overcentralized decision making within United Russia. The party was being run, he complained, by "people who have never commanded so much as three chickens." As for the Duma, he fumed: "Can you really call it a parliament? It's embarrassing to watch! The population is laughing!" To hear Rakhimov defending democracy was curious given the authoritarian choke hold he had established over Bashkortostan, but his decision to speak out said much about the political moment. When that year a psychotic policeman went on a drunken rampage in a Moscow supermarket, killing two and wounding seven, the public outcry was furious enough to prompt talk of serious police reform.

Yet, just as the various foci of discontent threatened to link up into something more general, the economy rebounded. From below $35 a barrel in early January 2009, the oil price jumped to $72 in December. By spring 2010, stocks had made up more than half their losses. Despite declining GDP, the government managed to buffer the population, raising pensions by 11 percent in real terms in 2009, and by another 13 percent in January 2010. Real disposable incomes rose by a small but nevertheless positive 2.3 percent. The tandem's approval ratings stabilized above 70 percent.

For the various disaffected minorities and frustrated elites, the sudden switch was infuriating. They had sensed the Kremlin's momentary confusion, had been preparing challenges, only to have the opportunity snatched away. Business people sick of paying off the bosses, regional elites chafing at Moscow's diktat, media personalities tired of biting their tongues, indignant liberals, drivers harassed by the traffic police, even honest policemen disgusted at the corruption around them—all were growing increasingly resentful. Were the Kremlin's popular support to slip, they were ready to pile on.

For their part, the country's leaders seemed to recognize how dependent they had become on economic growth. Medvedev, determined to refire the engines and demonstrate his usefulness, was swept up in an almost comical frenzy of technocratic initiatives. To boost productivity, he abolished two of the country's eleven time zones, ordered officials to install energy-efficient light bulbs, and founded an "innovation city" in a Moscow suburb, where Russia's top scientists and entrepreneurs were to brainstorm on products of the future. With his video blog, his Twitter micro-blog, his i-Phone, and his Facebook page, Medvedev seemed determined to turn Russia into a haven of high technology by force of personal example.

If the recovery of 2010 gathered speed, it seemed unlikely that Medvedev would do more than fiddle with the controls, as he had done during his first two years. The consummate professional, he would play his part as scripted, resisting the temptation to ham it up or ad lib. He would sign decrees sent his way, turn in his annual income declaration, wink at his foreign guests, deliver well-crafted speeches, all the while hinting, without specifics, that he was a little more liberal than those around him. In a few years' time, he would leave the Kremlin with a gold watch and the gratitude of the siloviki, to be invited back to annual reunions to drink champagne, clink glasses with the Surkovs, Markovs, and Zubkovs, and maybe, when his turn came, give another toast to the rebirth of private law in Russia.

But if the economic crisis resumed, setting off a storm the technocrats could not contain, if the Putin script itself fell flat, then it would be up to the understudy, as the audience shifted in their seats and started hurling tomatoes, to improvise a new ending. Would he rise to the occasion and grasp his moment in the limelight? Would he capture the audience's sympathies, building a bridge from the Kremlin to the heartland, from the suddenly discredited security agents to the democrats and populists, gathering together the discontented regions, casting off the familiar hypocrisy like a worn Armani jacket, fighting the corruption and incompetence around him rather than shuffling around abstractions? Would he finally start on reforms that the liberals he admired would have believed in? Would he betray his mentor and steal the show?

It was hard to imagine. But in Russian politics, nothing could be called impossible.

CHAPTER 5

The Unraveling

Almost two decades later, the surprising thing is not that the Soviet Union came apart but how it did so. Many multiethnic states and empires have disintegrated. Their final acts tend to be barbaric, tearing up previously peaceful communities in unexpected ways. The Habsburg Empire's attachment to its Balkan provinces plunged Europe into a war that cost 15 million lives. Ottoman Turkey's collapse engendered massacres of Armenians and Kurds. Europe's colonists left bloody footprints retreating from Africa and Asia—more than 300,000 dead in both French Indochina and Algeria, hundreds of thousands murdered in the riots that split British India. More recently, Yugoslavia's dissolution unleashed waves of savagery. In Bosnia-Herzegovina alone, somewhere betwen 97,000 and 250,000 people were killed, by different estimates, constituting from 2 to 6 percent of the population.

The Soviet Union's demise was not without casualties. However, compared to previous experience, it was remarkably peaceful. The ethnographer Valery Tishkov puts total deaths at 63,000—or 98,000 if one counts the first Chechen war, which began three years after the Soviet disintegration and arguably had little to do with it. About 24,000 died in fighting between Armenians and Azerbaijanis in Nagorno-Karabakh, and another 24,000 in Tajikistan's civil war. In Georgia, the separatist province of Abkhazia was the site of 12,000 deaths; other trouble spots had smaller losses.

There is something disconcerting—indeed, shocking—about referring to the killing of "only" 63,000 people as "remarkably peaceful." Yet, taking everything into account, it is clear the outcome could have been much, much worse. As of 1991, the Soviet continent was a minefield of potential conflicts. Hundreds of ethnic groups had been jumbled together by Stalin's whims and historical chance, scattered across the land as unevenly as the oil, gas, gold, and diamonds beneath it. In their midst, the world's largest military was breaking up. About ten thousand strategic nuclear weapons were lodged in four of the fifteen Union republics, and thousands of tactical nuclear weapons were spread across many more. Inexperienced commanders-in-chief scrutinized each other across their disputed borders. Twenty-five million ethnic Russians—plus another 11 million Russian speakers—suddenly found themselves on the wrong side of a barbed wire fence, a "beached diaspora" left high and dry by the retreating tide of Russian expansion. In Kazakhstan, Latvia, and Estonia, ethnic Russians made up a larger share of the population than had Sudeten Germans in Czechoslovakia in the 1930s. Russians in the Baltic states felt, in David Laitin's phrase, as New Yorkers would if suddenly forced to choose between "learning Iroquois or being deported to England."

Yet, even as Russian patriots—from the ethno-nationalist Aleksandr Solzhenitsyn to the jingoistic imperialist Vladimir Zhirinovsky—demanded the creation of a Greater Russian state incorporating large adjacent territories, the new diaspora remained calm. Only in a strip of Moldova between the Dniester River and the Ukrainian border did local Russians take up arms. In a remarkable act of maturity, three of the successor states agreed to surrender their nuclear weapons to a country some viewed as their former colonizer. The Second Soviet Civil War could have been the bloodiest of the late twentieth century. It was one of the deadliest wars never to happen.

The disintegration had not been predicted. But, after the fact, it was all too easy to explain. There were too many reasons. The Soviet Union collapsed because of the economic inefficiency of communism. Or was it the innate human desire for freedom? Or the force of ethnic nationalism? Or military competition from the West? Or simply the character flaws and mistakes of the country's leaders? The challenge is not to identify causes but to sort through them. As I will argue, none of the simple answers works by itself. One must understand how many of these factors interacted to produce a result that five years earlier had been highly unlikely. Only then can one answer the more puzzling question: what kept the breakup from generating the carnage many had feared?

Belovezhskaya Pushcha

The Ukrainians were the first to arrive. By the time Yeltsin's motorcade turned up the snow-packed driveway to the hunting lodge near the Polish border, President Leonid Kravchuk and his prime minister, Vitold Fokin, were somewhere in the ancient pine forest shooting at wild boar. The estate's director was waiting at the front door. While he showed the Russian president to his suite, Stanislav Shushkevich, still at heart more physics professor than Belarusan head of state, retired to the more modest cottage he had chosen for himself.

It was December 7, 1991. When the guests assembled that evening, Yeltsin posed, for the sake of propriety, the question whose answer everybody knew already. Was there any form of refashioned Soviet Union that the Ukrainians would agree to join? Kravchuk, puffed up by his presidential landslide, reminded them that 90 percent of Ukrainian voters—76 percent of those eligible—had opted in a referendum days before for complete independence. There could be no going back. The Russian foreign minister, Andrey Kozyrev, wrote later that visions of Yugoslavia—where Serbian shells were ripping through Dubrovnik—flashed before his eyes. Gingerly, the three leaders began to feel each other out. If a Union was impossible, was there some other legal structure in which all three Slavic states might coordinate their actions? Someone brought up the idea of a British-style commonwealth.

And then, while the principals dined on game and toasted each other in the local herb-flavored vodka, Yeltsin's aides—Kozyrev, Yegor Gaidar, Gennady Burbulis, and Sergey Shakhray—retired to a cabin with their Belarusan counterparts to hammer out the elements of an agreement. All sides would recognize existing borders and respect the political, social, economic, and cultural rights of each other's citizens. They would adhere to international treaties and commitments of the USSR. There would be a common currency and unified control over all the Soviet Union's nuclear weapons. The Ukrainians—curious, but preserving their neutrality—hovered outside the cabin, sending emissaries every now and then for updates.

By morning, the aides had a draft for Yeltsin, Kravchuk, and Shush-kevich to comb through and rewrite, sentence by sentence, word by word, sending pages back to the specialists to reformulate. A frazzled secretary, press-ganged from a neighboring village, typed it out in time for the afternoon press conference, when, as cameras clicked, the three heads of state and their prime ministers added their signatures. A local newspaper reporter fixed the time—2:17 p.m.—on his hammer-and-sickle watch. "We, the Republic of Belarus, the Russian Federation, and Ukraine," the document read, "state that the USSR as a subject of international law and a geopolitical reality is ending its existence."

The Forest Coup?

Same place, almost ten years later. A man in a leather cap is walking in the woods. His wife and younger daughter linger behind.

"Why does Papa never want to walk on the road that leads to that house in the distance," the daughter asks.

"It's not a good house, and so Papa doesn't like it," her mother replies. But this does not satisfy the girl's curiosity, and she presses for a better answer.

"You understand," her mother begins, "we used to have a big country. And it was very varied. Very many people lived in it. People spoke in different languages. It could be winter at one end of the country and already summer at the other. Somewhere it could be day, and somewhere else already night. But everyone lived in one country. All understood each other, because they had lived together for a very long time. And they lived together in order to help each other, so things would be better for everyone."

The man in the cap looks back and sees his daughter listening intently.

"That's what sort of country it was," his wife continues. "Big and strong, respected by everyone. It was called the Soviet Union. And the country had one president—the most important person. He led the country, and to do that he had power. He decided what needed to be done, and how. People listened to him."

"And what happened?" asks the daughter, turning towards the "bad house."

"What happened is that three men came along who also wanted to have power, who wanted people to listen to them and not the president of the big country. And in that same 'bad house' they wrote a paper to make it so that the big country did not exist, and to replace it with some smaller countries in which they would be the most important people."

Suddenly, the girl frowns—and runs. Not to her father but to her older sister who is walking on the road to that "house." She runs to her sister and shouts: "Don't go there. Over there three blockheads tore the country apart."

Belovezhskaya Pushcha—the Belovezha Forest. The name itself has become infamous in Russian nationalist circles. There, hiding in the woods, "without even sobering up," as one writer put it, the three power-hungry conspirators ripped up the map they had inherited. Lands imperial armies had conquered, cossacks homesteaded, Bolshevik engineers industrialized, Red Army troops defended—all signed away, with a few strokes of a borrowed pen. Not just the Baltic border states and the Transcaucasus, but the Slavic heartland of Belarus and Ukraine, the birthplace of Russian civilization. So outrageous had the agreement come to seem by the late 1990s that a band of former Soviet army officers was said to be planning to kidnap Kravchuk and force him to recant. Vladimir Zhirinovsky, the ultranationalist firebrand, waved a pair of handcuffs at his colleagues in the Russian Duma and demanded that the perpetrators be arrested.

The Commonwealth of Independent States (CIS) that emerged from the Belovezha meeting satisfied no one. In Alma-Ata, Kazakhstan, two weeks later, the heads of eight more republics agreed to join. In 1993, Georgia signed on as well. Only the Baltic republics remained aloof. But the hopes for a solid coordinating body never panned out. Although nuclear weapons were transferred to unified command under Russia, the idea of a common army failed in the face of Ukraine's determination to form its own armed forces. The common currency lasted only until 1993.

And as time passed, anger about the deed done at Belovezha seemed to grow. To the writer Aleksandr Solzhenitsyn, the three leaders' accord was a "crazy conspiracy." To Belarus's authoritarian leader, Aleksandr Lukashenko, it was "a crime." Russia's president, Vladimir Putin, speaking in 2005, described the Soviet dissolution as "the greatest geopolitical catastrophe of the century." The tale of the three blockheads was told and retold around kitchen tables, and not just by extreme nationalists or communists. The young girl walking in the snow, Olga Luzhkova, heard it from her mother, Yelena Baturina, the new Russia's most successful businesswoman. The man in the leather cap was Moscow's redoubtable mayor, Yury Luzhkov.

Although it is often repeated, there is one problem with this story of geopolitical murder in the woods. Almost all witnesses agree: the victim was already dead. By the time of the Belovezha meeting, most Soviet citizens, and almost all politicians and officials, had already concluded that the Soviet state in its old form could not be revived. Overwhelming evidence supported this belief. A far more urgent question, by this point, was how to manage the collapse and reduce its human cost.

To review a few facts, as of December 7, 1991, when the three leaders met, thirteen of the fifteen Union republics had already declared independence, all except Russia and Kazakhstan, both of which did so right afterwards. The international community—and even the Soviet Union— had recognized the Baltic states' independence. Poland had recognized Ukraine's, and the United States, Canada, Hungary, Sweden, and Czechoslovakia had announced their intention to do so. All fifteen republics had announced they were sovereign states whose laws took supremacy over Soviet ones. One by one, they had been dropping out of central institutions. By November, only seven of the fifteen republic leaders bothered to attend meetings of Gorbachev's State Council, the last Soviet executive body, and only seven republics still sent deputies to the Soviet parliament.

Financially, the Soviet government was bankrupt. In early December, the state bank had stopped making payments on its behalf. Soldiers' wages, pensions, and other obligations went unpaid. The republics had almost completely halted contributions to the Soviet budget. The ruble's value was collapsing. Estonia, Lithuania, Latvia, and Ukraine were preparing to launch their own currencies. Other republics had authorized their central banks to issue rubles, and they were racing to see who could extend credit the fastest. In the first nine months of 1991, the Soviet state bank issued more rubles than in the previous five years, and the state mint could not print bank notes quickly enough. As Soviet administrative organs imploded, starved of cash and increasingly deserted by their demoralized staffers, the republic governments had stepped into the gap. Most had created customs posts on their borders and were appropriating federal property on their territory. Russia had taken control of most Soviet ministries and was funding them directly from its budget.

Ukraine had begun turning Soviet army troops and equipment into a Ukrainian national army, and had asserted control over police and border troops as well. The Baltic republics, Armenia, Azerbaijan, Georgia, and Moldova were all creating national military formations. More and more young men were simply refusing to serve in the Soviet army. Even in Moscow, only about half the draftees were showing up, and thousands later deserted. As of June 1991, the army was short by about 353,000 conscripts. In the words of one expert, the military had fallen into a state of "disorder, decay, and, especially in lower-level units, disintegration."

By late 1991, the commander of Soviet armed forces, Marshal Shaposhnikov, was "convinced that the Union in fact no longer existed and that there would be nothing like it in the future . . . no functioning Union structures remained by that time except, perhaps, the USSR President and several ministers, including myself." Had Gorbachev ordered him to use force, he says he would have disobeyed. Asked in a poll in November 1991, shortly before the Belovezha meeting, whether the Soviet Union still existed, only 17 percent of Russian respondents said that it did; two-thirds said it did not. Had the three leaders signed only autographs in Belovezha, it would not have changed the fact that by this time the Soviet Union was in pieces.

The final countdown had begun right after the August coup. Gorbachev, back from Foros, had tried to restart negotiations on a Union treaty, initially with Yeltsin's support. Yeltsin pushed vigorously for an economic agreement between the republics, which was signed on October 18. But the prospect of a political Union dimmed as ever more republics dropped out of the talks at Novo-Ogaryovo. Finally, these deadlocked when, on November 25, Gorbachev insisted on a "confederal state." Yeltsin, knowing neither the Ukrainians nor the Russian parliament would agree to this, and supported by the leaders of Turkmenistan, Uzbekistan, and Belarus, insisted on a "confederation of states." Gorbachev stormed out of the room. At this moment, Yeltsin wrote later, "as a heavy, oppressive silence hung over the room, we suddenly realized that it was over. . . . The Novo-Ogaryovo saga had drawn to a close. . . . We would have to seek and conceive of something new." After a while Yeltsin and Shushkevich went to find Gorbachev. A couple of weeks later, Shushkevich welcomed Yeltsin to Belovezha.

Yeltsin and Gorbachev

If the Soviet Union was beyond rescuing by December 1991, that merely pushes the question back. What had brought things to this point? Could different policies at some earlier date have prevented the disintegration?

For some, the cause could be reduced to a clash of personalities. In Gorbachev's retelling, the key factor was Yeltsin's hunger for power at any cost: "The Russian President and his entourage . . . sacrificed the Union for the sake of realizing their ardent desire to reign in the Kremlin." In his view, Russia's declaration of sovereignty in June 1990 catalyzed the explosion of separatist demands that followed: "I am certain that, had it not been for this fatal step, the Union could have been preserved." Then, as Gorbachev labored to put together a more democratic federal system, the Russian leaders undercut him at every turn, whipping up fears about an "imperialist" center, attacking his authority, exerting "every effort to incite the Balts to secede." The final stab in the back came at Belovezha. This section in Gorbachev's memoirs carries the one-word heading "Perfidy." "I was shocked by such treacherous behavior of the people who ruined the country and cut whole peoples into pieces in order to settle scores, in order to secure themselves the royal status," he later complained.

Surprisingly, in his own memoirs Yeltsin provides considerable support for this interpretation. Recalling the Belovezha meeting, he sounds positively gleeful. "It was an excellent winter evening—a light frost, quiet snowfall, a real crisp December," he begins. "I well remember how a sensation of freedom and lightness suddenly came to me in the Belovezhsky Nature Reserve." A few lines later comes another remarkable confession: "Perhaps I did not completely fathom the prospects opening up before me, but I felt in my heart that such major decisions had to be made easily." He had considered other courses, he says.

I had not lost sight of the option of attempting to take Gorbachev's place lawfully. To stand at the head of the Union, to begin his reform "from above" once again. To travel down the same path that Gorbachev could not take because of the treachery of those closest to him. To gradually, systematically dismantle the imperial machine, as Gorbachev had tried to do.

There were ways to achieve this. We could fight for popular elections for president of the USSR. We could make the Russian parliament the legal heir of the dissolved Soviet legislature. We could persuade Gorbachev to make me acting president, and so on.

Yet he rejected all of these. "For me, that path was already occupied," he writes. "Psychologically, I could not take Gorbachev's place. Just as he could not take mine."

The candor is refreshing. Yeltsin was the sort of client a wise defense lawyer would never allow to take the stand. But were things really so simple? The evidence suggests otherwise.

First, the actions for which Gorbachev criticized Yeltsin were not the idiosyncratic whims of a power-hungry egotist. All were strongly supported by the voters who had elected Yeltsin and by the elected members of the Russian parliament. He was not striking out on some adventure. He was doing something revolutionary for a Soviet politician: listening to—and heeding—public opinion.

Between 1989 and 1992, Russians' views about the future of their country underwent a series of changes. Of course, opinions within Russia were varied and often ambivalent; still, the trend is clear. From 1989, when the first polls were taken, through the summer of 1991, the majority of Russians favored preserving the Soviet Union, in a more decentralized form, rather than Russian independence. In one poll in late 1989, 63 percent agreed that Russians should "above all be concerned about the unity and cohesion of the Union." Only 10 percent thought the best course was to "struggle for the full political independence of republics, not excluding secession." In mid-1991, a Times-Mirror survey found that 64 percent preferred that "Russia remain part of the Soviet Union but with much more independence and authority," compared to 19 percent who favored secession. Still, Russians did not favor forcing the other republics to stay. For instance, in a poll in mid-1990, 60 percent agreed that "a republic should be allowed to leave the USSR if this is the choice of that republic's people." After the violent crackdown in Lithuania in January 1991, 150,000 Russians demonstrated in Moscow against the Soviet action—a level of opposition that shocked the Soviet leaders.

But then, after the August coup, as central authority dissolved, the preferences of Russians about their republic's future changed. By late 1991, 58 percent supported an independent Russian state, either within a Commonwealth of Independent States or outside it, compared to only 41 percent of respondents who wanted a restored USSR. Although the mood would shift later, a large majority of Russian citizens at the time approved Yeltsin's diplomacy to create the CIS. In a December 1991 poll of fourteen Russian cities, 64 percent of respondents said they welcomed the signing of the CIS agreement, compared to 11 percent who disapproved. A month later, another poll found that 72 percent of Russians approved, while 12 percent disapproved.

Support for Russian independence was never enthusiastic and was always tinged with regret. Although most Russians did not want to preserve the Union by force, they have nevertheless lamented its passing ever since. In a popular saying picked up by President Putin: "Those who do not regret the end of the Soviet Union have no heart; those who want to rebuild it have no brain." Throughout the years from 1989 to 1991, Yeltsin's positions on this were in tune with those of the Russian public, even as Gorbachev grew increasingly out of touch.

Yeltsin was also closely aligned with the Russian political elite. Gorbachev is probably right that Russia's sovereignty declaration in June 1990 stimulated other republics to follow. The pace of such declarations picked up. But declaring sovereignty was not a notion Yeltsin dreamed up by himself: it was a goal shared by Russian politicians across the spectrum. In the Russian Congress, the vote for the declaration was 907 to 13. Even the Communists were overwhelmingly in favor. Yeltsin was also correct that the Russian parliament would not have ratified Gorbachev's watered down, confederal Union treaty. When Shushkevich presented this document, with its split hairs and squared circles, to his own Belarusan parliament, the deputies berated him for wasting their time with "such an absurdity" and asked if he had ever read a dictionary.

The parliaments of Russia, Belarus, and Ukraine quickly ratified the Belovezha Agreement with overwhelming majorities. In Russia, 188 voted in favor, with 6 against, and 7 abstaining; not a single deputy spoke against the motion, which passed "with a roar of approval." In Belarus, only one deputy voted against (the future president, Aleksandr Lukashenko, was in the restroom at the time, and so can also deny complicity). In Ukraine, the vote was 288 to 10, with 7 abstentions. Although many Russians had misgivings which would ripen into nostalgia, the Russian political elite and most ordinary citizens were solidly behind Yeltsin at every step.

Yeltsin's assertion of control over the Soviet state bank and ministries can easily be portrayed as a grab for power and property motivated by personal ambition. But the economy—and, most critically, the food supply system—was collapsing in late 1991. The Soviet bureaucrats who had administered it now listened to neither Gorbachev nor Yeltsin. "No one decides anything," wrote KGB head Vadim Bakatin of the atmosphere of greedy irresponsibility. "One can't get through to anyone on the phone, but everyone demands a telephone in his car." They were too busy stealing the assets they controlled, setting up commercial firms to which state property could be transferred. If the Russian authorities did not get control of economic administration, there would be no hope for a price reform that could avert severe food shortages. To negotiate such a reform with fourteen other heads of government plus a Soviet president still talking up the "socialist choice" was certain to fail. In the Russian parliament, deputies criticized Yeltsin for not moving faster to dissolve all Union-level bodies and absorb their property. Rather than grabbing for power, one might say Yeltsin was grabbing for the steering wheel of a car careening out of control.

Indeed, most accounts suggest that after the August coup Yeltsin, like Gorbachev, wanted to preserve a confederal state led from Moscow. Bakatin, a Gorbachev ally often critical of Yeltsin, was sure the latter had wanted a stronger commonwealth than the one that emerged. Boris Nemtsov, the reformist governor of Nizhny Novgorod, was certain that for Yeltsin the collapse of the USSR was "a personal tragedy." Shaposhnikov, the CIS military commander, said Yeltsin always backed his attempts to keep the Soviet armed forces united. The Russian president gave up on a closer union when the Ukrainian movement for independence convinced him this was simply not attainable.

Had Yeltsin decided at this point to "stand at the head of the Union," and had Gorbachev—against all prior indications—agreed to let him, this would only have increased the determination of other republics to secede. A change of heart on Yeltsin's part would not have changed the minds of the 29 million Ukrainians who voted for independence. Indeed, after the August coup, anxiety in many republics had come to focus on the prospect of Great Russian revanchism. And, as Yeltsin correctly realized, to recreate a Union without Ukraine would damage his country's most important and potentially dangerous relationship. At the time, Ukraine still housed the world's third largest nuclear arsenal. The two countries were at odds over the future of the Soviet Black Sea Fleet, based on the Crimean peninsula, a region inhabited mostly by Russians. The Crimea had been part of the Russian Republic, but had been transferred to Ukraine in 1954 by Khrushchev as a gift on the three hundredth anniversary of the unification of Russia and Ukraine, a decision that continued to outrage Russian nationalists. Denuclearizing Ukraine and avoiding violence over the fleet and the Crimean question were Yeltsin's priorities—and among his greatest achievements.

Other writers have pinned the blame for Soviet disintegration more evenhandedly on both Yeltsin and Gorbachev, with their equally oversized egos and personal resentments. "In the end," writes the historian Stephen Kotkin, "the Russian president proved too spiteful and the Soviet president too vain for the two to embrace each other and save some form of the Union." To say "plague on both their houses" has its appeal. But this, too, risks overemphasizing the superficial and missing the context. Yeltsin could be spiteful, Gorbachev could be vain, and vice versa. Such qualities are common in high level politics; state disintegration is not.

To their credit, both Gorbachev and Yeltsin tried for a surprisingly long time to find a common position. They sat, hour after hour, with a dwindling band of colleagues at Novo-Ogaryovo, talking about federations and confederations as the leaves turned yellow on the birches outside the window. Until the August coup, Yeltsin had been ready to sign Gorbachev's Union Treaty. Both were maneuvering within political constraints—for Yeltsin, the views of those in the Russian parliament, Russian public opinion, and the positions of the Ukrainian leadership; for Gorbachev, the demands of hard-line Communists. Yeltsin was probably right that an economic agreement and the CIS were all that were possible at that time. Had Gorbachev overcome his vanity, it is not clear what he could have done after August 1991 to save the Union.

Neither leader was innocent of ambition, and their mutual animosity was legendary. One evening, two days after the Ukrainian referendum, an anxious Gorbachev phoned Yeltsin to plan yet another session on saving the USSR. Gorbachev's aide Chernyaev recounts the conversation in his diary. Yeltsin does not want to meet. "Nothing will come of it," he says, "Ukraine is independent." He suggests they return to the idea of a four-way combination of Russia, Ukraine, Belarus, and Kazakhstan. "And where's my place in that?" Gorbachev explodes.

> "In that case, I'll resign. I'm not going to hang around like a piece of shit in an ice-hole. I'm not worried about myself. But understand: without the Union you'll ruin everything and destroy all the reforms. You need to get a fix on this. Everything crucially depends on us two."
>
> "How could I manage without you, Mikhail Sergeyevich!" Yeltsin drunkenly persuaded him.

The antagonism and rivalry between these two men gave the Soviet collapse its air of heightened melodrama. But they do not explain why it happened.

Nationalist Revival

To some observers, the underlying cause seems simple. The Soviet Union was torn apart by a resurgence of minority nationalisms. A second "springtime of nations" had swept Eastern Europe in 1989. The million Balts who stretched in a human chain from Vilnius to Tallinn via Riga that summer were just the northernmost outgrowth. It seemed only natural that non-Russian nationalities, imprisoned for decades within the Soviet police state, would, when given a chance, race to liberate themselves. Nationalism could be powerful. A wounded *Volksgeist*, said Isaiah

Berlin, "is like a bent twig, forced down so severely that when released, it lashes back with fury." When Gorbachev loosened censorship and political terror, the nationalist twigs sprang back together, shattering the machinery that had kept them bent. Or, in another metaphor common at the time, minority nationalisms were what bubbled over when the end of the cold war knocked the lid off "a cauldron of long-simmering hatreds."

But there are problems with this. First, many of the "nationalist" heroes who led their countries' fights for independence turn out on examination not to have been nationalists at all—or, at least, not until the last minute. There were exceptions. Lithuania's first post-Soviet leader, Vytautas Landsbergis, was an expert on Lithuanian composers whose grandfather had written the first Lithuanian grammar and whose father had fought for the country's independence in 1918. But what to make of the champion of Uzbek sovereignty, Islam Karimov, a career Communist, who had viciously repressed the spontaneously formed movement of Uzbek nationalists, *Birlik* (Unity), before stealing their agenda? After rediscovering his roots, Karimov had to get coaching in the Uzbek language, which apparently was not used much in the republic's state planning committee where he spent most of his career. Or what about the Turkmen leader, Saparmurat Niyazov, head of the republic's Communist Party, who also crushed the local separatist movement before declaring sovereignty and independence himself? Or Ayaz Mutalibov, the Azerbaijani Communist Party boss, who suddenly revealed in late 1991 that he was actually an "anti-Communist" and a "secret Muslim"? Having come out of the closet, so to speak, Mutalibov restored the country's crescent-and-star pre-Soviet emblem, renamed streets in honor of national heroes, and transferred the Communist Party's property to the Azerbaijani state.

Leonid Kravchuk, the father of Ukrainian independence, had been a loyal hack in the party's agitprop department, pressuring his compatriots to take courses on "developed socialism" and harassing independent-minded newspaper editors. In 1989, as the nationalist movement Rukh got organized, he was advising the Communist leaders on how to stifle it. But then he underwent "a breathtaking political metamorphosis" from "enemy of Ukrainian nationalism to Ukrainian nationalist par excellence." It worked. In November 1990, Kravchuk did not even make the list of the twenty most popular politicians in the capital, Kiev. By June of the next year, astride the horse of sovereignty, he had become the favorite to win the Ukrainian presidency. When the former political prisoner, Vyacheslav Chornovil, was asked what distinguished Kravchuk's platform from his own, he had a simple answer: "Nothing, except that my programme is thirty years old, and Kravchuk's three weeks old."

In short, many of the "nationalist" leaders who championed independence for their republics had until days before been typical apparatchiks, focused on climbing the Communist ladder. Of the fifteen heads of state that led their republics to independence, twelve were longtime party members, and ten had spent their careers in the party or state apparatus. Some had themselves attacked local nationalists with either propaganda or police. Some had difficulties speaking their national language. For these opportunists, nationalism became the latest opportunity, a means of legitimizing themselves with the local population and thus preserving their power and access to resources.

It was not only party leaders that were suddenly discovering their national identities. Rank and file party members were also defecting. Almost half the leaders of the Estonian Popular Front were members of the Communist Party, as were 30 percent of participants in the Latvian Popular Front's founding congress, and one-third of the Belarusan Popular Front's organizing committee. Around one-quarter of the delegates to the founding congress of the Ukrainian Rukh were Communists, as were four of the ten members elected to the organization's secretariat.

If many supporters of national self-determination were recent converts to the cause, some supporters were not even of the nationality seeking self-determination. Many of the ethnically Russian residents of the non-Russian republics also came to favor secession. In Estonia, as of spring 1991, 37–40 percent of ethnic *non*-Estonians supported independence, and by the time of the August coup so did 55 percent of the republic's Russian speakers. In Latvia, surveys from around that time suggested that from 38 to 45 percent of residents of non-Latvian descent favored independence. The Russian writer Vladlen Dozortsev served on the Governing Board of the Latvian Popular Front and helped to write its program. In April 1990, a poll asked residents of Vilnius whether the Lithuanian parliament should retract its decision to reestablish an independent state. Forty-two percent of Russians and 58 percent of Polish residents said no.

In Ukraine, too, it was not just ethnic Ukrainians who wanted to secede. In the December 1991 referendum, 55 percent of ethnic Russian voters supported independence as well. The Western regions of Ukraine had been part of Poland before World War II, and not surprisingly support for independence was highest there. But even in the country's heavily russified East, more than 80 percent favored independence, as did a majority in the Crimea, which had been Russian territory until 1954. The ethnically Russian deputy speaker of the Ukrainian parliament, Vladimir Grinev, was a vociferous secessionist.

Another problem with the image of nationalist explosion is that most people in most republics remained unmoved by nationalist appeals until just months before the Soviet Union's end. Although small groups of diehard nationalists existed almost everywhere, to become politically significant, demands had to spread to the general public. Years after the start of glasnost, polls found surprisingly little national consciousness and still less support for separatism. As late as the fall of 1989, a survey found that in the Baltics only 47 percent favored a "struggle for the full political independence of republics, not excluding secession." In Ukraine, the percentage was just 20 percent, and in Armenia it was 17 percent. As of May 1990, 52 percent of ethnic Moldovans in the Moldovan Republic still supported remaining within the USSR over independence or reunification with Romania. In March 1991, Gorbachev held a referendum that asked: "Do you consider it necessary to preserve the USSR as a renewed federation of equal sovereign republics, in which the rights and freedoms of an individual of any nationality will be fully guaranteed?" Of course, the question cast the alternative to separation in the most attractive light. Georgia, Armenia, Moldova, and the Baltic states refused to participate. But in the nine republics that did, large majorities supported the USSR's preservation. In Belarus, this was the choice of 83 percent (69 percent of eligible voters), and in Russia 71 percent (54 percent of eligible voters). In each of the five Central Asian republics and Azerbaijan, the vote in favor was over 90 percent.

But then, in what seemed less like an explosion than a relay race, the mood turned in one republic after another. First, in April 1989, the killing by Soviet troops of nineteen unarmed protesters provoked a sudden hardening of opinion in Georgia: by September, 89 percent thought the republic should be independent. The Baltics followed. By the summer of 1990, at least 80 percent of ethnic Estonians, Latvians, and Lithuanians favored complete independence. During the next year, other republics piled on. By August 1991, 79 percent of Moldovan residents, of all ethnicities, favored secession. That October, 94 percent of Turkmen voters endorsed independence in a referendum, just 4 percent fewer than had voted to preserve the Union in March. In Ukraine, where 70 percent had voted to keep the USSR in March, 90 percent voted to leave it in December.

What can explain these sudden reversals? It could be that until mid-1991 most Soviet citizens were too afraid to admit separatist inclinations to pollsters. However, in the same polls they freely criticized almost every feature of the governing regime. It seems more likely that the mood simply changed. Glasnost did not unleash nationalist sentiments that had been waiting under the surface. It somehow generated separatist aspirations that—in most places—had not been widespread. And as the boundaries of what was conceivable shifted outward, so too did public demands.

These changes in public opinion are mirrored in the pattern of street demonstrations. Mark Beissinger collected information on more than six thousand mass protests that occurred in the Soviet Union between 1987 and 1992. His data, the most comprehensive available, show how the number participating rose from close to zero in January 1987 to a peak of around 7.7 million a month in November 1988, when hundreds of thousands took to the streets of Yerevan, Baku, Tbilisi, and Riga. The demands made at protests changed in waves between 1987 and 1990, as shown in Figure 5.1, from human rights and political freedom to the preservation of historical monuments and respect for non-Russian languages and cultures, to outright secession from the USSR. As the economy deteriorated from early 1989, a new wave of demonstrations on economic issues began. And as anti-Soviet agitation escalated, it provoked counter-demonstrations in support of Soviet rule. Such waves were not uniform across the country. Large demonstrations for secession occurred first in Georgia, then spread to the Baltics, followed by Armenia, Ukraine, and eventually Moldova (see Figure 5.2). Such actions never quite got off the ground in Central Asia.

Figure 5.1 Number of demonstrations per month, classified by main demand of demonstrators, USSR, 1987–1992

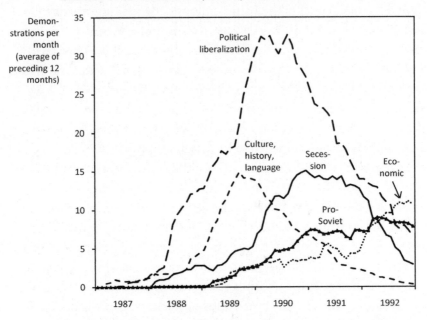

Source: Dataset for Mark R. Beissinger, *Nationalist Mobilization and the Collapse of the Soviet State* (New York: Cambridge University Press, 2002).

Ethno-Federal Structure and Electoral Politics

To recapitulate, the struggle for secession did involve a few thousand committed anti-Soviet nationalists. But almost all the leaders who declared independence were career Communists who had only recently rediscovered their national identity. The mainstream public felt little desire to leave the Union until years after the beginning of glasnost, and then the demand spread in waves, drawing in local Russians as well as the minority nationalities. Given this, it does not seem quite enough to say the USSR was destroyed by nationalism. One must explain what made the half-formed dreams of a few thousand activists suddenly so explosive in 1989–1990. To understand this one must move beyond nationalism itself to consider the ways it was nurtured and manipulated, shaped by inherited state structures, and mismanaged by the Kremlin.

Figure 5.2 Number of participants per month in demonstrations for secession from the USSR, selected republics, 1988–1992

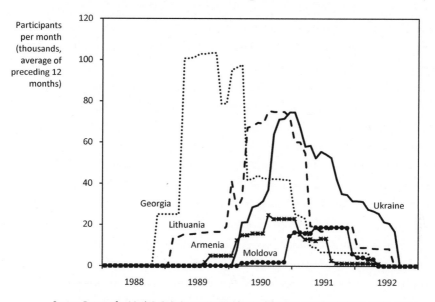

Source: Dataset for Mark R. Beissinger, *Nationalist Mobilization and the Collapse of the Soviet State* (New York: Cambridge University Press, 2002).
Note: Demonstrations where "secession from the USSR" was one of the five main demands of demonstrators.

National divisions were so dangerous to the Soviet state, some experts argue, because of the way they were embedded in its architecture. For this, one could blame history. As the Bolsheviks struggled to defeat the White counterrevolutionary armies in 1918–1922, Lenin found it expedient to appeal to the nationalist movements that had taken power in the territories vacated by the tsar's gendarmes. Later, policies were devised to incorporate and coopt non-Russian nationalities, while keeping them strictly subordinate to the central leadership.

The Union, created in 1922, was structured as a federation in which many non-Russian nationalities had their own ethnically defined units. As of 1990, these ranged from the fifteen Union republics, which even enjoyed—on paper—a constitutional right to secede, to twenty autonomous republics, in which the locally dominant nationality's language generally had official status, to autonomous regions and districts for some smaller ethnicities. In the 1920s, the Bolsheviks introduced a kind of affirmative action to educate members of the titular nationalities and promote them into the party, government, industry, and culture. Schools were established to instruct students in everything from Ukrainian and Kirghiz to Evenk and Chukchi. By the late 1970s, mathematics and science were being taught in thirty-five languages, and literature in fifty-three. This policy of indigenization (*korenizatsiya*) created non-Russian, educated middle classes that themselves helped block the growth of an independent nationalist counter-elite. Non-Communist nationalists were brutally repressed.

When they found no nationalities to incorporate, the Bolsheviks invented them. In Central Asia, they combined small clans and tribes to form the Kazakh, Kirghiz, and Turkmen "nations." One ethnographer said she had "given birth to thousands of Tajiks," registering individuals in this way during the first Soviet Census of 1926. Linguists crafted written languages for about fifty ethnic groups, often using Latin rather than Arabic or Cyrillic scripts. Soviet theorists expected national consciousness to disappear as society developed. But, good dialecticians, they argued that before the "inevitable fusion (*sliyanie*) of nations," nationalities would have to pass through phases of blossoming (*rassvet*—literally "dawn") and convergence (*sblizhenie*). The policy of cooptation was interrupted by Stalin's paranoid deportations and mass killings. But with Khrushchev, the effort at control through incorporation returned.

Under Brezhnev, this approach proved remarkably successful. Very little force was actually needed. Tensions remained under the surface. But through close KGB monitoring, preemptive arrests of dissidents, and sentencing of nationalist activists to long penal terms, the authorities managed to avoid almost any mass protests over national issues. The human rights activist Lyudmila Alekseyeva collected reports of 185 demonstrations within the Soviet Union between 1965 and 1986 in which one hundred or more people participated. Of these, only twenty concerned secession, and all were in the Baltic republics. Only three times during the Brezhnev period did the authorities have to use guns to disperse protesters.

The legacy of these policies meant that as Gorbachev liberalized, ready-made political units existed for nationalists to seize. Each of the fifteen Union republics had its own council of ministers, parliament, academy of sciences, higher education system, writers' union, native language television stations, newspapers, and book publishers. As the sociologist Rogers Brubaker put it, the Soviet Union could disappear so rapidly only because it already contained its successors—fifteen "quasi-nation-states, with fixed territories, names, legislatures, administrative staffs, cultural and political elites, and—not least—the constitutionally enshrined right to secede." Two other communist states—Yugoslavia and Czechoslovakia—were also ethno-federations. Both fell apart, giving birth to nation-states congruent with the former administrative units.

Still, although the Soviet Union's structure empowered the separatists, it did not make disintegration inevitable. Within the Soviet Union, the Russian Republic was also an ethno-federal state, containing thirty-one ethnically defined units alongside fifty-seven nonethnic ones as of 1991. In the early 1990s, some worried that it too might splinter. Yet, for reasons I discuss in Chapter 8, it survived, with only one serious threat of secession, Chechnya.

Other scholars argue that the key destabilizing factor was the republic-level elections of 1990. As a country democratizes, the first few elections can be critical in structuring the field of competition. If elections are held early for central offices, activists face incentives to build countrywide parties and focus on issues relevant to the whole population. The winner enjoys a countrywide mandate to decide on the state's territorial and administrative structure. By contrast, if early elections are in regional units, this encourages candidates to emphasize anti-center, local, or ethnic issues, and weakens the legitimacy of central officials.

In the spring of 1989, several hundred reformers won seats in the USSR Congress of People's Deputies. To unite democrats from around the country, they formed a coalition, the Interregional Group, co-chaired by Andrey Sakharov, Boris Yeltsin, an Estonian activist called Viktor Palm, and several others (see Chapter 1). Assuming the Communist Party would be in power for some time, they concentrated on learning the tricks of parliamentary opposition—inquiries, amendments, exposés, and other maneuvers. But development of a Union-wide reform party was cut short by the republic and local legislative elections of 1990. Russian activists realized they could win more influence at subnational levels. "From the tactics of opposition . . . we went over to tactics of the

struggle for power on its lower floors," recalled Gavriil Popov, a reformist economist later elected mayor of Moscow. In the heat of battle, the
rhetoric tilted from democracy and markets to national self-determination. Nationalism became a way of stumping for votes, of channeling
the public's disenchantment with its rulers. As the philosopher Grigory Pomerants put it: "Nationalities have turned into political parties."
Yeltsin, whose rhetoric until then had focused on reform, now began to
emphasize the demand for Russian sovereignty.

A Union-wide reform movement never emerged. Local separatists
were the only cohesive opposition in most places. So when discontent
boiled over, even when motivated by consumer shortages and economic
crisis, the separatists were the main beneficiaries. Support for democracy and market reform became linked to the demand for national independence.

Moscow's Miscalculations

The Soviet state's structure and the logic of electoral competition catalyzed the growth of minority nationalism. But why were Gorbachev and
the other Soviet leaders so helpless before this challenge?

Any strategy to contain minority nationalisms must consist of two
elements: force and economic inducements—in the Russian phrase, the
whip and the gingerbread. Gorbachev's hard-line critics were sure that a
tough response could have silenced separatist demands. As early as 1988,
Yegor Ligachev insisted it was time "to use force, to restore order, show all
these scoundrels. . . ." Many in the military and security services agreed.
In March 1990, General Varennikov presented to the Politburo an elaborate plan to break Baltic resistance, modeled on the effective Soviet intervention to end the Prague Spring of 1968.

Force was used on several occasions, with considerable success. In
December 1986, riots erupted in the Kazakh capital Alma-Ata after Gorbachev replaced the republic's party leader, a Kazakh, with an ethnic
Russian. Security forces arrested thousands of demonstrators and jailed
more than six hundred; an unknown number were killed. Repression
was so potent that the republic remained quiet for the next two and a
half years, even as unrest surged elsewhere. In Uzbekistan, Karimov used

interior ministry troops to rough up demonstrators, driving the separat-ist organization Birlik "to the sidelines of politics."

Yet, in other places, attempts to intimidate demonstrators turned into violent fiascos. In Tbilisi in April 1989, Baku in January 1990, and then Vilnius and Riga in January 1991, Soviet special forces or army troops were sent into tense situations with poorly defined missions, then recalled and accused of indiscriminate violence. In the Tbilisi and Vilnius cases, Gorbachev equivocated on how deeply he was involved, hesitating to either defend or denounce the attacks. Meanwhile, reac-tionaries in the security forces were engaging in counterproductive dirty tricks. In December 1990, General Varennikov sent orders to the Kiev military garrison to destroy "fascist monuments." Shortly afterwards, a nationalist statue in the Western Ukraine was mysteriously blown up. The pattern of halfhearted, inadequately planned, bloody interventions undermined faith in Gorbachev's leadership, exacerbated divisions in Moscow, angered both liberals and Soviet loyalists, and did not subdue the waves of protest.

Why the failure? Beissinger argues that repression could have worked, but only before mid-1989. By the time Gorbachev recognized the dan-ger, it was simply too late: he had lost control of the streets. To intimidate potential protesters, the authorities must convince them that demon-strating is risky. Each must believe there is a significant chance he will be arrested, injured, or harmed in some other way. But as the number of demonstrators rises, unless the government can overwhelm them with additional troops, the danger to each individual falls. Regime opponents start to feel safety in numbers. Just as it is less risky to join a million-man march than to picket with a handful of dissidents, as demonstrations spread across the country the risk of staging an additional one declines. The center has to marshal its troops and manage the many crises erupt-ing simultaneously.

Knowing this, the secret policemen who protected Brezhnev were careful never to let down their guard. Not even a small demonstration could be tolerated because it might inspire imitators. Citizens had to know that sanctions would be swift and unavoidable. Demonstration organizers were bundled into vans, tried, and sentenced to prison terms.

Early in the Gorbachev era, the fear of arrest was still strong. In Alma-

Ata in 1986, thousands had been taken into custody. But as demonstrations proliferated, the odds of arrest dwindled. Between early 1987 and early 1989, the percentage of demonstrators arrested fell from about one in ten to just one in eighty, and then in 1990 it fell to about one in four hundred. Of course, this varied from place to place; repression remained more systematic in Central Asia. But in most other regions, citizens no longer lived in fear when it came to public shows of political opposition.

And when violence does not intimidate, it tends to enrage. Creating victims or martyrs helps nationalists attract recruits, shocks the regime's erstwhile supporters, and demoralizes its defenders. Beissinger's statistical analysis suggests that before April 1989, when Soviet troops beat to death nineteen Georgian protesters in Tbilisi, declaring a local state of emergency reduced the frequency of demonstrations. But after April 1989, states of emergency made protests grow even faster. Moderate force had become counterproductive.

The Politburo hard-liners were not alone in recognizing the danger of contagion. Nationalists in the Baltics understood the logic and from early on set out to "export their revolutions." They published Russian language newspapers to report on protests throughout the Union, advised other separatist groups on tactics, sent lawyers to help them draft documents, and hosted delegations from Uzbekistan, Armenia, Moldova, and various Russian cities. Algirdas Brazauskas, the reformist Lithuanian Communist leader, had to field complaints from Moscow about the Lithuanian activists agitating in parts of the Caucasus.

After 1988, force might still have saved the Union. But it would have required a massacre rather than a limited police operation. Gorbachev was not prepared to order this. Nor, it turned out, were defense minister Dmitry Yazov or KGB chief Vladimir Kryuchkov, who eventually pulled the plug on the disastrous August 1991 coup.

When one lacks the capacity to deter, the only hope may be to coopt. If enough of the demonstrators had been bought off with economic concessions, this might have isolated the diehard nationalists. Could central authorities have quelled the protests with gingerbread? To some, the idea that economic inducements can weaken nationalism seems far-fetched. People, it is said, will not sacrifice their identity for sausage. Once violence begins, economic promises cannot undo the mutual insecurity it creates. "There is no food rationing in Ulster," Yeltsin's nationalities adviser Galina Starovoytova observed: "but ethnic conflict has been going on there for more than a decade."

Of course, some nationalist true-believers cannot be coopted with any quantity of economic benefits. But, as the opinion polls show, most supporters of independence were at best lukewarm separatists. They came to favor secession reluctantly after concluding that the Soviet leadership could not solve the most basic problems of daily life.

A cooptation strategy would not have been easy to implement. Most critically, by the late 1980s the central authorities had little gingerbread to offer. The economic meltdown had undermined the state budget. Even had they been able to target fiscal concessions at potentially separatist republics, the opaqueness of Soviet economic relations meant such gestures might not have had the desired psychological effect. Even net recipients of resources often believed they were being victimized. Nationalists saw in consumer shortages not evidence of a system-wide failure but proof their surpluses were being "stolen" by Moscow. Gorbachev was shocked to discover, when he flew to Vilnius in 1990 to plead for unity, that his interlocutors thought they were being exploited. In fact, he argued, the Baltic republics were massively subsidized through the pricing system, under which Russia and Turkmenistan sold oil and gas to their neighbors at a fraction of the world price, while the Baltics sold expensive food and consumer products back to Russia. "You get independence and switch to world prices, and you'll end up in the soup," he told the Lithuanians.

Gorbachev was right. Lucjan Orlowski estimates that in 1990, Lithuania, Estonia, and Latvia received net indirect transfers through such pricing worth, respectively, 17, 12, and 10 percent of their GNPs. Yet this was only part of the story. Baltic nationalists could concentrate instead on flows through the state budget. Here, it was the richer republics—Russia, Belarus, Estonia, and Lithuania—that were subsidizing the less developed Central Asian states, and, after the 1988 earthquake, Armenia. The nontransparency of interrepublican relations allowed even Uzbeks, whose budget received subsidies worth almost 10 percent of GNP, to feel exploited by their "colonial" relationship with Moscow. In 1989, one Birlik leader compared the Uzbek cotton workers to slaves in the American plantations of the antebellum South.

Given the confusion about who was subsidizing whom, public opinion was probably more sensitive to economic changes than to arguments about absolute levels. Had the authorities managed to improve living conditions in the Baltics in 1986–1988, convincing residents of the benefits of integration, nationalists might have found it harder to attract mainstream support. For this to work, economic improvements would have had to be felt before the population mobilized and they would have had to be combined with effective policing of demonstrations. Discontent might then have stayed focused on campaigns for cultural and civic rights. Seeing that the general public was not angry enough to follow them into the streets, Baltic nationalists might have settled on demands for gradual liberalization. Without the Baltic sparks, and perhaps Georgia as well, the long fuse to Soviet disintegration might never have been lit. One cannot know for sure if such an approach would have worked. It would certainly have been hard to find the necessary resources. And, as the crisis deepened and prospects of a serious Union-wide economic reform dwindled, the attraction for the Balts of independently racing to join the European market grew ever stronger.

Gorbachev's actual economic strategy towards the Baltic states was as counterproductive as his irresolute use of force. Rather than channeling resources to the region when the rise of separatism might have been forestalled, he tried to punish Lithuania economically once people were already mobilized to resist. When the Lithuanians declared independence in 1990, Gorbachev announced an economic blockade and demanded billions of rubles in compensation for the industries developed under Soviet rule. Shipments of oil, gas, and some other products were cut sharply, leading to shortages of hot water and heat. Politburo member Vitaly Vorotnikov warned that economic sanctions against the Balts could backfire. "But we must show them," Gorbachev shot back. "Whoever takes the path toward a rupture dooms his people to vegetation. They need to feel this." The embargo was an embarrassing failure. It emboldened the Lithuanian nationalists and aroused sympathy for them worldwide. Gorbachev called it off as soon as a face-saving opportunity arose. It might have had some effect had Gorbachev been able to cut electricity to the republic—the party leader Brazauskas said this would have been a "catastrophe." But the republic actually exported electricity from its atomic power station to parts of Russia. Interdependence worked to the Balts' advantage even as they tried to secede.

The reasons for failure, then, lay both in objective circumstances and miscalculations. Objectively, especially after perestroika undermined the Soviet economy, the resources to engineer a consumer boom in the Baltics were not easy to find. A redirection of investment from Russia to the already relatively advanced Baltic states might have helped, but would have aroused protest within the central economic bureaucracy. Subjectively, Gorbachev did not understand the dangers that mass mobilization posed to the Soviet machinery of rule until too late. It is not that he ignored the issue; his aides Shevardnadze, Chernyaev, and Yakovlev badgered him to make more concessions, while Ligachev and Kryuchkov pressed for a tougher stance. He just had no idea what approach would work, and distrusted both the brutal bloodymindedness of the hard-liners and the seemingly unlimited flexibility of the liberals. Lacking a strategy, he temporized, responding—or, more often not responding—to crises as they arose.

A Synthesis

Putting all this together, we can now say what caused the Soviet Union, which to one Soviet dissident had seemed as "eternal as the Egyptian pyramids," to suddenly crumble. Was it economic crisis, political liberalization, the revival of minority nationalisms, cutthroat electoral competition, the greed of the local nomenklatura, the inept application of force by the central authorities, or the inherently fragile structure of the Soviet ethno-federation? None of these individually would have been sufficient. The combination, in which each exacerbated the effects of the others, was disastrous.

Economic crisis—caused by falling oil prices and Soviet policy mistakes—generated a discontent that might have found a variety of outlets. Gorbachev's political reforms weakened hierarchical authority, split the Communist elite, and opened unprecedented opportunities for autonomous organization. These opportunities were seized first by small groups of committed nationalists and anti-Soviet dissidents, who formed networks that spread from the Baltics to Uzbekistan. Competitive elections at the republic level encouraged both liberals and opportunistic local Communists to run on anti-Moscow nationalist platforms. Exploiting the center's weakness, nomenklatura nationalists in the republics set out to grab federal assets in the name of nationalities whose identities they had sometimes spent decades repressing. As consumer goods vanished and the Soviet authorities deadlocked, secession came to seem the only hope for rapid economic reform. The Kremlin's toleration of street demonstrations destroyed the centerpiece of Brezhnev-era social control. As more and more joined, the fear of punishment fell, and the spiral of escalation took hold. Unsure what to do, the central authorities used what tools they had in counterproductive ways—irresolute and unpredictable stabs of force along with unenforceable attempts at economic blackmail.

Given the complicated combination of mistakes and misfortunes that led to the collapse, it is not surprising that no one predicted it five years before. The unraveling of the Soviet order was not an accident waiting to happen. It was a series of accidents and bungling responses to them that—like the chain of events that led to World War I—diverted history down one of its least likely paths.

Why Not More Violent?

But why so relatively peaceful? When multiethnic states break up, violence can come from two directions. Central authorities may try to bludgeon secessionist groups and territories into submission. However, even worse brutality can occur after the center collapses, as suddenly vulnerable ethnic groups confront each other in conditions of anarchy. Whipped on by fear or geopolitical ambition, ethnic leaders seek to exploit historic resentments, to grasp temporary opportunities, or just to strike first out of insecurity. The danger is greatest when, as was the case for the post-Soviet Russians, a diaspora finds itself cut off from its ethnic homeland, suddenly a minority within a newly created foreign country.

The Soviet failure to use force to save the Union came down to the personal scruples and doubts of a few individuals. There was nothing inevitable about this. Gorbachev's equivocations and ambiguities served to hypnotize the army hard-liners. He held out just enough hope that he would side with them to keep them from major freelancing until it was too late. Had he not been genuinely confused and torn, he could not have neutralized the reactionaries so effectively. By 1991, it would have taken massive violence to reverse the tide of popular mobilization. Stalin, Khrushchev, Brezhnev, and Andropov would probably not have hesitated. But Gorbachev—and, more surprisingly, Yazov and Kryuch-kov—did. Why?

Beissinger argues that the leaders had become victims of their past successes. The effectiveness of previous control policy—which required little bloodshed—had left them psychologically unprepared: "government leaders failed to order the use of severe force against civilians because that way of reestablishing their authority was to them unimaginable." This rings true for Gorbachev, who knew that a crackdown would destroy his international reputation, end all talk of reform, and make him expendable to the old guard, which by this point detested him.

Yet, reestablishing order with tanks and AK47s was certainly imaginable to some of his colleagues. General Varennikov mocked the squeamishness of his fellow generals after the August coup: "Had I been here, I would have forced my colleagues to do the task, not to sit in their offices waiting." There were others of his ilk such as the anti-Semitic General Makashov, then in command of the Urals-Volga military district. A massacre was possible. One can only speculate about the motives of Yazov and Kryuchkov; their memoirs are not very helpful. In Chapter 1, I suggested they gave up during the coup because they felt their authority over subordinates melting away. The disorganization, delaying tactics, and deception that began one echelon down in the armed forces and KGB meant that violence, if unleashed, might have unpredictable consequences and would probably accomplish little.

After the coup, the moderation and responsibility of Marshal Shaposhnikov, the Soviet defense minister, was important. He firmly objected when Gorbachev, "thinking out loud," brought up the possibility of a military coup to save the Union. A possible danger point came when, after the failed coup, the Ukrainian government required all army officers in the country to pledge allegiance to Ukraine or be transferred to Russia. Had a large proportion refused the pledge and refused to leave, it is anyone's guess what would have followed. In fact, almost all made the pledge. As the commander of Soviet troops in Ukraine, General Andrey Nikolayev, later recalled: "When the majority of generals and officers pledged their loyalty to Ukraine, that ended conversations about the USSR."

Thus, Gorbachev's ambivalence, the willingness of most military officers to accept the split into national armies, and the fecklessness of those hard-liners who happened to be in key positions at the end explain the failure of the center to strike back. But what kept the Russian irredenta from catching fire? Why didn't the civil war in Moldova spread to the Baltics, Ukraine, and Kazakhstan? What stopped ultranationalists in the army from joining Russians in these republics to demand reunification with their homeland?

Although information on public opinion within the diasporas is patchy and attitudes were probably quite fluid, it appears that most local Russians had little desire to be reunified with their "homeland." By late 1991, majorities within the Russian diaspora communities—as elsewhere—had come to favor Soviet dissolution. As noted, in the December 1991 Ukrainian referendum, 55 percent of ethnic Russian voters supported independence, and large proportions of the Baltic Russian populations also favored breaking away. Despite being treated as second class citizens in Estonia and Latvia, Baltic Russians continued to identify with their new countries. Among Russians in Latvia surveyed in February 1995, 62 percent called Latvia their "native land," compared to 16 percent who said it was Russia. Forty-seven percent thought a "strong" Russia not desirable, almost twice as many as thought it was. Having seen what happened to the Russians "rescued" in Chechnya, few in the Baltics wanted a similar fate.

Many Russians in the new diaspora believed they enjoyed better economic and political prospects where they were than they would within Russia. In autumn 1993, 53 percent of Russians in Estonia, 43 percent in Lithuania, and 34 percent in Latvia thought that conditions for people like them were worse in Russia than in their current location. The percentages of Russians thinking this increased in all three republics throughout the 1990s. Larger proportions—64, 49, and 44, respectively—thought that living standards were more likely to improve in their republic than in Russia; again these proportions increased over time. In all three Baltic republics in the early 1990s, Russians evaluated their republic's political system more positively than they did Russia's. Common exposure to the economic crisis may have reduced tensions between Russians and the non-Russian native populations. In the past, occupational segregation and economic discrimination had caused ethnic resentment. But all suffered the rigors of transition to the market. Studying street demonstrations in Latvia and Ukraine, Stephen Bloom found that in the early 1990s protests against economic hardship—in which Russians and the native populations could march together—superceded demonstrations on nationalist issues.

In short, there was little desire in most parts of the diaspora for help from Russian nationalists. Polled in the spring of 1995, 54 percent of Russians in Estonia, 50 percent of those in Latvia, and 47 percent in Lithuania agreed that "hardline nationalist politicians in Russia are a threat to the peace and security of this country." The Pridnestrovyans in Moldova and the Crimeans in Ukraine were exceptional. Early on, many Russians in Ukraine and Kazakhstan also believed that the CIS would become a powerful, unifying institution, integrating most of the former Soviet republics. By the time the weakness of the Commonwealth became evident, the moment for a mass uprising had passed.

Opinion within Russia was more complicated. While the public sympathized with their co-ethnics when discrimination was reported, most thought their government should only negotiate peacefully on their behalf. Few supported the use of force. One poll in September 1991 found small pluralities in Moscow and large cities opposed to the transfer to Russia of territories in other republics where Russians predominated (the Crimea, Donbass, and Northern Kazakhstan were mentioned); in small towns and rural areas, the votes for and against such annexations were equal. When that December the nationalist Vladimir Zhirinovksy called a protest demonstration in Moscow against the Soviet disintegration, only about 3,000 showed up in a city where democratic activists could summon 100,000 at the drop of a hat. In 1996, a New Russia Barometer poll found that 92 percent of Russians favored negotiating with the governments of neighboring states about the conditions of Russian minorities, while only 16 percent supported military action.

The public's caution stood in contrast to the more aggressive nationalism of many in Russian political circles, including some often thought of as liberals. Vladimir Lukin, a former ambassador to the United States who in the early 1990s chaired the Russian parliament's foreign relations committee, demanded that Ukraine return the Crimea and the entire Black Sea Fleet to Russia. Moscow's Mayor Luzhkov enjoyed turning up in Sevastopol to champion Russia's claim to the port. Aleksandr Lebed, the popular general who ran for president in 1996, insisted that: "We must keep the glorious city of Sevastopol Russian, as is our legal right." Sergey Stepashin, the chair of the Russian parliament's defense and security committee, rejected the demand for a rapid withdrawal of Russian troops from Lithuania in 1992 on the ingenious grounds that this would violate the soldiers' human rights.

Against this backdrop, Yeltsin's patient diplomacy and restraint were crucial. While insisting the other republics recognize the political and legal rights of their Russian residents, he resisted pressures to intervene directly. In contrast to the Communist leader, Gennady Zyuganov, and the ultranationalist Zhirinovsky, who framed their support for Russian minorities in explicitly ethnic terms, Yeltsin sought to promote a kind of "liberal-secular nationalism." He made a point of speaking of Russians as *rossiyane*, a term that invokes citizenship of Russia, rather than *russkie*, the ethnic and linguistic category. When in 1994 the Crimea elected as its president Yury Meshkov, an ardent separatist who advocated the return of the Crimea from Ukraine to Russia, Yeltsin refused to meet with him. Instead, he negotiated a ten-year friendship treaty with Ukraine, which was signed in May 1997, formally recognizing existing borders and accepting Ukraine's sovereignty over Crimea. Under its terms, the Black Sea Fleet was split between the two countries, with Russia retaining a lease to its base in the port of Sevastopol.

In what nationalists saw as a humiliation, Russia withdrew its troops from Lithuania by August 1993, and from Estonia and Latvia by August 1994. Speed was of the essence. Where Russian troops lingered longer as popular nostalgia and imperialist aspirations grew, they sometimes seemed to generate instability. This was the case in both Georgia and Moldova. But by the time revanchist nationalism peaked in the late 1990s, the troops were already out of the Baltics, Ukraine, and Kazakhstan, and the potential for troublemaking was correspondingly smaller.

Had a leader like Serbia's Slobodan Milosevic been in the Kremlin, the guerrilla war that broke out in Moldova might have been the rule not the exception. The Crimean standoff could easily have escalated, dragging in the Russian troops of the Black Sea Fleet. The fact that some ships in the fleet were armed with nuclear weapons made the prospect of skirmishes over its control even more alarming. A more militant Russian leader might also have taken a stand in the Baltic, refusing to withdraw Russian forces and annexing border territories. The cautious policies of Ukraine's Kravchuk and Kazakhstan's Nazarbayev helped. While rejecting the Crimea's demands and removing its secessionist president, Kiev accorded the peninsula special economic status as well as tax breaks and disproportionate subsidies from the central budget in the early 1990s. Separatist passions subsided. Nazarbayev was careful to avoid alienating the large Russian communities in his republic's North. He encouraged use of the Russian language, ensured that Russian schools stayed open, and automatically extended Kazakh citizenship to all Russian residents.

Yeltsin's role in preserving the peace between Russia and its neighbors is one of his most underappreciated achievements. It stands in contrast to his bloody blundering in Chechnya. Disappointed that the Commonwealth turned out far weaker than he had hoped, Yeltsin nevertheless recognized the limits of what Russia could achieve through sabre rattling, and instead focused on avoiding a slide into unpredictable conflicts. For trying to build institutions that would manage the dissolution, and for rejecting calls to expand Russia's borders, he is—and will always be—reviled by Russian nationalists.

Yeltsin was surely sincere when he wrote after leaving office that he always hoped for and expected the republics to reunite. A peaceful disintegration was, in his mind, a necessary first step towards reintegration.

More than anything, I am deeply convinced that one day we will share a common finance system, common administration of law enforcement agencies, common international priorities, and perhaps even a common parliament. These prospects may frighten some people today, but our integration is inevitable. This is precisely why we Russians must not scare off our neighbors. We must not disrupt the ties we have established.

One may think this a naïve position, but it was a civilized one. Whether or not the former Soviet states will at some point move towards such a confederation, Yeltsin was right that any attempt at intimidation would have driven them apart. When in 2004 his successor tried too blatantly to influence Ukraine's presidential election, this merely strengthened anti-Russian forces. Just before leaving office, Yeltsin signed a treaty with the Belarusan leader Aleksandr Lukashenko on uniting their two states—the first concrete movement towards reintegration. But little progress had been made nine years later on defining what exactly this would mean. Lukashenko's ambitions to lead a united Greater Russia were at odds with the determination of Russia's leaders to prevent this from ever happening. If the tide had turned, it was sweeping in slowly.

CHAPTER 6

The Transformation

C risis is too mild a word to describe the economy that Yeltsin inherited in late 1991. It had an industrial sector that was too large, hopelessly inefficient, ecologically hazardous, hobbled by supply bottlenecks, and that was being stripped of assets by its state-appointed managers. Consumer goods and service sectors were anemic. The flood of rubles issued by Gorbachev's governments had devalued household savings and was poised to send prices shooting upwards. The state was bankrupt. Foreign debt had reached $97 billion, Western banks had cut off credit, and currency reserves were sufficient to finance imports for less than two hours. There were long lines even for bread, and economists feared widespread hunger within months. Trade with other Soviet republics was breaking down. Official measures of output were plunging.

Could any reform program solve all these problems simultaneously, quickly, and painlessly? Obviously not. What reforms were needed? Which were most urgent?

Preventing mass hunger was a sensible place to start. The basic problem was not lack of food. It was that producers were not shipping it to either the state warehouses or the market. Farmers had no use for rubles that, given the empty stores, would buy nothing. And as inflation began to break through the controls, they hoped for higher prices later. There were only two options. Had Yeltsin felt secure about his support within the army, he could have emulated Stalin and sent troops to requisition grain with bayonets. Barring this, the only way to motivate producers to supply goods was to set prices free and remove barriers to trade.

In fact, the government had little choice in the matter. Prices were already freeing themselves. To enforce a system of artificial prices, set at levels unprofitable for many sellers, one needs an apparatus of coercion. The old Soviet state could count on a disciplined ruling party, backed by a dependable police force and security service. By late 1991, this machinery was disintegrating. State enterprises were jacking up their prices, ignoring the planners. Even before Yeltsin's liberalization decree took effect, the consumer price index jumped 9 percent in November and 12 percent in December. The authorities could only legalize this spontaneous process, smoothing out the transition.

Given the inherited "overhang" of unspendable rubles, prices when freed were bound to leap upward. By how much was hard to guess since sellers might overshoot, asking too much at first and only lowering their demands when they found no buyers. A wave of inflation was, thus, unavoidable—a parting gift from the Communists. But no recovery would begin until price increases subsided. International experience shows that when inflation exceeds 40 or 50 percent a year, GDP almost never grows. Investment ceases because, given the uncertainty accompanying rapid price increases, investors cannot tell what projects will be profitable.

To reduce inflation, the authorities would have to control growth of the money supply. This, in turn, would require cutting the budget deficit to a level that could be covered by borrowing. If a government cannot finance its deficit with loans or reserves, its only option is to print more money, pushing prices higher. To balance the budget, the authorities would have to cut spending and build a modern tax system to collect revenues.

The next problem was that the potentially profitable parts of Russian industry were being looted by their managers. Not sure how long they would remain in control, the directors were squeezing profits as quickly as possible from their enterprises and stealing any moveable assets. They were selling their company's output cheaply to their own trading firms, which kept the profits but left the debts to accumulate on the state enterprise's ledger. Many managers had forged relationships with organized crime. An obvious solution was to order law enforcement bodies to prosecute such abuses. But, as often as not, corrupt law enforcers were conspiring with the looters.

As with price reform, privatization was not an ideological hobby-horse of the reformers—it was something that was happening already, in the most destructive way. The challenge was to get control of the process, to clarify property rights, make them easily tradeable, and persuade those currently looting for short-term gain to invest for the long term. Those with the power to develop or destroy the country's assets—mostly industrial managers, workers, and local government—needed to be given incentives to use these assets productively or sell out to those with greater entrepreneurial skill. New laws were needed to regulate the system of private property, along with an effective, honest bureaucracy to enforce them. Such a bureaucracy could not simply be wished into existence. The old corrupt officials had no desire to see it built. The reformers had to hope that new property owners would form a lobby for impartial law enforcement and secure property rights.

Finally, the dinosaurs of Soviet industry needed to be closed, liberating resources to provide the consumer goods, services, and high technology products the population demanded. Because tens of millions of Russians worked in unsalvageable enterprises, and many could not find new jobs without moving and changing careers, this could not be done quickly without major trauma. The temporarily unemployed would need to be provided with income and social services.

The first three candidates Yeltsin asked to head the government in late 1991 turned him down. One can understand why. The fourth, Yegor Gaidar, had no illusions that attempting to rescue the economy would make him popular. The running joke, he wrote, was that his government was like a potato—it would be either "chewed up in the winter or buried in the spring."

Gaidar, at thirty-five, was already known as one of the Russians best versed in Western economic theory. As a child, he had accompanied his father, a *Pravda* correspondent, to hot spots around the world. In Cuba, Che Guevara had visited them at the Hotel Riomar and taken the elder Gaidar target shooting. As a teenager in Belgrade, Gaidar found a copy of Adam Smith's *The Wealth of Nations*, along with Paul Samuelson's *Economics*, and became an economist. By 1991, he was heading an institute, whose conferences drew young scholars from the city's research centers, the kind who spoke foreign languages and had more to say about the quantity theory of money than Marx's labor theory of value. Among these was a former engineering student from Leningrad, author of a thesis on "The technology of magnetic-abrasive polishing of non-magnetic steel components," who had recently turned his thoughts to economic reform. Gaidar asked the young technocrat, whose name was Anatoly Chubais, to run the government's privatization program.

His colleagues planted in key ministries, Gaidar persuaded Yeltsin to sign a series of presidential decrees. From January 2, 1992, most prices were "unfrozen." Those for fuels and vital food goods—milk, ordinary bread, vodka—remained regulated, but for others sellers could choose their own price. Next, trade was legalized. Enterprises and citizens could buy and sell goods "without special permission . . . in any convenient place." Foreign trade was also liberalized—any firm could now export or import—although licenses and quotas remained for various exports. Quantitative limits on imports were abandoned in January, and a flat 5 percent tariff imposed in July.

Free prices and trade quickly transformed city streets. An enormous flea market stretched down central Moscow sidewalks. Treasures came out of the closets. On Tverskaya Street one morning, a dignified, middle-aged gentleman in spectacles and a cap was standing beside a two-meter-long, white, mounted telescope. One could pay 10 rubles to look through it, he said, or 10,000 to buy it. By the end of the year, almost all shortages had disappeared. The country got through the winter without hunger.

As expected—but faster—prices shot up. By June, the consumer price index was nine times higher than in January. For three and a half years, inflation surged out of control. On three occasions, the authorities forced the rate down, only to see it rebound a few months later. Only in late 1995 did they manage to stabilize price increases below 4 percent a month (see Figure 6.1). This then held for three years. In 1998, aftereffects of the financial tornado that had devastated Asia the previous year struck Russia's markets, forcing the government to devalue the ruble. Prices leapt 38 percent in one month. However, inflation quickly retreated. That the crisis had such a limited effect actually shows how solidly inflation had already been beaten.

The crisis of August 1998 was often blamed on the government's failure to balance its budget. In 1992, the general government deficit

Figure 6.1 Monthly inflation rate, Russia, 1991–2009

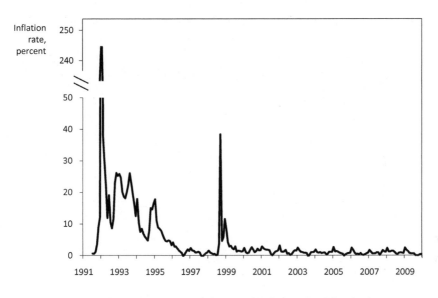

Sources: *Russian Economic Trends* dataset and Goskomstat Rossii downloads.

(including federal, regional, and local governments, plus extrabudgetary funds) came to a shocking 19 percent of GDP, and it ranged over the
next few years between 6 and 11 percent (see Figure 6.2). Several times,
the reformers managed to reduce spending sharply. In his first months
in power, Gaidar cut arms procurement by about 70 percent. Federal
spending fell by 5.3 percent of GDP in 1993 and another 4.9 percent of
GDP in 1995. But these savings were offset by an increasing failure of the
federal authorities to collect taxes.

Between 1992 and 1998, federal tax revenues fell from 18 percent of
GDP to just 9 percent, even as GDP itself shrank. Enterprises ran up
massive debts to the federal budget. In 1998, total unpaid federal taxes
equaled about 6 percent of GDP. In part, the tax take dropped because
of the economic contraction, which squeezed profits and thus profit tax
receipts. In part, the government let struggling enterprises get away with
not paying in order to avoid bankrupting them and driving up unemployment. Early on, more than 90 percent of the nonpayment of federal taxes reflected state-sanctioned exemptions. But another important

Figure 6.2 General government surplus or deficit, Russia, 1992–2008

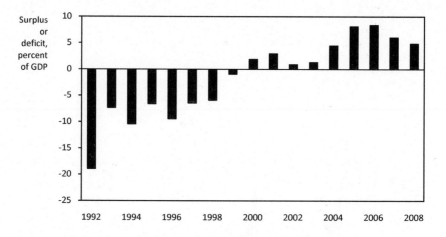

Source: European Bank for Reconstruction and Development, data downloaded in December 2009 from www.ebrd.com/country/sector/econo/stats/index.htm.
Note: General government includes the federal, regional, and local budgets and extrabudgetary funds, and excludes transfers.

cause was covert collusion between the regional governors and large businesses. The governors helped defend firms against the federal tax collectors and lobbied for tax breaks for them. In return, the firms paid their regional taxes more responsibly than their federal ones.

To finance its deficits, the federal government began selling short-term treasury bills called GKOs. As the market for these grew, their high rates of return attracted foreign investors. But the currency crises in Thailand and Indonesia in mid-1997 made investors nervous about emerging markets. Many rushed to sell their GKOs and cash out in dollars. To turn over the treasury bills, the government had to raise interest rates to 55 percent in May 1998 and 81 percent in July. By this point, the Central Bank was selling hundreds of millions of dollars a day of foreign currency reserves to support the ruble.

As more of the revenues from each GKO sale went to redeem previous issues, and as Central Bank reserves shrank, the expectations of a default or devaluation became self-fulfilling. Yeltsin sent Chubais to persuade the IMF to provide emergency funding, which it did, reluctantly, but the amount was too small and came too late to reassure the markets.

(While $22.6 billion was promised, only $4.8 billion was made immediately available.) On August 17, the Russian government announced a forced exchange of the GKOs for long-term bonds, a devaluation of the ruble, and, in an effort to save Russia's commercial banks, a ninety-day moratorium on their payments of foreign debt. The ruble's value quickly shot through the newly announced floor, and many banks—which could not pay back their foreign currency loans—went bankrupt. So did those that had borrowed heavily to buy GKOs.

The government's repeated failures managing inflation and the budget contrast with the smoothness with which privatization proceeded. From early 1992, stores, restaurants, and other small firms were auctioned. By April 1994, 70 percent had been sold, mostly to their managers. Citizens could also take ownership of the apartments they rented, usually for free or a nominal charge. Then, in late 1992, Chubais began selling off the country's large and medium-sized companies. Managers and workers were given the right to buy shares in their enterprises at low prices. In addition, for the equivalent of seven U.S. cents, each citizen was issued a voucher to bid for shares in privatizing companies. Most medium and large enterprises were required to sell 29 percent of their shares in "voucher auctions."

A steady stream of these auctions occurred between December 1992 and June 1994. By the end, more than 14,000 enterprises had sold shares, and around 98 percent of eligible Russians had claimed and used their vouchers (see Figure 6.3). By December 1995, 122,000 enterprises—including small ones—had been privatized. At that point, 62 percent of employed Russians worked in nonstate enterprises, and an estimated 40 million Russians owned shares either in companies or in investment funds.

The consistency with which privatization proceeded is puzzling at first sight. Opposition to "selling off Russia" was intense. Throughout the period, most Russians told pollsters they rejected private ownership of large enterprises and firms. While some critics just opposed the government's methods, others distrusted everything about the market. As one *Pravda* commentator complained: "vouchers, stocks, bonds, and privatization accounts are nothing more than another deception of the people." As late as March 1992, two advisors to the Russian reformers had

Figure 6.3 Privatization in Russia, 1992–1995

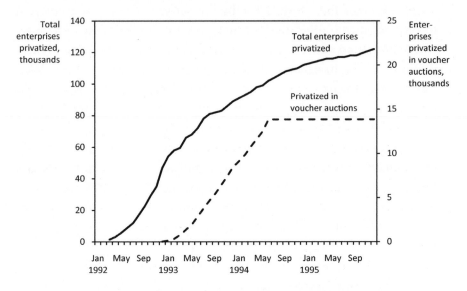

Sources: Anders Åslund, *How Russia Became a Market Economy* (Washington, DC: Brookings, 1995), 256; reports of State Property Committee, Russia; *Russian Economic Trends*, February 1997.

concluded that: "With a high probability, there will be very little privatization in Russia in the near future." And yet, privatization raced ahead. Even as the parliament and president engaged in armed confrontation in October 1993, the pace of voucher auctions hardly dipped.

The vouchers exhausted, the government switched to cash sales, hoping to raise revenues and attract outside investors. This proved much harder. By September 1995, privatization had brought in only about $36 million of the roughly $1.9 billion assumed in the budget. To complicate matters, the parliament had prohibited the sale of oil companies, and other privatizations were blocked on vague grounds of national security. Disappointed at the slow pace, and eager to get more of the economy into private hands before the expected Communist victory in the 1996 presidential election, the government changed its strategy, entering into a set of deals with certain large banks that came to be known as "loans for shares." The banks bid in auctions for the right to lend the government a total of around $800 million. As collateral, the government pledged shares in twelve major companies, including some large oil and metal producers. If the government did not repay the loans—and it did not intend to—these banks could auction off the shares and keep 30 percent of any profits. By dressing the transactions up as loans, the reformers bypassed the restriction on the sale of oil companies.

The scheme, designed and implemented by the bankers themselves, quickly became a scandal, arousing criticism in the parliament and the media. The same banks that organized the auctions usually won them, with bids just slightly above the starting prices. Foreign investors were discouraged from participating, and some Russian competitors were disqualified on what appeared to be technicalities (the authorities said they had not made the required cash deposits). After the deadline passed in September 1996, the banks sold the shares to themselves or affiliated firms. Control of the oil companies Yukos and Sibneft, along with that of the world's largest nickel producer, Norilsk Nickel, went to three of the bankers. Within a few years, their share prices had surged, generating huge capital gains for their new owners.

A crucial aspect of reform was creating the legal and regulatory infrastructure to govern a market economy. In a burst of legislative activity in the early 1990s, laws were passed to articulate basic rights, define rules of market exchange, and set up new agencies to enforce them. The Constitution of December 1993 guaranteed private property (Articles 8, 35), including private ownership of land (Articles 9, 36), and free movement of goods, services, and financial resources (Article 8). Parts 1 and 2 of the new Civil Code, passed in 1994–1995, protected freedom of contract. Laws on bankruptcy, intellectual property, insurance, and consumer protections were passed in 1992 and 1993, along with a customs code, and somewhat later a new criminal code that abolished penalties for private entrepreneurial activity. A 1995 law on the Central Bank defined its new role.

To implement these laws, a string of new agencies sprung to life in the early 1990s. A Federal Commission on Securities and Capital Markets, created in November 1994, was to regulate stock trading and protect investors' rights. A State Insurance Supervisory Committee (*Gosstrakhnadzor*), formed in 1992, was to monitor insurance companies and enforce solvency requirements. The Central Bank was given responsibility for regulating commercial banks. Unemployment had been virtually unknown under communism. In 1991, a new law had established an Employment Fund, into which enterprises paid two percent of their payroll. The next year, Yeltsin set up a State Employment Service to pay unemployment benefits, provide job training, help job seekers, and support job creation schemes. By the mid-1990s, the service had established a network of eighty-nine regional and roughly 2,300 local employment centers.

Transforming the politicized Soviet legal system into an independent judiciary was a particular challenge. To increase judicial independence— guaranteed in Article 120 of the new Constitution—a 1992 law established lifelong appointments for judges; they could now be fired only for cause, as determined by a panel of other judges. Jury trials were introduced in 1993 for serious cases, initially in a subset of regions, and a corps of court bailiffs was created in 1997. During 1991–1992, a system of commercial (*arbitrazh*) courts was established, replacing the Soviet state *arbitrazh* bodies. Although viewed skeptically at first, these courts appear to have been relatively successful. Between 1994 and 2003, their caseload increased fourfold.

Structural reform—the closing of unsalvageable enterprises and farms and reallocation of labor to new, productive activities—was slower, indeed much slower, in Russia than in many other postcommunist economies. Over time, as prices adjusted to reflect the market value of resources, the hopelessness of reviving vast parts of the economy became clear. By 1998, 53 percent of enterprises were running at a loss, outnumbering those that made a profit! Eighty-four percent of farms were in the red. In one-fifth of the country's regions—mostly in Siberia and the Far East—two-thirds or more of enterprises were unprofitable, and in Chukotka, 83 percent were. The total losses of unprofitable units in 1998 came to about 18 percent of GDP, more than the total profits made by profitable firms.

As their finances worsened, enterprises were closing—but slowly. Between 1991 and 2005, 21 million jobs in medium and large enterprises—one-third of the total—disappeared. Fifty-six percent of the industrial enterprises (with more than one hundred employees) that had existed in 1990 were gone by 2005. New companies were starting up, but not fast enough to absorb the discarded workers. Beginning in 1990 total employment fell by 8.7 million before stabilizing in 1999. Some Russians found new jobs in small family firms or as short-term laborers; the share of such workers rose from 1 to 12 percent of total employment between 1992 and 1999, an increase of about 6.6 million workers.

Compared to many other postcommunist countries, however, this adjustment was very gradual. It took seven years from the start of reforms for total Russian employment to fall by more than 13 percent. In Poland, Hungary, the Czech Republic, Latvia, Lithuania, and Estonia, decreases this large occurred within four years. Russia's total employment decline was also unusually small, never exceeding 15 percent. By contrast, employment fell by 19 percent in the Czech Republic, 20 percent in Poland, 26 percent in Estonia, 28 percent in Lithuania, 30 percent in Hungary, and 33 percent in Latvia. Unemployment in Russia was surprisingly moderate for a country undergoing such a major transition. Unusually flexible wages and working hours, along with a growing informal sector, help to explain this.

The Politics of Reform

The early reform years mixed successes and partial successes with failures. While some changes were made quickly and smoothly, others remained frozen for years. Some were still blocked when the August 1998 crisis struck. What explains the uneven results?

In a word, politics. To understand how politics retarded necessary changes, it helps to think about reform as a game. A number of players, each interested in promoting or blocking particular changes, interacted strategically, trying to anticipate their adversaries' responses. The game had a set of rules—primarily the Constitution—but it was always possible some player might try instead to kick over the board. While winning for Gaidar meant getting reforms implemented, for most other players the goals were money and power. Both skill and chance helped determine who won.

Besides top officials, several groups constituted the main players. First, there were the managers and employees of the unsalvageable enterprises and collective farms, who relied on the government aid that burst the budget. The industrial bosses and workers had many ways to get the government's attention—lobbying in parliament, picketing the Kremlin, staging strikes, blocking railway lines, and voting for the opposition. Each spring, the collective farm chiefs threatened food shortages if denied money for fuel and fertilizers. Since the Supreme Soviet was itself packed with collective farm bosses and industrial managers, such requests tended to hit their target. Second, the country's bankers—in both the Central Bank and the almost fourteen hundred new commercial banks—were getting rich channeling credits and speculating on currencies and commodities as inflation surged. Together, they controlled the arteries of the economy—the clearing system through which all payments and tax revenues passed.

Regional and local governments were seizing powers the weakened center had left unguarded. They feared losing federal subsidies. The governors could sabotage reforms by ignoring central directives, coopting federal agents, and pressuring courts to issue antireform rulings. They could play the central executive off against the parliament and rally opinion against Moscow. If local enterprises were privatized against their wishes, they could cut off electricity and water or harass them in other ways.

Fourth, although nominally under President Yeltsin's control, the federal bureaucracy—the police, security services, army, and economic ministries—was not always on his side. These agencies feared cuts to their budgets and limits on their influence and access to bribes. They enjoyed endless opportunities for disruption. Fifth, managers and workers in potentially *profitable* enterprises—mostly producing raw materials—had reason to favor reforms, but only those they controlled. They wanted to privatize their companies' assets to themselves, protect their firms from takeovers, and minimize their tax payments. The managers had cash to bribe corrupt regulators and law enforcement agents. Finally, ordinary Russians stood to gain from successful reform, but they had little way to judge whether current hardship was a temporary cost or the result of government incompetence, as the opposition claimed. They could vote the president and parliament out of office at election time. In between, the results of public opinion polls emboldened or discouraged the key players in their battles for power.

Yeltsin's reformers confronted these opponents in several settings. First, just about all reforms had to be enacted into law—or at least not overruled—by the parliament. Initially, this parliament had virtually unchecked constitutional power (see Chapter 2). It could overturn presidential vetoes or dismiss the prime minister by a simple majority vote (in both houses) and impeach the president or amend the constitution with a two-thirds majority. The new 1993 constitution strengthened the president vis-à-vis the parliament. The president could ignore a vote of no confidence in the government, and, if it voted no confidence again within three months, he could, in most circumstances, dissolve the Duma rather than surrender his prime minister. Parliament now needed a two-thirds majority in both chambers to override a presidential veto. The procedures for impeachment were made more complicated. Still, it remained impossible to enact economic reforms if the parliament was solidly opposed, as it very often was. Parliament could still overturn presidential decrees by passing laws. And economic legislation—the annual budget, laws on taxation, pensions, social benefits, the use of land, among other subjects—had to be passed by the Duma.

Key decisions on the money supply and interest rates were made by the Central Bank. Initially, the bank's chairman was appointed by and accountable to parliament, whose speaker had a hotline to his desk. The 1995 central banking law said the Central Bank was "independent," but the parliament still appointed and dismissed its chairman, on the president's nomination. The judges of the Constitutional Court—who could declare laws or presidential decrees unconstitutional—were similarly nominated by the president and appointed by parliament.

Getting reforms enacted was just the start. They would then need to be implemented by the bureaucracy, along with the regional and local governments. The bureaucrats were often conservative, corrupt, ineffective, and influenced by the parliament. Did they resist reforms? " 'Resistance' is not the word," said minister of foreign economic relations Pyotr Aven. "The state apparatus took us for the town madmen." Gaidar exaggerated only a little when he called the government in late 1991 "purely decorative."

> Nothing in it was connected to anything else. It had no army, no KGB [security service], no MVD [interior ministry], no control over other regions of the country whose local governments might

pull who knows what. It effectively had no central bank. No control over the greater part of industry. No customs service. In fact, nothing at all, except the name—the Russian State.

A functional bureaucracy had to be pieced together from the debris of the collapsing Soviet order. Gaidar expressed particular frustration with the Ministry of Security, successor to the KGB.

> I made repeated but as a rule fruitless attempts to get information from this agency on corruption in the ministries and the government apparatus as a whole. Beyond eloquent pronouncements on the theme of fighting corruption, I got nothing. . . . In general, if the security ministry was working at all, it wasn't working for us.

Opponents of reform lobbied tirelessly in parliament. Opposition could also surface, more dangerously, in the streets. From June 1992, neo-Bolsheviks picketed the Ostankino television center, sometimes clashing violently with police. Veterans from separatist struggles in Moldova and elsewhere turned up in the throng, and Yeltsin, watching the television footage, writes that he sensed in the disturbances "the hand of my old friends, the KGB." Meanwhile, in dozens of regions, many home to ethnic minorities, governors backed by crowds demanded greater local autonomy or even secession.

In this environment, the government's capacity to push through reforms came down to two things—Yeltsin's initial popularity and his determination to draw a line beneath the Communist past. Yeltsin has often been criticized for wavering and failing to support his reformist ministers sufficiently. This has been put down to his superficial understanding of economics, his greater personal rapport with old-style Soviet managers, or excessive populism. Although personal characteristics played a part, objective factors were more important.

While Gaidar and his lieutenants could, if they chose, focus single-mindedly on economic reform, Yeltsin had to worry also about order. He had seen how street protests could spin out of control, how secession movements could tear a state apart, how indecision at the top could inspire a hard-line coup. The danger of total breakdown of central authority was real. As in the late 1980s, disparate protests could feed upon each other, and one region's refusal to remit taxes could prompt others to follow, pushing federal agencies towards bankruptcy. A softening of loyalty within the law enforcement agencies, not necessarily visible from above, could hollow out the state's ability to resist challenges. Given the constitutional weakness of the presidency before 1994, Yeltsin had to balance the need for victory on any individual measure against the broader goals, fencing simultaneously against the parliament, courts, governors, and opposition leaders. With the parliament free to dump the government—indeed, amend the presidency out of existence—going for broke would have been counterproductive.

Initially awed by Yeltsin's stature after August 1991, the parliament rallied behind him, authorizing Yeltsin to issue decrees for a year, and approving his reform speech of October 28. Later, as hyperinflation sapped Yeltsin's popularity, ambitious politicians—led by the parliamentary speaker, Ruslan Khasbulatov, and Yeltsin's own vice president, Aleksandr Rutskoy—set out to exploit growing public discontent (see Chapter 2).

Yeltsin, sensing the changing balance of forces, sought to preempt and resist attacks, while keeping to the main strategic line—support for economic and political freedom. At times, he shielded his reformers. At others he gave them "a good horsewhipping," in the hope of deflecting pressures to fire them. From May 1992, he began balancing Gaidar's protégés in the government with traditional economic managers. That December, as the Congress held a gun to his head, he dismissed Gaidar and replaced him with the gas industry veteran Viktor Chernomyrdin. More changes followed. By 1995, not just the parliament was packed with lobbyists—some of the more brazen ones were in the government. Deputy Prime Minister Aleksandr Zaveryukha, loyal friend of the collective farms, saw nothing odd about insisting that: "The country must feed its peasants." Oleg Soskovets defended military industry and metal producers, while Chernomyrdin stuck up for oil and gas. Some ministers even lobbied against their own budget. The government, said former finance minister Boris Fyodorov, had turned into the partnership of "a swan, a crab, and a pike . . . all going in different directions."

Against this background, it is remarkable that Yeltsin's reformers managed anything at all. They relied, at different moments, on three distinct approaches to the politics of reform, approaches that have been used in many other times and places. Successes came when the tactics they chose were appropriate to the circumstances. Failures occurred when they chose badly. Sometimes, of course, no winning tactics were available.

The first approach might be called the *cavalry charge*. Plunging head-long at the enemy, the reformers sought a breakthrough by force of will, speed, and concentration. Such tactics worked wonders in postwar Japan, where General MacArthur, U.S. troops at his back, broke up the business empires of the prewar *zaibatsu* and imposed a democratic constitution. With similar cavalry attacks, Ataturk carved a modern Turkish state out of the Ottoman ruins, closing religious schools, suppressing opposition parties, and imposing European legal codes. General Pinochet crushed the Chilean labor unions to impose macroeconomic stability. Cavalry charges make for rousing theater and—sometimes—stunning victories. They make less sense when the valley one must charge down is surrounded by cannons.

The second approach—the *war of attrition*—involves neither speed nor surprise, nor overwhelming force, just a patient search for incremental gains. What victories occur result from painstaking preparation and periodic probing of the opposition's defenses. Reformers exploit moments when the opponent is distracted to make technocratic advances, which add up over time to more substantial change. In such a war, persistence is key. "Many of our decrees were overturned three or four times," Chubais later recalled of 1993, "but we would remake them phrased slightly differently." The war of attrition can work well when time is on the reformers' side. Often it is not.

Finally, reformers may seek progress through *creative recombination*—dividing and conquering their opponents, coopting some by designing reforms in ways that benefit them, while isolating others, who can then be crushed or ignored. Reformers help potential beneficiaries to organize, building a support coalition. Victories, in this approach, are always relative and costly, and to keep reforms moving the reformers must be ready to make sudden turns, striking out against their erstwhile allies. The timing of such reversals can be crucial. Too soon, and the first reform crumbles; too late, and the reformers end up hostage to their creations.

On two occasions, Yeltsin's reformers used creative recombination to good effect. The first was privatization. As of early 1992, majorities in the country and the parliament opposed selling off major enterprises. The directors, determined to keep control, announced through their chief lobbyist, Arkady Volsky, that they would "paralyze the country by calling their workers out on strike." Volsky's association claimed to include companies with 20 million workers. Many of the government's own ministers feared losing influence over "their" enterprises, while regional governors fumed at the prospect of carpetbaggers buying up local industry.

At first, Chubais hoped to avoid concessions. His priority was to attract entrepreneurial outsiders who could turn poorly run companies around. But the first framework for privatization he sent to parliament in March 1992 was torn apart by the industrial lobbyists. When it became clear the plan had no chance, Chubais tried again.

Turning to the politics of coalitions, he agreed to let managers and workers in most enterprises buy 51 percent of the voting shares at a discount, even using their companies' own funds. In return, the managers accepted that workers' shares would be individually held and freely tradeable (rather than collectively held by management), which made corporate takeovers possible. Regional and local governments got the right to sell most shops and small firms for cash, as well as tranches of shares in some local enterprises. Central ministries got to hold back some "strategic" enterprises for later sales. Finally, vouchers were issued to ordinary Russians to buy their acquiescence.

All this required a major reversal for Gaidar and Chubais, who in late 1991 had drafted plans to conduct privatization entirely by sales for cash. Four years earlier, both had scoffed when a visionary libertarian economist, Vitaly Nayshul, lectured on the idea of giving privatization vouchers to the public—too unrealistic, risky, socially unjust, and politically dangerous, Gaidar and Chubais had objected. Later, the two were blamed for all the problems they had anticipated. Still, without such concessions, privatization would not have occurred for some time, and without it the social base for many other reforms would not have emerged.

The second successful use of creative recombination made possible the victory against inflation in 1995. Previous attempts had run into opposition from powerful beneficiaries of inflationary policies. Bankers were earning billions from the flood of cheap credits to struggling enterprises, estimated in 1992 at 18.9 percent of GDP. The Central Bank itself made about $2 billion in profits that year from interest on such credits; about two-thirds of these profits went into a fund to pay bonuses to the bank's employees. Commercial banks channeled the credits, earning commissions and bribes. Besides this, they made an estimated 8 percent of GDP in 1992 from speculating on oil and currency with their depositors' cash. For their part, the inefficient enterprises and collective farms could not survive without credits and lavish government subsidies. By the summer of 1992, in Gaidar's words, these groups had formed a "powerful pro-inflation political coalition" that dominated parliament and repeatedly threatened to sack the government.

The war of attrition tactics Gaidar and his team attempted during the first three years achieved some incremental successes. Gradually, the reformers managed to cut off the other former Soviet republics, which had been issuing massive ruble credits, knowing most of the inflation would land in Russia. ("Why hold down the budget deficit when you've got your own printing press?" Gaidar quotes the Ukrainan prime minister, Vitold Fokin, as saying. In 1992, Russia's neighbors received ruble credits and currency worth almost 12 percent of Russian GDP. Yeltsin only allowed the government to unilaterally end the ruble zone in mid-1993.) There was even the occasional cavalry sortie, as in October 1993, when, fresh from his triumph over the Supreme Soviet, Yeltsin abolished subsidized Central Bank credits. However, the discipline did not last long. Spring and summer of 1994 saw a new flurry of Central Bank loans. A lasting victory required breaking the pro-inflation coalition.

What did this were policies that gave the banks a reason to like stable prices. As inflation fell, the government sold the banks GKOs at extremely high interest rates, providing an alternative source of profits. Twenty-five of the largest banks won the lucrative role of primary dealer, purchasing the bonds at auctions and reselling them to their clients. For the favored banks, incentives changed by 180 degrees. Now high inflation, rather than boosting their profits from currency speculation, cut into the value of the interest they earned on their GKOs. The Central Bank became the government's GKO dealer, and got to keep much of the profit. This came to $104 million in 1997, far less than the $2 billion in 1992, but still enough to pay bonuses averaging more than $1,000 to each of the Bank's roughly 90,000 employees. Meanwhile, by 1995 the largest banks had been drawn into privatization and hoped to attract inflation-shy foreign investors to the companies they were buying.

With the bankers coopted in this way, the government gave the inefficient enterprises and farms just enough relief to keep them from boiling over. It found a noninflationary way to pass on subsidies. Rather than transferring money, it pressured the oil, gas, and electricity companies to supply the terminally ill enterprises with fuel at low prices, or even, in effect, for free. In mid-1996, the gas monopoly Gazprom was being paid for only 23 percent of the gas it supplied. What payments the energy companies did receive were mostly in the form of "barter"—in goods worth much less than the enterprises claimed, if anything at all. One World Bank study estimates that, through such unpaid bills, the Russian energy sector extended subsidies worth $63 billion during 1993–1997. Such subsidies came to about 4 percent of GDP each year. To keep farmers in business, the government persuaded fuel and fertilizer suppliers to extend "commodity credits"—i.e., to supply the farms, with little hope of payment. The government also obliged the utilities to serve the public at a fraction of the true cost.

In return, the government allowed the energy companies to accumulate large tax arrears and pay their taxes with dubious promissory notes their delinquent clients gave them. The most important concessions, however, involved privatization. Gazprom was allowed to distribute 15 percent of its shares to its employees in return for privatization vouchers, and sell another 10 percent mostly to firms affiliated with management. Gazprom's director won the right to manage the 35 percent state holding in trust, with the prospect of eventually buying these shares. Lukoil and other cooperative oil companies were allowed to participate in the loans for shares deals.

This approach was less deliberate strategy than a messy improvisation that emerged from the collision between Yeltsin's political intuition, Gaidar's grasp of economic fundamentals, and Chubais's pragmatism. But it worked. It helped slow the rise in unemployment, and it stretched out the agony of restructuring over a less politically explosive, longer duration. And whereas subsidies paid in newly printed money would have fed inflation, canceling debts and providing free energy did not.

Not everyone agrees with this account. Anders Åslund, for instance, argues that stabilization worked in 1995 because finally the reformers got up the nerve to impose a dose of "true shock therapy." Instead of reaching counterproductive compromises with the enterprise directors and bankers, they "hit all important interest groups hard and fast." Chubais cut back subsidies sharply to reduce the deficit: "The key to macroeconomic stabilization was fiscal adjustment."

It is true that the government cut expenditures significantly in 1995 (as it had, for instance, in early 1992). However, a glance at Figure 6.2 shows that, in general, such bouts of heroic belt-tightening were not politically sustainable. The effects were fleeting. After falling to 6.6 percent of GDP in 1995, the general government deficit leapt back to 9.4 percent of GDP in 1996. Meanwhile, government aid—explicit and implicit—to the struggling enterprises did not fall but increased. Pinto and colleagues estimate that total government subsidies—including toleration of unpaid taxes—rose from 11 percent of GDP in 1994 to 16 percent in 1998. Rather than a sharp shock, the government provided a continuing lifeline. The point is that it found a way to do so that did not increase the money supply.

In contrast to this use of creative recombination to fight inflation, the government adopted a classic war-of-attrition approach to structural reform. Whether this was a qualified success or a failure is still debated. Thousands of doomed enterprises were kept alive for several years, producing goods that could be sold only by means of barter at cut-rate prices. This was a cost of the tactics used to weaken the pro-inflation lobby. A gradual reduction of the subsidies resulted in a slow cull of the worst enterprises. For the most part, the workers were left to decide for themselves when to give up on their enterprise, find another job, and sell their shares to whoever would buy them.

Some writers think Russia's reformers should have relied more on cavalry charges. On occasions, this did work well. In the five months after November 1991, Gaidar's team exploited the opposition's disarray to liberalize prices and trade and lay the foundations for other reforms.

However, most attempts to force the pace of change by the exercise of will power alone were far less effective.

A striking personification of the cavalry charge strategy was Boris Fyodorov, who served as finance minister in 1993. How had he got the inflationary central banker, Viktor Gerashchenko, to compromise, I asked Fyodorov in July 1997. "I am a dangerous individual (*vredny chelovek*)," he explained. He bombarded Gerashchenko with telegrams, insulted him in the press, wore down his nerves. Commercial bank lobbyists were not allowed into Fyodorov's reception area. He telephoned the heads of the ethnic republics of Tatarstan and Bashkortostan and told them firmly to pay their taxes. By early 1994, Fyodorov had been replaced in the ministry. On the eve of the 1995 parliamentary elections, he published at his own expense a book entitled *Achievements of the Chernomyrdin Government in 1994–5*. It contained thirty blank pages.

This was interesting because it was precisely in 1995—long after Fyodorov left government—that the authorities finally drove monthly inflation below 5 percent. Fyodorov's efforts in 1993 had scored some partial victories—the abuses of Russia's ruble by other republics had ended. Still, notwithstanding Fyodorov's phone calls, Tatarstan and Bashkortostan did not remit their taxes in full. Credits continued to sluice out in 1993 and 1994. Only one and a half years after he had left the finance ministry, after the banks had been coopted, did stabilization occur.

Then in 1998, Fyodorov was appointed to head the Federal Tax Service, and the cavalry rode into battle again. "I have been in Government twice and by the time I leave, a lot of people feel pain," he warned an interviewer. He threatened to investigate the country's celebrities for tax evasion and ordered his subordinates to start arresting and selling the assets of Gazprom to pay the company's tax debt. He blocked access to export pipelines for oil companies with tax arrears. As best one can tell, the consequence was that tax discipline weakened slightly. During Fyodorov's stint in power, total tax collections came to 160 billion rubles, compared to 173 billion in the same months of the previous year. Gazprom paid less right after Fyodorov's assault than before, and it started cutting supplies to various regions, forcing them to burn fuel stockpiled for winter.

Meanwhile, in the Duma, the government was trying to pass an emergency program to prevent the collapse of financial markets. On hearing of Gazprom's travails, the leaders of three factions—the Communists, Zhirinovsky's Liberal Democrats, and Our Home Is Russia—leapt to the company's defense. "Largely owing to the attack on Gazprom," the analyst Vyacheslav Nikonov reported, "a substantial proportion of the government's anticrisis package was torpedoed in the State Duma. . . . [O]n Friday [the parliament] voted down a number of draft laws that it had been prepared to support on Wednesday." In place of 71 billion rubles of additional revenues, the deputies approved only 3 billion. The humiliating dénouement arrived a few weeks later in the form of the default and devaluation.

Common Criticisms of the Reforms

Catastrophic fall in living standards

Most observers of Russia's reforms are convinced that the standard of living deteriorated drastically for most Russians in the 1990s. For some, it certainly did. However the evidence suggests a more complicated picture.

Gross domestic product per capita, as recorded by the state statistical agency, did fall sharply—by 42 percent between 1990 and 1998. However, in 1990 much of what was produced—redundant tanks and combine harvesters, defective shoes, unfinished construction projects—although entered positively into the GDP accounts, actually wasted resources. Conversely, the 1998 statistics missed much of the value created in the underground sector. Consequently, the true drop must have been considerably less than the headline figure. Consumption by households, estimated from surveys, fell only 11 percent between 1990 and 1998. Retail trade per capita dropped by less than 3 percent. Most of the output contraction evidently concerned goods that households did not consume.

Many other indicators suggest *improving* quality of life. Car ownership doubled by 1998 and tripled by 2006. The average living space per person rose every year, summing to an increase of 18 percent by the end of the 1990s. More households owned radios, televisions, tape recorders, refrigerators, washing machines, and electric vacuum cleaners in 2000 than in 1991, and the biggest increases came early in the decade, when living standards supposedly declined the most. Nor were these changes limited to major cities: even in the depressed Arctic outpost of Chukotka car ownership doubled.

The share of households receiving at least three television channels doubled and the share of Russians with home telephones almost doubled. In 2000, Russians made almost twenty times as many international phone calls as in 1990—more than five calls for each citizen. Between 1992 and 1994—the years of most intense crisis—the proportion of urban Russians owning a country house or vegetable plot increased from 18 percent to 30 percent. Millions of Russians came to own the state apartments they occupied. In Moscow and St. Petersburg, by 2008 these could be worth millions of dollars. An additional 132,000 kilometers of public paved roads were built in the 1990s, more than the entire length of paved roads in Norway and Finland combined.

This is not to say that no one suffered. The relatively small fall in average consumption conceals a rise in inequality and a redistribution of purchasing power away from some groups. The main beneficiaries were the educated, the young, and those living in the cities of European Russia—especially Moscow and St. Petersburg—as well as residents of the raw materials–producing regions of Siberia. Those hardest hit were not, as often claimed, pensioners, but families with many children, and those trapped in dead-end jobs in agriculture and the industrial rustbelt. Poverty rose from 1992 to 1998, before retreating to around its 1992 value by 2003 and falling below it in 2004.

In short, although hardships increased for a significant slice of the population, many Russians enjoyed a higher standard of living in the 1990s than ever before, and for many the decade brought a mixture of losses and gains. Since 1999, rapid increases in wages and pensions have improved the lives of all income groups.

"Shock therapy" too radical

Some contend that the transition would have been less painful if Russia's reformers had moved more slowly, enacting changes one after another, and giving people more time to adapt. Rather than "shock therapy," they argue, Yeltsin should have chosen "gradualism." He should have followed China's example, liberalizing prices incrementally, and using leaseholding and state-enterprise partnerships rather than privatization. Instead of focusing on macroeconomic stability, the government should have kept interest rates low to encourage the growth of new private businesses. Rather than closing down outdated industries overnight, it should have done so gradually, as new jobs appeared to replace the old. Finally, the reformers should have focused more on building institutions rather than relying on free markets to organize themselves.

This set of criticisms is peculiar for two reasons. First, much of the gradualists' program consists of *precisely* the perestroika reforms that Gorbachev had already tried and that had proved disastrous under Soviet conditions. Chinese-style gradual liberation of prices was the central element of Gorbachev's 1987 "Law on the State Enterprise," which let state enterprises sell on the free market what they produced in excess of state orders. Given the weakening of Soviet administrative levers, the planners could not control the implementation of this strategy, and coordination collapsed as each enterprise struck out for itself, its managers finding ways to appropriate the enterprise's profits. Leasing of enterprises, legalized by Gorbachev in 1989, became a main instrument of insider privatization, without improving productivity. What worked in China did not work in Russia because of the enormous differences between the two countries.

Second, these criticisms are odd because, in other ways, gradualism was exactly the strategy Yeltsin's governments ended up pursuing. The notion that Gaidar's team, motivated by monetarist ideology, imposed high interest rates is particularly strange. They tried to do so, but until late 1993, failed completely. Interest rates adjusted for inflation were not just low but *negative*. As already discussed, rather than forcing the liquidation of hopeless enterprises, the authorities continued to support them for years, first with credits and subsidies, later with tax write-offs and free energy. This stretched out restructuring and temporarily saved jobs. Unemployment rose even more slowly in Russia than in some countries such as Hungary that are usually considered models of "gradualism." In fact, in all but three of the years between 1992 and 2004, unemployment was lower in Russia that it was in France. It took Russia longer to bring inflation down because of the drawn-out way in which successive governments reduced their spending.

The claim that Russia's reformers neglected institutions does not square with the history of major initiatives to build market infrastructure and reform the judiciary. Within a few years, agencies to protect consumer rights, monitor insurance companies, and regulate the securities market were built from scratch, along with a nationwide network of employment centers. Of course, there were some failures—notably, the inability to pass a land code and a tax code until much later. But the government's efforts are impressive. Less impressive, however, was how these new and reformed institutions functioned. Enforcing the new laws to protect investors and consumers was an enormous problem, given widespread corruption and the growth of organized crime.

In many respects, the reformers were simply outgunned. Dmitry Vasiliev, a former privatization official who headed the Federal Securities Commission, tried hard to protect minority investors, but resigned in October 1999, complaining that the tax service and police were not responding to his requests to investigate cases of share dilution. Besides a lack of cooperation from law enforcement, the new market regulators often had insufficient funds due to the government's inability to collect taxes. They also had to combat efforts by regional governments to coopt their local branches. These limitations clearly had nothing to do with the radicalism of "shock therapy." They reflected the decision by Yeltsin, in the politically challenging setting in which he found himself, to work with existing law enforcement agencies rather than to attempt to fundamentally reform them (see Chapter 2). Gradualist critics have offered few concrete ideas about how enforcement could have been improved in such difficult circumstances.

Reforms too gradual

By contrast, others have criticized the reformers for being too measured in their approach, for making too many compromises with those opposed to reform. Instead of trying to coopt opponents, such critics say, the Russian government should have stuck to the cavalry charge, relentlessly cutting spending and subsidized credit. Since the public continued to support economic reform, they add, the soft approach must have arisen from some flaw in Gaidar's character. Even friends and associates took him to task. "He's not by nature a stubborn fighter," said Anders Åslund, a Swedish economist who was advising the team. "The problem is that Gaidar is a very pleasant man and a compromiser by instinct." Gaidar's own economics minister said he thought Gaidar "could be harder."

Gaidar admitted the government had compromised, permitting ministries to issue cheap credits, even instructing the Central Bank to do so as well. He attributed this to the requirements of operating in a democracy. "It is, without any doubt, a result of political pressure, political compromises. But what to do? Life in a democratic society does not permit the government to isolate itself." When I visited his aide Vladimir Mau in July 1992, he also invoked the limits imposed by democracy: "In his time, Pinochet gave his word that he would not receive industrialists during the period of stabilization, so as not to hear complaints. We did not give such a pledge."

It was not just democracy, but the particular, precarious position of the reformers in 1992 that accounts for their choices. As we have seen, the parliament was empowered to sweep the government away on a whim, even amend the presidency out of the Constitution, and it controlled the Central Bank. Yeltsin had simultaneously to maneuver around the parliament, manage the regional governors, and maintain enough popular support to prevent the extreme opposition from taking to the streets. He could not always give the defense of his reformers priority over the preservation of presidential authority, and attempting to push reforms too hard could have quickly undermined them.

At the time, opinion polls sent confusing messages that both sides could interpret in their own way. On one hand, support for reform remained quite robust through the end of 1993; throughout 1992, a majority said reforms should be continued. In early 1992, about twice as many respondents favored an economic system based on private property and market relations as preferred one based on state planning, although the proportions later evened out. On the other hand, as early as June 1992, 50 percent of Russians said the government's economic reforms had failed, while only 5 percent said they were proceeding quite successfully. And Yeltsin's approval rating dropped inexorably. In this context, attempts to force the pace worked only at unusual times such as the winter of 1991–1992 when Yeltsin still had popularity to burn, or after his victory in October 1993.

If the reforms were too gradual, one has to wonder what a truly radical approach would have entailed. There was both a practical and a political problem. The practical problem was that to formally bankrupt all the enterprises that were insolvent in early 1992 would have been too indiscriminate. Even potentially profitable companies had been ensnared in the web of interenterprise debts: unpaid by their clients, they lacked working capital to buy supplies. To sort out which enterprises were doomed and which merely temporarily insolvent was impossible since no one knew yet how demand for different products would develop.

Politically, the costs of a genuinely radical approach were forbidding. A study of the Soviet economy in 1989 had estimated that "if all prices were released at once and privatization was carried out within five years, 40 million people would lose their jobs in the very first year of this process." Slowing the transition, as the government did with its half-measures, gave at least some workers time to find new jobs or entrepreneurial pursuits before their enterprises crashed. An overnight change of this magnitude would have been extremely painful and politically explosive, especially since vital social services—housing, heating, medical care—were often provided by major enterprises rather than government. As the economy minister in 1998 put it, "carrying out structural reform slowly" was "the price we pay for social peace."

Whether or not it was politically feasible, were these critics right on technical economic grounds to favor a faster strategy? Among postcommunist countries, those that reformed most rapidly did generally experience a quicker turnaround and smaller drop in official output. Throughout the 1990s, the European Bank for Reconstruction and Development tracked the progress of specific reforms in each of twenty-eight countries. Those that had reformed more radically by 1994 grew faster on average between 1990 and 1998 than those that reformed more slowly. This is true whether one considers price liberalization, trade reform, banking reform, or privatization, and whether one examines the former Soviet countries alone or takes them together with Eastern Europe. It does not follow that radical reforms caused faster growth—it could be that some other factor (political consensus, perhaps, or effective government) both enabled some countries to reform rapidly and also caused them to grow faster. But in light of this pattern, it is hard to imagine that slower reforms are better for growth.

Problems with privatization

Russia's privatization has been criticized on many, often conflicting grounds. Some argue that the program entrenched insiders—managers and workers—who were more interested in saving their jobs than in improving productivity. Others say it was too generous to outsiders—the oligarchs and raiders who bought up privatization vouchers to secure large blocs of shares. Some contend that the shares were sold too cheaply and made certain people too wealthy; everything should have been auctioned for cash to the highest bidder. Others say more should have been given away to the public. Some think not enough was done to close down the bankrupt companies; others that not enough restructuring took place. Some argue that privatization should not have begun until a comprehensive body of laws and regulations was in force to protect investors.

There are too many criticisms to evaluate all in detail here. But consider the main ones. Giving "insiders"—workers and managers—too much control is often thought to slow restructuring and prompt excessive wages and overstaffing. Chubais was correct, however, that without major concessions to the workers and managers privatization would not have occurred at all, and restructuring would have been even slower. In practice, workers gradually sold their shares to outsiders, and a wave of takeovers broke out in the late 1990s. In 1994, workers owned 50 percent of the average Russian enterprise; by 1999, their share was down to 36 percent. The share of outsider private owners rose from 15 to 47 percent. Between 1992 and 1996, one-third of medium and large enterprises replaced their general directors, and 12 percent did so in 1995 alone. Consolidated ownership was also emerging. By 2005, in 71 percent of medium and large industry and communications enterprises a single shareholder owned more than half the stock.

Such concentration of ownership brings with it greater inequality of wealth and income. However, without consolidated authority, companies rarely make the difficult decisions necessary to restructure. The spread of dominant owners in Russia brought it in line with most other countries. Rafael La Porta and colleagues studied twenty-seven of the richest countries and found that in Argentina, Hong Kong, Belgium, Greece, Israel, and Mexico, single families or individuals were controlling shareholders in at least half of the twenty largest publicly traded firms. A single control-ling shareholder existed in at least half the medium-sized firms sampled in Argentina, Australia, Hong Kong, France, Greece, Israel, Italy, South Korea, Mexico, Portugal, Sweden, and Switzerland. The United States, where almost all companies are widely held, is actually quite exceptional.

Minority shareholders were often mistreated as unscrupulous entre-preneurs went about consolidating their stakes. Investors sometimes found the value of their shares diluted by new share issues, or company profits drained away through shady marketing arrangements. Sometimes they learned too late that key decisions had been made at secret share-holder meetings in remote locations. Vasiliev's Securities Commission struggled doggedly against such fraud for a time, but it was too poorly staffed, with too little backup from law enforcement, to make much dif-ference.

Did privatization improve performance? Some disagreement remains on this score. Just about all authors of scientific studies agree that priva-tization to foreigners—in Russia and elsewhere—had a positive effect. Regarding privatization to Russians, different scholars read the record in different ways. Some see clear evidence that privatization improved performance. For example, two OECD economists, after examining fifty studies, concluded that: "for all the opprobrium heaped on Russian privatization policies, it is difficult to find any serious empirical study that does *not* show positive effects of privatization on restructuring." Privatized firms had higher productivity and faster growth of produc-tivity and of sales; they shed excess labor faster than state-owned firms, changed product lines more often, invested more in new equipment, and more often instituted pay for performance schemes. Guriev and Rachin-sky studied a large dataset of Russian enterprises in 2002 and found that, other things equal, productivity grew much faster in firms privatized to oligarchs than in state-owned firms. Privatization to other Russian own-ers had less clear effects.

Others are more skeptical. One recent survey reports that, looking at the non-Baltic former Soviet countries, privatization to domestic own-ers generated a negative or insignificant effect on productivity. (Even this survey found that privatized enterprises in Russia tended to pay higher wages and to have lower wage arrears than their state-owned counterparts.) Another study found that productivity in enterprises privatized to Russian owners at first fell below that in state enterprises, and then recovered after a few years. Since the data ended soon after the start of Russia's economic recovery, it is possible that the privatized firms surged ahead of their state-owned counterparts in the boom of the late 2000s.

In short, there is still room for legitimate disagreement about whether—and if so how quickly—privatization improved performance in Russia. This is hardly surprising given the large number of basket-case enterprises that were bound to fail whoever ended up owning them. For companies located thousands of miles from international markets, with poor transportation links, obsolete capital stock, and an order book filled in the past by state contracts, privatization was unlikely to perform any magic. However, the empirical record provides absolutely no evidence to support the claim made by some critics that privatization made things disastrously worse.

Loans for shares

The loans for shares program, under which a handful of well-connected businessmen bought stakes in twelve major Russian companies, epitomized for critics the errors and sins of Yeltsin's team of reformers. It was a "Faustian bargain," wrote one journalist, a "fiendishly complicated scheme," in which the young liberal ministers sold their souls to a cabal of unscrupulous tycoons. The program "deformed" the economy, "impoverished" the population, and laid "a corrupt, inegalitarian foundation for everything that came after it." Under loans for shares, wrote one Nobel Prize–winning economist, the country's best firms were stripped of their assets and "left on the verge of bankruptcy, while the oligarchs' bank accounts were enriched."

The critics were surely right that the conduct of the auctions appeared blatantly corrupt. Winners often turned out to be front companies for the auctioneers. Winning bids came in barely above the minimum price. One firm held its auction in a remote Siberian location, and reportedly got the local airport to close to reduce competition. Some would-be participants were barred on technicalities or on grounds that might also have applied to the winners. Excluded investors sometimes ripped open their envelopes to reveal offers for tens of millions of dollars more than the winning bid.

Unseemly as the auctions were, the claim that they deformed the economy is hard to sustain. To begin with, loans for shares involved only a relatively small slice of the market. Journalists characterized the twelve companies as "crown jewels" and "behemoths" of the Russian economy. Some were, indeed, impressive properties. Still, all the shares pledged by the state, valued at their market prices in late 1995, amounted to just 8–10 percent of the stock market's total capitalization. All the stakes together were worth less than those shares in Gazprom that the government had given away in return for privatization vouchers. Revenues of all twelve companies in 1995 totaled less than those of the national electricity company, UES.

Critics claimed the stakes were sold at shockingly low prices. To support this, they pointed to the much higher prices—per barrel of oil reserves—that oil company shares fetched in other parts of the world. However, as accountants know, a firm's value is not just the sum of its assets—one must also factor in its liabilities and the risks. The main companies came with billions of dollars of debt. As for the risks, they were paralyzing. Berezovsky and Khodorkovsky both solicited partners in the West. Their business contacts would not gamble a dollar in the deals, even at what the critics labeled "bargain basement prices." George Soros advised Berezovsky not to risk his own money and instead to sell out and flee Russia.

The first layer of risk was political. Gennady Zyuganov, the Communist leader, seemed poised to win the presidency in June 1996 and annul the loans for shares contracts, most likely without compensation. Even if Zyuganov lost, making a profit from the deals required a long list of things to go right. Mineral prices would have to recover from the depressed levels of the mid-1990s. The government would have to refrain from punitive taxation. The new investors would have to force out entrenched Soviet-era managers and the criminal gangs that controlled marketing in some of the enterprises. They would need to overcome "greenmail" by minority shareholders, and succeed in restructuring the companies. Even at low prices, the government found no bidders at all for other properties. In 1997, auctions of stakes in Tyumen Oil, Eastern Oil, Slavneft, LUKoil, and Rosneft had to be postponed or cancelled.

Critics also claimed the stakes had been sold too cheaply because the companies' share prices later increased. Reporters were outraged that in late 1997 some loans for shares enterprises were valued at many times their 1995 capitalizations. This, again, ignores the risks involved. Of course, with the prospect of President Zyuganov removed, the shares were worth more. As it happened, the high prices of 1997 did not last long. Soon afterwards, the markets crashed. By 1998 and 1999, the capitalizations of some loans for shares companies had fallen far below their values when the auctions took place. Had the oligarchs sold out at that point—as most Western investors did—some would have *lost* millions of dollars from the program.

The standard way to value firms is to look at what others were willing to pay for them—their share price and market capitalization—at the relevant point in time. One assumes the average buyer takes into account the company's debt, the risks, and other relevant considerations. Based on the companies' capitalizations in late 1995, the total value of the loans for shares stakes was $1.5 to $1.9 billion. The discounts relative to market prices received by the oligarchs were about 45 percent for Yukos, 16 percent for Sibneft, 13 percent for Norilsk Nickel, and 2 percent for Novolipetsk Steel. Major discounts are universal in privatization share offerings around the world; research suggests an average discount of 34 percent in emerging market countries, rising as high as 57 percent in Malaysia. The oligarchs' discounts appear comparable. The discounts were larger on some of the deals. As for most aspects of economic policy in the 1990s, the biggest beneficiaries turn out to be the "red directors"—well-placed, Soviet-era industrial managers. The managers of the oil companies LUKoil and Surgutneft, who used the program to increase their stakes in their companies, received discounts of 89 percent and 69 percent respectively.

Did the new owners depress investment, squash growth, and strip their corporations' assets? Initially, the oligarchs used all kinds of tricks to squeeze out minority shareholders. But after consolidating control, the tycoons set out to restructure their companies and attract foreign investors. They introduced international accounting standards, appointed independent board members, hired experienced foreign executives. Yukos and Sibneft engaged the oil service firms Schlumberger and Halliburton to improve efficiency. The results were dramatic. Between 1996 and 2001, pretax profits of Yukos, Sibneft, and Norilsk Nickel rose by 36, 10, and 5 times respectively (this despite only a modest increase in the oil price from $21 to $24 a barrel). Productivity—measured in dollars of revenue per worker—rose much faster in oligarch-owned oil companies than in similar state-owned enterprises or firms led by "red directors." The stock prices of the privatized firms also exploded. Between late 1996 and late 2003, Sibneft's market capitalization increased by more than ten times, and that of Yukos grew by more than fifty times in dollar terms; in the same period, the RTS market index increased by about three times.

What about asset stripping? The oligarchs diluted the stakes of minority shareholders initially and defaulted on loans to Western banks during the 1998 crisis. But after that, the companies' audited accounts suggest they were investing hundreds of millions of dollars each year building plants, replacing equipment, and developing their property. Between 1998 and 2003, annual "upstream" investment in the two oligarch-controlled oil companies Yukos and Sibneft increased by about 140 percent, faster than in the red-director-owned LUKoil and Surgutneftegaz.

Did loans for shares depress economic growth? Quite the opposite. Surging oil production in the oligarchs' companies helped to catalyze Russia's recovery in 1999–2004. Between 1999 and 2003, revenues of Yukos, Sibneft, and Norilsk Nickel grew much faster than GDP. Between 1999 and 2003, output of oil and gas condensate in the oil companies sold to oligarchs in loans for shares (Yukos, Sibneft, Sidanko) rose by 62 percent; that in the two companies sold to red directors (LUKoil and Surgutneftegaz) rose by 46 percent; while that of the three state-owned oil companies Rosneft, Tatneft, and Bashneft rose by just 15 percent.

As for "impoverishing" the population, there is no evidence of this. The poverty rate fell from 28 percent in the four years before loans for shares to 24 percent in the four years after the program, and had dropped to 13 percent by 2008. The wealth of Russian big businessmen expanded dramatically in the 2000s, which must have exacerbated wealth inequality. However, most of the new rich had nothing to do with loans for shares. By 2008, there were eighty-seven Russians on *Forbes*'s list of the world's 1,125 billionaires. Of these, only eight had any link to the program. Fortunes were created by the rise in world commodity prices, the restructuring of Russian enterprises, and the consequent stock market boom. In fact, only three of the seven original oligarchs that Berezovsky mentioned in his famous 1996 *Financial Times* interview—in which he claimed that he and six other bankers controlled half the Russian economy—won anything in loans for shares. Two—Mikhail Fridman and Pyotr Aven—complained angrily about their exclusion. Even Berezovsky only got in at the last minute. The loans for shares winners were a small subset of Russia's wealthy at the time, and are an even smaller subset today.

In short, loans for shares was a public relations disaster. It gave the appearance of brazen cronyism. However, the claim that the program enabled upstart oligarchs to ravage the economy is contradicted by most evidence. The stakes were less than 10 percent of the market, the prices were mostly not outrageously low, the biggest beneficiaries were not oligarchs but members of the old elite, and although the oligarchs pitilessly squeezed out minority shareholders, their companies performed extremely well, becoming models of corporate governance, and helping to fuel Russia's post-1999 commodity-driven boom.

Misconceived reforms caused the financial crisis of August 1998

Many observers viewed Russia's 1998 financial crisis with a kind of moralistic gratification. To some, it seemed to show the foolishness of neoliberal reforms. Others drew the opposite conclusion: the authorities, overspending and running up irresponsible budget deficits, had not been neoliberal enough. Both sets of critics agreed on one thing—the crash was an inevitable reckoning for years of government mistakes.

In fact, there was nothing inevitable about it. It is true that when the Asian currency crises sowed panic among international investors, Russia's poor fiscal record and high level of very short-term debt made it particularly vulnerable. But it is also quite likely that had there been no Asian financial crisis, Russia would have managed to get its GKO "pyramid" under control, gradually reduce its debt, and adjust its exchange rate policy to achieve stability. Even given the Asian events, it is possible that with a larger and faster commitment of funds by international institutions or foreign governments, Russia could have withstood the pressure. Historians know that they must guard against the temptation to view what actually happened as inevitable. Sometimes it wasn't.

By mid-1997, Russia was headed along an encouraging path. The first hints of economic growth were appearing, stimulating an increase in foreign direct investment from $2.5 billion in 1996 to $6.2 billion in 1997. The stock market—although narrow—was booming and had risen by more than six times between January 1996 and August 1997. As for government finances, the federal budget deficit had been coming down— from 9.2 percent of GDP in the last quarter of 1996 to 5.5 percent in the last quarter of 1997 and 3.0 percent in the third quarter of 1998. In the first half of 1998, the federal budget even had a primary surplus of 0.3 percent of GDP. Government debt as a percentage of GNP was lower than in the average G-7 country. Central Bank reserves had risen to about $25 billion. Debt service due had fallen from 34 percent of exports in 1993 to 13 percent in 1997. The average interest rate on GKOs had dropped from 176 percent a year in June 1996 to just 18 percent in July 1997. And the average maturity of GKOs and the analogous OFZ savings bonds had risen from less than three months at the end of 1995 to nearly thirteen months in September 1997.

Pressures on the ruble were extreme in 1998 because the drop in Asian demand for oil, along with increased OPEC production, had caused the oil price to crash—from about $23 a barrel at the end of 1996 to $9 in the middle of June 1998. This converted the Russian trade surplus to a deficit. But, although of course no one knew this at the time, the oil price would be rising again by early 1999, reaching $25 by the end of the year. Had Russia been able to survive these challenging months, the inflow of dollars from oil revenues would have supported the ruble's value. As late as August 13, 1998, Rudiger Dornbusch of MIT, perhaps the world authority on exchange rate economics, thought the Russian government could avoid devaluation completely. So did many in the investment world, such as Deutsche Bank's head of emerging markets research, David Folkerts-Landau. Moreover, had the international financial world not been overtaken by panic over the Asian events, it might well have been possible to engineer a moderate devaluation in late 1997, adjusting the ruble corridor downwards without alarming investors.

Had the crisis not occurred, had the first hints of growth in 1997 strengthened in 1998, the course of Russian history might have been quite different. The financial crisis resulted in the final discrediting of the economic reformers still in government—Nemtsov, Chubais, and Kirienko. Nemtsov's prospects as a potential presidential candidate in 2000 dimmed, and the Yeltsin team's search for a successor focused even more than before on individuals with a martial background. Absent the August default, the odds would have been much higher of a regime emerging that would have reconciled the creation of a more effective state with liberal democracy.

The reformers contributed to bringing about the crisis, but not in the way usually supposed. They did not rely on high interest government bonds out of recklessness; the dangers were obvious from the start, and they recognized them. However, there were no better feasible alternatives. Nor did they run up budget deficits out of mere inability to balance a checkbook. To force the economic heavyweights to pay more taxes in 1997–1998 would have required a political strategy to divide opponents and mobilize potential allies. The strategy they chose, in very difficult circumstances, was counterproductive. It united all economic elites against them—from the governors to the oligarchs and the Gazprom barons. They might have tried to pick off the oligarchs, one by one, as Putin did later, applying the legal force necessary to obtain the back taxes owed. They might have temporarily enlisted the support of Gazprom, offering concessions in return for larger tax payments in the short run. Instead, from 1996, they fought a war of attrition against all taxpayers simultaneously—threatening and negotiating with the regional governors, the oligarchs, and Gazprom—followed in 1998 by Fyodorov's cavalry charge in all directions at once.

Putinomics

Russia's sudden—and remarkably robust—recovery after the crisis of 1998 took almost everyone by surprise. Official GDP grew 5.4 percent in 1999, shot up 10.0 percent in 2000, and then averaged 6.6 percent over the next seven years. In part, this represented underground production coming into the light, but new output was also surging. Productivity—as measured by real GDP per worker—rose at an average rate of 5.5 percent a year in 2000–2006. From a fiscal and monetary disaster zone,

Russia became one of the most macroeconomically stable emerging markets, running large surpluses instead of deficits, and paying down its foreign debt from $133 billion in 1999 to $30 billion in December 2009. By mid-2008, the Central Bank had built up the third largest international reserves in the world, totaling $570 billion.

At the same time, the country plunged into a consumer boom. Retail trade, adjusted for inflation, more than doubled between 1999 and 2007, while the average real wage tripled. The stock market rose by more than eighteen times between July 1999 and July 2008, swelling the ranks of the immensely wealthy. In 2002, just seven Russians made the magazine *Forbes*'s annual list of billionaires; by 2008, as noted, there were eighty-seven. The number of Russians with more than $1 million in financial assets reached 136,000 in 2008, by one very conservative estimate. But incomes also increased among the poor. In 2000–2006, the fifth of the population with the lowest incomes saw their real incomes rise by 10 percent a year on average, compared to 12 percent a year for the richest fifth. The explosive growth would reverse, at least temporarily, in the international financial crisis of 2008–2009; by 2009, the number of Russian billionaires on the *Forbes* list had fallen back to thirty-two. But this came after eight years of consistently rapid development.

What caused the growth? The president's supporters attributed it to the political stability Putin created and the expert economic policies chosen by his ministers. His critics saw it as the fortuitous result of a sudden shift in world economic conditions—in particular, the surge in oil, gas, and other commodity prices—as well as a rebound from a severe contraction. Who is right?

One way to begin looking for an answer is to determine which parts of the economy were driving the growth. This appears to have changed over time. In 1999–2001, growth was broad based. During these three years, value added increased by 69 percent in communications, 47 percent in agriculture, 37 percent in construction, 32 percent in financial services, and 28 percent in industry. Within industry, production grew fastest in textiles (74 percent), light industry (52 percent), petrochemicals (56 percent), machine building (48 percent), and chemicals (45 percent). Output of tractors and farm machinery recorded an amazing 226 percent spurt.

From these figures, it is clear that growth in 1999–2001 was not driven just by oil and raw materials. Rather, this was the period when some of the firms that had survived the 1990s got their second wind. The ruble's sharp devaluation in 1998—and the associated drop in real wages—suddenly made traditional sectors more competitive. Exports surged from $74 billion in 1998 to $105 billion in 2000. A lower ruble also protected the domestic market: Western foods and cars became much more expensive. Imports fell in 1998–2000 from $58 billion to $45 billion.

The 1998 crisis also stimulated a shakeout of many of the most hopeless enterprises and the poorly managed banks. The next few years offered great opportunities for corporate raiders, who took over bankrupt companies on the cheap, integrating what valuable assets they had into larger groups. Productivity rose briskly in 2000 and 2001, except in sectors such as gas and electric power where the state retained a large role.

But then, in 2002–2004, the pattern changed. Those sectors previously helped by devaluation now suffered as the exchange rate appreciated and competition from imports resumed. Instead, the driver of growth in these years was oil extraction, which rose by 32 percent in 2002–2004, along with surging oil exports. The boom was overwhelmingly concentrated in private oil companies, especially the largest three (Yukos, TNK, and Sibneft), owned by leading oligarchs. Output of oil and gas condensate in state-owned companies grew just 15 percent between 1999 and 2003. In the three largest oligarch-owned companies, the increase was 91 percent!

Rising oil wealth stimulated demand for services. Construction, trade, and financial services all boomed. Those parts of manufacturing and transport that serviced the oil sector also got a boost. Railway machine building grew by 157 percent in 2001–2004. Why? With limited pipeline capacity, the oil companies needed a huge number of railway container cars to ship oil out of the country. Demand for consumer goods such as refrigerators, washing machines, and microwave ovens also increased as those with new oil-fueled paychecks remodeled their apartments.

Finally, in 2005–2007, things changed again. The oil boom ran into production constraints. Having increased by 11 and 9 percent in 2003 and 2004, oil extraction grew at just 2 percent a year in the next three years. Gas production even fell. The engine of growth became the soaring world *prices* of oil and gas. Between December 2004 and January 2008, the price for Russian Urals crude rose from $33 to $94 a barrel. Various studies have found a link between the oil price and Russian growth. Oil income flooding in continued to support demand for services, extending the boom of previous years. Value added in construction and trade both grew by more than 40 percent in three years, while financial services grew 38 percent, and transport and communications 25 percent. Real estate prices in Russia's large cities followed the oil price upward.

Why did oil output stagnate after 2004? In part, the oligarch companies had managed impressive gains by importing techniques to harvest leftover oil from the dying West Siberian fields. But these opportunities were drying up, and the companies had invested too little in developing new fields. By 2005, increasing oil production substantially—or even maintaining current levels—would require major investments. In 1999–2001, upstream investment had increased greatly for all types of oil companies. But after 2001, it began to fall. By 2004, real investment in fixed assets in oil extraction was only 70 percent of the 2001 level. Overall, fuel extraction was attracting a smaller share of total investment: the sector's share in fixed investment fell from 17.5 percent in 2001 to just 12.4 percent in 2005, rising slightly in the following two years. After 2004, the number of new fields coming on line fell each year, from ten fields in 2004 to two fields in 2007.

This fall in investment just as the world oil price was soaring is puzzling. It probably did not help that the government had turned to renationalization, using criminal prosecutions and tax claims to force private entrepreneurs out of their companies. The share of oil output produced by state-controlled companies rose from 24 percent in 2003 to at least 37 percent in 2007, mostly because of the government takeovers of Yukos and Sibneft. High tax rates on the oil companies' windfall profits may also have discouraged investment.

In short, the initial jump in growth in 1999–2000 was fueled by the devaluation; growth in 2001–2004 was mostly associated with increased minerals extraction, especially by private companies; and that in 2005–2007 resulted from soaring world oil and gas prices. Higher oil prices increased Russians' incomes and boosted demand for real estate, hotel rooms, financial services, and consumer goods, a few of which were now competitively produced by Russian companies. Restarting growth in the minerals sector—or in others—would subsequently require large investments.

To what extent do Putin's policies explain the recovery? That fiscal management improved tremendously after 1999 is undeniable. Of course, balancing the budget is far easier when the economy is growing rapidly. And the dramatic fiscal reforms of Putin's first years—the new Tax Code, cuts in income and profit taxes—had been prepared in detail by Yeltsin's reformers in the late 1990s. Implementation had begun even before the crisis of 1998. In encouraging these initiatives, along with efforts to reduce the bureaucratic harassment of small firms, Putin helped boost business confidence at a time when he could have made things worse. The number of small businesses increased, although still not very rapidly, and employment in small enterprises rose by five million between 1999 and 2006. Putin's governments also kept inflation low, built up reassuring currency reserves, and prevented alarming changes in the exchange rate.

Beyond the introduction of those early policies, it is hard to credit much of the improvement to Putin. If high growth were caused by Putin's reforms and the stability he created, one would expect to see businesses investing more. But, as noted, in the oil sector, after an initial increase in 2000 and 2001, investment fell rapidly. Economy-wide, fixed investment grew as a share of GDP in 1999–2001, but then dropped slightly and stabilized around 18 percent of GDP. This was below the average during Yeltsin's presidency—19.5 percent of GDP. Following Khodorkovsky's arrest, the share of long-term investment in total investment fell from 23 percent in 2000–2003 to 18 percent in 2004–2006. This suggests less rather than more business confidence.

There were good reasons to be nervous. Under Putin, a practice of *reyderstvo* ("raiding") became common, in which rivals would conspire to take over private companies using the instruments of the state. Police might be paid to investigate the main shareholder and threaten him with criminal prosecution if he did not sell his shares cheaply. Or the raiders might bribe tax authorities to present exorbitant bills for back taxes, forcing the company into bankruptcy, from which it would emerge in the raider's hands. The true motive for prosecutions was often unclear, so there are no reliable statistics on the extent of raiding. Still, experts claimed that thousands of companies were being targeted annually. Such practices were not new. But under Putin, they emanated at times from the innermost circles of the Kremlin. Both Berezovsky and Gusinsky were threatened with criminal prosecution if they did not hand over their television company shares. They did. Later, Khodorkovsky was jailed, and his oil company broken up and sold off after the tax service alleged it owed $28 billion in back taxes.

By the end of Putin's term, growth had come to depend heavily on the combination of foreign investment into the oil sector and growth in oil prices, which boosted demand for services. Preserving this growth in the medium term would require either continuing growth in oil prices or changes in policies to make investing more attractive. The plunge in oil prices during the financial crisis of 2008–2009 showed how volatile an economy dependent on hydrocarbon exports could be. In 2009, GDP fell by almost 8 percent, prompting a feverish search for technocratic fixes that could modernize and diversify the economy without liberalizing politics in a way that might threaten the ruling team's control (see Chapter 4). At the same time, the creative destruction unleashed by the crisis was limited by the Kremlin's determination to keep large enterprises from going bankrupt or laying off workers.

Summing Up

The disaster Russia's reformers inherited in 1991 was worse than most people realized. It had been caused both by failures of the Soviet system and by Gorbachev's destructive muddling. The transition was painful for all the former Soviet countries. To different degrees, they all needed to scrap their old industrial base and start again. There turned out to be a tradeoff. In general, countries that were quicker to pull the plug on their unsalvageable enterprises recovered faster, but usually at the cost of higher unemployment. Russia phased out its industrial dinosaurs more gradually, keeping unemployment much lower, but at the cost of slower recovery, lower average wages, and considerable waste of resources.

This outcome was less a deliberate strategy than Yeltsin's improvisational reaction to the pressures and arguments that cascaded over him in the mid-1990s—from economic reformers, pragmatists, seasoned industrialists, and the panoply of self-interested lobbyists. Those who favored a more radical approach must consider the possibility that this would have led to tens of millions of unemployed at a time when the government had few resources to fund a generous social insurance system or contain civil unrest. It is not clear a better alternative was available. Although the transition was painful, the drop in average living standards was nowhere near that suggested by the contraction in official GDP. And, even as real wages fell, families somehow managed to buy ever more televisions, washing machines, cars, and garden plots. They were allowed to privatize their state apartments, many of which became extremely valuable within ten or fifteen years.

Russia failed to beat high inflation for three years because a powerful coalition of banks and inefficient enterprises was determined to keep the enormous benefits it derived from inflationary policies. The reformers overcame this coalition only by coopting the leading banks and appeasing the enterprises with cheap energy and tax writeoffs. To restore fiscal balance, they needed to turn on their erstwhile allies, owners of the new, successful privatized companies, and find a way to make them pay more tax. But by attacking all simultaneously, they forged a coalition against themselves, exacerbating the risk of financial crisis in 1998. Still, had it not been for the Asian events, it is quite possible Russia would have had time to solve this problem as well.

Privatization led to clear improvements in the performance of potentially profitable enterprises, although it could not help the many that were truly unsalvageable. It made possible enormous rewards for the quick witted, the adventurous, and for those who had accumulated cash exploiting the uncertainties of transition. By 2007, Russia had the tenth largest stock market in the world, ahead of Italy and South Korea. The enormous appreciation in Russian shares made early investors very rich. This would certainly have been true without the favoritism shown at times by the privatizers towards certain investors such as the beneficiaries of "loans for shares." Such favoritism—which was not even used effectively to forge reform coalitions—was the reformers' biggest mistake.

Russia's vigorous recovery after 1998 owed a little to Putin's early liberal reforms. But after 2001, it was driven by oil—first by expanded production, especially in the oligarch-owned companies, and later by rising oil prices and revenues, which fed demand for domestic services. Amid signs of increasing corruption and politicization of the legal system, investment stagnated in the late Putin years. By the time the financial crisis of 2008–2009 struck, the model of commodity-based growth seemed to be running out of steam.

CHAPTER 7

The Logic of Politics

An entrenched Marxist dictatorship, led by a clique of corrupt septuagenarians, suddenly opens up, choosing a young leader with new ideas. This leader encourages citizens to speak freely, introduces competitive elections (for others, not himself), and accidentally destroys the mechanism that coordinates the country's economy. The state he rules splits into fifteen pieces. A rival with the legitimacy of popular election takes over in the largest fragment and lays the foundations of a market economy, freeing prices and trade and privatizing state enterprises. He is fought to a standstill by revanchist forces, which prevent any more reform. Just as it seems this deadlocked system is sure to last a long time, a new leader appears and quickly recentralizes power. Obstacles evaporate. He further liberalizes the economy, and then whittles away civic freedoms while encouraging a clan of security service veterans to grab the commanding heights of business.

How to explain this cascade of events? The twists and turns of Russia's politics in the last twenty-five years seem to defy any simple accounting. Observers have pointed to a number of factors. While some of these certainly figure in the story, none by itself gets us very far.

First, looking at Putin's authoritarian turn, some see the influence of Russia's thousand-year history of autocracy. Subjected to princes, khans, tsars, and then commissars, Russians are said to have acquired a culture of "submission to strong and willful authority." At the same time, the struggle to survive in a harsh climate is thought to have bred a collectivist mentality and a suspicion of outsiders. These factors combined, so it is said, to produce a predilection for strong, unconstrained leaders. Russia, concludes the historian Richard Pipes, is "committed to authoritarian government."

A related argument puts the onus of Putin's reversion on Russia's geography: the country is simply too far east to have a liberal democracy. Lands beyond the Baltics missed the formative experiences of Europe—Roman law, feudalism, the Renaissance, the Reformation, and the Enlightenment. While serfdom ended early in the West, it lasted into the nineteenth century in the East. Moreover, the prospect of being welcomed into the European Union and other Western clubs provided a powerful incentive for the countries closest to the West to reform their politics quickly after the Berlin Wall fell. As a result, a spectrum of freedom runs today from West to East in Europe, and Russia is on the wrong side of the divide.

Other observers are convinced that the driving force behind political change in Russia is oil. Countries rich in hydrocarbons tend to have less democratic governments. Some also see a connection within particular countries between changes over time in world oil prices and cycles of freedom and repression. In states that have weak institutions and that are dependent on oil revenues, writes *New York Times* columnist Tom Friedman, "the price of oil and the pace of freedom always move in opposite directions." Russia, he argues, is a perfect example. After the oil price plunged in the early 1980s, Gorbachev began his political reforms; when the price soared after 1998, Putin began rolling back democratic freedoms.

Yet another way to understand Russia's abrupt transitions is to see in them the phases of a social revolution. The great revolutions—in England, France, Russia, and to some extent America—progressed through a common series of stages. First, the old regime falls and a moderate reformer takes power. He is overthrown by radicals, who introduce a reign of terror and mobilize the population behind a utopian ideology. The radicals are, in turn, deposed, initiating a period of stabilization ("Thermidor"), in which new elites, enriched by the redistribution of property, dominate. Nationalism replaces the radical ideology. Finally, a dictator appears who promises to restore a strong state. Applying this schema to Russia since 1985, one can see Gorbachev as the moderate reformer, Yeltsin as the radical, and Putin as the postrevolutionary dictator.

A fifth approach traces the varied outcomes to the personalities and ideas of the leaders in power. In the flux of postcommunist politics, writes the economist Anders Åslund, Russia's leaders had unusually broad opportunities to choose the country's direction: "Naturally, the political leaders did not decide everything themselves, but when they focused on a goal, the effect was truly amazing." The "ideas of the leaders were extremely important and were to mold their policies." A great deal depended, therefore, on the incumbent president's aims and his ability to focus. "The Russian capitalist revolution bears the imprint of one giant, Boris Yeltsin. Both successes and failures were direct consequences of his personal insights and frailties."

Most of these perspectives point to something important. But none by itself explains very much. A certain view of geography and history may make Putin's rollback of civic freedoms seem inevitable. If so, this renders the democratic breakthrough of the early 1990s all the more puzzling. The most remarkable thing about Russia's politics in the last twenty-five years is not that authoritarian features sometimes resurface but that freedom has made such inroads. Not since at least the fifteenth century have Russians lived as freely as they have in the last two decades.

Moreover, surveys do not suggest that "ancient authoritarian traditions" or anticapitalist collectivism have much influence over Russians today. Far from submitting quietly, citizens have expressed overwhelming opposition at times to their "strong and willful" rulers, condemning military adventures in Chechnya, and calling on their leaders to step down. Demonstrations and strikes were frequent in the 1990s. In 1999, 92 percent of Russians said they disapproved of their president, and 63 percent said they were ready to join protests demanding his resignation. Under Putin, from December 2002 a majority opposed the military operation in Chechnya and favored negotiating with the Chechen rebels. At least thirteen antiwar demonstrations in Moscow and St. Petersburg in the mid-2000s attracted more than one thousand participants. Rather than favoring autocracy, Russians have consistently told pollsters that their leaders should be chosen in free and fair elections (see Chapter 10). In December 1991, 29 percent of supposedly collectivist Russians said they wanted to open their own business, and 24 percent wanted to buy shares.

A spectrum of freedom does run from West to East. By 2010, the countries of Central and Eastern Europe were all stable democracies; the Central Asian states had different brands of autocracy. However, European Russia, along with its Western neighbors, lies in an ambiguous zone around the middle of this spectrum. Regimes there range from the dictatorship of Aleksandr Lukashenko to the relatively competitive democracy of Moldova, with Russia and Ukraine in between. Countries in this group are notable for the lack of geographical determinism. In some, regimes have changed markedly over time. At the same time, the dividing line between democracies and autocracies has been moving eastward, just as in the past democracy spread from the North of Europe to its South. In the 1990s, some of the Balkan states—Serbia, Croatia—had authoritarian governments. In the last decade, they have converged towards their more democratic Western neighbors. Even if democracy is unlikely soon to overtake Uzbekistan and Turkmenistan, there is little reason to think Russia's illiberal turn was predetermined by its location.

Oil and gas clearly feature in Russia's politics. However, they cannot by themselves explain the country's recent political changes. We need to distinguish between supposed effects of the oil *price* and those of the *income* a country receives from oil, which depends on both price and output. Scholars who have looked for a systematic relationship between the oil price and democracy have failed to find one. The two line up as predicted in a few countries. But it is not clear that they do so more often than they would purely by chance. By contrast, there is evidence that countries with significant oil and gas income tend to be less democratic than those without, at least under certain conditions. It turns out, however, that the effect is diminishing; it is much stronger for the first $100 per capita of oil revenues than for the fifth. In countries already receiving significant income from petroleum, even large increases or decreases have only a small impact on the nature of the regime. In 1985, Russia was already a major oil producer. Consequently, international experience suggests that changes in the country's oil income since 1985 can explain only a very small fraction of the observed change in the country's politics.

In some ways, the revolutionary template seems to fit Russia's recent history. There was something reminiscent of Aleksandr Kerensky—the dithering head of the 1917 Provisional Government—about Gorbachev, caught between reactionaries and radical reformers. But other details correspond less well. Applying the traditional stages, one finds that many of the key battles took place not in the streets but inside Gorbachev's or Yeltsin's head. Gorbachev is both the ruler of the ancien régime and the moderate revolutionary who overthrows him. Yeltsin starts out as the "radical," but, around 1994, has to guillotine his inner Robespierre to preside over the Thermidor. Unlike the classic revolutions, Russia's was mostly nonviolent and democratic. Instead of storming the Bastille or the Winter Palace, Russia's radicals spent their time running for election, holding referenda, and participating in endless parliamentary debates. This "revolution" was also an inside job. Both moderates and radicals were former Politburo regulars. They imposed no reign of terror, no utopian ideology. Theirs was an uprising *against* utopias and terror, which aimed only to make Russia more like other countries. Finally, even if Russia's transition were more like the historic revolutions, identifying the parallel would not reveal much about why events took the course they did.

The ideas of Russia's leaders certainly mattered. So, to a lesser degree, did their personalities. But what is striking in retrospect is how much more the president's ideas mattered at some moments than at others. At certain points, a leader's conceptions did change the course of history. Had any other Politburo member been chosen to succeed Chernenko in 1985, Russia would undoubtedly have developed quite differently, at least for a while. Yet at other moments leaders' proposals were rejected or simply ignored, buried in Duma committees or blocked by coalitions of hostile elites. The puzzle is why leaders' ideas sometimes find traction but at other times bounce off the hard surface of reality and disappear into the ether.

In this chapter, I offer a new interpretation of the logic that drove Russia's political transition, one that emerges from a close look at the data and which, I believe, fits the evidence better than any of those mentioned so far. Oil comes into the story, as do the ideas of leaders. History, geography, and revolutionary dynamics are in the background. The story begins with changes in public opinion and, specifically, the popularity of incumbent presidents.

The Popularity of Presidents

Plotted over time, the approval ratings of Russia's leaders resemble a mountain canyon (Figure 7.1). On the left, when polling starts in December 1989, Gorbachev is still extremely popular: 81 percent of Russians say they approve of his performance. But the next years see his support collapse. By February 1991, he is down to 49 percent, and, although he recovers a little, by late 1992 he is at 19 percent. As Russians abandon Gorbachev, they rally to Yeltsin, whose rating soars from 55 percent in December 1989 to almost 90 percent a year later. Then Yeltsin begins his own bumpy descent to a low of 6 percent in March 1999. Putin, appointed prime minister in August 1999, shoots up the scale during his first months, reaching 84 percent in mid-January 2000 as he settles in as acting president. Throughout his two terms, his approval remains between 61 and 87 percent. In 2008, Medvedev starts 10 points below his mentor and paces Putin—now prime minister again—from below.

The pattern in Figure 7.1 is quite unusual. Yeltsin's spectacular

Figure 7.1 Popular approval of Russian leaders, 1989–2009

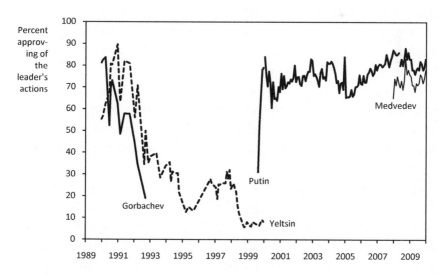

Sources: VCIOM and Levada Center polls, from http://sofist.socpol.ru/ and www.Russiavotes.org.
Note: The questions vary slightly in the 1990s, but all ask whether or to what extent the respondent "approves" of the president's performance, actions, or handling of his responsibilities.

plunge—from 90 to 6 percent—exceeds that of any U.S. president since World War II. Nor has any American president in this period equaled Putin's sustained popularity.

Thus, an obvious first question is whether the poll data can be trusted. The numbers in Figure 7.1 come from surveys taken by the organization VCIOM and later the Levada Center. VCIOM was founded in 1988 by two of the country's most respected sociologists and soon acquired a reputation as the most independent of the country's half dozen leading polling organizations. This was thought to be why, in 2003, the government repossessed VCIOM and forced out its director, Yury Levada. Levada and most of his colleagues set up the Levada Center, which continued the polls.

In late 1989, VCIOM began asking representative samples of voting-age Russians—at first sporadically, then from late 1996 more regularly—if they approved or disapproved of the country's political leaders. The respondents were interviewed in person, in their homes. VCIOM's professionalism is suggested by the many Western pollsters that have worked with Levada's team (such as World Public Opinion and the New Russia Barometer) and by the list of the center's international clients and partners (including the World Bank, the World Health Organization, the International Labor Organization, and the Ford Foundation). Given Levada's history as a semidissident—he was fired from Moscow State University in the 1960s for "ideological errors in his lectures"—and the takeover of VCIOM in 2003, it is hard to believe his team was slanting results to please the Kremlin. Nor does it seem plausible, given the poll results, that many of the respondents were inhibited from criticizing the country's leaders. In September 1999, for instance, more than 90 percent said they disapproved of President Yeltsin's performance.

Economic Underpinnings

What caused the dramatic changes in the ratings of Russia's leaders? Of course, individual Russians had various reasons to like or dislike their presidents. Some may have been motivated by ideology; others probably responded to the president's image. However, statistical analysis suggests that one set of factors was particularly important in determining changes in the average rating—the public's beliefs about the state of the economy. Approval of Russian presidents was higher when citizens saw the economy doing well, and lower when they saw it performing poorly. Like people in many parts of the world, Russians had greater confidence in their leaders during booms than in recessions.

Gorbachev's popularity survived the revelations of glasnost about the brutality and inefficiency of the Soviet system. But, as discussed in Chapter 1, his rating crashed in 1990 as shortages of consumer goods and food became critical. Viewed as a tribune of the opposition, Yeltsin soared in 1990. But after he was elected president of Russia, the deteriorating economy dragged his rating down as well. As Putin took over, the economy had already begun a vigorous recovery, which would last through his two terms. This helped sustain his extremely high approval. As the financial crisis of 2008–2009 sapped economic optimism, both Putin's and Medvedev's ratings dropped.

The link between perceptions of the economy and presidential approval can be seen in Figure 7.2. The dotted line plots an index of positive economic sentiment constructed by adding the percentage of respondents who said Russia's economic situation was "average," "good," or "very good" to the percentage that expected "some improvement" or a "significant improvement" in the next few months. Thus, the index captures both positive assessments of the current economy and optimism about the future. I have superimposed on this the approval ratings of the currently serving presidents (Yeltsin, Putin, and Medvedev). The parallel between the two lines is striking. Using more elaborate tests, I have confirmed that there is a strong, statistically significant link between perceptions of the economy and approval of the president, and that the former go a long way towards explaining trends in the latter.

Of course, economic perceptions do not explain everything. Other factors also mattered. Yeltsin's episodes of boorish behavior apparently cost him some popularity. When the television networks showed him in Berlin in August 1994 grabbing the baton and tipsily conducting a police band, his rating fell the next month. Putin's rating rose after he restored the Soviet-era music to the national anthem and after he arrested the oligarch Khodorkovsky. Putin's rise in the polls in late 1999 is particularly interesting. Most observers attributed this to Putin's resolute response to

Figure 7.2 Economic sentiment and presidential approval, Russia, 1991–2009

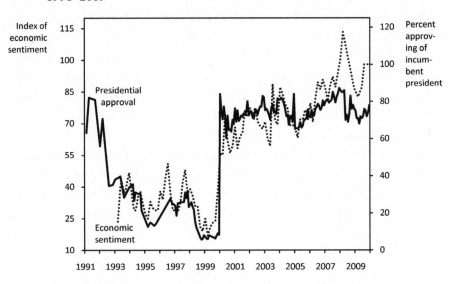

Sources: VCIOM, Levada Center, and author's calculations.
Note: Economic sentiment is percent saying "very good," "good," or "average," when asked "How would you evaluate Russia's economic situation?" plus percent saying "a significant improvement," or "some improvement," when asked "What awaits Russia in coming months in the economy?" Only available from 1993. Missing values interpolated.

the warlord Shamil Basayev's invasion of Dagestan and the subsequent bombing of Russian apartment buildings. "People believed that he, personally, could protect them," Yeltsin wrote in his memoirs. "That's what explains his surge in popularity."

This is quite plausible. However, support for Putin's tough policy on Chechnya cannot explain why his rating stayed so high. After initially rallying behind their commander in chief, Russians rapidly turned against the Chechen war. By October 2003, just 21 percent favored continuing the military operation, compared to 61 percent who wanted to start peace negotiations. On balance, the second war—like the first—seems to have weighed on the president's popularity rather than boosting it. At the same time, polls suggest Russians did *not* believe Putin could protect them from terrorists. Between 2002 and 2006, fewer than one-third said this on polls; from 53 to 76 percent said the authorities could not protect them.

As Figure 7.2 shows, economic sentiment also suddenly shot up at the end of 1999. The recovery had finally begun. Between August 1999 and June 2000, the average wage, adjusted for inflation, rose by about 20 percent. Simultaneously, wage arrears fell and the demand for workers increased by more than one third. As Russians began to feel the improvement, their assessment of the economy brightened. Simulations suggest that even without any terrorist attacks or Chechen war, the rating of Putin—or any other new Kremlin candidate for president—would have surged upwards, driven by the revival of economic confidence. The apartment bombings and Basayev's incursion seem to have hastened by a few months a jump in approval that would have occurred anyway.

It could be that Russians' perceptions of the economy reflected not its true state but a rosy image fed to them by government propagandists. Under Putin, after all, television news coverage was carefully managed from the Kremlin. I did find evidence of such media effects. During certain presidential campaigns—in 1996 and 2004, although not so clearly in 2000—average assessments of the economy improved by more than merited by objective conditions, and sank again after the vote. Russians also rated economic conditions slightly better when they had greater confidence in their president. On the whole, though, their views of the economy tracked objective economic indicators such as unemployment, job openings, the average real wage, the average pension, and wage arrears. For the most part, Russians were not fooled by propaganda; they correctly perceived the economic deterioration of the 1990s and the recovery of the 2000s. They blamed the first on Yeltsin, and credited Putin for the second.

One way to see the importance of economic conditions is to imagine what would have happened to Yeltsin's approval rating had he governed during a period when the public's view of the economy was as positive as it was under Putin. With statistics, one can make the thought experiment concrete. I estimated the relationship between the public's assessment of the economy and approval of Yeltsin during his time in office. Then, using this estimated relationship, I projected what Yeltsin's popularity would have been had Russians' assessments of the economy been the same as in the corresponding month of Putin's presidency. The results are in Figure 7.3, along with Yeltsin's actual rating (I use the public's average rating of Yeltsin on a 10-point scale here rather than the percent of respondents approving of the president's performance, since the latter series was only collected regularly from 1996). Of course, we need to take such artificial reruns of history with a grain of salt. Still, it seems that Yeltsin would have left office extremely popular. Similar simulations suggest that had the economy under Putin been rated as poorly as it was under Yeltsin, Putin's popularity would have been much lower.

If the economy's performance, as perceived by the public, shaped the president's popularity, what determined economic performance? Did booms and busts reflect the government's policies and management skills? Or were they caused by extraneous factors such as world market conditions?

This varied. As discussed in Chapter 1, Gorbachev bears considerable responsibility for the economic deterioration on his watch. He inherited a system in chronic decline that needed to adjust to a sharp fall in the oil price—a challenging predicament, for sure, but one that he made much worse. His improvisations led to the greatest expansion of political

Figure 7.3 What if perceived economic conditions under Yeltsin had been the same as under Putin?

Sources: VCIOM and author's calculations. See Treisman. "Presidential Popularity in a Hybrid Regime."

freedom in modern history. But they also produced the macroeconomic explosion that detonated just as his successor took over. Yeltsin inherited this mess from Gorbachev. One can debate the details of policy, but there was absolutely nothing he could have done from 1991 on that would have prevented a painful economic crash. Despite this, he managed to push through reforms that created the bases of a market economy and a democratic political system.

Putin, by contrast, had the good luck to come to office just as the positive effects of his predecessor's reforms and the ruble's devaluation were kicking in, and as the oil price was rising (see Chapter 6). By the time he reached the Kremlin, the economy had been rebuilt. Russia had a market system with free prices, private property, and rising stock values. Putin deserves credit for cutting tax rates, balancing the budget, and setting up reserve funds to save part of the windfall oil revenues. But his regime's expropriation of private businesses discouraged investment, slowing Russia's growth. And he used the leverage derived from favorable economic conditions to circumscribe political freedoms. He won his exceptional ratings in the lottery. Medvedev inherited most of this popularity, starting out as president with the approval of 70 percent of Russians.

Getting Things Done

As a leader's popularity rose or fell, so did his ability to enact change. Losing the public's confidence in 1990–1991, Gorbachev saw his authority drain away. Heads of the fifteen Soviet republics pressed ever more insistently for autonomy, calling hundreds of thousands of demonstrators into the streets and refusing to implement central policies. At the same time, orthodox Communists in the security forces started disregarding instructions and edging towards outright revolt. In 1987–1989, Gorbachev could carry the country with him as he singlehandedly decided to loosen the reins in Eastern Europe, begin rapid nuclear disarmament, and undercut the party's authority. By 1991, he had a hard time getting the leaders of the republics to take his phone calls.

In late 1991, close to the peak of his popularity, Yeltsin could get a parliament of moderate communists to approve the dissolution of the

Soviet Union, accept his plan for radical economic reform, and authorize him to rule by decree and appoint regional governors. Ninety-four percent of deputies voted to ratify the CIS accords, and 98 percent endorsed his economic reform proposal. By mid-1992, with his approval down to 35 percent, his reform efforts had been stymied. The fickle deputies attacked him on precisely the policies they had earlier approved. As his rating bumped still lower, he found himself constrained at every step by a hostile parliament, obstreperous governors, and unruly businessmen.

By contrast, opposition vaporized as Putin's ratings shot up in late 1999. Suddenly, the parliament was loyal, the governors docile, and the population quiescent. Some of the businessmen took a little longer to get the message, but those that risked offending the Kremlin found themselves isolated. Tax reform bills that had been blocked for years sailed through the Duma. Within two years, the opposition movement of mayor Yury Luzhkov, which had fought a propaganda war for the Duma in December 1999, had agreed to merge with Putin's party of acolytes.

Getting new policies enacted required, first of all, legislation in parliament. Yeltsin never had a reliable majority in either the Supreme Soviet or the Duma. But as his popularity dwindled, it grew harder and harder to get loyalists elected. In late 1990, pro-government factions held about 24 percent of the Supreme Soviet seats. In the 1993 election, pro-government blocs won 19 percent of the Duma seats, and in 1995 they won 14 percent. Even between elections, some deputies always defected to the opposition.

From 1999, the process went into reverse. Riding on Putin's coattails, the Unity bloc along with the loyalist Our Home Is Russia won 18 percent of the seats that December. In 2003, pro-government parties won 58 percent of seats, and in 2007 they managed 78 percent. Elections in this period were subject to increasing manipulation. But the surge in support for pro-Putin blocs reflected more than that. Credible polls by the Levada Center and other organizations showed a consistent rise for the pro-Kremlin parties and a sharp fall in the popularity of the opposition (see Chapter 10). Between elections, an avalanche of defections—both by individual deputies and, as in Luzhkov's case, whole blocs—increased Putin's advantage. Between December 2003 and October 2007—without any new parliamentary election—the rush to jump on Putin's bandwagon increased the pro-executive factions from 58 to 75 percent of the seats.

As Yeltsin's rating plunged, passing each scrap of legislation required the patience of Sisyphus. Chubais recalled bringing back the same decree three or four times with slightly different phrasing until it slipped past the Duma's defenses (see Chapter 6). Enacting the budget required creative deal making and tactical finesse. Deputies from regions where Yeltsin's ratings were falling fastest were particularly resistant. Those representing regions where support for Yeltsin had dropped in 1991–1993 were more likely to vote against the government's proposals at the March 1993 Congress session than those from regions where his support had held steady. Government bills that the Duma passed were sometimes vetoed by the Federation Council. This occurred 12 percent of the time under Yeltsin in 1994–1999, but only 6 percent of the time under Putin in 2000–2004.

Even when the reformers got their way, the delays grew ever longer. In 1994, it took less than six months on average to pass major, non-budgetary bills. By 1999, it took almost two years. Under Putin, the time required fell back to about six months. Momentous pieces of legislation made it through in just days. Putin's bill to replace the progressive income tax with a single, flat rate of 13 percent was signed into law just over two months after its introduction in the Duma. Yeltsin had to fight off repeated attempts to impeach him—in December 1992, March 1993, September 1993, July 1995, and June 1998 to April 1999. All failed, although the 1999 effort came quite close. No one dreamed of trying to impeach the more popular Putin.

The parliament was just one of the roadblocks in Yeltsin's path. A second set lay in the country's regions, where governors, emboldened by Yeltsin's plunging rating, ignored government instructions, appropriated federal property, and coopted locally based federal bureaucrats to their team. They remitted less tax revenue to the center, undermining the federal budget. Some actively supported the Communist opposition. Local politicians apparently took Yeltsin's local popularity into account. Where support for the president had been dropping relatively faster, the governors were apt to take a tougher line.

A critical moment came in September 1993, as Yeltsin declared a state of emergency and ordered the Supreme Soviet to dissolve. Khasbulatov and Rutskoy holed up in the White House with a collection of opposition deputies. In the midst of this national crisis, fifteen regional governors spoke out against Yeltsin's action or even rallied behind the parliament. Local trends in Yeltsin's popularity help to explain which governors took such a stand. In regions where Yeltsin's support had fallen during the previous two years, 30 percent of the governors publicly opposed him; where Yeltsin's support had risen, only 11 percent did.

Putin, his rating soaring above 80 percent, had no such problems. Previously defiant governors were suddenly his strongest supporters. They smiled sportingly and hardly emitted a peep as he stripped them of their seats in the Federation Council (and associated parliamentary immunity), sent presidential prefects to watch over them, cut their share of budget revenues from 54 percent in 1999 to 35 percent in 2005, and finally abolished popular elections for their posts.

Presidential approval did not reshape the political arena all by itself. The surge in Putin's rating was part of a self-reinforcing syndrome of positive developments—higher tax revenues, expanded government spending (in real terms), revived public optimism—all of which were fueled by the economic recovery and which together helped sustain the image of an effective president. The belief that the president was effective, in turn, increased his public support. But the president's popularity was not just a function of presidential power. His rating was a barometer that other actors used to gauge the political weather. High ratings signaled to opponents of the Kremlin that they would be foolish to stick their necks out. If they did, they would find themselves alone, easy prey for the president's enforcers. When the mercury sank, however, this signaled to the same self-interested elites that it was safe to pile on, ripping apart the president's plans and grabbing power and money for themselves.

Although it made enacting change much harder, low presidential popularity did not make it impossible. Even in the trying circumstances of the mid-1990s, Yeltsin's team managed to drive through some reforms. This required great tactical skill and the correct choice of techniques (as discussed in Chapter 6). Conversely, even with extremely high ratings, Putin failed to achieve many of his stated objectives. He was defeated not so much by political opposition as by the contradictions among his goals and the complexity of the problems.

A Few Implications

To recapitulate, Russia's severe economic contraction after 1989 and vig-orous recovery after 1998 reshaped the balance of political forces. As the economy shrank, so did support for Gorbachev and then Yeltsin; as it rebounded, this helped sustain Putin's soaring ratings. The president's ratings, and the economic performance that underlay them, determined whether the president was free to enact and implement new policies or was blocked by coalitions of opponents. When presidents were very pop-ular—Gorbachev in 1987–1989, Yeltsin in 1989–1991, and Putin from 1999 on—they enjoyed broad leeway to choose their country's path. When their ratings sank, they were reduced to running in place and fighting for survival.

Russia's oil and gas income mattered in this story, to the extent that it affected the economy's performance. But this was not uniform over time. For instance, the boom in 1999–2001, during which Putin's popu-larity first surged, owed more to the competitiveness created by devalu-ation (see Chapter 6). It was only after 2005 that the oil price became the principal driver of growth. (The growth in oil output and incomes in 2001–2003 benefited both the Kremlin and the remaining oil oli-garchs, setting up a clash between them.) At the same time, although the booming economy and higher tax revenues generated by oil and gas after 1999 gave the president considerable freedom of maneuver, they did not guarantee that he would use this freedom to make the govern-ment more authoritarian. This decision belonged personally to Putin. Had Russia in 2000 had a president with deep democratic convictions, he might have used the economic revival and the associated surge in support for the incumbent to entrench liberal institutions. Likewise, the oil price plunge of the 1980s did not make Gorbachev's political open-ing inevitable. On the contrary, a more pragmatic strategy of political self-preservation would have been to tighten control domestically, cut spending, and adjust painfully to the new international conditions. That is what Andropov would have done. That Gorbachev responded in the way he did must be attributed to him personally. At certain moments, leaders' ideas were extremely important.

My account here differs from conventional views of Russian politics in several ways. In characterizing political systems, most people start by looking at their institutions—the rules and structures of government. How does the constitution divide responsibilities among different branches of the state and between the central and regional authorities? Is parliament elected by a majoritarian or a proportional electoral rule? How great are the formal powers of the president vis-à-vis the parliament? Surprisingly, in Russia since 1991, such distinctions explain very little. The system has operated very differently at different times even without any significant change in institutions. Conversely, major reforms of institutions have occurred with hardly any visible effect on the outcomes of politics.

In December 1993, Yeltsin introduced a constitution with presidential powers so extensive that critics called it authoritarian. It replaced a constitution that had assigned sovereign—indeed, dictatorial—authority to the legislature. Did this mean that henceforth Yeltsin could enact and implement the reforms he favored? Not at all. He remained blocked at every step by the familiar coalition of opponents—the opposition majority in the new Duma, defiant governors, hostile bureaucrats, and self-interested business elites. There was no noticeable increase in the president's effectiveness. What victories he achieved were the result of painstaking preparation, persistence, and tactical skill.

The rules for selecting regional leaders changed twice. From late 1991, Yeltsin had the right to hire and fire the governors; during the mid-1990s, he gradually authorized gubernatorial elections; finally in 2004 Putin reinstated presidential nomination, subject to confirmation by the regional legislatures. Did the center's practical leverage over the governors rise and fall in line with these institutional changes? Elected governors were sometimes less cooperative than their appointed counterparts. But this was a relatively small effect. Context was far more important. The peak of regional challenges—autonomy demands, withholding of federal tax remittances, threats of local disorder—came in 1992–1993, precisely the years in which almost all governors were still appointed. Later, Putin's success in taming the governors came not after he reintroduced presidential nomination, but before that in 2000–2002, while they were still popularly elected.

Indeed, the greatest change in politics during this period—the major recentralization of authority and reassertion of presidential power—occurred between 1999 and 2002 with almost no simultaneous change in political institutions. Putin did not amend the constitution once during his presidency, although he could have done so quite easily. Between 1999 and 2002, he made only minor changes to the rules and procedures of government. And yet his ability to get his way was incomparably greater than Yeltsin's, and the pattern of political outcomes was completely different. There were no formal changes to speak of in the constitutional role and powers of the Duma. Yet by 2004, it had turned from a formidable obstacle blocking Kremlin projects into a rubber stamp. Putin's personal power rested less on an authoritarian state than on an authoritarian moment.

A second misconception concerns the importance of public opinion. In Russia, the political elite is often thought to be insulated from the population and unconcerned with the attitudes and preferences of ordinary citizens. I have argued that public opinion actually plays a central role, defining the president's freedom of maneuver. Popular presidents can achieve far more than unpopular ones. In this, Russia resembles many other countries, including the United States, where leaders' effectiveness rises and falls with their poll numbers.

From the dawn of Russia's democratic politics, officials have paid a great deal of attention to polling data. Running in the first competitive election in 1989, Yeltsin already claimed to be tracking all available polls "including those of the Americans" (see Chapter 2). Under Putin and Medvedev, the Kremlin commissioned numerous surveys and closely monitored changes in opinion in the country's regions. Besides keeping an eye on their own ratings, Russia's leaders have taken positions in line with the prevailing majority view on many policy issues. Both Yeltsin's initiation of radical economic reform in 1991 and his decision to slow its pace from late 1992 matched public opinion at the time. His dissolution of the parliament in September 1993 was supported by the public, as was his use of force to end the standoff. Yeltsin's main unpopular decisions were starting the first Chechen war (the public backed him both in ending this war in 1996 and in starting the next in 1999) and firing Primakov as prime minister in the spring of 1999.

Putin's emphasis on restoring order, attacking the oligarchs, and increasing the state's role in the economy were all extremely popular. His nods to nostalgia such as the reinstatement of the Soviet era music to the national anthem also bought him popularity. Both his cooperation with the United States after 9/11 and his gradual slide into resentful ambivalence also mirrored the evolution of Russian public opinion. In October 2001, 61 percent of Russians felt "very good" or "mostly good" about the United States, and 62 percent expressed willingness to give blood to help the victims of the 9/11 terrorist attack. By January 2009, after the Iraq war, the U.S. recognition of Kosovo, and Washington's support for Georgia in its 2008 war with Russia, the percentage feeling good about the United States had fallen to 38 percent, while 49 percent "felt bad" about the American superpower. Even Putin's decision to support Medvedev as his successor was in line with the polls: when Russians were asked for whom they would vote out of lists of possible contenders (not including Putin himself), Medvedev typically came first, beating the other Kremlin candidates Ivanov and Zubkov as well as the leaders of opposition parties. Just about the only Putin policies that were clearly unpopular were his economically liberal initiatives—introducing the flat income tax and monetizing the payment of social benefits.

On the one hand, that leaders' ratings—and their power to act—change with the economy's performance implies a certain accountability. Despite all imperfections in the electoral machinery, the public turns out to have an important role in politics. On the other hand, the mode of accountability is rather perverse. First, given the sensitivity of the Russian economy to international factors such as the price of oil, economic performance sometimes has little to do with the incumbent president's management skill. Leaders then end up revered or scorned on the basis of fortuitous factors. Second, the long lags between policies and their results mean that Russia's presidents, when they were not being judged on the basis of international market conditions, were often rewarded or penalized for the actions of their predecessors. Gorbachev was, in large part, responsible for the economic problems on his watch. But history played tricks on his two successors. Yeltsin was punished for the catastrophe bequeathed to him by Gorbachev, while Putin was rewarded for a boom caused in part by external factors and in part by the market reforms Yeltsin had introduced.

Economic Crisis and Future Scenarios

The financial crisis of 2008–2009, which sent growth rates and the stock market tumbling, struck at the central element of the system I have described. As expected, as public assessments of the economy grew gloomier, the ratings of both Medvedev and—now prime minister—Putin began to fall. The war in Georgia interrupted the decline—the poll numbers of both president and prime minister spiked in August and September 2008—but then the slide resumed. The economic crisis bottomed out around March 2009, and, as economic sentiment recovered a little in subsequent months, so did the ratings of the two leaders (see Figure 7.4).

From Figure 7.4, two additional points leap out. First, the ratings of Putin and Medvedev move in lockstep, Medvedev tracking Putin almost exactly, from a few points below. At the same time, Medvedev has been gradually gaining on Putin. The gap closed from 10 points early in his term to 5 points in late 2009. Second, even the severe shock to the eco-

Figure 7.4 Economic sentiment and approval of Medvedev and Putin, 2008–2009

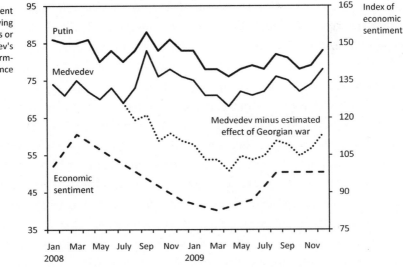

Source: Levada Center and author's calculations. Economic sentiment index calculated as in Figure 7.2.

nomic system of late 2008 only lowered the leaders' ratings by some 10–15 points, a drop that was almost completely offset by the rally caused by the war in South Ossetia. Since the two started at an astronomically high level, at this rate it would take a serious crisis lasting years to push their ratings down into dangerous territory. On the other hand, were the economy to crash, sensitivity to it might increase. In the Yeltsin-era contraction, assessments of the economy had a stronger impact on presidential popularity than in the Putin boom years, during which Russians apparently grew accustomed to the steady rise in wages.

Were the stabilization of late 2009 to end and the economy to deteriorate further, one might expect the slide in the ruling tandem's ratings to resume. This might well, in turn, prompt a gradual reemergence of opposition to the Kremlin. Citizens would begin to test the boundaries. Such resistance could take a variety of forms—more protest demonstrations around the country, a breaking of previous taboos in the media, more legal challenges against officials, resistance by governors and regional legislatures to unpopular central projects, some more vocal dissent from within the parliament, perhaps even public disagreements among cabinet members.

How Putin and Medvedev would react to such a trend cannot be confidently predicted. Fearing the erosion of their authority, they might either tighten or loosen administrative controls. The challenge could either strengthen or strain the bond between them. They might replace personnel at the top in an attempt to recapture the initiative. Most likely, they would continue trying to coopt potential allies in the intellectual and economic elite, while using targeted force to intimidate those held responsible for coordinating protests. If the momentum of disparate challenges grew, however, it would reduce their ability to implement any policies. In such circumstances, governments find themselves overstretched, trying to respond to diverse, simultaneous threats, without the time to devote to strategy. In the long run, assuming a sufficiently serious economic crisis, challenges could build to pressures for a turnover of control, and an unpredictable process of negotiation would begin between the Kremlin incumbents and representatives of the new protest movement. Needless to say, as of early 2010 such a prospect seemed very far away.

If, by contrast, oil and gas prices surge again and remain very high, the sense of urgency about reforms will likely dissipate. A resumption of boom times would keep the Kremlin incumbents popular and would quiet opposition to their rule. Finally, if oil prices remain at intermediate levels—around $60 to $80 a barrel—the Kremlin's most likely strategy is one of muddling through. This would probably result in somewhat slower growth, with gradually increasing public discontent and louder grumbling within the elite. But, barring some unexpected trauma, a gradual slide would probably not be enough to prompt a major departure from the established model.

CHAPTER 8

The Mountains

There is a romantic version of the wars in Chechnya. It goes something like this. An ancient nation of Muslim mountain dwellers, the Chechens, who lived self-sufficiently in their forest villages, valuing courage and independence above all else, was attacked in the nineteenth century and—after fighting valiantly for forty years against the army of Imperial Russia—brutally colonized. Despite attempts by the Russian and Soviet states to assimilate them, the Chechens preserved their culture and way of life for more than a century, along with an unquenchable desire for national self-determination. Finally, in the 1990s, the Chechens had a chance to break free. They united behind their elected president, Dzhokhar Dudayev, who tried to negotiate a peaceful secession. But Russia's leaders, determined to preserve the empire, invaded in 1994. Against overwhelming odds, the Chechens repelled the attackers and forced them in 1996 to sign a truce. Humiliated by this defeat, a revisionist Russian government invaded again in 1999, and, reducing the republic to rubble, established a puppet regime under a native strongman, who was loyal to Moscow but hated by the local population.

This story has much to be said for it. It is simple, coherent, and morally unambiguous. Variations on it inform much press coverage of the region. To scholars who study the Caucasus, however, its broad brushstrokes and perpendicular lines call to mind the kind of portrait in which one sees the artist but not the subject. Critics do not have a generally accepted alternative. Nor do they agree on who, if anyone, deserves their sympathies. What they do have is an accumulation of facts and voices that do not seem to fit, details that hang over the narrative like editors' scribbled queries, clues to a stranger story.

There is the nostalgia of the Chechen woman from a town outside Grozny who misses the way the Russians, Armenians, and Chechens on her street used to celebrate each other's religious holidays—first Ramadan, then Orthodox Easter—competing to cook the tastiest ceremonial dishes to impress the neighbors. There is the awkward way the separatist fighters kept changing their minds about for whom they were fighting— was it Vaynakhs, Chechens, Ichkeritsy, or Allah? There is fourteen-year-old Adi Sharon's penciled note to his father: "I feel very sick here. There is a very bad man. Please, please, give money now, and I shall go home." There are the statistics collected by courageous human rights advocates that show how, even as the collectors were being murdered, the number of killings and abductions was falling sharply under Chechnya's latest warrior king. And—an image that rises above the others, not because it does not fit but because it somehow fits too well—there is the solitary *lezginka*, a joyful Caucasus folk dance, tapped out on the tarmac by a Soviet general at the military airfield in Poltava, Ukraine.

By 1999, Chechnya had become a floating metaphor for everything that had gone wrong in Russia's troubled rebirth, a story with many imaginary beginnings and no ending. "Wherever one looks," a weary prime minister Vladimir Putin complained that October, "one sees Chechnya." What he saw was a morass of weakness and self-inflicted disorder, a country that was tearing itself apart. He was right. Wherever they looked, Russians did see Chechnya. And each one who looked saw something different.

Kavkaz

The Caucasus mountains stretch nearly seven hundred miles across the isthmus that separates the Black Sea from the Caspian. Starting above the pebbled beaches of Sochi, granite peaks extend southeast to the twin summits of Mount Elbrus, a snow-capped dormant volcano that, at 18,510 feet, is Europe's highest point. From there, the range curves down into Azerbaijan, ending near the coast, south of the ancient Dagestani port of Derbent.

Literate Russians know the scenery from the lush descriptions of Lermontov, Tolstoy, and others. Narrow gorges stretch into the mist, their slopes covered by forests of oak and maple, beech and pine. Wisps of cloud "coil and twist like snakes," above "gloomy, mysterious abysses." Rushing streams overflow their banks in summer, watering the meadows where a young Lev Tolstoy wandered, botanical primer in hand, picking out the

> ... red, white, and pink scented tufty clover; milk-white ox-eye daisies with their bright yellow centers and pleasant spicy smell; yellow honey-scented rape blossoms; tall campanulas with white and lilac bells, tulip-shaped; creeping vetch ...

and other flowers of all descriptions. Further north, the reedy Terek River bisects the steppe, redolent of wild grasses and acacia blossoms. Moors teem with grouse and rabbits, a hunter's paradise. And always in the distance, even in the heat of August, loom the bewitchingly white, snowy summits.

People have lived in these mountains for many thousands of years. Successive empires left their deposits of languages and legends, religions and customs. From the northern steppes came Scythians, Khazars, Mongols, and Russians; from the south, Romans, Persians, Arabs, Byzantines, and Ottoman Turks. The Caucasus range became a repository of tongues—the Arabs called it a "Language Mountain"—peopled by Persian-speaking Ossetians and Tats; Turkic-speaking Balkars, Karachays, and Kumyks; Circassian-speaking Adyghes, Kabardins, and Cherkess; and many others—such as the Avars and Ingush—whose languages had no relatives outside the Caucasus.

The Chechens lived in villages, or *auls*, of clay-plastered, windowless cottages with roofs of thatch and earth, grazing sheep, goats and cattle. They are said to have constituted a kind of warrior democracy, organized in clans governed by councils of male elders according to a system of customary law, which emphasized individual freedom, courage, and honor, and prescribed hospitality and respect for elders. From childhood, boys learned to handle weapons and ride horses. Farming income was supplemented by raids on the nearby villages of cossacks—Slavic freebooters and escaped serfs who had settled on the empire's edges where law enforcement was weak.

Some time after the eighth century, Islam spread west from the Arab communities of Dagestan. Sunni Islam, with its emphasis on the mosque and Sharia, proved less successful in attracting converts than Sufism—the mystical, inward-focused, ascetic branch of Islam—which was more easily blended with Chechen customary law. During the anti-Russian wars of the nineteenth century, the great Avar sheikh Imam Shamil used the networks of the Sufi brotherhoods to unite mountain tribes against the invaders.

The major Russian push to dominate the Caucasus began after Georgia was annexed in 1801, when control over the military highway through the mountains became critical. From 1816, General Aleksey Yermolov set out to subjugate the mountain peoples, building forts south of the Terek and founding the fortress city of Grozny ("Menacing"). To defeat the mountaineers, whose tactic was to descend in sudden bloody raids and then disappear up the impassable ravines, he adopted a scorched earth approach. Russian troops burnt villages and crops and cut swathes through the forests, driving the plains dwellers into the mountains. The war lasted from roughly 1817 to 1864, and cost the lives of at least 77,000 Russian troops and an unknown number of civilians.

The Caucasus—"Kavkaz" in Russian—was where nineteenth century Russian gentlemen went to confront the Orient in themselves. Exotic and dangerous, an anarchic playground on the margin of the tsar's police state, it exerted a powerful attraction on the cultivated daredevils of St. Petersburg and Moscow. Writers would come to observe and fight, and observe themselves fight. Lermontov, who served bravely at Grozny, wrote with compassion of the burning auls the Russian troops left behind, the murdered children and elders, the raped women. Tolstoy, as a guest of General Baryatinsky, watched a mountain village sacked, and came away disgusted with himself for failing to stop or report the abuses.

Many went native, adopting Caucasian dress—the *burka* (a sleeveless felt cloak), and *papakha* (lambskin hat)—seducing mountain women, learning local languages, entering into blood pacts with the mountaineers. Lermontov took to dressing à la Circassian. There were Kurtzes aplenty, like Major-General Grigory von Zass, a Baltic junker with piercing blue eyes and a sandy mustache that drooped to his chest, who, dressed in a Caucasian shirt, liked to pillage mountain villages and display the heads of his victims on stakes. Or the Polish artilleryman and freedom fighter Teofil Lapinsky, known to the Caucasians as Teffik Bey, who snuck into the mountains to attack the Russian invaders in the late 1850s. General Yermolov himself had three native "wives," one of whom he had had to kidnap from her first husband.

Such fun and games came to an end with the Revolution. In May 1918, the North Caucasus declared itself the "Mountain Republic," and was recognized as an independent state by Germany, Austria-Hungary, Turkey, Bulgaria, and Poland. A little later, it resurfaced as an Islamic emirate. In one of many miscalculations, the White forces of General Denikin chose to attack the Caucasians. Wooed by the Bolsheviks, in the person of Commissar of Nationalities Affairs Joseph Stalin, the Muslim peoples joined the Reds and rode into battle under the memorable slogan: "For the Soviet government, for Sharia!" However, as the Bolsheviks triumphed, the Red Army occupied the southern territories, crushing resistance. In 1921, the Mountain Republic was incorporated into the Russian Socialist Federative Soviet Republic (RSFSR), which would itself become the largest constituent of the Soviet Union, created in December 1922.

In 1922, Chechnya was split off from the Mountain Republic to form the Chechen Autonomous Oblast. Two years later, what was left of the Mountain Republic was divided into the North Ossetian and Ingush autonomous oblasts. Then in 1934 the Chechen and Ingush autonomous oblasts were joined in the Chechen-Ingush Autonomous Oblast, which was raised to the status of an autonomous republic in 1936. Anti-Soviet revolts broke out periodically—in particular in 1929–1930, as agriculture was forcibly collectivized—but they were put down by NKVD troops.

During World War II, Chechen partisans used the moment of Moscow's weakness to rebel again, inspired by the successes of the Finns' resistance to Stalin's 1940 invasion. As the Wehrmacht approached, thrusting south towards the Baku oil fields, a small number of Chechens defected to the Germans. After Hitler's defeat at Stalingrad, Soviet forces reoccupied the region, and Stalin took his revenge, claiming that the Chechens, along with their neighbors, the Ingush, and several other Caucasian nationalities, had collaborated with the Nazis.

Before dawn on February 23, 1944, in operation Chechevitsa ("Lentil"), Russian secret service officers drove into each Chechen town, firing flares into the night sky. They rounded up the inhabitants at gunpoint, herded them into American Studebaker trucks supplied under the lend-lease program, and drove them to the Grozny railway station, where they were packed into cattle wagons. Those too old or sick to travel were shot. In Khaybakh, a village near the Georgian border, more than six hundred of the "untransportables" were packed into a stable, which was then boarded up, doused with kerosene, and set on fire. Weeks later, those still alive after the train ride, clambered out over the corpses to find themselves in Kazakhstan. In Central Asia, they lived in mud huts and unheated barracks. A total of 387,229 Chechens and 91,250 Ingush were deported. Even by conservative estimates, more than one-third perished during their years in exile.

Only in 1957, four years after Stalin died, were the Chechens allowed to return, to find their houses destroyed or occupied by others. One whole district—Aukh, renamed Khasavyurt—had been transferred to Dagestan. The Ingush, deported at the same time, lost the Prigorodny district to North Ossetia. Chechens remained a suspect nationality. During the postwar period, the oil and petrochemicals industries developed rapidly around Grozny. However, almost all jobs went to ethnic Russians, relocated to the region. By 1989, Grozny's population had become 53 percent Russian. Even highly educated Chechens could not find work outside agriculture, and by the 1980s the labor surplus constituted some 200,000 young people. Most were forced to migrate to other regions in search of work, legal or illegal. In 1990, the republic of Checheno-Ingushetia, at 19.3 thousand square kilometers about the size of Slovenia, had a population of 1.3 million. Of these, 57.8 percent were Chechens, 12.9 were Ingush, and 23.1 were Russian.

Dudayev's Revolution

At first, the Chechen political awakening prompted by Gorbachev's reforms looked much like those occurring elsewhere. As in the Baltics, it started with ecology. In the summer of 1988, thousands protested against the construction of a biochemical plant in the city of Gudermes. Soon a

Popular Front of Checheno-Ingushetia had formed to advocate democratization, freedom of speech and the press, the revival of local culture, the honest retelling of history, and an end to anti-Caucasian discrimination. It was soon challenged by more explicitly nationalist groups like the Bart ("Concord") society, founded in the summer of 1989 and reformed into the Vaynakh Democratic Party (VDP) in 1990, which began demanding sovereignty and independence for the republic within the Soviet Union. Among the leaders of Bart and the VDP was the poet and children's magazine editor Zelimkhan Yandarbiev, a tall man with a bushy black beard, author of such collections as *Plant Saplings, People* (1981) and *Signs of the Zodiac* (1983). Inspired by the Baltic nationalists, Bart printed the first three issues of its party newspaper in Riga with the help of the Latvian Popular Front.

In June 1989, under pressure from below, the republic's Communists elected their first ethnically Chechen secretary, an agricultural bureaucrat called Doku Zavgayev. Hoping to coopt the nationalists, Zavgayev allowed them to convene a so-called Chechen National Congress in November 1990. During a weekend of stormy speeches, Yandarbiev and his radicals seized the agenda. They had persuaded the highest-ranking Chechen in the Soviet armed forces, General Dzhokhar Dudayev, to fly out from Tartu, Estonia, where he commanded a garrison of nuclear bombers. After a militant oration to the roughly one thousand delegates, Dudayev was elected chairman of the group's executive committee. A few days later, on November 27, struggling to catch up, the Chechen-Ingush Supreme Soviet issued a declaration of state sovereignty.

Sovereignty or no sovereignty, Zavgayev still believed in Gorbachev's project of saving the Soviet Union, and when the reactionary junta struck in August 1991 he was in Moscow to sign the Union Treaty. Back in Grozny, Dudayev spoke out in support of Yeltsin-led demonstrations against the coup. Then, as it collapsed, Dudayev's loyalists began occupying the city's government buildings, replacing red flags with green Islamic ones, storming the television and radio centers, taking control of the airport, and opening the prisons. Ruslan Labazanov, a murderer sprung from the Chechnya jail, formed a gang of his prison mates and merged them into Dudayev's newly formed "national guard." On September 6, the general's armed supporters burst into the regional parliament building, ordered the deputies to disperse, and forced Zavgayev to resign. The chairman of the Grozny City Council, Vitaly Kutsenko, was either thrown out of a window to his death or fell while trying to escape, depending on whose account one believes. Zavgayev fled to his home village in the North.

Until the fall of 1991, Russia's democratic leaders had looked with sympathy on the struggle for Chechen sovereignty. By some accounts, Yeltsin's own close aides had helped persuade Dudayev to return to Chechnya, hoping he would prove a popular but reasonable democratic nationalist with more charisma than Zavgayev. Yeltsin's deputy, Ruslan Khasbulatov, himself a Chechen, had visited Grozny in mid-September, met with Dudayev, and then told Zavgayev that if he continued trying to recover power, Khasbulatov would "take him to Moscow in an iron cage."

In the end, however, Yeltsin did not recognize Dudayev's coup. On October 19, he ordered Dudayev's forces to leave the buildings they had seized, dissolve their illegal armed formations, and hold elections and a referendum on the republic's future. Dudayev did hold elections on October 27 for a new parliament and president of the Chechen Republic, which would henceforth be separate from Ingushetia. To no one's surprise, he was announced to have won the presidency, receiving more than 80 percent of the vote, on turnout of 72 percent. Nationalists won most seats in the parliament. Other candidates complained of fraud, and it did not increase confidence that all members of the electoral commission were leading figures in Dudayev's National Congress, or that seven other presidential candidates had withdrawn in protest against the biased management of the election. On November 1, with his first decree in office, ratified the next day by the new parliament, Dudayev declared Chechnya's independence.

At the urging of his vice president Aleksandr Rutskoy, who had visited Grozny and concluded that Dudayev's entourage was no more than a "gang terrorising the population," Yeltsin authorized a military intervention. On November 9, 600 lightly armed interior ministry troops flew into the Khankala airbase outside Grozny, where they were quickly surrounded by crowds of Chechens with Kalashnikovs. Lacking reinforcements—Gorbachev, who still commanded local Soviet forces, refused to help, fearing a bloodbath—the Russian servicemen had to be ignominiously withdrawn, disarmed and bused out of the republic. A furious

Dudayev threatened to turn Moscow into a "disaster zone," and called on Chechens to "carry out 'terrorist acts' against installations on Russian territory, including nuclear power facilities." Right on cue, a young militant called Shamil Basayev hijacked a passenger airliner in southern Russia and forced it to fly to Turkey. In return for giving up his hostages, the authorities allowed Basayev to return to Chechnya, where he received a hero's welcome.

At this point, the Russian leadership, preoccupied with economic reforms and the power struggle in Moscow and demoralized by the November fiasco, chose to look the other way. Through the spring of 1992, Chechen guerrillas looted military bases in the republic, meeting only sporadic resistance. General Pyotr Sokolov, the commander of the North Caucasus military training center, later recalled how Basayev had sat in his office that February, nagging Sokolov to give him a machine gun. By mid-year, all Russian troops had been withdrawn, having either sold or simply abandoned much of their military hardware. The Russian defense minister, Pavel Grachev, after negotiations with Dudayev, ordered his troops to split the remaining weaponry equally with the Chechens. During this period, the Chechens reportedly acquired 42 tanks, 139 artillery pieces, and almost 40,000 firearms, although the figures could not be verified.

Grozny, as journalists described it, soon resembled a postindustrial wasteland. The federal government ended subsidies and cut oil shipments to the city's refinery; in 1993, it processed only 1.2 million tons of oil, down from 5.3 million tons in 1985. Moscow imposed a trade embargo, although it was ineffectively enforced. Together with the incompetence of Dudayev's government and the general economic crisis, these measures led to a 75 percent drop in per capita income between 1991 and 1993. Infrastructure fell apart. Roads decayed into patchworks of potholes; refuse lay uncollected; the telephone system disintegrated. "At night," wrote one frequent visitor, "the street lamps long since having failed, the bazaar was lit by heaps of burning garbage."

By many accounts, Chechnya under Dudayev became a haven for organized crime. Its airport, virtually devoid of customs or border guards, was a free transit point for drugs, arms, and other contraband entering and leaving Russia. Bank frauds netted hundreds of millions of dollars for Chechen criminals who, like their counterparts elsewhere in the former Soviet Union, exploited the rudimentary security arrangements of the inherited payments system. Trains crossing the republic were routinely plundered. In 1992–1994, police recorded 1,354 attacks on freight trains, and seventy passenger trains robbed; travelers were warned to lock themselves in their compartments. Many of the republic's illegal markets and schemes must have involved corrupt patrons in Moscow as well as organizers in Chechnya. And, no doubt, xenophobic Russians exaggerated the criminality of their swarthy southern neighbors. But the accumulation of anecdotes and interviews, many of them with ethnic Chechens, suggests there was something to exaggerate. In his memoirs, Yandarbiev, who became Dudayev's vice president, accuses one minister of stealing $8 million, and admits that: "all of the power [organs in Chechnya]—the MVD, the DGB, the *spetsnaz*, the OMON and DON, and the Shali tank regiment—participated in the plundering of petroleum products, under the guise of guarding them."

Whether because of the economic crisis or intimidation by armed thugs, much of the ethnically Russian population—including most highly skilled oil industry workers—left the republic during Dudayev's first years in power. In 1992–1994, 147,000 people migrated from Chechnya, 80 percent of them ethnically Russian. They took with them much of the republic's human capital.

By late 1992, Dudayev's support was dwindling. Much of the elite favored accommodation with Moscow. The former Soviet nomenklatura, the intelligentsia, those Russians still around, and many Chechens dismayed by the economic decline deserted the president, who now relied for support upon the countryside and socially conservative mountain strongholds. Advocates of compromise included the speaker of the Chechen parliament, Hussein Akhmatov, the chairman of its foreign relations committee, Yusup Soslambekov, the mayor of Grozny, Beslan Gantemirov, and Dudayev's own prime minister, Yaragi Mamodayev. In December 1992 and January 1993, Mamodayev, Soslambekov, and Akhmatov, together with Russian Nationalities Minister, Sergey Shakhray, and the chairman of the upper house of Russia's Supreme Soviet, Ramazan Abdulatipov, negotiated a draft "Treaty on the Delimitation and Mutual Delegation of Powers," between the Russian Federation and the Chechen Republic. This treaty, similar to one signed later with Tatarstan, would have left Chechnya's status ambiguous and established a loose confederative relationship. Chechnya could have kept its own armed forces and independently joined international Islamic organizations. The draft was supported by many leading Chechen politicians.

Dudayev, furious, refused to consider it because it did not explicitly recognize Chechnya's independence. Those who had printed the document were fired. According to Akhmatov, when Shakhray and Abdulatipov flew to Grozny in mid-January to continue negotiations, Dudayev wanted to prevent their plane from landing. They were kept circling above the airport for an hour before being given clearance. Dudayev's security service refused to guarantee the negotiators' safety.

The spring of 1993 saw the confrontation between Dudayev and his more moderate opponents turn unconstitutional and violent. In February, ignoring a parliamentary veto, Dudayev called a referendum on expanding presidential powers, but its legitimacy was undermined by low turnout. Two months later, after the parliament voted no confidence in Dudayev, he ordered both it and his cabinet of ministers to dissolve, saying he was introducing direct presidential rule. Refusing, the parliament began impeachment proceedings, and the Constitutional Court ruled Dudayev's decrees unconstitutional. The general then ordered the Court to dissolve as well. Finally, in early June, Dudayev sent Shamil Basayev with armed commandos to close the parliament and violently disperse opposition demonstrators who gathered regularly on Teatralnaya Square. At least seventeen people died in the fracas. Opposition members said they saw Dudayev's militants "shoot people on the square, kill members of parliament inside the parliament building, and, finally, shoot a dozen disloyal policemen at the city's police headquarters."

From this point, opposition groups retreated to the anti-Dudayev northern regions, set up their own administrations there, and began planning to storm the capital. Gantemirov went home to Urus Martan. In December 1993, Umar Avturkhanov, a former police officer and protégé of Zavgayev, formed a so-called Chechen Provisional Council in the Nadterechny region, two hours north of Grozny.

Still, negotiations with Moscow continued. In December 1993, Chechen Deputy Prime Minister Mairbek Mugadayev began talks with

Russian Prime Minister Viktor Chernomyrdin. They made progress on some practical issues. However, when Mugadayev returned to Grozny, Dudayev accused him of trying to cut a deal behind his back. Although denouncing the agreement, Dudayev *did* like the idea, which negotiators had floated, of a summit with Yeltsin. He even prepared a new uniform for the occasion. The summit never occurred. Analysts cite various reasons—conspiracies of Moscow hard-liners, an assassination attempt against Dudayev in May, Dudayev's gratuitous insulting of Yeltsin. The most logical is simply that, given Dudayev's intransigence on Chechnya's independence, which Yeltsin was not prepared to concede, the latter had no desire to legitimize the general. There was a basic impasse.

As battle lines hardened, Kremlin circles despaired of reaching agreement with Dudayev. In the summer of 1994, the Federal Security Service (FSK) persuaded Yeltsin to let it provide logistical support to the northern rebels. As the anti-Dudayev rhetoric increased in Moscow that fall, the flow of arms to the opposition accelerated.

Then, predictably yet unexpectedly, the volcano erupted. At military bases around Moscow, FSK agents had recruited tank crews, promising one or two thousand dollars for a few days work. Flown down to North Ossetia, the soldiers were relieved of identifying documents, fitted out with T-72 tanks, and sent across the border to Avturkhanov's stronghold in Tolstoy-Yurt. Shortly after dawn on November 26, three columns of tanks, about forty in all, entered Grozny. At first, all was peaceful. The tank drivers stopped at red lights and signaled politely as they merged into the morning traffic. But a few hours later, they were being incinerated by Dudayev's fighters, who ambushed the tanks, aimed rocket-propelled grenades at their vulnerable spots, and exploded their ammunition caches. Those quick enough to leap out were picked off by snipers on the rooftops.

By late afternoon, the survivors were withdrawing. Only eighteen of the roughly forty tanks reportedly made it out. Several dozen Russian soldiers, captured by Dudayev's forces, were imprisoned in the basement of the Presidential Palace. The Chechens threatened to shoot them as mercenaries if Moscow did not acknowledge them as its own.

The raid had been a fiasco, mangled so badly that some suspected sabotage. The Russian crews had been sent in without accurate maps, clear orders, air cover, or communications support. To find their way to the Presidential Palace, they had had to jump out and ask directions, in what must have resembled scenes from a Bunuel movie. (One imagines they were not told the shortest route.) Secrecy had been completely neglected; Dudayev's forces even knew what radio frequencies the attackers would use. Guns misfired so often that one soldier thought the cartridges must have been soaked in kerosene. The infantry, critical for protecting tanks in urban warfare, consisted of a rag-tag band of volunteers—"shepherds with assault rifles and their young sons," as one Russian described them—who had been issued telltale grey knitted hats to distinguish them from ordinary Grozny residents. Some did not know how to take the safety lock off their grenade launchers. Many simply melted into the city to rob kiosks and loot stores.

The next day, a mortifying charade began, as federal officials insisted on denying the obvious. Russian soldiers among the guerrillas storming Grozny? "Delirium," said the defense minister, Pavel Grachev on November 28. If the Russian military *were* to get involved, he could not help adding, "the whole matter could be settled in two hours with one paratrooper regiment." So it went, one denial following another, even as Dudayev's people threatened to execute the "mercenaries"; as Russian television broadcast the captured soldiers identifying their hometowns and units and showing their military dogtags; as their families appeared on the news having recognized their boys in the previous broadcast (one mother said her son's base had told her he was on a "business trip"); as soldiers from their units related how FSK agents had recruited them. Finally, on December 1, Grachev admitted federal participation, although the operation had not been under Defense Ministry control. The commander of the Kantemirov Division, General Boris Polyakov, whose men had been recruited out from under him, angrily resigned.

Eventually, through the efforts of liberal parliamentarians and certain behind-the-scenes negotiators, most of the captured Russians were released. But the die had been cast. On November 29, Russian planes bombed Grozny's airport. Two weeks later, on December 11, the land invasion began.

Mikhail Gorbachev, general secretary of the Soviet Communist Party, speaking at the U.S.S.R. Congress of People's Deputies, May 1989.

President Ronald Reagan and General Secretary Gorbachev at the Hofdi House in Reykjavik, Iceland, during the Reykjavik Summit, October 1986.

Russian president Boris Yeltsin and Soviet president Mikhail Gorbachev, October 1991.

Yeltsin campaigning for reelection, Belgorod Region, April 1996.

Yeltsin speaking from on top of a tank during the putsch, August 19, 1991.

Leonid Kravchuk, president of Ukraine, Stanislav Shushkevich, chairman of Belarus's Supreme Soviet, and Boris Yeltsin, president of Russia, in Belovezhskaya Pushcha after signing the agreement establishing the Commonwealth of Independent States, December 1991.

Yegor Gaidar (top left) and Anatoly Chubais (top right) in the Duma, May 1994.

The Russian White House on fire after being assaulted by government troops, October 4, 1993.

Chechen president and former Soviet air force general Dzhokhar Dudayev (left), December 10, 1994, shortly before the start of the first Chechen War.

A Chechen man prays during the battle for Grozny, January 1995. The flame in the background is from a gas pipeline hit by shrapnel.

Prime minister Viktor Chernomyrdin (left) meets with the "oligarchs" Mikhail Khodorkovsky (second from left), Boris Berezovsky (second from right), and Aleksandr Smolensky (right), January 1998.

12

Russian ex-president Boris Yeltsin (right) leaving the Kremlin after resigning early and transferring his powers to acting president Vladimir Putin (left), December 31, 1999. Kremlin chief of staff Aleksandr Voloshin is in the middle.

13

President Putin speaking to the relatives of sailors who died in the Kursk nuclear submarine disaster, August 22, 2000, Vidyaevo.

14

President Putin (left) and President-elect Medvedev (right), election night, March 2, 2008, Moscow.

Dmitry Medvedev at work, July 17, 2007.

Barracks of the Russian Peace-Keepers, Tskhinvali, South Ossetia, after Georgian attack, August 24, 2008.

Russia's Ethnic Revival

Before returning to the war, it is worth considering the context in which it occurred. With its vast size, its history of migrations and conquests, Russia contains a myriad of small ethnic groups—from the reindeer-herding Chukots and the shamanistic Nentsy to the Muslim Avars and the throat-singing Tuvans. The 1989 Russian census identified 105 nationalities with more than one thousand members. Ethnic Russians dominated, with 81.5 percent of the population, followed by Tatars (3.8 percent), Ukrainians (3.0 percent), Chuvash (1.2 percent), and Bashkirs (0.9 percent). The Chechens, with 899,000 members in 1989, came in eighth.

Designing Russia's administrative architecture, Stalin gave the largest non-Slavic ethnic groups their own "autonomous republics." By 1992, after the Chechen-Ingush split, there were twenty-one of these. On paper, the republics had broader rights than the country's other sixty-eight regions. They were entitled to their own constitutions and official languages; their heads of government served *ex officio* in the Russian government; and their borders could not be changed without their governments' consent. Eight republics, clustered in the Northern Caucasus and along the Volga River, were traditionally Muslim (Adygeya, Karachayevo-Cherkessia, Kabardino-Balkaria, Chechnya, Ingushetia, Dagestan, Tatarstan, and Bashkortostan). Another three (Kalmykia, Buryatia, and Tuva) were historically Buddhist.

The other sixty-eight regions broke down into several categories. First, there were forty-nine *oblasts*, or provinces, and six *krays*, or territories—categories that in practice had the same status and rights. The only difference was that krays might contain sparsely populated autonomous *okrugs*, or districts, of which there were ten in 1992. Although named in honor of smaller non-Russian ethnicities, the autonomous okrugs had no additional rights and were subordinate to both the federal government and the surrounding kray. The two federal cities of Moscow and St. Petersburg had the same status as oblasts and krays. Finally, the Jewish Autonomous Oblast, on the border with Chinese Heilongjiang, existed to prove that Stalin's Soviet Union did not engage in anti-Semitism. Located in one of the swampiest corners of the Far East, it was inhabited mostly by non-Jewish ethnic Russians.

As glasnost dissolved previous inhibitions, a gale of nationalism seemed to sweep in from Eastern Europe and the Baltics. From Karelia on the Finnish border to Sakha in Eastern Siberia, leaders of autonomous republics began demanding new cultural and political rights, adopting their own constitutions, anthems, and flags, asserting the superiority of their laws over federal ones, even declaring themselves sovereign states. Checheno-Ingushetia's sovereignty declaration actually came quite late; it was the fourteenth republic within Russia to make one. Some nationalists called for changes in borders. In southern Siberia, a Buryat party agitated to unite Russian Buryatia with Mongolia, while some Altays and Khakass dreamed of a Turkic Siberian Republic. In Tatarstan, nationalists quite seriously demanded that Moscow begin "peace negotiations" to end the "state of war" that had existed since Ivan the Terrible sacked the capital Kazan in 1552. In March 1992, in a referendum called by the Tatar government, 61 percent of voters endorsed the republic's assertion of sovereignty. Moscow is said to have moved troops up to the republic's border.

To those who saw a surge of primordial nationalism in the uprisings of Lithuanians and Georgians, Russia's ethnic awakening looked similar. Nationalities that had been squelched and assimilated by the Russian—and then Soviet—occupiers were now bursting out. From up close, the process looked a little less spontaneous. Had a powerful, historically forged sense of nationhood prompted demonstrations and autonomy demands, one might expect the strongest pressures from groups that were the most culturally and linguistically distinct from Russians and that had been victimized the most. In fact, republics where most people spoke Russian at home were no less likely to press for autonomy than those where almost everyone spoke a minority language. Oddly enough, the more ethnic *Russians* a republic had, the quicker it declared sovereignty. Nor were groups that had been deported by Stalin or that had experienced recent violent ethnic clashes with local Russians more separatist. It is true that two traditionally Muslim republics—Tatarstan and Chechnya—were the most assertive autonomy seekers. But among the other republics, Muslim traditions were not clearly associated with greater activism.

Nor did most of the republic leaders resemble the prototypical nationalist. Like the nomenklatura nationalists in Uzbekistan and Ukraine who had discovered their ethnic roots as the Soviet glue came unstuck (see Chapter 5), many presidents of Russia's autonomous republics had shortly before been typical apparatchiks. The second region to declare sovereignty, in August 1990, was the Komi Republic, an expanse of virgin forest and tundra in Russia's North. The firebrand championing the indigenous Komi people was none other than Yury Spiridonov, an ethnically Russian oil miner and party worker, born in Omsk and educated in Sverdlovsk, who had once gotten into trouble for snapping at someone who tried to address him in Komi: "Speak in a way that can be understood." Komis were one of the most assimilated minorities. By the early 1990s, they made up only 23 percent of the local population; almost two-thirds of them spoke Russian at home. On the other hand, Komi did have deposits of coal, oil, gas, gold, and diamonds, which local leaders, understandably, hoped to control. Among other early sovereignty declarers, longtime apparatchiks such as Tatarstan's Mintimer Shaymiev and Karelia's Viktor Stepanov were common.

Economics seemed to come up frequently in these outbursts of micro-nationalism. Ethnic groups that happened to live above mineral deposits or whose republics contained valuable industrial assets tended to push harder for self-government than those dependent on federal subsidies. Many demands were explicitly economic rather than cultural or even political. Republics claimed ownership of local resources and federally owned factories and mines. They demanded tax breaks or transfers, and insisted on remitting less revenue to the central budget.

By 1993, Russia's "springtime of nations" had, in any case, metamorphosed into a "springtime of regions." Jealous of their ethnic neighbors, homogeneously Slavic oblasts joined the struggle for decentralized power. Vologda, a sleepy region in the northern forests known mostly for its butter and cheese, became the "Vologda Republic." Sverdlovsk, Yeltsin's old stomping ground, rebranded itself the "Urals Republic" and announced plans to replace the ruble with a "Urals franc." Like their ethnic counterparts, many regions began reducing the tax they remitted to the federal budget. Moscow's attempts to force compliance achieved little. By this point, local agents of the tax inspectorate, police, security service, and procuracy had been coopted by the governors, who supplemented their wages, found them housing, and in practice had a say in local appointments.

In short, the wave of miniature nationalisms that swept Russia in the early 1990s had less to do with distinctive cultures and historically rooted identities than with bargaining over resources. That is not to say local nationalists were not sincere; many were. But the seasoned bureaucrats who usually ended up on top knew how to use the nationalists' sincerity to practical effect.

What these professionals understood was how the little explosions—a dramatic street demonstration, a week-long strike—could be used to scare the Moscow politicians into concessions. Ethnic grievances were a potent fuel to keep the explosions coming. A wheeler-dealer like Shaymiev could fly to Moscow with pictures of the Tatar nationalists demonstrating in Kazan and warn that things might slip out of control if he was not given more room for maneuver and cash to subsidize depressed enterprises. Those regions that did not have nationalists were tempted to invent them. The deputy governor of Tambov Oblast, a solidly Russian agricultural region, joked to me in 1996 that the most valuable commodity he could import to improve the oblast's economic prospects would be several thousand Tatars.

The sight of numerous regions declaring sovereignty and barraging Moscow with demands was unsettlingly familiar to those who had just watched the Soviet Union fall apart. Many politicians, in government and opposition, started to warn that Russia might meet the same fate. Russia, said Supreme Soviet Chairman Khasbulatov, was "threatened with Balkanization." The country was about to fracture, said Vice President Rutskoy, into "more than 100 banana republics." Yeltsin himself would later agree that in 1992 the danger of disintegration had been "rather serious." Various scholars concurred. According to one Western analyst writing in 1994, the Russian Federation was "not sustainable as a state." Another sketched "explosion" and "implosion" scenarios. The Russian public, too, seemed to consider Russia fragile. In November 1991, 53 percent agreed there was a "high probability that the RSFSR will break up into several independent states in the near future."

Pessimists could point to recent parallels and historical precedents. By 1993 Russia was the last remaining postcommunist federation; the other three—Yugoslavia, Czechoslovakia, and the Soviet Union—had vanished from the map. Much earlier, the postrevolutionary Civil War had given birth to a number of small statelets on Russian territory. Besides the Caucasus Mountain Republic, a Far Eastern Republic had formed east of Lake Baikal in 1920, with an elected parliament and government, and even its own postage stamps and currency. In 1918, several groups had tried to found a Siberian Republic, although without great success.

Separatism, per se, was not the greatest danger. In few regions did a serious faction press for complete independence. The danger was that the economically motivated challenges of individual regions might, in the aggregate, starve the central state of resources, rendering it powerless and irrelevant. By September 1993, one-third of regions were withholding some or all of their assessed taxes, threatening the government with what Finance Minister Boris Fyodorov called "financial asphyxiation." Such tax revolts create a logic of contagion; no region wants to contribute while its neighbors ride for free. Eventually, as the central state atrophies, regional associations and local bodies are forced to take over functions previously handled by central bodies, in the process forming the skeleton of new, smaller states.

And yet, the Russian Federation survived. That so much of the population was ethnically Russian no doubt helped. The small size of most regions, many of which were nowhere near a border, must also have given potential separatists pause, although larger groupings of Siberian, Far Eastern, North Caucasus, or even Volga regions might have been quite viable. A great deal of credit for reversing the centrifugal trend must, nevertheless, go to the particular strategy employed by Yeltsin's administration. Knitting together the regions in the mid-1990s, despite the government's desperate lack of resources, was one of Yeltsin's greatest achievements.

The irony is that most observers at the time, including Yeltsin's aides, thought his approach misguided. Even he often seemed embarrassed. In essence, he selectively gave in. He appeased the regions where, for historical, cultural, or other reasons, the public was most predisposed to defy Moscow. Regions that had demonstrated disaffection by declaring sovereignty, staging strikes, or voting for opposition candidates were paid off with larger subsidies and tax breaks. From 1994, Yeltsin began negotiating "power-sharing agreements" with individual regions, conceding some of the rights they demanded. The first, with Tatarstan in February 1994, gave the republic more control over its natural resources and greater freedom to engage in foreign trade; it authorized the Tatar government to create a national bank and to exempt its young men from conscription. The agreement with Bashkortostan, concluded some months later, gave that republic authority over its budget, prosecutor, and judiciary. By early 1996, Yeltsin had signed similar agreements with several ordinary Russian regions.

By then, the strategy had succeeded brilliantly. Paradoxically, Yeltsin's earliest supporters when he ran for president in 1996 were precisely the nationalist hotheads who had defied the center several years earlier. Tatar President Shaymiev endorsed him in February, because, in his words, Yeltsin "adheres to democracy more than others, and guarantees the current relationship between Tatarstan and the center." Bashkir President Rakhimov followed suit. Even Eduard Rossel—founder of the famous "Urals Republic," whom Yeltsin had fired, but whom the voters had then reelected—showed no hard feelings, announcing: "I, as governor of his native province, will do everything I can to promote Boris Nikolayevich's victory."

Greasing the squeaky wheel is dangerous if wheels can choose to squeak. Rewarding defiance risked encouraging other regions to defy. What made this policy work was how accommodation changed the regions that were accommodated. Where governments were able to sustain or even increase public spending during the early 1990s, attitudes towards Yeltsin and his reformers remained more positive and there was less support for anti-Moscow confrontations. Knowing this, the governors of such regions chose not to push things too far—if they did, Yeltsin could fire them without sparking local protests. (And Yeltsin did fire recalcitrant governors like Rossel from time to time.) By cooling the political temperature in previously rebellious regions, Yeltsin's selective appeasement prevented a bandwagon from forming that even moderate regions might have been tempted to join.

For Yeltsin, all this was more improvisation than conscious design, an intuitive manipulation of carrots and sticks. He would fly out to problem regions, listen to the complaints, and sign decrees on the spot, ordering his ministers to find the money. His advisers viewed the concessions as a bad habit, a character flaw, a lack of personal discipline. Yeltsin was sensitive to such criticism:

I have repeatedly heard rebukes along the lines that the president takes a bag of money with him on his trips and certain lucky enterprises receive support. I admit that I don't like that idea either. The president is not an ambulance. You can't salvage the situation or cure the country like that. You can't visit everyone who's in a bad way.

Still, he continued to drive the ambulance. Government experts devised complicated formulas to measure regions' needs for financial aid. Then Yeltsin or his ministries would poke holes through the budget. Yeltsin's adviser on political geography said that when the president traveled his aides were told never to leave him alone with local officials. One governor reportedly ditched the chaperones by inviting Yeltsin for a row on the lake in a boat with room for only two. When the pair returned, the governor had a freshly signed decree in his pocket.

The bilateral agreements proved particularly controversial. To the nationalist writer Aleksandr Solzhenitsyn, they were "a form of direct capitulation by the center before the autonomies and a violation of the rights of the remaining oblasts of Russia." Yegor Stroyev, chairman of the Federation Council, said the treaties were "pulling the country apart." In fact, they helped stitch it back together. By the late 1990s, with the separatist bandwagon parked in the garage, the federal government could start retracting the privileges some regions had won.

Against this background, Chechnya stands out as a unique exception. Rather than appease the nationalists, the Kremlin cut subsidies and attempted to impose an economic embargo. Its negotiators tried to craft a bilateral agreement like those signed later with Tatarstan and Bashkortostan, but Dudayev would not settle for less than complete independence. In the face of Grozny's intransigence, Yeltsin's indiscipline then showed a less benign side as he let himself be provoked into war without any clear conception of what it might achieve. I will return in a few pages to the question what made Chechnya different.

The First War

After the debacle of November 26, 1994, events seemed to speed up. When, on November 29, Yeltsin's adviser Yury Baturin tried to talk him out of using force, the president "fixed him with a long, testing look" and sent him off to Sweden to busy himself negotiating a minor maritime issue. The same day, at Yeltsin's strong urging, Russia's Security Council approved a full-scale military operation to overthrow Dudayev. The Justice Minister, Yury Kalmykov, an ethnic Cherkess, expressed reservations and resigned soon afterwards. But the vote was unanimous. Almost immediately, Russian planes started bombing the Grozny airport and other sites. Then on December 11, after some hurried planning by the military brass, an army of about 38,000 men crossed into Chechnya.

On New Year's Eve, the federal forces attacked Grozny. Artillery pounded the capital, as bombers circled overhead. At the height of the Serb shelling of Sarajevo, the city had taken 3,500 detonations a day. In Grozny, the rate reached, by one estimate, 4,000 an hour. Dense layers of smoke from the burning oil refinery covered the city as a cold drizzle fell. It was, wrote one lyrical observer, "like being at the bottom of a grey, turbid sea, watching great grey sharks wheeling and diving above your head."

In the first few days, the poorly trained federal ground troops were slaughtered. The generals had apparently learned little from the November disaster. Tanks were bottled up in city streets, trapped and methodically incinerated by teams of guerrillas with antitank missiles and grenades, who navigated via the sewer system and popped out unannounced. The crews, terrified eighteen- and nineteen-year-olds with no training in urban warfare, raced into basements, apartments, toilets, seeking cover, where the Chechen fighters finished them off with knives, pistols, even swords. Two whole battalions of the 131st Maykop brigade were wiped out within a few days around the Grozny train station.

Only after more than two months of heavy fighting did the much larger federal contingent manage to force Dudayev's defenders out of Grozny, occupying the final parts on March 7th. Much of the city had been pulverized—the university and oil institute completely destroyed, the museum and archive badly damaged. The Chechen fighters retreated to the mountains, from where they would descend to ambush Russian troops in the towns. Through the spring, the federal forces pushed south. By May the Chechens were in bad shape, driven back to Vedeno and running low on ammunition. Russian bombers circled "like a swarm of flies" above them, Aslan Maskhadov, the Chechen military commander, later recalled.

To regain the initiative, the defenders turned to terror. Shamil Basayev, eleven of whose relatives had just been killed by Russian bombs, led a gang of fighters into Stavropol in June 1995. Disguised as Russian mercenaries in army fatigues and black headscarves, they were escorted by a car with fighters in police uniforms. At the checkpoints, they swore at the soldiers who wanted to inspect their trucks, said they were carrying "Cargo 200," the code for corpses of Russian servicemen, and bribed their way through. Their true target is not known, but about one hundred miles into Russia proper they were stopped by a line of police cars amid the golden wheatfields. Basayev, with his 148 commandos, shot his way into the nearby town of Budyonnovsk, raised a Chechen flag above the telephone exchange, and took some 1,200 hostages, herding them into the hospital.

For several days, officials tried to negotiate, while law enforcement surrounded the building. Basayev, demanding an immediate withdrawal of Russian troops from Chechnya, executed twelve of the prisoners. On the fourth day, the authorities tried to storm the hospital, and rescued some hostages, but many were killed. Eventually Prime Minister Chernomyrdin, negotiating by phone with Basayev, struck a deal in which the government agreed to restart peace talks and call a ceasefire and the terrorists were allowed to escape, driving in buses to Chechnya, where the final hostages were released.

Six months later, another field commander, Salman Raduyev, hoping to equal Basayev's feat, took more than two thousand hostages in Kizlyar, Dagestan. The terrorists began driving prisoners back to Chechnya in buses, but were stopped by a helicopter gunship at the village of Pervomayskoe, where they took cover with their hostages in the empty houses, strafing with machine guns the Russian troops that tried to storm the village. Eventually, the Chechens made a dash for freedom, walking across a minefield at night, using their prisoners as human mine-sweepers. Many, including Raduyev, made it. Sixty-nine people, including twenty-eight civilians, were reported to have died.

In April 1996, Dudayev, hiding in the Chechen forests, talked for too long on a satellite telephone. A Russian guided missile homed in on the signal, killing him. By this point, Yeltsin, campaigning for reelection, had begun peace talks, and they continued, somewhat bizarrely unaffected by Dudayev's death. On May 27, Yeltsin met with acting Chechen president Yandarbiev in the Kremlin and agreed to a ceasefire and exchange of prisoners. Then, on June 10, Yeltsin promised to withdraw Russian troops by the end of August. The peace held until after Yeltsin's reelection. But on July 9, as Yeltsin recovered from a heart attack, Russian planes bombed a mountain village where Chechen leaders were meeting, forcing them to flee on foot through the ravines. Despite restarting hostilities, the Russians proved unprepared when a Chechen offensive in August, led by Basayev, swept back and retook Grozny. On August 31, Maskhadov and General Aleksandr Lebed, whom Yeltsin had appointed Secretary of the Security Council, signed the Khasavyurt Accords, which provided for an immediate armistice and put off consideration of Chechnya's final status until 2001. All federal troops withdrew.

Although they had killed Dudayev, the Russians had achieved none of their objectives. Chechnya had not renounced its claim to independence. The security threat to southern Russia was worse than before. The Chechens were widely considered to have won, defeating a much larger and stronger enemy, although at terrible cost. In Russian military circles, many thought Lebed, who had negotiated the accord with Maskhadov, a traitor who had stabbed the army in the back.

Casualty figures are still disputed. The Russian authorities admit to having lost 5,500 troops, although others give figures as high as 14,000. Tallies of civilian deaths are even more controversial. Among more believable estimates, the ethnographer and former Russian nationalities minister Valery Tishkov puts the death toll at around 35,000, with some 400,000 refugees forced from their homes. The human rights organization Memorial assesses total civilian deaths somewhat higher, at 50,000.

Why it Happened

Fifteen years after its outbreak, the first Chechen war remains puzzling. Given how masterfully Yeltsin's governments had managed other potentially dangerous, ethnically charged confrontations, why was Chechnya different?

To adherents of the romantic view sketched earlier, the war is not puzzling at all. An ancient nation, intensely conscious of its identity, the Chechens had been fighting Russian colonialism for centuries. When Moscow's capacity for repression weakened, it was only natural that they would fight for their freedom. The martial culture of the mountain clans and the priority they placed on liberty made compromising on independence unthinkable.

The Chechens were culturally distinct from most other citizens of Russia. Although almost all could speak Russian, 94 percent in 1989 spoke Chechen at home. The vast majority were active Muslims, who gave their children Muslim first names, and married other Chechens. In 1994, four thousand made the pilgrimage to Mecca. But this does not by itself explain why war broke out. The neighboring Avars were even less assimilated than the Chechens, with slightly higher rates of native language usage and observant Muslims. Yet Avar nationalism was kept in check by Dagestan's political institutions.

To say the Chechens were an ancient nation that had been fighting for self-determination for centuries is misleading. They fought the Russians in the nineteenth century not as Chechens but as Muslims and inhabitants of particular mountain villages, under the Avar holy warrior Imam Shamil. A Chechen national identity began to emerge during this war, and was later solidified by policies of the Soviet regime, which printed the word "Chechen" in local inhabitants' passports, and deported them as a suspect "nationality." Despite this, it is striking that leading "nationalists" in the early 1990s seemed confused at first about which nation they represented. Yandarbiev named his party not the Chechen Democratic Party but the *Vaynakh* Democratic Party. Dudayev, in early speeches, also called for the creation of a "single Vaynakh statehood." Chechen nationalism seems to have been a fallback position once schemes for Vaynakh unity faltered.

Even once they settled on Chechen nationalism, the leaders could not decide what to call themselves. "Chechen," most experts agreed, was a term chosen by Russian colonists after the name of a local village that, ironically, bore the name of thirteenth century Mongol conqueror. Some favored "Nokhchii," a variant of a name found in a seventh century Armenian chronicle, but it had only recently been used by Chechens themselves. In office, Dudayev rechristened the republic "Ichkeria," and some Chechens called themselves Ichkeritsy. This was what nineteenth century Russian mapmakers had labeled the mountainous southern part of today's Chechnya, a name picked up by the poet Lermontov. It came from the Kumyk—the Turkic lingua franca of the Caucasus—and literally meant something like "hinterland" or "that place over there."

All nations live in counterpoint with their neighbors, defined in part by their "others." Still, the embarrassment over names in the early 1990s shows that Chechen identity was not as ancient and natural as the romantics imagined. The intense separatist nationalism of the early 1990s was a relatively short-lived phenomenon, cooked up by local politicians from convenient myths and misremembered history. By the late 1990s, it had largely evaporated, replaced by a brand of transnational Islamic fundamentalism.

As for the clans, the culture of the mountain auls, the blood feuds, they had faded into the background as the republic modernized. Some "ancient" practices and attitudes that journalists observed were probably products of the war rather than causes of it. In 1990, most Chechens disapproved of blood vengeance, according to one survey, and showed little religious prejudice. By 1995, prejudice against non-Muslims and support for vendettas had increased dramatically. Even in 1995, Chechens were not intensely anti-Russian, at least judging by this survey. They apparently blamed the politicians, not the people. Nor did Chechen culture make compromise unthinkable, as demonstrated by the fact that in 1993 much of the population and elite appeared to favor a compromise. As noted, the leaders of parliament and Grozny city government, supported by many other politicians, had been working on a bilateral treaty with Moscow.

Of course, some Chechens were consumed by historical grievance. But others had a more pragmatic outlook, focused on the benefits of modernization, the improvements in lifestyle achieved in preceding decades, and hopes for continued development, for which integration with Russia remained necessary. In fieldwork in the republic, the sociologist Ekaterina Sokirianskaia found a third image competing with these two—surprisingly, one of cosmopolitan harmony and nostalgia for the multicultural 1970s and 1980s. "Life was much more interesting back then," recalled one of her interviewees, from the village of Sernovodsk, outside Grozny. The five Chechen and four Ingush families on her street, along with one Armenian and one Russian couple, celebrated each other's religious holidays. "Everyone tried to cook the best of their cuisine and invite the neighbors." In school, she was taught by Russians, Jews, and Armenians. "This monoethnic environment is very bad for us," she complained to Sokirianskaia. "We need people of other nationalities around." After the Russian bombing of residential areas in 1995, such perspectives went into hibernation.

If Chechnya's history and culture did not make conflict inevitable, why did it occur? Some point to particularities of Chechnya's social structure. Unlike in Tatarstan or Bashkortostan, where Soviet leaders had sought to coopt potential nationalists by creating a caste of indigenous apparatchiks, Chechens and Ingush received no affirmative action. Even after 1957, they remained "traitor nations," always distrusted. Russians were moved in to fill the important administrative and industrial jobs. Grozny's Oil Institute was staffed by Russians, Armenians, and Jews, but not Chechens. Chechens also faced discrimination in higher education. What native intelligentsia developed was small and embittered. Those who managed to break in, like the poet Yandarbiev, had little hope of climbing the ladder to Moscow.

In other places, the nomenklatura nationalists—careerists trained in bureaucratic maneuver and tactful deception—proved skilled at mediating between their regions and Moscow while fortifying their own positions. Those that grabbed the controls of Union republics helped dissolve the Soviet Union (see Chapter 5). Within Russia, it was precisely these seasoned machine politicians—Shaymiev of Tatarstan; Spiridonov, the honorary Komi; Yeltsin himself—that found a way, anarchic as it looked to outsiders, to reintegrate the country while reallocating power and disarming the authentic nationalists. In Chechnya, a native bureaucrat only took charge in 1989 with the appointment of Zavgayev. Whether for lack of skill, resources, or just time, he failed to coopt the Chechen National Congress and was himself displaced by Yandarbiev's radicals.

Besides an embittered intelligentsia, anti-Chechen barriers in higher education and industry, along with the high birth rate, generated a large "subproletariat" of underemployed, rural young men, dependent on migratory work. The Soviet economic crisis destroyed the demand for migrant labor. Tens of thousands of youths who would have been building private cottages in Siberia were stuck at home during the summer of 1991, with little to do other than populate the nationalist crowds and militias.

The legacies of Soviet discrimination increased the odds that someone like Dudayev—who, could fire up the rural masses with the help of angry local intellectuals—would rise to the top. But that does not explain why he proved so intransigent. The contrast with Ingushetia is striking. It too had almost no native nomenklatura and a mass of underemployed young men. And there, as in Chechnya, an outsider ended up as regional leader—like Dudayev, a military officer and Afghan war hero, General Ruslan Aushev. Yet Ingushetia was careful not to get dragged into Dudayev's adventure. Aushev negotiated ably with Moscow, avoiding a flare-up of Ingush nationalism, which at times risked sparking a war with North Ossetia over the disputed Prigorodny district.

Could Dudayev have imitated Aushev or Shaymiev? Could he have pushed Yeltsin to the brink, extracting Tatarstan-like concessions, but then settled for a confederative status within the Russian Republic? Here we need to consider Dudayev's character.

Given his earlier life and career, Dudayev's absolutism seems strange. He would appear the perfect candidate to strike a deal. The first Chechen to make general in the Soviet armed forces, he was the republic's best example of successful assimilation. Indeed, Dudayev had spent only a few years of his life in Chechnya, and, according to many contemporaries, while fluent in Russian, he spoke Chechen haltingly. His wife was the ethnically Russian daughter of a Soviet army officer. Hardly an Islamic fundamentalist, he once "told an interviewer that Muslims must pray three times a day," and when informed that it was actually five, replied "Oh, well, the more the merrier." In Afghanistan, he loyally carpet bombed the Islamic militants fighting Soviet occupation, winning the Order of the Red Star and the Order of the Red Banner. A Ukrainian air force officer who commanded him, Konstiantyn Morozov, was impressed by Dudayev's discipline and professionalism, his "real military backbone."

Who better to work out a compromise with Russia's ruling circles, men like Defense Minister Pavel Grachev, whom Dudayev had known in Afghanistan? And yet, the climb itself must have taken a toll. As a Chechen, he had been under the microscope, watched constantly for any sign of unreliability. Morozov was at the military airfield when Dudayev got the news of his promotion to general.

> He was absolutely ecstatic, carried away by his emotions, which probably got the better of him. Right there on the tarmac he danced the *lezginka*, a traditional folk dance of Chechnya and much of the Caucasus region. . . . He understood . . . that at that particular moment in our history it was impossible for a top military man to speak out in defense of one's national identity. That moment would come, all in due time, but for the moment he simply danced the *lezginka*. Very well, I might add.

Morozov's recollection may be colored by his own national awakening—he would later serve as independent Ukraine's first defense minister. But in that defiant and somewhat risky *lezginka* perhaps one glimpses the chronic tension that must have accompanied Dudayev's efforts to blend into the chauvinistic officer corps. Perhaps the emotional price he paid for his successful assimilation helps explain the prickly sensitivity he showed later towards Yeltsin and his generals.

In the portraits of reporters, Western and Russian, Dudayev appears almost a caricature of a third world dictator. He would emerge for interviews, usually late at night, in an impeccably ironed uniform, and harangue the journalists with rhetorical questions and hour-long tirades against "Russism"—an ideology that was "a form of Satanism" and "worse than Nazism." With his delicate mustache, his "mirthless, artificial smile," and his "theatrical, metallic laugh," he reminded the British journalist Anatol Lieven, of "a well-groomed but irritable Siamese cat." Even as he sought meetings with Yeltsin, Dudayev could not help goading the Russian president, calling him a "drunkard," the "leader of a gang of murderers." He threatened to attack nuclear power plants and send Basayev to blow up the Kremlin. He chose to read out a demand from demonstrators that after every air raid he hang a Russian prisoner in the street using captured parachute cords.

Besides the counterproductive rants, there was an element of plain

strangeness about Dudayev's behavior. Some suspected psychological infirmity—paranoia or megalomania. After an explosion killed the
Chechen interior minister in 1993, Dudayev's men abducted the mayor of
a nearby village "whom Dudayev suspected of complicity because he had
been seen to glance at his watch fifteen minutes before the explosion." He
claimed to have discovered that Islam emerged not in the Arabian desert
but in Chechnya, and that his people were descendants of Noah, whose
Ark had landed in the Chechen mountains. According to his economics
minister, Taymaz Abubakarov, Dudayev "spoke with the conviction of a
man who knows mysteries that are concealed from others."

Asked why he would not compromise on complete independence,
Dudayev sometimes claimed to be a hostage of his radical supporters. On
the eve of war, Grachev met Dudayev and urged him to back down. "I do
not belong to myself," Dudayev exploded, according to Grachev. "If I take
such a decision, I won't be there any longer, but others will." There may
be some truth to this. However, it is not clear that accommodating Russia would have been more dangerous than the alternative. Basayev and
Yandarbiev would have called him a traitor. Yet if he stuck to his guns, he
would face Gantemirov, Labazanov, Avturkhanov, and the entire Russian
army. In fact, he survived just sixteen months after the war's outbreak.

My guess is that, to put it bluntly, Dudayev did not reach a deal with
Moscow because he did not know how. A competent air force commander, he had been thrust into a politically treacherous environment,
with no useful experience and no allies he could trust. He knew how to
manage a fleet of bombers, but had no idea how to negotiate political
agreements or run a government, no intuition about when to bluff and
when to fold his cards. He had, as Georgi Derluguian writes, "the military
belief in the power of stern commands." This was of little use for dealing
with Yeltsin or building a functional state. Caught between a grandiose
self-image and a lack of administrative ability, he relied on aggressive
rhetoric because he knew no other way to build support, and ended up a
hostage not so much of his surroundings as of his own limitations.

On the other side, Yeltsin's resort to force also requires explaining.
A permissive factor was his very success in calming other centers of
unrest. Two years earlier, as regions from Arkhangelsk to Chukotka were
declaring sovereignty, even the hawks felt queasy. "At that time," Nation-

alities Minister Nikolay Yegorov admitted, "the use of force against the Chechen leadership could have caused an explosion throughout the Northern Caucasus as well as in other parts of the country." Abdulatipov thought military intervention in 1992 would have prompted "several Chechnyas." After agreements were signed with other Muslim republics such as Tatarstan, Bashkortostan, and Kabardino-Balkaria, the danger of a broader conflagration was much weaker. In the event, the Tatar and Bashkir presidents made only muted criticisms and offered to mediate.

Moscow's successful accommodation of regional challenges casts doubt on one common rationale for the intervention. Allowing Chechnya independence, some said, would have encouraged other republics to secede. However, by late 1994 no other regions wanted to. As Yeltsin himself announced that August: "The danger of Russia falling apart has passed."

Some claimed Yeltsin's main concern was oil. Although Chechnya's own reserves had shrunk to insignificance—in 1985, it produced less than one percent of Russia's oil—a major pipeline crossed the republic, running from Azerbaijan to Novorossiysk. However, given the war's enormous cost—estimated at $5.5 billion, not including rebuilding—it would have been much cheaper to construct a new stretch of pipeline bypassing the republic than to fight. In 1999 a plan to do this was priced at $100 to $350 million.

Others suggest that Yeltsin's aides hoped to boost his popularity with a lightning military campaign. One lawmaker said Security Council Secretary Oleg Lobov told him the Kremlin needed "a small victorious war to raise the President's ratings." Although popular with commentators, this interpretation is not based on much evidence. Lobov later denied making any such statement. Polls before the war showed the public solidly against the use of force, and Yeltsin's advisers actually argued against it.

Liberals sometimes cast the Chechen adventure as a conspiracy of hard-liners. In fact, the picture is more complicated. One early advocate of support for the anti-Dudayev opposition was the president's chief of staff, Sergey Filatov, a leading Kremlin democrat. The liberal foreign minister Andrey Kozyrev favored military intervention. Within the security service, it was Sergey Stepashin, the FSK head, usually seen as a relative liberal, and his deputy, Yevgeny Savostyanov, one of the founders of

Democratic Russia, that got the Russian authorities into the disastrous November attack on Grozny. While some of the Moscow liberals—Gaidar, Kovalyov—consistently opposed military intervention, it was not only hard-liners who supported it.

Hawks favored a military strategy for reasons that were transparent—to strengthen the image of the Russian state, enhance the role of the armed forces, even to create an environment for restricting freedoms elsewhere. But why would liberals favor force? This gets to one of the most fundamental, if sometimes neglected, motivations. In Stepashin's telling, the key factor was not Dudayev's insistence on Chechen independence but the security problem Chechnya had become for its neighbors. In early 1994, terrorist gangs struck repeatedly across the border in Stavropol Kray, taking hostages and demanding ransom. By summer, the attacks were occurring with what Stepashin called "provocative regularity." On May 26, four gunmen hijacked a bus full of school children in the city of Mineralnye Vody, and then fled to Chechnya in a helicopter with several million dollars the authorities had provided. On June 28, three guerrillas stormed a bus, again in Mineralnye Vody, and, after collecting $3 million, flew in another helicopter to Chechnya. Exactly one month later, on July 28, four masked Chechens seized a bus with forty-one passengers near Pyatigorsk, demanding $15 million and a helicopter. Four hostages were killed when police stormed the vehicle. In mid-August, Chechen gunmen kidnapped a young man in Kizlyar, Dagestan, and demanded ransom.

In Yeltsin's own account, the insecurity loomed large. His memoir (written later and with the obvious aim of self-justification) says little in this context about Russia's territorial integrity. His main points concern the security vacuum in the failing Chechen state.

> A black hole of criminality had opened within Russia. Here the Chechens looked no worse and no better than other people—every nation has its bandits. But it was only in Chechnya that this banditry became a virtually legal form of income and a matter of civic pride. It's one thing when a state tries to fight organized crime in its cities and its territory where the law enforcement agencies have some sort of authority. It's another matter when the local govern-

ment helps the bandits, and they disappear with their cash, hostages, and weapons into that black hole.

Dudayev either could not or would not prevent the cross-border raids.

Most likely, he could not. By this point, the institutions of law enforcement in Chechnya were barely functional and no match for the many armed groups in the territory. The state's implosion had not been inevitable. It resulted from Dudayev's actions. First, he helped arm the Chechen population, making it legal, in one of his first decrees, for all Chechens to own firearms, and helping to force the departing Soviet troops to sell or surrender their stocks, on the theory that universal gun ownership was the most effective national defense. Soon one could buy a grenade launcher in the Grozny market for the price of a television. Second, unlike the wary nationalists who took power in other ethnic republics, Dudayev sought not so much to capture local state institutions as to replace them.

Alongside the police, Dudayev established his new "National Guard." In March 1992, he liquidated the Russian tax inspectorate and created his own. He abolished the commercial court system and reorganized the ministry of justice, first into a committee on legal reform, then back into a justice ministry, which was then merged with the procuracy. He suspended the criminal inspections committee. In April 1993, he dissolved the cabinet of ministers, the parliament, the constitutional court, and the Grozny City Council, imposing unconstrained presidential rule. That month he also suspended the Interior Ministry, and in June the National Security Service. The constant reorganizations aimed to consolidate personal power. Along the way, Dudayev quarreled with almost all his former supporters.

In place of Soviet era institutions, Dudayev relied on charismatic appeal, nationalistic slogans, and armed young men from the countryside. He sought to reanimate elements of traditional social structure and to employ institutions like the Council of Elders, formed in 1991, which occupied the building of the disbanded parliament. As his authority waned in 1994, he tried to revive the Chechen National Congress. These organizations were of little use for implementing policy, and, for all their romantic appeal, were not even effective forums for deliberation or bridges to the public. The Council of Elders, with some seven thousand members, was too unwieldy and did not control the armed bands.

This strategy of undermining the state while arming tens of thousands of unemployed men had predictably destructive consequences. It fostered the emergence of centers of violent economic crime and terrorism. It left the ethnic Russians and educated, professional Chechens vulnerable to intimidation by armed thugs, prompting an exodus. And it eliminated mediating structures between the president and the population. Without effective vehicles to mobilize and control his supporters, Dudayev could not lead them in a moderate direction. His only way to rouse a crowd was through extreme—even paranoid—rhetoric. In place of political mechanisms, he was reduced to using force to address all problems. By the end he had become, in Tatar President Shaymiev's apt phrase, "a general in whose hands remained nothing but weapons."

Some observers argue that war might have been averted had Yeltsin agreed to meet personally with Dudayev. But by late 1994 the deeper problem was no longer Dudayev and his demands for independence, although of course these remained irritating. Had Yeltsin and Dudayev met and become the best of friends, that would not have eradicated the pockets of lawlessness south of the border, which Dudayev no longer seemed able to control.

If the security threat was the ultimate justification for Russia's intervention, that it occurred so haphazardly has to do with the way Yeltsin let himself get drawn into the conflict and humiliated. As recently as August 11, he had insisted that: "Intervention by force is impermissible. . . . Were we to apply pressure by force against Chechnya, this would rouse the whole Caucasus, there would be such a commotion, there would be so much blood that nobody would ever forgive us." In August and September 1994, both the FSK and military intelligence, the GRU, strongly advised against direct military intervention. Even the rebel leader Gantemirov said a federal invasion would be "a disaster," uniting all Chechens against the invaders. Right up until the November debacle, Yeltsin had not decided to use force, according to Filatov. But when Dudayev paraded the captured tank crews before the press, threatening to execute them, this seems to have been more than Yeltsin could take.

Speed was suddenly of the essence. The whole military operation was planned in eleven days, largely bypassing the senior generals. It showed. Tanks were sent in without the necessary infantry and air support or even accurate maps. The brigades were a "salami" of bits and pieces patched together from up to seven units, soldiers who had never trained together if they had trained at all. There were too few of them. World War II experience showed that in urban combat the attacker needs a six-to-one manpower advantage; but only about 6,000 troops entered Grozny on January 1, 1995, probably fewer than Dudayev had on hand. During the war, the troops were underfed and, according to General Lebed, crawling with lice. Early on, they received only one quarter liter of water a day.

Yeltsin appeared genuinely shocked by the apalling state of his military and the incompetent planning. On January 4, he met with Grachev, Interior Minister Yerin, and Security Council chairman Lobov, and peppered them with angry questions. He had become hostage, he later wrote, to "the stereotype of the might of the Russian army." But, having given Grachev just days to plan the assault, he had no cause to be surprised. There had been plenty of signs. On December 19, Grachev had removed the operation's commander, General Aleksey Mityukhin, after the latter reported that the troops were not ready. His replacement, General Eduard Vorobyov, resigned when he saw the mess the plans were in. Other leading generals also openly opposed the operation. Lieven writes that 557 officers of all ranks were disciplined, fired, or resigned in protest.

The problem was not just poor preparation. There was a basic incompatibility between the operation's goal and the instrument with which it was pursued. At this point, the Russian armed forces knew how to do three things: launch a nuclear armada, refight the Battle of Stalingrad, and march into a rebellious capital (Budapest in 1956, Prague in 1968) to intimidate the locals. None of these was useful for dealing with a collapsed state degenerating into a terrorist haven. After their columns of tanks failed to cow the Chechen defenders, the generals fell back on the second option. Nothing could have been more counterproductive. Besides the enormous human tragedy, a World War II–style offensive was guaranteed to accelerate the decay, razing the last foundations of the old order, further militarizing the population, destroying trust, and spreading trauma.

All large powers have trouble fighting insurgencies and dealing with the emotional blow of terrorism. But there were alternatives, some proposed by Yeltsin's own advisers. Moscow might have tightened economic pressure on Dudayev, restricting outside funding, while assisting local leaders in Chechnya. By creating islands of security and relative prosperity, it could have competed for the hearts and minds of Chechens outside Grozny. To defend against terrorist attacks, it might have reinforced policing in adjacent regions, improved intelligence gathering, and retrained the Alfa quick response teams. Instead, old-style military muscle was used on a massive scale, with horrific consequences for civilians, destroying far more than all previous terrorist attacks, and actually exacerbating the security threat to Stavropol and Dagestan. The use of force was justified by the danger Chechnya posed to its neighbors. But there was no justification for the *way* force was used. This was Yeltsin's greatest blunder, and, with apologies to Talleyrand, it was worse than a mistake: it was a crime.

The Short Peace

In Chechnya, the war's end prompted a surge of hope. Citizens queued in the January chill to vote in the republic's second presidential election. The results, pronounced free and fair by OSCE observers, seemed to yield a mandate for pragmatism. The relatively moderate military commander Aslan Maskhadov won with 59.3 percent of the vote, far ahead of Basayev, with 23.5 percent, and Yandarbiev, with 10.1 percent. That May, Yeltsin and Maskhadov signed a treaty agreeing to "reject forever the use of force, or threat to use force, to resolve any disputes."

Maskhadov's challenges were enormous. The republic's economy and infrastructure had been crushed by Russian bombs. What social and political institutions had survived Dudayev's demontage had been torn apart by war. Hundreds of thousands had been forced from their homes. Violence had been decentralized to a dozen warlords, who proved unwilling to let it become once again the monopoly of the state. The ideals of modernity and development, cultivated by Soviet rule, had disappeared, along with most of the professors, teachers, doctors, and engineers. About 250,000 people had left Chechnya between 1994 and 1996. Grozny's population had shrunk from 400,000 in 1989 to 186,000 in 1996.

Despite the exodus of intellectuals, those scholars that remained made some remarkable breakthroughs. Researchers discovered that Chechnya was, in fact, the world's oldest state; that the Vikings had originated not in Scandinavia but in the Caucasus; that the names for Kiev and the Dnieper River derived from the Chechen language; that 'Rus' was not, as previously thought, a Germanic word but actually a Chechen name; and that the best generals in the Jordanian, Iranian, and Turkish armies were of Chechen nationality.

To make money, the warlords trafficked narcotics, weapons, and people. Probably the biggest business was kidnapping foreigners, Russians from neighboring regions, and ordinary Chechens, to be ransomed to their families. Thousands were kidnapped each year. Ransoms ranged from $10,000 for an ordinary Russian soldier to millions of dollars for a major figure; the total take between 1997 and 2000 was estimated at $200 million. One top official, Valentin Vlasov, was sold to the Russian authorities for $5 million after six months in captivity. Prisoners were kept in pits or dungeons and often tortured, with videos or body parts sent to relatives to encourage them to send money. Some were traded as slaves—markets operated openly in Grozny and Urus Martan—and performed menial work for Chechen families. Four Western telephone engineers were brutally decapitated in December 1998.

Maskhadov first tried to coopt Basayev, but soon found himself fighting him and his radical allies. The struggle for power merged with a battle between different brands of Islam. Yandarbiev, as acting president in 1996, had replaced ordinary courts by Sharia ones. A Sharia criminal code was quickly translated from Sudan's and enacted—so quickly, in fact, that fines were listed in Sudanese pounds and compensation for killings measured in camels. In April 1997, executions began, and Chechen television showed a convicted murderer having his throat slit. Drunks received forty strokes of the rod.

Such measures attracted the interest of purists from the Persian Gulf, who helped finance a growing movement of fundamentalists, known in Russia as Wahhabis. The Wahhabis, who had no clear connection to the Saudi sect, favored a literal interpretation of the Koran, advocated theocratic rule, and accused Sufis, who worshiped at saints' shrines, of polytheism. During the first war, Chechen links to Al Qaeda had been tenuous—a Saudi-born guerrilla and Afghan war veteran, Emir al Khattab, turned up to lead an Arab battalion—but later the contacts increased. Khattab set up camps in Chechnya to train militants, and sold gruesome videos of the execution of Russian soldiers over the Internet. In 1997, bin Laden's deputy, Ayman al Zawahiri, tried to enter Chechnya with false documents, but was arrested at the border and imprisoned for six months.

By the summer of 1998, Basayev had joined Khattab and the Wahhabis in open confrontation with Maskhadov and the Sufis. Their ambitions now extended beyond Chechnya to the creation of an Islamic caliphate across the North Caucasus. In May 1998, Wahhabis associated with Basayev and Khattab occupied several mountain villages in Dagestan, hoisting green flags above the government building, forcing out the local police and creating a "Chiapas-like revolutionary enclave." Repulsing a police force sent to retake the village, the Wahhabis set up their own Sharia patrols and posted signs around the villages that read: "You are entering independent Islamic territory."

In Chechnya, by late 1998, Maskhadov's rule did not extend much beyond Grozny. In a last bid to regain control, he fired his vice president, dissolved parliament, and began cooperating with the Russian authorities. According to Stepashin, then interior minister, Moscow provided Maskhadov with intelligence information, training for some of his guards, bulletproof vests, and an armored limousine that, reportedly, saved his life more than once. At home, Maskhadov remained almost completely isolated. "There are criminals around me," he complained to his sister-in-law. "I can do nothing." He lost even Moscow's support when, in March 1999, another top official, Major General Gennady Shpigun, was kidnapped from his plane on the runway at Grozny's airport. A year later, Shpigun's body was discovered in a mass grave.

Repeat Engagement

The incidents that began the second war had been planned for months, on both sides. After the brazen abduction of General Shpigun, the federal authorities started tightening a noose around the republic. Stepashin sent more Interior Ministry troops to the borders in Stavropol and Dagestan with orders to shoot suspected terrorists on sight; air and train communications were shut off. A plan was developed for troops to advance to the Terek River by August or September.

In Chechnya, anyone who paid attention knew a major operation was coming. In April, Basayev's associates had called for the "decolonization of Dagestan." Throughout the summer, rumors of the impending attack circulated. The anthropologist Valery Tishkov recalls talking to a Chechen scholar at a conference in Geneva in June 1999. "Don't you know that a big war will start in Dagestan no later than September? This is perfectly obvious," the scholar told him. Stepashin said the authorities had received intelligence of a planned offensive in June.

Given this, claims that Basayev's incursion was organized by the Russian security services to boost support for Putin seem implausible. Both the incursion and the federal response were planned months before Putin's appointment as prime minister. Nor does it appear that Basayev and Khattab needed any encouragement. On August 6 and 7, the two led more than one thousand guerrillas across the border to the Wahhabi-occupied villages, from where they announced the creation of an "independent Islamic State of Dagestan" with Basayev as its emir. The Chechens apparently expected Dagestanis to join the jihad against the Russian "colonists." In fact, the local tribesmen, who had grown tired of paying ransom to Chechen kidnappers, formed militias to fight the invaders. By August 24, the volunteers, with Russian air support and ground troops, had forced Basayev's band back across the border. As the defenders started reclaiming the Wahhabi villages, Basayev struck again further north, prolonging fighting for another month. Putin, who as prime minister sent the army to repel Basayev, became a hero in Dagestan.

Meanwhile, on September 4, terrorists exploded a car bomb beside an apartment building in the Dagestani city of Buinaksk, not far from the conflict, killing sixty-eight people. Over the next two weeks, explosions destroyed apartment buildings in Moscow and Volgodonsk, bringing total deaths to about three hundred and spreading panic. The central authorities blamed Chechen and Wahhabi militants associated with Basayev and Khattab, but the lack of clear evidence and the strange events in Ryazan—where what looked like a similar bomb was found in an apartment building, having been planted there by FSB agents who then said it was part of a "training exercise"—left many unsure just who was responsible (see Chapter 3).

On September 29, Putin offered to negotiate with Maskhadov if he condemned terrorism "clearly and firmly," ejected armed bands from Chechnya, and agreed to extradite "criminals." Maskhadov, although disavowing the Dagestan adventure, would not go this far. Meanwhile, following Stepashin's plan, Putin moved troops to Chechnya's borders and then to the Terek. Sukhoi bombers and fighter jets destroyed bridges and blocked mountain roads and passes. But the troops did not stop at the Terek. To establish a cordon sanitaire would be "pointless and technically impossible," Putin said. In the South and East, the terrain was too rugged, and in the North Stepashin's efforts to seal the border had not stopped attacks. The troops continued south, surrounded Grozny, and started bombing.

From a technical standpoint, the generals had learned from their previous mistakes. This time their reenactment of Stalingrad was quite proficient. Instead of shelling Grozny for just a few hours before sending in ground troops, they bombed for four weeks, showering the city with Grad, Uragan, Tochka, and Tochka-U ballistic missiles that could cover seven hectares with cluster shrapnel. "The Russians have decided that the best way to handle urban combat is not to engage in urban operations in the first place," wrote one military analyst. By the time they had finished, there was very little left. The civilian population suffered more than even in 1995. Why Grozny was such a target is not entirely clear since it was still controlled by Maskhadov, who even the Russians agreed had not been organizing terrorist attacks or cross-border incursions.

By February 2000, the federal troops had taken Grozny, and a month later they had occupied all the main towns, forcing the defenders into the mountains. As in the first war, action then shifted to guerrilla ambushes, minor skirmishes, anti-rebel operations, reprisal killings, and terrorist attacks. The federal troops established garrisons in around two hundred towns and villages. From there, they conducted *zachistki* ("security sweeps") of villages to uncover hidden guerrillas, rounding up males and taking some to filtration camps, from which many never returned.

As in the first war, the Chechens turned to terrorist attacks within

Russia proper. Already in June 2000, "black widows" began appearing, young Chechen women who—whether voluntarily or not—became suicide bombers, setting off explosions that killed themselves and their targets. Such attacks initially focused on military installations in Chechnya but then spread to Moscow, where a rock concert, a subway station, and two Russian passenger planes were bombed. In the siege of Moscow's Dubrovka Theater in October 2002, the terrorists included nineteen women wearing belts packed with explosives. All forty-one hostage takers were executed by the Russian troops that stormed the building, and 129 hostages died, almost all killed by the anesthetic gas piped in to incapacitate the terrorists (see Chapter 3). An even more traumatic case came in September 2004, when terrorists captured a school in Beslan, North Ossetia; 334 hostages, including many children, were killed when special forces stormed the building after three days. Basayev took credit for both incidents.

Such attacks aimed not just to terrify Russians but to attract funding from jihad supporters abroad. Before seizing the Dubrovka Theater, the terrorists sent a video to the Al Jazeera television station. In Chechnya women customarily dress in Western fashion. But in the video, the female terrorists appeared shrouded in black chadors, in front of a banner with the Arabic words "Allahu Akbar" (God is great). Speakers recited slogans including one taken verbatim from Osama bin Laden: "We yearn for death even more than you yearn for life."

Such international connections seemed increasingly important. In the late 1990s, the Pankisi Gorge, across the border in Georgia, had been a refuge for drug dealers, kidnappers, and some 450 fighters of the warlord Ruslan Gelayev. Early in the second war Al Qaeda set up an outpost there of Arab technicians, who, using encrypted satellite communications, assisted the Arab fighters in Chechnya as well as terrorist operations elsewhere. About sixty specialists in computer programming, communications, finance, poisons, and explosives, from Saudia Arabia, Jordan, Morocco, Algeria, and Egypt, hid out in the village of Omalo, near Duisi, training new recruits for Khattab's battalion and delivering cash from foreign donors.

Whereas the first war had seemed unnecessary to many Russians, public opinion initially strongly favored Putin's offensive. The kidnapping, the televised executions in Grozny, and then the shock of Basayev's attack on Dagestan and the apartment bombings left Russians with little sympathy for their southern neighbors. In March 2000, 70 percent of respondents thought Russia should continue the military operation, and only 22 percent favored beginning peace negotiations. But enthusiasm drained away. By January 2001, a majority favored negotiating. In 2003–2004, as support for the military option sank into the low double digits, thousands of people demonstrated against the war each month in Moscow and St. Petersburg.

Putin moved fast to reestablish political institutions in Chechnya, even if cynics saw them as fig leaves for Moscow rule, and to turn practical management over to Chechen partners. This became known as "Chechenization." From the start, the federal invasion was called not a war but a "counterterrorism operation." In January 2001, control was passed from the military to the FSB, which in July 2003 handed it over to the Interior Ministry. In March 2003, a referendum on a new draft Chechen constitution reportedly received 97 percent of the vote, with 89 percent participating. In October 2003, a new president was elected, followed by parliamentary elections in November 2005.

Putin's search for Chechen partners prompted one of his biggest personal gambles. In November 1999, Chechnya's former chief mufti, Akhmat Kadyrov, had defected to the federal side. Kadyrov, a Sufi cleric who had studied Islam in Bukhara, Tashkent, and Jordan, had supported Dudayev in the first war, urging his compatriots to: "Kill as many Russians as you can." After the armistice, he had backed Maskhadov. But he grew disenchanted with Maskhadov's inability to check the Arab fundamentalists. When the new war started, together with the local warlord Sulim Yamadayev, Kadyrov arranged for federal forces to occupy his home city of Gudermes without a fight. Maskhadov fired him from the post of chief mufti, calling him an "enemy of the Chechen people" who "should be eliminated." Shamil Basayev put a price of $100,000 on his head. Putin, on the other hand, appointed Kadyrov head of an interim Chechen government in June 2000. He put Sulim Yamadayev in charge of an elite military unit, the Vostok ("East") Battalion, set up to absorb rebels who accepted amnesty and switched sides.

Kadyrov remained faithful to his Moscow patron, consolidating control with the help of a militia known as the Kadyrovtsy led by his son Ramzan. Some rebel fighters accepted amnesties to join his forces. Others assassinated members of his administration. At times, Kadyrov pressed Putin to reduce the wanton violence federal troops inflicted on the Chechen population. In the presidential election of October 2003, no one was surprised that Kadyrov won by a landslide—or that rivals alleged fraud.

But six months later, on May 9, 2004, Kadyrov was killed when a massive explosion destroyed the stand where he was observing a Victory Day parade. Power passed to his son, Ramzan, who was chosen by parliament as the republic's president when he reached the constitutionally required minimum age of thirty in March 2007.

From 2003, Moscow began turning over the hunt for insurgents to the Kadyrovs and the Yamadayevs. Human rights organizations had accused the federal forces of the torture, abduction, and extrajudicial killing of civilians, as well as of theft and house burning. They reported similar abuses by the pro-Moscow Chechen forces. One scholar, using a broad set of sources, found reports of 22,253 cases of individual abuse during sweep operations between 2000 and 2005. The abuses included extrajudicial killings, injuries, forced disappearances, kidnapping for ransom, sexual assault, torture, property damage, and theft. Sweeps conducted by Chechen commandos prompted fewer counterattacks by insurgents than sweeps by Russian troops, perhaps because the Chechen raiders had superior intelligence or were better able to deter revenge attacks (under Kadyrov, the relatives of insurgents were held responsible for rebel actions). Kadyrov rejected the allegations that his subordinates engaged in torture.

One by one, the warlords were picked off. Khattab died in March 2002, reportedly poisoned by a letter sent by the Russian secret services. Raduyev, captured in March 2000, died in prison two years later from "internal bleeding," the cause of which was never convincingly explained. Yandarbiev, in exile in Qatar, was assassinated in February 2004 by Russian secret agents. A few weeks later, Gelayev was shot while trying to cross into Georgia. Maskhadov died in March 2005 after special forces threw a grenade into the basement where he was hiding. Then Basayev was killed in Ingushetia in July 2006 when a truck filled with explosives that he was escorting detonated. Russian special forces claimed to have set off the explosion by remote control; the Chechen rebels blamed a pothole. By 2009, Russian authorities said about five hundred Chechen militants remained. Their new leader, Doku Umarov, was fighting not for an independent Chechnya but for a Caucasian Emirate. "Our enemy is not only Russia," he was quoted as saying in 2007, "but also America, England, and Israel; all those who conduct war against Islam and Muslims." When in March 2010 "black widow" suicide bombers detonated explosives on two Moscow subway trains, killing thirty-nine, a video surfaced in which Umarov claimed responsibility.

With massive financial assistance from Moscow—which paid for 85 percent of the Chechen budget in 2008—Ramzan Kadyrov rebuilt Grozny from a rubble-strewn wasteland to a bustling city. Bullet-ridden shells of houses were replaced by neat, nine-storey blocks of flats, flanked by cafés, ice cream parlors, and luxury shopping malls. In October 2008, Europe's largest mosque opened in central Grozny, surrounded by manicured lawns. The old Lenin Prospekt had been reborn as Akhmat Kadyrov Prospekt, and Victory Prospekt was now Putin Prospekt.

Kadyrov also succeeded in concentrating power. Bad things seemed to happen to his enemies. The Yamadayev brothers had become rivals. In September 2008, the eldest, Ruslan, was assassinated in Moscow, apparently in a contract killing. Then, in March 2009, Sulim Yamadayev was shot dead in Dubai. The Vostok and Zapad battalions, associated with the Yamadayevs, were dissolved. In November 2006, Movladi Baysarov, an outspoken critic of Kadyrov, was shot and killed by Chechen policemen in central Moscow while apparently resisting arrest. A former Kadyrov bodyguard who became a regime critic, Umar Israilov, was murdered in Vienna in January 2009. Three other former insurgents were shot dead in Istanbul in 2008 and 2009.

Within Chechnya, as the leader's grip tightened and the insurgents were worn down, a kind of relative stability emerged. Although the details of human rights abuses by rebels and law enforcement remained horrific, the frequency of such abuses seemed to be declining. The organization Memorial monitored cases of abduction and murder in the republic. Its experts estimated that, taking into account nonreporting by victims and the group's limited geographical coverage, their figures captured from one-quarter to one-third of the total. These figures are shown in Table

Table 8.1 Memorial's count of abductions and murders in Chechnya

	2002	2003	2004	2005	2006	2007	2008	2009*
Abductions	544	498	450	325	187	35	42	77
Murders								
total	724	447	312	195	101	54	72	16
of noncombatants	557	297	122	79	33	16	24	7

Source: Memorial, *Statistika pokhishcheny i ubiystv v Chechne i Ingushetii* (figures for Chechnya), http://memo.ru/hr/hotpoints/caucas1/index.htm.
Note: * First six months of 2009

8.1. They show a very dramatic decrease in the number of abductions and murders between 2002 and the first six months of 2009.

Could it be that victims' families were growing more reluctant to reveal such crimes? The human rights workers believed that, at least in part, the statistics reflected a genuine improvement. Memorial attributed the sharp fall in abductions in 2007 to an effort by Kadyrov, as he sought to outmaneuver his rivals and consolidate public support, to improve the republic's record: "There is evidence that in January 2007, R. Kadyrov gave strict instructions to the leaders of the security services he controls to halt the abductions." A certain police investigation bureau, ORB-2, subordinate to federal, not Chechen, authorities, had been accused of engaging in systematic torture of detainees. Its leadership was purged in the summer of 2007, after an unusual joint campaign by local human rights advocates and the Kadyrov administration. "Since then Memorial has not received any reports of torture in ORB-2 and, in general, the number of cases of torture by law enforcement structures in the Chechen Republic has declined sharply," Memorial noted in April 2008. However, the situation worsened again from late 2008, with seventy-seven abductions reported in the first six months of 2009.

Some Chechens were undoubtedly glad of the growing stability. But it was stability of the kind Saddam Hussein provided to Iraqis. There were fewer deaths, fewer abductions than during the war. But there was fear. Giant Ramzan Kadyrovs stared down from massive billboards throughout Grozny. The original lived in a lavish complex in the family home of Tsentoroy, with a menagerie of black swans, pelicans, ostriches, lions, leopards, and tigers. Playing to conservative opinion, Kadyrov banned foreign music from the Grozny radio station, and female professors at the university were told to cover their heads in lectures. As everyone realized but no one said out loud, the whole construction rested on a single point. Should something happen to Kadyrov, nobody knew what would follow.

Criticizing the regime's human rights record continued to be dangerous. Nataliya Estemirova, Memorial's chief human rights advocate in Grozny, was kidnapped and murdered in July 2009. The journalist Anna Politkovskaya had been murdered in Moscow in 2006. She had been about to publish an article on kidnappings and torture by agents of the Chechen government. Other brave journalists and professionals who had looked into the Chechen abyss met similar fates. Paul Klebnikov, the editor of the Russian edition of *Forbes*, was shot dead in Moscow in 2004 in a contract hit. The Russian procurator general's office accused a Chechen warlord about whom Klebnikov had written an unflattering book of having ordered the killing.

As the jihadi militants were forced out of Chechnya, they spread to other parts of the North Caucasus, increasingly destabilizing Ingushetia and Dagestan. Data collected by the National Counterterrorism Center show that as the number of terrorist incidents in Chechnya fell after 2005, the number in Ingushetia and other North Caucasus republics soared. Reported attacks in Ingushetia rose from five in 2004 to 227 in 2008; those in Dagestan increased from twenty-nine to eighty-nine in the same period. Indeed, despite the decline in terrorist incidents in Chechnya, the total for the four republics of Chechnya, Ingushetia, Dagestan, and Kabardino-Balkaria rose from 230 in 2005 to 398 in 2008.

By the summer of 2009, Ingushetia was teetering on the edge. On June 10, the deputy head of the republic's supreme court was assassinated by terrorists, followed days later by Ingushetia's former vice premier. Then, on June 22, the republic's president, Yunus-Bek Yevkurov, was severely injured by a car bomb driven by a suicide bomber. Medvedev immediately called Kadyrov to the Kremlin, and asked him to personally take charge of the investigation.

Was the resort to Kadyrov's methods the only hope for stability in the North Caucasus? The irony was that Yevkurov, in his eight months in power, had come to symbolize the hope for a more intelligent, less brutal strategy. A tough career officer and paratrooper from military intelligence, he combined a readiness to use force against the jihadis with political flexibility and sensitivity to public opinion. He had included members of the political opposition in his government, paid his personal condolences to the family of a murdered human rights campaigner, and set up a hotline for citizens to complain about police abuses. He had required recertification of police officers and fired the head of the republic's interior ministry, who was accused of involvement in abductions. He had offered amnesty to corrupt officials who returned stolen money and to insurgents who had not committed major crimes. He had taken measures to reduce torture in Ingush jails. Shortly before he was attacked, Yevkurov had announced his cell phone number to the public, asking people to report abuses of power to him directly. Human rights campaigners, not a group prone to giddy optimism, were impressed. "Yevkurov consistently tried to reduce the gap between the people and the authorities, to make people believe that state agencies are defending the public interest," wrote Tatyana Lokshina of Human Rights Watch. "Today . . . people with sinking hearts are reading the bulletins about the president's health."

At the end of August, after months in the hospital, Yevkurov did return to office, a new scar visible on his right cheekbone. In October, he sacked his entire government for failing to make progress against the republic's deep-rooted problems. Yet he appeared unable to control the various special forces operating on the territory. Abductions by the secret services continued. To his outrage, all those arrested after the terrorist attack against him were freed by judges within two weeks.

Chechenization

Chechnya had started out in 1990 quite similar to other Muslim regions such as Tatarstan or Kabardino-Balkaria. Events took it down a different path. A secular nationalist movement—inspired by historical grievances and bad poems—dismantled the state it had seized, armed a volatile population of unemployed young men, and released criminals from the prisons to lead them. Responding to a genuine—although limited—danger, Russia's leaders sent thousands of poorly trained nineteen-year-olds with Kalashnikovs and Grad missiles to terrorize the local population, causing the nationalists to metamorphose, first into a collection of battle-hardened warlords, financed by kidnapping and donations from Middle Eastern jihadis, and then into an underground terrorist network of Islamic fundamentalists with cells across the North Caucasus. Unable to seal the borders, the Russians pulverized the region again, and then delivered it to a ruthless strongman, who imposed a stability based on ubiquitous fear.

One could sympathize with the victims and admire the only heroes in this story—the human rights advocates who tried to help the helpless and record the abuses, knowing the personal risks involved—but there was little edification to be had in the dismal chronicle of failures. It was not, primarily, a story of noble nationalists denied their right to self-determination. Nor was it simply a tale of externally financed Islamic terrorists attacking the Russian state. Rather, a series of mistakes and crimes, committed by many individuals, had amplified the effects of previous crimes and mistakes, liberating the human capacity for unimaginable cruelty that emerges in conditions of structured anarchy when men with guns grow accustomed to using them.

Historians used to ask whether the militaristic state of Prussia had been dissolved into modern Germany or whether Germany itself had been Prussianized, the whole remade in the image of the part. In Russia, some saw the pathologies of Chechnya infecting the country's entire democratic experiment. The violence, corruption, and crime that flourished in the republic in the early 1990s seemed to spread northwards, year by year. It was not, some said, Chechnya that had been "Chechenized." It was Russia.

Putin viewed Chechnya as, if not a cause of disorder elsewhere, an emblem of it. Chechnya appeared before him wherever he looked: "And not only in the North Caucasus. . . . Everywhere there is some kind of gaping hole. Problems."

Others saw Chechnya not in the problems that afflicted Russia but in the specious solutions that the country's leaders found for them. The empowerment of the security services, the quick resort to military means, the intimidation of the press, the progressive hollowing out of civic and political freedoms—all were justified by the threat of terrorism, the unscrupulousness of Russia's enemies. Lingering wars rarely improve the quality of government, but in a new democracy fighting an insurgency on its own territory rather than across the ocean, the effects were bound to be particularly pernicious. Other young democracies— Spain, Turkey, Indonesia—had struggled with similar challenges, some more successfully than others. Rarely did democracy emerge completely unscathed.

By 2009, the Chechenization of Russia had taken on a more direct meaning. With the decrease in violence in Chechnya itself and the sharp rise in terrorist attacks and police abuses in neighboring Ingushetia and Dagestan, the much-feared spread of war across the Caucasus was no longer hypothetical. Even the Kremlin leadership seemed to recognize that the crude application of security service methods by Ingushetia's previous governor had fueled the fire rather than extinguishing it, driving more local men into the mountains to join the jihad. For a region short on good news, and even shorter on optimists, the miraculous survival of Yunus-Bek Yevkurov was an unexpected piece of good luck. Expecting him to fail, one could still hope that he would not.

CHAPTER 9

Falling Apart

For the world's statesmen, the early 1980s was a time of clenched knuckles and insomnia. A new and dangerous cycle of the cold war had burst through the respite of *détente*. In 1977, Moscow had begun deploying intermediate range SS-20 missiles in Eastern Europe, prompting fears of a surprise nuclear strike. Two years later, Moscow had ordered tanks into Afghanistan, confirming the West's darkest suspicions about Soviet expansionism. President Reagan, who took office in 1981, increased U.S. defense spending from 6 to 7 percent of GDP, branded the Soviet Union an "evil empire," and announced a plan to develop lasers that would shoot down its missiles in space. To counter the SS-20s, Washington stationed nuclear-armed Cruise missiles in Britain and Germany. Warsaw Pact leaders, rattled by this response, drew up a classified plan in May 1985 to transport themselves to secret international bunkers in the event of nuclear war. Not since the 1962 Cuban Missile Crisis had relations been so tense.

Into this overcharged atmosphere stepped Gorbachev, a new kind of Soviet leader, part Nikita Khrushchev, part Mahatma Gandhi. Not content just to further his country's interests, he set out to change how the world thought about interstate relations. Instead of national interests, foreign leaders were to prioritize the "interests of humanity"; all states, he said, should abjure the threat or use of force and adopt "universal human values." At first, Western leaders and many of Gorbachev's own aides assumed the pacifist rhetoric must be some kind of propaganda ploy. Over time, they realized he was sincere. To the delight of Western observers and the horror of some of his own generals, Gorbachev launched into an elaborate geostrategic striptease.

It began with nuclear disarmament. At Reykjavik in October 1986, Gorbachev proposed the complete elimination of all strategic nuclear weapons. Reagan, himself attracted by big ideas, almost went along. The deal fell through only because Reagan refused to limit development of his Strategic Defense Initiative to laboratory experiments, foregoing those conducted in the atmosphere or space. But this proved only a minor setback. In December 1987, the two sides agreed not just to remove their intermediate range nuclear missiles from Europe but to eliminate such missiles entirely. In 1991, the Soviets and the United States pledged, in the START treaty, to reduce their arsenals to six thousand deployed nuclear warheads apiece.

Simultaneously, Gorbachev began cutting his country's conventional forces, sometimes in agreements with the West, sometimes unilaterally. In December 1988, he announced the immediate demobilization of half a million troops. In fact, between 1988 and 1991, active duty Soviet soldiers fell by 900,000. Then in the Conventional Forces in Europe Treaty, signed in 1990, he agreed to destroy 19,000 tanks, while NATO only had to destroy 4,000.

Along with arms reductions, Gorbachev began repatriating troops from around the world. He withdrew Soviet forces from Afghanistan, cut military aid to Nicaragua, and began removing personnel from Cuba. Glasnost and perestroika, where introduced in Eastern Europe, weakened the cohesion of ruling communist parties, as they had done in the Soviet Union. As opposition emerged, Gorbachev made it clear he would not use military force—or even threats and moral pressure—to defend Moscow's local client regimes. Warsaw Pact countries, he said, could "choose their own paths to socialism." True to his word, he kept the Soviet soldiers in their bases in the fall of 1989 as governments crumbled and the previous dictators were imprisoned, exiled, or executed.

Gorbachev even settled for a reunified Germany within NATO. He did not use the nearly 400,000 Soviet troops still stationed there to make trouble or delay the process. On the contrary, he began bringing home the forces deployed across Eastern Europe. The Warsaw Pact was dissolved. And then, against Gorbachev's wishes but as a result of his policies, the Soviet Union itself disintegrated. Russia, in turn, began recalling its troops behind its own borders.

Within a few years, the world had changed so utterly that even sea-soned diplomats felt disoriented. History contained no precedent for such a peaceful, voluntary surrender by a global empire, such a stunning retreat, motivated by a leader's philosophical conversion. For a moment, euphoria reigned. The West had lost its nuclear-armed enemy of forty years. Russians could not help hoping the new peace would enable their country to flourish. Liberals on both sides could believe they now shared a common goal—a "Europe whole and free," as Bush put it, or a "com-mon European home," in Gorbachev's phrase.

For a while in the early 1990s, it did not seem fanciful to think the West might draw Russia into its orbit just as it had incorporated Ger-many after World War II, binding its former enemy to it with a network of treaties and agreements, cultural and economic ties. This would take diplomacy and good will, not to mention a certain amount of financial aid to ease Russia's economic transformation and prevent the discredit-ing of pro-Western, democratic, and free market ideas. But if an Ameri-can president could conceive of a world without nuclear weapons, why not a peaceful, united Europe including Russia? In Boris Yeltsin, Russia had a leader who believed his country's destiny lay in the West.

For those who dared to hope, the next two decades were disheart-ening. Disappointment followed disappointment. Russia was not inte-grated into the West. Twenty years later, relations between the two were so frosty that some saw the outbreak of a new cold war.

What went wrong? How did the optimistic projects of 1990 turn into the competitive schadenfreude of 2010? To a great extent, the answer one gives depends on where one spent the intervening years. History always has many sides. But in this case, the versions diverge so much that it is not easy to fit them together. Even those inclined to see opposing view-points—America's Russia hands and Russia's pro-Western experts—have quite different interpretations of how and why efforts to integrate Russia into the West failed.

These contrasting understandings of recent history color interactions between Moscow and Washington. They influence how both sides con-strue the other's behavior, and how each defines its goals. Such percep-tions cannot simply be reset by pushing a metaphorical button. They must be taken into account in the formation and presentation of new policies if those policies are to have a chance of success. The radical split in perceptions also makes it hard to tell the story of the last twenty years as a single narrative. Instead, I present two versions—one recounting how recent experience looks to many moderate, pro-Western Russians; the other from the perspective of an American believer in the possibilities of mutual accommodation.

The View from Moscow

Economic aid

As seen from Russia, the trail of disappointments begins with economic aid. Although they claimed otherwise, Western leaders proved unprepared to invest more than symbolic amounts into the reconstruction of their former adversary.

The "peace dividend" Gorbachev's disarmament entailed for the West was enormous. In 1986, at the height of Reagan's arms buildup, U.S. defense spending had reached 7.0 percent of GDP. By 1999, it had fallen to just 3.6 percent. Had Washington had to keep spending 7 percent of GDP on defense, the additional burden would have added up by 1999 to $1.9 trillion. The cost of the Marshall Plan, which helped rebuild Western Europe after World War II, had equaled 5 percent of 1948 GDP. In 1991, five percent of GDP would have been about $300 billion. Even a tenth of that amount, if invested in stabilizing the ruble, balancing the federal budget, and paying pensions and unemployment relief for a couple of years, might have radically changed the situation in Russia, undercutting nostalgia for communism, forestalling the political struggles of the 1990s, and entrenching democracy and pro-Western policies.

The West had other concerns. Yeltsin was about to introduce comprehensive reforms to create an open market economy. However, the U.S. Treasury official sent to confer with Russia's leaders, David Mulford, was not interested in discussing reform. His mission was to pressure the Soviet republics to pay the huge foreign debt the last communist governments had run up. If the successor states did not make payments, Mulford threatened to halt shipments of American grain. The contrast with the treatment of Poland was striking. The West had written off $15 billion of the Polish debt and given the Poles a $1 billion stabilization fund to restore confidence in the zloty. For Russia, there was no write-off and no stabilization fund. Quite the opposite—Russia was bullied into taking responsibility for the entire Soviet debt.

The tone seemed to be changing when, in April 1992, President Bush announced a Western package of $24 billion to help Russia reform. How-ever, the headline figure turned out to be a massive deception. As Bush himself explained, the plan did not contain "a lot of new money." Old loans had been repackaged and repromised. More than half the total consisted of short-term credits at market rates to buy Western agricul-tural products that Russia was not sure it needed—that is, export sup-ports for Western farmers dressed up as "aid." (The IMF would use these loans later as an excuse not to provide Russia with the kind of financing it *did* need.) Excluding such credit to buy Western exports, only $2.5 bil-lion was actually provided in 1992. Of this, $1 billion consisted of an IMF loan—issued in August, just after Russia's first attempt to stabilize the ruble had failed—and $1.5 billion of Western government grants.

Washington's goal, at least as it appeared from Moscow, was to pre-tend to help while contributing as little money as possible. Some in the administration disliked and distrusted Yeltsin; others thought him a transitional figure on whom the White House should not place too many chips. As Bush's national security adviser, Brent Scowcroft, put it later, giving Russia money at that time would have been akin to stuffing it "down a rathole." It would be unwise, Vice President Dan Quayle opined in February 1992, "to create a stabilization fund just for the sake of creat-ing one." Even the humanitarian food aid that Washington did provide was not entirely humanitarian. The pilots making shipments were simul-taneously spying out targets for the U.S. nuclear bombing plan.

President Clinton, who took over in 1993, urged his aides to "think bigger" on Russia and come up with bolder proposals. But he, too, proved unwilling or unable to provide significant aid. Russia was withdrawing its armies from Germany and the Baltics and had only tents to put them in. In four years, Moscow brought home 800,000 troops, 400,000 civilian personnel, and 500,000 of their family members—about 1.7 million peo-ple in all. In response to Yeltsin's urgent plea for help building housing, Clinton pledged to construct a total of 450 apartments, and he promised to find funding for another 5,000. Even that was trimmed by Congress, whose members did not see why the United States should pay to house Russian soldiers when some American servicemen had subpar accommodations. The hundreds of thousands of surplus Russian soldiers, left in decrepit quarters, with meager and often unpaid wages, furnished a reservoir of embittered, militarily trained patriots to fill out the ranks of radical nationalist movements and criminal enterprises.

Although Clinton never found the missing money promised by his predecessor, he did encourage the IMF to lend Russia $6.8 billion in 1995, which helped the authorities restore confidence in the ruble. By that point, three years of hyperinflation had discredited market reforms among many Russians. Still, had Yeltsin not managed to bring inflation down in 1995, the Communists would most likely have won the presidency in 1996 and taken a harder line against the West. So this was a sensible investment.

In total, the IMF provided loans to Russia of about $20 billion between 1990 and 2000. By March 2005, Russia had repaid the IMF in full. The World Bank lent about $12 billion, three quarters of which had been repaid by 2009. By that year, Russia had also paid down the Soviet debt, for which it had assumed responsibility, from $97 billion at its peak to less than $5 billion. The interest payments on this debt were an enormous burden on Russia's public finances. During the eight years after 1991, Russia's interest payments on the foreign debt came to more than all the aid and new loans the country received. Even in those difficult years, Russia was supplying the West with net flows of capital.

The actual amount of aid—as opposed to loans, which had to be repaid with interest—that the West provided to Russia was tiny. Total grants between the fall of communism and 2001 came to about $5 billion—roughly the same as U.S. aid to Egypt and Israel in a single year. Put another way, the West's total investment of aid in securing Russia's transition and supporting its turn towards democracy was less than the cost of three B-2 bombers.

Military expansion

Clinton's aides may not have "thought bigger" when it came to aid. But they did in one other respect.

Picking up where Gorbachev had left off, Russia under Yeltsin was executing the biggest retreat and demilitarization in the country's history. All Russian forces were leaving Eastern Europe and the Baltics. The Soviet army was being dismantled at breakneck speed. Between 1990 and 1996, the number of active troops under Moscow's command fell from 3.4 million to 1.3 million. Russia cut its military spending by almost four-fifths. It was rapidly destroying nuclear weapons, and it helped negotiate the denuclearization of Ukraine, Belarus, and Kazakhstan. It renounced its claims to Ukrainian territory, signed a Treaty of Friendship, Cooperation, and Partnership with the Ukrainian government, and gave Kiev part of the Black Sea Fleet.

And yet, year after year, Russians saw the military alliance that had been created to oppose them expanding, modernizing, and moving closer to their borders. First, Poland, Hungary, and the Czech Republic joined NATO in 1999. Then, in 2004, another seven countries followed. These even included the three former Soviet Baltic republics Estonia, Latvia, and Lithuania. Even to pro-Western Russians, this race by NATO, a historically hostile military alliance, to occupy the territory Russian troops were leaving came as a shock. Despite all the rhetoric about demilitarizing Europe and preventing the emergence of new dividing lines, the United States seemed intent on encircling the new democratic Russia even more tightly than it had contained the totalitarian USSR.

Some in Russia believed Western leaders had lied to Gorbachev about their intentions regarding NATO. In early 1990, as the West sought Gorbachev's acceptance of NATO membership for a reunified Germany, the U.S. secretary of state, James Baker, told Gorbachev that if he agreed to this, "there would be no extension of NATO's jurisdiction or NATO's forces one inch to the East." A year later, British prime minister John Major told the Soviet defense minister he did not "anticipate conditions under which the East European countries could join NATO at present or in the future." However, Gorbachev never got this in writing. Both Yevgeny Primakov, Gorbachev's foreign policy aide, and Jack Matlock, the U.S. ambassador to Russia at the time, thought NATO would have agreed to put this into a formal agreement in 1990. But Gorbachev never insisted.

The motives of the East Europeans were simple and transparent. Russia was their historic enemy. For decades, Soviet ambassadors had laid down the law in Budapest and Warsaw. Naturally, the Poles and Hungarians wanted the United States to commit to use its nuclear weapons if necessary to defend them. At the same time, their democracies were young, and it was always tempting for officials to seek votes by stirring up anti-Russian nationalism. From under the American nuclear umbrella, politicians could score points domestically by agitating against Russian interests in international arenas, without having to worry about a Russian response.

U.S. motives for expanding NATO were less easy to decipher. From the memoirs of those involved, the alliance seemed to have expanded, as Lord Palmerston said of the British Empire, "in a fit of absent-mindedness." The subject of discussions changed from *why* and *if* to *when* and *how* without anyone seeming to notice. Walesa and Havel made emotional appeals to Clinton. And suddenly the decision seemed to have been made. The leading Russia expert in the administration, Strobe Talbott, went from being nervous about the idea to just trying to slow it down, to insisting that: "it was the right thing to do"—all, apparently, within a matter of months.

Opponents suggested the alternative of developing the Partnership for Peace program. Within this, the Hungarians and Poles could have deepened their cooperation with NATO almost to the point of membership. If that were not enough, the Central European countries could have joined the European Union's new defense arm, which was being developed under the aegis of the Western European Union. This would have been far less threatening to Russia. Eighteen former U.S. ambassadors and State Department officials, including Matlock and Paul Nitze, thought this arrangement would have achieved the best of both worlds. They begged the Clinton administration to consider it. Their proposal was rejected.

Clinton sometimes sounded as though his real motive was to win the support of Polish voters in Detroit. He told Yeltsin that he was facing a tough reelection fight in 1996 and that the Republicans were emphasizing the NATO issue. He said he needed to win in Wisconsin, Illinois, and Ohio, states which "have a lot of Poles and others who like the idea of NATO expansion." Later, he campaigned on this platform in the Midwest. Western spokesmen said NATO was needed to "anchor" the East European states in the West—as though they were about to float off into the Baltic Sea—and to support their democratic reforms. To Russians, the idea that NATO was a club for democracies had the virtue of original- ity. NATO had overlooked such concerns when Greece and Turkey were ruled by military juntas. Portugal, under the dictator Antonio Salazar, had been a founding member. In any case, by 1997 when the decision was made to admit Poland and Hungary, there was no possibility that either would revert to totalitarian communism. Democracy did not seem to have much to do with it.

Then there was talk of "new threats" that might arise—terrorism, rogue states, and so on. But in many ways, enlarging NATO made it harder for the West to fight these. For almost all, Russia's help was needed. To pressure Iran and North Korea to give up their nuclear programs, to fight the Taliban in Afghanistan, even to make peace in Kosovo, Russian coop- eration was important. Apparently extending NATO into Eastern Europe was a higher priority.

Of course, adding the Poles and Czechs to NATO did little to change the military balance. It was no doubt irritating for Russian generals to see NATO fighter jets buzzing the border with Estonia, just 100 miles from St. Petersburg. And the use of AWAC planes to spy deep into Russian territory was annoying, although not necessarily illegal. Not even Rus- sia's hard-liners thought NATO was planning to invade. Still, the hypoc- risy was galling. Year after year, as the Western military alliance advanced toward Russia, as new weapons systems were moved in and armies mod- ernized, and as Russia shrank back into its seventeenth century borders, authoritative voices from Washington repeatedly warned that the great- est threat to peace in Europe was *Russian* expansionism.

NATO was defensive, Russians were told. Yet had Russia formed a "defensive" alliance with Cuba, Grenada, Haiti, Nicaragua, and Venezu- ela, trained and modernized its partners' armies, and proposed placing antiballistic missile batteries near the U.S. border, all while criticizing the U.S. regime as undemocratic, funding American opposition groups, and accusing the United States of imperial ambitions, Russians found it hard to imagine that Washington would have simply turned the other cheek.

It almost made it worse that Western leaders kept insisting that Rus- sia was not excluded, that there was always the possibility that Russia too could one day join NATO. Nobody honestly believed that this could happen. The offer was understood as the kind of *politesse* with which Truman offered Marshall Plan aid to Stalin—knowing, of course, that Congress would withdraw funding immediately were Stalin to accept. Article 10 of the North Atlantic Treaty stated that NATO's members must agree unanimously to admit a new member. After Poland—not to mention Estonia—joined, the chance that the members would unanimously agree to invite Russia was essentially zero. President Clinton called this "blue-sky stuff"—suggesting something one sees in the distance but which retreats as one approaches. In December 1991, Yeltsin had sent a letter to NATO "raising the question of Russia's membership" although calling this a "long-term political aim." He received no reply. In February 1992, at his first official meeting with Bush, Yeltsin pressed the U.S. president to say in public that the two countries were on the way towards becoming allies. Bush agreed to "friends and partners," but "moving towards becoming allies" was going too far, he said, because: "we don't want to act like our problems are solved."

The minor concessions Washington made to soften the blow of Russia's exclusion were more insulting than anything else. The Conference on Security and Cooperation in Europe—which included all the European countries plus North America—had been little more than a pan-European debating society. Russian leaders proposed building a Europe-wide security system under its aegis. Instead, the West agreed only to change the body's name to the more imposing sounding Organization for Security and Cooperation in Europe. The West set up a Permanent Joint Council to consult with Russia on NATO activities—not so permanent, it turned out: it was soon replaced by the NATO-Russia Council, which was supposed to deepen the interactions. Russia was, indeed, consulted on a variety of insignificant matters, but not on such questions as which wars NATO should fight.

Kosovo

Then, just a few weeks after the first new NATO members were admitted, the alliance began bombing the Serbs in Yugoslavia. In fact, this was the second time. In 1995, NATO aircraft had bombed Serb forces fighting for territory in Bosnia. In 1999, they bombed the Serbian heartland to pressure Milosevic to withdraw from the Serbian region of Kosovo.

Even to Russians who agreed that Milosevic was a brutal dictator, whose forces had been massacring Albanian Kosovars, the NATO operation touched a raw nerve. The West did not intervene in a way that could have stopped the ethnic cleansing. That would have required ground troops in Kosovo, something Clinton was not prepared to order. Instead, the West intervened by bombing the military in Serbia proper. And not just the military. The bombs NATO planes dropped on the Chinese Embassy in Belgrade were no doubt a tragic accident. But NATO planes deliberately bombed the Serbian television station, knowing this would kill civilians. They bombed the electricity grid, aware that this would cut off patients on life support and babies in hospital incubators. NATO's commanders could not not know that Article 14 of the 1977 Protocol to the 1949 Geneva Conventions prohibits attacking "objects indispensable to the survival of the civilian population."

Bombing civilians was only part of it. The British Parliament's Foreign Affairs Committee found the whole operation to be at best of "dubious" legality. As for preventing ethnic cleansing, it was probably true that Milosevic was planning another offensive. But the worst ethnic cleansing happened *during* the NATO intervention. Before the bombing began, about 2,500 people had been killed in Kosovo. During the eleven weeks NATO was bombing, at least 4,400 and maybe as many as 10,000 more died, mostly Albanians murdered by Serbs. Before the war, about 350,000 Kosovars had been displaced; by the end, 800,000 had been forced out of the country, mostly to refugee camps in Albania and Macedonia, and 500,000 more were displaced within Kosovo. The humanitarian catastrophe might have been even worse had NATO not intervened. But the operation did not prevent a horrific increase in bloodshed.

And after NATO had forced the Serb troops out, the Kosovars it was protecting took revenge on the defenseless Serb population. They destroyed Serbian churches and monasteries and "conducted reverse ethnic cleansing of the Serbs—under the noses of NATO troops." The West's main ally in Kosovo, the Kosovo Liberation Army, had been branded a "terrorist organization" in 1998 by one of the U.S. State Department's own officials. It was funded in part by heroin trafficking; some Western intelligence linked it to Osama bin Laden; Islamic mujahideen were turning up to enlist in it from across the Arab world. Despite this, the West welcomed it as a partner.

And nine years later the United States broke international law again to recognize Kosovo as an independent state. Even those in Moscow who believed in the West's good intentions found the whole Kosovo saga hard to understand. In the first major military engagement since NATO's founding, it had broken international law to dismember a country, taking the side of a group of guerrillas with links to terrorists and the heroin trade, who then ethnically cleansed defenseless civilians "under the noses of NATO troops." NATO had illegally bombed civilians and civilian infrastructure. The operation, whatever its motivation, made a mockery of the claim that NATO's military forces were for "defensive or deterrent purposes only." And, by choosing to bomb from above the clouds rather than intervene on the ground, the West did not prevent—and may even have catalyzed—the massacres that were used to justify its intervention.

Kosovo was a shock to Russian public opinion. And then came Iraq. The United States invaded another country on a mistaken or trumped-up charge that it had secretly developed weapons of mass destruction. The result was the death of more than 100,000 Iraqis. From Moscow, this seemed like another example of the careless way the United States exercised its power in places its policymakers did not understand, causing massive casualties.

This pattern made even America's friends in Russia extremely nervous about U.S. pressures to extend NATO into the Caucasus and Ukraine. The greatest danger was not so much Western aggression as Western ignorance combined with overconfidence. Across the board, Americans seemed to have lost their inhibitions about the use of violence. Democratic administrations intervened for "humanitarian" reasons. Republicans intervened to fight "preventive wars." Both fired missiles at suspected terrorists. The old restraints—respect for state sovereignty, fear of nuclear escalation—had disappeared.

The world was getting more dangerous. In Kosovo, according to one common view, NATO had let itself be used by the Albanian guerrillas. The KLA's strategy had been to provoke the Serbs into overreacting so that the West, outraged by Belgrade's brutality, would defend the Kosovars. If that was the KLA's thinking, it had worked brilliantly. This did not excuse the Serbs. But the West's actions sent a dangerous message to those elsewhere in Europe who were ready to cynically inflame ethnic conflicts.

As NATO moved into Russia's periphery, all it would take was for a radical nationalist group in the Baltics or Ukraine to start terrorizing the local Russian minority, perhaps hoping to drag in U.S. forces. Russia would be pressured by public opinion to protect its coethnics across the border. And overnight a military crisis could erupt between the nuclear-armed "humanitarian" West and the nuclear-armed "imperialist" East. Even without NATO membership, as the United States sent its military trainers and special forces officers to Russia's sensitive borders, the chances of an accident or a mistake in which Russian soldiers shed American blood was increasing. In both countries, the public had been fed a one-sided view of the rivalry. Both governments were unprepared to calm passions when the shooting started.

The moral seemed to be that—since Russia and the West had failed to build a stable structure for cooperation—it was vital to keep their forces far apart. Yet they kept getting closer. Suddenly Ukraine and Georgia were next. Despite the fact that only 22 percent of Ukrainians wanted to join NATO and 59 percent opposed it. Despite the fact that more Ukrainians wanted to live in a union with Russia, Belarus, and Kazakhstan—35 percent—than wanted to become NATO members. Despite the fact that moves towards NATO membership for Ukraine were likely to reignite the separatist movement in the Crimea. Despite all this, the United States had decided that the minority of Ukrainians who wanted NATO membership should be encouraged. To do any less, some pundits said, would be "appeasement."

Georgia

As for Georgia, the NATO admission criteria required that countries demonstrate willingness to resolve conflicts with their ethnic minorities peacefully. By 2009, Russians felt they had a pretty good idea of how the incumbent Georgian government believed in settling ethnic conflicts. Even those who were dismayed by their own government's discriminatory overreactions—the trade embargo, deportations, raiding of Georgian restaurants, petty harassment of Georgian individuals—found the

American tolerance for the forcible reunification project of the Tbilisi authorities mystifying.

In 2004, a young, presentable lawyer, trained in New York, called Mikheil Saakashvili, had become Georgia's leader. He had tolerable credentials as a democrat, at least until he closed down the only independent television station, sent riot police to beat unarmed demonstrators, arrested political opponents, and won reelection in an election marred by irregularities. From the start, this leader made it clear he had two objectives. First, he was determined to regain control over three autonomous regions within Georgia, two of which contained ethnic minorities that wanted to secede. "Georgia's territorial integrity is the goal of my life," he said right after his inauguration. Second, he was committed to getting Georgia admitted to NATO.

To fight the separatists, Saakashvili built up his army, with the help of the United States, Israel, and some East European states. In 2006 and 2007 alone, he bought 109 tanks, 49,000 assault rifles, and 18,000 missiles, mostly from new or prospective NATO members. In 2007, Georgia spent on its military twelve times what it had spent in 2002. The U.S. government sold Georgia five times as much weaponry in 2003–2007 as in 1998–2002, and the arms sales of private dealers that the U.S. government licensed also mushroomed.

And, systematically, Saakashvili set about subjugating his ethnic minorities and decreasing regional autonomy. Within months of his inauguration, he forced out the leader of the southern autonomous region of Adjara, and began decreasing the province's independence. That summer, he sent troops to fire mortars into South Ossetia, but the fire was returned and they were eventually withdrawn. In 2006, his police troops cleared out local guerrillas in the Kodori Gorge in Eastern Abkhazia and he installed a puppet Abkhaz government there. He also set up a puppet government on the edge of South Ossetia. Finally, on August 7, 2008, he sent about 12,000 heavily armed troops back to the South Ossetian border. They shelled the region's capital, Tskhinvali, and then attacked it with tanks.

Russia had had peacekeepers in South Ossetia and Abkhazia since the early 1990s, when the Georgians fought brutal but unsuccessful wars against both. In what the EU fact-finding mission later characterized as an "open challenge to Georgian sovereignty," Moscow had issued Russian passports to the local populations to demonstrate its commitment to defend them. Both regions had bad reputations as centers of smuggling and other crime. Still, given the history of Georgian invasion and Saakashvili's threats, it seemed justifiable to Russians for their country to offer to protect local civilians. During the early fighting, Saakashvili's troops fired on the Russian peacekeepers' headquarters, set it ablaze, killed two Russian soldiers, and wounded five others.

Why did Saakashvili attack? He said he was responding to an incursion by Russian troops that had started moving south through the Roki Tunnel, which connects Russia to South Ossetia. The Russian military said it moved only after the shelling of Tskhinvali began. Even taking Saakashvili at his word, the goal of stopping Russian troops does not explain why it was necessary to shell Tskhinvali with Grad BM-21s—powerful missiles never intended for use in inhabited areas because they destroy everything within a large radius. The EU fact-finding mission would later characterize this response as "illegal," and the Georgian attack on Russian peacekeepers as "contrary to international law." The report characterized Russia's initial intervention to defend its peacekeepers as legal, but its subsequent attacks within Georgia proper as incommensurate with the threat faced. Russia drove the Georgians out, destroyed much of the Georgian army, and eventually withdrew its forces back into Abkhazia and South Ossetia.

Historians will have to sort out Saakashvili's true motives. Perhaps he thought Russia was bluffing when it promised to defend the South Ossetians. He cannot have expected to win against Russia's much larger and better equipped army. Whatever his calculations, the defeat partially served his purposes. He restored, at least temporarily, his falling popularity at home. And, at least at first, he won the sympathy of the West. After the war, even German Chancellor Angela Merkel, who had resisted a final decision on Georgian membership in NATO until shortly before, flew to Tbilisi to declare that: "Georgia will become a member of NATO if it wants to." Saakashvili crowed that the Georgian "position has been strengthened." In the past, the world told him to negotiate over South Ossetia, he said, but now Georgia's separatist regions had become "a problem for the world."

Even to those inclined to believe Washington's assertions that it had not encouraged the Georgians, the picture that unfolded was disconcerting. The United States had trained and helped to equip Saakashvili's army, despite his clear intention to use it against his ethnic minorities. Just weeks before the attack, 1,200 U.S. troops had conducted joint military exercises with the Georgians near Tbilisi. About 160 U.S. military advisers stayed in Georgia throughout the war. In July, Condoleezza Rice, the U.S. secretary of state, had flown to Tbilisi to assure Saakashvili that the United States would fight to get his country admitted to NATO. "We always fight for our friends," she told him. She shook hands with the head of Saakashvili's puppet government of South Ossetia. Right before the Georgians attacked, a top aide to Vice President Richard Cheney, Joseph Wood, visited Tbilisi. When the Georgian troops entered Tskhinvali after bombing it, they were driving American jeeps and wearing uniforms and helmets that had been made in the United States. In the midst of the battle, the United States flew 2,000 more Georgian troops back from Iraq.

In the West—both in the press and in politics—Russia's incursion into Georgia was taken as evidence of Russia's imperial ambitions. Yet Russia's peacekeepers had been killed by Georgian guns, and the civilians Russia had promised to defend were being shelled with heavy ordnance. Some in the West placed the blame on Russia for somehow "tricking" Saakashvili into bombing the civilians of Tskhinvali. They pointed out that, like the Georgians, Russia had been conducting military exercises nearby. But to Russians it seemed only natural—indeed, responsible—for the military to prepare given Georgia's evident desire to retake the region by force.

Had the Russian leaders been imperialist, some asked, why would they have waited so long? They could have annexed the South Ossetian and Abkhaz enclaves years earlier, before Saakashvili started modernizing his army. And why would Russia have withdrawn without deposing Georgia's government and installing a pro-Moscow regime?

It rankled for Russians to be called expansionist by the Americans. Since 1991, Russian troops had intervened in civil wars in four countries on their borders, as well as serving as peacekeepers in Bosnia and Kosovo after NATO had finished bombing there. During the same years, the United States had intervened militarily in eleven countries across the globe, some of them more than once. It rankled for Russians to be told that they should not think of the former Soviet states as their sphere of interest by the country that had invented the Monroe Doctrine, whose currently serving defense minister had said some years earlier that the United States should not hesitate to bomb Nicaragua because: "The fact is that the Western Hemisphere is the sphere of influence of the United States." It rankled to be told that the Russian defense of South Ossetia was "disproportionate" because Russian planes attacked bases inside Georgia proper. Was it not U.S. military strategy to strike with overwhelming force? In Washington was this not referred to as the "Powell Doctrine"?

And what, Russians wondered, was disproportionate, in any case? When President Reagan had decided in 1983 that some American students might be in danger on the island of Grenada, U.S. forces had invaded the country to "rescue" them, killing ninety-four soldiers and civilians. When in July 2006, Hezbollah guerrillas killed three Israeli soldiers and took two hostage on the Lebanese border, Israel had blockaded Lebanon, shelled the country for weeks, and invaded, killing more than eight hundred Lebanese citizens. Not only did Washington not consider that disproportionate, it had shipped the Israelis precision-guided bombs for them to use. Yet when Russian peacekeepers were attacked, two killed, many wounded, and scores of local civilians killed by artillery, Russia's intervention and occupation of some northern parts of Georgia for about a month was deemed disproportionate aggression.

Russia was bent on rebuilding its empire, the Americans said. And Putin was the imperialist in chief—Putin, who, early in his term, had closed down the Russian military bases in Vietnam and Cuba, acquiesced to the United States stationing troops in Central Asia, and provided intelligence and overfly rights to NATO forces fighting in Afghanistan. He had even reopened the question of Russian membership in NATO, only to be told in private that such ideas were not to be pursued.

It rankled, also, when Russians were accused of using sales of oil and gas to intimidate their neighbors. For years they had been subsidizing the Ukrainians, selling them gas at a fraction of the West European price. Yet when they raised the price a little closer to the market level, the West called this economic blackmail, even though the price continued to include a large subsidy. And this accusation came from a country that, for forty-six years, had imposed a complete economic and financial embargo on Cuba, an embargo that had been condemned by the UN, denounced by the European parliament, and criticized by the Pope. From a country that continued to impose economic sanctions on Russia—the famous Jackson-Vanik amendment—to punish it for not permitting free emigration, even though everyone knew that Russia had permitted free emigration for more than fifteen years!

Personal dynamics

For Russia's foreign policy elite, the way the United States presented its policies was almost as difficult to stomach as the content of those policies.

Yeltsin worked hard at not noticing the condescending tone and repeated snubs. In the first Bush administration, some thought him a crude demagogue and hardly bothered to conceal this opinion. Although respecting him somewhat more, Clinton mostly humored Yeltsin. He and his aides seemed to regard Russian opposition to NATO enlargement as a kind of psychopathology. When, in Budapest in 1994, Yeltsin used forceful language, reminding Clinton that "NATO was created in Cold War times" and that expanding it would "sow the seeds of distrust," the U.S. delegation was "stunned," and concluded that Yeltsin had become "erratic." Clinton started to worry about his counterpart's "emotional stability."

From the president down, administration officials seemed to define their task as being to manage Yeltsin's mood, as though the cure for encirclement by a historically hostile alliance was a mix of therapy and antidepressants. Yeltsin had to "absorb" or "internalize" enlargement, Clinton said, as "one of those things in life that you can't avoid—you just have to get used to and learn to live with." Of course, Yeltsin could be moody and unpredictable. But NATO enlargement was an objectively bad thing for Yeltsin and for Russia.

Rather than argue the merits, the American team often seemed to be trying to intimidate their Russian counterparts into silence. Enlargement was "going to happen," they said, and fighting it would "only intensify the darkest suspicions about Russia's intentions and future." If Yeltsin's people opposed NATO's growth, they warned, this would "strengthen the hard-liners" in Russia—as though it were the opposition of Moscow liberals to NATO, not NATO enlargement itself, that was empowering the anti-Western crowd.

Well intentioned and sincere, confident in their own judgments, the Americans did not always take their interlocutors very seriously. They joked among themselves about how hard it was to get the Russians to "eat their spinach." They were the patient parents, their interlocutors the difficult children. Russia was weak, and so they stuffed the spinach down their counterparts' throats. And sometimes, to the Russians, it did not taste very much like spinach.

And then the self-assured tone of the Clinton people gave way to the bizarre transitions of the Bush administration. One minute, the president was laying on the folksy charm and Texan bonhomie, as if he thought he could turn a trained intelligence agent like Putin with declarations of friendship. The next, some other official was sputtering cold war style denunciations. The only thing constant was the lack of attention American policymakers seemed to pay to Russian views and interests.

Finally, President Obama arrived with his "reset button," a leader who seemed genuinely eager to improve relations. Yet Russians soon heard again that characteristically American mixture of good intentions and arrogance, enthusiasm and superficiality. After all the talk of a new beginning, the president, on the eve of his first summit with Medvedev, made a point of insulting Russia's prime minister—Mr. Putin, he said, still had "one foot in the old ways of doing business." Obama's aim at the meeting, well-placed journalists reported, was to "build up" President Medvedev at Prime Minister Putin's expense. What exactly the White House had in mind was left for readers—and the Kremlin—to guess. To Russian ears, this sounded about as scatterbrained as if Putin had announced he was flying to Washington to give Vice President Biden a boost vis-à-vis Obama. It was all the more odd since Obama's approval rating trailed that of the Russian president he planned to "build up" by 12 percentage points.

The Moscow summit accomplished little. Everyone agreed to things they had already agreed to, and smiled through gritted teeth. And then, a few weeks later, the American vice president turned up in Kiev to announce that if Ukraine chose to join NATO, "which I believe you have, we strongly support that." Once again, Russian observers were at a loss. Was the U.S. government unaware that only 22 percent of Ukrainians said in polls that they wanted to join NATO? Did it not know that whereas 81 percent of Ukrainians had a favorable view of Russia, only 54 percent had a favorable view of the United States? Did it realize that the main Ukrainian cheerleader for NATO, President Yushchenko, was so unpopular that only 4 percent planned to vote to reelect him?

In September 2008, right after the Georgian war, Russian public attitudes toward the United States reached a new low. Only 23 percent said they felt good about the country, compared to 67 percent who said they felt bad about it. The irony was that, at heart, Russians wanted to like Americans; they were attracted by their economic power, innovation, optimism, personal warmth. Even in 2007, Russians remained more pro-American than the citizens of some U.S. allies such as France, Spain, Germany, and Turkey. But every few years, another unilateral thunderbolt—Bosnia, Iraq, Kosovo, support for Georgia—turned opinion against the trigger-happy superpower. Over time, Russians had become afraid of Washington's aproach. By 2008, 62 percent thought they had good reason to fear NATO.

For Russia's pro-Western elites, by 2010 the infatuation was long past. Those dreamers who had once thought a close partnership possible had become pragmatists. After the economic boom of Putin's years, the United States had become much less important to Russian aims. Indeed, the main concern was simply to avoid getting dragged into one of Washington's military adventures. Russia was integrating not so much with the West as with the world. It was developing its relationship with China, via the Shanghai Cooperation Organization and expanding trade, and that with Europe, via its pipelines. Russia invested more in the United States in 2008 than the U.S. invested in Russia. American officials still liked to fly over and tell their Russian counterparts why they should support American priorities. But even the most pro-Western experts no longer thought Moscow should do more than listen politely.

The View from Washington

To a sympathetic American observer, one who had also hoped in the early 1990s that Russia could be integrated into the West, the frustrations of Russian liberals would be understandable. Such an observer would admit to certain mistakes and insensitivities in Western policy. Yet the catalog of Western errors and shortcomings would seem to him only part of the picture.

Hopes for a full-fledged partnership between Russia and the United States failed, he would contend, not because Washington betrayed such hopes with its penny-pinching and determination to expand NATO, but because the hopes themselves were simply unrealistic. Russia's interests diverged too much from those of the United States and Europe. It was not disrespect that led the West to treat Russia differently from Poland. It was a recognition of the country's scale and importance. At the same time, some of the problems Russia faced and continues to face would seem, even to such an observer, largely self-inflicted. Especially in the last decade, Moscow had never missed an opportunity to shoot itself in the foot.

Western aid

The U.S. response in the early 1990s was inadequate, many in the West would admit. More could, no doubt, have been done to support Russia's transition. And yet, there were reasons—some of them good ones—why more aid was not quickly forthcoming.

First, the problem lay not so much in the pusillanimity of American leaders as in the preferences of the American public. Washington did not provide more aid, in large part, because the American voters did not want it to. In one poll taken in August 1991, for instance, 75 percent opposed providing cash grants to the Soviet Union. Had President Bush or President Clinton proposed larger amounts, they would not have made it through Congress. Had they suggested some kind of new Marshall Plan, they would have been laughed out of the Capitol. It is possible a more determined effort to educate the public would have worked; but it is far from certain.

At the same time, skeptics surely had a point: given the political conflict and apparent chaos in Moscow, the efficacy of aid was open to question. Even had Washington conjured up a stabilization fund of several billion dollars in early 1992, there was reason to doubt it would have enabled Yeltsin to stabilize the ruble. The government and parliament were already dueling. Russia's federal budget was revised quarterly throughout the year. Had the United States helped Yeltsin balance the budget, the parliament would have unbalanced it again. Until Russia resolved the political impasse, money would have solved nothing. And, to add to the confusion, Boris Fyodorov, the former finance minister, was practically begging the West *not* to send aid in the early 1990s because Yeltsin only reformed when his back was against the wall.

By providing some assistance to pensioners and the poor, the United States could probably have bought some good will. But there was no infrastructure to administer such programs without major corruption. There were many stories, sometimes exaggerated but often true, of humanitarian aid enriching middlemen. The strongest argument was that the West should have written off at least part of the Soviet debt. In 1991–1992, Western officials mistakenly believed the economic crisis would be short lived, and that Russia's oil and gas wealth would enable it to pay. By 1993, such misperceptions had surely passed. Yet debt writeoffs were still not forthcoming.

NATO

Russia was insulted that its former Warsaw Pact allies felt the need to be defended against a possible Russian invasion. Russia had turned over a new leaf. It was moving towards democracy. It offended Russians to be suspected and feared.

And yet, even those sympathetic to Russia had to admit, the West could not close its eyes to the legitimate concerns of the East Europeans. Given the history, surely protecting the vulnerable was more morally compelling than satisfying Russia's desire for respect and leadership in its neighborhood. When Talbott said enlarging NATO was "the right thing to do," surely that was what he meant.

Citizens of Prague or Warsaw could not be blamed for seeing the future through the mist of history. The Poles had watched their country repeatedly dismembered, its intellectuals exiled to Siberia, its population butchered by the Nazis on one side and the Red Army on the other. The country had been picked up—like a prefabricated house on a truck—and moved west in 1945, turned into a "people's democracy," and run under Soviet tutelage. The Czechs had been Nazified, then communized, their Prague Spring crushed by Russian tanks. After that, they could not be expected to simply take it on faith that Russia had reformed. U.S. leaders could not look Havel and Walesa in the eye and say: you are on your own.

One could not pretend that history had not happened. The West sold out the East at Munich, at Moscow in 1944—when Churchill divided up the countries on a scrap of paper and Stalin checked them off with a blue pencil—and then again at Yalta. It was wrong, many thought, for the United States to have accepted the subjugation of the East Europeans by the Soviet Union. Churchill had bargained them away in return for Greece. If the idea of spheres of influence in Europe was particularly sensitive, perhaps that history was the reason.

Even advocates of NATO enlargement agreed that the Russia of Yeltsin should not be punished for the sins of Stalin. Russians had suffered from Soviet totalitarianism as much as any nation. But the West could not begin as though from a blank slate. The map of Europe had been drawn by Stalin. So when Walesa and Havel came to Clinton and said "never again," they had the right to appeal to America's guilt, to ask for insurance.

Yeltsin, being anti-Soviet himself, understood this. Or so American leaders thought. He was shocked by the secret documents on Stalin's massacre of the Polish officers at Katyn. He knelt in Warsaw at the monument to them in 1993. Walesa took him for a long walk in the Presidential Palace gardens, and Yeltsin came back to tell the press: "Poland and Russia are two sovereign states and must respect each other's sovereign decisions." Russia would not object to Poland joining NATO, he said. This blindsided his aides. But to those watching from the West, this seemed a moment of greatness.

The Russians wanted the West to dissolve NATO and build a Europewide security structure out of the CSCE. But even Russophiles recognized that this could never have worked. Such an organization could not have agreed on issues such as the future of Yugoslavia. When required to act, it would have split. The acrimonious breakup would surely have created more ill will than a careful attempt to create looser but more durable links between Russia and the West. As for Russia joining NATO, it was not for lack of respect that the United States could not see a place for Russia inside the alliance. It was *because* the United States considered Russia a major power. Russia was not Poland or Hungary. NATO had always worked as a military alliance because, although it was never said out loud, the members knew that informal leadership came from Washington. The alliance had one undisputed leader. Poland and Hungary were happy to join on those terms. But Russia was too big, too focused on its own distinct interests, to accept the role of second fiddle.

Global in its scale, Russia had concerns that were global as well. Its interests in Asia diverged from those of the NATO members. Its positions on the Middle East were different by virtue of its location. Even with a fully democratic Russia, there would not be enough commonality of purpose with the United States to cohere in an alliance. The elder President Bush was right to resist making unrealistic promises on this score. The challenge was to forge some other structure within which the United States and Russia could cooperate on issues of mutual agreement and act separately when their interests and views diverged.

And then, beyond the practicalities and logistics, what made it so hard to imagine Russia within NATO was Russians' permanent ambivalence about their relations with the West. They did not want to be integrated in the same way that Poland did. Poland was eager to lose itself in Europe, to become just another European country. Russia wanted to be part of Europe, part of the West, but at the same time outside it. That ambivalence was not easy to deal with, month after month. If Clinton was upset by Yeltsin's outburst in Budapest in 1994, it was not because he did not realize that NATO enlargement was sensitive but because he was so tired of the infantile guessing game, always having to wonder whether Yeltsin would be playing good cop or bad cop on a given day.

Still, the United States did not realize quite *how* traumatic NATO enlargement would be. Perhaps the negotiators were too glib in their attempts to smooth things over. Yeltsin and Kozyrev did not make it easy with their continual mood changes. It often seemed they had accepted NATO enlargement and were just eager to slow down the process and make sure a framework for cooperation with Russia was built in parallel. Washington worked hard at this. It got Russia invited to the Council of Europe and the G7, which became the G8. Naysayers thought Russia did not belong among the leading industrial democracies. But Clinton insisted. The United States negotiated the 1997 NATO-Russia Founding Act. It created the Permanent Joint Council and then the NATO-Russia Council. It encouraged the European Union to sign its partnership and cooperation agreement with Russia. No doubt this all happened more slowly than it should have, the consultation was not as deep as had been hoped. Perhaps Washington should have tried harder. But it did try.

And surely Moscow could not be as worried as it pretended about the East Europeans' military potential. Together, the Czechs, Hungarians, and Poles spent only about one-seventh of what Russia spent on defense. Russians complained about the United States's selling arms to their neighbors. But it was not just the United States. Russia's own Rosoboronexport had been upgrading the fighter jets and military helicopters of the new European NATO members of whom Moscow pretended to be afraid.

Kosovo and Georgia

Even defenders of NATO's operation in Kosovo would admit that not all went according to plan. Humanitarian intervention is hard to do right when one is not willing to take casualties (although that does not mean that one should never try). The Kosovars' reprisals against local Serbs deeply disappointed their Western backers. Still, the scale of the violence against Serbs in Kosovo never approached the savagery organized by Milosevic against the Kosovars. Of course, it is true that the West's Kosovar allies were no choir boys (one could say the same about the militias that Russia befriended in South Ossetia). But, defenders would argue, NATO worked in good faith to stop a clear attempt at genocide. In the fall of 1998, there were 50,000 civilians—mothers with children, frail old men, and so on—in the forests and mountains, without shelter. Many remained outdoors through the winter as the ceasefires came and went. Many more were in refugee camps across the borders. The West could not let this continue. For all the messiness, ten years later Kosovars no longer lived in fear of massacre by the Serbs. That was something.

Was NATO manipulated by the KLA into fighting its war for it? Perhaps. And was Russia drawn into the Georgian conflict by the South Ossetians in a similar way? Those who have humanitarian concerns, or just allies they have promised to defend, are always subject to the hostage ploy. It is easy to say one should let the hostages die rather than allow oneself to be manipulated. It is harder to watch this play out.

NATO tried to involve Russia as soon as possible. The West welcomed Chernomyrdin's help persuading Milosevic to withdraw from Kosovo.

But then came Russia's mad dash to occupy the airport in Pristina. That seemed more in the style of Rutskoy than of Yeltsin. Western leaders worried that the generals were running wild and that Moscow's foreign policy was completely out of control.

As for Georgia, it was hard to say at times who was the hostage and who the provocateur. Were the South Ossetians trying to provoke an attack by the Georgians in order to get Russia involved? Were the Georgians trying to provoke Russia in order to draw in the West? Was Russia trying to provoke the Georgians in order to smash their army? Too many parties had a motive for war.

It was true that Saakashvili struck first, with at least a shameful lack of concern for civilian casualties. Even his supporters in the West found this hard to defend. Russia cast its intervention as humanitarian and compared it to NATO's in Kosovo. But unlike in Kosovo, there had been no good faith attempt at negotiation with the Georgians to prevent the humanitarian crisis before the Russian military went in. Russia's aggressive attitude toward the Saakashvili regime in preceding years had made a negotiated settlement considerably harder. And there were reports that Russia had been infiltrating troops into the region beyond the number allowed under the peacekeeping agreement.

Russian truculence

Even Russia's Western supporters often wondered at the government's apparent determination to be difficult at times for the sake of being difficult. More and more frequently after 2000 Moscow seemed to do things that were costly but brought little in return. There was Russia's cozying up to dictators such as Milosevic, Saddam Hussein, and Kim Jong-Il, its support for Belarus's Lukashenko, its dealings with Hamas. There were its weapons sales, continually upgrading the capacities of the world's tyrants, whether in Syria, Iran, or Venezuela.

What did Moscow gain from such policies, its Western friends wanted to know. During the cold war, supporting third world dictators had been a matter of global competition. But why, in the twenty-first century, did Russia damage its international reputation to befriend all the rogue states? Why side with the likes of Chavez and Castro rather than the people of Latin America? Some of the arms sales were for large amounts of money. But often Moscow seemed just out to make mischief. A nuclear North Korea or Iran would threaten Russia as well. And yet the Russian diplomats did nothing but obstruct and delay in the six-party talks with Pyongyang and they blocked almost every attempt at UN-backed pressure on Tehran.

The position on Iran was particularly puzzling. Was it all about commercial interests? Moscow built the Iranian nuclear station at Bushehr. It pretended to believe Iran wanted nuclear power just for civilian purposes—a country with 10 percent of the world's oil reserves. In 1995, Russia had been planning to sell Tehran centrifuges that its engineers could use to enrich uranium. The Clinton administration had had to lean on Yeltsin to get him to reconsider. Every time U.S. leaders raised the Iran issue, Moscow told them not to worry. Russia refused to support tough economic sanctions. And each year, Tehran got closer to nuclear weapons, which, as Moscow could not help but know, would destabilize the region to its south and probably start a nuclear arms race in the Middle East.

And what did Russia accomplish by interfering in the Ukrainian election in 2004? The Kremlin had sent consultants like Vyacheslav Nikonov and Gleb Pavlovsky over to run Yanukovich's campaign; Putin had visited Kiev; and then the world blamed Russia for Yanukovich's ballot-stuffing. There might have been less support in Western Europe for Ukraine's admission to NATO if Moscow did not seem so keen to manipulate its neighbor's political process.

A little attention to public relations would have gone a long way. Treating foreign journalists as something close to spies did not help them to see Moscow's side. When asked about the bombing of Grozny, surely the rhetorically effective response would have been to talk about the atrocities of the warlords, the victims of Basayev, the Grozny slave market. Instead, the headline of the day became that President Putin wanted to circumcise a French journalist. Did this really help? And, in Georgia, what was to stop the army taking an embedded journalist or two from CNN, the BBC, or even Al Jazeera with the troops as they went through the Roki tunnel? If Russia was acting legitimately, why not show the world the craters the Georgians had made in Tskhinvali? The Kremlin's instinct for secrecy made the world think it had something to hide.

When confronted on such points, the response of Russian diplomats was always to accuse the West of doing the same dubious things for which Russia was criticized. Any Russian misstep was justified by a similar American blunder. But why, some wondered, did Russia's leaders insist on making all America's mistakes? NATO failed to control the KLA, which commited atrocities on its watch. Russia then felt licensed to let Ossetian militias rampage in the occupied Georgian villages. Washington weakened the commitment to territorial integrity of states by recognizing Kosovo. Moscow condemned this, and then weakened the principle further by recognizing South Ossetia and Abkhazia.

Then there was the crudeness, the *thuggishness*, of the way the Kremlin operated at times. Supposedly independent nationalist youth groups were sent to picket embassies and intimidate ambassadors. Gazprom cut off gas supplies to Europe in the dead of winter. Russia sheltered suspects in a nuclear poisoning after they had left radioactive trails across Europe. It allowed cyberterrorists to assault the networks of its neighbors. It agreed to withdraw its troops from Moldova and Georgia, and then acted as if it had never agreed to this. It assigned high school students Chekist shmaltz to read in place of history, with rosy portraits of Stalin and anti-Western distortions.

It might seem in Moscow that such small acts of defiance had little cost. But they gradually recast Russia's image in the West. They made the case for those pushing for NATO enlargement, and silenced Russia's friends.

What next?

The dialogue of the deaf into which relations had degenerated by the end of the Bush administration provided little reason for optimism. Still, sympathetic American observers were not without hope.

If nothing else, the previous twenty years had lowered expectations. A more realistic view of the limits of partnership might make it easier to build on opportunities that were available. Yanukovich's election in February 2010 had taken the question of Ukraine's admission to NATO off the agenda, at least for a while. Meanwhile, in small ways, the Obama administration had begun opening doors previously closed. In September 2009, the president had canceled his predecessor's plan to install an antimissile defense in Eastern Europe, replacing it with a system of smaller interceptors to be based at first on ships. Putin had furiously denounced the previous program, seeing it as aimed against Russia.

Under Bush, the spectrum of interactions between the Russian and U.S. governments had narrowed to little more than the periodic meetings between the two presidents. With Medvedev, Obama set up thirteen interstate working groups on everything from nuclear energy and drug trafficking to space cooperation. The two countries resumed active military-to-military contacts. For the generals who might have to react fast to unclear and menacing situations, developing personal acquaintance with their counterparts was clearly invaluable.

In Washington, more and more people seemed to recognize that, when it came to encouraging the deepening of democracy, patience was in order. Most now accepted that lectures did not work. Although not specifically focused on democracy at all, the kind of regularized, multidimensional contacts between states and societies that Obama seemed keen to develop were the best hope for gradually changing the culture within bureaucracies and spreading knowledge about democratic procedures and methods. Broad, nonideological business and educational exchanges were the most effective way of transmitting Western values. Of course, such contacts worked slowly and would not necessarily prompt convergence. But they had a better chance of success than isolation. The promotion of democracy in a country like Russia worked best when it was not called the promotion of democracy.

Arms control talks had been reinvigorated—none too soon, given the wear and tear the regime had undergone. A replacement for the START treaty had been signed, reducing the number of each country's deployed nuclear warheads to 1,550. There was room for progress elsewhere as well. As Iran moved close to developing nuclear weapons, the major nuclear powers needed to think how to prevent this unraveling the nonproliferation regime. Since Bush's 2001 withdrawal from the Anti-Ballistic Missile Treaty, missile defense had been a source of tension—it went back to the old Russian fear, familiar since Reykjavik, that American technological breakthroughs would undermine the architecture of deterrence on which the other nuclear powers relied. The challenge was for Washington to find a way to include Moscow in the process that would allay such fears.

Conventional arms control was in disarray. The Conventional Forces in Europe Treaty, signed in 1990, had placed limits on conventional weapons within the members of NATO and the Warsaw Pact. It aimed to balance the forces of the two blocs. But the Warsaw Pact had dissolved and many of its former members had joined NATO. A treaty that counted the troops and weaponry of these countries on the Russian side was patently absurd. In 1999, an adapted version of the treaty, imposing limits on individual countries, was signed at a conference in Istanbul. But the NATO countries had refused to ratify it until Russia withdrew about 2,000 of its military personnel who remained in Moldova and Georgia. After waiting eight years, Putin had given up and announced in 2007 that Russia was suspending its compliance. The question for Western statesmen was whether there was a way to prevent disagreement on these few thousand Russian troops from ending all conventional arms control in Europe.

Russia was not about to make concessions for nothing. But it stood to benefit as much as the West from a robust arms control regime, with effective controls against nuclear proliferation, and collaborative programs to fight international terrorism. There remained significant opportunities to work together for a safer world, Russia's Western friends believed, despite the disappointments of the previous two decades.

CHAPTER 10

The Russia That Has Returned

T o most Russians, the consternation that their country's tentative revival arouses in the West is quite bewildering. As they see it, Russia has never been so weak. For two decades, it has been in retreat, vacating Eastern Europe, casting off its third world allies, and withdrawing into its borders, even as its new neighbors discriminate against their Russian-speaking minorities and its old rival, the United States, strikes out with missiles and infantry brigades all over the globe. Yet authoritative voices in the West portray Russia as on a rampage, bent on rebuilding an empire. "In these long winter nights, a headless horseman is roaming Russia's 'near abroad,' threatening independent countries," the columnist Nicholas Kristof complained in December 2004. The menacing equestrian, Russia's president Vladimir Putin, was not "a sober version of Boris Yeltsin," Kristof warned, but rather a "Russified Pinochet or Franco" set on guiding his country "into fascism." To Zbigniew Brzezinski, a former U.S. national security adviser, Putin's geopolitical agenda appeared "ominously similar to Stalin's and Hitler's in the late 1930s."

Most Russians believe that, for all its faults, their political system has been gradually stabilizing in recent years, leaving more space than ever before for individuals to live independent, private lives. By contrast, when the historian Niall Ferguson looks at Russia, he sees shades of Nazi Germany:

> Hitler's power was consolidated after 1933 by the emasculation of both parliamentary and federal institutions. Putin has already

done much to weaken the Duma. . . . Hitler's regime also rested on the propaganda churned out by state-run media; Putin already controls Russia's three principal television channels. . . . And Hitler believed firmly in the primacy of the state over the economy. The Kremlin's systematic destruction of the country's biggest oil company, Yukos—like its effective renationalization of the entire energy sector [sic]—suggests that Putin takes the same view and that, like Hitler, he regards both private property rights and the rule of law with contempt.

To the political scientist Alexander Motyl, Putin resembles not Hitler so much as the Führer's Italian ally:

Like Mussolini, Putin favors stylish black clothing that connotes toughness and seriousness. Like Mussolini, Putin likes being photographed in the presence of weapons and other instruments of war. And like Mussolini, Putin likes to show off his presumed physical prowess.

Other Western commentators have likened Putin to the dictators Ferdinand Marcos, Anastasio Somoza, Park Chung Hee, and Kim Jong Il. I searched the Internet for Idi Amin and Genghis Khan, but comparisons to these are apparently not yet so common.

The respected nonprofit advocacy group Freedom House evaluates countries annually on the extent of political freedom and civil liberties that their residents enjoy. Since 2005, it has rated Russia's political rights at 6 on a scale that runs from 1 (the most freedom) to 7 (the least freedom). This puts the country's political system on a level with that of the United Arab Emirates. The United Arab Emirates, according to Freedom House's report, is a federation of seven absolute dynastic monarchs whose appointees make all legislative and executive decisions. There is no hint of democracy anywhere in the system. The only "parliament" is a consultative assembly, whose members are either appointed by the emirs or chosen by a college of electors whom the emirs appoint. There are no political parties. Court rulings are "subject to review by the political leadership." It is illegal to publish "negative material about presidents, friendly countries, [and] religious issues." There is "compelling evidence," Freedom House writes, that "members of the royal family and the country's police have used torture against political rivals."

Freedom House gives Russia's civil liberties a score of 5, the same as Yemen, a country where the state has a complete monopoly over television and radio, where criticizing the president or publishing material that "might spread a spirit of dissent and division among the people" is illegal, where the authorities block websites they consider offensive, where the constitution declares Sharia the "source of all legislation," where the penal code "allows lenient sentences for those convicted of . . . assaults or killings of women for alleged immoral behavior," where more than forty people were killed and hundreds more injured recently when the authorities forcibly dispersed a protest demonstration, where citizens are flogged as punishment for drinking alcohol or for sexual offenses, and where in 2008 an eight-year-old girl turned up at the courthouse in the capital to ask a judge to grant her a divorce. Her father had forced her to marry a thirty-year-old man. Ironically in the circumstances, the law did not allow her to bring charges against her father because she was underage; mercifully, the judge made an exception.

Do conditions in Russia these days really justify comparisons to Hitler's Germany, Mussolini's Italy, and some of the more repressive regimes of the Persian Gulf? In this chapter, I examine some common criticisms of Russia's economic and political record, evaluating the claims in light of available statistics, opinion surveys, and other relevant information. Some of the criticisms are valid, as documented in previous chapters. However, examining the facts and comparing Russia not to an idealized image of a capitalist democracy but to the kind of regimes found in other countries around its level of economic development and to its peers in the transition from communism, I reach a more measured assessment.

For instance, it is true that Putin has reduced the role of parliament, increased state control over the media, and overseen the renationalization of two major oil companies. It is also true that Hitler strengthened the power of the executive, and expanded state control over the press and the economy. At the same time, weak parliaments, state ownership of and interference in the broadcast media, and imperfect enforcement of property rights turn out to be common phenomena, found in scores if not hundreds of other countries today. What distinguishes these countries' governments from Hitler's is that they do not plan to murder six million Jews and conquer Europe in search of *Lebensraum* for the Aryan race, details which surely are not inconsequential when it comes to choosing historical analogies.

Russia's future is uncertain. It is not impossible that it will turn into a murderous fascist dictatorship, an expansionist empire, or even a hereditary autocracy ruled by seven emirs. Somewhat more plausibly, the current leaders might seek to tighten the screws if the economy plunges again, reviving opposition to them. At present, however, the common comparisons to historical villains seem greatly overstated. In almost all respects, Russia has become quite similar to other countries around its level of income in Latin America and Asia. In the few respects in which it differs from these, it is comparable to other postcommunist countries. No two countries are identical, and Russia resembles its middle income peers also in that it is in some ways unique. As will become clear—if it has not yet— life in a normal middle income country is not easy for most of its citizens, who generally wish their country could graduate to the club of boring rich democracies. Nevertheless, given Russia's starting point, to become normal in this way in the course of two decades is quite an achievement.

Markets Emerging

To evaluate Russia's economy, one needs to consider what typical middle income economies look like. The group of countries with GDP per capita around Russia's level—averaging $9,700 at 2005 prices in the years 1991 to 2007, at purchasing power parity—includes Venezuela, Malaysia, Argentina, Latvia, and Turkey. Such emerging market economies tend to be turbulent, vulnerable to swings in international prices and investor sentiment, and to have currencies that often come under pressure and sometimes crash. In many, income inequality is high and a few families dominate big business. Officials intervene in corrupt or merely populist ways, and it is not uncommon for the state to expropriate foreign or domestic private investors. Property rights are relatively insecure.

Russia fits into this group all too well. In the 1990s, the ruble's value leapt around, and in August 1998 it collapsed (see Chapter 6). Some saw this as a sign that there was something uniquely wrong with Russia and

the economic reform strategy it had chosen. For middle income economies, however, such crises are not unusual. Between 1992 and 2007, forty-
eight countries had years in which their currency lost at least 50 percent
of its value against the dollar. The fall in Russia's ruble was exactly as large
as the drop in the value of the currency in neighboring Belarus, which
had adopted a completely different economic strategy based on preserving the state economy. Russia that year was just one in a line of dominoes
that began with Thailand and Indonesia and ended with Brazil.

Russia is also often singled out for its "crony capitalism," dominated
by powerful tycoons, its high income inequality, and its widespread corruption. To explain these, commentators point to particularities of Russia—its long history of centralized autocracy, or the personal foibles of
individuals in the leadership. But the unattractive features of Russia's
business world are typical of middle income capitalist systems. Concentrated ownership and flamboyant, politically connected tycoons are
ubiquitous in such countries. Russia's billionaire count is high due to its
natural resource wealth. Still, even at the peak of the commodity boom,
Russia's wealthiest magnate looked like a pauper besides Mexico's Carlos
Slim Helú or India's Lakshmi Mittal. From Mexico and Brazil to South
Korea, Malaysia, and South Africa, large slices of GDP are controlled by
a few families via financial-industrial groups. In Argentina, Hong Kong,
Mexico, Greece, Israel, and Belgium, at least ten out of the twenty largest
firms by market capitalization had a single controlling shareholder in the
1990s—and in Mexico all twenty did. In middle income countries, the top
businessmen always have connections in government who provide loans,
subsidies, special treatment in privatization, and other favors; sometimes the tycoons hold office themselves. Measuring income inequality
in developing and middle income countries is difficult (see Chapter 6).
In all these, surveys tend to miss the superwealthy. Still, the best available figures suggest Russia's income inequality—which did increase in
the early 1990s—was in recent years close to that of the United States,
Turkey, and China; a little below that of Venezuela and Argentina; well
below that of Brazil or South Africa; and higher than that of Latvia.

As for corruption, all agree that in Russia it is widespread. But this is
also true in many other middle income capitalist economies. The best
data to assess this come from surveys that ask businessmen and citizens

resident in the country whether they or their acquaintances have recently been asked to pay bribes. (Other surveys which ask international business-men for their assessments of corruption in particular countries, whether or not they have themselves done business there, are more vulnerable to distortions based on press portrayals of these countries. Ratings that rely on experts' judgments are similarly susceptible to the media-influenced group-think of the experts, most of whom have not themselves tried to register a business or negotiate a tax break in the countries they study.) For instance, the anti-corruption group Transparency International sur-veys the residents of many countries, asking whether they or anyone in their household has "paid a bribe in any form" during the previous twelve months. When this was asked in Russia in the years 2004 to 2009, those saying "yes" averaged 18 percent. (This was close to the propor-tion—16.6 percent—that said in another survey, taken in the late 1990s, that a government official had asked or expected them to pay a bribe for his service.) Figure 10.1 shows the Russian response compared to those in other countries, also averaged over these years.

Figure 10.1 Frequency of bribery around the world, 2004–2009

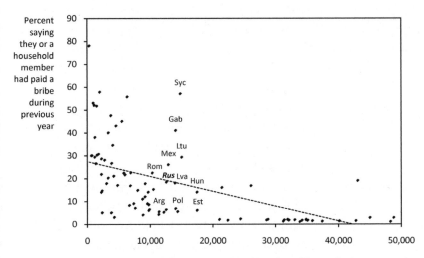

Percent saying they or a household member had paid a bribe during previous year

GDP per capita in dollars, average 2004-2007, adjusted for purchasing power parity

Sources: Transparency International, *Global Corruption Barometer* surveys, averaged for 2004-2009; World Bank, *World Development Indicators*.

As can be seen, richer countries tended to have lower rates of reported bribery. Among countries around Russia's level of GDP per capita, the percentage saying someone in their household had paid a bribe ranged from 4 percent in Turkey to 57 percent in the Seychelles. The dashed trend line shows the level of bribery that, given these data, one would expect to find at each level of national income, assuming a linear relationship. Russia's 18 percent lies almost directly on the line: corruption is exactly as common as one would expect given the country's level of economic development. Russians reported paying bribes a bit more often than Hungarians or Latvians, but less often than Mexicans and Lithuanians.

Politics in the Foggy Zone

Before reviewing Russia's political institutions, it is useful to consider the kinds of democracy that have evolved in other middle income countries. Such polities tend to come a little rough around the edges.

There is democracy à la mexicaine, in which citizens get their news from a show called "The Morning Quickie" hosted by a clown named Brozo, who a few years ago regaled viewers with footage of an aide to the capital's mayor stuffing banknotes into a suitcase in the office of a notorious businessman; in which a state governor—or perhaps, as he claims, an impostor with a voice similar to his—was caught on tape boasting of having jailed a journalist who dared accuse one of the governor's friends of connections to a child sex ring; where election losers call millions into the streets and citizens must judge between credible allegations of fraud and perhaps more credible allegations of sour grapes; where a state-of-the-art electoral commission struggles to monitor the armies of experienced *mapaches*—ballot stuffers, literally "raccoons"—who have fixed past votes; where recently institutions have been corroded by the drug trade, criminal kingpins bribe their way out of prison, headless bodies turn up on back streets, police officers kidnap children to ransom to their parents, drug cartels plant spies in the president's inner office, and the country's top narcotics agents leave office in handcuffs, charged with accepting enormous payoffs from the drug lords they were fighting.

Further south, there is Argentina, which has muddled along from crisis to crisis since the military junta left power in 1983; where, according to a U.S. government lawsuit, two successive presidential administrations accepted million dollar bribes from the German company Siemens; where one former president is on trial for arms smuggling; where the current president, who goes by the nickname "Queen Cristina," and the former president, her husband, reportedly hope to "tag-team the presidency for at least twelve more years," alternating in office to evade term limits; where fire wardens on a routine inspection found $64,000 stashed in the bathroom of the economics minister; where the president's former chauffeur is now one of the country's leading media magnates, owning two television stations, one radio station, and one daily newspaper, which, helped by millions of dollars of public advertising, adopt an editorial line fiercely supportive of the magnate's former passenger; where the government has taken to "Argentinizing" the stakes of foreign investors in "strategic" companies (and sometimes those of domestic investors as well), a process that often ends with the shares owned by tycoons close to the president.

Or perhaps the correct reference point is Turkey, in which democracy is a game umpired by the military, which has repeatedly intervened to keep things on the right track; a country whose inner workings seemed tellingly exposed when a speeding Mercedes crashed in 1996 and the passengers turned out to be a police chief, a prominent parliamentarian, an internationally wanted hitman, and a former beauty queen; a democracy, so many believe, in which ultimate power is held by a shadowy network of security agents, ultranationalist politicians, crime bosses, arms traffickers, assassins, and journalists—a "deep state" operating beneath the visible institutions, conducting kidnappings, murders, even, on occasion, "false flag" terrorist attacks that the media then blame on Kurdish separatists; a country where the current prime minister, a moderate Islamist, who was once imprisoned for reciting a religious poem, reacts furiously to criticism in the press; where, after a newspaper reported on government corruption, the authorities suddenly fined its owners $525 million for alleged tax irregularities, detained one of the press conglomerate's executives on suspicion of links to underground paramilitaries, and banned the group from bidding for state tenders for a year.

Considered beside states like these, around the same level of economic development, does Russia's political system stand out as less effective and democratic? Are its defects so severe that it can be compared only to fascist states and the harshest Middle Eastern dictatorships? Overall, politics in Russia as of 2010 was quite comparable to that in other middle income countries—a group whose regimes span a broad range, straddling the divide between illiberal democracy and soft authoritarianism. In the last ten years, Russia has been moving from the former toward the latter.

The most compelling criticism of Russia's democracy concerns the evidence of increasing electoral fraud and pressure on voters to support incumbents. Especially since 2000, journalists have reported numerous cases of ballot stuffing, falsification of results, and bullying of voters. Simultaneously, the number of localities and regions with implausibly high turnout and support for the incumbents has soared, and the distributions of results have become quite bizarre from a statistical point of view. Oddly enough, such fraud and pressure seem to have been almost entirely redundant, generating outcomes that were close to those predicted by credible preelection polls. Moreover, the official results fit well with the long-term trends of support for different parties evident in repeated polls. Figure 10.2 shows the percentage of respondents who said in VCIOM/Levada Center polls that they would vote for particular parties if a Duma election were held the following Sunday. The letters "CP," "U," "UR," and "RC," indicate the share of the valid vote received by the Communist Party, Unity, United Russia, and Russia's Choice (or the Union of Right Forces) in elections between 1993 and 2007. The electoral results for each party lie close to the lines showing the trajectories of support for them in the polls.

It could still be that voters were brainwashed by pro-Kremlin media, as some critics claimed; I consider this below. But Figure 10.2 suggests that pressures on voters and falsification did not change the results much. Had votes for the main contenders exactly matched their levels of support in opinion polls, it would have made no difference at all to the outcomes of presidential elections and very little to the distribution of power in the Duma. Of course, stealing what one could have obtained honestly is still stealing. But in all the national elections since 1991, the results roughly reflected the stated preferences of the voters.

Another valid criticism concerns the way authorities have harassed opposition candidates, denying them public spaces to campaign, and

Figure 10.2 Support for parties in opinion polls and official election results, Russia, 1993–2007

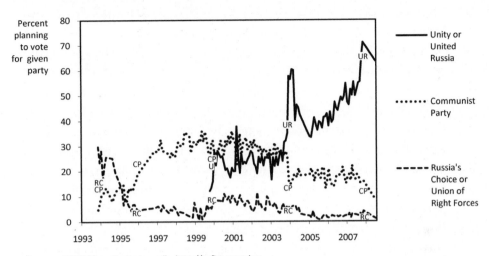

Sources: VCIOM/Levada Center polls, http://sofist.socpol.ru.
Note: Lines indicate percent choosing the party when asked how they would vote if a Duma election were held next Sunday, excluding those who would not vote or were undecided; some values interpolated. Letters indicate percent of valid vote for party in elections; U: Unity; UR: United Russia; CP: Communist Party; RC: Russia's Choice or Union of Right Forces.

sometimes striking them from the ballot on technicalities or invented pretexts. Such abuses are not unique to Russia. Indeed, far worse occur in various middle income countries. In Malaysia, Venezuela, and Argentina, rivals of the current officeholders have been imprisoned after questionable or at least selective prosecutions. In the Philippines and Thailand, parliamentary candidates are often murdered. It is puzzling that Russia's central authorities have bothered to disqualify reformist candidates whose vote totals were unlikely to make it into the double digits. Despite such manipulation, the positions represented by candidates on the ballot in many national elections have spanned the spectrum from utranationalism to orthodox communism.

One claim that has some validity but is often exaggerated is that freedom of the press has disappeared in Russia. I return to the broader issue below, but focus here on press bias during election campaigns. On the one hand, the main television channels have provided disproportionate coverage of Kremlin-connected parties and candidates, violating election laws. Reporting on Kremlin favorites has been lavish and uncritical. On the other hand, the same networks have, as required by law, provided large amounts of free airtime to all opposition candidates on the ballot. In 2008, for example, the four presidential candidates received a total of forty-two hours—seven on each of three national television stations and three radio stations—to debate each other and run advertisements. No Russian who wanted information about the programs of opposition candidates had the slightest difficulty obtaining it. Whether the candidates helped or hurt themselves with their television appearances is another question.

Did biased television coverage swing the vote? The most sophisticated analysis of this is in a paper by Ruben Enikolopov, Maria Petrova, and Ekaterina Zhuravskaya, who exploited the fact that certain regions did not receive the signal of the NTV network during the 1999 election to estimate how much difference a pro-opposition channel made. Other things equal, in regions that had access to NTV, the vote for the pro-government Unity party was 2.6 percentage points lower, and the total vote for the three other parties 2.4 points higher. Thus, the state takeover of NTV in 2001 may have increased the vote for Kremlin candidates in subsequent elections—but probably by at most a few percentage points. Had Putin's or Medvedev's totals in 2004 and 2008, or United Russia's in 2003 and 2007, been 2.6 percentage points lower, this would have changed little in practice. Each would still have won in a landslide.

Putin's administration has been rightly criticized for making it harder for the opposition to hold street rallies and for sending large numbers of police troops to club and arrest demonstrators. What is less often reported is how ineffective and partial such intimidation has been. Jason Lyall studied antiwar protests held in Moscow and St. Petersburg during the first and second Chechen wars. Somewhat surprisingly, he found that more protests were held—with larger total attendance—under Putin than under Yeltsin, although in part this might reflect the second war's longer duration. He also found that the frequency and scale of protests increased over time despite the authorities' efforts to discourage them. Two other researchers collected data on demonstrations between January 2007 and March 2009, and also found the number of protests and participants increased during this period, especially protests against the central government. The number of suppressed demonstrations decreased, which conflicts with the image of tightening restrictions.

Other criticisms of Russia's politics single out features considered unobjectionable in other countries. From the election of 2007, the authorities replaced a hybrid system for Duma elections with pure proportional representation (PR), ostensibly to encourage consolidation of the party system. Many of the world's most respected democracies—including Austria, Denmark, Spain, and Switzerland—use the same party-list PR system to elect their parliaments. The philosopher John Stuart Mill called proportional representation a "great practical and philosophical idea, the greatest improvement of which the system of representative government is susceptible." Yet Putin's reform was viewed by some as yet another step along the road to autocracy. With slightly more justification, critics attacked as antidemocratic Putin's raising of the threshold for seats from 5 to 7 percent of the vote, also intended to encourage party consolidation. In fact, Putin's 7 percent was about halfway between the 5 percent of Germany and Poland and Turkey's 10 percent. A number of countries have high thresholds for blocs that consist of multiple parties—10 percent for a two-party bloc in the Czech Republic and 8 percent in Poland and Romania. My point is not that these were desirable changes. Clearly, they were adopted because Kremlin operatives thought that, under current conditions, they would make the system more manageable. But the institutions themselves were hardly incompatible with democracy.

Increasing the presidential term from four to six years reduced the frequency with which presidents could be held to account. Yet until 2000 France's president had a seven-year term and Mexico's president serves for six years (although he is limited to one term whereas the Russian president can serve two). Putin's replacement of direct gubernatorial elections with a system of presidential nomination and confirmation by regional legislatures was cast as a grave threat to democracy. However, among European Union members, a number—including Portugal, Bulgaria, Estonia, and Lithuania—have regional executives that are centrally appointed. None of these countries is typically criticized for this. In 2007, editorialists waxed indignant about Putin "anointing his successor," as if an incumbent endorsing a colleague was something unique to Russia. The same writers apparently saw nothing untoward about Tony Blair "anointing" Gordon Brown to succeed him or President Bill Clinton endorsing Al Gore in 2000.

How much does the kind of flawed democracy or soft authoritarianism that we see in Russia differ from the regimes of other countries around Russia's level of economic development? A more systematic comparison requires some international metric. At a minimum, an acceptable cross-national rating of democracies should be able to distinguish between the kind of system observable in Russia and government by a federation of dynastic monarchs free from any checks whatsoever, as in the United Arab Emirates. This rules out the Freedom House index. Instead, I make comparisons using the widely used Polity IV database, compiled by a team of political scientists; this evaluates the authority characteristics of national regimes, rating them on a 21-point scale that runs from -10 (pure autocracy) to +10 (pure democracy).

Between 1992 and 2007, Russia's Polity score ranged between 3 and 6, averaging 4.5. In 2007 it was 4, putting Russia between Malaysia and Venezuela. The UAE received a score that year of -8. Saudi Arabia was rated -10, a fully consolidated autocracy, and the United States +10, a fully consolidated democracy.

Figure 10.3 shows countries' 2007 Polity scores plotted against their GDP per capita, adjusted for purchasing power parity. In general, higher income is associated with a higher level of democracy, the major exceptions being the oil-rich countries and Singapore. Countries around Russia's income level exhibit a broad range of political regimes—from the highly authoritarian Libya to the consolidated democracy of Poland. The dashed trend line shows the level of democracy that might be expected at each level of economic development, given the data plotted in the graph and assuming a linear relationship. Russia's Polity score is close to the line, suggesting that Russia's political practice, as evaluated by the Polity team, is well predicted by its income alone. Russia is certainly not the outlier some of the comments quoted in the introduction to this chapter suggest.

Like many other countries, Russia lies in what Andreas Schedler calls "the foggy zone" between states that all would accept as democratic, like Switzerland, and those that are clearly authoritarian, such as China or the old Soviet Union. Could Russia have done better? To get a sense of the range of possibilities, we can compare it both to countries at similar levels of economic development and to others that were also transitioning

Figure 10.3 Economic development and democracy, 2007

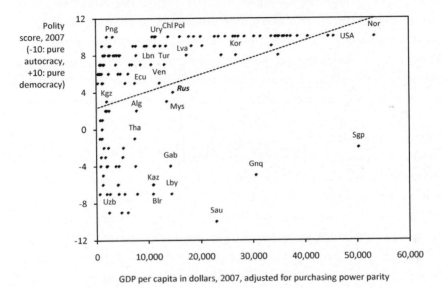

Sources: Polity IV (after September 2009 revision), and World Bank, *World Development Indicators*, 2009.

from communism. Countries in the same rough income bracket show a range of political regimes. Some, such as Chile, achieved a perfect Polity rating of 10 in 2007; others, such as Iran, were close to consolidated autocracies; Venezuela was at a level similar to Russia's. Looking at the political trajectories of postcommunist countries, there are strong geographical patterns. The East European, Baltic, and Balkan states almost all achieved high levels of democracy by 2007; by contrast, almost all the Central Asian countries had become consolidated authoritarian states. States in the Caucasus (Georgia, Armenia, Azerbaijan) and in the continental European part of the former Soviet Union (Russia, Ukraine, Belarus, Moldova) were in between, with a range of outcomes in each group. Russia was third in its group, behind Moldova (8) and Ukraine (7), but far above Belarus (-7).

Thus, it seems reasonable to conclude that Russia might have done somewhat better. In 2000, Russia had a Polity score of 6, equal to Ukraine's. But whereas the sustained antidemocratic tinkering of Putin's

Kremlin eventually drove Russia's rating down to 4, Ukraine's climbed to 7 by 2008. Under a president with deeper democratic convictions, it is plausible that Russia could have done the same. On the other hand, Russia could also have done much worse. In 1992, Belarus was rated 7 on Polity's scale, higher than any of the other three countries in its group. But after the election of and consolidation of power by President Lukashenko, its rating plummeted to -7, where it has remained ever since.

Freedom of the Press

Putin's critics condemn his handling of the country's media. To Ferguson, the Kremlin's control over the three main television channels recalls Hitler's use of propaganda. As well as rating democracy in general, Freedom House publishes evaluations of the media environments in different countries. In 2008, it rated press freedom in Russia equal to that in Yemen. In Yemen, according to Freedom House's report, *all* television and radio stations are owned by the state. It is a crime to criticize the president, to publish material that "undermines public morality" or that "distorts the image of the Yemeni, Arab, or Islamic heritage." Journalists can be sentenced to flogging for defamation or executed for apostasy. Throughout 2007, according to Freedom House, Yemeni "journalists were fined, arrested, imprisoned, abducted, threatened, subjected to home and office raids, and prevented from reporting on a spectrum of issues and events." Numerous websites were blocked.

The press certainly operates under constraints in Russia, and to pursue a career in investigative journalism requires considerable courage. But are conditions *that* bad? The three main television channels are all controlled by the state or businessmen loyal to the Kremlin, and media executives are given detailed guidance on how current events are to be covered (see Chapter 3). Even without this, journalists clearly censor themselves. International companies own some other channels—CTC, Domashny, TV3, DTV, MTV—but these focus on entertainment rather than news. Criticism of the president and prime minister are largely absent from national television, although free-ranging debate of controversial issues and attacks on ministers and local politicians continue. At the same time, various newspapers and magazines are independent and their coverage is increasingly professional. Putin and Medvedev seem—with some exceptions—to react philosophically to the often biting attacks found in these. Indeed, one columnist was surprised to find that one of his newspaper columns blaming the "catastrophic failure of economic policy in 2009" on Putin's destruction of the electoral process had been reposted on Putin's own official website. All flavors of news, information, gossip, and commentary on the authorities—from the polite to the abusive—are available on the Internet, to which almost 40 percent of Russian households are now connected, more than two-thirds of households in Moscow and St. Petersburg. Then there are local and cable television stations, not to mention satellite TV. One radio station, Ekho Moskvy, despite being owned by Gazprom, remains a haven for liberal Putin critics, who are outspoken in their analysis and opinions. It broadcasts to forty cities around the country.

Focus groups show that Russians, trained in the Soviet Union, are sophisticated television viewers, conscious of the need to read between the lines. As one scholar puts it:

> . . . the Russian audience well understands that the "news" they receive from sources such as Vremya on The First Channel or Segodnya on NTV is an arrangement of information through strong political filters. As long as they understand the type of filter, they feel that they can understand the news. They are also quick to say that anyone who believes that this filter does not exist, in any media system, is merely naive.

One perhaps overly optimistic view is that the dramatic increase in advertising revenues—which grew by a factor of six between 1999 and 2007—is beginning to undermine the state's control. In the 1990s, almost all media companies relied on state subsidies, which left them dependent. A recent study found that in regions of Russia where advertising revenues were higher, media analysts judged the press to be freer.

How unusual among middle income countries is this combination of state interference and partial press freedom? Sadly, Russia's use of administrative levers and economic threats to cow the press is not at all unique. As the Kremlin pursued Berezovsky and Gusinsky in 2000–2001, similar events were occurring in South Korea. In what was widely viewed as a politicized campaign to punish publications that criticized the government, the Korean tax agency investigated twenty-three media conglomerates and ordered them to pay multimillion-dollar fines. The owners of three of the largest newspapers were arrested and held in solitary confinement. President Kim Dae-jung's aide, Roh Moo-hyun, who succeeded him as president, was quoted calling the newspapers "no different from organized crime" and threatening to nationalize them. In Turkey in September 2009 the authorities imposed a $2.5 billion fine for alleged tax evasion on the Dogan media group, which had criticized the prime minister. Two other Turkish media companies had already been bankrupted after their owners were charged with fraud. One of these ended up owned by a firm managed by the prime minister's son-in-law. In both Korea and Turkey, the government insisted that these actions were simple law enforcement matters that had nothing to do with editorial policy. Many had doubts.

Nor is there anything unusual about the use of state funds to support friendly media and encourage sympathetic coverage. In Argentina, the government spent $100 million in 2008 advertising in loyal companies. Among recipients was ex-President Ernesto Kirchner's former chauffeur. Such carrots do not exclude the use of sticks. In 2009, the head of Argentine state intelligence filed criminal charges against the director and owner of an anti-Kirchner paper, alleging he had been slandered by editorials on the intelligence agency. In September 2009, the tax authorities sent two hundred inspectors to question the employees of another newspaper, Clarin, which had also been critical of the Kirchners. The newspaper's director was charged with having illegally adopted orphans. Simultaneously, the president was pushing a bill through parliament that would limit the access of private television and radio companies to the digital spectrum.

The most serious attempt to quantify levels of press freedom in multiple countries is the "media sustainability index" constructed since 2001 by the International Research and Exchanges Board (IREX) in collaboration with the U.S. Agency for International Development. In each country, a panel of editors, reporters, media executives, advertising specialists, lawyers, professors, and human rights activists evaluates the extent to which the country's media environment meets five objectives—"Legal and social norms protect and promote free speech and access to public information; journalism meets professional standards of quality; multiple news sources provide citizens with reliable, objective news; independent media are well-managed businesses, allowing editorial independence; supporting institutions function in the professional interests of independent media." In 2009, IREX constructed such ratings for twenty-one countries in the Balkans and the former Soviet Union.

In 2001, Russia's media environment was rated the highest of any of the twelve former Soviet republics covered and higher than almost all the Balkan states. It was surpassed only by Croatia, Romania, and Bulgaria. By 2009, it had fallen significantly. Russia now rated below Ukraine, Kyrgyzstan, and—just—Georgia. Nevertheless, the Russian media was still judged more independent and professional than those of eight other former Soviet republics plus Macedonia.

The "most dramatic barometer of press freedom," according to one official of the Committee to Protect Journalists (CPJ), an advocacy group based in New York, is "the number of journalists killed." Each year, the CPJ publishes lists of journalists killed for reasons related to their work in a large number of countries, as does the organization Reporters Without Borders. Both consider the Russian government's record in this regard unusually bad. According to the CPJ, fifty-two journalists were killed in Russia in the line of duty between January 1992 and December 2009, twenty-one of them since Putin came to power in March 2000. That puts Russia fourth on the list of countries dangerous for journalists, surpassed only by Iraq, with 141, the Philippines, with sixty-eight, and Algeria, with sixty. In July 2009, Reporters Without Borders counted "at least 20" journalists who had been killed "in connection with their work" since Putin became president. The organization characterized Presidents Putin and Medvedev as "Predators of Press Freedom," along with Libyan President Muammar Gaddafi, Uzbekistan's Islam Karimov, and North Korea's Kim Jong-Il. The figures of these organizations are quoted in almost every article lamenting the lack of press freedom in Russia.

This would seem to justify a close look at the numbers. Are they, in fact, a meaningful barometer of freedom of the press, and do they provide a basis on which to characterize the leaders of some countries as

"predators"? One should first acknowledge that collecting internationally comparable statistics on journalist killings is extremely difficult. The
killers do not usually explain their motives, and the extent to which such
cases are publicized varies across countries. Documenting the dangers
journalists face is tremendously important. Still, the figures are only useful if accurate, transparent, and correctly interpreted. An examination of
the data suggests some problems.

First, if the death statistics constitute a "barometer of press freedom,"
this is a barometer that, by construction, can only record the pressure
accurately within a certain range. Both in countries with very high and
with very low press freedom, deaths occur extremely rarely—in the first
case because journalists are protected, in the second because very few
journalists are suicidal enough to antagonize the powerful. Countries
with high death statistics are likely to be those in which there *is* some
intermediate level of press freedom, where the power structures are in
flux and the rules of the game are unclear, and where journalists are
unusually brave.

Second, the published statistics are not adjusted in any way for the
number of journalists working in a given country. Other things equal,
in a country with many large cities, each with a major daily newspaper,
there will be more opportunities (and more reporters) to get into trouble
investigating crime and corruption than in a country with only one or
two large cities. Even if the small country is much more dangerous for
journalists, there are still likely to be more deaths in the large one. To
judge countries on the basis of the raw figures is about as meaningful
as comparing the absolute numbers of highway fatalities in Afghanistan
and the United States. Besides penalizing countries with moderate press
freedom, fluid power structures, unclear rules of the game, and brave
journalists, this index will also penalize large, urbanized countries with
many newspapers and reporters. In a word, Russia.

UNESCO publishes statistics on the number of newspaper journalists in different countries. According to its figures, Russia, with 102,300
in 2005, had more newspaper journalists than any other country. China
came second, with 82,849, followed by the United States, with 54,134.
Unfortunately, figures for television and radio journalists were not available for most countries. If we assume that the number of broadcast jour-

nalists varies across countries roughly in proportion to the number of newspaper journalists, this casts the journalist death statistics in a different light. In the CPJ's lists, Russia, with fifty-two journalists killed since 1992, looks much worse than Turkey, with twenty. But, according to UNESCO, whereas Russia has more than 100,000 newspaper journalists, Turkey has only 8,652. In Russia, one journalist was killed for every 1,967 newspaper journalists; in Turkey one was killed for every 433 newspaper journalists. The ratio of deaths to newspaper journalists was one in 1,300 in Lithuania, one in 731 in Zimbabwe, one in 711 in Croatia, one in 432 in Brazil, one in 371 in Nepal, and one in 186 in Lebanon. Of course, these figures are only a rough approximation—for instance, many foreign journalists work in the given countries—but they show how misleading the raw statistics can be. Based on these simple adjustments, it seems likely that the rate at which journalists are killed in Russia is actually *not* near the top of the list.

Third, even if the widely quoted absolute death statistics were cross-nationally comparable, the implication that they are a reliable measure of press freedom—and, more specifically, an indicator of "predatory" attitudes of the government towards the press—is simply wrong. Consider how the fifty-two cases of journalists confirmed killed by the CPJ because of their work in Russia since 1992 break down. First, five journalists died in October 1993 as Russian special forces sought to *defend* the Ostankino television center against a crowd of armed Communist extremists who were attempting to storm it with guns and Molotov cocktails (see Chapter 2). Four were caught in the crossfire and one suffered a heart attack. These deaths certainly do not indicate a desire by the authorities to intimidate the press; the government was trying to protect the journalists. Second, a number of the journalists on the list were murdered by Islamic terrorists or in Grozny under the Dudayev regime at a time when the federal government had no control over the republic. Adlan Khasanov was killed by the bomb that assasinated the pro-Moscow Chechen president Akhmat Kadyrov in 2004, for which Shamil Basayev claimed responsibility. Vladimir Yatsina was "killed in Chechnya by Chechen militants who had taken him hostage," according to the CPJ's own report. Dmitry Krikoryants was murdered in Grozny in 1993, most likely in retribution for his investigative reporting into corruption in the Dudayev regime. Telman Alishayev was believed killed by Islamic extremists. It is ironic that such atrocities committed by forces fighting *against* the Russian government would be used to impugn the government.

Another thirteen journalists were caught in the crossfire during the wars in Chechnya or as Russian forces attempted to rescue civilian hostages who had been seized by Chechen terrorists. Tragic as such deaths are, they reveal the danger of reporting on a civil war and terrorist attacks and tell us very little about freedom of the press. Two more journalists were killed in the crossfire as federal troops stormed the parliament building on October 4, 1993. One can hold various opinions about Yeltsin's decision to use force against the parliamentary opposition, but it was certainly not an attempt to cow the press. Other cases appear connected to the high crime rate in Russia, for which the government of course bears some responsibility. At least eight journalists seem to have been killed by local criminal groups enraged by their reporting on organized crime. Although these cases may reveal something about the government's inability to control crime and protect citizens, they show little about the government's policies towards the press. (Even as measures of how the crime rate affects journalists, the total number killed is meaningless unless one adjusts for the vast differences in countries' populations of journalists, as discussed above.) Another victim, Vladislav Listyev, was a television executive, whose murder was believed to be related not to reporting but to the business affairs of the station. One journalist died after being run over while filming illegal drag racing. Two more appeared to be robbery victims.

Including ambiguous cases is particularly likely to distort the figures in Russia's case. Given the very large number of journalists in Russia and the country's relatively high rates of murder and accidental death, one should expect a considerable number of journalists to be killed in Russia each year for reasons that have nothing to do with their work. Just multiplying the number of newspaper journalists—102,300—by the average murder and accidental death rates yields the prediction of twenty-nine homicides and twenty-eight accidental deaths per year, or a total of 493 homicides and 459 accidental deaths between 1992 and 2008. In a pool this large, some of the deaths, even when unrelated to journalism, are bound to look suspicious.

By the time one whittles the list down to those cases in which it is somewhat plausible to imagine that the journalist was killed by some associate of the state—whether from the military, government, or police—in order to punish or intimidate journalists, the total has fallen from fifty-two to about fifteen, and the total under Putin from twenty-one to around twelve. I include in this list the big-name cases familiar to Western readers of Anna Politkovskaya, Yury Shchekochikhin, Nataliya Estemirova, and Paul Klebnikov, although in the last case the killer seems more likely to have come from the worlds of business or crime. Even without allowing for the number of journalists in the country, this total is now only slightly greater than that for Brazil after one also excludes the Brazilian cases that appear linked to crime rather than to the authorities. Needless to say, Brazil's president Luiz Lula da Silva does not appear on Reporters Without Borders' list of Press Predators.

The danger of misperceptions creeping into the discourse over press freedom in Russia is illustrated by the sad case of Ilya Zimin, a journalist for NTV who was found beaten to death in his apartment in February 2006. The director-general of UNESCO was prompted to express his concern about "reports of violence against journalists in Russia," adding that: "Attacks against journalists . . . undermine society as a whole." Freedom House mentioned the Zimin murder in its account of problems for freedom of the press in Putin's Russia. It later emerged that Zimin had been killed in a drunken brawl by a homophobe angered by his amorous advances. Tragic as this murder was, the one thing that was completely clear was that it had nothing to do with freedom of the press.

Russia is often criticized, with justification, for its failure to successfully prosecute and convict the perpetrators of attacks on journalists. One fact rarely publicized by advocacy groups is that the record of prosecutions has been improving under Putin's presidency. As a report by the International Federation of Journalists (IFJ) puts it: "The total impunity that prevailed until 1997 has steadily receded." The number of trials of the killers of journalists has increased since the late 1990s. A milestone of sorts was reached in 2007 when for the first time more trials of accused journalist killers were held, four, than journalists were killed, three. Of the 165 homicides of journalists between 1993 and 2009 (including those not related to the journalist's work), trials had been held in forty-six of the cases, resulting in thirty-seven convictions, according to the IFJ. In the last six years of Yeltsin's presidency, there were eleven convictions; in the last six years of Putin's there were twenty.

Another issue is the imprisonment of reporters to punish or intimidate them. In 2009, according to the CPJ, one journalist was jailed in Russia. A radical sympathiser with the Chechen militants, he was convicted of "inciting ethnic hatred and making public calls to extremist activity." "To kill, to kill, to kill!" he had written. "To cover the whole of Russia in blood, not to give the slightest mercy to anybody, to try to arrange by any means even one nuclear explosion on the territory of the Russian Federation—that should be the program of radical resistance." He had praised the Chechen terrorists for "blowing up this stupid and senseless Russian population." Opinion divided in the commentariat between those who thought that freedom of the press should be absolute and others who thought that if one punished hate speech similar to that quoted when aimed at Jews, one had to punish it also when aimed at Russians.

It seems distasteful to quibble over the number of dead journalists. Even one is obviously too many. The courage and commitment of reporters such as Anna Politkovskaya and Yury Shchekochikhin command admiration. But exaggerations that—even if innocently arrived at—look politically motivated do not help the cause of press freedom in Russia. They discredit the critics and reinforce cynicism within the Russian elite about the objectivity and independence of Western nongovernmental organizations. Even some of Russia's homegrown press freedom advocates are embarrassed by the slipshod zeal of their Western champions. A better way to honor the journalistic values of those killed might be to insist on accuracy and meticulous reporting, even when the results do not fit the prevailing story line.

Petrocracy

In one respect, Russia does seem different. Under its tundra lie enormous reserves of oil and gas, gold and diamonds, nickel and iron ore. Many scholars see in such natural abundance a paradoxical burden. Governments that can rely on income from the sale of mineral resources have no need to develop the complex institutions of conflict management and political exchange that are the hallmark of modernity. Instead of bargaining with the public over taxation, rulers can simply buy citizens' acquiescence—or buy enough machine guns and mercenaries to keep them in check. Natural resource wealth, it is said, produces unfree politics.

This idea is often seen as the key to Russia's predicament. "Russia's future," writes Moisés Naím, editor-in-chief of *Foreign Policy* magazine and a former trade and industry minister of Venezuela, "will be defined as much by the geology of its subsoil as by the ideology of its leaders. . . . A lot of oil combined with weak public institutions produces poverty, inequality, and corruption. It also undermines democracy." According to *New York Times* columnist Tom Friedman, the noxious consequences of oil increase as its price rises. The higher the oil price, the less freedom one should expect to see in Russia.

In Chapter 7, I pointed out that the international evidence for Friedman's claim is weak. Examining the world's oil producers, there is no clear sign that the price of oil is related to the extent of democracy. High oil prices and authoritarianism do not coincide significantly more often than one would expect them to by chance. Oil and gas *income* may be related to political freedom—at least in certain times and places (although not before the 1980s, not among rich countries, and not in Latin America). Russia may be less democratic than it would have been had it had no oil or gas. That said, the effect of oil income is diminishing. Given Russia's level of production in the early 1980s, changes in its oil income since then probably explain very little of the subsequent changes in its political institutions.

Even this may be saying too much. There are reasons to wonder whether Russia is really comparable to the mostly Middle Eastern, African, and Central Asian countries where oil income seems to have a clear negative impact. In many ways, Russia is more like the Latin American countries, where no "oil curse" is to be found. (Among Latin American countries, oil and gas have actually been associated with *more* democracy.)

Compared to the oil-rich autocracies of the Persian Gulf, Russia's income per citizen from hydrocarbons looks rather meager. In Qatar, if the value of all oil and gas produced in 2006 had been divided among the emirate's residents, each would have received a check for $45,000. In Russia, the check would have been for only $2,800, about the same as in Venezuela. Qatar's rulers can keep citizens cocooned in a system of cradle-to-grave benefits—ranging from free health care, education, and telephone service to guaranteed civil service jobs and free plots of land—while eschewing most taxes. This is far from the case in Russia, where social services are much less generous and oil and gas contribute only about one-third of government revenues.

At the same time, Russia's economic and social structure is far more like that in Latin America than it is like those of the Middle Eastern or African oil states. Developed in the distinctive Soviet manner, Russia has rates of educational achievement and scientific infrastructure that are closer to those of developed countries. Literacy is universal. Female participation in the workforce is higher than in Norway or Denmark. The proportion of workers in research and development is close to that in Canada and forty-five times that of Kuwait. Among the world's twenty leading oil and gas producers, Russia has the highest share of GDP in manufacturing and the third highest share in services. Maintaining political control over a literate, urbanized population, rich in scientists, where women are integrated into the workforce, is bound to be more challenging than imposing an authoritarian regime on traditional communities of farmers, traders, or migrant workers.

Finally, petrodollars are only likely to entrench autocracy if they accrue to the regime. However, since the mid-1990s Russia has been one of very few oil-rich countries in which most oil has been produced by independent, private companies rather than in projects dominated by the state (with or without foreign partners). It is easy to forget this amid the furor over the Kremlin's efforts to increase the state's role. The attacks on Putin for nationalizing "the entire energy sector" are mystifying for two reasons. First, he didn't, and, second, most others did.

Between 1960 and 2006, private oil companies were nationalized in: Algeria, Angola, Argentina, Bahrain, Bangladesh, Bolivia, Burma, Cambodia, Chad, Colombia, Congo-Brazzaville, Ecuador, Egypt, Ethiopia, Gabon, Ghana, Guyana, India, Indonesia, Iran, Iraq, Kuwait, Libya, Malaysia, Morocco, Mozambique, Nepal, Nigeria, Oman, Pakistan, Peru, the Philippines, Qatar, Saudi Arabia, Sudan, Trinidad and Tobago, Uganda, UAE, Venezuela, Yemen, and Zambia. In other oil-producing countries like Mexico, nationalization was ruled out only because the state could not nationalize what it already owned. About three-quarters of oil drilled around the world is now produced by state-owned national oil companies.

By contrast, since the privatizations of the 1990s, Russia has belonged to a small club of countries including the U.S.A. and Canada where most of the oil sector is private. Even after the expropriation of Yukos, the repurchase of Sibneft, and Moscow's renegotiation of production shar- ing agreements with foreign oil companies, the proportion of oil pro- duced in majority state-owned companies was estimated at from 37 to 43 percent. In the gas sector, the Kremlin brought the state stake in Gazprom up to just over 50 percent through the repurchase of shares. Yet simulta- neously, Putin made it legal for foreigners to own the other 50 percent of Gazprom shares. Of course, Russia's private oil firms can hardly ignore the Kremlin's wishes. They rely on licenses from the state and on the state-owned pipeline system to ship their output. Still, the Russian oil sector has created concentrations of private wealth that could, were the Kremlin's position to weaken, finance the rebirth of opposition and the regeneration of civil society.

Even if Russia's surging oil income did not make Putin's authoritar- ian turn inevitable, it might be responsible for stimulating corruption. Steven Fish agrees that Russia's oil revenues were insufficient for leaders "to play the role of the Kuwaiti rulers, showering the people with ser- vices without taxing them." But in Russia, he writes, there was "more than enough money to corrupt the state apparatus."

But was there? And was that what corrupted the state apparatus? This turns out to be a difficult question to answer. Oil rich states such as Qatar and Equatorial Guinea are perceived by international business- men and country experts to be more corrupt than others at their income level. However, the views of such businessmen and experts are likely to be influenced by images in the world media, which may be inaccurate or out of date. A better way to assess the reality is to use corruption measures that reflect direct experience of citizens or local businessmen. I looked for such effects using the results of two surveys. First, I used the question on bribery in Transparency International's Global Corruption Barome- ter—the same survey of citizens shown in Figure 10.1. Second, I used the World Business Environment Survey (WBES), a poll of company managers in eighty countries conducted by the World Bank in 1999–2000. The WBES interviewers read out the statement: "It is common for firms in my line of business to have to pay some irregular 'additional payments' to get things done," and then asked the respondent whether this was true. The respondent could pick among six answers ranging from "always" to "never." Plotting the reported frequency of bribery against the logarithm of countries' oil and gas income per capita, I found similar patterns for both surveys: bribery was slightly *less* frequent in countries where oil and gas income per capita was higher. Figure 10.4 shows the relationship for the WBES data. (To make interpretation more intuitive, I reverse the scale so that 1 equals "never" and 6 equals "always.")

There is no evidence in these surveys that mineral wealth corrupts lower level officials. Such officials are corrupt in resource-poor developing countries as well. On the other hand, it is possible that mineral wealth makes a difference higher up in the bureaucracy, where the effects will not be captured by surveys of the population or average businessmen.

Figure 10.4 Oil and gas income and corruption, 1997–2000

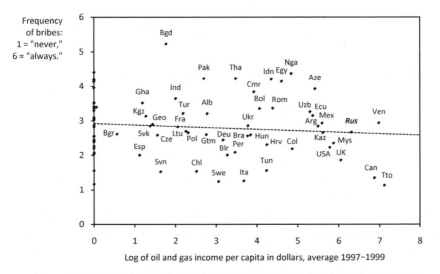

Sources: Michael Ross dataset on oil and gas income; World Bank, *World Business Environment Survey*, 1999–2000; "It is common for firms in my line of business to have to pay some irregular 'additional payments' to get things done." This is true: 6 = always, 1 = never, country averages (I have reversed the scale for easier interpretation).

In Russia, as the oil price rose anecdotes circulated of brazen venality among top officials, involving mind-boggling sums. Unfortunately, we have no reliable measures of such high-level corruption.

In sum, Russia does not appear doomed by its mineral endowments to a future of authoritarian politics. Its relatively moderate income per capita from oil and gas, its modernized economy and society, and the important role of private companies in the energy sector make Russia look more similar to Latin American oil-rich states than to the Middle Eastern and African countries in which oil has been linked to dictatorship. Moreover, international evidence suggests that changes in the country's oil and gas income since 1985 can explain only a very small part of the transformations of its political order. It is possible that higher oil incomes stimulated corruption, but there is little reliable evidence of this.

If Russia's oil and gas do not preclude democracy, they do have some more complicated effects. If an incumbent president has authoritarian inclinations, rapid economic growth, which boosts the president's popularity, makes it easier for him to act on them. Although surging oil prices are not the only cause of growth, they do provide a major stimulus. Thus, at times in Russia one sees the logic of the "oil curse" in action: in 2005–2007, rising hydrocarbon prices sustained growth, which permitted Putin to continue concentrating power. However, between 2000 and 2004, Putin strengthened executive authority without any significant increase in the oil price. And in the early 1980s oil prices fell sharply without stimulating any move towards democracy.

Besides such contingent, occasional effects, dependence on commodity exports subjects countries to considerable economic turbulence since the prices of commodities are more volatile than those of manufactured goods and services. In countries such as Russia, where the income from oil per capita is not too large, the result is likely to be not so much autocracy as instability. Such instability may not always be bad for democracy. If it is moderate, it could even facilitate turnover at the top of the state. In Latin America, the boom-bust cycles of the 1970s and 1980s arguably helped to dislodge authoritarian regimes and promote the return to democracy. It may be overly optimistic to imagine something similar in Russia, but such a turn of events seems more plausible than that oil rents will consolidate a Persian Gulf style–dictatorship.

Demographic Catastrophe

Any reader of Western newspapers knows that Russia's population is imploding. "Russia's demography befits a country at war," thundered *The Economist* in November 2008. "The population of 142m is shrinking by 700,000 people a year. By 2050 it could be down to 100m." "The drop in population in Russia," says a World Bank health economist and co-author of a recent study, *Dying Too Young in the Russian Federation*, "is unprecedented among industrialized countries."

Perhaps so, if by "industrialized" one means rich. But it is hardly unprecedented among Russia's neighbors. Among twenty-eight postcommunist countries for which the World Bank publishes data, Russia had only the *fourteenth* largest fall in population between 1989 and 2007 (see Table 10.1). While Russia's population decreased by 3.8 percent during this period, Georgia's shrank by almost 20 percent, and Latvia's, Estonia's, and Armenia's by around 15 percent. In this company, Russia's population problems—which *are* serious—seem somewhat less imposing.

Russia's figures would look worse were it not attracting hundreds of thousands of immigrants each year; conversely, Georgia and the Baltics would look better if so many of their residents were not choosing to leave. But even subtracting out the net immigration to Russia of 4.2 million people during these years would only increase the fall in Russia's population to 6.6 percent, putting it between Kazakhstan and Romania in Table 10.1. Russia would still be nowhere near the top of the list.

Surveying the demographic challenges faced by postcommunist countries, several compete for attention with Russia's. There is the breakdown of the traditional family in Estonia, where today almost 60 percent of babies are born to unmarried mothers. Within Europe, only Iceland, with 64 percent in 2007, beats Estonia's record for illegitimate births. Perhaps this is less worrisome than it sounds since many of the unmarried parents nevertheless live together. There is no such reassurance about a horrifying problem developing in the Caucasus. In Georgia, Armenia, and Azerbaijan, demographers have recorded a huge imbalance in the numbers of male and female infants. In almost all countries, more boys are born than girls—in the United States and most developed countries, the ratio of boys to girls among children under age five is about 1.05. In

Table 10.1 Percentage change in population, 1989–2007

Georgia	-19.6
Latvia	-15.2
Armenia	-15.1
Estonia	-14.4
Bulgaria	-13.7
Bosnia and Herzegovina	-13.5
Moldova	-12.9
Ukraine	-10.2
Lithuania	-8.5
Croatia	-6.9
Romania	-6.9
Kazakhstan	-4.7
Belarus	-4.6
Russian Federation	**-3.8**
Hungary	-3.3
Albania	-2.3
Czech Republic	-0.3
Poland	0.4
Slovenia	0.9
Slovak Republic	1.9
Montenegro	2.8
Macedonia, FYR	7.6
Kyrgyz Republic	20.6
Azerbaijan	20.8
Mongolia	26.1
Tajikistan	30.4
Uzbekistan	34.1
Turkmenistan	39.0

Sources: World Bank, *World Development Indicators*, 2009, adapted from Elizabeth Brainerd, "The Demographic Transformation of Post-Socialist Countries: Causes, Consequences, and Questions," Brandeis University: manuscript, August 2009, 43.

China and India, the high ratio of infant boys to girls is taken as indirect evidence of the selective abortion of female fetuses, mistreatment and neglect of female babies, and even female infanticide. In China and India in recent years, there were respectively 1.15 and 1.11 boys aged under five for every girl. In Azerbaijan, Armenia, and Georgia, the number of boys per girl in this age group is 1.17, 1.15, and 1.13. Demographers do not know why this is happening.

This is not to say that Russia does not have severe demographic problems. Its mortality rate is unusually high. In 2007 there were 14.6 deaths per 1,000 people in Russia, compared to 8.1 in the United States and 10.1 in Germany. The rate is higher than those in most Latin American and Asian middle income countries—8.0 in Argentina, 4.3 in Venezuela, 4.3 in Malaysia, and 5.1 in South Korea. A number of other postcommunist countries have rates similarly high—16.4 in Ukraine, 14.8 in Bulgaria, 14.5 in Latvia, 13.9 in Serbia, 13.7 in Belarus, 13.5 in Lithuania, and 13.2 in Hungary—so the problem is not unique to Russia, but it does appear to be a crisis of the postcommunist transition rather than one common to middle income countries.

Why are so many Russians dying? Most experts agree that a large part of the increase since 1990 in Russia—and much of the postcommunist world—resulted from abuse of alcohol, in particular hard liquor. Alcohol is thought to have caused from one-quarter to more than half of the additional deaths. Various clues point in this direction. First, the mortality rate is much higher—and rose more—among groups known to drink heavily. The big increase in deaths struck not the old or the very young but the middle aged. Infant mortality *fell* from 17.4 to 9.4 deaths per 1,000 live births between 1990 and 2007, and the death rate for those over 70 also fell. But mortality for those aged 30–34 rose by more than 70 percent. At the same time, mortality was much higher and rose faster for men—who, in Russia, tend to drink much more—than for women. Second, most of the additional deaths were attributable to diseases and conditions associated with alcohol abuse—accidents, suicides, homicides, liver disease, and, most importantly, heart attacks (myocardial infarction), which research has linked to excessive consumption of hard liquor, especially binge drinking. Many deaths attributed to other causes may also have been alcohol related. In the early 1980s, 58 percent of a sample of autopsies performed in twenty-five regions of Russia showed alcohol in the blood of the deceased. Another study of 25,000 autopsies found that one-fifth of all the Russian men whose death had been attributed to circulatory diseases had lethal or near-lethal levels of ethanol in their blood.

Measuring alcohol consumption is difficult, especially in Russia where home brewing is a tradition in the countryside and dedicated alcoholics turn to eau de cologne or brake fluid when vodka is unavailable. But the rises and falls in estimated liquor consumption have corresponded quite closely to the rises and falls in mortality. During Gorbachev's anti-alcohol campaign in the late 1980s, the death rate plummeted, only to start rising again as drinkers switched to home brew and liquor gradually became more available again (see Figure 10.5). Between 1987 and 1994, the leading Russian expert estimates that drinking by the average Russian rose from 10.6 liters of pure alcohol a year (or 26.5 liters of 40 percent proof vodka) to 14.6 liters. He estimates that the decrease in consumption during the Gorbachev anti-alcohol campaign saved 1.22 million lives, at least temporarily. The timing of deaths even correlates with the timing of binges on a smaller scale: deaths from alcohol poisoning, accidents, violence, and cardiovascular diseases are all significantly higher during and right after the weekend in Moscow than on work days. Among thirty-five to thirty-nine-year-olds, there are almost 25 percent fewer deaths on Tuesdays than on Saturdays.

Figure 10.5 Drinking and death, Russia, 1970–2001

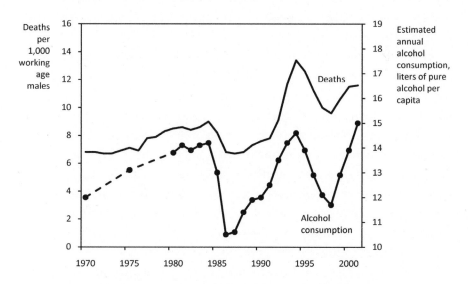

Sources: A.V. Nemtsov, "Alcohol-related human losses in Russia in the 1980s and 1990s," *Addiction* 97 (2002): 1413-25, and A.V. Nemtsov, *Alkogolnaya istoriya Rossii: noveyshy period* (Moscow: Librokom, 2009), for alcohol consumption estimates; Goskomstat Rossii for mortality data.

A final clue is linked to geography. Mortality—and increases in it—
tended to be lower in those postcommunist countries, and those regions
within Russia, that had large Muslim populations, whose religion and
culture discouraged alcohol consumption. In the southern Russian
region of Dagestan, for instance, despite high poverty and unemployment, the crude mortality rate actually fell from 6.2 per thousand people
in 1990 to 5.9 per thousand in 2005, while the national rate was soaring.
Between 1992 and 2005, the death rate fell in Uzbekistan from 6.5 to 5.3
per 1,000 and in Azerbaijan it fell from 7.1 to 6.3 per 1,000.

Some other possible causes do not seem to have been important.
Smoking is widespread in Russia and may have increased in the 1990s.
However, the death rate from lung cancer fell during this period. Environmental pollution, although serious in some places, has been improving. Between 1990 and 2005, the emission of pollutants from stationary
sources into the air decreased by 41 percent and discharges of sewage
and industrial waste into rivers fell by 36 percent. TB and HIV have been
spreading, but still account for only a tiny fraction of total deaths. Despite
the economic crisis of the 1990s, surveys have failed to find any sign of
serious malnutrition in Russia—more gained than lost weight during
the period—and the quality of diets improved as Russians reduced animal fats. There is also no clear evidence that mortality rose because of a
decline in the quality of health care.

Some attribute the surge of deaths to the effects of stress and despair
in the period of wrenching economic change. There may be some truth to
this. However, the evidence is limited and indirect. It is based mostly on
correlations across Russia's regions between certain economic variables
such as job turnover and regional mortality rates. However, job turnover
is bound to correlate with numerous factors, and there is no clear evidence that across regions it correlates with average levels of stress. Nationwide, the degree of social tension and stress expressed in opinion polls
correlates *negatively* over time with the death rate: anxiety was greatest in
the late 1990s, when mortality was falling, and then sank sharply during
the Putin presidency, as mortality once again began to rise.

Why were middle-aged Russian men bingeing on dangerous quantities
of liquor? One reason was probably that the relative price of vodka dropped
very sharply in the early 1990s. At the end of 1990, the average monthly

income was enough to buy ten liters of vodka. In December 1994, it would buy forty-seven liters. By this point, vodka was selling for the equivalent of $2–3 a liter. Other things equal, in regions of Russia where the price of vodka fell more, the death rate rose faster. Vodka prices may have been held down by competition from underground alcohol producers, which proliferated in the relative openness of the 1990s. However, the main reason for the fall in relative vodka prices appears to have been misguided populism. Under both Gorbachev and Yeltsin, increases in the price of ordinary vodka were capped at a time when the prices of other goods—and eventually nominal wages—were soaring. This led to a dramatic increase in the number of liters of vodka the average wage would buy.

Controlling alcoholism is one of the greatest challenges Russia faces over the next decade. Many European countries experienced alcohol problems as they industrialized. Workers' incomes rose, enabling them to consume unhealthy amounts, before policies were put in place to limit problem drinking. In late–nineteenth century Germany, schnapps was ubiquitous in the factories and some laborers brought kegs of beer to work. The American expression "There is no free lunch" referred originally to the late–nineteenth century practice of saloons offering complimentary food to lure industrial workers in for a midday schooner of beer. Bringing alcohol abuse under control often required the combined pressures of temperance leagues, employers concerned about industrial discipline, religious campaigners, and, sometimes, price increases.

In Russia, there are many obstacles to restraining alcohol consumption, including a politically influential vodka producers lobby. Perhaps the greatest perceived impediment, however, is the almost sacred place vodka occupies in the Russian imagination. Invented—so legends say— by monks in the late fifteenth century, sold in the nineteenth century not in bottles but in pails, vodka came into its own as the great social unifier in the Soviet period, dissolving all class and geographical barriers. "At nine o'clock in the morning," wrote Joseph Brodsky, describing Leningrad in the early 1970s, "a drunk is more frequently seen than a taxi." He could have said the same of almost any Russian city. Inebriation was one of very few means of escape. Even the shape of the vodka bottle, wrote the novelist Viktor Yerofeyev, "resembled the cosmic rocket on which one could fly away into space."

This history—along with the opprobrium that met Gorbachev's attempts to sober up the workforce—has inhibited reformers. However, it is not clear how great public opposition to moderate price increases or restrictions on vodka sales would be these days, especially if accompanied by efforts to encourage substitution of vodka by beer, which far less often results in alcohol poisoning or sudden cardiac failure. Awareness of the serious social problems associated with vodka is growing. In January 2007, 40 percent of respondents to one poll said they had at least one alcoholic among their acquaintances and relatives, and 65 percent said they looked negatively upon alcoholics. Asked on the World Values Survey whom they would not like to have as a neighbor, 89 percent of Russians chose "a heavy drinker"—a higher rate of disdain for alcoholics than in any other country surveyed except for Muslim Jordan and Iran. Russians, not known for their tolerance towards sexual minorities, even preferred to live next to homosexuals and AIDS patients. The only category of potential neighbors less popular than heavy drinkers was drug addicts.

Crime and Punishment

Russia and crime have become twinned in the Western subconscious. Whole library shelves have been taken over by books with titles such as *Comrade Criminal, The Rise of the Russian Criminal State,* and *Bandits, Gangsters, and the Mafia.* More are no doubt in the works.

As discussed in previous chapters, crime was a significant aspect of Russia's transition, and remains a matter of concern. The official statistics make for quite terrifying reading. The number of major crimes registered in Russia surged after the end of communism. Between 1990 and 2007, burglaries more than tripled, from 83,000 to 295,000; thefts increased from 913,000 to 1.6 million; drug crimes rose by more than fourteen times, from 16,000 to 231,000.

All this sounds extremely alarming—until, that is, one compares Russia's rates with those of other countries. Overall, Russian police registered two crimes for every 100 people in 2000 and by 2007 the number had risen to 2.5. That marked the country out as a haven of legality compared to the criminal paradises of New Zealand, with eleven crimes per 100 people, Finland, with ten, or even the United States, with nine. Felon-infested New Zealand had almost four times as many thefts and drug crimes per capita as Russia. Canadian women, it turns out, were sixteen times as likely to be raped as their Russian counterparts—and, for that matter, twice as likely to be raped as American women! The obvious con-clusion is that comparing officially reported crime rates across countries is quite meaningless given the very different frequencies with which vic-tims report crimes in different countries, not to mention the practice of some governments of distorting the statistics to improve their reputa-tions. Similarly, the dramatic increase in the official Russian crime rate in the 1990s must be treated with considerable caution.

So what did happen to Russian crime during the transition? A better way to assess this is by means of victimization surveys, in which represen-tative samples of the inhabitants of different countries are asked whether they have been victims of particular crimes, defined in standardized ways. Such surveys are not distorted by the widely divergent rates at which peo-ple in different countries report crimes to the police. Nor are they eas-ily manipulated by the authorities. Since 1989, a consortium of research teams with funding from the Dutch Ministry of Justice has been conduct-ing repeated crime victims surveys in urban areas in about forty-six coun-tries. The group surveyed the population of Moscow in 1992, 1996, and 2000. Their results suggest that crime did increase in the mid-1990s, but by 2000 was around the level of 1992 or below it. The frequency of bur-glaries rose from 1.8 per 100 respondents in 1992 to 3.2 in 1996, before falling back to 1.8 in 2000. Thefts of personal property rose from 10.8 per 100 respondents to 12.7, before falling to 8.2. Assaults and threatened assaults rose from 4.9 per 100 respondents to 5.7, then fell to 3.4.

How does Russia compare to other countries in the project? The latest results that include Russia are from the late 1990s and early 2000s. Rus-sia does not stand out as particularly criminalized in these statistics. Of the forty-six countries for which data were available, Russia had only the thirty-seventh highest rate of victimization by burglary, the twenty-third highest for theft of personal property, and the twenty-fourth highest for assault with force. People were more likely to become victims of serious crimes in a number of developed and middle income countries. Whereas 1.8 percent of Moscow respondents said they had been burgled in the previous year, 4.8 of urban respondents in England and Wales reported this, and 3.2 percent did in Denmark. In Moscow, 1.1 percent had been forcibly assaulted, compared to 4.1 percent in England and Wales, 2.9 percent in Finland, and 1.3 percent in Sweden. In many ways, Muscovites appeared safer than residents of Copenhagen.

There is one crime for which more reliable official statistics can be recovered (and for which victims' surveys do not work so well). Murder rates—especially those recorded in the demographic statistics—are less subject to underreporting, in part because most bodies tend to turn up. The World Health Organization collects data on the rates of death from various causes. In 2004, the latest year for which figures were available, Russia had the fourteenth highest rate of death from violence (excluding wars and self-inflicted violence) in the world. Among middle income countries, Russia's violent death rate—29.7 deaths per 100,000 people— was exceeded by those of Brazil, Jamaica, Venezuela, South Africa, and Colombia, which topped the list at 82.6 deaths per 100,000 people.

As in many large countries, Russia's murder rate varies greatly from region to region. In the Siberian republic of Tuva, an amazing 133 murders occurred per 100,000 people in 2004, while in the Caucasus republic of Kabardino-Balkaria there were only six per 100,000. In general, rates of violence increase as one moves north or east. Moscow and St. Petersburg actually had relatively low homicide rates—11 and 18 per 100,000 respectively. For comparison, the rate of murder and nonnegligent manslaughter in U.S. cities per 100,000 people in 2007 was 46 in Detroit, 45 in Baltimore, 40 in St. Louis, 31 in Washington, D.C., and 27 in Philadelphia. Assuming U.S. "murder and nonnegligent manslaughter" statistics are roughly comparable to those on homicides in Russia—which they may not be—Moscow's rate would put it on a level with Boston or Oklahoma City.

Why is the murder rate so high in certain parts of Russia? Many factors are probably involved, but an important one appears to be alcohol abuse. Studies have found that about 80 percent of those arrested for murder and 60 percent of murder victims had been drinking immediately before the crime. In regions where alcohol consumption increased in the 1990s, the murder rate also rose. As Figure 10.6 shows, the nationwide trend in homicides has tracked the trend in estimated alcohol consumption closely.

When it comes to punishment, Russia does stand out. As of 2000, the latest year for which comparative data were available, Russia incarcerated 6.3 people per 1,000 inhabitants. This was the third highest level among the countries for which the UN had figures, behind only Swaziland, with 8.9 people per thousand, and the United States, with 6.4 people per thousand.

Figure 10.6 Alcohol consumption and homicides, Russia, 1980–2001

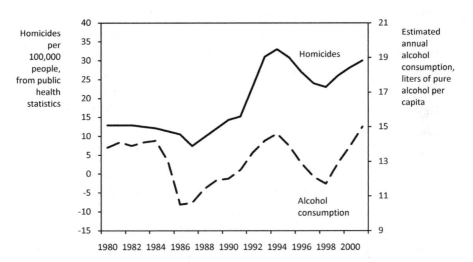

Sources: A.V. Nemtsov, "Alcohol-related human losses in Russia in the 1980s and 1990s," *Addiction* 97 (2002): 1413-25, and A.V. Nemtsov, *Alkogolnaya istoriya Rossii: noveyshy period* (Moscow: Librokom, 2009), for alcohol consumption estimates; Goskomstat Rossii and www.demoscope.ru for homicide data.

What Do Russians Want?

Russia's economic and political systems do not seem radically different from those in other middle income countries. But it could be that Russians themselves are different. Perhaps their culture, aspirations, and understanding of the meaning of life mark them out as a unique civilization, determined to march along a different path, intrinsically at odds with the West.

To the question "What do Russians want?" the only reasonable answer is: many things. Russians are as varied as the citizens of any nation. Finding common threads in the thousands of opinion polls taken since 1989 requires as much art as science. Still, some interpretations fit the evidence better than others.

Do Russians want to live in a democracy? Perhaps the dominant Western view in recent years has been that they are at best lukewarm democrats, who under Putin willingly traded freedoms for a greater sense of social order. This is then blamed on the country's thousand years of autocracy, the experience of serfdom, and the other usual suspects.

But what do the opinion surveys say? At first sight, the evidence seems contradictory. On the one hand, various scholars report strong, stable support for democratic government. Richard Rose and colleagues have been polling Russians regularly since 1992. "When asked to state a preference between a democratic regime or a dictatorship," they write, "more than two-thirds positively endorse democratic rule and less than one in ten endorses even a mild form of dictatorship. . . . The endorsement of democracy as an ideal fluctuates little with the passage of time." The Levada Center has also asked respondents whether they think "Russia needs democracy." In recent years, from 55 to 67 percent of respondents have said yes, compared to 17 to 27 who have said no.

On the other hand, the newspapers brim with reports of polls that seem to confirm the public's authoritarian proclivities. Summing up what they took to be the consensus in 2005, two American journalists wrote that democracy was not then, and perhaps had never been, "a goal supported by much of the population." As they read them, the polls had "consistently found that no more than a third of the population considered themselves democrats . . . while an equally large number believed authoritarianism was the only path for their country."

In part, the confusion can be blamed on the sociologists, whose choices of questions sometimes seem almost designed to confuse the respondents or lead them into "authoritarian" positions. One common approach is to ask if the country needs a "strong leader" or a leader "with a strong hand" and to take agreement as a sign of authoritarian leanings. Of course, since the phrase "strong leader" could equally well suggest a Saddam Hussein or a Winston Churchill, the answers to this question are meaningless. There was no reason for Russian respondents to assume a strong leader could not also be a democrat—and, as discussed below, Russians did not assume this. If the point was to detect a taste for dictatorship, a more direct approach would have been to ask respondents whether the country needed "a dictator." The vast majority would almost certainly have said no.

Other questions set up false dichotomies that implicitly disparaged democracy. "Which is more important for Russia: democracy or order?" some asked, as though the two could not exist together, as though the most orderly countries in the world were not also democracies, and as though restricting civil and political rights was in general an effective means of producing greater order. Or, to take another example, "Which better provides for the welfare of the population—worthy people in the country's leadership or reliable, effective laws?" the pollsters asked, as though worthy people in the country's leadership would not themselves choose to govern by means of reliable, effective laws. From such leading and misleading questions, it is impossible to draw any firm conclusions at all.

Another problem, at times, was a failure to compare the responses of Russians to responses of citizens in established democracies. When sociologists did this, the results were often enlightening. In collaboration with German colleagues, the Levada Center asked respondents in both Russia and Germany whether they agreed that "in order to be defended against crime and terrorism, we should in the future limit our freedom." Sixteen percent of Russians agreed but so did 19 percent of Germans. Thirty-seven percent of Russians were willing to accept "less freedom in return for more justice," but so were 30 percent of the German respondents. After the terrorist attacks of 9/11, large majorities of Americans and Britons were willing to compromise civil liberties in the interest of safety. In a YouGov poll of British adults, 70 percent said they were "willing to see some reduction in our civil liberties in order to improve security in this country." A New York Times/CBS poll around the same time found that 64 percent of U.S. respondents thought that in wartime "it was a good idea for the president to have authority to change rights usually guaranteed by the Constitution."

But, in part, the confusion over Russians' political attitudes reflects a basic lack of agreement among Russians about what democracy means. Surveys show that some believe that it refers to effective economic management. Others associate it with the so-called "Democrats"—Gaidar,

Chubais, and other economic and political liberals, who are widely blamed for the pain of the transition in the 1990s. Such associations do not increase the concept's appeal.

In a clever piece of sociological sleuthing, Henry Hale has now tied up many of these loose ends. Surveying Russians in 2008, he first asked respondents what they understood by "democracy." Forty-one percent correctly referred to such things as "rights, freedoms, the rule of law, honest politics, people power, elections, or political competition." The other 59 percent had no idea what the word meant, refused to answer, or gave the term their own more exotic interpretations. Across all the respondents, 74 percent thought Russia "should be a democratic country." But among those who correctly understood what democracy meant, the rate was as high as 85 percent in favor. Of those who said they opposed democracy, it turned out that 60 percent misunderstood the term's meaning or had no idea what it meant!

What about the supposed Russian soft spot for "strong leaders"? Mimicking previous polls, Hale asked whether to solve its problems Russia needed a head of state "with a strong hand." Fifty-five percent "fully" agreed, and 34 percent did so "more or less." Rather than stopping at this point and lamenting the benighted Russian voter, Hale asked another question of those in favor of the "strong hand": should the people have the right to choose this head of state or should he "appear without the participation of the people"? Ninety-six percent said the people should choose, and 87 percent of these said they should do so "by means of free and fair elections" between several candidates with different views. If the leader managed the country successfully should he be allowed to "deal with his opposition by any available means, even illegal means," Hale asked? No, said 74 percent. In short, Russians do not "see strong-hand leadership and democracy as being incompatible, but instead tend to expect them to go together." They want a version of democracy with a powerful presidency, but in which the president is constrained by the constitution and the laws, and is subject to periodic, free, and fair elections. Other polls confirm that, while favoring democracy, a large majority think the president should have more power than the parliament. After the enervating deadlock of the 1990s, Russians want a system with effective executive power.

Another way to get beyond Russians' uncertainty about the meaning of the word "democracy" is to ask about particular elements of it. Did they consider it important that Russians had the freedom to elect the country's leaders, Timothy Colton and Michael McFaul asked in a 1999 survey. Eighty-seven percent of respondents said yes. The same percentage considered freedom "to have one's own convictions" and freedom of expression important; freedom of the press, radio, and television was judged important by 81 percent. A Levada Center poll in January 2008 found that 60 percent thought there should be television channels independent of the state reporting on social and political events. In 2008, Hale found that 59 percent thought that competition among political parties made the political system stronger, compared to 29 percent who disagreed. Among those who correctly understood what democracy is, Hale found, only 24 percent were willing to consider sacrificing it either to improve the economy or to strengthen the state.

While committed to democracy as an ideal, Russians are unhappy about "the actual practice of democracy in Russia." Asked to rate this on a five-point scale, on which 1 is the lowest and 5 the highest, the average since 1993 has remained stably around 2.5. Most Russians think their current regime is neither a pure democracy nor a pure autocracy but something in between. More judged the 2008 election to be neither completely fair nor unfair (48 percent) than thought it was either completely fair (28 percent) or unambiguously unfair (14 percent). Most do not consider the press either completely free or completely controlled by the state (only 12 and 10 percent, respectively, chose these extreme options). In July 2008, about one-third said it was "mostly free" and a third said it was "mostly controlled."

However, in contrast to most Western experts, who see a slide towards authoritarianism under Putin, Russians tend to think their system has become more democratic over time. This might, once again, reflect confusion over what democracy means; those who equate it with economic performance might see progress for this reason. But in part, many Russians seem to feel that conditions in the 1990s were simply too volatile and tumultuous for them to meaningfully exercise the new rights and freedoms that existed on paper. The violent confrontations of the early 1990s did not appear to them highly democratic. In January 1999,

63 percent thought that Russia was heading towards "chaos, anarchy, or the threat of a state coup." Nine years later, only 9 percent said this, and 54 percent said Russia was heading towards democracy. Only 8 percent thought the country was "recreating the old Soviet order" and another 16 percent thought it was heading toward dictatorship.

Since 1997, the proportion of Russians who say they feel "a free person" has risen from 42 to 70 percent. Asked how the situation had changed in the previous year with regard to "the possibility of expressing one's opinion freely," more Russians saw an improvement than a deterioration in every year between 2000 and 2007 except for 2004. The highest number perceiving an improvement in freedom of expression—36 percent—came in 2007. But Russians saw their increase in freedom as coming at some cost: they felt that social bonds had loosened. Asked in 2008 about the previous five years, 66 percent said that freedom had increased; but majorities saw decreases in justice (64 percent), legality (59 percent), order (58 percent), solidarity between people (68 percent), and mutual trust (74 percent).

This picture could hardly be more different from that usually suggested by Western observers, who tend to assume Russians back Putin thinking he has brought greater order, albeit at the expense of freedom. In fact, surveys suggest just the opposite: on balance, Russians see the Putin years as ones in which freedom increased, at the expense of order and social solidarity. As argued elsewhere in this book, the underlying reason why Russians rallied behind Putin was the dramatic improvement in the economy, which also—to some extent—created a sense of greater predictability. However, Russians saw no decrease in corruption or increase in the effectiveness of the state.

What can Russians mean when they say freedom increased in the last decade? This is not entirely clear. But it seems likely to relate, again, to the country's economic progress. Rising incomes enabled Russians to begin enjoying some of the freedoms granted in the 1990s. More traveled abroad, surfed the Internet, and set up their own businesses. The preoccupation with survival gave way, for many, to the crafting of a private life—a luxury that requires both civic liberties and a certain level of income. More Russians were able to move out of cramped family and multifamily apartments into individual ones. The menu of leisure options broadened with the development of an increasingly professional entertainment industry. At the same time, there were some new freedoms that Russians appreciated less. Many felt abandoned to markets that were *too* free, without effective consumer protections or reliably enforced labor rights. If these were the freedoms respondents had in mind, it was not surprising they would feel an associated loosening of social bonds and solidarity. The liberties that come with modernization, marketization, and integration into the world economy are precisely those that, for better or worse, increase mobility and dissolve the traditional ties of dependence that connect individuals to families, communities, and their birthplaces.

In short, a large majority of Russians favor democracy, specifically one with a powerful executive. Most do not consider their government to be completely democratic; rather, they view it as an often ineffective and corrupt hybrid, in which recent elections have been only partly free and fair. Yet they see progress during the past decade and disagree with Western scholars and activists who see freedom being sharply curtailed. On the contrary, most think freedom has increased, but alongside a decline in social solidarity, legality, and mutual trust. They hope that progress toward democracy will continue, and associate such progress with the incumbent regime.

This picture is not completely coherent, and questions remain. Yet it makes far better sense of Russians' declared opinions than a simple characterization of them as undemocratic. It also casts recent attempts of Western well-wishers to stimulate democracy in Russia in a somewhat new light. After 2004, the goal of deepening Russia's political freedoms became largely identified with the notion of revolution. Georgia's "Rose Revolution" and Ukraine's "Orange Revolution" inspired democracy advocates in the West and seemed to promise a broader wave of advances across the region. To those with revolution in their sights, the reluctance of Russian youths to do their part came as a disappointment. "No dramatic revolution in Russia is likely to come soon from below or outside," two scholars concluded in late 2005, because "many Russians are simply too ambivalent about democracy for any revolutionary scenario to be plausible."

But was it that they were ambivalent about democracy? Or was it perhaps that they did not share the questioners' enthusiasm for revolu-

tionary scenarios? Or doubted that it would make Russia more democratic if they were to try to seize power—unconstitutionally and possibly
violently, fighting heavily armed police—from an elected president who
remained overwhelmingly popular? Since 2005, doubts have grown about
whether Georgia's and Ukraine's "revolutions" produced a major breakthrough. But to Western observers in 2005, it seemed that the young Russians who expressed skepticism about the Orange Revolution—and the
89 percent who said they did not want anything similar in Russia—must
be either apathetic or dupes of a distorted Kremlin line.

In economics, Russians accept the reality of free markets. But they
long for a state that they could feel is honest, effective, and capable of
regulating the cutthroat competition that they see around them. Only 24
percent would like to return to a Soviet-style planned economy. But even
fewer—15 percent—favor a pure market economy. The most popular
choice, that of 47 percent, is a mixed economy combining both markets
and planning. Most Russians would like to be protected by a generous
welfare state that would guarantee jobs and regulate prices of food, fuel,
housing, and utilities—something like the Swedish model of the 1960s.
They do not want to hear that this model no longer works so well, even
in Sweden.

It has been a painful transition, not made easier by the sight of con-
spicuous wealth being spent conspicuously. About 65 percent of Russians
think they are in the bottom half of the income distribution. They feel
that privatization was deeply unfair; 81.5 percent of Russians favor either
renationalizing the privatized enterprises or at least requiring owners to
"pay the privatized assets' worth." But Russians are not unusual in this.
In fact, the proportion in favor of revisiting privatization is lower in Russia than the average for the postcommunist states; in sixteen of twenty-
eight such countries—including Hungary and Slovakia—an even higher
percentage would like privatization redone in some way. In Croatia and
Macedonia, only 6 percent think assets should simply be left in the hands
of their new owners.

Disaggregating, one can make out three groups within Russian society today, although at times they seem more like three moods that pass
across the same individuals. There are those—primarily the elderly, but
not just the elderly—who live with a great deal of nostalgia. There is a

material basis for this. Many draw pensions that have still not caught up to their pre-transition level. But there is also a purely psychological aspect. They resent being told that the scenery against which they came of age, loved, married, and raised children, the songs and catchphrases, rituals and campaigns, were all part of an ugly lie that is in bad taste now to recall. Their memories have been devalued like their bank accounts.

Second, there is the emerging middle class, with its dishwashers and domestically manufactured washing machines, its compact cars and one cell phone per person, its determination to be entertained and apolitical, to thrive. Finally, there are the many in between, the ones who live from day to day, pragmatists by necessity if not conviction, who have adapted to the new world, who would like to believe that they are middle class too, who are ambivalent, envious, exhausted by the struggle, yet at times still hopeful, not innocent, having made many compromises, the walking wounded, who in a stable world would have to blame themselves or fate, but who still have the alibi of transition.

Most Russians are preoccupied by the new realities around them. Yet when they look outside, beyond Russia's borders, the dominant mood is one of anxiety. They feel threatened by the United States, with its sense of global mission, its push to expand NATO, its support for revolutions in the former Soviet Union, and its sometimes intimidating rhetoric. On the list of countries considered "most unfriendly and hostile to Russia," the United States comes second, chosen by 45 percent, behind only Georgia with 62 percent. Almost two-thirds of Russians say their country has "good reason to fear Western countries in NATO." In September 2008, 68 percent said that Ukraine's joining NATO would constitute a "serious threat" or "some threat" to the security of Russia, and 74 percent said the same about Georgia.

They do not want well-intentioned foreigners turning up with cash, like a new sect of Leninists, to foment revolution in their country in the service of some eschatological ideology. In light of U.S. actions around the world, American lectures about democracy and legality are taken with a grain of salt. In 2008, 76 percent of Russians agreed that: "The USA hypocritically tries to force other countries to observe international law, although it does not always follow it itself." Fifty-one percent thought that Western criticism of Russia's democracy and observance of human rights was interference in the country's internal affairs. Russians do not want Western presidents telling them which of their leaders they should like. They are tired of being patronized and feeling bullied. They would like to be taken seriously again.

But rather than being great, most Russians would be content now just to fit in. The loss of global status rankles. But overall, they are mostly just tired of all the drama. Would they rather see Russia "first and foremost a great power, respected and feared by other countries, or a country with a high standard of living, even if not one of the strongest countries in the world," the pollsters asked in 2003. Fifty-four percent opted for the high standard of living. Are Russians "the same as other people" or "very much a special people"? Two-thirds answered: "the same as other people." Do they agree that: "Sooner or later, Russia will proceed along the path common to all civilized countries"? In 1994, 58 percent agreed. In 2008, 65 percent did.

And, more than at any point since the end of perestroika, Russians say they are happy. At roughly five-year intervals since 1990, the World Values Survey (WVS) has asked Russians: "Taking all things together, would you say that you are: very happy, quite happy, not very happy, not at all happy?" The Russian pollsters VCIOM and the Levada Center have posed a similar question—"In life, all sorts of things happen, both good and bad, but overall, are you happy?"—allowing respondents to choose between "yes, completely," "yes, mostly," "mostly not," and "completely not." In Figure 10.7, I combine the WVS and VCIOM/Levada Center polls, and plot the percentage of respondents saying that they were "very" or "quite" happy (on WVS polls) and "completely" or "mostly" happy (on VCIOM/Levada Center polls). The percentage that were "happy," after falling slightly in the early 1990s, has risen dramatically since then, reaching a peak of 76 percent in 2008. The proportion that were mostly or completely unhappy peaked at 49 percent in 1999, falling to 13 percent in 2008. The WVS also asks: "All things considered, how satisfied are you with your life as a whole these days?" Respondents rate their satisfaction on a scale that runs from 1 ("dissatisfied") to 10 ("satisfied"). The percentage rating their satisfaction above five started out at about 43 percent of respondents in 1990. It fell quite substantially in the early 1990s, but then it too recovered. By 2006, 58 percent were more satisfied than dissatisfied with their lives.

Unfortunately, there are no comparable polls from before 1990, a year in which the Soviet system was already in crisis. It is possible that Russians were happier still and more fulfilled by their lives before Gorbachev began tinkering with the system. But based on their own responses—and not on nostalgic recollections—it appears that Russians have become substantially happier and more satisfied with their lives since 2000 than they were during the final years of communism.

This refers to the average. Happiness and life satisfaction were strongly affected by age. The young became much happier from early in the transition, and, as best we can tell, suffered no subsequent, even temporary, decline in life satisfaction. In 1990, about one-third of Russians between the ages of sixteen and thirty said they were "not very" or "not at all" happy. By 2006, this had fallen to just 14 percent. Those over fifty became considerably less happy in the 1990s, and only relatively recently have they surpassed their happiness scores of 1990. The pattern is similar for life satisfaction.

Figure 10.7 Self-reported happiness and life satisfaction, Russia, 1990–2006

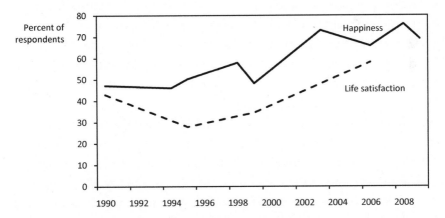

Sources: 1990, 1995, 1999, 2006: World Values Survey, "Taking all things together, would you say that you are: very happy, quite happy, not very happy, not at all happy?"--percent saying very or quite happy--and "All things considered, how satisfied are you with your life as a whole these days?"--percent choosing greater than 5 on scale from 1 = "dissatisfied" to 10 = "satisfied" (www.worldvaluessurvey.org). 1994, 1998, 2003, 2008, 2009: VCIOM/Levada Center, "In life, all sorts of things happen, both good and bad, but overall, are you happy?"--percent choosing "yes, completely" or "yes, mostly" (Levada Center, *Obshchestvennoe mnenie 2008*; http://sofist.socpol.ru for VCIOM *Kurer*-2, 1998; www.wciom.ru for March 2009 poll).

In one other way, Russians have been converging to global norms. After decades of officially prescribed atheism, the country has undergone a religious resurgence. The percentage of Russians who said they were "religious people" rose between 1990 and 2006 from 52 to 65 percent. The increase was particularly marked for thirty- to forty-nine-year-olds, among whom the share of "religious people" increased from 45 to 64 percent. By 2006, the proportion of Russians who called themselves "religious"—65 percent—was close to the average for all countries in the WVS. Asked to rate how important God was in their lives on a 10-point scale from 1 ("not at all important") to 10 ("very important"), the average Russian answer rose from 4.0 in 1990 to 6.1 in 2006. Russians were not going to church more frequently, or even praying more often, but stronger belief in God might help to explain why happiness did not fall further during the transition.

Taking Stock

The Russia that has returned, after its twentieth century misadventure, is not the "petro-fascist" state depicted in much recent writing, where mafiosi roam the streets and citizens hide in their apartments, literally dying of chagrin as they see the country's wealth corruptly privatized, while the prime minister, clad in black, preens before the mirror, envisioning his own triumphant March on Rome. Nor is it the old Soviet Union in disguise, a Marxist bureaucratic meat grinder of a state, bristling with missiles aimed at the United States, and determined to use all tricks at its disposal to weaken the Western world.

It is something more prosaic—a country struggling with a combination of challenges, governed under a system that is part democratic, part authoritarian; informed by a press that is only partly free; powered by an economy cued to world commodity cycles; inhabited by citizens who judge their leaders on the basis of economic performance; where alcoholism, encouraged by the extremely low cost of vodka, is taking an extraordinary toll on life expectancy and aggravating crime. It is a country with problems that are painful but not unusual for middle income states, and with medium-run prospects that remain relatively promising.

Russia's current leaders face some pressing questions. Can they devise a model of relations with society that will work in bad times as well as good? Can they mount a real fight against corruption despite the many trails that lead to their door? Can they trace for themselves a route out of power that will safeguard their personal security and avoid the Suharto scenario, while preserving their international reputation and their claim to have brought stability to Russia? Or, when push comes to shove, will they destroy all that they have built and, giving up on respectability, try to turn their country into a snowy version of Robert Mugabe's Zimbabwe?

Those in the West who deal with Russia face questions of their own. Too large to ignore, too large to coopt, Russia, with its Security Council veto, its intelligence networks in Central Asia and the Middle East, its nuclear arsenal, its oil and gas deposits, sits at the epicenter of the major issues that the West must confront in the next generation—from Islamic terrorism and nuclear proliferation to energy security and global warming. In many ways, the interests of Russia and of the United States and its allies diverge. But on some issues, there is overlap. Whether this overlap develops into cooperation in addressing these existential challenges will depend on whether the United States and Russia can build a more constructive relationship than they have managed in the last two decades.

Building a constructive relationship depends in large part on Russia. But it will also require some careful thinking on the Western side. Does it really serve the West's long-run interests to assume some unproven imperial agenda, to exaggerate the authoritarian features of the current regime, to demonize those in the Kremlin and romanticize its liberal opponents, to identify progress toward democracy with revolution, to jump to the defense of Russia's international adversaries before the facts are clear, and to publicly patronize leaders whose help we need in world affairs? Or does this pattern of behavior—part deliberate, part inadvertent—merely discredit us in the eyes of Russia's leaders and its citizens, making it that much harder to begin a mutually useful conversation?

Year by year, month by month, Russians are waking up. Their country's journey continues. The new Russia will find its place in the world. To increase the chance that the role it defines for itself in coming decades is compatible with Western interests will require an approach that combines patience, humility, and a painstaking attention to the facts as they are rather than as we have imagined them.

NOTES

PREFACE

x *drunks, idolaters, and sodomites*: See the writings of George Turberville and others collected in Lloyd E. Berry and Robert O. Crummey, eds., *Rude and Barbarous Kingdom: Russia in the Accounts of Sixteenth Century English Voyagers* (Madison: University of Wisconsin Press, 1968).

x *breeding ground for witches*: M. S. Anderson, "English Views of Russia in the 17th Century," *The Slavonic and East European Review* 33, no. 80 (1954): 140–60, at 145.

x *"blank page in the intellectual order"*: Pyotr Chaadaev, "Pismo pervoe" (from *Filosoficheskie pisma*), in *Apologia sumasshedshego* (St. Petersburg: Azbuka-Klassika, 2004), 23–49.

x *certain peculiarities that verge on the fantastic*: Tatyana Tolstaya, "President Potemkin," *New Republic*, May 27, 1991, 27–35.

xi *"In the Russian soul"*: Nicolas Berdyaev, *The Russian Idea* (Boston: Beacon Press, 1947), 2–3.

xi *"mysterium of Russia"*: Orlando Figes, *Natasha's Dance: A Cultural History of Russia* (New York: Picador, 2002), 265–87; the phrase "mysterium of Russia" is that of Diaghilev's collaborator, the artist and critic Aleksandr Benois.

CHAPTER 1: THE CAPTAIN

1 *Soviet ship of state*: The nautical metaphor was one Gorbachev favored. "One might say that I had to assume the role of the captain of a ship riding out a storm," he wrote later. "Indeed the . . . 'ship' veered to port and to starboard, occasionally turning so sharply that I thought the wheel would be ripped from my hands. I admit that I felt proud at being able to keep control of the situation, without being driven off course" (Mikhail Gorbachev, *Memoirs* [New York: Doubleday, 1996], 256).

1 *revive the Soviet political and economic order*: Although the two are obviously related, the fate of the USSR's political and economic system can be distinguished

from the question of the territorial integrity of the state. I return to the latter in Chapter 5.

1 *"can only be dismantled and replaced"*: Martin Malia, "Leninist Endgame," *Daedalus* 121, no. 2 (1992): 57–75.

1 *"highly contingent process"*: Mark Kramer, "The Collapse of the Soviet Union, Part 1," *Journal of Cold War Studies* 5, no. 1 (2003): 3–16, at 5. See also Mark Almond, "1989 without Gorbachev," in Niall Ferguson, ed., *Virtual History: Alternatives and Counterfactuals* (New York: Basic Books, 1999), who sketches some alternative ways things might have gone.

2 *"fiery arrows"*: Gorbachev, *Memoirs*, 29.

2 *executed in the street*: Jonathan Steele, "Mikhail Gorbachev: The Russian Revolutionary," *The Guardian*, August 18, 2001.

3 *Kuybyshev Street*: Kuybyshev Street, named after the Bolshevik revolutionary and Politburo member Valeriyan Kuybyshev, was later renamed Ilinka.

4 *46,000 industrial companies*: Figures for 1986 from Nikolai Shmelev and Vladimir Popov, *The Turning Point: Revitalizing the Soviet Economy* (London: I.B. Tauris, 1990), 114.

4 *provincial outpost*: Vyacheslav Molotov, Stalin's revolutionary comrade and foreign minister, found himself in 1957 appointed the new Soviet ambassador to Mongolia.

5 *"Just don't whistle!"*: Aleksandr Yakovlev, *Sumerki* (Moscow: Materik, 2003), 306–8.

5 *up to 750,000 goods*: Michael Ellman and Vladimir Kontorovich, eds., *The Destruction of the Soviet Economic System: An Insiders' History* (New York: M.E. Sharpe, 1998), 109.

5 *police horses and dogs*: Yakovlev, *Sumerki*, 560.

5 *"install a toilet"*: Anatoly S. Chernyaev, *My Six Years With Gorbachev*, trans. Robert English and Elizabeth Tucker (University Park: Pennsylvania State University Press, 2000), 98.

5 *underground torture chamber*: David Remnick, *Lenin's Tomb: The Last Days of the Soviet Empire* (New York: Vintage, 1994), 186.

6 *"collaborator of the NKVD"*: Yakovlev, *Sumerki*, 547.

6 *owning a typewriter*: F.J.M. Feldbrugge, *Samizdat and Political Dissent in the Soviet Union* (Amsterdam: Sijthoff, 1975), 3.

6 *"Nothing doing!"*: Gorbachev, *Memoirs*, 147.

6 *two powerful jamming stations*: Yakovlev, *Sumerki*, 278.

6 *shortwave radios*: Yegor Gaidar, *Collapse of an Empire: Lessons for Modern Russia* (Washington, DC: Brookings Institution Press, 2007), 72.

6 *"the main telegraph agency"*: Boris Yeltsin, *Ispoved na zadannuyu tyemu* (Moscow: Ogonyok, 1989).

7 *murder by ricin pellet*: Oleg Kalugin, *The First Directorate* (New York: St. Martin's Press, 1994), 178–79.

7 *"indifference to luxury"*: The characterization of Georgy Arbatov, director of the

USA and Canada Institute and an Andropov confidant, in Arbatov, *The System: An Insider's Life in Soviet Politics* (New York: Times Books, 1992), 257.

7 *could write passable verse*: Georgy Shakhnazarov, *S vozhdyami i bez nikh* (Moscow: Vagrius, 2001), 103, 116–18.

7 *a way out of Afghanistan*: Karen Brutents, "Origins of the New Thinking," *Russian Social Science Review* 47, no. 1 (2006): 73–102, at 76. Soviet troops had invaded to rescue a socialist regime in 1979.

7 *grew up in his shadow*: The list would include Arbatov, Nikolay Ryzhkov, and Yegor Ligachev, as well as Gorbachev. Others with ties to Andropov included Oleg Kalugin, Georgy Shakhnazarov, and Aleksandr Bovin. It is peculiar how this orthodox communist and secret police chief could have been admired by so many with far more liberal inclinations, and says something about the dearth of talent in the rest of the Politburo. Andropov also promoted some who would later oppose reform, such as Kryuchkov; others, such as Ryzhkov and Ligachev, supported early reforms but thought Gorbachev later went too far.

7 *"no trees without saplings"*: Gorbachev, *Memoirs*, 10–14.

7 *"poking his nose into political affairs"*: Boris Ponomaryov, Secretary of the International Department, quoted in Chernyaev, *My Six Years*, 4.

7 *"shared his ideas"*: Gorbachev, *Memoirs*, 14.

8 *evening of heavy drinking*: The official cause of death was "heart failure." The more detailed description was reportedly told by Gorbachev to his aide, Valery Boldin (see Valery Boldin, *Krushenie pedestala: Shtrikhi k portretu M. S. Gorbacheva* [Moscow: Respublika, 1995], 228). Although Boldin may not be a reliable witness on all matters, there is no reason he would invent this detail.

8 *"Is it really that bad?"*: Gorbachev, *Memoirs*, 15, 133.

8 *"met Brezhnev on a railway platform"*: Gorbachev's future nemesis, Boris Yeltsin, then party chief of Sverdlovsk Province, had a less rewarding experience of waiting to meet Brezhnev on one of his whistlestop train tours. Yeltsin was standing with flowers on the platform the night of March 29, 1978, only to watch as Brezhnev's train sped through the junction without stopping (Timothy J. Colton, *Yeltsin: A Life* [New York: Basic Books, 2008], 86).

8 *channel of secret negotiation*: Details of these negotiations are in Yakovlev, *Sumerki*, 460–62, and Anatoly Gromyko, *Andrey Gromyko: v labirintakh kremlya* (Moscow: Avto, 1997), 87–96.

9 *"the use or threat of force"*: Gorbachev, *Memoirs*, 462.

9 *"the basis of human co-existence"*: Gorbachev, *Memoirs*, 421.

10 *"messianic enthusiasm"*: Brutents, "Origins," 78.

10 *five million copies*: Brutents, "Origins," 83.

10 *"Any reasonable person"*: David Pryce-Jones, *The Strange Death of the Soviet Empire* (New York: Metropolitan Books, 1995), 364.

10 *At a summit with Reagan*: Henry Kissinger, *Diplomacy* (New York: Simon & Schuster, 1994), 782–83.

10 *500,000 troops and 10,000 tanks*: Kissinger, *Diplomacy*, 791.

11 *"They're sick of us"*: Anatoly Chernyaev, "Problems of the Foreign Policy of M.S. Gorbachev: Its Historical and Future Significance," report to Conference on "Gorbachev Readings," June 28, 2002, Moscow, The Gorbachev Foundation, www.gorby.ru/rubrs.asp?rubr_id=200&art_id=16303.

12 *failed to extract enforceable commitments*: In the view of Jack Matlock, U.S. Ambassador to Moscow from 1987 to 1991, Western leaders would probably have agreed to make a written pledge not to expand NATO further in return for Soviet acquiescence to German reunification (comments to the Los Angeles World Affairs Council, November 19, 2007). Gorbachev settled for an oral assurance that was later reinterpreted.

12 *Gorbachev talked to Bush, Major, Andreotti*: Anatoly Chernyaev, *1991 god: dnevnik pomoshchnika prezidenta SSSR* (Moscow: Terra, 1997), 104.

12 *compared him to Chamberlain at Munich*: Gromyko, *Andrey Gromyko*, 190.

12 *thirteen times as many medium-range missiles*: Brutents, "Origins," 86.

13 *98.5 percent of Russians*: Literacy rate as of 1959 census, from Boris N. Mironov, "The Development of Literacy in Russia and the USSR from the Tenth to the Twentieth Centuries," *History of Education Quarterly* 31, no. 2 (1991): 229–52, at 243.

13 *produced them badly*: See Clifford Gaddy, "Has Russia Entered a Period of Sustainable Economic Growth?" in Andrew Kuchins, ed., *Russia after the fall* (Washington, DC: Carnegie Endowment, 2002), 125–46.

13 *women's underwear*: United Nations, *Industrial Commodity Statistics Yearbook*, 1992.

13 *"a steak, a piece of unprocessed cheese"*: Leon Aron, "Was Liberty Really Bad for Russia?" American Enterprise Institute, *Russian Outlook*, Summer 2007.

13 *no indoor toilet*: Goskomstat Rossii, *Sotsialnoe polozhenie i uroven zhizni naseleniya Rossii* (Moscow: Goskomstat Rossii, 1996).

13 *appendectomies using safety razors*: Murray Feshbach and Alfred Friendly, Jr., *Ecocide in the USSR: Health and Nature Under Siege* (New York: Basic Books, 1992), 3–4.

13 *one-third as many personal computers*: World Bank, *World Development Indicators*, downloaded May 8, 2008.

13 *60 percent more steel*: S. Kheinman, "O problemakh nauchno-tekhnicheskoy politiki," *Voprosy Ekonomiki* 3 (1989): 65–74.

14 *Even Soviet cows*: figures for 1989, from Yegor Gaidar, *Gibel imperii: uroki dlya sovremennoy Rossii* [Collapse of an Empire: Lessons for Modern Russia] (Moscow: Rossiyskaya Politicheskaya Entsiklopediya, 2006), 211.

14 *Two-thirds of Russian industrial equipment*: A. Akopian, *Industrial Potential of Russia: Analytical Study Based on Fixed Assets Statistics to 1992* (Commack, NY: Nova Science Publishers, 1992).

14 *about seventeen years*: Shmelev and Popov, *The Turning Point*, 145.

14 *12,000 combine harvesters*: Shmelev and Popov, *The Turning Point*, 256.

14 *"mountains of defective shoes"*: Anders Åslund, "How Small Is Soviet National

Income," in Henry S. Rowen and Charles Wolf, Jr., *The Impoverished Superpower: Perestroika and the Soviet Military Burden* (San Francisco: ICS Press, 1990), 13–62, at 21, quoting a Soviet economist.

14 *it would have been cheaper to relocate*: quoted in Fiona Hill and Clifford Gaddy, *The Siberian Curse: How Communist Planners Left Russia Out in the Cold* (Washington, DC: Brookings Institution Press, 2003), 168.

14 *unsalvageable enterprises*: Even in 1998, after maybe 30 percent of these industrial enterprises had been closed, a careful Western study estimated that 25 percent of Russian industrial capacity was "currently in sub-scale or obsolete assets, which are still operating and fully staffed, but should be shut down" (Vincent Palmeda and Bill Lewis, "Unlocking Economic Growth in Russia," in John Hardt, ed., *Russia's Uncertain Economic Future* [Armonk, NY: M.E. Sharpe, 2003], 47–80, at 48).

14 *60 percent of regional and local party secretaries*: Chernyaev, *My Six Years*, 153.

14 *investment in civilian machine building*: Anders Åslund, *Gorbachev's Struggle for Economic Reform* (Ithaca: Cornell University Press, 1991), 75.

14 *Production of vodka*: Åslund, *Gorbachev's Struggle*, 78.

14 *volume of vodka sold*: Sergey Sinelnikov, *Byudzhetny krizis v Rossii: 1985–1995 gody* (Moscow: Yevraziya, 1995), 37.

15 *20 percent of retail sales*: Ellman and Kontorovich, *Destruction*, 107.

15 *vineyard owner committed suicide*: Arkady Vaksberg, *The Soviet Mafia* (London: Weidenfeld and Nicolson, 1991), 232–33.

15 *20 million people*: Shmelev and Popov, *The Turning Point*, 198–99.

15 *smash hundreds of greenhouses*: Åslund, *Gorbachev's Struggle*, 160.

15 *Not one automatic lathe*: Leon Aron, *Yeltsin: A Revolutionary Life* (New York: St. Martin's Press, 2000), 183.

15 *"polluted by bribery"*: Ellman and Kontorovich, *Destruction*, 124.

15 *"How then can we control ourselves?"*: "Gorbachev on the Future: 'We Will Not Give In,'" *New York Times*, December 22, 1986, 20.

16 *told to fire a young reporter*: Vitaly Korotich, *Zal ozhidaniya* (New York: Liberty Publishing House, 1991), 32–33.

16 *"the Chinese model in Russia"*: in Ellman and Kontorovich, *Destruction*, 168–69.

16 *elected by the workers*: Ellman and Kontorovich, *Destruction*, 145–46.

17 *88 percent were party members*: Vadim Medvedev, *V kommande Gorbacheva: vzglyad iznutri* (Moscow: Bylina, 1994), 85.

17 *"someone to the left of us"*: Medvedev, *V kommande Gorbacheva*, 46.

17 *"purple with rage"*: Boldin, *Krushenie pedestala*, 328. Boldin at the time of writing was hardly on good terms with Gorbachev, having betrayed him in August 1991, so it is possible he is exaggerating. Still, the intensity of Gorbachev's anger is evident in his words in the official transcript as well as the accounts of other participants.

18 *"It's not enough for you"*: the quotations are from the official transcript of the Plenum, published in *Izvestia TsK KPSS* 2 (February 1989): 209–87. My translation is based on Matlock's apt rendering.

18   *"I will not let you back into politics!"*: Yeltsin, *Ispoved*, 1. Gorbachev, in his memoir, reports a somewhat softer sentence: he would not let Yeltsin back into "big-time politics [*sfera bolshoy politiki*] any time soon" (quoted in Colton, *Yeltsin*, 154). Mikhail Poltoranin notes that the meeting ran more than four hours in *The Second Russian Revolution*, a Discovery Channel documentary, produced by Norman Percy.

18   *prize fighter*: Matlock, *Autopsy*, 115.

18   *"'infantile' disease of leftism"*: Chernyaev, *My Six Years*, 136. *The Infantile Disease of 'Leftism' in Communism* was a pamphlet written by Lenin in 1920, in which he attacked those communists who were too extreme in rejecting old forms and insufficiently flexible in tactics.

19   *"five times a day"*: Shatalin and Yeltsin, interviewed in Norman Percy, *The Second Russian Revolution*, "The End of the Beginning."

19   *"I'm going around in circles"*: David Remnick, "Dead Souls," *New York Review of Books* 38, no. 21 (December 19, 1991). It is not clear from the context whether this answer was meant to ridicule the question or expressed irony about himself. Gorbachev's aide Boldin memorably characterized Gorbachev's style as: "two steps forward, three to the side, and one step back" (quoted in Yu. M. Baturin et al., *Epokha Yeltsina: Ocherki politicheskoy istorii* [Moscow: Vagrius, 2001], 224).

19   *plan for a state of emergency*: Yevgeniya Albats, *Mina zamedlennogo deystviya: politichesky portret KGB* (Moscow: Russlit, 1992).

20   *blueprint for such an intervention*: Chernyaev, *My Six Years*, 264–65.

20   *occupying buildings in Vilnius*: Gaidar, *Gibel imperii*, 373.

20   *"bourgeois system"*: James Rosen, "Gorbachev threatens Lithuania," UPI, January 10, 1991.

20   *attacked the city's television and radio stations*: For a useful account, see Brian D. Taylor, "The Soviet Military and the Disintegration of the USSR," *Journal of Cold War Studies* 5, no. 1 (2003): 17–66. Already in April 1989, Soviet troops had brutally clubbed peaceful demonstrators who were occupying the central square of Tbilisi, Georgia, resulting in nineteen deaths (see Chapter 5).

20   *knew about the ongoing operations*: Ainius Lasas, "Bloody Sunday: What Did Gorbachev Know About the January 1991 Events in Vilnius and Riga," *Journal of Baltic Studies* 38, no. 2 (2007): 179–94.

20   *"do the job myself"*: Lasas, "Bloody Sunday," 189.

20   *army to patrol cities*: Gerald Nadler, "Army Patrols Soviet Streets," UPI, February 1, 1991.

20   *"Mind your own business!"*: Chernyaev, *My Six Years*, 335.

21   *shortage of ropes*: Yakovlev, *Sumerki*, 507–8.

21   *"I can't run to the President"*: Vitaly Vorotnikov, *A bylo eto tak?* (Moscow: Soviet Veteranov Knigoizdaniya, 1995), 434.

21   *"The coup is over."*: Bill Keller, "Soviet Turmoil: A Coup Gone Awry," *New York Times*, August 25, 1991.

21   *generals were meeting suspiciously often*: Yakovlev, *Sumerki*, 427.

21 *"What a chicken!"*: Chernyaev, *My Six Years*, 353.

22 *"temporary phenomenon"*: Chernyaev, *My Six Years*, 383.

22 *"You, the military, take power"*: Yevgeny Shaposhnikov, *Vybor*, 2nd Edition (Moscow: Nezavisimoe izdatelstvo pik, 1995), 137–38. Shaposhnikov did not include this incident in the first edition of his memoir, but has repeated it on several occasions. When a scholar asked Gorbachev about this in 2002, he "denied that he was actually proposing the introduction of martial law in November 1991, but he acknowledged that he 'did consider a number of options, including the use of force,' as the dissolution of the Soviet Union approached." See Kramer, "The Collapse," 9, and Taylor, "The Soviet Military," 59.

23 *"play the army card"*: *Nezavisimaya gazeta*, December 12, 1991, excerpted in M. Gorshkov and V. Zhuravlev, eds., *Nesokrushimaya i legendarnaya: v ogne politicheskikh batalii 1985–1993 gg.* (Moscow: Terra, 1994), 261.

23 *"You see, Sasha. That's how it is."*: Yakovlev, *Sumerki*, 518, my translation.

23 *"inefficient but stable"*: See the analysis of Gennady Zoteyev, one of Gosplan's long-range planners, in Ellman and Kontorovich, *Destruction*, 13, 87–94.

24 *spontaneously combusted*: Aganbegyan, quoted in Åslund, *Gorbachev's Struggle*, 19.

24 *one-third of potatoes*: N.K. Baybakov, *Sorok let v pravitelstve* (Moscow: Respublika, 1993), 140.

24 *Per capita consumption of meat*: Goskomstat SSSR, *Narodnoe khozyaystvo SSSR v 1990 g.* (Moscow: Finansy i Statistika, 1991); see also Vladimir Shlapentokh, "Standard of Living and Popular Discontent," in Ellman and Kontorovich, eds., *Destruction*, 30–40.

24 *how many windows were lit*: Oleg Gordievsky, *Next Stop Execution: The Autobiography of Oleg Gordievsky* (London: Macmillan, 1995), 261.

24 *defense spending had stabilized*: Federal outlays on national defense reached $273.4 billion in 1986, remained around that level in real terms until 1989, then fell by 16 percent in 1989–1991 (my calculations from Government Printing Office, *The Budget for Fiscal Year 2004, Historical Tables* [Washington: U.S. Government Printing Office, 2003], Table 3.1, deflated by the GDP deflator from the World Bank's *World Development Indicators*).

24 *Soviet experts were confident*: Gorbachev's science adviser Roald Sagdeyev reportedly laughed at the notion the USSR should try to build its own missile defense. Archie Brown, *Seven Years that Changed the World: Perestroika in Perspective* (New York: Oxford University Press, 2007), 246.

24 *According to his advisor, Georgy Arbatov*: Arbatov, *The System*, 321–22.

25 *When Andropov broached*: Brown, *Seven Years*, 247.

25 *to live as before was unacceptable*: "Mikhail Gorbachev: ya spokoyno khozhu po ulitsam v kepke i tyomnykh ochkakh," *Komsomolskaya Pravda*, March 2, 2006. Brown discusses this in *Seven Years*, 5.

25 *"inescapable generational change"*: Stephen Kotkin, *Armageddon Averted: The Soviet Collapse, 1970–2000* (New York: Oxford University Press, 2001), 176.

25 *"just hope"*: Chernyaev, *1991 god*, 320.

26 *"impossible, project from the beginning"*: Martin Malia, "The Highest Stage of Socialism," in Lee Edwards, ed., *The Collapse of Communism* (Stanford: Hoover Institution Press, 2000), 71–92.

26 *"collapsed like a house of cards"*: Martin Malia, "A Fatal Logic," *The National Interest*, 31 (Spring 1993): 80–91.

26 *Ligachev casts Gorbachev as the pawn*: Yegor Ligachev, *Inside Gorbachev's Kremlin* (New York: Pantheon, 1993), 348–51.

26 *a savage form of capitalism*: Nikolay Ryzhkov, *Desyat let velikikh potryaseny* (Moscow: Assotsiatsiya Kniga, Prosveshchenie, Miloserdie, 1995), chapter 17.

27 *"enjoyed maneuvering too much"*: quoted in Remnick, *Lenin's Tomb*, 447.

27 *"it was emotions"*: Chernyaev, *My Six Years*, 295. For the analyses of Gorbachev's liberal aides, see for instance, Yakovlev, *Sumerki*, 505, and Chernyaev, *My Six Years*, 276.

27 *"Enough blackmail!"*: Chernyaev, *My Six Years*, 249.

28 *"Self-interested scum"*: Chernyaev, *My Six Years*, 280.

28 *"muddying people's minds"*: Chernyaev, *My Six Years*, 141.

28 *"It seems that the minister is in a panic."*: Chernyaev, *My Six Years*, 262–63.

28 *"to gather citrus fruits"*: "Mikhail Gorbachev: ya spokoyno khozhu."

28 *stretched the meaning of the term*: His conception of the "socialist idea," in the words of former U.S. Ambassador Jack Matlock, was "so general and vague that it defies precise description." Jack F. Matlock, "The Dreamer: The World According to Gorbachev," *Foreign Affairs*, January/February 2000, 168–72.

29 *"The conditions required guile"*: Yakovlev, *Sumerki*, 28.

29 *All-Union Center for Public Opinion Research*: It later changed its name to the Russian Center for Public Opinion Research and then to the Levada Center.

30 *two-thirds of respondents believed the party*: Matthew Wyman, *Public Opinion in Post-Communist Russia* (London: Macmillan, 1997), 58. Along these lines, in December 1989 a majority said they wholly or partly supported the party's political line. This probably did not reflect mere reluctance to criticize the regime since only 25 percent said the influence of ministries and government departments should increase or stay the same.

30 *52 percent of Russians fully approved*: for results mentioned in this paragraph, see VCIOM Omnibus Survey, 1989–8, 1,609 respondents, July–August 1989; 1989–17, 1,013 respondents, November–December 1989; 1989–19, 2,943 respondents, December 1989–January 1990; 1989–18, 2,521 respondents, December 1989; 1989–20, 2,706 respondents, January 1990; results available at: http://sofist.socpol.ru.

30 *But then during 1990*: For polls cited in this paragraph, see VCIOM Omnibus Survey, various issues for Gorbachev ratings; 1991–5, 2,665 respondents, April–May 1991; 1990–12, 2,953 respondents, August–September 1990.

30 *4.2 million members*: *Pravda*, July 26, 1991, quoted in Graeme Gill, *The Collapse of a Single-Party System* (New York: Cambridge University Press, 1994), 154. For the earlier figures, see Gill, *The Collapse*, 101.

30 *Ninety-three percent said food supplies*: VCIOM poll, cited in Wyman, *Public Opinion*, 34.

31 *In Chelyabinsk*: Aron, *Yeltsin*, 397–98.

31 *"scale unprecedented in peacetime"*: Gertrude Schroeder, "Soviet Consumption in the 1980s: A Tale of Woe," in Michael Ellman and Vladimir Kontorovich, eds., *The Disintegration of the Soviet Economic System* (New York: Routledge, 1992), 86–105, at 99.

31 *Frightened by the empty store shelves*: for poll results cited in this paragraph, see VCIOM, Omnibus 1991-15, November 1991–January 1992, 3,453 respondents and VCIOM Omnibus Survey, 1991-1p, 2,263 respondents, February–March 1991, at http://sofist.socpol.ru; Yury Levada, "Social and Moral Aspects of the Crisis," in Ellman and Kontorovich, eds. *The Disintegration*, 65, 69; Vera Nikitina, "God za godom: 1991," *Informatsionny byulleten monitoringa*, VCIOM, 6, no. 32 (November–December 1997), 46–51. A majority still opposed privatizing large enterprises. Some supporters of radical reform changed their minds later, but at this time the public was far more market-oriented than the Soviet leader.

31 *Yeltsin was so close to the people*: Gorbachev, in retrospect, accepts this interpretation of Yeltsin's rise. "If we hadn't made primary errors, such as allowing gaps to develop between purchasing power and supplies in the shops which created those massive shortages, then these adventurists, including Yeltsin, wouldn't have appeared," he said in a 2001 interview. "Yeltsin is basically a result, a tendency" (Steele, "Mikhail Gorbachev").

31 *price of oil fell*: British Petroleum, *Statistical Review of World Energy*, June 2009.

31 *grain prices soared*: Gaidar, *Gibel imperii*, 252.

31 *increasing Soviet foreign debt*: IMF et al., *A Study of the Soviet Economy* (Paris: IMF, World Bank, OECD, and EBRD, 1991), 59; OECD, *Economic Surveys: Russian Federation* (Paris: OECD, 1997), 72.

32 *German banks would lend*: Ellman and Kontorovich, *The Disintegration*, 3. Gaidar, in *Gibel imperii*, emphasizes the role of the oil price and the hard-currency gap in creating the financial crisis that erupted in 1991.

32 *"bacchanalia of local protection"*: Schroeder, "Soviet Consumption," 99–100.

32 *estimated at 30 percent*: for 1985–90, from IMF et al., *A Study*, 55–56; for 1991, Gaidar, *Gibel imperii*, 386. Estimates vary slightly across sources, but the trend is the same.

32 *spent the public's accumulated savings*: Baybakov, *Sorok let*, 135.

32 *including Gorbachev's own book royalties*: Gaidar, *Gibel imperii*, 368.

32 *cash in circulation*: calculated from Michael Ellman, "Money in the 1980s: From Disequilibrium to Collapse," in Ellman and Kontorovich, eds., *The Disintegration*, 106–33, at 121, and Gaidar, *Gibel imperii*, 402.

33 *Twelve hours a week*: Schroeder, "Soviet Consumption," 99.

33 *His aides repeatedly urged him*: Vorotnikov, *A bylo*, 138, 346; Medvedev, *V kommande Gorbacheva*, 55.

33 *Ryzhkov considered*: Ryzhkov, *Desyat let*, 249.

33 *"about twenty years late"*: Chernyaev, *My Six Years*, 226. A halfhearted and poorly designed price reform was tried in April 1991, but was too little and too late to help much.

34 *more than seven thousand generals and admirals*: William Odom, *The Collapse of the Soviet Military* (New Haven: Yale University Press, 1998), 38–39.

34 *cut defense procurement*: Taylor, "The Soviet Military," 23.

34 *"The army is no longer with you"*: Odom, *The Collapse*, 168.

34 *may have inoculated the system*: As Kotkin puts it, Gorbachev's "temporizing, including his repeated instructions for these groups to prepare plans for martial law, paralysed them until the summer of 1991, by which time the Russian republic, and a Russian president, had become authoritative sources of allegiance for the central Soviet elite" (*Armageddon Averted*, 104).

35 *not well respected*: See Albats, *Mina*.

35 *"drunk prostitute"*: Andrey Uglanov, "Smertelnaya rana KGB," *Argumenty i fakty*, August 15, 2001.

35 *even bugged the conversations*: Yevgenia Albats, *The State Within a State: The KGB and Its Hold on Russia—Past, Present, and Future* (New York: Farrar Straus and Giroux, 1994), 281.

35 *"We tried"*: Odom, *The Collapse*, 339.

35 *visited the Tula airborne troops*: He writes that at this lunch he obtained a promise from Grachev to come to the Russian government's aid if it was ever threatened by "a terrorist act, a coup, efforts to arrest the leaders." He was able to remind Grachev of this conversation when he called on the morning of August 19th (Yeltsin, *The Struggle for Russia* [New York: Times Books, 1994], 58).

36 *farcical provocation*: Aleksandr Lebed, *Spektakl nazyvalsya putsch* (Tiraspol: Lada, 1993).

36 *"extraordinary amateurism"*: Pryce-Jones, *The Strange Death*, 410.

36 *"like toys"*: Albats, *The State*, 289.

36 *did not order his arrest*: This is the version advanced in the account of the Russian procurators, V. Stepankov and E. Lisov, *Kremlyevsky zagovor* (Moscow: Ogonyok, 1992), 121. Some other accounts (e.g., those of Yeltsin's bodyguard, Aleksandr Korzhakov, *Boris Yeltsin: Ot rassveta do zakata* [Moscow: Interbuk, 1997], 84–85, and Vadim Bakatin, *Izbavlenie ot KGB* [Moscow: Novosti, 1992], 20–21) claim that an order was given, but that some members of the KGB unit refused to carry it out. Yeltsin, in his memoir (*The Struggle*, 53), says an order was given, but quickly rescinded by Kryuchkov himself.

36 *stopped politely at traffic lights*: Leonid Shebarshin, *Ruka Moskvy: zapiski nachalnika sovetskoy razvedki* (Moscow: Tsentr-100, 1992).

36 *not initially meant to be a military coup*: Oleg Kharkhordin, "A byl li putsch na samom dele?" *Neprikosnovenny zapas* 5, no. 19 (2001), discusses this possibility. See also Odom, *The Collapse*, who points out that a "coup" by members of the government itself is something of a contradiction.

37 *that Yeltsin's dislike of Gorbachev would prove stronger*: Yelena Skvortsova, "My ne dumali chto Gorbachev predatel," *Sobesednik*, August 20, 2007.

37 *probably could not get the two-thirds of votes*: Stepankov and Lisov, *Kremlyevsky zagovor*, 121, 157.

37 *"I understood how far I was"*: Stepankov and Lisov, *Kremlyevsky zagovor*, 261.

37 *"tacking between the army leadership"*: quoted in Taylor, "The Soviet Military," 47.

38 *suffer heavy losses*: Stepankov and Lisov suggest that, given the lack of surprise and the armed defenders, the Alfa unit might have lost 50 percent of its men (Stepankov and Lisov, *Kremlyevsky zagovor*, 171–73).

38 *"They were too naïve"*: Geoffrey York, "Revenge of the Commissars," *Globe and Mail* (Toronto), August 11, 2001.

38 *"I am an old fool"*: Valentin Stepankov, "The Kremlin Plot," *Newsweek International*, August 31, 1992.

39 *"give the authorities a harder shake"*: Gorbachev, *Memoirs*, 270.

39 *"They say we need to thump our fists"*: Marietta Chudakova, "Itogi i perspektivy sovremennoy Rossiyskoy revolutsii," *Obshchestvennie nauki i sovremmenost 2* (2002): 5–27, at 25.

39 *"I was never afraid of him"*: Korotich, *Zal ozhidaniya*, 137.

39 *"the televised replay of a game"*: Korotich, *Zal ozhidaniya*, 142.

39 *like Christopher Columbus*: quoted in Pryce-Jones, *The Strange Death*, 102–3.

39 *"Not so much every year"*: Korotich, *Zal ozhidaniya*, 141.

40 *"that latent, demonic cheerfulness"*: Yury Luzhkov, *My deti tvoi, Moskva* (Moscow: Vagrius, 1996), 185.

40 *"All revolutions end in failure"*: Chernyaev, *1991 god: dnevnik*, 104.

CHAPTER 2: THE NATURAL

41 *a vital strength*: Yeltsin, *Zapiski prezidenta* (Moscow: Ogonyok, 1994), 293.

41 *six foot two and 227 pounds*: Height from Colton, *Yeltsin*, 83; weight from Interfax, "Official doctor expects Yeltsin to recover rapidly from his heart operation," Moscow, November 23, 1996, which quotes Yeltsin's doctor to the effect that as of mid-1996, he weighed about 103 kgs, or 227 lbs.

41 *One night in 1934*: Much information on Yeltsin's early life can be found in his first two books of memoirs, *Ispoved na zadannuyu tyemu* (Moscow: Ogonyok, 1990), and *Zapiski prezidenta*, translated as *Against the Grain* (New York: Summit Books, 1990), and *The Struggle for Russia* (New York: Times Books, 1994). The best accounts are in two excellent biographies—Aron, *Yeltsin*, and Colton, *Yeltsin*, which makes sense of various contradictions and inaccuracies in Yeltsin's own version.

42 *the yellowing case file*: Yeltsin, *The Struggle*, 94–98.

42 *"I'm hu-u-u-u-ngry"*: from an interview of Klavdiya Yeltsina by Andrey Goryun, quoted in Colton, *Yeltsin*, 38.

42 *discover how a hand grenade worked*: Playing with ammunition seems to have been a common pastime for boys of the wartime generation. Yury Luzhkov, later mayor of Moscow, recalls disassembling artillery shells and rigging them to explode (Luzhkov, *My deti tvoi*, 129–30).

43 *striking a volleyball*: Yeltsin, *Zapiski prezidenta*, 253.

43 *wore his helicopter pilot out*: The source for details in this and the next paragraph is Aron, *Yeltsin*, 58, 92.

44 *"Permanent filth"*: Luzhkov, *My deti tvoi*, 151.

44 *Yeltsin worked punishing hours*: Details in this and the next paragraph come from Aron, *Yeltsin*, 147, 152, 159, 162, 166, 173, 190–91.

45 *eight hundred store directors*: Yeltsin, *Ispoved*.

46 *"burned-out cinder"*: Yeltsin, *Against the Grain*, 204.

46 *staring at the silent phone*: Yeltsin, *The Struggle*, 15–16.

46 *"Letters to Boris Yeltsin"*: Aron, *Yeltsin*, 227.

46 *He lambasted the "hungry nomenklatura"*: See Aron, *Yeltsin*, 241–42.

46 *Nominated by more than fifty districts*: Aron, *Yeltsin*, 275.

47 *"Only Yeltsin, with his animal instinct"*: Chernyaev, *My Six Years*, 279.

47 *"eternal night"*: Aron, *Yeltsin*, 448.

47 *promised some improvement*: "Speech by Boris Yeltsin," *BBC Summary of World Broadcasts*, October 30, 1991.

47 *"We should create"*: quoted in Oleg Moroz, *Tak kto zhe rasstrelyal parlament?* (Moscow: ID Rus-Olimp, 2007), 16.

48 *deputies voted for Yeltsin's proposal*: Aron, *Yeltsin*, 491. The parliament had a week in each case to overturn a presidential decree; if it did not do so, the decree went into effect.

48 *"found the courage to speed up reform"*: quoted in Leonid Mlechin, *Kreml, prezidenty Rossii: strategiya vlasti ot B.N. Yeltsina do V.V. Putina* (Moscow: Tsentr Poligraf, 1992), 280.

48 *whose articles Gaidar*: Yegor Gaidar, *Days of Defeat and Victory* (Seattle: University of Washington Press, 1999), 144.

49 *"scholarly boys in pink shorts"*: Moroz, *Tak kto zhe*, 25–29.

49 *A network of informers*: Sergey Filatov, *Sovershenno nesekretno* (Moscow: Vagrius, 2000), 150.

50 *With reforms blocked by the parliament*: source for this and the next paragraph: Aron, *Yeltsin*, 504, 507.

50 *The referendum's results*: results from the Russian Central Electoral Commission, available at www.electoralgeography.com/en/countries/r/russia/1993-referendum-russia.html.

50 *sixty people were injured*: Mlechin, *Kreml*, 364.

51 *"a colossal omission"*: quoted in Mlechin, *Kreml*, 360.

51 *five-thousand man force*: Filatov, *Sovershenno nesekretno*, 185.

51 *many in Moscow assumed*: Aron, *Yeltsin*, 514.

51   *changes were to be adopted*: Yury Baturin, *Konstitutsionnye etyudy* (Moscow: Institut Prava i Publichnoy Politiki, 2008), 36.

51   *he did so in the paradoxical belief*: Yeltsin, *Zapiski prezidenta*, 361.

51   *"fruitless and senseless fight to the death"*: Aron, *Yeltsin*, 515–17, quoting from Yeltsin's address to the nation, September 21, 1993.

52   *more than four hundred amendments*: Filatov, *Sovershenno nesekretno*, 180.

52   *Khasbulatov believed support was rallying*: Ruslan Khasbulatov, *Velikaya Rossiyskaya tragediya* [The Great Russian Tragedy] (Moscow: SIMS, 1994), 126.

52   *Yeltsin's "criminal orders"*: Filatov, *Sovershenno nesekretno*, 289.

53   *prescribing the death penalty*: Gaidar, *Days*, 237.

53   *163 submachine guns*: Moroz, *Tak kto zhe*, 612.

53   *"wash their faces in their own blood"*: Aron, *Yeltsin*, 525–26.

53   *studied Mein Kampf*: John B. Dunlop, "Alexander Barkashov and the Rise of National Socialism in Russia," *Demokratizatsiya* 4, no. 4 (1996): 519–30.

53   *others they suspected of being Jewish*: Aron, *Yeltsin*, 527–32; Veronika Kutsyllo, *Zapiski iz belogo doma* (Moscow: Kommersant, 1993).

53   *the Kremlin tried to negotiate*: Filatov, *Sovershenno nesekretno*, 294–97.

53   *rioted on Smolensk Square*: Aron, *Yeltsin*, 537.

53   *leading out disarmed policemen*: Kutsyllo, *Zapiski*, 115.

53   *"time to finish off the fascist dictator"*: Aron, *Yeltsin*, 538.

54   *pulled programming off the air*: Moroz, *Tak kto zhe*, 639–42.

54   *toasted his health, shouted "Hurrah"*: Baturin et al., *Epokha Yeltsina*, 350.

54   *"picking potatoes"*: Yeltsin, *Zapiski prezidenta*, 385.

54   *"Will you fulfill my orders?"*: Baturin et al., *Epokha Yeltsina*, 369.

54   *Four T-80 tanks fired twelve shells*: Gaidar, *Days*, 251; Colton, *Yeltsin*, 278.

54   *Of the 187 killed*: Mlechin, *Kreml*, 378, quoting Yevgeny Savostyanov, deputy chairman of the security service.

55   *"more powers than the tsar"*: Colton, *Yeltsin*, 280. For a more persuasive assessment, by one of the Constitution's moderate critics, see Viktor Sheinis, "The Constitution," in Michael McFaul, Nikolai Petrov, and Andrei Ryabov, eds., *Between Dictatorship and Democracy: Russian Post-Communist Political Reform* (Washington, DC: Carnegie Endowment, 2004), 56–82.

55   *55 percent of the electorate voted*: Stephen White, Richard Rose, and Ian McAllister, *How Russia Votes* (Chatham, NJ: Chatham House Publishers, 1997), 99. The 57 percent is of all votes, not just valid votes.

55   *the evidence was circumstantial*: See the discussion in Richard Sakwa, "The Russian Elections of December 1993," *Europe-Asia Studies* 47, no. 2 (1995): 195–227, at 218–20. Two political scientists examined the evidence and concluded that, although fraud could have occurred, the method used by the critics was "inadequate" to prove such claims (see Mikhail Filippov and Peter C. Ordeshook, "Who Stole What in Russia's December 1993 Elections," *Demokratizatsiya* 5, no. 1 [1997]: 36–52).

55 *the figures had been "corrected"*: Vyacheslav Kostikov, *Roman s prezidentom* (Moscow: Vagrius, 1997), 266–67.

56 *declaring themselves sovereign states*: Daniel Treisman, *After the Deluge: Regional Crises and Political Consolidation in Russia* (Ann Arbor: University of Michigan Press, 1999).

56 *"financial asphyxiation"*: *Moskovskie Novosti*, September 19, 1993.

57 *a center of lawlessness*: Carlotta Gall and Thomas de Waal, *Chechnya: Calamity in the Caucasus* (New York: NYU Press, 2000), 129–31.

57 *took more than two thousand hostages*: Gall and de Waal, *Chechnya*, 292.

57 *"the most botched war"*: quoted in Colton, *Yeltsin*, 291.

57 *other estimates run as high as 14,000*: Jamestown Foundation, "Casualty Figures," *Chechnya Weekly*, February 20, 2003.

57 *35,000 Chechen civilians were killed*: Valery Tishkov, *Chechnya: Life in a War-Torn Society* (Berkeley: University of California Press, 2004), xvi. The human rights organization Memorial put the total at 50,000.

57 *"I don't think this was a game"*: Yevgeny Primakov, *Russian Crossroads: Toward the New Millennium* (New Haven: Yale University Press, 2004), 231.

58 *Yeltsin "suffered terribly"*: Mlechin, *Kreml*, 16.

58 *"monstrous lack of preparation"*: Boris Yeltsin, *Midnight Diaries* (New York: Public Affairs, 2000), 59.

58 *Korzhakov had adopted*: On Korzhakov's phone-tapping and interventions in economic policy and personnel matters, see the various sources cited by Colton, *Yeltsin*, 342–3 and 560–1. Colton refers to interviews with Yeltsin and several of his aides as well as articles in the Russian press. In his memoir, Korzhakov himself gives various examples of his contributions to personnel decisions (*Boris Yeltsin: ot rassveta do zakata*, e.g., 240, 274–75).

58 *below 40 percent a year*: He found an unexpected ally in the acting Central Bank head, Tatyana Paramonova.

58 *only 14 percent of Russians*: VCIOM poll, September 14–19, 1995, 1,527 respondents, available at http://sofist.socpol.ru.

59 *"best present to the Communists"*: Filatov, *Sovershenno nesekretno*, 378.

59 *Nemtsov convinced him the only option*: Nemtsov, interviewed in Lyudmila Telen, *Pokolenie Putina* (Moscow: Vagrius, 2004), 31.

59 *"Sometimes I have a feeling"*: Eldar Ryazanov, interview with Yeltsin, Ostankino Channel 1, November 16, 1993, transcribed in *BBC Summary of World Broadcasts*, November 19, 1993.

59 *behind in payments*: Government wage arrears made up 13 percent of the total in 1997. Most arrears were accumulated by private enterprises (*Russian Economic Trends* 7, no. 3 [1998], 56).

59 *almost failed to collect*: Aron, *Yeltsin*, 580.

59 *After one visit to Stavropol*: Baturin et al., *Epokha*, 565.

60 *Korzhakov offered them cabinet posts*: Yekaterina Deyeva, "Russkaya ruletka—96.

Kak delali prezidenta," *Moskovsky Komsomolets*, July 6, 2001, interviews with Korzhakov, Sergey Lissovsky, and Sergey Zverev.

60 *a nationwide network of twenty thousand party cells*: Leon Aron, *Russia's Revolution: Essays 1989–2006* (Washington: AEI Press, 2007), 181.

60 *"insatiable carnivores"*: Aron, *Yeltsin*, 598, 602.

60 *draft a decree dissolving the Duma*: Baturin et al., *Epokha Yeltsina*, 559.

60 *Gaidar, alerted by a call from Chubais*: Andrey Kolesnikov, *Neizvestny Chubais* (Moscow: Zakharov, 2004), 50; Colton, *Yeltsin*, 357.

60 *Three individuals were key*: Yeltsin, *Midnight Diaries*, 24–25.

61 *"Russians have already forgotten"*: *Rossiyskaya Gazeta*, June 11, 1996.

61 *Yeltsin slipped past Zyuganov*: A runoff election was required if no candidate received 50 percent of the votes in the first round. For more on the campaign, see Daniel Treisman, "Why Yeltsin Won," *Foreign Affairs*, September/October 1996, 64–77.

62 *71 percent evaluated the pre-perestroika economic system positively*: Polls from *New Russia Barometer*, at www.Russiavotes.org. Only 29 percent evaluated the current economic system positively, and 38 percent did so for the current political system.

64 *left the Kremlin in his hands*: Yeltsin enjoyed a quiet retirement, rarely speaking out about political matters. He died of heart failure in April 2007, at age seventy-six.

64 *"by nature a destroyer"*: Gorbachev, *Memoirs*, 346. The Lebed quote is from Alexander Lebed, *My Life and My Country* (Washington, DC: Regnery Publishing, 1997), 357.

64 *still studying the work of Feliks Dzerzhinsky*: Lev Ponomarev, "Has Reform Hit Security Organs?" *Perspective* (Institute for the Study of Conflict, Ideology, and Policy, Boston University) 2, no. 5, (1992).

64 *moonlighting as guards for organized crime*: In 1997, when the godfather of the Koptevo crime family was shot in central Moscow, it turned out that members of an elite police unit were moonlighting as his bodyguards (Maksim Barybdin, "Skandal v militsii: koptevskogo 'avtoriteta' okhranyal militseysky spetsnaz," *Kommersant*, March 1, 1997).

65 *"If either Gorbachev or Yeltsin"*: Albats, *State*, 310.

65 *"preparing for self-liquidation"*: Baturin et al., *Epokha*, 150.

65 *"provoked a tirade"*: Albats, *State*, 301.

65 *froze her out*: "Yeltsin Misread the Elections" (interview with Galina Starovoytova, February 4, 1994), *Demokratizatsiya* 2, no. 2 (1994), 184–85.

65 *perish defending the Communists*: Mlechin, *Kreml*, 273. On Yeltsin avoiding vengeance, see Yeltsin, *Zapiski prezidenta*, 166.

66 *taken their networks*: In Albats' view, this was pretty much what the KGB veterans did anyway. Interview with Yevgeniya Albats, Moscow, June 5, 2008.

66 *enlarged the security service's powers*: Jeremy R. Azrael and Alexander G. Rahr,

The Formation and Development of the Russian KGB, 1991–1994 (Santa Monica: Rand Corporation, 1993), 6; *Zakon Rossiyskoy Federatsii "O vnesenii izmeneny i dopolneny v Zakon Rossiyskoy Federatsii, 'O federalnykh organakh gosudarstvennoy bezopasnosti,' "* N. 5306-1, July 1, 1993; *Ukaz Prezidenta RF "O neotlozhnykh merakh po zashchite naseleniya ot banditizma i inykh proyavleny organizovannoy prestupnosti,"* N. 1226, June 14, 1994.

66 *"even shed a few tears"*: Baturin et al., *Epokha Yeltsina*, 451.

66 *"not thought through everything"*: Colton, *Yeltsin*, 260.

67 *"pure fiction"*: Paul Klebnikov, *Godfather of the Kremlin: Boris Berezovsky and the Looting of Russia* (New York: Harcourt, 2000), 283.

67 *According to David Hoffman*: David Hoffman, *The Oligarchs: Wealth and Power in the New Russia* (New York: Public Affairs, 2003), 348–50.

67 *40 percent of poll respondents*: VCIOM poll, reported June 10, 1996; information from VCIOM at http://wciom.ru/zh/print_q.php?s_id=458&q_id=35460&date=10.06.1996.

68 *"I never liked Boris Berezovsky"*: Yeltsin, *Midnight Diaries*, 97–98.

68 *never had dinner*: Telen, *Pokolenie*, 180; Colton, *Yeltsin*, 424. David Hoffman, in his generally authoritative book on the oligarchs, squares the circle by writing that it was not "Berezovsky's style to whisper directly into Yeltsin's ear" (Hoffman, *The Oligarchs*, 392). It was *exactly* Berezovsky's style to whisper into Yeltsin's ear. The problem was he couldn't get near it.

68 *"There were a few fleeting meetings"*: Yeltsin, *Midnight Diaries*, 98.

68 *"It's past time"*: Telen, *Pokolenie*, 33.

68 *firing him with a minor executive order*: Colton, *Yeltsin*, 406, 424.

69 *"claptrap"*: Colton, *Yeltsin*, 424–25.

69 *Berezovksy had "lobbied furiously"*: Michael Gordon, "Behind the Battle for Russian Post, Economic Control," *New York Times*, April 21, 1998.

69 *As Chubais campaigned*: Aleksandr Malyutin, "Tax Delinquents' Assets Seized, Ordered Sold," *Kommersant-Daily*, December 9, 1997.

69 *He lost again*: Gordon, "Behind the Battle."

69 *procurator general raided Berezovsky's offices*: Yekaterina Zapodinskaya, "Berezovsky Is Placed Under Arrest," *Kommersant*, April 7, 1999.

70 *They sat together*: source for this paragraph is Yeltsin, *Midnight Diaries*, 330.

71 *"stifling of freedoms"*: BBC, "Yeltsin Fears for Russia Freedoms," September 16, 2004, at http://news.bbc.co.uk/2/hi/europe/3663788.stm.

71 *"the state of the country"*: Guy Chazan, Alan Cullison, and Gregory L. White, "For Russians, Yeltsin Leaves Tarnished Legacy," *Wall Street Journal*, April 24, 2007.

71 *who, in Sobchak's view, could reintegrate*: See Chapter 3.

72 *"He shielded the Leningrad security service"*: Nataliya Gevorkyan, Nataliya Timakova, and Andrey Kolesnikov, *Ot pervogo litsa: razgovory s Vladimirom Putinym* (Moscow: Vagrius, 2000), 129.

72 *how he described himself*: Yeltsin's self-descriptions from Yeltsin, *Ispoved; The Struggle*, 205, 141; *Zapiski prezidenta*, 270; and Vladimir Polozhentsev, "Privet

Pribaltitsy," interview with Yeltsin from June 1988, at http://podolsk-news.ru/statelcin.php.

72 *no longer be useful*: The best example was Yeltsin's loyal aide Lev Sukhanov, fired without a parting meeting, who died without having received a word of thanks from Yeltsin. See Mlechin, *Kreml*, 16.

73 *the phone already disconnected*: Filatov, *Sovershenno nesekretno*, 241.

73 *"man of sober mind"*: Joseph Brodsky, *Less Than One* (New York: Farrar, Straus and Giroux, 1987), 72.

73 *"Do you have the green stuff?"*: Colton, *Yeltsin*, 310; Kostikov, *Roman s prezidentom*, 25.

73 *five shot glasses*: Mlechin, *Kreml*, 20.

73 *Barannikov, whose wife shopped*: In his memoir, *The Struggle for Russia* (232), Yeltsin reports that he asked Barannikov if there was any truth to an allegation that his wife had traveled abroad at the expense of a Swiss firm and, together with the wife of another official, spent $350,000 shopping in three days. He writes that Barannikov "lowered his head and muttered yes" but promised that "it wouldn't happen again."

73 *in Korzhakov's conspiracies*: For instance, Korzhakov writes that he included Barsukov in the planning of the incident in December 1994 when Korzhakov sent a team of unidentified commandos to intimidate the businessman Vladimir Gusinsky, following Gusinsky's car and disarming his bodyguards (see Korzhakov, *Boris Yeltsin: ot rassveta do zakata*, 285–88; Remnick, *Resurrection: The Struggle for a New Russia* [New York: Random House, 1997], 184–214).

73 *occupied a shorter period*: See Colton, *Yeltsin*, 88–89, 310, 383.

73 *"You and Chubais laugh"*: Boris Nemtsov, *Ispoved buntarya* (Moscow: Partizan, 2007), 59.

74 *fewer vacation days*: Colton, *Yeltsin*, 382–83.

74 *"not in long, elaborate blocks"*: Aron, *Yeltsin*, 108.

74 *No evidence contradicting this*: See Carlotta Gall, "Pacolli Admits Credit Card Role," *Moscow Times*, January 22, 2000.

75 *Pavel Borodin, was indeed convicted*: Robin Munro, "Switzerland Fines Borodin $177,000," *Moscow Times*, March 7, 2002.

75 *"Yeltsin won't give up"*: Chernyaev, *My Six Years*, 416–67.

75 *immediately approved the request*: This is recounted by Yevgeny Kiselyov in Mikhail Kasyanov, *Bez Putina* (Moscow: Novaya gazeta, 2009), 293–94.

75 *amazed at his fastidiousness*: Shaposhnikov, *Vybor*, 130.

75 *to engage the Swedish crown princess*: Yelena Tregubova, *Bayki kremlyovskogo diggera* (Moscow: Ad Marginem, 2003), 50–51; on his formality in the office, see Colton, *Yeltsin*, 83.

75 *an introvert*: Mlechin, *Kreml*, 11, 21.

75 *"greed for self-realization"*: Lev Sukhanov, *Tri goda s Yeltsinym* (Riga: Vaga, 1992), 305; on the pronoun "I," Mlechin, *Kreml*, 21.

76 *"stupid monotony"*: Yeltsin, *Prezidentsky marafon* (Moscow: ACT, 2000), 413.

76 *pull out a pencil*: Colton, *Yeltsin*, 83; Mlechin, *Kreml*, 13.

76 *fired such weak individuals quickly*: Baturin et al., *Epokha*, 435.

77 *Yeltsin himself wondered about this*: Yeltsin, *Zapiski prezidenta*, 165.

77 *unanimously overturned his decree*: Aron, *Yeltsin*, 471–72.

77 *Kremlin aides estimated*: Michael McFaul and Nikolai Petrov, "Elections," in McFaul, Petrov, and Ryabov, *Between Dictatorship and Democracy*, 307.

77 *cutting strategic nuclear warheads*: Arms Control Association, "US and Soviet/Russian Strategic Forces," http://www.armscontrol.org/act/1997_03/factmr97, downloaded October 19, 2008. These are "Start-accountable" deployed warheads.

78 *"the first leader"*: Peter Rutland, "Boris Yeltsin: Judging the Legacy," *Transitions Online*, April 24, 2007.

78 *"Yeltsin is a know-nothing"*: quoted in David Remnick, "Ability to Mobilize Public a Key to Yeltsin's Comeback," *Washington Post*, May 30, 1990.

78 *"Each pillowcase must be justly distributed!"*: Details in this paragraph from Aron, *Yeltsin*, 80, 83, 87.

79 *"all the official and unofficial public opinion polls"*: Yeltsin, *Ispoved*, 1.

79 *"sociologists, economists, scholars"*: Sukhanov, *Tri goda*, 346.

79 *"I see the eyes of many people"*: Yeltsin, *Zapiski prezidenta*, 368.

79 *"As for popularity"*: Yeltsin, *Ispoved*.

79 *"When I am constantly asked"*: quoted in Richard B. Dobson and Steven A. Grant, "Public Opinion and the Transformation of the Soviet Union," *International Journal of Public Opinion Research* 4, no. 4 (1992): 302–20.

CHAPTER 3: UNREASONABLE DOUBT

81 *Hitler's plan*: quoted in the Nuremberg trials; see Konstantin Dushenko, *Tsitaty iz Russkoy istorii ot priznaniya varyagov do nashikh dney* (Moscow: Eksmo, 2005).

81 *Families burned their books*: this and the following details are from Alexander Werth, *Russia at War: 1941–1945* (New York: Carroll & Graf Publishers, 1964), 323–25.

82 *one of its defenders, Vladimir Spiridonovich Putin*: This account is Putin's from his collection of interviews (Gevorkyan, Timakova, and Kolesnikov, *Ot pervogo litsa* 10–11). Of course, there is little way to check the veracity of such war stories.

82 *third and only surviving child*: A first son had also died in infancy.

82 *average abilities, said his eighth grade teacher*: Vera Gurevich, *Vospominaniya o budushchem prezidente* (Moscow: Mezhdunarodnie Otnosheniya, 2001).

82 *remembers him on the rooftops*: quoted in the RTR documentary "The Unknown Putin," broadcast March 17, 2000.

82 *134 million people saw it*: N.A. Zenkovich, *Putinskaya Entsiklopediya* (Moscow: Olma-Press, 2006), 232.

83 *"romantic ideas"*: Gevorkyan et al., *Ot pervogo litsa*, 39.

83 *380,000 Soviet troops*: David Hoffman, "Putin's Career Rooted in Russia's KGB," *Washington Post*, January 30, 2000.

83 *"we have nothing to restructure"*: Gorbachev interviewed by CNN, at www
.cnn.com/SPECIALS/cold.war/episodes/23/interviews/gorbachev/, downloaded
August 30, 2007.

83 *pseudonym Vladimir Usoltsev*: Vladimir Usoltsev, *Sosluzhivets* (Moscow: EKSMO,
2004). See also the interview with Vladimir Bragin on the website Strana.ru,
March 9, 2004. Needless to say, some aspects of these can not be taken at face
value, but there is no obvious reason why these sources would misrepresent the
details of daily life.

83 *one of his informers was later arrested*: Christian Neef, "A Complete Conformist,"
Der Spiegel (English version), October 20, 2003, at www.spiegel.de/international/
spiegel/0.1518.270555.00.html.

83 *catalogs from West German mail order outlets*: Usoltsev, *Sosluzhivets*, 105, 210–11.

84 *broke the stove*: Gevorkyan et al., *Ot pervogo litsa*, 69.

84 *the two sat in Sobchak's office*: Gevorkyan et al., *Ot pervogo litsa*, 79.

86 *"If the mafia did not pay me"*: interview with Oleg Utitsyn, Moscow, August 2,
1993.

86 *Yury Shutov, a reputed criminal authority*: Mikhail Alekseyev, "Klan," *Sovershenno
Sekretno*, December 2001; *Russia & CIS General Newswire*, November 21, 2006,
available via Lexis.

86 *an office on the same floor as his boss*: John Thornhill, "Russia's Regions Prepare to
Bow Again to the Centre," *Financial Times*, March 15, 2000; Mlechin, *Kreml*, 48.

87 *his KGB bosses asked*: Gevorkyan et al., *Ot pervogo litsa*, 81–2.

87 *at least five intelligence or KGB veterans*: Valery Golubev, Oleg Safonov, and Viktor Ivanov all listed their KGB past in their official biographies (see www.gaz-
prom.ru/eng/articles/article8872.shtml; http://archive.kremlin.ru/state_subj/
149806.shtml; http://president.kremlin.ru/state_subj/27809.shtml). Two others—Igor Sechin and Sergey Naryshkin—had served overseas in jobs that
almost always required an intelligence background. Sechin reportedly told a
Western scholar that he had served in intelligence (see Alan Cullison, Gregory L. White, and David Crawford, "The Leningrad Enigma: In Putin's Past,
Glimpses of Russia's Hardline Future," *Wall Street Journal*, December 21, 2007).
Naryshkin has been reported by various publications to have served in foreign
intelligence (e.g., Radio Free Europe, "Russia: Siloviki Take the Reins in Post-
Oligarchy Era," September 17, 2007). Mlechin (*Kreml*, 631) mentions another
KGB agent in the Smolny, but I have not found independent confirmation of
his KGB affiliation.

87 *a former Stasi officer, Matthias Warnig*: Guy Chazan and David Crawford, "In
From the Cold: A Friendship Forged in Spying Pays Dividends in Russia Today:
Top Dresdner Banker's Ties To Putin Go Back to Days When They Were Agents,"
Wall Street Journal, February 23, 2005. The *Wall Street Journal* quoted former col-
leagues of the two men and Stasi documents. Warnig denies having worked with
Putin in Germany and says he met the future president in St. Petersburg in 1991.

87 *export more than $90 million worth of raw materials*: Andrew Higgins, "No Party

Animal: Putin's Only Record of Public Office Is One Full of Paradoxes," *Wall Street Journal*, March 24, 2000.

88 *Putin carried a gun*: Mlechin, *Kreml*, 48.

88 *Putin met a Russian businessman, Vladimir Smirnov*: Mark Hosenball and Christian Caryl, "A Stain on Mr. Clean: How a Money-laundering Indictment in Europe Could Haunt Putin," *Newsweek*, September 3, 2001.

88 *Putin himself served on SPAG's unpaid advisory board*: Agathe Duparc and Vladimir Ivanidze, "Le nom de M. Poutine apparaît en marge des affaires de blanchiment au Liechtenstein," *Le Monde*, May 26, 2000; Hosenball and Caryl, "A Stain on Mr. Clean"; Catherine Belton, "Putin's Name Surfaces in German Probe," *Moscow Times*, May 19, 2003; Derek Scally, "Putin Sat on Board of Firm in Russian Mafia Inquiry," *Irish Times*, May 15, 2003.

88 *German prosecutors accused SPAG*: Belton, "Putin's Name Surfaces in German Probe."

88 *Rudolf Ritter, was indicted*: Elizabeth Olson, "Europe: Liechtenstein; Money-Laundering Charges," *New York Times*, July 20, 2001. Ritter was eventually acquitted of money laundering. The German authorities did not file charges against SPAG.

88 *the Kremlin has denied*: Belton, "Putin's Name Surfaces in German Probe."

88 *contracts to supply the city's ambulances*: Information from the Petersburg Fuel Company's website at www.ptk.ru/s/2/240/full.html, downloaded April 10, 2008.

89 *Barsukov was later arrested*: Michael Schwirtz, "A Mobster Trial, and a Flash of a Violent Past," *New York Times*, May 14, 2009. In November 2009, Barsukov was convicted of fraud and sentenced to 14 years in prison ("Court Finds Eight People Guilty in High-Profile Hostile Takeover Case," *Russia & CIS Business and Financial Newswire*, November 13, 2009).

90 *"unite around himself"*: Mlechin, *Kreml*, 563.

90 *"blended masterfully"*: Tregubova, *Bayki*, 142.

90 *is said to have tried to talk Yeltsin out of appointing Putin*: on this, see Tregubova, *Bayki*, 200, and also Yeltsin's own account in *Midnight Diaries*, 332–33. However, since the source for both these accounts may very well be Voloshin himself, perhaps one should reserve judgment. Chubais subsequently expressed strong support for Putin.

90 *Berezovsky came to view Putin as someone*: Author's interview with Mikhail Margelov, senior official in Putin's election campaign and head of Rosinformtsentr, Moscow, March 24, 2000.

91 *sacks contained the explosive hexogen*: Anna Dolgov, "Police Find Possible Prank Bomb in Apartment Building in Western Russia," Associated Press, September 23, 1999.

91 *part of a training exercise*: Anatoly Medetsky, "Sacks in the Basement Still Trouble Ryazan," *Moscow Times*, September 24, 2004.

91 *"kill them even in the toilets"*: Putin's phrase, *"my i v sortire ikh zamochim,"* which became an often repeated catchphrase, has been translated in many ways. The

verb *mochit*, which literally means "to make wet," is criminal slang for to kill; the wetness connotes blood. *Sortir* is a crude colloquialism for outhouse.

91 *16 percent supported Primakov*: VCIOM poll of 1,545 respondents, taken September 17–21, 1999, at http://sofist.socpol.ru. The Communist leader, Gennady Zyuganov, was even higher at this point, with 19 percent, but his support was less likely than Primakov's to grow by attracting the uncommitted, center voters.

92 *freeing up jail cells*: Mlechin, *Kreml*, 592.

92 *slung mud at Putin's opponents*: For Dorenko's various claims, see: Andrei Zolotov, "Media Wars Turn to Blood and Guts," *Moscow Times*, October 26, 1999; Oksana Yablokova, "ORT Accuses Mayor of Paul Tatum's '96 Murder," *Moscow Times*, November 9, 1999; PBS, "The Newshour with Jim Lehrer," December 17, 1999; Interfax, "Moscow Mayor Files Libel Suit Against Russian Public Television," Moscow, October 15, 1999. On the fact that the attacks were instigated by Berezovsky, see Jen Tracy, "Berezovsky: My Media Wars Can End," *Moscow Times*, December 23, 1999, in which Berezovsky is quoted admitting that he "closely directed Dorenko in formulating media assaults on Luzhkov." Luzhkov, claiming to be "stunned by the enormity of lying" about him in the press, brought a series of libel suits against Dorenko. In three rulings in February 2000, October 2000, and February 2001, Moscow courts found in favor of Luzhkov and ordered ORT to run retractions and pay small amounts of compensation to Luzhkov and his wife, Yelena Baturina. The suits concerned the allegations that Luzhkov had been involved in the 1996 contract killing of an American businessman, that Baturina owned an apartment in Manhattan, and that Luzhkov had demanded reimbursement for supplies provided by Moscow to the Stavropol region during the Budyonnovsk terrorist attack (Viktor Loshak, "I Was Stunned by the Enormity of Lying," *Moscow News*, October 11, 2000; Anna Badkhen, "ORT Gets License, Vote of Support," *Moscow Times*, May 25, 2000; RIA News Agency, Moscow, October 23, 2000; Russian Public TV ORT, Moscow, 18:00, February 10, 2001).

92 *42 percent said they planned to vote for him*: VCIOM Express poll of 1,600 respondents, December 24–27, 1999, at http://sofist.socpol.ru.

92 *"What do you think—am I not capital?"*: *Vedomosti*, March 24, 2000.

92 *"Berezovsky knows how to pick his moment!"*: Author's interview with Margelov, Moscow, March 24, 2000.

93 *"fantastically free"*: Telen, *Pokolenie Putina*, 58.

93 *scholars who counseled him nervous*: The rector of the Academy of the National Economy, Vladimir Mau, worried at the time that Putin's expectations of economic reforms were so high that disillusion might follow if reforms failed to deliver fully. Personal communication, March 2000.

93 *"I asked him respectfully"*: Author's interview with Leontyev, March 22, 2000.

93 *Within a few years, they replaced*: OECD, *Economic Surveys: Russian Federation* (Paris: OECD, 2004), 37.

93 *Currency reserves grew*: Central Bank of Russia, *Bulletin of Banking Statistics*, various issues.

93 *reforms sought to reduce regulation*: OECD, *Economic Surveys: Russian Federation* (Paris: OECD, 2002), 101; OECD, *Economic Surveys: Russian Federation* (Paris: OECD, 2006), 125.

94 *did lighten the burden on small business*: Yevgeny Yakovlev and Ekaterina Zhuravskaya, *Reforms in Business Regulation: Evidence from Russia* (Moscow: Center for Economic and Financial Research, 2008).

94 *Between 2001 and 2006, the proportion*: CEFIR, *Monitoring the Administrative Barriers to Small Business Development in Russia, Rounds 1–6* (Moscow: Center for Economic and Financial Research, 2002–07); CEFIR, *Presentation on the Results of Monitoring the Administrative Barriers to Small Business Development in Russia, Round 6*, at http://www.cefir.ru/index.php?1=eng&id=261.

94 *extended the use of jury trials*: Peter H. Solomon, Jr. "Assessing the Courts in Russia: Parameters of Progress under Putin," *Demokratizatsiya* 16, no. 1 (2008), 63–73.

94 *The right to approve searches*: Sakwa, *Putin*, 156.

94 *arrests initially fell by a third*: Mark McDonald, "Russia Begins New Twist On Trials: Juries," Knight Ridder Newspapers, February 17, 2003.

95 *"class of oligarchs will cease to exist"*: Barry Renfrew, "Putin Urges Russia's Voters to Elect Him in First Round," Associated Press, March 18, 2000.

95 *Putin set new rules*: Peter Baker and Susan Glasser (*Kremlin Rising: Vladimir Putin's Russia and the End of Revolution* [New York: Scribner, 2005], 86–87) quote the businessman Oleg Kiselyov, a participant in the meeting, to this effect. It remains a matter of some debate just how explicit Putin was at this meeting, but most seem to have got this message.

95 *stormed onto the tycoon's plane*: for the details, see Baker and Glasser, *Kremlin Rising*, Chapter 14.

96 *had jumped from the country's sixth largest oil producer*: Pavel Romanov, "Rosneft Passes LUKoil on Output, not Profit," *Energy Tribune*, May 12, 2008; "Yukos Sale a Mix of Auction Pomp, Russian Bureaucracy," Associated Press, December 27, 2004.

96 *35 percent of government revenues*: Goskomstat Rossii, *Finansy Rossii* (Moscow: Goskomstat Rossii, 2000, 2006).

96 *"for sale down to its hair roots"*: Vladimir Solovyov, *Putin: putevoditel dlya neravnodushnykh* (Moscow: Eksmo, 2008), 340.

96 *Planting untrue stories for a fee*: Lev Kadik and Gleb Pyanykh, "Rossiyskaya pressa okazalas prodazhnoy," *Kommersant*, February 24, 2001.

97 *"But who reads it, your press?"*: Solovyov, *Putin*, 15.

97 *"not in prime time"*: Sergey Ivanenko, deputy chairman of Yabloko, author's interview, State Duma, Moscow, July 31, 2002.

97 *"How dare you!"*: Tregubova, *Bayki*, 270.

97 *summoned to the Kremlin every Friday*: Baker and Glasser, *Kremlin Rising*, 294.

97 *A number of journalists*: According to the International Federation of Journalists, however, the rate of successful prosecution of the killers of journalists increased under Putin (International Federation of Journalists, *Partial Justice: An Inquiry*

into the Deaths of Journalists in Russia, 1993–2009 [Brussels: IFJ, 2009], 12). On this, see Chapter 10.

98 *benefited from such electoral manipulation*: In Russia, extremely high turnout in a given district or region has often been taken as a sign of irregularities. High turnout correlated geographically with higher votes for the Communists in 1993, 1995, and the first round of 1996; Luzhkov and Primakov's Fatherland–All Russia in 1999; and United Russia, Putin, or Medvedev in 2000–2008.

98 *redundant fraud*: for some thoughts on this, see Daniel Treisman, "What Keeps the Kremlin Up All Night," *Moscow Times*, February 18, 2008.

99 *One died after apparently being poisoned*: Nabi Abdullaev, "Mystery Surrounds Shchekochikhin's Death," *Moscow Times*, July 3, 2008; BBC, "Russian MP's Death Sparks Storm," April 18, 2003, http://news.bbc.co.uk/2/hi/europe/2958997.stm.

99 *"If there is no party"*: *Moscow Times*, April 2, 2007.

99 *"just vote like you're told"*: Gregory L. White and Alan Cullison, "Putin's Pitchman: Inside Kremlin as It Tightens Its Grip: Ex-Aide to Tycoons," *Wall Street Journal*, December 19, 2006.

99 *two judges accused Moscow's chief judge*: Francesca Mereu, "Yegorova Rejects Criticism of Her Court," *Moscow Times*, June 21, 2005.

99 *a Kremlin official had made her reappointment*: Natalya Krainova, "Judge Tells of Kremlin Threat," *Moscow Times*, May 14, 2008.

99 *still acquitted only 1 percent*: Solomon, "Assessing the Courts."

99 *about 363,000 additional bureaucrats were hired*: calculated using Goskomstat Rossii, *Rossiysky statistichesky yezhegodnik* (Moscow: Goskomstat Rossii, 2008). These figures do not include the police, secret services, or the army. I have adjusted the Goskomstat figures for 2005 and subsequent years to take into account a classification change, noted in OECD, *Economic Surveys: Russian Federation* (Paris: OECD, 2006), 119. Instead of the 10.9 percent increase found in the Goskomstat statistics for 2005, I have used the 2.1 percent figure suggested by the OECD.

99 *Law enforcement mushroomed*: Estimates for the United States from c. 2000: about 9.5 prosecutorial personnel and 11.0 judges per 100,000 inhabitants, from UN, *United Nations Surveys of Crime Trends and Operations of Criminal Justice Systems, 1990–2002* (New York: United Nations Office on Drugs and Crime, Division for Policy Analysis and Public Affairs), at http://www.unodc.org/pdf/crime/eighthsurvey/5678svr.pdf. For Russia, court and prosecutorial employees from Goskomstat Rossii, *Rossiya v tsifrakh* (Moscow: Goskomstat Rossii, 2008); spending calculated from the federal budget laws at http://www1.minfin.ru/ru/budget/federal_budget/.

99 *It built less housing*: Figures from various Goskomstat Rossii publications. I compare annual averages for 1991–99 (or a shorter period, when data start later) to those for 2000–2007.

100 *less corruption and stealing*: Figures as of September 2006 (Levada Center, "Privatizatsiya, vlast i biznes," http://www.levada.ru/sborniki.html).

100 *crimes related to corruption had doubled*: Andrey Sharov, Nataliya Kozlova, "Vslukh o taynakh sledstviya," *Rossiyskaya Gazeta*, January 30, 2007. Of course, it could be that enforcement had tightened, but this seems unlikely given other evidence.

100 *Each year under Putin*: Levada Center, "Silovye strukturi i pravokhranitel-nye organi," http://www.levada.ru/sborniki.html, and http://www.levada.ru/press/2007120703.html.

100 *The number of crimes registered*: compiled from Goskomstat Rossii, various publications, reports of Interior Ministry.

100 *not by the terrorists but by the gas*: BBC News, "Gas 'Killed Moscow Hostages,'" October 27, 2002, http://news.bbc.co.uk/2/hi/europe/2365383.stm.

100 *After Beslan, local residents said*: Delphine Thouvenot, "Many Beslan Hostages Were Killed by Russian Forces, Residents Say," Agence France Presse, May 18, 2005.

100 *52 percent of respondents agreed*: VCIOM polls, see http://www.levada.ru/sborniki.html.

100 *terrorist attacks were much more frequent*: Interior Ministry of the Russian Federation, statistics at www.mvd.ru/stats/, downloaded April 17, 2008 and Goskomstat Rossii, www.gks.ru statistics, downloaded April 17, 2008. Data were only available from 1997.

101 *only 38 percent of Russians believed the authorities*: VCIOM polls, see Levada Center, *Obshchestvennoe mnenie 2006*, Table 11.6, www.levada.ru/sborniki.html. Despite this, the share of the population that said they were at least somewhat worried about becoming victims of terrorists did fall a little—from 86 percent in September 1999 at the height of the apartment bombing scare to 74 percent in August 2006. Chechnya was one area in which Russians might think the state had increased the level of order, although of a brutal form, by supporting the consolidation of power of Ramzan Kadyrov (see Chapter 8).

101 *423 soldiers killed themselves*: Vitaly Tsimbal and Vasily Zatsepin, "Reforma armii," *Vlast*, October 29, 2007.

101 *growing use of commercial (arbitrazh) courts*: Kathryn Hendley, "Are Russian Judges Still Soviet?" *Post-Soviet Affairs* 23, no. 2 (2007): 240–74, at 246, and information from the Supreme Arbitrage Court at www.arbitr.ru/_upimg/333C5BE19C913A9C6E308ED47DE59BCB_VAS_pz_2007.pdf, downloaded April 17, 2008.

101 *contested decisions of the tax authorities*: Figures for 2005–2007, from a survey by the consultancy Ernst and Young (*Survey of Taxation Issues in Russia 2005, 2007*, at http://www.ey.com/global/content.nsf/Russia_E, downloaded April 15, 2008). Of course, firms might only choose to sue if they had clear-cut cases, rendering these statistics somewhat ambiguous.

101 *"cumbersome, slow-moving, ineffective state apparatus"*: from Putin's 2002 annual address to the parliament, quoted in Viktor Martyanov, "Zhidky terminator novogo pokoleniya," *Ekspert*, December 3, 2007.

101 *disposable income, adjusted for inflation, increased by 12 percent*: Goskomstat Rossii, www.gks.ru, downloaded January 19, 2010.

101 *nine members of Putin's inner circle*: The nine I have in mind are Igor Sechin (Rosneft), Viktor Ivanov (Aeroflot, Almaz-Antey), Sergey Chemezov (Rostekhnologii),
Aleksey Miller (Gazprom), Vladimir Yakunin (Russian Railroads), Nikolay Tokarev
(Transneft), Andrey Kostin (VTB), Sergey Ivanov (United Aircraft Corporation),
and Yury Kovalchuk (Bank Rossiya, Sogaz, Gazprombank, OMZ). Not all of these
served in the security services, but all had close connections with others who did.
From the *Ekspert* database and company websites and statements, I estimate total
revenues of these companies in 2007 at $221 billion. GDP in 2007 was about $1,258
billion. Due to some missing data, this is a low estimate of revenues.

102 *scripted and staged in excruciating detail*: Mikhail Fishman and Konstantin Gaaze,
"Kreml upravlyaet telekanalami v 'ruchnom rezhime'," *Russky Newsweek*, August
4, 2008.

103 *"feed off foreign embassies like jackals"*: Vladimir Isachenkov, "Crowd Calls on
Putin to Stay as Russia's 'National Leader' After Presidential Term Ends," Associated Press, November 21, 2007.

104 *"I have come home"*: Vladimir Grigoriev and Inessa Slavutinskaya, "Putin
naverkh," *Profil*, April 5, 1999.

104 *laid flowers at the grave of Yury Andropov*: Andrew Jack, *Inside Putin's Russia: Can
There Be Reform Without Democracy?* (New York: Oxford University Press, 2004),
14.

104 *"I want to report that the group of FSB operatives"*: Olga Kryshtanovskaya, "Operatsiya 'Vnedrenie' zavershena!" *Novaya Gazeta*, August 30, 2004.

104 *bursts of cold war invective*: For instance, after the Beslan tragedy, he practically
accused the West of helping Basayev's terrorists (see "Putin Tells the Russians:
'We Shall Be Stronger,'" *New York Times*, September 5, 2004). At his United Russia
rally in November 2007 he said his democratic opponents, having "gotten a little
training from Western specialists," were planning "provocations" to try to restore
a "regime based on corruption and lies" (Andrey Kolesnikov, "Yedinstvo foruma
i soderzhaniya," *Kommersant*, November 22, 2007, at http://www.kommersant
.ru/doc.aspx?DocsID=828086).

104 *33 percent of government ministers*: Olga Kryshtanovskaya and Stephen White,
"Putin's Militocracy," *Post-Soviet Affairs* 19, no. 4 (2003): 289–306, at 294.

105 *The generals had been shocked*: Grigoriev and Slavutinskaya, "Putin naverkh."

105 *Putin was having him tailed*: Yeltsin, *Midnight Diaries*, 203.

105 *unsure of his reception among the KGB barons*: As the head of the State Security
Veterans Association put it right after Putin's election: "We are watching what his
next steps will be. And if in the next three to four months or half a year we are
convinced that what he does serves the state, then he will have many supporters
among the veterans. Yes, we did help him during a first stage, during the election
campaign. But now, it's time to wait. Putin can go one way and continue working
for the Family. . . . Or he can work for the state. Or he can work for himself. For

the moment, he hasn't shown anything yet" (Sophie Lambroschini, "KGB Veterans Head Has High Hopes for Putin," *RFE/RL Newsline*, June 30, 2000).

105 *its own chief rabbi*: Michael Freund, "Russian Army Gets First Chief Rabbi Since the 1917 Revolution," *Jerusalem Post*, December 17, 2007.

106 *which had collected 40 percent of Russia's intelligence on the United States*: See, for instance, "Press Conference with State Duma Committee for Defense Chairman Andrey Nikolayev," Official Kremlin International News Broadcast, March 21, 2002, via Lexis. The army general Leonid Ivashov accused Putin of making Russian foreign policy "subservient to American and Western policy" (Associated Press, "Putin's Plan to Revamp a Troubled Military Faces Stiff Resistance from Top Brass," December 29, 2001).

106 *"keep rootin' for Putin"*: Thomas Friedman, "Russia's Last Line," *New York Times*, December 23, 2001.

106 *must all have aggravated the FSB*: The procurator general complained publicly on the odd grounds that: "Many civilized countries have given up on jury trials. They belong to another century" (Agence France Presse, Moscow, May 23, 2001).

106 *Primakov had proposed exactly this*: Melissa Akin, "Primakov Knows What Governors Want," *Moscow Times*, February 24, 1999.

106 *arrest warrants were issued*: Bill Powell, "Indicting the Oligarchs," *Newsweek*, April 19, 1999, 42; Igor Denisov, "Property Issue as Dividing Line Between Putin and Primakov," Interfax, Moscow, November 22, 1999. The charges against Berezovsky were dropped in November 1999 after Primakov was replaced as prime minister, but new charges were filed and an arrest warrant for him issued in October 2001 (Interfax, "Russia Issues Arrest Warrant for Berezovsky," Moscow, October 19, 2001). The charges against Smolensky were also canceled.

106 *he took a list of oligarchs*: quoted in Padma Desai, *Conversations on Russia: Reform from Yeltsin to Putin* (New York: Oxford University Press, 2006), 125–26.

107 *trying to pack the Russian state-owned media*: Andrei Zolotov, "Primakov Spy Ally in Battle for RTR," *Moscow Times*, January 21, 1999.

107 *"build a tough, strong system"*: "Boris Yeltsin Calls on the Congress to Strengthen Executive Power," *Izvestia*, October 30, 1991, translated in *Current Digest of the Soviet Press* 43, no. 44 (1991).

107 *Yeltsin's aides had drafted*: Baturin et al., *Epokha Yeltsina*, 398.

107 *Yeltsin had called for such a law*: See Edwin Bacon and Bettina Renz, with Julian Cooper, *Securitising Russia: The Domestic Politics of Putin* (New York: Manchester University Press, 2006), 183.

107 *An early draft of the law had been introduced*: Bacon, Renz, and Cooper, *Securitising Russia*, 115–21.

107 *According to Kryshtanovskaya*: Kryshtanovskaya and White, "Putin's Militocracy," 294.

108 *"It was not just Putin"*: Kryshtanovskaya, "Operatsiya 'Vnedrenie.'"

109 *"It would be awkward"*: Celestine Bohlen, "Gray Eminence Compels Respect and Even Fear," *New York Times*, August 10, 1999.

109   *Yeltsin clings to Putin's arm*: The footage can be seen in a documentary *Rise and Fall of the Russian Oligarchs*, Part 9, from TVO Human Edge, available for instance on the website of the lawyer Robert Amsterdam, at www.robertamsterdam .com/2007/11/video_the_rise_fall_of_the_rus.htm.

109   *"literally grey-green"*: Stanislav Belkovsky, *Biznes Vladimira Putina* (Yekaterinburg: Ultra.Kultura, 2006), 10.

110   *"palaces, airplanes, limousines"*: Belkovsky, *Biznes Vladimira Putina*, 10.

110   *Shamil Basayev's shinbone*: Maksim Kononenko, *Vladimir Vladimirovich™* (Moscow: KoLibri, 2005), 451.

110   *At moments he seemed genuinely to fear*: For instance, see his statement in September 2004: "There are Muslims along the Volga, in Tatarstan and Bashkortostan. Chechnya isn't Iraq. It's not far away. It's a vital part of our territory. This is all about Russia's territorial integrity" (Jonathan Steele, "Angry Putin Rejects Public Beslan Inquiry," *The Guardian*, September 7, 2004).

110   *He appeared to believe*: Putin told a group of foreign journalists that he had raised this issue with Western leaders but had been brushed off: "It's a replay of the mentality of the cold war. There are certain people who want us to be focused purely on our internal problems. They pull strings here so that we don't raise our heads internationally" (John Kampfner, "Special report—A President Craves Understanding," *New Statesman*, September 13, 2004).

110   *a Moscow-based newspaper published a list*: See "Veliky severoamerikansky turan," *Rossiya*, reprinted on the website agentura.ru (http://www.agentura.ru/ terrorism/turan/).

111   *agreed with the United States to cut nuclear arsenals*: See David Sanger and Michael Wines, "Bush and Putin Sign Pact for Steep Nuclear Arms Cuts," *New York Times*, May 24, 2002.

112   *"There are no former spies"*: Gevorkyan et al., *Ot pervogo litsa*, 75.

112   *Yuliya Latynina described a session*: Yuliya Latynina, "Yest takie partii!" *Yezhednevny Zhurnal*, October 4, 2007, www.ej.ru/?a=note&id=7444; *Russky Newsweek*, "Shchit i kit," November 13–19, 2006.

112   *claimed that the security services had blown up*: Alex Goldfarb and Marina Litvinenko, *Death of a Dissident: The Poisoning of Alexander Litvinenko and the Return of the KGB* (New York: Simon & Schuster, 2007).

113   *Sergey Yushenkov, was shot*: BBC, "Russian MP's Death Sparks Storm," April 18, 2003, http://news.bbc.co.uk/2/hi/europe/2958997.stm.

113   *Shchekochikhin, died three months later*: Nabi Abdullaev, "Mystery Surrounds Shchekochikhin's Death," *Moscow Times*, July 3, 2008.

113   *As of early 2010, Kovalyov*: Sergey Kovalyov interviewed on *Ekho Moskvy*, July 25, 2002, http://echo.msk.ru/programs/beseda/19169.phtml.

113   *three days after Seleznyov's announcement*: Igor Vandenko, "Prikazano zabyt: Gennady Seleznyov otrekaetsya ot sobstvennykh slov," *Novie Izvestia*, April 3, 2002. Strange as this was, it does not necessarily fit the theory of an FSB plot. Were there an FSB conspiracy, one might have expected that after Selenyov's

announcement the organizers would call off this attack or redirect it somewhere else.

115 *vocation not politics but business*: Belkovsky (*Biznes Vladimira Putina*, 76) makes an argument to this effect.

115 *one might call these new magnates silovarchs*: On their emergence, see Daniel Treisman, "Putin's Silovarchs," *Orbis* 51, no. 1 (2007): 141–53.

115 *Gazprom was a personal obsession*: Two journalists who investigated in 2007 wrote that all the top Gazprom managers they interviewed insisted that: "Gazprom is personally managed by Vladimir Vladimirovich Putin" (Valery Panyushkin and Mikhail Zygar, *Gazprom: novoe russkoe oruzhie* [Moscow: Zakharov, 2008], 251). Mikhail Kasyanov, prime minister from 2000–2003, said that the affairs of Gazprom and Rosoboronexport, the arms exporter headed by Putin's Dresden friend Chemezov, were among the few areas of government business on which Putin personally intervened. He claims that Putin personally secured tax breaks for Gazprom (Kasyanov, *Bez Putina*, 136, 194–95).

115 *along with his old acquaintance, Matthias Warnig*: Panyushkin and Zygar, *Gazprom*, 115, 159, 192, 199.

115 *old Putin acquaintance, Gennady Timchenko*: See, for example, Andrew Higgins, Guy Chazan, and Alan Cullison, "The Middleman: Secretive Associate of Putin Emerges as Czar of Russian Oil Trading," *Wall Street Journal*, June 11, 2008.

116 *"Under Putin, this is different"*: Author's interview July 31, 2002, Moscow.

116 *As Putin explained in February 2008*: Interfax, "State Corporations Will in the Future Be Privatized—Putin," February 14, 2008.

117 *"Some parts might be sold"*: Jeremy Ventuso, "Chemezov Granted Stakes in 426 Firms," *Moscow Times*, July 15, 2008.

117 *an attempt to expand Russia's geopolitical influence*: for details of Putin's involvement, see Panyushkin and Zygar, *Gazprom*, 156–63.

117 *no proof Putin had more than a few hundred thousand dollars*: His income declaration in October 1997 said he owned two very old cars, a 1,500 square meter plot of land in the Moscow Region, a 78 square meter apartment in St. Petersburg, and bank deposits worth about $149,000 (Prime Tass, "Election Commission Reports Putin's 2006 Income at 2 ml Rs," October 26, 2007).

118 *stocks almost doubled during the following two years*: The RTS stock index rose by 96 percent between November 2003 and November 2005.

118 *Alan Greenspan, Chairman of the Federal Reserve*: Patrice Hill, "Oil Prices to Stay High, Greenspan Predicts; US Must Rethink Consumption," *Washington Times*, April 28, 2004.

118 *Was it true, Gref wanted to know*: Personal communication, Vladimir Milov, February 2008.

118 *"There can be no superpower"*: Bobo Lo, *Vladimir Putin and the Evolution of Russian Foreign Policy* (London: Royal Institute for International Affairs, 2003), 65–71.

118 *"We're not threatened by dictatorship"*: Vladimir Solovyov, "Anatoly Sobchak:

Vladimir Vladimirovich Putin—chelovek lisheny zhazhdy vlasti," interview with Anatoly Sobchak, February 9, 2000, http://www.vsoloviev.ru/orange/text .mhtml?PubID=138.

120   "*The people sitting at the table*": Andrey Kolesnikov, *Razdvoenie V.V.P.: Kak Putin Medvedeva vybral* (Moscow: Biblioteka Kommersant, 2008), 250.

120   *as his Chechen protégé Ramzan Kadyrov*: Megan Stack, "Chechen Tiger Without a Chain," *Los Angeles Times*, June 17, 2008.

121   *Once, flying from Barnaul to Moscow*: Kolesnikov, *Razdvoenie V.V.P.*, 14–21.

121   *28 percent of Russians thought it at least possible*: Public Opinion Foundation, February 16, 2000, at http://bd.fom.ru/report/cat/reg_ros/mos/o000601#.

CHAPTER 4: THE UNDERSTUDY

123   "*fell upstairs*": Mark Aldanov, "Count Witte," *The Russian Review* 1, no. 1 (1941): 56–64, at 58.

123   "*Englishman from a good family*": Vladimir Solovyov, *Russkaya ruletka: zametki na polyakh noveyshey istorii* (Moscow: Eksmo, 2008), 192. For a sketch of Witte, see Richard Pipes, *The Russian Revolution* (New York: Vintage, 1991), 31–32.

124   *doubled state revenues*: Aldanov, "Count Witte," 57.

124   "*Russian revolt, senseless and merciless*": the phrase is from Pushkin's "The Captain's Daughter."

124   "*peace of mind*": Aldanov, "Count Witte," 64.

124   "*Withdraw the troops?*": S. Yu. Tyutyukin, "Sergey Yulyevich Witte i revolutsiya 1905–1907 gg. v Rossii," in T.I. Zaslavskaya, ed., *Kuda idyot Rossiya? . . . Vlast, obshchestvo, lichnost* (Moscow: MVShSEN, 2000), 29–36, at 34.

124   *the hangman's noose*: To fight the revolutionary terrorists, who had bombed, among other targets, his own St. Petersburg residence, injuring his two children, Stolypin introduced military courts that were required to reach verdicts within forty-eight hours, without any right of appeal. In the eight months this system remained operative, up to 1,000 death sentences were handed down (Pipes, *The Russian Revolution*, 169–70).

125   *His father, Anatoly Afanasyevich*: Nikolay Svanidze and Marina Svanidze, *Medvedev* (St. Petersburg: Amfora, 2008), 110.

125   *Yuliya Venyaminovna, had studied Russian language*: When Medvedev ran for president in 2008, certain extreme nationalists tried to discredit him by claiming that he had Jewish ancestry on his mother's side. There is no evidence in the public record that this was, in fact, the case, and such claims are a common tactic of the anti-Semitic right, which has accused many other Russian leaders of having Jewish origins. Medvedev chose not to speak to this question directly, but he has said that he was baptized into the Orthodox Christian Church at the age of twenty-three. He has spoken out in favor of religious tolerance (see Angela Charlton, "Russian Extremist Seeks to Sully Presidential Favorite with Claim He Has Jewish Roots," Associated Press, Moscow, February 28, 2008).

125   *a "purposeful child"*: Larisa Kaftan, "Vera Smirnova, pervaya uchitelnitsa pervogo vitsepremyera: Dmitry byl bolshim pochemuchkoy," *Komsomolskaya Pravda*, December 11, 2007.

125   *racing off to do his homework*: Denis Yermakov, "Vitse sterty, kraski tuskly," *Moskovsky Komsomolyets*, November 18, 2005.

126   *the three Medvedevs would flee the dusty city*: Svanidze and Svanidze, *Medvedev*, 111.

126   *received a golden watch*: Svanidze and Svanidze, *Medvedev*, 113.

126   *In the second and third grades*: Svanidze and Svanidze, *Medvedev*, 204–5.

127   *stowing away with friends*: Gevorkyan et al., *Ot pervogo litsa*, 28–9.

127   *the music of Engelbert Humperdinck*: Svanidze and Svanidze, *Medvedev*, 128, 161. His musical tastes evolved from Engelbert Humperdinck to heavy metal rock bands such as Deep Purple and Black Sabbath.

127   *"without fanaticism"*: Andrey Vandenko, "Prostye istiny," *Itogi*, February 19, 2008.

127   *Medvedev dreamed of owning*: Vandenko, "Prostye istiny."

127   *"law (Recht) and other trash"*: Karl Marx, *Critique of the Gotha Programme* (London: Central Books Limited, 1978), Chapter 1.

127   *laws that served the working class*: Pipes, *The Russian Revolution*, 797.

128   *"political elasticity" of the law*: Robert Sharlet, "Stalinism and Soviet Legal Culture," in Robert C. Tucker, ed., *Stalinism: Essays in Historical Interpretation* (Piscataway, NJ: Transaction Publishers, 1998), 155–79.

129   *"I could tell you about the influence that Stalin's work"*: Svanidze and Svanidze, *Medvedev*, 136.

129   *"Soviet law proclaims democracy"*: Olimpiad S. Ioffe, *Soviet Law and Soviet Reality* (Boston: Kluwer, 1985), 1.

129   *Back in St. Petersburg*: Medvedev says that in January 2000, at his suggestion, Putin, who had attended Ioffe's lectures in the 1970s, sent the professor a telegram to congratulate him on his eightieth birthday (Svanidze and Svanidze, *Medvedev*, 135).

129   *something of a dissident*: Anton Ivanov, "Anatoly Sobchak—prepodavatel," in Olga Guseva, ed., *Anatoly Sobchak: kakim on byl* (Moscow: Gamma-Press, 2007), 106–7.

130   *"political conversations and jokes"*: Svanidze and Svanidze, *Medvedev*, 134.

130   *correct, diplomatic in argument*: Svanidze and Svanidze, *Medvedev*, 42–43, offers accounts of fellow student Marina Lavrikova and Professor Yury Tolstoy.

130   *a positive example*: Ilya Yeliseyev, quoted in Svanidze and Svanidze, *Medvedev*.

130   *"public and not private law"*: quoted in Piers Beirne, *Revolution in Law: Contributions to the Development of Soviet Legal Theory, 1917–1938* (Armonk, NY: M.E. Sharpe, 1990), 78.

130   *slowed down Medvedev's graduate career*: Svanidze and Svanidze, *Medvedev*, 38–39.

130   *"No one wins an election singlehandedly"*: Anatoly Sobchak, *For a New Russia* (New York: The Free Press, 1992), 15.

131 *"drunk with the air of freedom"*: Svanidze and Svanidze, *Medvedev*, 217.

131 *on an old mimeograph machine*: Owen Matthews and Anna Nemtsova, "From a Mouse to a Tsar," *Newsweek*, March 3, 2008, www.newsweek.com/id/114679.

131 *co-authored a three volume textbook*: Larisa Kaftan, "Kak Kozak borolsya s pyanstvom, a Medvedev gruzil snaryady. Studencheskie bayki," *Komsomolskaya Pravda*, December 14, 2005.

131 *"strict, but not harsh"*: Nataliya Shatikhina, quoted in Svanidze and Svanidze, *Medvedev*, 160.

131 *comments in Latin*: Svanidze and Svanidze, *Medvedev*, 158.

131 *dilapidated couch*: Svanidze and Svanidze, *Medvedev*, 169.

131 *Russia's early democratic politics*: Viktor Rezunkov, "Karyera Dmitriya Medvedeva," Vremya Gosti, Radio Svoboda, February 6, 2008.

132 *"having seen the Putin style"*: Quoted in Darya Pylnova and Dmitry Shkrylev, "Zanimatelny Medvedev," *Novaya Gazeta*, December 14, 2007.

132 *mistook him for the receptionist*: Alan Cullison, Gregory White, and David Crawford, "The Leningrad Enigma: In Putin's Past, Glimpses of Russia's Hardline Future," *Wall Street Journal*, December 21, 2007; Matthews and Nemtsova, "From a Mouse to a Tsar."

132 *"It was then that I first visited"*: Svanidze and Svanidze, *Medvedev*, 212.

132 *"I was free and helped them"*: Svanidze and Svanidze, *Medvedev*, 172.

132 *half a billion dollars*: *Ekspert* database, www.expert.ru/ratings/, revenues for 2000.

132 *sixth largest timber reserves*: Company website, at www.ilimpulru/about-company/business-profile/, June 2009.

132 *own 20 percent of it*: According to Russia's Accounting Chamber, the state auditing agency, as of September 1994 IPE was owned by a Swiss company Intertsez (40 percent), the Ust Ilim works (10 percent), the Kotlassky Cellulose and Paper Combine (10 percent), and a private firm Fintsell (40 percent). Fintsell, registered in December 1993, belonged to three entrepreneurs in the lumber business—Zakhar Smushkin (21.25 percent), Boris Zingarevich (21.25 percent), and Mikhail Zingarevich (7.5 percent)—and to Dmitry Medvedev (50 percent). Thus, Medvedev owned 50 percent of 40 percent—or 20 percent—of IPE. See V.S. Sokolov, "Otchet Schetnoy Palaty 'O rezultatakh proverki zakonnosti prodazhi Rossiyskim fondom federalnogo imushchestva v 1994 godu paketa aktsii Kotlasskogo tsellyulozno-bumazhnogo kombinata zakrytomu aktsionernomu obshchestvu "Ilim Palp Enterprayz" i realizatsii investitsionnoy programmy ukazannym obshchestvom," *Byulleten Schetnoy Palaty* 7, no. 31 (2000), www.ach.gov.ru/user-files/bulletins/8-buleten_doc_files-fl-315.pdf. Medevedev has acknowledged that he owned a stake in the company (Svanidze and Svanidze, *Medvedev*, 173).

132 *assessed by auditors at $400 million*: Vladimir Pronin, "600 dney lesnoy voiny: 'Bazovy Element' protiv 'Ilim Palp Enterprayz'," *Sliyaniya i pogloshcheniya* 5–6 (2003), 46–59, at 51, www.ma-journal.ru/archive_new/articles/1166.

133 *worth $300 million*: Andrey Litvinov, Ilya Zhegulev, and Aleksandr Gordeyev, "Tretim budet. Rossiysky biznes mozhet ne dozhdatsya milostey ot Dmitriya

Medvedeva," *SmartMoney*, December 17, 2007, www.vedomosti.ru/smartmoney/article/2007/12/17/4640.

133 *has said that he sold all his shares*: Svanidze and Svanidze, *Medvedev*, 173.

133 *invest about $77 million in fixed capital*: That is, 180 billion rubles, at an average exchange rate for September 1994, the month of the auction, of 2,350 R/$.

133 *less than one percent of the required investment*: The report concluded that of a required investment of 180 billion rubles in 1994–1997 in fixed capital for the enterprise, a total of 0.83 billion rubles was actually invested in fixed capital by IPE. In order to give the appearance that the conditions had been fulfilled, money had been wired into the enterprise's account, but then withdrawn again on the same day. The report noted numerous other irregularities in the privatization of the enterprise. See Sokolov, "Otchet Schetnoy Palaty."

133 *"These days one can get mad"*: Svanidze and Svanidze, *Medvedev*, 174–75.

134 *Medvedev was seconded*: Pronin, "600 dney," 51.

134 *a Bratsk deputy prosecutor*: "Bratskomu sprutu prishchemili shchupaltse," *Argumenty i Fakty*, June 9, 2004.

134 *Some referred to rumors*: Igor Stepanov, "Kak tikhy Medvedev prevratilsya v materogo politicheskogo volka," *Sobesednik*, January 21, 2008.

134 *Others saw in Medvedev's hasty departure*: Irina Vyunova, "Kremlyevsky vizir," *Profil*, November 17, 2003.

135 *like Snickers or Tampax*: AFP, "Putin Compares Election TV Spots to Tampax Ads," Moscow, March 8, 2000.

135 *"It was a test of strength"*: Svanidze and Svanidze, *Medvedev*, 222.

135 *"a quick learner"*: Natalya Gevorkyan, "Ne budet nikakoy uzurpatsii vlasti prezidenta," *Kommersant*, February 19, 2008.

135 *"He is capable of smooth talking"*: Nikolay Petrov, quoted in Alex Nicholson, "Medvedev Was Waiting in the Wings," *Moscow Times*, November 3, 2003.

135 *economic advisor Andrey Illarionov*: Anatoly Medetsky, "Medvedev Would Tip Scales in Gazprom's Favor," *Moscow Times*, December 17, 2007.

135 *increasing judges' salaries*: RIA Novosti, "Judges Salaries Set to Increase Again," Moscow, February 1, 2005.

135 *Kremlin's 2003 attempt at administrative reform*: OECD, *Economic Surveys: Russian Federation* (Paris: OECD, 2006), 125–28.

135 *"all people, irrespective of their posts"*: RIA Novosti, "The New Chief of Administration Interviewed on Rossiya TV Channel," Moscow, November 3, 2003.

135 *Kremlin-connected political consultants*: Nikolai Petrov and Andrei Ryabov, "Russia's Role in the Orange Revolution," in Anders Åslund and Michael McFaul, eds., *Revolution in Orange* (Washington, DC: Carnegie Foundation, 2006), 145–64, at 151.

136 *grew from $7 billion to $244 billion*: This is the change from the end of 2000 to the end of 2007, from the *Ekspert* database, www.expert.ru/ratings.

137 *investigated by the U.S. Justice Department's Organized Crime Unit*: Glenn Simpson, "U.S. Probes Possible Crime Links to Russian Natural-Gas Deals," *Wall Street*

Journal, December 22, 2006; Lynn Berry, "Russia Slaps Tax Evasion Charges on Suspected Crime Boss Sought by FBI," Associated Press, Moscow, January 30, 2008.

137 *Chuychenko earned $12.5 million*: Marina Tsvetkova, Yevgeniya Pismennaya, and Aleksey Nikolsky, "Kremlyevskie bogachi," *Vedomosti*, April 10, 2009.

137 *Valeriya Adamova, served as vice president of Sibur*: Henry Meyer, "Medvedev May Tap Leningrad Grads to Build Power Base," Bloomberg, February 27, 2008.

137 *Ilya Yeliseyev served as deputy CEO*: Gazprom-Media's website at www.gazprom-media.com, June 16, 2009. Same source for Anton Ivanov.

137 *When Valery Musin*: Gazprom's website at http://www.gazprom.com/management/directors/musin/, June 30, 2009.

137 *Ruslan Linkov, an old acquaintance*: Rezunkov, "Karyera Dmitriya Medvedeva."

138 *too low to fuel a breakthrough*: Iika Korhonen, Seija Lainela, Heli Simola, Laura Solanko and Pekka Sutela, *The Challenges of the Medvedev Era* (Helsinki: Bank of Finland, 2008), 14–15.

138 *"little islands of support"*: Maria Levina, "National Projects Under Crisis Watch," *Moscow Times*, November 14, 2008.

138 *53 percent of Russians*: Levada Center, *Obshchestvennoe Mnenie 2008*, www.levada.ru, 53.

138 *quietly disbanded*: Anatoly Medetsky, "National Projects Moved to Back Seat," *Moscow Times*, March 10, 2009.

138 *"Dmitry Anatolyevich, have you been consulted"*: Andrey Kolesnikov, "Independent Politicians Nominate Medvedev," *Kommersant*, December 11, 2007.

138 *"I am confident that he will be"*: Interfax, *Russia & CIS Business and Financial Newswire*, February 14, 2008. Medvedev was also beating Ivanov in hypothetical matchups in the polls (see Chapter 7).

139 *a large suite had been renovated*: Konstantin Gaaze and Mikhail Fishman, "Sluzhili dva tovarishcha," *Russky Newsweek*, December 24, 2008.

139 *"as if by mistake"*: Kolesnikov, *Razdvoenie V.V.P.*, 272.

139 *"Freedom is better"*: Dmitry Medvedev, speech to the Fifth Krasnoyarsk Economic Forum, February 15, 2008, at http://www.medvedev2008.ru/performance_2008_02_15.htm.

140 *"to overcome legal nihilism"*: Ilya Barabanov, "Luchshaya rol vtorogo plana," *New Times*, May 11, 2009.

140 *"We are all legal nihilists"*: Svanidze and Svanidze, *Medvedev*, 46.

140 *One Yukos lawyer*: TASS, "Ex-Yukos Lawyer Granted Early Conditional Release," Moscow, April 21, 2009; "Aleksanyan Discharged from Hospital," *Russia & CIS General Newswire*, January 16, 2009.

140 *One much-criticized judge*: "Fired Judge Loses Appeal," *Moscow Times*, June 10, 2009.

140 *eliminated the use of juries*: Peter Solomon, "Can President Medvedev Fix the Courts in Russia? The First Year," *Russian Analytical Digest* 59, no. 5 (2009).

140 *Special police units*: Konstantin Gaaze and Aleksandr Raskin, "Sledstvie vedut svoyaki," *Russky Newsweek*, September 15, 2008.

140 *monitoring and harassing the political opposition*: Irina Pavlova, "Who is Mr. Medvedev?" *Grani.ru*, May 27, 2009.

140 *"harsh, depraved, and aggressive"*: Svanidze and Svanidze, *Medvedev*, 138; Nabi Abdullaev, "Commission to Guard Against False History," *Moscow Times*, May 20, 2009; RIA Novosti, "Russia Sets Up Commission to Prevent Falsification of History," May 19, 2009.

141 *unlawful "raiding"*: "D. Medvedev prizval zhestko karat za reyderstvo," *Vedomosti*, February 27, 2008.

141 *Raiding continued*: Olga Kryshtanovskaya, director of the Center for Elite Studies of the Russian Academy of Sciences, singled out Deputy Premier Igor Sechin as the champion of such raiding. "He is the state's main raider," she told *The New York Times* in December. "He organizes these raider seizures, sometimes to the benefit of the state, or sometimes to the benefit of companies that are friendly to him" (Clifford J. Levy, "In Hard Times, Russia Tries to Reclaim Industries," *New York Times*, December 8, 2008).

141 *poor husbands of rich wives*: Barabanov, "Luchshaya rol vtorogo plana."

141 *"these Potemkin declarations"*: Owen Matthews and Anna Nemtsova, "Medvedev's Moscow Spring," *Newsweek*, May 4, 2009.

141 *declared ownership of one Moscow apartment*: Anna Malpas, "Medvedev and Putin Declare Their Earnings," *Moscow Times*, April 7, 2009, 1–2. President's income and wealth declaration, at http://www.kremlin.ru/eng/text/news/2009/04/214779.shtml.

141 *"The state bureaucracy is guided"*: Dmitry Medvedev, "Message to the Federal Assembly of the Russian Federation," November 5, 2008, at www.kremlin.ru/appears/2008/11/05/1349_type63372type63374type63381type82634_208749.shtml.

142 *stifling media freedom*: See Mikhail Fishman and Konstantin Gaaze, "Efir dlya dvoikh," *Russky Newsweek*, August 4, 2008, http://www.runewsweek.ru/country/9021/.

142 *"Experience has shown that"*: Dmitry Medvedev, "Message to the Federal Assembly," November 5, 2008.

142 *Medvedev would "recommend to judges"*: Vandenko, "Prostye istiny."

142 *"a free society of free people"*: Viktor Martyanov, "Zhidky terminator novogo pokoleniya."

142 *"someone in epaulettes"*: Vladimir Putin, "Poslanie Federalnomu Sobraniyu Rossiyskoy Federatsii," Moscow, April 25, 2005, http://www.kremlin.ru/appears/2005/04/25/1223_type63372type63374type82634_87049.shtml.

142 *"There is no Problem No. 1"*: Andrew McChesney, "A Private Lunch with Medvedev," *Moscow Times*, June 7, 2006. Of course, he would not have wanted at this point to seem critical of Putin, but he could still have indicated some general directions. Even Putin acknowledged there was more to do.

143 *"I just hope he doesn't spoil anything!"*: Svanidze and Svanidze, *Medvedev*, 246.

143 *Medvedev's people had tried*: Gaaze and Fishman, "Sluzhili dva tovarishcha." It is another question whether the particular reforms they chose—for instance, the

planned reorganization of the law enforcement system—would have had a significant, positive impact on the quality of government.

143 *privatize the state-owned*: Fishman and Gaaze, "Efir dlya dvoikh."

144 *"His main strength"*: Catrina Stewart, Anna Smolchenko, and Miriam Elder, "Investors Breathe a Sigh of Relief," *Moscow Times*, December 11, 2007.

144 *If the Duma refused three times*: Article 111 of the Russian Constitution.

145 *"That has engendered confidence"*: Leonid Velekhov, "Prioritety i avtoritety," *Sovershenno Sekretno* 3 (2008), 3–6.

146 *the former president was maneuvering*: See Vitaly Yaroshevsky, "The 'Chancellor' Version," *Novaya Gazeta*, August 11, 2008, interview with Olga Kryshtanovskaya. Nikolay Patrushev moved from FSB head to chair of the Security Council, a largely advisory position; Viktor Ivanov left the Kremlin to lead the drug control agency; Sergey Ivanov remained first deputy prime minister; Igor Sechin, while made a deputy prime minister, lost his previous role as gatekeeper to the president.

146 *tired and bored*: Pavel Sedakov, Mikhail Fishman, and Konstantin Gaaze, "Vlast yemu k litsu," *Russky Newsweek*, May 12, 2008.

146 *"We're in challenging times."*: David Cho and Neil Irwin, "Crises of Confidence in the Markets; Federal Reserve's Rescue of Bear Stearns Exposes Cracks in Financial System," *Washington Post*, March 18, 2008.

147 *Nor did they have much direct exposure*: World Bank, *Russian Economic Report*, November 2008, 17.

147 *"island of stability"*: Russia Today, "Russia is an 'Island of Stability': Finance Minister," January 24, 2008, http://www.russiatoday.ru/Business/2008-01-24/Russia_ is_an_island_of_stability_Finance_Minister.html.

147 *Russia's current account surpluses*: calculated from EBRD Current Account Balance Database, at http://www.ebrd.com/country/sector/econo/stats/index.htm, downloaded June 1, 2009.

147 *contained $157 billion*: Ministry of Finance of the Russian Federation, www1. minfin.ru/ru/stabfund/statistics/volume/, accessed June 17, 2009.

147 *"like a slave in the galleys"*: *Rossiyskaya Gazeta*, February 14, 2008, http://www. rg.ru/2008/02/14/putin-rezultaty-anons.html.

147 *"Everything happening now"*: Agence France Presse, "US 'Irresponsibility' Sparked Financial Crisis: Putin," October 1, 2008.

147 *"The authorities in that country"*: Russia Today, "Putin Looks Forward to Positive Relations with the US," December 4, 2008, www.russiatoday.com/Top_News/2008-12-04/Putin_looks_forward_to_positive_relations_with_US.html?page=70.

147 *forced to pay higher interest rates*: Denis Maternovsky, "Hedge Funds Foment Russia Credit Crunch With 16% Puts," Bloomberg, May 28, 2008.

148 *"the only financiers visiting"*: Melissa Akin, "Corporate Debt No Longer Russia's Achilles Heel," Reuters, January 21, 2009.

148 *to prevent hysterical selling*: World Bank, *Russian Economic Report*, 22.

148 *MICEX stock index fell 17.5 percent*: Jason Bush, "Behind the Russian Stock Market Meltdown," *Business Week*, September 17, 2008.

148 *RTS share index fell by 78 percent*: World Bank, *Russian Economic Report*, 18.

148 *threatened to send Zyuzin a "doctor"*: *Economist*, "Mechel Bashing," July 31, 2008.

149 *The price of Urals crude*: Data from the U.S. Energy Information Administration, at http://tonto.eia.doe.gov/dnav/pet/hist/wepcuralsw.htm.

149 *Russia's stock slide*: Between June 1, 2008 and March 1, 2009, the fall in stock indexes in a few emerging markets was: 78 percent (RTSI, Russia), 57 percent (Kuwait Stock Exchange market index, Kuwait), 50 percent (Ibovespa, Brazil), 46 percent (BSE Sensex, India), 46 percent (IPC, Mexico), 39 percent (SSE Composite, China). My calculations from data of the various stock exchanges.

149 *Industrial production fell*: Goskomstat Rossii, information downloaded, December 2009, http://www.gks.ru/bgd/free/B04_03/IssWWW.exe/Stg/d02/83.htm; http://www.gks.ru/bgd/free/B09_00/IssWWW.exe/Stg/d04/6-0.htm; http://www.gks.ru/bgd/free/b04_03/IssWWW.exe/Stg/d02/93.htm.

149 *provided $50 billion*: Sergei Balashov, "Every Banker for Himself: While Businesses Must Now Swim on Their Own, the Government Is Reluctant to Economize on Social Spending," *Russia Profile*, May 27, 2009.

149 *AvtoVAZ received a Loan*: RIA Novosti, "Putin Instructs Government to Extend $806 Million Loan to AvtoVaz," June 4, 2009; RIA Novosti, "Aluminum Giant RusAl Confirms $4.5 bln Loan from VEB," November 5, 2008.

149 *To prevent bank runs*: Reuters, "Russia Cuts Banks' Deposit Insurance Burden," Moscow, September 23, 2008.

149 *prop up the market by buying shares*: Ira Iosebashvili, "Medvedev Slams State Stock Purchase," *Moscow Times*, May 6, 2009.

149 *the government's various stimulus measures*: Zeljko Bogetic, "Russia: Reform After the Great Recession," Carnegie Moscow Center, March 20, 2010, http://carnegieendowment.org/publications; Reuters, "Factbox: How US Stimulus Plan Ranks Against Other Programs," February 13, 2009.

150 *Georgian forces began bombarding*: C.J. Chivers and Ellen Barry, "Georgia Claims on Russia War Called into Question," *New York Times*, November 7, 2008.

151 *"should be chopped up"*: Quoted in Robert English, "Georgia: The Ignored History," *New York Review of Books*, November 6, 2008. See also Stephen Jones, "Georgia: The Trauma of Statehood," in Ian Bremmer and Ray Taras, eds., *New States, New Politics: Building the Post-Soviet Nations* (New York: Cambridge University Press, 1997), 505–44, at 512.

151 *500 or 600 people died*: Christopher Zürcher, *The Post-Soviet Wars: Rebellion, Ethnic Conflict, and Nationhood in the Caucasus* (New York: NYU Press, 2007), 152.

151 *For twelve years*: International Crisis Group, *Georgia's South Ossetia Conflict: Make Haste Slowly*, Crisis Group Europe Report 183, June 7, 2007, 1.

151 *"Georgia . . . will restore its wholeness"*: Steve Gutterman, "Georgia Leader Starts Inauguration Weekend," Associated Press, Gelati, Georgia, January 24, 2004.

151 *"the unification and strengthening of Georgia"*: Agence France Presse, "Saakashvili

Vows to Steer Georgia Westward at Inauguration," January 25, 2004.

151 *retrained and reequipped the Georgian army*: Agence France Presse, "NATO Aspirant Georgia Boosts Military Budget," September 26, 2007.

151 *South Ossetians held a referendum*: Simon Saradzhyan, "S. Ossetians Strongly Back Independence," *Moscow Times*, November 14, 2006.

151 *Tbilisi sent security forces*: International Crisis Group, *Abkhazia Today*, Crisis Group Europe Report 176, September 15, 2006, 19–22.

152 *issued Russian citizenship*: RIA Novosti, "South Ossetia Conflict FAQs," September 17, 2008, http://en.rian.ru/russia/20080917/116929528.html.

152 *about 12,000*: Ralf Beste et al., "Did Saakashvili Lie? The West Begins to Doubt the Georgian Leader," *Der Spiegel* (English Edition), September 15, 2008.

152 *they did not hear outgoing missiles*: Peter Finn, "A Two-Sided Descent Into Full-Scale War," *Washington Post*, August 17, 2001; Chivers and Barry, "Georgia Claims on Russia War." It is still possible that some of the Georgian villages were being shelled from somewhere else.

152 *shot Grad BM-21 rockets*: Finn, "A Two-Sided Descent." Finn quotes the Georgian Defense Minister Davit Kezerashvili on the use of Grad BM-21s. Catherine Belton, "Tskhinvali Bears Scars of Military Maelstrom," *Financial Times*, August 18, 2008. Saakashvili said he had "strictly ordered" the troops not to fire on civilians ("Saakashvili's Account of Events that Led to Conflict," Civil Georgia, August 25, 2008, http://www.civil.ge/eng/article.php?id=19282).

152 *Two of the Russian peacekeepers*: European Union, *Independent International Fact-Finding Mission on the Conflict in Georgia Report*, vol. 1, 2009, 21, www.ceiig.ch/Report.html; Chivers and Barry, "Georgia Claims on Russia War"; Uwe Klussmann, "Georgian Tanks vs. Ossetian Teenagers," *Der Spiegel* (English Edition), August 26, 2008; Peter Finn, "For South Ossetians, Bitterness Follows Attacks; Residents of Separatist Zone Describe Georgian Assault That Destroyed Houses and Apartment Buildings Across Their Capital," *Washington Post*, August 17, 2008.

152 *The next morning, a column of Russian troops*: The Georgians initially said the Russians had moved into Georgia in the morning of August 8, after their own attack on Tskhinvali had begun (see statement of Georgian representative to the U.N. Security Council, August 8, 2008, minutes are at www.undemocracy.com/5_PV_5952.pdf). Later they changed their story, claiming that Russian troops had begun driving through the Roki Tunnel at 11:30 p.m. on the previous night. Georgian intelligence released a taped phone conversation between sentries at the tunnel purporting to show that some Russian armored vehicles had passed through the tunnel even before that, before dawn on August 7. The Russians said that this was just a small, routine rotation of peacekeeping forces. Western intelligence analysts interviewed by *Der Spiegel* believed that Russian troops had begun moving through the Roki Tunnel only around 11 a.m. on August 8 (Beste et al., "Did Saakashvili Lie?"). The EU fact-finding mission reported in September 2009 that Georgian claims of a large-scale Russian incursion into South Ossetia

before the Georgian offensive "could not be substantiated" (European Union, *Independent International Fact-Finding Mission on the Conflict in Georgia*, 23).

153 *South Ossetian militias marauded*: Bruno Waterfield, "Georgians Still Fear Life in the Russian 'Zone,'" *Daily Telegraph*, September 19, 2008.

153 *a list of 365 Ossetians*: online at http://osetinfo.ru/spisok.

153 *Georgian authorities said 228 Georgian civilians*: European Union, *Independent International Fact-Finding Mission on the Conflict in Georgia Report*, 5.

153 *The Russian military said it lost forty-eight soldiers*: RIA Novosti, "Semi pogib-shikh v Yuzhnoy Osetii rossiyskikh voennykh poluchili po $100 tys." Moscow, February 10, 2009, http://www.rian.ru/defense_safety/20090210/161623452.html. Earlier, the military had put the number of Russian dead in the sixties (e.g., Interfax, "SKP ustanovil tochnoe chislo rossiyskikh voennykh, pogibshikh v Yuzhnoy Osetii," Moscow, September 11, 2008, http://www.interfax.ru/news.asp?id=32196&sec=1484.)

153 *the loss of 170 servicemen*: European Union, *Independent International Fact-Finding Mission on the Conflict in Georgia Report*, 5.

153 *Around 200,000 people were reportedly*: Amnesty International, *Civilians in the Line of Fire: The Georgia-Russia Conflict*, November 2008, 5; European Union, *Independent International Fact-Finding Mission on the Conflict in Georgia Report*, 5.

153 *Georgian defense minister assessed damage*: International Crisis Group, *Georgia: The Risks of Winter*, November 26, 2008, 9.

153 *Nazi invasion of the Czech Sudetenland*: Robert Kagan, "Putin Makes His Move," *Washington Post*, August 11, 2008.

154 *"unreconciled to the new map"*: David Miliband, "There Is No Such Thing as a Post-Soviet Space," *Moscow Times*, September 2, 2008.

154 *U.S. presidential candidate John McCain*: Agence France Presse, "McCain to Work with Russia, Won't Ignore 'Aggression,'" St. Paul, Minnesota, September 4, 2008.

154 *"Russia had to respond"*: Mikhail Gorbachev, "A Path to Peace in the Caucasus," *Washington Post*, August 12, 2008.

154 *flying more than 38,000 missions*: Anthony H. Cordesman, *The Lessons and Non-Lessons of the Air and Missile Campaign in Kosovo* (Santa Barbara: Praeger, 2001), 56–58.

154 *the* New York Times *had to retreat*: On August 11, the newspaper reported: "Vladimir V. Putin, who came to office brooding over the wounds of a humiliated Russia, this week offered proof of its resurgence. So far, the West has been unable to check his thrust into Georgia. He is making decisions that could redraw the map of the Caucasus in Russia's favor" (Ellen Barry, "Russia, and Putin, Assert Authority," *New York Times*, August 11, 2008). Then, on November 7: "Newly available accounts by independent military observers of the beginning of the war between Georgia and Russia this summer call into question the longstanding Georgian assertion that it was acting defensively against separatist and Russian aggression. Instead, the accounts suggest that Georgia's inexperienced military attacked the isolated separatist capital of Tskhinvali on Aug. 7 with indiscriminate artillery

and rocket fire, exposing civilians, Russian peacekeepers and unarmed monitors to harm" (Chivers and Barry, "Georgia Claims on Russia War").

154 *about 160 American military advisers*: Manfred Ertel et al., "Road to War in Georgia," *Der Spiegel* (English Edition), August 25, 2008.

155 *Condoleezza Rice*: U.S. Department of State, "Remarks with Georgian President Mikheil Saakashvili," Tbilisi, Georgia, July 10, 2008, at http://merln.ndu.edu/archivepdf/EUR/state/106912.pdf; *Russia & CIS General Newswire*, "Rice meets head of 'provisional Tskhinvali authorities' at reception in Tbilisi," July 10, 2008; Dan Eggen, "Cheney To Visit Georgia Next Week; Ukraine, Azerbaijan Also on Itinerary," *Washington Post*, August 26, 2008.

155 *74 percent of Russians*: Levada Center, at http://www.levada.ru/press/2008082100.html.

155 *"constant reorganizations improve nothing"*: Vladimir Putin, "Pochemu trudno uvolit cheloveka," *Russky Pioner*, May 28, 2009.

155 *overwhelmed by a burst of nationalism*: Gaaze and Fishman, "Sluzhili dva tovarishcha."

156 *needed to borrow a satellite phone*: Aleksandr Raskin and Konstantin Gaaze, "Brigadny podryad," *Russky Newsweek*, November 1, 2008.

156 *Medvedev got quick consent*: Raskin and Gaaze, "Brigadny podryad."

156 *"emotional center"*: Mikhail Fishman, "Nas khotyat vsyekh ubit," *Russky Newsweek*, September 1, 2008.

156 *Washington's "selfish" and "unilateral" approach*: Ellen Barry and Sonia Kishkovsky, "Russia May Deploy Missiles to Baltic, Medvedev Says," *New York Times*, November 5, 2008.

156 *"We should admit"*: Iosebashvili, "Medvedev Slams State Stock Purchase."

157 *jet engine producer NPO Saturn*: Anna Smolchenko, "Crisis Opens Door to Reprivatization," *Moscow Times*, November 18, 2008.

157 *Amur Shipbuilding Plant, renationalized*: RIA Novosti, "United Shipbuilding Corp. to Get Controlling Stake in Amur Plant," May 11, 2009.

157 *"they are not little girls"*: Reuters, "Yakunin Urges State to Buy Weak Firms," July 1, 2009.

157 *the whole event had been staged*: Darya Guseva, Artyom Vernidub, and Nadezhda Ivanitskaya, "Na Deripasovskoy khoroshaya pogoda," *Russky Newsweek*, June 8, 2009.

157 *an extra $8.1 million*: "Putin Has Pikalevo Jumping, Money Flying," *Moscow News*, June 5, 2009.

158 *On June 24, he leapt up*: See the good account of Putin's trip in Adrian Blomfield, "Vladimir Putin Humiliates Russian Supermarket Chiefs over Expensive Sausages," *Daily Telegraph*, June 25, 2009. Film of the visit is also available at http://www.youtube.com/watch?v=EtSRdqszT5Q.

159 *closed down the country's casinos*: Clifford Levy, "Exiled by Russia: Casinos and Jobs," *New York Times*, June 28, 2009.

159 *The idea suddenly appeared in Medvedev's speech*: Gaaze and Fishman, "Sluzhili dva tovarishcha."

159 *twenty-one changes of prime minister in thirty-five years*: Government of Italy website at http://www.governo.it/Governo/Governi/governi.html. I refer to the thirty-five years from 1946 to 1981.

160 "*one-and-a-half party system*": Many Russian analysts have noted this apparent course of development. In 2004, the politician and political scientist Vladimir Lysenko predicted that a one-and-a-half party system would emerge four years later, with United Russia, led by Putin, dominating parliament, flanked by the rump Communist Party (comments at Seminar on "Proposals for Transition to a Proportional Electoral System and the Prospects for Multi-partisanship in Russia," Moscow Carnegie Center, May 24, 2004, www.carnegie.ru/en/pubs/media/70524.htm, downloaded April 2, 2009). See also Vladimir Mau, "Politics vs. Economics: Economic and Political Challenges in Russia in 2003," *Russia in Global Affairs*, February 18, 2004.

160 *Every year from 1945 to 1975*: Angus Maddison, *The World Economy: Historical Statistics* (Paris: OECD, 2003); GDP per capita measured in dollars.

160 *Riot police had to be flown to Vladivostok*: "Moscow Riot Police Flown in to Smash Protests against Car Tariffs in Vladivostok," *The Times* (London), December 22, 2008.

160 *a similar demonstration*: Brian Whitmore, "Kremlin Stumbles in Regions as Unrest Mounts," Radio Free Europe/Radio Liberty, February 16, 2010.

160 *In a scathing interview*: Dmitry Bulin, "Torzhestvo plyuralizma," *Politichesky klass*, May 21–June 6, 2009.

162 *Surkovs, Markovs, and Zubkovs*: Vladislav Surkov remained first deputy chief of the presidential administration under Medvedev; Sergey Markov was an advisor to the Kremlin and Duma member; Viktor Zubkov, a former prime minister, was in 2010 a deputy prime minister. All three were Putin loyalists.

CHAPTER 5: THE UNRAVELING

163 *cost 15 million lives*: Unless otherwise noted, all casualty estimates come from Micheal Clodfelter, *Warfare and Armed Conflicts: A Statistical Reference to Casualty and Other Figures, 1500–2000*, 2nd Edition (Jefferson, NC: McFarland, 2001). These are mostly conservative estimates.

163 *In Bosnia-Herzegovina*: U.S. Department of State, *Bosnia and Herzegovina Country Report on Human Rights Practices for 1996* (Washington, DC: U.S. State Department, 1997); Balkan Investigative Reporting Network, "Justice Report: Bosnia's Book of the Dead," June 21, 2007, http://birn.eu.com/en/88/10/3377/. The one major exception—a multiethnic state that disintegrated with almost no violence—was Czechoslovakia. For many reasons the likelihood of violence as the Soviet Union came apart seemed far greater.

163 *Valery Tishkov puts total deaths*: Valery Tishkov, "Ethnic Conflicts in the Former USSR: The Use and Misuse of Typologies and Data," *Journal of Peace Research* 36 (1999): 571–91, at 578.

164 *10,000 strategic nuclear weapons*: Anthony H. Cordesman, *Western Military Balance and Defense Efforts* (Washington, DC: CSIS, 2002).

164 *Twenty-five million ethnic Russians*: For ethnic Russian and Russian-speaking populations as of the 1989 Census, see Igor Zevelev, *Russia and Its New Diasporas* (Washington, DC: U.S. Institute of Peace, 2001), 96–97. "Beached diaspora" is David Laitin's phrase.

164 *"learning Iroquois"*: David Laitin, *Identity in Formation: The Russian-Speaking Populations in the Near Abroad* (Ithaca: Cornell University Press, 1998), 85.

164 *had not been predicted*: Except by some who gave the wrong date, or none at all, and the wrong reasons. An exiled Soviet writer, Andrey Amalrik, wrote that the USSR would be torn apart in a war with China in 1984. Hélène Carrère d'Encausse, an eminent scholar of Soviet nationalities, thought the Muslims of Central Asia would rise up. Many, of course, saw growing strains in the Soviet system that increased the odds of crises in future decades. In 1986, the sociologist Randall Collins published a perceptive account of Soviet overextension and vulnerability to ethnic protest, but was wisely imprecise in his predictions, saying only that "precipitous losses of territorial power" might occur "within the next thirty years" (Randall Collins, *Weberian Sociological Theory* [New York: Cambridge University Press, 1986], 187). My point is not to belittle social scientists who failed to predict the date of Soviet disintegration. My point is that they were *right* not to make such a prediction. There was no solid basis on which to make one.

165 *the more puzzling question*: To be precise, in this chapter I seek to explain not so much why the Soviet Union disintegrated as why it disintegrated *when it did*. There were many reasons to think it would come to end at some point in the next few decades—the chronic economic problems discussed in Chapter 6, growing disillusion with the official ideology, the inhospitable climate for empires in the late twentieth century, to name a few. But, as with humans, it is easier to predict a declining state's eventual mortality than to identify in advance the year and particular cause of death.

165 *The Ukrainians were the first to arrive*: Sources for this section include: V.T. Loginov, ed., *Soyuz mozhno bylo sokhranit*, 2nd Edition (Moscow: AST, 2007); Boris Yeltsin, *The Struggle*; Andrey Kozyrev, *Preobrazhenie* (Moscow: Mezhdunarodnie Otnosheniya, 1994), 168–87; Andrey Lobanov, "Shushkevich: Belovezhskie soglasheniya byli podpisany na trezvuyu golovu," *Belorusskie Novosti*, November 30, 2006; Olga Tomashevskaya, "Ekonomicheskie problemy nevozmozhno reshit bez politicheskikh," *Vremya novostey*, December 7, 2006; Sergey Shakhray, "Raspad Soyuza SSR: mify i fakty," *Argumenty nedeli*, December 10, 2006; Yury Zaynashev, "Belovezhskaya Pushcha: chto eto bylo?" *Novye Izvestia*, December 8, 2006; Mechislav Dmukhovsky, "Belovezhskie tayny," *Sovetskaya Belorussiya: Sobesednik*, December 12, 2003; Lyudmila Maslyukova, "Za pominalny stol po Sovetskomu Soyuzu selo 45 chelovek," *Sovetskaya Belorussiya*, December 8, 2001. Where accounts differ on the details, I have used the one supported by more independent observers or participants in the events.

165 *Yeltsin posed, for the sake of propriety, the question*: In one interview (in Loginov, *Soyuz mozhno bylo sokhranit*, 440), Kravchuk remembers this conversation as occurring on the morning of the 8th. However, he must be confusing this with the previous evening, since it would have been absurd for the three leaders to charge their aides with drafting an agreement on a new commonwealth of republics if they had not yet decided whether Gorbachev's Union Treaty could be acceptably revised. Others (e.g., Kozyrev, *Preobrazhenie*, 170–71) report this conversation as occurring on the first evening.

166 *three heads of state*: Burbulis, Yeltsin's first deputy prime minister, was the second to sign for Russia as Yeltsin had adopted the role of prime minister himself.

166 *hammer-and-sickle watch*: Loginov, *Soyuz mozhno bylo sokhranit*, 462.

166 *A man in a leather cap is walking*: I have retold this story, with slight condensation, from Yury Luzhkov, *Tayna gostinogo dvora: o gorode, o mire, o sebe* (Moscow: Olma Media Group, 2006), 145–46.

167 *"without even sobering up"*: According to the Russian ultra-nationalist Aleksandr Prokhanov: "In Belovezhskaya Pushcha, where everyone had been binge drinking for several days, Yeltsin, without even sobering up, finished off the Soviet Union." Quoted in "Kak otsenivaetsya rol vodki v istorii otechestva," *Profil*, May 16, 2005, www.profile.ru/items/?item=11502.

167 *a borrowed pen*: From the account of Valery Drozdov, a reporter who was present at the signing: "Finally, the main characters began to come out onto the stage. At that moment, everyone looked proud: they were changing the direction of history. One last obstacle remained. . . . I heard someone's irritated voice: "Where are the pens!" And then something unprintable. They set about borrowing them from anyone who had one. I gave my pen. After the signing, I did not see it again: one of the three put it in his pocket, by habit—I believe it was Yeltsin" (Maslyukova, "Za pominalny stol").

167 *planning to kidnap Kravchuk*: Kravchuk recalls this in Yaroslav Shapochka and Aleksandr Galukh, "Leonid Kravchuk: kogda Belovezhskie soglasheniya byli podpisany, Yeltsin pozvonil Bushu i skazal: 'Gospodin prezident, Sovetskogo Soyuza bolshe net'," *Fakty*, December 8, 2006.

167 *Vladimir Zhirinovsky, the ultranationalist*: Robin Lodge, "Duma Votes to Restore Soviet Union," *Moscow Times*, March 16, 1996.

167 *Only the Baltic republics*: Georgia withdrew from the CIS in August 2009, after the war with Russia. Turkmenistan changed its status to that of an associate member in 2005. Ukraine never formally ratified the CIS Charter, adopted in January 1993, but continued to participate in practice.

167 *"crazy conspiracy"*: Vitaly Tretyakov, "Aleksandr Solzhenitsyn: Sberezhenie naroda—vysshaya izo vsekh nashikh gosudarstvennykh zadach," *Moskovskie Novosti*, April 28, 2006.

167 *"a crime"*: Tatyana Ryabchikova, "Aleksandr Lukashenko: 15 let nazad proizoshlo prestuplenie," *Krymskaya Pravda*, December 7, 2006.

167 *"the greatest geopolitical catastrophe"*: Vladimir Putin's Annual Address to

the Federal Assembly, Moscow, April 25, 2005, http://www.kremlin.ru/appears/2005/04/25/1223_type63372type63374type82634_87049.shtml.

168 *recognized the Baltic states' independence*: In the case of the United States, what was recognized was the restoration of de facto independence, since independent statehood had been recognized since 1922.

168 *only seven of the fifteen republic leaders*: Ann Sheehy, "A Bankrupt System, Nationalism and Personal Ambitions," in Vera Tolz and Iain Elliot, eds., *The Demise of the USSR: From Communism to Independence* (London: Macmillan, 1995), 3–20.

168 *Soldiers' wages*: Gaidar, *Gibel imperii*, 405.

168 *preparing to issue their own currencies*: Gaidar, *Gibel imperii*, 348, 391.

168 *the Soviet state bank issued*: Gaidar, *Gibel imperii*, 402, 406.

169 *Ukraine had begun*: See Konstiantyn Morozov, *Above and Beyond: From Soviet General to Ukrainian State Builder* (Cambridge, MA: Harvard University Press, 2000); Taras Kuzio, *Ukraine: Perestroika to Independence*, 2nd Edition (New York: St Martin's Press, 2000), 190.

169 *The Baltic republics, Armenia*: Odom, *The Collapse*, 280–81.

169 *only about half the draftees*: Stephen Foye, "Student Deferments and Military Manpower Shortages," *Report on the USSR*, August 2, 1991, 5–8; Odom, *The Collapse*, 302.

169 *short by about 353,000 conscripts*: Odom, *The Collapse*, 296.

169 *"disorder, decay"*: Odom, *The Collapse*, 297.

169 *Marshal Shaposhnikov, was "convinced"*: Shaposhnikov, *Vybor*, 126–27.

169 *only 17 percent of Russian respondents*: Fakt 1991-11, VCIOM, November 10–20, 1991, 1,915 respondents, at http://sofist.socpol.ru.

169 *Yeltsin pushed vigorously*: Vadim Bakatin, a Gorbachev ally, writes that at a meeting of the State Council on September 16, he "was struck by the energetic position of Yeltsin, who in a well-argued but laconic way, getting right to the essence, called for the urgent signing of an economic agreement, a quick (by the end of September) conclusion of an agreement on food produce, and also the creation of an interrepublican economic committee" (Bakatin, *Izbavlenie*, 202–3).

170 *"as a heavy, oppressive silence"*: Yeltsin, *The Struggle*, 110.

170 *"The Russian President"*: Gorbachev, *Memoirs*, 658, 347, 580.

170 *"I was shocked"*: Official Kremlin International News Broadcast, December 21, 2001, "Press Conference with Mikhail Gorbachev."

170 *"It was an excellent winter evening"*: Boris Yeltsin, *The Struggle*, 111–16, and *Zapiski prezidenta*, 143–51.

171 *In one poll in late 1989*: Wyman, *Public Opinion*, 152–53. Although the number of respondents—387—is low, the result is consistent with other surveys.

171 *In mid-1991, a Times-Mirror survey*: Wyman, *Public Opinion*, 164.

172 *For instance, in a poll in mid 1990*: Wyman, *Public Opinion*, 157–58.

172 *150,000 Russians demonstrated*: Mark Kramer, "The Collapse of the Soviet Union: Introduction," *Journal of Cold War Studies* 5, no. 4 (2003): 6.

172 *In a December 1991 poll of 14 Russian cities*: Wyman, *Public Opinion*, 166.

172 *stimulated other republics to follow*: Henry Hale finds this in a statistical analysis

(see Henry Hale, "The Parade of Sovereignties: Testing Theories of Secession in the Soviet Setting," *British Journal of Political Science* 30 [2000)]: 31–56).

172 *907 to 13*: Carey Goldberg, "Russian Republic Passes Non-Binding Sovereignty Measure," Associated Press, June 12, 1990.

172 *"such an absurdity"*: Stanislav Shushkevich, "Monolog o pushche," *Ogonyok*, December 2, 1996.

173 *"with a roar of approval"*: Jeff Berliner, "Russian Parliament Approves New Commonwealth," UPI, Moscow, December 12, 1991. All fifteen of the Communist deputies participating voted to approve the Agreement (seven did not take part). See Vladimir Pribylovsky and Grigory Tochkin, "Kto i kak uprazdnil SSSR?" *Novaya Yezhednevnaya Gazeta*, December 21, 1994, at www.sssr.su/demons .html , and "10 Dekabrya 1991—rezultaty poimennogo golosovaniya deputatov Verkhovnogo Soveta Ukrainy," *Chetvyertaya Sessiya Verkhovnogo Soveta Ukrainy Dvenadtsatogo Sozyva*, Bulletin No. 45, 1991, 58–62.

173 *"No one decides anything"*: Bakatin, *Izbavlenie*, 220.

173 *too busy stealing*: Yegor Gaidar, *Days*, 65. On the apparatchiks' grab for power and property, see Steven L. Solnick, *Stealing the State: Control and Collapse in Soviet Institutions* (Cambridge, MA: Harvard University Press, 1998).

173 *deputies criticized Yeltsin for not moving faster*: Bakatin, *Izbavlenie*, 215.

173 *Bakatin, a Gorbachev ally*: Bakatin, *Izbavlenie*, 232.

173 *Boris Nemtsov, the reformist*: Boris Nemtsov, *Provintsial v Moskve* (Moscow: Vagrius, 1999), 244.

173 *Shaposhnikov, the CIS military commander*: Shaposhnikov, *Vybor*, 113.

174 *"the Russian president proved too spiteful"*: Kotkin, *Armageddon Averted*, 111–12.

175 *an anxious Gorbachev phoned Yeltsin*: Chernyaev, *1991 god*, 284.

175 *A wounded Volksgeist*: Nathan Gardels, "Two Concepts of Nationalism: An Interview with Isaiah Berlin," *New York Review of Books*, November 21, 1991.

176 *"a cauldron of long-simmering hatreds"*: The quote is from President Clinton, in U.S. Newswire, "Remarks by President at Naval Academy Graduation Ceremony," May 25, 1994.

176 *an expert on Lithuanian composers*: "The Man Who Is Playing for Time," *Time*, April 2, 1990.

176 *champion of Uzbek sovereignty, Islam Karimov*: For a good discussion, see Mark R. Beissinger, *Nationalist Mobilization and the Collapse of the Soviet State* (New York: Cambridge University Press, 2002), 258–60.

176 *Karimov had to get coaching*: Felix Corley, "Uzbekistan: Islam Karimov's Everlasting First Term," *Transitions*, October 1998.

176 *"secret Muslim"*: Bill Keller, "Soviet Turmoil: Provincial Communist is Born (Again) Free," *New York Times*, September 4, 1991.

176 *advising the Communist leaders on how to stifle it*: Bohdan Nahaylo, *The Ukrainian Resurgence* (London: Hurst & Company, 1999), 178.

176 *"a breathtaking political metamorphosis"*: Alexander J. Motyl, "The Conceptual President: Leonid Kravchuk and the Politics of Surrealism," in Timothy J. Colton

and Robert C. Tucker, eds., *Patterns in Post-Soviet Leadership* (Boulder, CO: Westview Press, 1995), 103–22, at 108.

177 *favorite to win the Ukrainian presidency*: Alexander Motyl and Bohdan Krawchenko, "Ukraine: From Empire to Statehood," in Bremmer and Taras, eds., *New States*, 235–75, at 252.

177 *Vyacheslav Chornovil, was asked*: Kuzio, *Ukraine*, 63.

177 *Of the fifteen heads of state*: See David C. Brooker, "Founding Presidents of Soviet Successor States: A Comparative Study," *Demokratizatsiya* 12, no. 1 (2004): 133–45. The nonparty members were Landsbergis (Lithuania), Levon Ter-Petrossian (Armenia), and Zviad Gamsakhurdia (Georgia). These three, as well as Askar Akayev (Kyrgyzstan) and Stanislav Shushkevich (Belarus) were academics.

177 *Around one-quarter of the delegates*: Beissinger, *Nationalist Mobilization*, 98.

177 *In Estonia, as of spring 1991*: Neil Melvin, *Russians Beyond Russia: The Politics of National Identity* (London: Royal Institute of International Affairs, 1995), 36.

177 *In Latvia, surveys*: Nils Muiznieks, "Latvia: Restoring a State, Rebuilding a Nation," in Bremmer and Taras, eds., *New States*, 376–403, at 391.

177 *The Russian writer Vladlen Dozortsev*: Bill Keller, "Latvians Seek Freedom and Fret for Gorbachev," *New York Times*, October 9, 1989. After Latvian independence, Dozortsev would become disillusioned with the new state's treatment of Russians.

178 *Forty-two percent of Russians*: *Moskovskie Novosti*, April 22, 1990.

178 *55 percent of ethnic Russian voters*: Kuzio, *Ukraine*, 199.

178 *Vladimir Grinev, was a vociferous secessionist*: Serge Schmemann, "Ukraine Is Now Getting Serious About Its Drive for Independence," *New York Times*, October 30, 1991.

178 *only 47 percent favored a "struggle"*: Wyman, *Public Opinion*, 153. The number of respondents in each republic was low, so the figures should be treated with some caution.

178 *52 percent of ethnic Moldovans*: Beissinger, *Nationalist Mobilization*, 148.

178 *Gorbachev held a referendum*: In Kazkhstan, the question was changed slightly to: "Do you consider it necessary to preserve the USSR as a Union of equal and sovereign states?" In Ukraine, another question was added asking whether the country should remain in the USSR "on the basis of the Declaration of State Sovereignty of Ukraine." See Valery Tishkov, *Ethnicity, Nationalism and Conflict in and after the Soviet Union* (Thousand Oaks: Sage Publications, 1997), 50; Kuzio, *Ukraine*, 167.

178 *majorities supported the USSR's preservation*: Tishkov, *Ethnicity, Nationalism and Conflict*, 51.

179 *the killing by Soviet troops of nineteen unarmed protesters*: Beissinger, *Nationalist Mobilization*, 185, 351.

179 *at least 80 percent of ethnic Estonians*: Juan J. Linz and Alfred Stepan, *Problems of Democratic Transition and Consolidation: Southern Europe, South America, and Post-Communist Europe* (Baltimore: Johns Hopkins University Press, 1996), 413.

179 *79 percent of Moldovan residents*: Beissinger, *Nationalist Mobilization*, 148.

181 *embedded in its architecture*: for instance, Philip Roeder, "Soviet Federalism and Ethnic Mobilization," *World Politics* 43, no. 2 (1991): 196–232.

181 *Lenin found it expedient*: Tishkov, *Ethnicity, Nationalism, and Conflict*, 28–29.

182 *affirmative action*: Terry Martin, "An Affirmative-Action Empire: The Emergence of the Soviet Nationalities Policy, 1919–1923," in Ronald G. Suny, ed., *The Structure of Soviet History: Essays and Documents* (New York: Oxford University Press, 2003), 93–102.

182 *taught in thirty-five languages*: Barbara A. Anderson and Brian D. Silver, "Equality, Efficiency, and Politics in Soviet Bilingual Education Policy, 1934–1980," in Rachel Denber, ed., *The Soviet Nationality Reader: The Disintegration in Context* (Boulder, CO: Westview, 1992), 353–86, at 379.

182 *This policy of indigenization*: Roeder, "Soviet Federalism."

182 *"given birth to thousands of Tajiks"*: Tishkov, *Ethnicity, Nationalism, and Conflict*, 20.

182 *"inevitable fusion (sliyanie) of nations"*: The quote is from Lenin, writing in 1916, quoted in Martin, "An Affirmative-Action Empire," 96.

182 *Lyudmila Alekseyeva collected reports*: Beissinger, *Nationalist Mobilization*, 54.

182 *Only three times during the Brezhnev period*: Gaidar, *Collapse of an Empire*, 72.

183 *fifteen "quasi-nation-states"*: Rogers Brubaker, *Nationalism Reframed: Nationhood and the National Question in the New Europe* (New York: Cambridge University Press, 1996), 41.

183 *the key destabilizing factor*: Juan J. Linz and Alfred Stepan, "Political Identities and Electoral Sequences," *Daedalus* 121, no. 2 (1992): 123–39.

183 *learning the tricks of parliamentary opposition*: Gavriil Popov, *Snova v oppozitsii* (Moscow: Galaktika, 1994), 67–68.

183 *"From the tactics of opposition"*: Popov, *Snova v oppozitsii*, 78.

184 *"Nationalities have turned into political parties"*: quoted in Victor Zaslavsky, "Nationalism and Democratic Transition in Postcommunist Societies," *Daedalus* 121, no. 2 (1992): 97–121, at 107.

184 *Ligachev insisted it was time*: Chernyaev, *My Six Years*, 188.

184 *riots erupted in the Kazakh capital*: Bruce Pannier, "Kazakhstan: Zheltoqsan Protest Marked 20 Years Later," Radio Free Europe/Radio Liberty, December 14, 2006, http://www.rferl.org/featuresarticle/2006/12/1b31a151-3c74-413b-909c-876e8f3020a9.html.

185 *Karimov used interior ministry troops*: Beissinger, *Nationalist Mobilization*, 259–60.

185 *General Varennikov sent orders*: Kuzio, *Ukraine*, 162–63.

185 *a nationalist statue in the Western Ukraine*: S. Romanyuk, "Less Than Six Months Later," *Komsomolskaya Pravda*, January 4, 1991.

185 *Beissinger argues that*: Beissinger, *Nationalist Mobilization*, 96.

186 *the percentage of demonstrators arrested fell*: To estimate these odds, I use the data from Beissinger's dataset for *Nationalist Mobilization* and divide the number of demonstrators arrested each month by the total number of demonstrators.

186 *states of emergency made protests grow even faster*: Beissinger, *Nationalist Mobilization*, 366.

186 *"export their revolutions"*: Nils R. Muiznieks, "The Influence of the Baltic Popular Movements on the Process of Soviet Disintegration," *Europe-Asia Studies* 47, no. 1 (1995): 3–25.

186 *published Russian language newspapers*: Muiznieks, "The Influence."

186 *Algirdas Brazauskas*: Beissinger, *Nationalist Mobilization*, 84–5.

187 *"There is no food rationing in Ulster"*: Galina Starovoiteva, "Nationality Policies in the Period of Perestroika: Some Comments from a Political Actor," in Gail Lapidus, Victor Zaslavsky, and Philip Goldman, eds., *From Union to Commonwealth: Nationalism and Separatism in the Soviet Republics* (New York: Cambridge University Press, 1992), 114–21.

187 *the opaqueness*: On the opaqueness of the Soviet economy, see Yoshiko Herrera, *Imagined Economies: The Sources of Russian Regionalism* (New York: Cambridge University Press, 2005).

187 *Nationalists saw in consumer shortages*: Richard Ericson, "Soviet Economic Structure and the National Question," in Alexander J. Motyl, ed., *The Post-Soviet Nations: Perspectives on the Demise of the USSR* (New York: Columbia University Press, 1992), 265.

187 *"you'll end up in the soup"*: Anatol Lieven and Daniel Treisman, "Vilnius Acts to Reclaim Economy," *Times* (London), March 13, 1990.

187 *Lucjan Orlowski estimates*: Lucjan T. Orlowski, "Indirect Transfers in Trade among Former Soviet Union Republics: Sources, Patterns and Policy Responses in the Post-Soviet Period," *Europe-Asia Studies* 45, no. 6 (1993): 1001–24, at 1006.

187 *slaves in the American plantations*: Marie Bennigsen Broxup, "The Riots in Uzbekistan," *Index on Censorship* 1 (1990): 30.

188 *Gorbachev announced an economic blockade*: Lieven and Treisman, "Vilnius Acts."

188 *Shipments of oil, gas, and some other products*: Alfred Erich Senn, *Gorbachev's Failure in Lithuania* (New York: St. Martin's Press, 1995), 103–5.

188 *"But we must show them"*: Loginov, ed., *Soyuz mozhno bylo sokhranit*, 99.

188 *Brazauskas said this would have been a "catastrophe"*: Senn, *Gorbachev's Failure*, 104.

189 *"eternal as the Egyptian pyramids"*: Sergey Kovalyov, "Why Putin Wins," *New York Review of Books*, November 22, 2007.

191 *"government leaders failed"*: Beissinger, *Nationalist Mobilization*, 371.

191 *"Had I been here"*: Yelena Skvortsova, "My ne dumali chto Gorbachev predatel," *Sobesednik*, August 20, 2007.

191 *He firmly objected when Gorbachev*: Shaposhnikov, *Vybor*, 137–38. See discussion in Chapter 1.

192 *"When the majority of generals and officers"*: quoted in Mlechin, *Kreml*, 291.

192 *62 percent called Latvia their "native land"*: Laitin, *Identity in Formation*, 319.

192 *In Autumn 1993, 53 percent of Russians*: New Baltic Barometer survey, www.balticvoices.org/admin/single_slide_display.php?sld=130.

192   *The percentages of Russians thinking this increased*: New Baltic Barometer survey, www.balticvoices.org/admin/single_slide_display.php?sld=131.

192   *Russians evaluated their republic's political system more positively*: New Baltic Barometer survey, www.balticvoices.org/russia/trends.php.

193   *in the early 1990s protests against economic hardship*: Stephen Bloom, *Economic Reform and Ethnic Cooperation in Post-Soviet Latvia and Ukraine*, Ph.D. dissertation (Los Angeles: UCLA, 2004). Another reason might be that the more extreme anti-Baltic Russians emigrated to Russia. In 1990–1994, the flow of migrants from the three Baltic republics to Russia equalled 13.7 percent of the 1989 ethnically Russian population of the three republics [my calculations from Goskomstat Rossii, *Demografichesky yezhegodnik* (Moscow: Goskomstat Rossii, 1996)].

193   *agreed that "hardline nationalist politicians in Russia"*: New Baltic Barometer survey, www.balticvoices.org/admin/single_slide_display.php?sld=36. Of course, the factions that instigate violence rarely insist on waiting until they have majority support. Sometimes very small groups can set off a spiral of escalating attacks. Still, had opinion in the diaspora communities been more radically opposed to their host nations, violence would have been more likely.

193   *One poll in September 1991*: Wyman, *Public Opinion*, 169.

193   *Zhirinovsky called a protest demonstration*: Agence France Presse, "3000 Demonstrate in Moscow Against 'end of USSR,'" December 22, 1991. In fact, the demonstrators also included some protesting the government's economic policies.

193   *92 percent of Russians favored negotiating*: Aurel Braun, "All Quiet on the Russian Front? Russia, Its Neighbors, and the Russian Diaspora," in Michael Mandelbaum, ed., *The New European Diasporas: National Minorities and Conflict in Eastern Europe* (New York: Council on Foreign Relations Press, 2000), 81–158, at 148.

194   *"We must keep the glorious city"*: Lebed, *My Life*, 359.

194   *Sergey Stepashin*: Peter Vares, "Dimensions and Orientations in the Foreign and Security Policies of the Baltic States," in A. and K. Dawisha, eds., *The Making of Foreign Policy in Russia and the New States of Eurasia* (Armonk, NY: M.E. Sharpe, 1995), 157–74, at 165.

194   *"liberal-secular nationalism"*: Braun, "All Quiet," 97.

195   *Kiev accorded the peninsula special economic status*: Stephen Bloom, "Which Minority Is Appeased? Coalition Potential and Redistribution in Latvia and Ukraine," *Europe-Asia Studies* 60, no. 9 (2008): 1575–1600.

195   *"More than anything"*: Yeltsin, *Midnight Diaries*, 239.

CHAPTER 6: THE TRANSFORMATION

197   *producers were not shipping*: See Gaidar's television interview from mid-December 1991, quoted in Filatov, *Sovershenno nesekretno*, 117.

198   *when inflation exceeds 40 or 50 percent*: See Michael Bruno and William Easterly, "Inflation Crises and Long-Run Growth," *Journal of Monetary Economics* 41 (1998): 3–26. Moderate inflation has less clear effects.

199 *form a lobby for impartial law enforcement*: Of course, creating an effective system of law enforcement would have been at least as necessary—and just as hard—if property had been left under nominal state ownership.

199 *The first three candidates*: These were Svyatoslav Fyodorov, a famous eye surgeon and entrepreneur; Yury Ryzhov, the rector of the Moscow Aviation Institute and a leader of the democratic movement; and Mikhail Poltoranin, a newspaper editor and longtime Yeltsin supporter (Colton, *Yeltsin*, 224). Yury Skokov, an industrialist, was thought to be next in line.

199 *"chewed up in the winter"*: Gaidar, *Days*, 100.

199 *Che Guevara had visited*: Gaidar, *Days*, 8.

199 *"without special permission"*: Baturin et al., *Epokha Yeltsina*, 195.

200 *limits on imports were abandoned*: Rudiger Ahrend and William Tompson, *Fifteen Years of Economic Reform in Russia: What Has Been Achieved? What Remains to Be Done?* (Paris: OECD, 2005).

200 *The country got through the winter*: Among Russians asked in surveys what domestic problems worried them most, the proportion choosing "shortage of foods, essential goods" fell from 76 percent in November 1991 to 50 percent in February 1992, 26 percent in November 1992, and 14 percent in November 1993 (VCIOM "Fakt" surveys, 1991-11, 1992-2, 1992-11, and "Monitoring sotsialno-ekonomicheskikh peremen" 1993-11, at http://sofist.socpol.ru).

200 *consumer price index was nine times higher*: Goskomstat Rossii, *Tseny v Rossii* (Moscow: Goskomstat Rossii, 1996). Goskomstat's data collection and methodology for constructing a consumer price index were not perfected until the mid-1990s, so estimates of inflation in earlier years should be considered highly approximate (see V.E. Gimpelson and R.I. Kapelyushnikov, eds., *Zarabotnaya plata v Rossii: evolutsiya i differentsiatsiya* [Moscow: GUVshE, 2007], 28–29).

201 *Federal spending fell by 5.3 percent of GDP*: Alexander Morozov and Mark Sundberg, *Russia: Issues in Public Expenditure Policy* (Washington, DC: IMF, 2000), 1.

201 *more than 90 percent of the nonpayment of federal taxes*: *Ekspert*, June 3, 1996, 16–19.

202 *selling hundreds of millions of dollars a day*: Hoffman, *The Oligarchs*, 420.

203 *While $22.6 billion was promised*: Homi Kharas, Brian Pinto, and Sergey Ulatov, "An Analysis of Russia's 1998 Meltdown: Fundamentals and Market Signals," *Brookings Papers on Economic Activity* no. 1 (2001): 1–50.

203 *By April 1994, 70 percent had been sold*: *Russian Economic Trends*, Monthly Update, April 30, 1994, 14.

203 *98 percent of eligible Russians had claimed*: Alfred Kokh, *The Selling of the Soviet Empire* (New York: SPI, 1998); *Russian Economic Trends* 3, no. 2 (1994), 82.

203 *62 percent of employed Russians*: Goskomstat Rossii, *Rossiysky statistichesky yezhegodnik* (Moscow: Goskomstat Rossii, 1996). The source on the 40 million share owners is Chubais, from a news conference in mid-1994 (see TASS, "Voucher Privatization: First Stage of Transition to Market," Moscow, July 8, 1994).

203 *most Russians told pollsters*: VCIOM, *Monitoring obshchestvennogo mneniya* 2, no. 22 (1996): 72.

203 *"another deception of the people"*: *Pravda*, June 18, 1992, translated in *Current Digest of the Post-Soviet Press* 44, no. 24 (1992), 30.

204 *"there will be very little privatization"*: Andrei Shleifer and Robert W. Vishny, "Privatization in Russia: First Steps," in Olivier Blanchard, Kenneth Froot, and Jeffrey Sachs, eds., *The Transition in Eastern Europe*, vol. 2 (Chicago: University of Chicago Press, 1994), 137–64.

204 *By September 1995*: Rose Brady, *Kapitalizm: Russia's Struggle to Free its Economy* (New Haven: Yale University Press, 1999), 135.

204 *parliament had prohibited the sale*: Andrey Kolesnikov, *Neizvestny Chubais*, 107.

205 *Laws on bankruptcy, intellectual property*: Vladimir Mau, *Ekonomicheskaya reforma: skvoz prizmu konstitutsii i politiki* (Moscow: Ad Marginem, 1999), 121.

206 *2,300 local employment centers*: Vladimir Gimpelson and Douglas Lippoldt, *The Russian Labour Market: Between Transition and Turmoil* (Lanham, MD: Rowman and Littlefield, 2001), 149.

206 *To increase judicial independence*: Peter H. Solomon and Todd S. Foglesong, *Courts and Transition in Russia: The Challenge of Judicial Reform* (Boulder, CO: Westview Press, 2000), 11.

206 *their caseload increased fourfold*: Kathryn Hendley, "Handling Economic Disputes in Russia: The Impact of the 2002 Arbitrazh Procedure Code" (Madison: University of Wisconsin, unpublished paper, 2006).

206 *enterprises were running at a loss*: Some of the "loss making" was for tax evasion purposes, but the incentive to avoid taxes was strong in 1992 as well as in 1998, so it is hard to believe this explains the vast increase in these years. It is possible the true performance of enterprises was somewhat better. Still the steady closure of the larger enterprises and the drop in employment in larger enterprises is consistent with the view that many could not survive.

206 *The total losses*: Goskomstat Rossii, *Rossiysky statistichesky yezhegodnik* (Moscow: Goskomstat Rossii, various years); 1998 was a year of financial crisis, but in 1997, a year of positive growth, the total losses still equaled 44 percent of total profits, and more than 5 percent of GDP.

206 *Fifty-six percent of the industrial enterprises*: See Goskomstat Rossii, *Rossiysky statistichesky yezhegodnik*, 1996, for the number of industrial enterprises in 1990; Goskomstat Rossii, *Promyshlennost Rossii* (Moscow: Goskomstat Rossii, 2000 and 2005) gives figures for the number of industrial enterprises still in existence that had been founded before 1991 of 18,246 and 11,749 respectively.

207 *the share of such workers rose*: V. Gimpelson and R. Kapelyushnikov, *Nestandartnaya zanyatost v rossiyskoy ekonomike* (Moscow: GUVshE, 2006), 195.

207 *In Poland, Hungary*: I use the EBRD *Macroeconomics Database*, downloaded April 21, 2008, and use 1991 as the start of transition for the former Soviet States and 1989 for the East European ones. Employment fell by more than 13 percent after two years in Estonia, Hungary, and Latvia, and after four years in the Czech Republic, Lithuania, and Poland. To ensure comparability, I compare the first fourteen years of transition for all countries.

207 *constituted the main players*: In a previous book, Andrei Shleifer and I called these the "stakeholders," since most had a stake in the existing, inefficient arrangements (Andrei Shleifer and Daniel Treisman, *Without a Map: Political Tactics and Economic Reform in Russia* [Cambridge, MA: MIT Press, 2000]).

209 *It could overturn presidential vetoes*: *Konstitutsiya (Osnovnoy zakon) Rossiyskoy Sovetskoy Federativnoy Sotsialisticheskoy Respubliki ot 12 aprelya 1978 g., v redaktsii ot 3 yuliya 1991 g.*, at http://constitution.garant.ru/DOC_894079.htm.

209 *Parliament could still overturn*: Thomas Remington, *The Russian Parliament: Institutional Evolution in a Transitional Regime, 1989–1999* (New Haven: Yale University Press, 2001), 169.

209 *And economic legislation*: Thomas Remington, "The Evolution of Executive-Legislative Relations in Russia since 1993," *Slavic Review* 39, no. 3 (2000): 499–520.

209 *speaker had a hotline to his desk*: Gaidar, *Days*, 162.

209 *"'Resistance' is not the word"*: Dmitry Itskovich and Boris Dolgin, "Pyotr Aven: 'My nikogda ne budem lyubimy v nashey strane,'" interview with Pyotr Aven, December 12, 2006, http://www.polit.ru/analytics/2006/12/12/aven1.html.

209 *"purely decorative"*: Gaidar, *Days*, 66, 180–81.

210 *"the hand of my old friends, the KGB"*: Yeltsin, *The Struggle*, 178. On the separatist fighters from Moldova, see Moroz, *Tak kto zhe*, 54.

211 *"a good horsewhipping"*: Yeltsin, *The Struggle*, 165.

211 *"The country must feed its peasants"*: Aleksandr Bekker, "Center of Gravity," *Segodnya*, March 28, 1995, translated in *Current Digest of the Post-Soviet Press* 47, no. 13 (1995), 3–4.

211 *"a swan, a crab, and a pike"*: Ivan Rodin, "You Have to Take Risks If Power Is Going to Fall Into Your Hands," interview with Boris Fyodorov, *Nezavisimaya Gazeta*, March 17, 1995, translated in *Current Digest of the Post-Soviet Press* 47, no. 11 (1995), 6–7. The image comes from a fable by Krylov.

212 *"Many of our decrees were overturned"*: Kolesnikov, *Neizvestny Chubais*, 99.

213 *their chief lobbyist, Arkady Volsky*: Elizabeth Teague, "Russia's Industrial Lobby Takes the Offensive," *RFE/RL Research Report* 1, no. 32 (1992): 1–6, at 2.

213 *20 million workers*: Philip Hanson and Elizabeth Teague, "The Industrialists and Russian Economic Reform," *RFE/RL Research Report* 1, no. 19 (1992): 1–7.

213 *entirely by sales for cash*: Kolesnikov, *Neizvestny Chubais*, 94, quotes Dmitry Vasiliev, Chubais's deputy at that time, on this.

213 *too unrealistic, risky, socially unjust*: Kolesnikov, *Neizvestny Chubais*, 67.

214 *Bankers were earning billions*: The World Bank, *Russian Federation: Toward Medium-Term Viability* (Washington, DC: World Bank, 1996), 54.

214 *Central Bank itself made about $2 billion*: Aleksandr Bekker, "Money Begets Money: The Central Bank Has Made a Trillion Rubles in Profits," *Segodnya*, July 13, 1993.

214 *made an estimated 8 percent of GDP*: William Easterly and Paulo Vieira da Cunha, "Financing the Storm: Macroeconomic Crisis in Russia," *Economics of Transition* 2, no. 4 (1994): 454–55. For details of their calculations, see their footnote 13.

214 *"powerful pro-inflation political coalition"*: Gaidar, *Days*, 145; Teague, "Russia's Industrial Lobby."

214 *"Why hold down the budget deficit"*: Gaidar, *Days*, 155.

214 *neighbors received ruble credits*: Brigitte Granville, "Farewell, Ruble Zone," in Anders Åslund, ed., *Russian Economic Reform at Risk* (New York: Pinter, 1995), 65–88, at 81.

214 *Yeltsin abolished subsidized Central Bank credits*: Yegor Gaidar, ed., *The Economics of Transition* (Cambridge, MA: MIT Press, 2003), 135.

215 *Gazprom was being paid for only 23 percent*: See Daniel Treisman, "Fighting Inflation in a Transitional Economy: Russia's Anomalous Stabilization," *World Politics* 50, no. 2 (1998) for details.

215 *subsidies worth $63 billion during 1993–1997*: Brian Pinto, Vladimir Drebentsov, and Alexander Morozov, *Give Growth and Macroeconomic Stability in Russia a Chance: Harden Budgets by Eliminating Non-Payments* (Washington, DC: World Bank, 2000).

215 *pay their taxes with dubious promissory notes*: On such rings of promissory notes, see Clifford G. Gaddy and Barry Ickes, "Russia's Virtual Economy," *Foreign Affairs*, September–October 1998, 53–67, and David Woodruff, *Money Unmade: Barter and the Fate of Russian Capitalism* (Ithaca, NY: Cornell University Press, 1999).

215 *Gazprom was allowed to distribute*: See Leslie Shepherd, "Russia Moves to Privatize Natural Gas Monopoly," Associated Press, April 5, 1993.

215 *Gazprom's director won the right*: Panyushkin and Zygar, *Gazprom*, 36.

216 *Anders Åslund, for instance, argues*: Åslund, *Russia's Capitalist Revolution: Why Market Reform Succeeded and Democracy Failed* (Washington, DC: Peterson Institute, 2007), 143–44.

216 *Pinto and colleagues estimate*: Pinto et al., *Give Growth a Chance*, Table A-1.

216 *did not increase the money supply*: The IMF's $6.8 billion loan also helped. However, previous IMF aid had not been enough to offset the government's political problems. In another article, Åslund and co-authors argue that stabilization occurred because as economic actors reduced their cash holdings this rendered the inflation tax a less efficient way for the government to raise money [Anders Åslund, Peter Boone, and Simon Johnson, "How to Stabilize: Lessons from Post-Communist Countries," *Brookings Papers on Economic Activity* 1 (1996): 217–313]. However, the big decreases in money in circulation came in 1992–1993, without prompting the government to stop inflating. The drop in money demand in 1994–1995 was much smaller.

217 *"I am a dangerous individual"*: Boris Fyodorov, author's interview, Moscow, July 24, 1997.

217 *Achievements of the Chernomyrdin Government*: Filatov, *Sovershenno neskretno*, 95.

217 *"I have been in Government twice"*: Michael Gordon, "Brash Russian Tax Chief Takes on Land of Evasion," *New York Times*, July 4, 1998.

217 *investigate the country's celebrities*: Boris Fyodorov, *10 bezumnykh let: pochemu v Rossii ne sostoyalis reformy* (Moscow: Sovershenno sekretno, 1999), 205.

217 *total tax collections came to 160 billion rubles*: calculated from *Russian Economic Trends*, Monthly Update, January 2000, Tables 11 and 12, for the months of June through September. Collection of federal taxes increased slightly (from 63 billion to 67 billion rubles), but this was offset by a larger drop in regional and local tax revenues.

217 *Gazprom paid less*: RFE/RL *Newsline*, July 7, 1998.

218 *the analyst Vyacheslav Nikonov reported*: Vyacheslav Nikonov, "Government and Gazprom Tied at One All," *Izvestia*, July 7, 1998, translated in *Current Digest of the Post-Soviet Press* 50, no. 27 (1998): 7–8.

218 *the deputies approved only 3 billion*: RFE/RL *Newsline*, July 20, 1998.

218 *However the evidence suggests*: This section draws on Andrei Shleifer and Daniel Treisman, "A Normal Country: Russia After Communism," *Journal of Economic Perspectives* 19, no. 1 (2005): 151–74.

218 *less than the headline figure*: See Åslund, "How Small," and Evgeny Gavrilenkov and Vincent Koen, "How Large Was the Output Collapse in Russia: Alternative Measures and Welfare Implications" (Washington, DC: IMF, 1994). On the other hand, the statistics may not have fully captured the decrease in inexpensive or free services provided under the old system, such as child care and cheap vacations.

218 *Retail trade per capita dropped*: Goskomstat Rossii, *Rossiysky statistichesky yezhegodnik* (Moscow: Goskomstat Rossii, 2000, 2001); Goskomstat Rossii, *Rossiya i strany mira* (Moscow: Goskomstat Rossii, 2000).

218 *Car ownership doubled by 1998*: statistics in this paragraph are from Goskomstat Rossii, *Rossiysky statistichesky yezhegodnik*, 2001, 2007; Goskomstat Rossii, *Sotsialnoe polozhenie i uroven zhizni naseleniya Rossii*, 2002.

219 *The share of households receiving*: statistics in this paragraph are from Goskomstat Rossii, *Sotsialnoe polozhenie i uroven zhizni naseleniya Rossii*, 2002; Goskomstat Rossii, *Svyaz v Rossii*, 2003; the Russian Longitudinal Monitoring Survey (see T.A. Mroz, L. Henderson, and B.M. Popkin, *Monitoring Economic Conditions in the Russian Federation: The Russia Longitudinal Monitoring Survey 1992–2004* [Carolina Population Center, University of North Carolina at Chapel Hill, 2005], 14; Goskomstat Rossii, *Transport i svyaz v Rossii*, 2001. Figures for Norway and Finland are for 1997).

219 *these could be worth millions of dollars*: Listings on a commercial brokerage for three-room Moscow apartments as of July 2008 ranged from $630,000 to $3.8 million.

219 *Poverty rose from 1992 to 1998*: Comparative rates of poverty for different groups are in Mroz et al., *Monitoring Economic Conditions*, 17.

219 *He should have followed China's example*: Joseph Stiglitz, *Globalization and Its Discontents* (New York: Norton, 2002). Many of the gradualists' criticisms are rehearsed in Lawrence R. Klein and Marshall I. Pomer, eds., *The New Russia: Transition Gone Awry* (Stanford: Stanford University Press, 2001).

220 *What worked in China*: A few of these differences would include the continuing rule of a dictatorial party in China; the undeveloped, mostly agricultural Chinese economy; and the greater initial macroeconomic balance in China. For more, see Jeffrey Sachs and Wing Thye Woo, "Structural Factors in the Economic Reforms of China, Eastern Europe, and the Former Soviet Union," *Economic Policy* 9, no. 18 (1994): 102–45.

220 *Interest rates adjusted for inflation*: Real interest rates rose later, as inflation was brought down, but precisely because of the authorities' *gradual* approach to reducing the budget deficit. The high budget deficits had to be financed by government borrowing at whatever rates the markets demanded.

220 *unemployment was lower in Russia than it was in France*: World Bank, *World Development Indicators* database, downloaded July 4, 2008. The exceptions were 1998, 1999, and 2001.

221 *"He's not by nature a stubborn fighter"*: Anders Åslund and Andrey Nechayev, quoted in Steven Erlanger, "Reform School," *New York Times Magazine*, November 29, 1992.

22 *"In his time, Pinochet"*: Vladimir Mau, author's interview, July 6, 1992, Moscow.

222 *On one hand, support*: VCIOM "Fakt" and "Monitoring" surveys, various issues, at http://sofist.socpol.ru/; VCIOM "Fakt-6", June 10–20, 1992, 2,711 respondents.

222 *after his victory in October 1993*: Gaidar, with some justification, criticizes Yeltsin for not doing more in October 1993 (*Days*, 266–67).

223 *"if all prices were released at once"*: Andrey Denisov, "Reform: Effective but Painful" (interview with Economy Minister Yakov Urinson), *Moscow News*, May 28–June 3, 1998.

223 *As the economy minister in 1998 put it*: Denisov, "Reform: Effective but Painful."

223 *This is true whether one considers*: It is also true for the East European countries taken separately, except that for price liberalization and trade liberalization all the countries for which growth data were available had already achieved virtually perfect reform scores, and so there was no variation on which to compare them.

224 *Giving "insiders"—workers and managers*: Among large U.S. companies, measures of enterprise performance fall as management ownership rises above about five percent. See Randall Morck, Andrei Shleifer, and Robert Vishny, "Management Ownership and Market Valuation: An Empirical Analysis," *Journal of Financial Economics* 20 (1988): 293–325.

224 *In 1994, workers owned 50 percent*: Estimates from Raj Desai and Itzhak Goldberg, "The Politics of Russian Enterprise Reform: Insiders, Local Governments, and the Obstacles to Restructuring," *The World Bank Research Observer* 16, no. 2 (2001): 219–40, at 223; where the authors give a range of estimates, I report the midpoint.

224 *one-third of medium and large enterprises replaced*: Joseph R. Blasi, Maya Kroumova, and Douglas Kruse, *Kremlin Capitalism: Privatizing the Russian Economy* (Ithaca: Cornell University Press, 1996), 135.

224 *By 2005, in 71 percent of medium*: Tatiana G. Dolgopyatova, "Realities of Russian Companies: Corporate Control Under Concentrated Stock Property" (Moscow: Higher School of Economics, 2006).

224 *Rafael La Porta and colleagues studied*: Rafael La Porta, Florencio Lopez-de-Silanes, and Andrei Shleifer, "Corporate Ownership around the World," *Journal of Finance* 54 (1999): 471–517.

225 *Minority shareholders were often mistreated*: For some stories, see Hoffman, *The Oligarchs.*

225 *two OECD economists, after examining fifty studies*: Ahrend and Tompson, *Fifteen Years*, 32–33.

225 *Guriev and Rachinsky studied*: Sergei Guriev and Andrey Rachinsky, "The Role of Oligarchs in Russian Capitalism," *Journal of Economic Perspectives* 19, no. 1 (2005): 131–50.

225 *One recent survey reports that*: Saul Estrin, Jan Hanousek, Evzen Kocenda, and Jan Svenar, "Effects of Privatization and Ownership in Transition Economies" (London: London School of Economics, 2008).

226 *Another study found that productivity*: J. David Brown, John Earle, and Almos Telegdy, "The Productivity Effects of Privatization: Longitudinal Estimates from Hungary, Romania, Russia, and Ukraine," *Journal of Political Economy* 114, no. 1 (2006): 61–99.

226 *The loans for shares program*: For a more detailed version of the following analysis which documents the various claims, see my "Loans for Shares Revisited," *Post-Soviet Affairs* 26, no.3 (2010).

226 *"Faustian bargain"*: Chrystia Freeland, *Sale of the Century: Russia's Wild Ride from Communism to Capitalism* (New York: Crown Books, 2000), 22–23, 169–89.

226 *firms were stripped of their assets*: Stiglitz, *Globalization and Its Discontents*, 160.

226 *conduct of the auctions*: See Hoffman, *The Oligarchs*, 312–20.

226 *barred on technicalities*: Some of the apparent technicalities may not have been so technical; it is not clear that some of the bidders actually had the cash to pay the amounts they said they wanted to bid.

226 *Excluded investors*: Kokh, *The Selling*, 121–22, 126.

227 *"crown jewels" and "behemoths"*: See, e.g., Freeland, *Sale of the Century*, 170.

227 *8–10 percent of the stock market's total capitalization*: Treisman, "Loans for Shares Revisited."

227 *In 1997, auctions of stakes in Tyumen Oil*: Russian Economic Trends 1 (1998): 90.

228 *Reporters were outraged*: For example, Klebnikov, *Godfather of the Kremlin*, 207.

228 *By 1998 and 1999, the capitalizations*: According to the *Ekspert* database, www.expert.ru/ratings/, at the end of 1999 the capitalization of Yukos was $235 million (compared to $646 million in October 1995); that of Norilsk Nickel was $472 million (compared to $694 million in October 1995); that of LUKoil was $5.4 billion (compared to $7.7 billion in 1995). The lower valuations could reflect mismanagement by the winning bidders. However, they were most likely caused

largely by lower commodity prices and a fall in international investors' interest in emerging markets.

228 *Major discounts are universal*: Claude Laurin, Anthony E. Boardman, and Aidan R. Vining, "Government Underpricing of Share Issue Privatizations," *Annals of Public and Cooperative Economics* 75, no. 3 (2004): 399–429, at 415; Mohammad Ariff, Dev Prasad, and George S. Vozikis, "Are Government-linked IPOs Underpriced? A Three Country Privatization Effort Comparison," *International Entrepreneurship and Management Journal* 3 (2007): 293–307.

229 *Between 1996 and 2001, pretax profits*: profits calculated from figures in *Ekspert* database, www.expert.ru/ratings/, deflating by the CPI; oil price is annual average price for Brent crude, from *BP Statistical Review of World Energy*, June 2009.

229 *stock prices of the privatized firms*: calculated from *Ekspert* database, www.expert. ru/ratings/, which gives capitalization for Sibneft and Yukos respectively in 1996 as $1.29 billion and $646 million, and in 2003 as $13.2 billion and $32.8 billion. Peter Boone and Denis Rodionov ("Rent seeking in Russia and the CIS" [Moscow: Brunswick UBS Warburg, 2001]) also found superior performance in the oligarch firms.

229 *revenues of Yukos, Sibneft, and Norilsk Nickel grew much faster*: My calculations from the *Ekspert* database, www.expert.ru/ratings/.

229 *output of oil and gas condensate*: OECD, *Economic Surveys: Russia* (Paris: OECD, 2004), 85.

229 *The poverty rate fell*: Goskomstat Rossii, *Rossiysky statistichesky yezhegodnik*, various years.

229 *only eight had any link to the program*: These were Boris Berezovsky, Roman Abramovich, David Davidovich (of Abramovich's Millhouse), Vladimir Potanin, Potanin's partner Mikhail Prokhorov, Vagit Alekperov and Leonid Fedun of LUKoil, and Vladimir Bogdanov of Surgutneftegaz. See http://www.forbes. com/2008/03/05/richest-people-billionaires-billionaires08-cx_lk_0305billie_ land.html.

230 *his famous 1996 Financial Times interview*: Chrystia Freeland, John Thornhill, and Andrew Gowers, "Moscow's Group of Seven," *Financial Times*, November 1, 1996. The seven bankers mentioned were Berezovsky, Mikhail Khodorkovsky (of Bank Menatep), Mikhail Fridman and Pyotr Aven (of Alfabank), Vladimir Gusinsky (of Most Bank), Aleksandr Smolensky (of Stolichny Bank), and Vladimir Potanin (of Oneksimbank). Berezovsky's claim was demonstrable nonsense. Even if we assumed—wrongly—that they had full control already over the companies in which they were managing stakes under loans for shares, the total revenues of the seven tycoons' main industrial properties in 1996 would come to about 6 percent of GDP. This is the total for Norilsk Nickel, Novolipetsk Metal Works, Sidanko, Yukos, Sibneft, AvtoVAZ, Mechel, Apatit, and Aeroflot, calculated using the *Ekspert* database. Including the revenues of their banks, television companies, and shipping companies (for which figures were not available) would increase the total, but it is hard to imagine it would end up above 10 percent of

GDP. Still, the 50 percent claim was widely repeated as if credible by both the tycoons' promoters and their detractors.

230 *the crash was an inevitable reckoning*: The crisis also prompted an odd burst of hyperventilation. The usually sober financial journalist Paul Blustein, for example, claimed that Yeltsin's government had created, in the GKOs, "a threat more destabilizing to the West than anything the fiends of communism had ever concocted during their decades in the Kremlin" (Paul Blustein, *The Chastening* [New York: Public Affairs, 2001], 238).

230 *Russia could have withstood the pressure*: It is interesting to compare the international commitment made to Russia ($22.6 billion) to those made to other countries facing similar crises. Mexico received a $50 billion package in 1995. Indonesia received a $33 billion package and South Korea a $55 billion package in 1997. Brazil received a $41.5 billion package in 1998 and another $30 billion IMF program in 2002. Argentina got a $40 billion package in December 2000 (see Blustein, *The Chastening*, 18, 178, 354; *New York Times*, February 2, 1995).

231 *lower than in the average G-7 country*: Lawrence Summers, "Comment," *Brookings Papers on Economic Activity* 1 (2001): 51–68.

231 *The average interest rate on GKOs*: *Russian Economic Trends*, no. 2 (1998); *Russian Economic Trends*, Monthly Update, November 11, 1998, 29; *Russian Economic Trends* database.

231 *average maturity of GKOs*: It is also worth noting that Russia struggled through the 1990s under the burden of the USSR's foreign debt, which Russia had assumed. This debt, another parting gift from Gorbachev, was about twice the size of the government's entire GKO and OFZ debt as of December 1997. Had Western governments agreed to write this down as odious debt accrued by a tyrannical regime, Russia's fiscal position throughout the 1990s would have been considerably easier. The burden of the Soviet debt and the aid Russia continued to provide to the other republics in the form of ruble credits and cheap fuel may help to explain Russia's greater vulnerability and slower recovery than some of its neighbors.

231 *As late as August 13, 1998, Rudiger Dornbusch*: interviewed on National Public Radio, "All Things Considered," August 13, 1998.

231 *David Folkerts-Landau*: Blustein, *The Chastening*, 274.

232 *the dangers were obvious*: On the obviousness of the dangers, see Daniel Treisman, "Contemplating a Postelection Financial Crisis," *Transition*, October 4, 1996, 30–33: "Paradoxically, the increased confidence and the inflow of foreign capital that the government is hoping for is exactly what might increase its vulnerability to a Mexican scenario later.... Too rapid an inflow of foreign capital into the still rickety bond and money markets could leave the entire financial system unusually vulnerable." I quoted finance minister Aleksandr Livshits, who said the government had decided at that time not to sell GKOs at rates above 30 percent a year. Brave words!

232 *no better feasible alternatives*: Perhaps one could criticize the government for not moving faster in the spring and summer of 1997 to convert GKOs into Eurobonds, before the Asian crisis made such swaps risky or counterproductive.

232 *Instead, from 1996, they fought*: Pressure from the IMF may have limited the reformers' leeway to select effective tactics for dividing their adversaries. For instance, the fund both required that all tax debtors be targeted simultaneously and that the government get the Duma's approval for its emergency measures (Blustein, *The Chastening*, 257). As Summers acknowledges: "One could argue that giving the Duma a knife to hold at the throat of the Russian administration undermined rather than bolstered confidence" (Summers, "Comment," 54). In the view of Martin Gilman, who was then the IMF's senior representative in Russia, without an improvement in tax collection by the Russian authorities, foreign investors would not have believed that even a large infusion of cash could provide more than a temporary reprieve. And tougher implementation of administrative measures against tax debtors might have worked (see his lucid and well-reasoned *The Accidental Default: Its Enduring Legacy for the New Russia* [Cambridge, MA: MIT Press, forthcoming 2010]). My view is that improving tax administration at a time of extreme weakness of the authorities was very difficult and would have required a political strategy to divide and conquer. But revenues would have picked up somewhat as growth returned with the 1999 rise in oil prices, and economic improvements would have boosted the government's popularity, strengthening it in its fight with the major corporations. I also believe that foreign investors could have been reassured at that time by a somewhat larger aid package. This would have had to come from the G7. Even if the IMF had believed it advisable to extend more loans, it did not have the resources to do so at that time. The G7 was not willing to provide political loans to prevent a meltdown.

232 *Productivity—as measured by real GDP per worker*: my calculation from data in Goskomstat Rossii, *Rossiysky statistichesky yezhegodnik*, various issues.

233 *paying down its foreign debt*: Central Bank of Russia, "External Debt of the Russian Federation in 1993–2003," and "External Debt of the Russian Federation as at the End of December 2009," online at www.cbr.ru/eng/, downloaded February 6, 2010.

233 *Retail trade, adjusted for inflation*: Goskomstat Rossii, *Rossiysky statistichesky yezhegodnik*, 2001, 2007.

233 *stock market rose*: RTS index, data downloaded from RTS July 13, 2008, at www.rts.ru/ru.

233 Forbes's *annual list of billionaires*: Details at www.forbes.com. In 2002, *Forbes* identified 497 billionaires worldwide; in 2008, it found 1,125.

233 *Russians with more than $1 million*: Capgemini and Merrill Lynch & Co., *World Wealth Report 2008* 35 (2008), at www.ml.com/media/100502.pdf, downloaded July 13, 2008; *Moscow Times*, March 7, 2008.

233 *fifth of the population with the lowest incomes*: calculated from figures in Goskomstat Rossii, *Sotsialnoe polozhenie i uroven zhizni naseleniya Rossii*, various issues.

234 *Exports surged from $74 billion*: Goskomstat Rossii, *Rossiya v tsifrakh*, 2004.

234 *Productivity rose briskly in 2000 and 2001, except*: Ahrend and Tompson, *Fifteen Years*, 19.

234 *In the three largest oligarch-owned companies*: OECD, *Economic Surveys: Russian Federation* (Paris: OECD, 2006), 85.

235 *the price for Russian Urals crude rose*: U.S. Energy Information Administration, at http://tonto.eia.doe.gov/dnav/pet/hist/wepcuralsw.htm.

235 *Various studies have found a link*: See, for instance, Roland Beck, Annette Kamps, and Elitza Mileva, *Long-Term Growth Prospects for the Russian Economy*, Occasional Paper No. 58 (Frankfurt: European Central Bank, 2007); Jouko Rautava, "The Role of Oil Prices and the Real Exchange Rate in Russia's Economy: A Cointegration Approach," *Journal of Comparative Economics* 32, no. 2 (2004): 315–27; Paavo Suni, "Oil Prices and the Russian Economy: Some Simulation Studies with NiGEM" (Helsinki: Research Institute of the Finnish Economy, 2007). Most find a statistically significant relationship between the two. But it is harder to say just how big the effect is. Estimates of the elasticity range from .15 to .22—that is, a permanent 10 percent increase in the oil price should lead to a 1.5–2.2 percent increase in GDP in the long run. The difficulty is that the rising oil price, by increasing the value of the ruble, decreases the competitiveness of Russia's other exports, and so depresses growth in other industries. That—and the difficulty of knowing how long is the long run—makes it hard to pin down the size of the impact.

235 *Value added in construction and trade*: Figures for the trade sector may exaggerate its contribution to GDP because of transfer pricing; still reweighting to take this into account would not change the general picture (see OECD, *Economic Surveys: Russian Federation*, 2006).

235 *In 1999–2001, upstream investment*: OECD, *Economic Surveys: Russian Federation*, 2006, 43.

235 *By 2004, real investment in fixed assets*: calculated from Goskomstat Rossii, *Investitsii v Rossii*, 2005, using the index of the physical volume of investment in fixed capital.

235 *sector's share in fixed investment fell from 17.5 percent*: Goskomstat Rossii, *Rossiya v tsifrakh*, 2008.

235 *number of new fields coming on line*: Philip Hanson, "The Resistible Rise of State Control in the Russian Oil Industry," *Eurasian Geography and Economics* 50, no. 1 (2009): 14–27, at 20.

235 *The share of oil output produced by state-controlled*: Hanson, "The Resistible Rise of State Control in the Russian Oil Industry," 15.

235 *High tax rates on the oil companies' windfall profits*: According to Gaddy and Ickes: "Oil companies, whether privately owned, state-owned, or 'quasi-state' entities, paid roughly 10 times more in taxes in 2004 than in 1999. Taxes as a share of total corporate revenue grew from 10–15 percent to 30–35 percent for most companies" (Clifford Gaddy and Barry Ickes, "Resource Rents and the Russian Economy," *Eurasian Geography and Economics* 46, no. 8 [2005]: 559–83, at 564.) On the other hand, the high oil taxes and buildup of revenues in the stabilization fund slowed down the appreciation of the ruble, thus reducing Russia's problems with the "Dutch Disease."

236 *prepared in detail by Yeltsin's reformers*: According to Gaidar in 2002: "We started to prepare these [tax] reforms in 1996–7" (Yegor Gaidar, presentation at UCLA, June 14, 2002.)

236 *This was below the average during Yeltsin's presidency*: World Bank, *World Development Indicators*, downloaded July 24, 2008.

236 *Following Khodorkovsky's arrest, the share*: Goskomstat Rossii, *Investitsii v Rossii*, 2007.

237 *experts claimed that thousands*: Jason Bush, "Russia's Raiders," *Business Week*, June 5, 2008.

238 *tenth largest stock market in the world*: World Bank, *World Development Indicators*, 2009.

CHAPTER 7: THE LOGIC OF POLITICS

241 *"committed to authoritarian government"*: Richard Pipes, *Russian Conservatism and Its Critics: A Study in Political Culture* (New Haven: Yale University Press, 2005), xii, and Richard Pipes, "Is Russia Still an Enemy?" *Foreign Affairs*, September/October 1997, 65–78.

241 *Countries rich in hydrocarbons*: Michael Ross, "Oil and democracy revisited" (UCLA: manuscript, 2009), www.sscnet.ucla.edu/polisci/faculty/ross.

241 *"the price of oil and the pace of freedom"*: Thomas L. Friedman, "The First Law of Petropolitics," *Foreign Policy*, May–June, 2006, 28–36.

241 *a common series of stages*: The classic study is Crane Brinton, *The Anatomy of Revolution* (New York: Vintage, 1938).

241 *Applying this schema to Russia*: A sophisticated analysis along these lines is presented in Vladimir Mau and Irina Starodubrovskaya, *The Challenge of Revolution: Contemporary Russia in Historical Perspective* (New York: Oxford University Press, 2001).

242 *Russia's leaders had unusually broad opportunities*: Åslund, *Russia's Capitalist Revolution*, 1–2, 126, 285–88.

242 *92 percent of Russians said they disapproved*: VCIOM Kurer 1999-3, March 27–30, 1999, 1,600 respondents; VCIOM, Monitoring sotsialno-ekonomicheskikh peremen 1999–3, March 5–22, 1999, 2,385 respondents, http://sofist.socpol.ru.

242 *a majority opposed the military operation*: See www.russiavotes.org.

242 *At least thirteen antiwar demonstrations*: Jason Lyall, "Pocket Protests: Rhetorical Coercion and the Micropolitics of Collective Action in Semiauthoritarian Regimes," *World Politics* 58, no. 3 (2006): 378–412, at 390.

242 *29 percent of supposedly collectivist Russians*: VCIOM Omnibus, 1991-15, December–January 1991, 3,453 respondents, http://sofist.socpol.ru.

243 *regimes have changed markedly*: The Caucasus, at a similar longitude to European Russia, has shown similar variation and swings back and forth.

243 *Scholars who have looked*: Romain Wacziarg, "The First Law of Petropolitics"

(UCLA: manuscript, April 2009), http://www.anderson.ucla.edu/faculty_pages/romain.wacziarg/downloads/petropolitics.pdf.

243 *the effect is diminishing*: See Daniel Treisman, "Is Russia Cursed by Oil?" *Journal of International Affairs* 63, no. 2 (2010), for the details. I return to this issue in Chapter 10.

243 *something reminiscent of Aleksandr Kerensky*: See Mau and Starodubrovskaya, *The Challenge of Revolution*, 110, 146–47.

244 *The story begins with*: For another presentation of the argument, which draws on this account, see Daniel Treisman, "Russian Politics in a Time of Economic Turmoil," in Anders Åslund and Andrew Kuchins, eds., *Russia After the Financial Crisis* (Washington, DC: Peterson Institute for International Economics, 2010). I am grateful to the Peterson Institute for permission to draw on this material here.

246 *exceeds that of any U.S. president*: for ratings of U.S. presidents, see http://www.presidency.ucsb.edu/data/popularity.php. Harry Truman comes closest to Yeltsin's decline, his rating falling from 92 percent after Japan's surrender in August 1945 to 22 percent in February 1952 as the Korean War bogged down. Eisenhower is closest to Putin's performance, but even his rating fell into the fifties and occasionally the forties.

246 *disapproved of President Yeltsin's performance*: Matthew Wyman (*Public Opinion*, 5–19) provides an excellent discussion of the difficulties and common criticisms of polling in Russia, and concludes that most of these problems are those faced by survey researchers everywhere; he found "no evidence specific to Russia that respondents . . . engage in self-censorship." It is also reassuring that the various polling organizations that ask Russians about their attitudes towards their leaders get results that correlate with each other strongly over time.

247 *The parallel between the two lines is striking.*: The peak in economic sentiment in 2008 does not cause as large a jump in the president's rating, perhaps because the rating—at 87 percent in December 2007—is already so high. The last 13 percent of the population were likely ideological opponents of Putin and Medvedev, who could not be swayed by improved economic performance.

247 *there is a strong, statistically significant link*: Daniel Treisman, "Presidential Popularity in a Hybrid Regime: Russia Under Yeltsin and Putin" (UCLA: manuscript, 2010), http://www.sscnet.ucla.edu/polisci/faculty/treisman/Papers/Pres%20popdf.

248 *"People believed that he"*: Yeltsin, *Midnight Diaries*, 338.

248 *By October 2003, just 21 percent*: VCIOM data, at www.russiavotes.org.

248 *weighed on the president's popularity rather than boosting it*: Treisman, "Presidential Popularity in a Hybrid Regime."

248 *from 53 to 76 percent said the authorities*: Levada Center, *Russian Public Opinion 2007* (Moscow: Levada Center, 2007), 127; and www.levada.ru/press/2010042604.html. The proportion saying the authorities could protect them did subsequently rise to 45 percent in August 2009, but fell again to 35 percent in April 2010.

249 *hastened by a few months a jump in approval*: Treisman, "Presidential Popularity in a Hybrid Regime."

252 *Ninety-four percent of deputies voted to ratify*: See Chapters 2 and 5. On the CIS accords, the vote (in the Supreme Soviet) was 188 in favor, six opposed, seven abstaining. On the economic reform plan, the vote (in the Congress of People's Deputies) was 876 in favor, sixteen opposed.

252 *pro-government factions held*: I classify pro-government parties as follows. In the RSFSR Supreme Soviet (1990–1993): the "Coalition for Reform" bloc, including Democratic Russia, Radical Democrats, Left of Center, Non-Party Faction, and Free Russia (for discussion of this classification, see Josephine T. Andrews, *When Majorities Fail: The Russian Parliament, 1990–1993* [New York: Cambridge University Press, 2002], 128; Richard Sakwa, *Russian Politics and Society* [New York: Routledge, 1993], 67; and Thomas Remington, *Politics in Russia* [New York: Pearson, 2004, Third Edition], 175). In the Duma, 1994–1995: Russia's Choice, Party of Russian Unity and Accord; 1995–1999: Our Home Is Russia, Russia's Democratic Choice, Party of Russian Unity and Accord; 1999–2003: Unity, Our Home Is Russia, United Russia; 2003–present: United Russia, Fair Russia. Other sources on the balance of parliamentary factions include: Anders Åslund, *How Russia Became a Market Economy* (Washington, DC: Brookings Institution, 1995), 201; Remington, *The Russian Parliament*, 178–79, 195, and the website www.russiavotes.org.

252 *Riding on Putin's coattails*: If one classified the Union of Right Forces (URF), the successor to Russia's Choice, as a pro-government party, the pro-government bloc would swell to about 24 percent. The URF won 6.4 percent of the seats in 1999. However, the URF was not a reliable partner of the government by this point.

253 *more likely to vote against the government's proposals*: Treisman, *After the Deluge*, 122–31, 234.

253 *This occurred 12 percent of the time*: calculated using dataset on Russian bills from 1994–2004, collected by Moshe Haspel and Tom Remington. I am grateful to Tom Remington for sharing this. Since the executive is unlikely to introduce bills it expects the Federation Council to veto, it is not surprising that the absolute number of vetoes is relatively low. The contrast, however, suggests that the Putin administration was less frequently subjected to unpleasant surprises.

253 *it took less than six months*: See Paul Chaisty, "The Legislative Effects of Presidential Partisan Powers in Post-Communist Russia," *Government and Opposition* 43, no. 3 (2008): 424–53, at 448–49.

253 *Putin's bill to replace the progressive income tax*: Yegor Gaidar, speech on current Russian politics at UCLA, June 14, 2002.

254 *In regions where Yeltsin's support had fallen*: Treisman, *After the Deluge*, 122–31, 234.

254 *budget revenues from 54 percent*: Goskomstat Rossii, *Finansy Rossii* (Moscow: Goskomstat Rossii, 2000 and 2008).

255 *they enjoyed broad leeway*: This may push back the importance of public opinion in time too far. It was only in the period of mass mobilization, competitive elec-

tions, and widely published opinion polls—that is, after 1988—that this logic fully applied.

256 *critics called it authoritarian*: See, for instance, Pavel Felgenhauer, "Yeltsin—The Man Who Created Contemporary Russia," *Eurasia Daily Monitor* (Jamestown Foundation), April 24, 2007, at www.jamestown.org/single/?no_cache=1&tx_ttnews[tt_news]=32700, accessed December 10, 2009.

257 *unconcerned with the attitudes*: For instance, Stephen Holmes, "Simulations of Power in Putin's Russia," in Kuchins, ed., *Russia After the Fall*, 79–89.

257 *resembles many other countries*: See, for instance, Brandice Canes-Wrone and Scott de Marchi, "Presidential Approval and Legislative Success," *Journal of Politics* 64, no. 2 (2002): 491–509.

257 *Both Yeltsin's initiation of radical economic reform*: The creation of a market economy was favored by 74 percent of Russians, according to one poll in late 1991, although slightly more favored a "gradual" than a "rapid" transition. Fifty-one percent favored speeding up the privatization of state enterprises, compared to 21 percent who opposed this, and 56 percent liked the idea of distributing part of state property among all citizens, the essence of voucher privatization (VCIOM, Omnibus 1991-15, December 1991–January 1992, 3,453 respondents, see http://sofist.socpol.ru). Only 13 percent thought that private enterprises were not necessary at all (VCIOM, Fakt 1991-11, November 1991, 1,960 respondents, http://sofist.socpol.ru). Between December 1991 and December 1992, the percentage of respondents favoring a transition to the market "as fast as possible" fell from 33 to 19 percent, and the percentage favoring a gadual transition increased from 41 to 51 percent (VCIOM Omnibus 1991-15, December 1991–January 1992, and 1992-15, December 1992–January 1993, http://sofist.socpol.ru).

257 *dissolution of the parliament in September 1993*: Fifty-two percent approved the dissolution; 25 percent opposed it (VCIOM, Kurer 1993-18, September–October 1993, 1,966 respondents, http://sofist.socpol.ru). Asked about the use of force, 35 percent of respondents—this time from an exclusively urban sample—said he should have done so earlier, 20 percent said he used force at the right time, 11 percent said he should have waited; only 20 percent said he should not have used force at all (VCIOM, Kurer 1993-19, October 1993, 1,597 respondents, http://sofist.socpol.ru).

257 *starting the first Chechen war*: VCIOM Kurer 1995-2, January 1995, 1,506 respondents, http://sofist.socpol.ru; VCIOM Kurer 1999-5, May 1999, 1,581 respondents, http://sofist.socpol.ru.

257 *increasing the state's role*: In August 2001, 62 percent of Russians thought the state had "too little" role in the economy, compared to 3 percent that said it had "too much." In July 2003, 37 percent thought all privatized property should be returned to the state and another 31 percent thought this should be done in cases in which illegality in the privatization process was proven. See www.russiavotes .org/national_issues/privatisation.php.

258 *nods to nostalgia*: Treisman, "Presidential Popularity in a Hybrid Regime."

258 *61 percent of Russians felt "very good"*: Levada Center polls, at www.russiavotes.
org/security/security_trends.php#443 (accessed on November 15, 2009).

258 *Medvedev typically came first*: VCIOM Kurer 2007-17, December 7–11, 2007,
1,601 respondents, http://sofist.socpol.ru.

258 *introducing the flat income tax*: VCIOM Kurer 2000-17, June–July 2000, 1,600
respondents, http://sofist.socpol.ru; VCIOM Kurer 2004-16, December 2004,
1,601 respondents, http://sofist.socpol.ru.

259 *the ratings of Putin and Medvedev move in lockstep*: Their correlation in this
period is r = .86.

260 *In the Yeltsin-era contraction, assessments*: Treisman, "Presidential Popularity in a
Hybrid Regime."

CHAPTER 8: THE MOUNTAINS

262 *inform much press coverage*: And the opinions of commentators. For example, see
André Glucksmann: "The Chechen nation opposed the colonization of czarist
Russia, suffered in the Soviet gulag concentration camps, and now it is opposing
a new kind of red and black fascism" (Bogdan Turek, "Chechnya Awards French
Philosopher," UPI, Warsaw, June 7, 1995).

263 *competing to cook the tastiest ceremonial dishes*: Ekaterina Sokirianskaia, "Ideology and Conflict: Chechen Political Nationalism Prior to, and During, 10 Years
of War," in Moshe Gammer, ed., *Ethno-Nationalism, Islam and the State in the
Caucasus: Post-Soviet Disorder* (New York: Routledge, 2008), 102–38, at 109.

263 *fourteen-year-old Adi Sharon's penciled note*: Tishkov, *Chechnya*, 117.

263 *the solitary lezginka*: Morozov, *Above and Beyond*, 75–76.

264 *Narrow gorges stretch*: The quotations are from Lev Tolstoy, *Hadji Murad*, trans.
Louise and Aylmer Maude, 1904, and Mikhail Lermontov, *A Hero of Our Time*,
Moscow, 1840.

264 *many thousands of years*: Archaeological evidence from mountain cave settle-
ments suggests humans were living there 583,000 years ago (Anatoly Molodkov,
"ESR Dating Evidence for Early Man at a Lower Palaeolithic Cave-Site in the
Northern Caucasus as Derived from Terrestrial Mollusc Shells," *Quaternary Science Reviews* 20 [December 2001]: 1051–55).

264 *a repository of tongues*: Michael Reynolds, "Myths and Mysticism: A Longitudinal
Perspective on Islam and Conflict in the North Caucasus," *Middle Eastern Studies*
41, no. 1 (2005): 31–54, at 33.

264 *warrior democracy, organized in clans*: Amjad Jaimoukha, *The Chechens: A Hand-
book* (New York: Routledge, 2005), 123–24; the Chechen customary law was
called the nokhchalla.

265 *Sunni Islam, with its emphasis*: Galina Yemelianova, *Russia and Islam: A Historical
Survey* (Basingstoke: Palgrave Macmillan, 2002), 15.

265 *cost the lives of at least 77,000 Russian troops*: Mikhail Mamedov, " 'Going Native'

in the Caucasus: Problems of Russian Identity, 1801–64," *Russian Review* 67 (April 2008): 275–95, at 281.

265 *Lermontov, who served bravely at Grozny*: There is a good discussion in Figes, *Natasha's Dance*, 388.

265 *Tolstoy, as a guest*: Thomas Sanders, Ernest Tucker, and Gary M. Hamburg, eds., *Russian-Muslim Confrontation in the Caucasus: Alternative Visions of the Conflict Between Imam Shamil and the Russians, 1830–1859* (New York: Routledge, 2004), 212–14.

265 *Major-General Grigory von Zass*: Mamedov, "'Going Native'"; the description of Zass comes from the reminiscence of the exiled Decembrists N.I. Lorer and A. Belyaev, quoted in Lyudmila Belova, "General Zass: 'Otstupleniya so mnoy net, i ne budet!'" (Alekseyetenginskaya, 2007, unpublished paper). Mamedov gives Zass's first name as Petr, but other sources suggest it was in fact Grigory. His interest in the heads of dead Circassians seems to have been quite serious. Lorer describes how, visiting Zass at his home on one occasion, he noticed a strange smell. As Belova recounts: "Zass said, laughing slightly: 'My people must have put a box of heads under the bed.' And sure enough, two hefty cossacks pulled out an enormous chest with several heads, which nightmarishly 'observed' those present with their glassy eyes. 'Why do you have these here?' Lorer gasped. 'I am drying them out and cleaning them to send to various academic laboratories and to my friends who are professors in Berlin,' Zass replied, directly but pedantically." It was a German anthropologist, Johann Blumenbach, who had deduced some years earlier that the "Caucasian" race present in Western Europe must have originated in the Caucasus Mountains, on the basis of the attractive dimensions of the skulls of local inhabitants.

266 *General Yermolov himself*: Mamedov, "'Going Native,'" 291, 293.

266 *"For the Soviet government, for Sharia!"*: Emil Souleimanov, *An Endless War: The Russian-Chechen Conflict in Perspective* (New York: Peter Lang, 2007), 71, 73.

266 *Russian Socialist Federative Soviet Republic*: In 1937, the name was changed from Russian Socialist Federative Soviet Republic to Russian Soviet Federative Socialist Republic.

267 *They rounded up the inhabitants*: Souleimanov, *An Endless War*, 74.

267 *In Khaybakh, a village near the Georgian border*: Gall and de Waal, *Chechnya*, 64–65.

267 *more than one-third perished*: Zürcher, *The Post-Soviet Wars*, 73; Tishkov, *Chechnya*, 27.

267 *population had become 53 percent Russian*: Valentin Mikhailov, "Chechnya and Tatarstan: Differences in Search of an Explanation," in Richard Sakwa, ed., *Chechnya: From Past to Future* (London: Anthem Press, 2005), 43–66, at 50.

267 *labor surplus constituted some 200,000 young people*: Tishkov, *Chechnya*, 41.

267 *57.8 percent were Chechens*: Goskomstat Rossii, *Regiony Rossii*, 1998, vol. 1, 331; Jane Ormrod, "The North Caucasus: Confederation in Conflict," in Bremmer and Taras, eds., *New States*, 96–139, at 117.

267 *a biochemical plant in the city of Gudermes*: Dzhabrail Gakaev, "Put k chechen-skoy revolyutsii," in D.E. Furman, ed., *Chechnya i Rossiya: obshchestva i gosudarstva* (Moscow: Polinform-Talburi, 1999).

268 *Soon a Popular Front*: Stephen Shenfield, "Tataria and Chechnya—A Comparative Study," July 2009, http://www.circassianworld.com/new/north-caucasus/1366-tataria-chechnya.html; Gakaev, "Put k chechenskoy revolyutsii."

268 *Vaynakh Democratic Party*: "Vaynakh"—meaning "our people"—is a collective term for several Caucasian ethnic groups that speak closely related languages. Scholars disagree on exactly which groups are included. According to Johanna Nichols ("The Origin of the Chechen and Ingush: A Study in Alpine Linguistic and Ethnic Geography," *Anthropological Linguistics* 46, no. 2 [2004]: 129–155, at 131), the term includes the Chechen, Ingush, Melxii, Kisti, and Arshtxoi. According to Jaimoukha (*The Chechens*, 13), the group includes just the Chechens, Ingush, and Kisti. General Dudayev included also the Akkin Chechens of Dagestan. While most scholars view "Vaynakh" as an old, indigenous term, Shnirelman argues that it was a neologism coined by Soviet linguists in the late 1920s after officials decided that the Chechens and Ingush should be encouraged to form a common national identity (Victor Shnirelman, "The Politics of a Name: Between Consolidation and Separation in the Northern Caucasus," *Acta Slavica Iaponica* 23 [2006]: 37–73). See also Yan Chesnov, "Byt chechentsem: lichnost i etnicheskie identificatsii naroda," in Furman, ed., *Chechnya i Rossiya*.

268 *issues of its party newspaper in Riga*: James Hughes, *Chechnya: From Nationalism to Jihad* (Philadelphia: University of Pennsylvania Press, 2007), 19.

268 *elected their first ethnically Chechen first secretary*: Shenfield, "Tataria and Chechnya."

268 *Dudayev's loyalists began occupying*: Zürcher, *The Post-Soviet Wars*, 78.

269 *Vitaly Kutsenko, was either thrown out of a window*: Tishkov, *Chechnya*, 61; Anatol Lieven, *Chechnya: Tombstone of Russian Power* (New Haven: Yale University Press, 1998), 60.

269 *By some accounts, Yeltsin's own close aides*: Sergey Filatov, a member of the Supreme Soviet and later Yeltsin's chief of staff, makes this claim in a 2004 interview ("Sergey Filatov: Dudayeva podobrala Moskva," *BBC Russian.com*, December 8, 2004, http://news.bbc.co.uk/hi/russian/russia/newsid_4079000/4079537.stm).

269 *"take him to Moscow in an iron cage"*: Gakaev, "Put k chechenskoy revolyutsii."

269 *On October 19, he ordered*: Baturin et al., *Epokha Yeltsina*, 586; Tracey C. German, *Russia's Chechen War* (New York: Routledge, 2003), 45.

269 *receiving more than 80 percent*: German, *Russia's Chechen War*, 46.

269 *Other candidates complained of fraud*: Gakaev, "Put k chechenskoy revolyutsii."

269 *"gang terrorising the population"*: Souleimanov, *An Endless War*, 88.

270 *threatened to turn Moscow into a "disaster zone"*: Agence France Presse, "Hundreds of Thousands Reported in Grozny Demo," November 9, 1991.

270 *Basayev hijacked a passenger airliner*: John Dunlop, *Russia Confronts Chechnya: Roots of a Separatist Conflict* (New York: Cambridge University Press, 1998), 121.

270 *Basayev had sat in his office*: Quoted in Tishkov, *Chechnya*, 63.

270 *Grachev, after negotiations with Dudayev*: Dunlop, *Russia Confronts Chechnya*, 165; Grachev provides his account in a 2001 interview ("Pavel Grachev: 'Menya naznachili otvetstvennym za voynu,'" *Trud*, March 15, 2001). According to Grachev, all the equipment could have been withdrawn, but it would have required one additional division of paratroopers to fight off the guerrillas. He says his proposal to send one was turned down in favor of continuing negotiations with Dudayev.

270 *the figures could not be verified*: See the discussion of different lists published in the Russian press in Dunlop, *Russia Confronts Chechnya*, 167–68.

270 *only 1.2 million tons of oil*: Dunlop, *Russia Confronts Chechnya*, 126; Mairbek Vatchagaev, "Oil in Chechnya: A Brief History," *Jamestown Foundation: North Caucasus Analysis* 9, no. 15 (2008).

270 *75 percent drop in per capita income*: Monica Duffy Toft, *The Geography of Ethnic Violence* (Princeton: Princeton University Press, 2003), 76.

270 *"was lit by heaps of burning garbage"*: Lieven, *Chechnya*, 40.

271 *police recorded 1,354 attacks*: Vladimir Ustinov, *Obvinyaetsya Terrorizm* (Moscow: Olma Media Group, 2002), 135.

271 *accumulation of anecdotes and interviews*: For a variety of stories and press reports, see Robert Seely, *Russo-Chechen Conflict, 1800–2000* (New York: Routledge, 2001), 183–84.

271 *Yandarbiev, who became Dudayev's vice president, accuses*: Quoted in Dunlop, *Russia Confronts Chechnya*, 128–29. The MVD refers to the Interior Ministry, the DGB to the Department of State Security, the *spetsnaz*, OMON, and DON to special police forces.

271 *In 1992–1994, 147,000 people migrated*: Sergey Markedonov, "Sistemnye separatisty," Agenstvo politicheskikh novostey, December 28, 2006, www.apn.ru/publications/article11239.htm.

271 *Much of the elite favored accommodation*: Hughes, *Chechnya*, 73.

271 *"Treaty on the Delimitation"*: Shenfield, "Tataria and Chechnya," 70.

272 *refused to guarantee the negotiators' safety*: Dunlop, *Russia Confronts Chechnya*, 180–81; Seely, *Russo-Chechen Conflict*, 137.

272 *Dudayev called a referendum*: Interfax news agency, Moscow, February 21, 1993.

272 *At least seventeen people died*: Gall and de Waal, *Chechnya*, 120.

272 *Opposition members said they saw Dudayev's militants*: Tishkov, *Chechnya*, 91, referring to reports by Yavus Akhmadov and Dzhabrail Gakaev, who participated in the anti-Dudayev meetings on Teatralnaya Square.

272 *Chechen Provisional Council*: Shenfield, "Tataria and Chechnya," 55.

273 *prepared a new uniform*: Shenfield, "Tataria and Chechnya," 51, citing the memoir of Dudayev's economics minister, Taymaz Abubakarov on the Mugadayev mission. Shenfield provides a valuable account of the negotiations; Gall and de Waal, *Chechnya*, 182.

273 *agents had recruited tank crews*: S. Mostovshchikov, "FSK khorosho platit ofitseram, zaverbovannym dlya tainoy pomoshchi chechenskoy oppozitsii," *Izvestia*, January 21, 1995.

273 *The Chechens threatened to shoot them*: Agence France Presse, "Dudayev Vows to Crush Rebels Amid New Clashes around Grozny," Grozny, November 27, 1994.

273 *The raid had been a fiasco*: I have taken details from Petrovsky, "Desyat let pozornomu shturmu Groznogo"; Mostovshchikov, "FSK khorosho platit ofitseram"; Maria Eismont, "Chechnya: Seeds of the Debacle," *Jamestown Foundation Prism*, March 8, 1996; "Russia" TV channel, Moscow, December 3, 1994, 20:20, Captain Andrey Vasilievich Kryukov, interviewed in captivity, translated in BBC *Summary of World Broadcasts*, December 6, 1994; Leonty Bennigsen, "Izmena rodiny vozmutila samykh loyalnykh deputatov," *Kommersant*, December 6, 1994; Ostankino Radio Mayak, Moscow, December 3, 1994, 16:30, translated in BBC *Summary of World Broadcasts*, December 5, 1994.

274 *The next day, a mortifying charade began*: sources for this paragraph: Radio Rossii, "Novosti," November 29, 1994, 11:00; Deutsche Presse-Agentur, "Chechenia 'Threatening to Shoot Russian Prisoners,'" November 28, 1994, 14:47 Central European Time; RTR, "Podrobnosti," November 30, 1994, 20:25; RTR, "Vesti," December 1, 1994, 20:00; NTV, "Segodnya," December 3, 1994, 19:00, quoted in Aleksandr Cherkasov, "Predannye: kak nachinalas pervaya chechenskaya," polit. ru, December 3, 2004, http://www.polit.ru/analytics/2004/12/03/chech.html.

274 *On November 29, Russian planes*: Chris Bird, "Jets Attack Grozny after Yeltsin Issues Ultimatum," Associated Press, Grozny, November 29, 1994.

275 *considering the context in which it occurred*: Throughout this section, I draw on Treisman, *After the Deluge*.

275 *The 1989 Russian census identified*: Goskomstat Rossii, *Rossiysky statistichesky yezhegodnik*, 1996.

276 *Checheno-Ingushetia's sovereignty declaration actually*: Treisman, *After the Deluge*, 203. It was also beaten by five autonomous okrugs and one oblast.

276 *In southern Siberia*: Gail Fondahl, "Siberia: Assimilation and Its Discontents," in Bremmer and Taras, eds., *New States*, 190–234, at 207; Michael Hertzer, "Russia: Yeltsin Reviews Revolution in One Corner," Inter-Press Service, May 29, 1992.

276 *In Tatarstan, nationalists quite seriously demanded*: Michael Dobbs, "Ethnic Strife Splintering Core of Russian Republic," *Washington Post*, October 29, 1991.

276 *In March 1992, in a referendum*: Remarks of Rafael Khakimov, an advisor to President Shaymiev, reported in Peter Rutland, "Tatarstan: A Sovereign Republic Within the Russian Federation," *OMRI Russian Regional Report*, September 25, 1996. The details are a matter of some dispute.

276 *In fact, republics where most people spoke Russian*: I base this on my article "Russia's 'Ethnic Revival': The Separatist Activism of Regional Leaders in a Postcommunist Order," *World Politics* 49, no. 2 (1997): 212–49. To measure "separatist activism," I collected data on eleven indicators—including whether a republic declared sovereignty, claimed the status of a Union republic, adopted its own constitution, asserted the precedence of regional over federal law, held a referendum on sovereignty, declared independence, declared the right to have an independent foreign policy, among others—and added up the total to form an index.

I then looked at how this index correlated with various indicators of primordial nationalism.

277 *"Speak in a way that can be understood"*: Vladimir Ilin, "Respublika Komi: natsionalnye problemy i konstitutsionnaya reforma," *Politichesky monitoring* (Syktyvkar) 1 (1994).

277 *By the early 1990s, they made up only 23 percent*: Iurii Shabaev, "Peculiarities of Nation-Building in the Republic of Komi," in Pal Kolsto and Helge Blakkisrud, eds., *Nation-Building and Common Values in Russia* (Lanham, MD: Rowman & Littlefield, 2005), 59–88, at 62.

277 *Ethnic groups that happened to live above mineral*: Treisman, "Russia's 'Ethnic Revival.'" Henry Hale ("The Parade of Sovereignties"), studied the speed with which a broader set of ethnic republics—both the USSR's fifteen Union republics and the autonomous republics within them—declared sovereignty. He found, similarly, that more economically developed units tended to declare sovereignty earlier. Higher initial administrative status increased separatist activism (Union republics tended to declare sovereignty earlier than republics within them). In this broader set of units, linguistic assimilation *was* associated with a later declaration of sovereignty. But, as among Russia's autonomous republics, dramatic histories of ethnic victimization—such as deportation under Stalin—did not predict a stronger push for self-government.

278 *The deputy governor of Tambov Oblast*: Yury Blokhin, author's interview, Tambov, June 26, 1996.

278 *"threatened with Balkanization"*: Ruslan Khasbulatov, "Crisis of the State and Ways Out of It," *Rossiyskaya Gazeta*, May 15, 1993. Rutskoy's quote is from Aleksandr Rutskoy, "In Defense of Russia," *Pravda*, January 30, 1992. Yeltsin's is from "Ya uveren v svoey pobede" (interview with President Yeltsin), *Delovie Lyudi*, May 1996, 8–11.

278 *Various scholars concurred*: Jessica Stern, "Moscow Meltdown: Can Russia Survive?" *International Security* 18, no. 4 (1994): 40–65; Leon Gouré, "The Russian Federation: Possible Disintegration Scenarios," *Comparative Strategy* 13, no. 4 (1994): 401–18.

278 *In November 1991, 53 percent agreed*: Izvestia, December 6, 1991.

279 *Boris Fyodorov called "financial asphyxiation"*: Moskovskie Novosti, September 19, 1993.

279 *He appeased the regions*: Treisman, *After the Deluge*, chapter 3.

279 *The first, with Tatarstan*: Elizabeth Teague, "Russia and the Regions: The Uses of Ambiguity," in John Gibson and Philip Hanson, eds., *Transformation from Below: Local Power and the Political Economy of Post-Communist Transitions* (Cheltenam, UK: Edward Elgar, 1996), 13–36.

280 *Tatar President Shaymiev endorsed*: Interfax, Kazan, February 2, 1996, published in FBIS-SOV-96-024, February 5, 1996, 47.

280 *Even Eduard Rossel*: Rossiyskie Vesti, "Compact with the Urals Is a Guarantee of the Federation's Stability (Interview with Eduard Rossel, Governor of Sverdlovsk

Province and Leader of the Transformation of Russia Movement)," January 19, 1996, translated in *Current Digest of the Post-Soviet Press* 48, no. 3 (1996), 21.

280 *By cooling the political temperature*: For the evidence, see Treisman, *After the Deluge*, chapters 4 and 5.

281 *"I have repeatedly heard rebukes"*: "Boris Yeltsin: Danger of Russia's Collapse Has Passed" (Interview with President Boris Yeltsin), *Trud*, August 26, 1994, translated in FBIS-SOV-94-166, 10–15.

281 *Yeltsin's adviser on political geography*: Leonid Smirnyagin, author's interview, Moscow, July 9, 1996.

281 *To the nationalist writer Aleksandr Solzhenitsyn*: Aleksandr Solzhenitsyn, "Traditsii rossiyskoy gosudarstvennosti i perspektivy federalizma" (Traditions of Russian Statehood and Prospects of Federalism), *Obshchaya Gazeta*, June 6–12, 1996.

281 *Yegor Stroyev*: Oleg Medvedev, "Federation Council Plays Stabilizing Role," *Business in Russia* 69 (September 1996): 16–18.

282 *"fixed him with a long, testing look"*: Baturin et al., *Epokha Yeltsina*, 598–99.

282 *The Justice Minister, Yury Kalmykov*: for Kalmykov's version, see Gall and de Waal, *Chechnya*, 158–60. No minutes were kept, and accounts of what was said, based on recollections of different participants, do not exactly correspond. For other versions, see Primakov, *Russian Crossroads*, 230; Seely, *Russo-Chechen Conflict*, 170; Mlechin, *Kreml*, 427–29.

282 *Then on December 11*: Zürcher, *The Post-Soviet Wars*, 81; Pavel Felgenhauer, "The Russian Army in Chechnya," *Central Asian Survey* 21, no. 2 (2002): 157–66, at 158–59.

282 *At the height of the Serb shelling of Sarajevo*: Remnick, *Resurrection*, 264; Tom de Waal, "Chechnya: The Breaking Point," in Sakwa, ed., *Chechnya: From Past to Future*, 181–98, at 182.

282 *"at the bottom of a grey, turbid sea"*: Lieven, *Chechnya*, 44.

282 *Two whole battalions of the 131st Maykop brigade*: Gall and de Waal, *Chechnya*, 8–10; Petrovsky, "Desyat let pozornomu shturmu Groznogo."

282 *Much of the city had been pulverized*: Gall and de Waal, *Chechnya*, 227; de Waal, "Chechnya: The Breaking Point," 183.

283 *"like a swarm of flies"*: Maskhadov interview, *Small Wars Journal*, June 1999, http://smallwarsjournal.com/documents/maskhadovinterview.pdf.

283 *At the checkpoints*: Gall and de Waal, *Chechnya*, 264.

283 *For several days, officials tried to negotiate*: Gall and de Waal, *Chechnya*, 262–75, provides a detailed account of the events.

283 *Six months later, another field commander*: Gall and de Waal, *Chechnya*, 289–304.

284 *signed the Khasavyurt Accords*: Gall and de Waal, *Chechnya*, 318–30.

284 *figures as high as 14,000*: "Casualty Figures," *Chechnya Weekly*, Jamestown Foundation, February 20, 2003.

284 *Tallies of civilian deaths*: Tishkov, *Chechnya*, xvi; Gall and de Waal, *Chechnya*, 399. Some give much higher figures, but these do not seem credible.

285 *The vast majority were active Muslims*: Mikhailov, "Chechnya and Tatarstan," 53, citing the 1989 census. On religion: Susan Goodrich Lehmann, "Islam and Ethnicity in the Republics of Russia," *Post-Soviet Affairs* 13, no. 1 (1997): 78–103.

285 *four thousand made the pilgrimage to Mecca*: Ormrod, "The North Caucasus," 103.

285 *The neighboring Avars*: Lehmann, "Islam and Ethnicity."

285 *They fought the Russians*: In the nineteenth century, "the concept of ethnicity, or nationality, in the western sense, was foreign to the inhabitants of this region" (Ronald Wixman, *Language Aspects of Ethnic Patterns and Processes in the North Caucasus* [Chicago: University of Chicago, 1980], 100).

285 *national identity began to emerge*: Sokirianskaia, "Ideology and Conflict," 104.

285 *Dudayev, in early speeches, also*: Quoted in Tishkov, *Chechnya*, 50. Of course, it is not so unusual for ambitious nationalists to have broader and narrower conceptions of their nation; in some ways, the Ingush were for Chechen nationalists what the Ukrainians were for their Russian counterparts. The difference was that the Russian nationalists wanted to absorb the Ukrainians into the Russian nation, whereas the Chechens recognized a broader identity into which both Chechens and Ingush could be folded.

285 *"Chechen," most experts agreed*: Shnirelman, "The Politics of a Name," 60–61.

286 *Some favored "Nokhchii"*: The ethnographer Yan Chesnov thought the term "Nokhchii" had "only just completed its general dissemination among Chechens" (Chesnov, "Byt chechentsem"); Tishkov believed that Chechens had only called themselves Nokhchii since 1991 (Tishkov, *Chechnya*, 53–54).

286 *It came from the Kumyk*: See Georgi Derluguian, *Bourdieu's Secret Admirer in the Caucasus* (Chicago: University of Chicago Press, 2005), 36–38; Shnirelman, "The Politics of a Name," 61.

286 *As for the clans*: See the fascinating sociological investigations of Ekaterina Sokirianskaia (e.g., in "Families and Clans in Ingushetia and Chechnya. A Fieldwork Report," *Central Asian Survey* 24, no. 4 [2005]: 453–67).

286 *In 1990, most Chechens disapproved*: Zalpa Bersanova, "Sistema tsennostey sovremennykh chechentsev (po materialam oprosov)," in Furman, ed., *Chechnya i Rossiya*. Bersanova conducted surveys in 1990, 1992, and 1995; in each year, the sample included about four hundred old and four hundred young respondents, divided more or less evenly between the mountain, plains, and city regions. The difficulties involved in polling a community at war result in various methodological imperfections; nevertheless the large differences reported are likely to reflect social reality.

286 *Chechens were not intensely anti-Russian*: Only 15 percent of old respondents and 32 percent of young ones considered "the Russian people to be guilty of the tragedy taking place with the Chechens."

286 *others had a more pragmatic outlook*: Sokirianskaia, "Ideology and Conflict"; Tishkov (*Chechnya*, 219) contends that the main concerns of most prewar Chechens were not their ethnic identity, clan, or the history of deportation but their earn-

ings, quality of life, and chances of getting a good education and a professional career.

286 *In fieldwork in the republic*: Sokirianskaia, "Ideology and Conflict," 109.

287 *Grozny's Oil Institute was staffed*: Shenfield, "Tataria and Chechnya," 63.

287 *a large "subproletariat" of underemployed*: Derluguian, *Bourdieu's Secret Admirer*, 150–51.

288 *"Oh, well, the more the merrier"*: Gall and de Waal, *Chechnya*, 85.

288 *"real military backbone"*: Morozov, *Above and Beyond*, 74.

289 *"He was absolutely ecstatic"*: Morozov, *Above and Beyond*, 75–76.

289 *almost a caricature of a third world dictator*: Were the unsympathetic journalists' accounts the result of ethnic bias, as some Dudayev defenders hint? The same journalists offered respectful descriptions of the less bombastic Maskhadov, and even saw an element of charisma in the terrorist Basayev.

289 *He would emerge for interviews*: for details in this paragraph, see Angus Roxburgh, "'I Warned my People the Russians Would Use Planes and Tanks against Us, but that We Would Triumph Because of the Spirit of Our Nation,'" *Guardian*, December 9, 1995; Lieven, *Chechnya*, 65–69; Gall and de Waal, *Chechnya*, 147; Thomas de Waal, "Yeltsin Softens Chechen Ultimatum," *Moscow Times*, December 2, 1994.

290 *paranoia or megalomania*: Lieven, *Chechnya*, 67; Angus Roxburgh, "'I Warned my People'"; Seely also quotes Yeltsin's adviser on nationality issues, Galina Starovoytova, to this effect (*Russo-Chechen Conflict*, 207).

290 *After an explosion killed*: the following details are from Tishkov, *Chechnya*, 51–52, 77, 79.

290 *"the military belief in the power of stern commands"*: Derluguian, *Bourdieu's Secret Admirer*, 20.

291 *"At that time," Nationalities Minister Nikolay Yegorov admitted*: OMRI *Daily Digest*, March 29, 1995.

291 *Abdulatipov thought*: Ramazan Abdulatipov, author's interview, Moscow, July 8, 1996.

291 *"The danger of Russia falling apart has passed"*: Colton, *Yeltsin*, 287.

291 *Yeltsin's main concern was oil*: for example, Elaine Holoboff, "Bad Boy or Good Business? Russia's Use of Oil as a Mechanism of Coercive Diplomacy," in Lawrence Freedman, ed., *Strategic Coercion: Concepts and Cases* (New York: Oxford University Press, 1998), 179–248, at 206.

291 *Although Chechnya's own reserves*: Mairbek Vatchagaev, "Oil in Chechnya: A Brief History," *Jamestown Foundation: North Caucasus Analysis*, April 17, 2008; Goskomstat Rossii, *Promyshlennost Rossii* (Moscow: Goskomstat Rossii, 1996).

291 *it would have been much cheaper*: Emil Pain, "The Chechen War in the Context of Contemporary Russian Politics," in Sakwa, ed., *Chechnya: From Past to Future*, 67–78, at 67; Sergei Kolesnikov, "Pipeline Project Set to Bypass Chechnya," *The Russia Journal*, October 17, 1999.

291 *One lawmaker said Security Council Secretary Oleg Lobov*: Gall and de Waal, *Chechnya*, 160–65.

291 *Lobov later denied*: Colton, *Yeltsin*, 290.

291 *Polls before the war*: Baturin et al., *Epokha Yeltsina*, 626.

291 *The liberal foreign minister Andrey Kozyrev*: Of course, it is difficult to pin down exactly what positions officials took since few claimed credit later for advocating force. In his memoir, Filatov writes that right after the November 26 attack, he shepherded through all the agencies a draft decree to impose a "state of emergency in Chechnya" and introduce Interior Ministry troops to help Avturkhanov "remain in control of Grozny," but that the president, apparently persuaded by Interior Minister Yerin, refused to sign it. Filatov was not at the Security Council meeting on November 29. He says in a 2004 BBC interview that Kozyrev was a "supporter of the force option" (*BBC Russian.com*, "Sergey Filatov: Dudayeva podobrala Moskva"). Kozyrev, in an interview, said that he had backed the military option, and he resigned from the Russia's Choice party after it took an antiwar position (Gall and de Waal, *Chechnya*, 158).

291 *it was Sergey Stepashin, the FSK head*: See, for instance, Gall and de Waal, *Chechnya*, 155; Mlechin, *Kreml*, 426–27.

292 *"provocative regularity*: Telen, *Pokolenie Putina*, 88–89.

292 *four gunmen hijacked*: Associated Press, "Previous Hijacking Incidents in Southern Russia with BC-Russia-Hijacking," October 27, 1994; Itar-TASS, July 29, 1994.

292 *Chechen gunmen kidnapped a young man in Kizlyar*: TASS, August 18, 1994.

292 *"A black hole of criminality"*: Yeltsin, *Midnight Diaries*, 55.

293 *one could buy a grenade launcher*: Markedonov, "Sistemnye separatisty"; Derluguian, *Bourdieu's Secret Admirer*, 253.

293 *In March 1992, he liquidated*: For following details, see Markedonov, "Sistemnye separatisty"; Timur Muzayev, "Chechenskaya Respublika Ichkeria: Obshchy Obzor," www.igpi.ru/monitoring/1047645476/oct_97/chechen.html.

293 *institutions like the Council of Elders*: Zürcher, *The Post-Soviet Wars*, 111–12; Jaimoukha, *The Chechens*, 62; Thomas de Waal, "Chechen Elders Aim to Lead in Land of Leaders," *Moscow Times*, December 7, 1994; Lieven, *Chechnya*, 79.

294 *"a general in whose hands"*: Interview with Mintimer Shaymiev, Russian TV, "Moment Istiny," August 2, 1997.

294 *"Intervention by force is impermissible"*: Russia TV channel, Moscow, August 11, 1994, 12:00, translated in BBC Summary of World Broadcasts, August 13, 1994.

294 *In August and September 1994*: Lieven, *Chechnya*, 88; *BBC Russian.com*, "Sergey Filatov: Dudayeva podobrala Moskva."

294 *Speed was suddenly of the essence*: Details for this paragraph are from Remnick, *Resurrection*, 283, quoting General Vorobyov; Felgenhauer, "The Russian Army in Chechnya," 158; Timothy Thomas, "The Battle of Grozny: Deadly Classroom for Urban Combat," *Parameters* (summer 1999): 87–102; Michael Specter, "How

the Chechen Guerrillas Shocked Their Russian Foes," *New York Times*, August 18, 1996; Gall and de Waal, *Chechnya*, 209.

295 *Yeltsin appeared genuinely shocked*: Details from Baturin et al., *Epokha Yeltsina*, 633, 618; Yeltsin, *Midnight Diaries*, 59–60; Mlechin, *Kreml*, 431; Remnick, *Resurrection*, 281; Lieven, *Chechnya*, 106.

296 *won with 59.3 percent of the vote*: BBC Summary of World Broadcasts, "Official Results of Chechen Presidential Elections Announced," February 3, 1997.

296 *"reject forever the use of force"*: Laurence Peter, "Yeltsin Signs Landmark Peace Treaty with Chechen Leader," Agence France Presse, May 12, 1997.

296 *About 250,000 people had left*: My calculations from Goskomstat Rossii's estimates of migration rates and initial population in Goskomstat Rossii, *Regiony Rossii* (Moscow: Goskomstat Rossii, 2001) and Goskomstat Rossii, *Rossiysky statistichesky yezhegodnik*, 1999.

297 *some remarkable breakthroughs*: Tishkov, *Chechnya*, 198–99.

297 *To make money, the warlords*: Details in this paragraph are from Ustinov, *Obvinyaetsya Terrorizm*, 135; Larisa Kislinskaya, "How Much Is a Russian Slave on Chechen Market?" *Sovershenno Sekretno*, March 15, 1999; David Filippov, "Kidnappers of All Stripes Thrive on Chaos in Chechnya," *Boston Globe*, July 4, 2000; Nabi Abdullaev, "Chechnya: Puppet State or Failed State?" *Transitions Online*, August 17, 2004, www.ceeol.com; Dzhabrail Gakaev, "Chechnya in Russia, and Russia in Chechnya," in Sakwa, ed., *Chechnya: From Past to Future*, 21–42, at 32; Robert Parsons, "Chechen President Orders Kidnap Crackdown," BBC News, December 13, 1998, http://news.bbc.co.uk/2/hi/europe/234180.stm.

297 *A Sharia criminal code*: R. Bekkin, V. Bobrovnikov, "Severny Kavkaz—ne tsarstvo blagorodnykh razboynikov," *Tatarsky mir*, December 2003; Associated Press, "Chechen Man Executed on Orders of Islamic Court," Grozny, April 23, 1997; Tishkov, *Chechnya*, 195.

298 *Such measures attracted the interest*: Paul Murphy, *The Wolves of Islam: Russia and the Faces of Chechen Terror* (Dulles, VA: Brassey's, 2004), 40, 33–34; Lorenzo Vidino, "How Chechnya Became a Breeding Ground for Terror," *Middle East Quarterly* 12, no. 3 (2005): 57–66.

298 *In May 1998, Wahhabis associated with Basayev*: Derluguian, "Che Guevaras in Turbans," *New Left Review* 1, no. 237 (1999): 3–27, at 11–12; Gammer, "Between Mecca and Moscow," *Middle Eastern Studies* 41, no. 6 (2005): 833–48, at 840.

298 *Maskhadov's rule did not extend*: Zürcher, *The Post-Soviet Wars*, 91–92.

298 *According to Stepashin*: Telen, *Pokolenie Putina*, 91–92; David Hoffman, "Miscalculations Paved Path to Chechen War," *Washington Post*, March 20, 2000.

298 *"There are criminals around me"*: quoted in Sokirianskaia, "Ideology and Conflict," 122.

298 *He lost even Moscow's support*: Telen, *Pokolenie Putina*, 91–92; Valery Yaremenko, "General Shpigun: pokhishchenie i smert," polit.ru, March 22, 2006, http://polit.ru/analytics/2006/03/22/shpigun.html.

299 *A plan was developed*: UPI, "Russia Closes Borders with Chechnya," April 26, 1999.

299 *anyone who paid attention*: Details in this paragraph are from Robert Bruce Ware, "A Multitude of Evils; Mythology and Political Failure in Chechnya," in Sakwa, ed., *Chechnya: From Past to Future*, 79–116, at 82; Tishkov, *Chechnya*, 4; Hoffman, "Miscalculations Paved Path to Chechen War."

299 *On August 6 and 7, the two led*: Souleimanov, *An Endless War*, 147.

299 *became a hero in Dagestan*: Ware, "A Multitude of Evils," 83.

300 *On September 29, Putin*: Ware, "A Multitude of Evils," 85; Quentin E. Hodgson, "Is the Russian Bear Learning? An Operational and Tactical Analysis of the Second Chechen War, 1999–2002," *Journal of Strategic Studies* 26, no. 2 (2003): 64–90, at 68.

300 *"pointless and technically impossible"*: Gevorkyan et al., *Ot pervogo litsa*, 135. Stepashin said in interviews that, after the terrorist attacks in Volgodonsk and Moscow, he too would not have stopped at the Terek (e.g., Telen, *Pokolenie Putina*, 88).

300 *had not stopped attacks*: As recently as early August, four Chechens on horseback had kidnapped a shepherd while another gang had fired grenades at a local police car. See ITAR-TASS, "Police Release Shepherd from Captivity in Stavropol Region," August 12, 1999; ITAR-TASS, "Chechens Fire on Police Patrol Car in Stavropol Territory," August 9, 1999.

300 *bombed for four weeks*: Felgenhauer, "The Russian Army in Chechnya," 159; Hodgson, "Is the Russian Bear Learning?," 73.

300 *By February 2000, the federal troops*: Zürcher, *The Post-Soviet Wars*, 93; Hodgson, "Is the Russian Bear Learning?" 68; Felgenhauer, "The Russian Army in Chechnya," 163.

301 *"black widows" began appearing*: Irina Lagunina, "Russia: Nord-Ost Anniversary Recalls Ascent of Female Suicide Bomber," RFE/RL, October 27, 2006, http://www.rferl.org/content/Article/1072365.html.

301 *then spread to Moscow*: Vidino, "How Chechnya Became a Breeding Ground for Terror."

301 *Speakers recited slogans*: Mark Kramer, "Guerrilla Warfare, Counterinsurgency and Terrorism in the North Caucasus: The Military Dimension of the Russian-Chechen Conflict," *Europe-Asia Studies* 57, no. 2 (2005): 209–90, at 251.

301 *Al Qaeda set up an outpost there*: Paul Quinn-Judge, "Inside Al-Qaeda's Georgian Refuge," *Time*, October 19, 2002; Vidino, "How Chechnya Became a Breeding Ground for Terror."

302 *In March 2000, 70 percent of respondents*: VCIOM poll data, from russiavotes.com.

302 *thousands of people demonstrated*: Lyall, "Pocket Protests."

302 *In March 2003, a referendum*: Gakaev, "Chechnya in Russia," 36.

302 *"Kill as many Russians"*: Yelena Samoilova, "Pervuyu mashinu mne kupil Basayev," *Vlast*, 21, June 4, 2002.

302 *Shamil Basayev put a price*: "Biografia Akhmata Kadyrova," May 9, 2004, http://www.newsru.com/russia/09may2004/terakt.html.

303 *At times, Kadyrov pressed Putin*: "Akhmat Kadyrov: yesli by diktatorom v Chechne byl ya ...," *Novaya Gazeta*, March 21, 2002.

303 *In the presidential election*: Seth Mydans, "Russia's Chechnya Chief Wins Election, but Many Experts Cry Foul," *New York Times*, October 7, 2003.

303 *Kadyrov was killed*: There are several theories about who did this. Basayev and the Islamic mujahideen are obvious suspects. Some have suggested it might have had something to do with ongoing conflicts with Russian military interests over the control of Chechen oil (John Russell, "The Geopolitics of Terrorism: Russia's Conflict with Islamic Extremism," *Eurasian Geography and Economics* 50, no. 2 [2009]: 184–196, at 190.)

303 *Human rights organizations had accused*: See, for instance, Human Rights Watch, *Swept Under: Torture, Forced Disappearances, and Extrajudicial Killings During Sweep Operations in Chechnya* (Washington, DC: Human Rights Watch, 2002), http://www.hrw.org/en/node/77296/section/1; Amnesty International, *The Russian Federation: Denial of Justice* (London: Amnesty International, 2002).

303 *One scholar, using a broad set of sources*: Jason Lyall, "Are Coethnics More Effective Counterinsurgents? Evidence from the Second Chechen War," *American Political Science Review* 104, no. 1 (2010): 1–20.

303 *Kadyrov rejected the allegations*: Andrew Osborn, "Ramzan Kadyrov: The Warrior King of Chechnya," *The Independent*, January 4, 2006. For chilling accounts of alleged violence by the Kadyrovtsy, see, for instance Åsne Seierstad, *The Angel of Grozny: Inside Chechnya* (London: Virago, 2008).

303 *Yandarbiev, in exile in Qatar*: A Qatar court convicted the two Russians of the murder in June 2004; Russian authorities denied any involvement, but negotiated an agreement with Qatar under which the two were returned to Russia to serve out their sentences there (Steven Lee Myers, "Qatar Court Convicts Two Russians in Top Chechen's Death," *New York Times*, July 1, 2004).

303 *Then Basayev was killed*: C.J. Chivers, "Putin Honors Russia Agents After Death of Terrorist," *New York Times*, July 21, 2006.

304 *"Our enemy is not only Russia"*: Andrei Smirnov, "Is the Caucasian Emirate a Threat to the Western World?," *North Caucasus Analysis*, Jamestown Foundation, December 7, 2007.

304 *Kadyrov rebuilt Grozny*: Simon Saradzhyan, "Chechnya Vow Cast a Long Shadow," *Moscow Times*, February 26, 2008. The state auditing agency, the Accounting Chamber, has accused the Chechen government of mismanaging federal assistance. In 2007, it announced that "an estimated R1.9 billion (US$71.7 million) had been either embezzled or misspent by pro-Moscow Chechen officials" (Kevin Leahy, "Putin-Kadyrov Spat Overshadows Grozny's Conflict with Russia's Economic Ministries," *Central Asia-Caucasus Institute Analyst*, April 8, 2009).

304 *Europe's largest mosque*: Russell, "The Geopolitics of Terrorism," 194.

304 *Movladi Baysarov, an outspoken critic*: Osborn, "Ramzan Kadyrov."

304 *Umar Israilov, was murdered*: Richard Spencer, "The Chechen Warlords Murdered Across the World," *Daily Telegraph*, March 31, 2009.

305 *A certain police investigation bureau, ORB-2*: Memorial Human Rights Center, *The Situation in the North Caucasus, Autumn 2007–Spring 2008* (Report by the Memorial Human Rights Centre dedicated to the new round of consultations between the EU and Russia, Ljubljana, April 16, 2008), http://www.memo.ru/2008/04/18/1804083.html.

305 *"Since then Memorial has not"*: Memorial Human Rights Center, *The Situation in the North Caucasus.*

305 *a lavish complex in the family home of Tsentoroy*: Megan Stack, "Chechen Tiger Without a Chain," *Los Angeles Times*, June 17, 2008.

306 *Playing to conservative opinion, Kadyrov*: Sokirianskaia, "Ideology and Conflict," 132.

306 *Anna Politkovskaya*: Tom Parfitt, "Putin Silent as Fiercest Critic Is Murdered," *Guardian*, October 9, 2006, www.guardian.co.uk/world/2006/oct/09/topstories3.russia.

306 *Paul Klebnikov*: Henry Meyer, "Prosecutor Says Chechen Ordered Slaying of *Forbes* Editor," Associated Press, Moscow, June 16, 2005. Both Klebnikov and Politkovskaya had written critically about various other powerful people and conducted numerous investigations, so there was no proof their deaths were Chechnya related. However, this was a leading theory in both cases.

306 *rose from 230 in 2005 to 398 in 2008*: Worldwide Incidents Tracking System, National Counterterrorism Center Database, http://wits.nctc.gov.

306 *Yunus-Bek Yevkurov, was severely injured*: Orkhan Dzhemal, Stepan Kravchenko, and Aleksandr Raskin, "Vaynakh na oba vashikh doma," *Russky Newsweek*, June 29–July 5, 2009.

307 *Yevkurov had announced his cell phone number*: Dzhemal, Kravchenko, and Raskin, "Vaynakh na oba vashikh doma."

307 *"Today . . . people with sinking hearts"*: Tatyana Lokshina, "Ochen tyazheloe nasledstvo," *Russky Newsweek*, June 29–July 5, 2009.

307 *In October, he sacked his entire government*: Dmitry Solovyov, "Ingush Leader Sacks His Cabinet over Poverty, Crime," Reuters, October 5, 2009, www.reuters.com/article/latestCrisis/idUSL570436.

307 *all those arrested after the terrorist attack*: Yekaterina Grigoreva, "Prezident Ingushetii Yunus-Bek Yevkurov: 'Ya boyus, chto iz-za menya mogut pogibnut nevinnye lyudi,'" *Izvestia*, October 30, 2009.

308 *"And not only in the North Caucasus"*: Vladimir Putin interviewed on "Sergey Dorenko's Program," First Channel, October 31, 1999.

CHAPTER 9: FALLING APART

310 *increased U.S. defense spending*: Data from President's Budget, as in www.usgovernmentspending.com/index.php, for defense spending in 1980 and 1986.

310 *a classified plan in May 1985*: Brutents, "Origins of the New Thinking," 75.

311 *Reagan refused to limit*: See Jack F. Matlock, Jr., *Reagan and Gorbachev: How the Cold War Ended* (New York: Random House, 2005), 215–50.

311 *eliminate such missiles entirely*: In the Intermediate-Range Nuclear Forces Treaty, signed in Washington in December 1987.

311 *START treaty*: Amy F. Woolf, *Nuclear Arms Control: The U.S.–Russian Agenda* (Washington, DC: Congressional Research Service, 2006).

311 *active duty Soviet soldiers fell*: Anthony Cordesman, *Western Military Balance and Defense Efforts* (Washington, DC: CSIS, 2002), 129.

311 *in the Conventional Forces in Europe Treaty*: F. Stephen Larrabee, "The New Soviet Approach to Europe," *Proceedings of the Academy of Political Science* 38, no. 1 (1991): 1–25, at 19.

313 *I present two versions*: These accounts are composites of the positions of various individuals, expressed over the years in the press and in conversations. I have synthesized them, in the process trying to avoid factual inaccuracies and emphasize those points that seem to me most persuasive. The goal is not to present a comprehensive review of thought on the relationship between Russia and the West, but just to articulate two opposing, influential points of view.

313 *Mulford threatened to halt shipments*: Gaidar, *Days*, 119; James M. Goldgeier and Michael McFaul, *Power and Purpose: US Policy Toward Russia After the Cold War* (Washington, DC: Brookings Institution, 2003), 71. Under pressure from the G7, the new finance ministers of the former Soviet states agreed to take "joint and several responsibility" for the debt. Eventually, Russia agreed to take full responsibility. The creditors agreed to defer payments on the principal for a year.

314 *The West had written off*: Jeffrey Sachs, *The End of Poverty: Economic Possibilities for Our Time* (New York: Penguin, 2005), 126.

314 *did not contain "a lot of new money"*: See Goldgeier and McFaul, *Power and Purpose*, 81–83; Sachs, *The End of Poverty*, 141.

314 *The IMF would use these loans*: Åslund, *How Russia Became a Market Economy*, 218.

314 *only $2.5 billion was actually provided*: Richard Layard and John Parker, *The Coming Russian Boom: A Guide to New Markets and Politics* (New York: The Free Press, 1996), 90.

314 *thought him a transitional figure*: See, for instance, Charles Krauthammer, "Who Is Losing Russia?" *Washington Post*, February 14, 1992.

314 *"down a rathole"*: General Brent Scowcroft, quoted in Goldgeier and McFaul, *Power and Purpose*, 61.

314 *Vice President Dan Quayle opined*: Jim Hoagland, "Little Help for Yeltsin," *Washington Post*, February 11, 1992.

314 *spying out targets*: According to Andrew Carpendale, Deputy Director of Policy Planning in the State Department in 1989–1992, interviewed by Goldgeier and McFaul, the cities where the U.S. military pilots landed to deliver humanitarian aid were chosen to enable them to get a closer look at targets in the U.S. strategic bombing plan (*Power and Purpose*, 78).

314 *"think bigger"*: Strobe Talbott, *The Russia Hand: A Memoir of Presidential Diplomacy* (New York: Random House, 2002), 53.

314 *Moscow brought home 800,000 troops*: Aron, *Russia's Revolution*, 59.

314 *450 apartments*: Talbott, *The Russia Hand*, 63; U.S. Department of State Dispatch, "Fact Sheet: Russia and U.S. Assistance—Group of Seven 1994 Economic Summit and G-7 Plus One Political Meeting, Naples, Italy, July 8–10, 1994," July 1994.

315 *trimmed by Congress*: Goldgeier and McFaul, *Power and Purpose*, 172.

315 *from $97 billion at its peak to less than $5 billion*: Anders Åslund, *Russia's Capitalist Revolution*, 299; Central Bank of Russia, "External Debt of the Russian Federation," 2005, 2007, 2009, www.cbr.ru/eng/statistics; the $97 billion figure comes from OECD, *Economic Surveys: Russian Federation* (Paris: OECD, 1997), 72.

315 *supplying the West with net flows of capital*: From 1992 to 1999, the Russian government paid $50.3 billion in foreign debt service (*Russian Economic Trends*, no. 3 [1999], 101, and no. 1 [2000], 71; *World Development Indicators* database for 1992 debt service). Net aid plus loans from other governments and international organizations came to about $36 billion during this period (*World Development Indicators* database).

315 *Total grants between the fall of communism*: Anders Åslund, "Russia," *Foreign Policy*, July–August 2001, 20–25.

315 *less than the cost of three B-2 bombers*: The total program unit acquisition cost of a B-2 bomber was $2.1 billion in 1996 (U.S. General Accounting Office, "B-2 Bomber: Cost and Operational Issues," August 14, 1997, www.fas.org/man/gao/nsiad97181.htm).

316 *Between 1990 and 1996, the number*: Cordesman, *Western Military Balance*, 128–29.

316 *"there would be no extension of NATO's jurisdiction"*: This is the wording recorded by the U.S. note taker, Dennis Ross. See Mark Kramer, "The Myth of a No-NATO-Enlargement Pledge to Russia," *Washington Quarterly* 32, no. 2 (2009): 39–61, at 48. Kramer makes a strong case that Gorbachev and Baker were discussing only the disposition of forces within Germany, not the possible admission of new countries to NATO.

316 *John Major told the Soviet defense minister*: from Dmitry Yazov's report to Gorbachev on his conversation with Major, March 6, 1991, quoted in Primakov, *Russian Crossroads*, 129–30.

316 *Both Yevgeny Primakov, Gorbachev's foreign policy aide, and Jack Matlock*: See Primakov, *Russian Crossroads*, 130; Matlock, the U.S. ambassador to the Soviet Union at the time and longtime State Department insider, said he thought the Western powers would have been willing to sign such an agreement in 1990, while answering questions at a talk on "Living with Russia," World Affairs Council, Los Angeles, November 19, 2007.

316 *Gorbachev never insisted*: He seems to have failed to anticipate then that expansion beyond Germany would become an issue. Asked in 2001 why he did not ask for a commitment not to expand NATO further, Gorbachev replied: "The Warsaw Pact still existed. How could you get anything in writing on that? Expansion of NATO at that stage would have meant the third world war" (Jonathan Steele, "Mikhail Gorbachev: The Russian Revolutionary," *Guardian*, August 18, 2001). Gorbachev did, nevertheless, feel that Western leaders had promised him that

NATO would not expand to the east, and called those who broke these promises "devoid of morality" ("Mikhail Gorbachev's Interview to the Editor-in-Chief of Aachener Zeitung," November 22, 2008, at www.gorby.ru/en/rubrs.asp?art_id=26383&rubr_id=307&page=1, accessed February 22, 2010). Western participants in the talks deny that any concrete promises were made.

317 *changed from why and if*: In Prague, in January 1994, President Clinton said that: "now the question is no longer whether NATO will take on new members but when and how" (quoted in James M. Goldgeier, "NATO Expansion: The Anatomy of a Decision," *Washington Quarterly* 21, no. 1 [1998]: 85–102, at 94).

317 *The leading Russia expert*: Talbott, *The Russia Hand*, 92. On Talbott's changing positions, see Goldgeier, "NATO Expansion."

317 *Partnership for Peace*: Partnership for Peace, launched in 1994, was a program under which all European countries, including Russia, could cooperate with NATO on a bilateral basis.

317 *Eighteen former U.S. ambassadors*: See Richard T. Davies, "Should NATO Grow?— A Dissent," *New York Review of Books*, September 21, 1995.

317 *he needed to win in Wisconsin*: See Goldgeier and McFaul, *Power and Purpose*, 197, quoting from an interview with Talbott. The quotation is from Talbott, recalling what Clinton had said to Yeltsin. In October 1996, campaigning in Detroit, Clinton promised to bring Poland and Hungary into the alliance by 1999 (John Harris, "Clinton Vows Wider NATO In 3 Years; Foreign Policy Stands Defended as Challenger Alleges 'Foot-Dragging'," *Washington Post*, October 23, 1996).

318 *Western leaders kept insisting*: In September 1994, Clinton told Yeltsin that Russia was eligible for NATO membership (Goldgeier and McFaul, *Power and Purpose*, 189). Vice President Albert Gore repeated this in December 1994 (Talbott, *The Russia Hand*, 145).

319 *"blue-sky stuff"*: Talbott, *The Russia Hand*, 132.

319 *In December 1991, Yeltsin had sent*: Thomas L. Friedman, "Soviet Disarray; Yeltsin Says Russia Seeks to Join NATO," *New York Times*, December 21, 1991.

319 *"we don't want to act like our problems are solved"*: Goldgeier and McFaul, *Power and Purpose*, 54.

320 *Chinese Embassy in Belgrade*: On May 7, 1999, NATO bombs struck the Chinese Embassy in Belgrade, killing three Chinese citizens. NATO said this was a mistake and apologized. Some newspapers reported claims that NATO bombed the embassy deliberately because it was providing communications assistance to the Serbian army (John Sweeney and Ed Vulliamy, "NATO Bombed Chinese Deliberately," *Observer*, October 17, 1999).

320 *They bombed the electricity grid*: Timothy Garton Ash, "Kosovo: Was It Worth It?" *New York Review of Books*, September 21, 2000.

320 *"objects indispensable to the survival"*: Michael Mandelbaum, "A Perfect Failure: NATO's War Against Yugoslavia," *Foreign Affairs*, September/October 1999, 2–8.

320 *of "dubious" legality*: Garton Ash, "Kosovo: Was It Worth It?"

320 *Before the bombing began, about 2,500 people*: Mandelbaum, "A Perfect Failure."

320 *During the eleven weeks NATO was bombing*: The exact casualty figure is disputed. The 4,400 refers to individuals identified as killed. Estimates including deaths not reported to authorities run as high as 10,000–12,000. See Patrick Ball et al., *Killings and Refugee Flow in Kosovo, March–June 1999* (Washington, DC: American Association for the Advancement of Science, 2002).

320 *Before the war, about 350,000 Kosovars*: Ivo H. Daalder and Michael E. O'Hanlon, *Winning Ugly: NATO's War to Save Kosovo* (Washington, DC: Brookings Institution Press, 2000), 41, 109.

320 *"conducted reverse ethnic cleansing of the Serbs"*: Garton Ash, "Kosovo: Was It Worth It?"

320 *branded a "terrorist organization"*: In early 1998, the U.S. special envoy to the Balkans, Robert Gelbard, said the KLA were terrorists (BBC News, "The KLA—Terrorists or Freedom Fighters?" June 28, 1998, http://news.bbc.co.uk/1/hi/world/europe/121818.stm).

320 *It was funded in part by heroin trafficking*: for this and the following claims, see, for example, Tom Walker, "US Alarmed as Mujahidin Join Kosovo Rebels," *Times* (London), November 26, 1998; Jerry Seper, "Clinton Urged to Justify KLA Funding: Senator Wants Report on Rebels' Drug, Terror Ties," *Washington Times*, May 8, 1999, A1; Colin Brown, "Attack on Afghanistan: Bin Laden Linked to Albanian Drug Gangs," *Independent on Sunday*, October 21, 2001, 6.

321 *the death of more than 100,000 Iraqis*: Associated Press, using Iraqi Health Ministry information and its own reports, estimated that at least 110,600 Iraqis had died violent deaths between the start of the war in 2003 and April 2009 (Kim Gamel, "AP Impact: Secret Tally Has 87,215 Iraqis Dead," Associated Press, Baghdad, April 23, 2009). Other sources give much higher figures.

321 *The KLA's strategy had been to provoke*: Tim Judah ("Impasse in Kosovo," *New York Review of Books*, June 10, 2004) makes this argument.

322 *only 22 percent of Ukrainians wanted to join NATO*: Judy Dempsey, "NATO Tests Ukraine's Readiness to Join," *International Herald Tribune*, June 16, 2008.

322 *more Ukrainians wanted to live in a union*: Poll by the Kiev-based R&B Group of a representative sample of 2,079 respondents from twenty-five Ukrainian regions, conducted in May 2009 (www.rb.com.ua/rus/politics/research/2009/4480.html.)

322 *their own government's discriminatory overreactions*: In March 2006, Russia placed an embargo on Georgian wine. After the Georgian authorities detained four alleged Russian spies in September 2006, the Russian authorities deported a number of Georgians, ordered schools to compile lists of children with Georgian names, and raided Georgian restaurants (Paul Willis, "Georgians Deported amid Spying Row," *Guardian*, October 6, 2006).

323 *"Georgia's territorial integrity is the goal of my life"*: International Crisis Group, *Abkhazia Today*, 2.

323 *In 2006 and 2007 alone, he bought*: United Nations Register of Conventional Arms, Report of the Secretary General (New York: UN, 2007, 2008), http://disarmament.un.org/cab/register.html#item1a.

323 *twelve times what it spent in 2002*: According to the Military Expenditure Database of the Stockholm International Peace Research Institute, at http://milexdata. sipri.org/result.php4, Georgian military spending in 2002 was $49 million and in 2007 was $592 million.

323 *sold Georgia five times as much*: U.S. sales to Georgia in 2003–2007 were $64 million, compared to $12 million in 1998–2002; commercial weapons exports licensed by Washington increased from nothing in 2003 to $57 million in 2006; see U.S. Department of Defense, *Foreign Military Sales, Foreign Military Construction Sales and Military Assistance Facts (DSCA FACTS BOOK)* at www.fas.org/programs/ ssp/asmp/factsandfigures/government_data/section655_FY2006.html for foreign military sales deliveries for 1998–2006 and commercial exports licensed, and, for 2007, the 2007 report on *Foreign Military Sales (FMS)* at www.fas.org/programs/ ssp/asmp/factsandfigures/government_data/section655_FY2007.html.

323 *sent troops to fire mortars into South Ossetia*: International Crisis Group, *Georgia: Avoiding War in South Ossetia*, ICG Europe Report 159, November 26, 2004, 16.

323 *cleared out local guerrillas in the Kodori Gorge*: International Crisis Group, *Abkhazia Today*, 19–20.

323 *sent about 12,000 heavily armed troops*: Ralf Beste et al., "Did Saakashvili Lie? The West Begins to Doubt the Georgian Leader," *Der Spiegel* (English Edition), September 15, 2008.

324 *"open challenge to Georgian sovereignty"*: European Union, *Independent International Fact-Finding Mission on the Conflict in Georgia Report*, 2009, vol. 1, 21, www.ceiig.ch/Report.html.

324 *killed two Russian soldiers and wounded five*: See Chapter 4. The Georgians said they were returning fire from the peacekeepers. Main sources for background on this include: C.J. Chivers and Ellen Barry, "Georgia Claims on Russia War Called into Question," *New York Times*, November 7, 2008; Uwe Klussmann, "Georgian Tanks vs. Ossetian Teenagers," *Der Spiegel* (English Edition), August 26, 2008; Peter Finn, "For South Ossetians, Bitterness Follows Attacks; Residents of Separatist Zone Describe Georgian Assault That Destroyed Houses and Apartment Buildings Across Their Capital," *Washington Post*, August 17, 2008; European Union, *Independent International Fact-Finding Mission*, 21.

324 *said he was responding to an incursion*: Ralf Beste et al., "Did Saakashvili Lie?"

324 *shell Tskhinvali*: See Chapter 4 for sources. As noted there, Saakashvili said he had "strictly ordered" the troops not to fire on civilians and that they were responding to fire coming from the center of Tskhinvali ("Saakashvili's Account of Events that Led to Conflict," Civil Georgia, August 25, 2008, www.civil.ge/eng/article. php?id=19282). However, monitors from the Organization for Cooperation and Security in Europe who were based in Tskhinvali did not record any outgoing fire that evening before the Georgian assault, and firing BM-21 rockets into a densely populated area could not help but kill civilians (Peter Finn, "A Two-Sided Descent Into Full-Scale War," *Washington Post*, August 17, 2001; European Union, *Independent International Fact-Finding Mission*, 23–4).

324 "*Georgia will become a member of NATO if it wants to*": UPI, "Merkel Meets with Georgian President," Tbilisi, August 17, 2008.

324 "*a problem for the world*": "Saakashvili's Account of Events that Led to Conflict," Civil Georgia.

325 *1,200 U.S. troops had conducted*: "Georgian, U.S. Troops Start Military Exercise Amid Escalating Tensions with Russia," Associated Press, Tbilisi, July 15, 2008.

325 *160 U.S. military advisers*: Ertel et al., "Road to War in Georgia." The following details are from U.S. Department of State, "Remarks with Georgian President"; *Russia & CIS General Newswire*, "Rice Meets Head of 'Provisional Tskhinvali Authorities'"; Eggen, "Cheney To Visit Georgia."

325 *driving American jeeps and wearing uniforms*: Klussmann, "Georgian Tanks vs. Ossetian Teenagers."

325 *the United States had intervened militarily in eleven countries*: Russian troops intervened in Tajikistan, Georgia, Moldova, and Nagorno-Karabakh (Azerbaijan). Not including training missions and evacuations, the U.S. military intervened with ground troops or airstrikes in Iraq (1991, 1998, 2003–), Somalia (1992–1995, 2007), Macedonia (1993–1994), Haiti (1994–1995), Bosnia (1995), Sudan (1998), Afghanistan (1998, 2001–), Serbia (1999), East Timor (1999–2001), Yemen (2000, 2002), and Pakistan (2006).

326 "*The fact is that the Western Hemisphere*": Robert Gates, then CIA deputy director, speaking in 1984, quoted in Gaddis Smith, *The Last Years of the Monroe Doctrine, 1945–1993* (London: Macmillan, 1995), 201.

326 *Grenada, U.S. forces had invaded*: Ronald H. Cole, *Operation Urgent Fury: The Planning and Execution of Joint Operations in Grenada 12 October–2 November 1983* (Washington, DC: Joint History Office of the Chairman of the Joint Chiefs of Staff, 1997), 6.

326 *shipped the Israelis precision-guided bombs*: David S. Cloud and Helene Cooper, "U.S. Speeds Up Bomb Delivery for the Israelis," *New York Times*, July 22, 2006.

326 *embargo on Cuba*: Joaquin Roy, *Cuba, The United States, and the Helms-Burton Doctrine: International Reactions* (Miami: University Press of Florida, 2000), 102, 114–16.

327 *thought him a crude demagogue*: One of the most negative was National Security Adviser Brent Scowcroft (Goldgeier and McFaul, *Power and Purpose*, 22).

327 *the U.S. delegation was "stunned"*: The president's top advisor on Russia at the National Security Council, Nicholas Burns, said of Yeltsin's speech that: "The President and all of us were stunned by it as there had been no advance warning." Strobe Talbott, Clinton's top advisor on Russia in the State Department, said that Yeltsin was being "erratic" (Goldgeier and McFaul, *Power and Purpose*, 192–93). Clinton, according to Talbott, said this had "rattled his confidence in Yeltsin's emotional, physical and political stability" and that Yeltsin had been "scoring cheap points" at his expense (Talbott, *The Russia Hand*, 154).

327 "*one of those things in life*": Clinton, as quoted by Talbott (*The Russia Hand*, 217).

327 *Enlargement was "going to happen"*: Strobe Talbott, "Why NATO Should Grow," *New York Review of Books*, August 10, 1995.

328 *"eat their spinach"*: from Talbott, *The Russia Hand*, 76:

> I had prepared for the encounter by writing out in advance a detailed argument on how it was in Russia's own interest to join us in threatening military retribution against the Serbs. . . . Halfway through my presentation, Kozyrev, with a look of exasperation, cut me off.
>
> "You know," he said, "it's bad enough having you people tell us what you're going to do whether we like it or not. Don't add insult to injury by also telling us that it's *in our interests* to obey your orders."
>
> Afterward, in the car riding back to the U.S. embassy, my assistant Toria Nuland could tell I was rattled. "That's what happens when you try to get the Russians to eat their spinach," she said. "The more you tell them it's good for them, the more they gag." Among those of us working on Russia policy, "administering the spinach treatment" became shorthand for one of our principal activities in the years that followed.

328 *"build up" President Medvedev*: Peter Baker, "Preparing for Trip to Russia, Obama Praises Putin's Protégé, at Putin's Expense," *New York Times*, July 2, 2009.

328 *Obama's approval rating trailed*: A Washington Post/ABC News poll had Obama in mid-July at 59 percent approval (www.washingtonpost.com/wp-srv/politics/polls/postpoll_072009.html); the latest available Levada Center poll had Medvedev at 71 percent approval (www.russiavotes.org).

328 *"which I believe you have, we strongly support that"*: Maria Danilova, "Biden: U.S. Supports Ukraine's NATO Bid, Says Kiev Free to Choose Its Own Alliances," Associated Press, Kiev, July 21, 2009.

328 *22 percent of Ukrainians*: Judy Dempsey, "NATO Tests Ukraine's Readiness to Join," *International Herald Tribune*, June 16, 2008.

328 *Did it not know that whereas 81*: Pew Research Center, *47-Nation Pew Global Attitudes Survey* (Washington, DC: Pew Research Center, 2007), at http://pewglobal.org/reports/pdf/256.pdf.

329 *Only 23 percent said they felt good*: Levada Center poll at www.russiavotes.org.

329 *Russians remained more pro-American*: In the spring of 2007, 41 percent of Russian respondents had a favorable view of the United States, compared to 39 percent in France, 34 percent in Spain, 30 percent in Germany, and 9 percent in Turkey. See Pew Research Center, *47-Nation Pew Global Attitudes Survey*.

329 *had good reason to fear NATO*: Levada Center poll, July 18–21, 2008, www.russiavotes.org.

329 *Russia invested more in the United States in 2008*: Goskomstat Rossii, *Rossiysky statistichesky yezhegodnik*, 2009.

330 *75 percent opposed providing cash grants*: Richard Morin, "Most in Poll Reject Giving Soviets Cash," *Washington Post*, August 29, 1991.

331 *Boris Fyodorov, the former finance minister*: See, for instance, Boris Fyodorov, "Moscow Without Mirrors," *New York Times*, April 1, 1994.

332 *"Poland and Russia are two sovereign states"*: "Yeltsin in Poland," *Polish News Bulletin*, August 26, 1993, via Lexis.

334 *Together, the Czechs, Hungarians, and Poles*: Estimated for 2006 from International Institute for Strategic Studies, *The Military Balance* (London: IISS, 2008); according to the IISS, Russia spent on defense $70 billion in 2006, Poland spent $6.2 billion, Hungary $1.3 billion, and the Czech Republic $2.5 billion.

334 *Russia's own Rosoboronexport*: "Rosoboronexport Upgrading Russian-made Aircraft in NATO Nations' Inventory," *Russia & CIS Military Newswire*, December 5, 2006.

336 *with 10 percent of the world's oil reserves*: Oil reserves data calculated from U.S. Energy Information Administration, *Iran Energy Profile*, at http://tonto.eia.doe.gov/country/country_energy_data.cfm?fips=IR, downloaded December 5, 2008.

336 *planning to sell Tehran centrifuges*: Goldgeier and McFaul, *Power and Purpose*, 181.

336 *The Kremlin had sent consultants*: See Petrov and Ryabov, "Russia's Role in the Orange Revolution," 145–64. Vyacheslav Nikonov and Gleb Pavlovsky were two (of several) political consultants sent to Ukraine by the Kremlin to help the presidential campaign of the pro-Russian Viktor Yanukovich in 2004. When Yanukovich was declared the winner, thousands of supporters of his opponent, Viktor Yushchenko, took to the streets of Kiev to protest widespread electoral fraud in what became known as the "Orange Revolution." Eventually, a new vote was ordered by the Supreme Court, which Yushchenko won.

337 *Then there was the crudeness*: Details for this paragraph are from Peter Finn, "Protesters in Moscow Harass Estonian Envoy over Statue," *Washington Post*, May 3, 2007; Andrew Kramer, "Russia Cuts Off Gas to Ukraine as Talks on Pricing and Transit Terms Break Down," *New York Times*, January 2, 2006; Luke Harding, "Russia Unwilling to Hand Over Litvinenko Suspect to Yard," *Guardian*, January 27, 2007; Adrian Blomfield, "Estonia Calls for NATO Strategy on 'Cyber-Terrorists' after Coming Under Attack," *Daily Telegraph*, May 18, 2007; Marc Champion, "How Russia Seeks to Shape Europe's Security Posture," *Wall Street Journal*, June 12, 2007; Leon Aron, "The Problematic Pages," *New Republic*, September 24, 2008.

338 *thirteen interstate working groups*: "U.S.–Russia Bilateral Presidential Commission," White House, July 6, 2009, www.whitehouse.gov/the_press_office/FACT-SHEET-US-Russia-Bilateral-Presidential-Commission/.

338 *military to military contacts*: "United States–Russia Military to Military Relations," White House, July 6, 2009, www.whitehouse.gov/the_press_office/United-States-Russia-Military-to-Military-Relations/.

339 *NATO countries had refused to ratify*: In early 2008, Russia had about 1,000 troops in Georgia and about 1,200 in Moldova (International Institute for Strategic Studies, *The Military Balance*, 2008, 222).

CHAPTER 10: THE RUSSIA THAT HAS RETURNED

340 *"a headless horseman"*: Nicholas Kristof, "The Poison Puzzle," *New York Times*, December 15, 2004.

340 *"ominously similar to Stalin's and Hitler's"*: See Nathan Gardels's August 2008 interview with Brzezinski in *New Perspectives Quarterly*, Fall 2008, at http://www.digitalnpq.org/archive/2008_fall/11_brzezinski.html.

340 *"Hitler's power was consolidated"*: Niall Ferguson, "Look Back at Weimar—and Start to Worry about Russia," *Daily Telegraph*, January 1, 2005. On "renationalization of the entire energy sector," see below.

341 *"Like Mussolini, Putin favors stylish black"*: Alexander J. Motyl, "Inside Track: Is Putin's Russia Fascist?" *The National Interest* online, December 3, 2007, www.nationalinterest.org/Article.aspx?id=16258. The "presumed" is a particularly nice touch.

341 *Ferdinand Marcos, Anastasio Somoza, Park Chung Hee, and Kim Jong Il*: Robert Kagan, "Stand Up to Putin," *Washington Post*, September 15, 2004; Daniel Schor, reviewing the week's news on NPR's "Weekend Edition", c. 8:15 a.m., October 2, 2003, www.npr.org/rundowns/rundown.php?prgDate=02-Oct-2004&prgld=7.

341 *Since 2005, it has rated Russia's*: See Freedom House's website at www.freedomhouse.org/template.cfm?page=15.

341 *The United Arab Emirates*: See "United Arab Emirates 2009" in Freedom House, *Freedom in the World 2009* (New York: Freedom House, 2009) www.freedomhouse.org/template.cfm?page=22&year=2009&country=7727. Freedom House states on its website that its ratings for Russia do *not* include Chechnya, where political rights and civil liberties are in much worse shape than in most other parts of the country. I contacted Freedom House in September 2009 to inquire whether it genuinely considered Russia under Putin no more democratic than a federation of absolute monarchs. A representative explained that in the finer-grained sub-scores, Russia was rated slightly higher than UAE, with a total for political rights of 8 out of a possible 40, compared to UAE's 5. Looking at the sub-scores does not entirely resolve the puzzle, however. On these, it turns out that Russia is rated lower for political rights than Mauritania, a country ruled by a military junta that had just overthrown the elected president in a coup, arresting top civilian officials and taking over the state broadcast media. On "electoral process," Russia is rated equal to Oman, where the only elections are for a consultative council with no legislative power.

342 *Yemen*: Freedom House, *Freedom in the World 2009*, "Yemen 2009," www.freedomhouse.org/template.cfm?page=363&year=2009&country=7735; Amnesty International, *Amnesty International Report 2009* (London: Amnesty International, 2009), "Yemen," http://thereport.amnesty.org/en/regions/middle-east-north-africa/yemen; Hamed Thabet, "Yemen: 8-Year-Old Girl Asks for Divorce in Court," *Yemen Times*, March 14, 2008, online at www.wluml.org/english/newsfulltxt.shtml?cmd[157]=x-157-561353. In fairness, in its sub-scores Freedom House does rate Yemen slightly lower than Russia in two of the four civil rights areas; in the other two, the countries' scores are the same.

343 *Russia has become quite similar*: For a similar analysis written in 2003–2004, see "A Normal Country: Russia after Communism," *Journal of Economic Perspectives*

19, no. 1 (2005), co-authored with Andrei Shleifer. I am grateful to Andrei for his thoughts and continuing inspiration on this subject. Being normal does not mean being average in all regards; if it did, few, if any, countries could be considered normal. Nor is it abnormal for an individual to be below average in most or all regards—in any classroom, one will find some perfectly normal students who fit this description. Normal individuals may also stand out from the crowd in one or two ways. What makes a person or country abnormal is if they are outliers in more dimensions than the others or if their scores on one dimension are so far from those of others as to render them fundamentally different. In the classroom analogy, one might classify as abnormal the extremely gifted or those with learning disabilities. The prevailing Western view in recent years seems to be that Russia belongs in the latter category.

343 *Some saw this as a sign*: See, for example, the Congressional hearings held around this time. For instance, U.S. House of Representatives, "An Examination of the Russian Economic Crisis and the International Monetary Fund Aid Package," September 10, 1998, http://commdocs.house.gov/committees/bank/ hba51201.000/hba51201_0f.htm.

344 *forty-eight countries had years in which*: calculated from the World Bank's *World Development Indicators*, 2009.

344 *in neighboring Belarus*: calculations from the EBRD's *Macroeconomics Database*.

344 *Mexico's Carlos Slim Helú*: According to *Forbes*'s research, in 2008 Russia's richest citizen, Oleg Deripaska, was worth $28 billion. Slim Helú had assets worth $60 billion, and Mittal $45 billion. Among the world's ten richest individuals, there were three Indians and one Russian.

344 *From Mexico and Brazil*: La Porta, Lopez-de-Silanes, and Shleifer, "Corporate Ownership around the World."

344 *connections in government*: Mara Faccio, "Politically Connected Firms," *American Economic Review* 96, no. 1 (2006): 369–86. Billionaires—such as Silvio Berlusconi—also serve in government in developed countries.

344 *Russia's income inequality*: These comparisons are based on the World Income Inequality Database (http://62.237.131.23/wiid/wiid-documentation1.php). It gives the following Gini indexes (in each case, I list the most recent estimate available): Latvia .390 (2006), Turkey .450 (2003), Russia .451 (2006), USA .466 (2004), China .469 (2004), Venezuela .476 (2005), Argentina .483 (2006), Brazil .564 (2005), South Africa .578 (2000).

345 *those saying "yes" averaged 18 percent*: calculated from Global Corruption Barometer surveys, available at www.transparency.org/policy_research/surveys_indices/gcb.

345 *close to the proportion—16.6 percent*: UN International Crime Victims Survey; UN *Human Development Report*, 2002, Table 21, and Anna Alvazzi del Frate and J. van Kesteren, "Some Preliminary Tables from the International Crime Victim Surveys," *Criminal Victimisation in Urban Europe* (Turin: United Nations Interregional Crime and Justice Research Institute), www.unicri.it/wwd/analysis/icvs/ statistics.php.

346 *democracy à la mexicaine*: Details in this paragraph are from Alma Guillermoprieto, "'The Morning Quickie,'" *New York Review of Books*, August 12, 2004; Sam Enriquez, "Scandal? DC's Got Nothing on Mexico," *Los Angeles Times*, February 18, 2006; James McKinley, Jr., "Mexico Says Drug Cartel Had Spy in President's Office," *New York Times*, February 7, 2005; Joel Kurtzman, "Mexico's Instability Is a Real Problem," *Wall Street Journal*, January 16, 2009; Sam Quinones, "State of War," *Foreign Policy*, March/April 2009; Sophie Nicolson, "Desperate Families Snub Corrupt Police in Mexico Kidnap Epidemic," AFP, Mexico City, August 18, 2008.

346 *Further south, there is Argentina*: Details in this paragraph are from AFP, "Siemens Admits Corruption with Former Argentine Leaders," Buenos Aires, December 17, 2008; Alexei Barrionuevo, "In Argentina, the Campaign of 'Queen Cristina' Focuses on Global Relations," *New York Times*, September 25, 2007; Alexei Barrionuevo, "Cash-stuffed Suitcase Splits Venezuela and Argentina," *New York Times*, August 14, 2007; Carlos Lauría, "News for Sale: CPJ Special Report," Committee to Protect Journalists, October 23, 2007, http://cpj.org/reports/2007/10/news-for-sale-in-argentina.php; Reuters, "Factbox: 'Argentinization' of Companies," July 10, 2008, http://uk.reuters.com/article/idUKN1047883020080710; Celia Szusterman, "The Kirchner Model: King and Queen Penguin," *Opendemocracy.net*, July 17, 2007, www.opendemocracy.net/article/kirchner_model_king_queen_penguin.

347 *correct reference point is Turkey*: Details in this paragraph are from Zeyno Baran, "Corruption: The Turkish Challenge," *Journal of International Affairs* 54, no. 1 (2000): 127–46, at 137; Sarah Rainsford, "'Deep State' Plot Grips Turkey," BBC News, Istanbul, February 4, 2008, http://news.bbc.co.uk/2/hi/europe/7225889.stm; Gareth Jenkins, *Between Fact and Fantasy: Turkey's Ergenekon Investigation* (Washington, DC: School of Advanced International Studies, 2009), 10, 12–13, 20.

348 *ballot stuffing, falsification of results, and bullying of voters*: Considerable evidence is summarized in M. Steven Fish, *Democracy Derailed in Russia: The Failure of Open Politics* (New York: Cambridge University Press, 2005), chapter 3.

348 *quite bizarre from a statistical point of view*: For analyses, see, for instance, Mikhail Myagkov, Peter Ordeshook, and Dmitrii Shakin, "Fraud or Fairytales? Russian and Ukrainian Electoral Experience," *Post-Soviet Affairs* 21, no. 2 (2005): 91–131, and Andrei Beryozkin, Mikhail Myagkov, and Peter Ordeshook "Location and Political Influence: A Further Elaboration of Their Effects on Voting in Recent Russian Elections," *Eurasian Geography and Economics* 44, no. 3 (2003): 169–83.

348 *almost entirely redundant*: As the following table shows, in almost all elections the forecasts for the Kremlin-favored parties have been very close to the actual results. Unity and United Russia did several percentage points better than the average forecast, but Putin and Medvedev did slightly worse than predicted. It could be that the way in which the pollsters computed their forecasts already factored in expected levels of falsification or pressures on election day. But the straight poll results from preelection polls also predict the outcomes well (with the one exception of 1993, when VCIOM's polls were still being perfected).

Forecasts of pollsters and election results, Russia 1993–2008

	1993	1995	1996*	1999	2000	2003	2004	2007	2008
Kremlin favorite:	Russia's Choice	OHIR	Yeltsin	Unity	Putin	United Russia	Putin	United Russia	Medvedev
Forecasts of:									
FOM		9.2	34	20	53	33.6	73	63	70.0
VCIOM	15	10	35–9	17	53–55	33–35	73.6	62.1	72.6
Levada Center						33.7	73.7	62.8	73.8
Average forecast	15	9.6	35.5	18.5	53.5	33.8	73.4	62.6	72.1
Actual percent of total votes	14.5	10.1	35.1	23.3	52.9	37.6	71.3	64.3	70.3

* First round in 1996

Sources: 1993: VCIOM: Yury Levada, Nashi desyat let: itogi i problemy, www.levada.ru/levadaocherki.html, 248.

1995: FOM: http://bd.english.fom.ru/report/map/oslon/ed034726. VCIOM: Yury Levada, Nashi desyat let: itogi i problemy, http://www.levada.ru/levadaocherki.html, 249.

1996: FOM: http://bd.english.fom.ru/report/map/oslon/ed034726. VCIOM: Yury Levada, Nashi desyat let: itogi i problemy, http://www.levada.ru/levadaocherki.html, 249.

1999: FOM: http://bd.english.fom.ru/report/map/oslon/ed034726. VCIOM: http://www.yabloko.ru/Press/1999/9912154.html.

2000: FOM: http://bd.english.fom.ru/report/map/oslon/ed034726. VCIOM: www.polit.ru/news/2000/03/22/ (March 21, 2009, Polit.ru).

2003: Levada: party vote is percent of those intending to vote, from November 13–16 survey, adjusted to exclude those planning to vote but who say "don't know" for whom, www.levada.ru/press/2003112104.html. FOM: http://bd.english.fom.ru/report/map/oslon/ed034726. VCIOM: http://wciom.ru/arkhiv/tematicheskii-arkhiv/item/single/29.html?no_cache=1&cHash=febd77c4a5.

2004: Levada: www.levada.ru/press/2004031802.html. FOM: http://bd.fom.ru/report/map/o040802. VCIOM: http://wciom.ru/arkhiv/tematicheskii-arkhiv/item/single/623.html?no_cache=1&cHash=3944901775.

2007: Levada: www.levada.ru/press/2007120301.html. FOM: http://bd.fom.ru/report/cat/prognoz261107. VCIOM: http://wciom.ru/arkhiv/tematicheskii-arkhiv/item/single/9240.html?no_cache=1&cHash=378e108cc3.

2008: All: www.cikrf.ru/rcoit/news/politprogn_2008.pdf. Electoral results: Central Electoral Commission of the Russian Federation.

348   *The electoral results for each party*: I interpolated where data were missing. Where possible, I used fitted values from a regression of voting preferences for a given party on answers to another VCIOM/Levada question that asked with which party respondents "sympathized." (For instance, I regressed the percent saying they would vote for the Communists on the percent saying they sympathized with the Communists and used fitted values to fill gaps in the first series.) The series on voters' sympathies started later than that on vote preferences but had fewer gaps. The correlations between sympathy and voting for a given party were high. Where this was not possible, I simply interpolated linearly from the surrounding values in the series. Interpolations represent 41 percent of the data for the Communists and Russia's Choice and 23 percent for Unity/United Russia.

348   *the results roughly reflected*: Even the opposition seemed to accept this. After the 2003 vote, Zyuganov accused the Kremlin of rigging the election. Nevertheless, his party's

parallel vote tally had it winning just .03 percentage points more than it did officially ("Communists Say Duma Vote Was Rigged," *Gazeta.ru*, December 10, 2003).

349 *In Malaysia, Venezuela, and Argentina*: See Shleifer and Treisman, "A Normal Country."

349 *In the Philippines and Thailand*: See, for example, Michael Buehler, "Suicide and Progress in Modern Nusanatara," *Inside Indonesia*, July–September 2009, http://insideindonesia.org/content/view/1217/47/.

349 *disproportionate coverage of Kremlin-connected parties*: See, for example, Scott Gehlbach and Konstantin Sonin, "Government Control of the Media," University of Wisconsin, Madison: manuscript, July 2009.

350 *a total of forty-two hours*: In this connection, Freedom House's claim in its report on Russia in 2008 that "debate was absent" from the 2008 campaign is a little puzzling. There were forty-two hours of debate on the national airwaves, funded by the state. It is true that Dmitry Medvedev opted not to participate in the debates; this did not stop his opponents from criticizing him in his absence. To compare with one more venerable democracy, it is hard to recall the last time the U.S. government paid the national networks to broadcast hours of debate between a communist, an ultranationalist, and a centrist presidential candidate, all of them from parties with minority support.

350 *The most sophisticated analysis*: Ruben Enikolopov, Maria Petrova, and Ekaterina Zhuravskaya, "Television and Political Persuasion in Young Democracies: Evidence from Russia," Moscow: CEFIR, 2007.

350 *Jason Lyall studied*: Lyall, "Pocket Protests." Lyall attributes the relative ineffectiveness of these demonstrations to the inability of their organizers, rooted in the old dissident intellectual culture, to frame the protests in terms that would have broad appeal.

350 *Two other researchers*: Tomila Lankina and Alexey Savrasov, "Growing Social Protest in Russia," *Russian Analytical Digest*, May 19, 2009, www.res.ethz.ch/analysis/rad/details.cfm?lng=en&id=100499.

351 *"great practical and philosophical idea"*: John Stuart Mill, *Autobiography* (New York: Henry Holt & Co., 1887), 258.

351 *Yet Putin's reform was viewed*: For instance, Michael McFaul ("Sovereign Democracy and Shrinking Political Space," *Russia Business Watch*, April–June 2006, www.usrccne.org/news2.phtml?m=244) includes "eliminating the single mandate ('district') elections that formerly contributed one-half of the State Duma's composition" in a list of signs that Russia was moving "in an autocratic direction."

351 *editorialists waxed indignant*: For example, the *Boston Globe*'s editorial "Anointed by the Kremlin Boss," December 11, 2007, www.boston.com/bostonglobe/editorial_opinion/editorials/articles/2007/12/11/anointed_by_the_kremlin_boss/. Of course the way Putin announced his support for Medvedev, pretending that the suggestion had come autonomously from a group of party leaders, was farcical (see Chapter 4).

352 *rules out the Freedom House index*: Another set of country ratings is the "voice and accountability" index compiled by the World Bank on the basis of a number of expert ratings and surveys. However, this also gives Russia almost exactly the same score as the United Arab Emirates, which is not surprising since the strongest-weighted source used by the World Bank is the Freedom House political rights rating. The two indexes are correlated at r = –.95.

352 *Russia's Polity score ranged*: See the Polity website www.systemicpeace.org/polity/polity4.htm. Even the Polity coders may not be immune to outside pressure. Until September 2009, Polity had scored Russia between 4 and 7 in 1992–2007. In September 2009, however, the group published an "update" of some of its figures. These reduced Russia's Polity scores by one point for the entire period from 1992. They also raised the rating of Estonia, which had been given only a 6—less than a perfect democracy score, because of its continued disenfranchisement of part of its population by means of a demanding language exam—to 9, close to a perfect score. The only explanation Polity provided for these changes referred to information that had been widely known for years and already mentioned in previous Polity reports. When I contacted the director of the Polity team, he explained that an ongoing reevaluation of democracy scores was in progress. Despite my repeated inquiries, he did not give any specific explanation for the changes to Russia's and Estonia's scores. When I asked if these changes might have something to do with the fact that since the late 1990s the project has relied on funding from the U.S. government's Political Instability Task Force, which is itself funded by the Central Intelligence Agency (see www.systemicpeace.org/polity/polity4.htm), he replied: "As regards my response to pressure from our U.S. Government supporters, you can be sure that I consider their perspectives as seriously as the many inquiries and criticisms I receive from academics and other experts. There has never been any serious arm-twisting from either side; not that such tactics would be strong enough to induce me to make changes that I did not feel were warranted by the evidence." While I have confidence in the integrity of the individual involved, I remain baffled by why the project would be unwilling or unable to explain why the scores of these countries were changed, purportedly on the basis of information that had been well known for years. The one-point reduction in Russia's rating does not affect my argument. On Figure 10.2, I show Russia's and Estonia's positions with the new, revised Polity scores. The old score would place Russia slightly higher.

352 *Russia is certainly not the outlier*: Even if one excludes the major oil and gas producers apart from Russia, as well as the outlier Singapore, Russia remains close to the trend line.

352 *Andreas Schedler calls "the foggy zone"*: Andreas Schedler "The Menu of Manipulation," *Journal of Democracy* 13, no. 2 (2002): 36–50.

354 *To Ferguson, the Kremlin's control*: Ferguson, "Look Back at Weimar."

354 *In Yemen*: Freedom House, *Freedom of the Press 2008* (New York: Freedom House, 2008), www.freedomhouse.org/template.cfm?page=251&year=2008; Human Rights

Watch, "Yemen: Closure of Newspaper, Journalist Flogging," June 19, 2001, www .hrw.org/en/news/2001/06/19/yemen-closure-newspaper-journalist-flogging.

354 *CTC, Domashny, TV3, DTV, MTV*: Ivan Zassoursky, "Free to Get Rich and Fool Around," in Birgit Beumers, Stephen Hutchings, and Natalia Rulyova, eds., *The Post-Soviet Russian Media: Conflicting Signals* (London: Taylor and Francis, 2009), 31.

355 *Indeed, one columnist was surprised to find*: Konstantin Sonin, "Pravila igry: teoria praktikov," http://premier.gov.ru/premier/press/ru/4417/, downloaded May 2,2010.

355 *"the Russian audience well understands"*: Sarah Oates, "The Neo-Soviet Model of the Media," *Europe-Asia Studies* 59, no. 8 (2007): 1279–97, at 1285. See also Ellen Mickiewicz, *Television, Power, and the Public in Russia* (New York: Cambridge University Press, 2008).

355 *increase in advertising revenues*: Gehlbach and Sonin, "Government Control of the Media."

355 *in regions of Russia where advertising revenues*: Maria Petrova, "Political Economy of Media Capture," in Roumeen Islam, ed., *Information and Public Choice: From Media Markets to Policy Making* (Washington, DC: World Bank, 2008), 132.

356 *the Korean tax agency investigated*: Shleifer and Treisman, "A Normal Country."

356 *In Turkey in September 2009*: *Economist*, "Dogan v Erdogan," September 12, 2009, 72.

356 *In Argentina, the government spent*: Mary Anastasia O'Grady, "Kirchner vs. the Press," *Wall Street Journal*, June 15, 2009; Associated Press, "Kirchner and Clarin: Argentina Media Fight Gets Personal," Buenos Aires, September 13, 2009.

356 *"media sustainability index"*: See details on the IREX website at www.irex.org/ msi/index.asp.

357 *"most dramatic barometer of press freedom"*: Emma Gray, testimony before the Commission on Security and Cooperation in Europe's hearing, "The Deteriorating Freedom of Media and Speech in OSCE Countries," Washington, April 4, 2000, www.csce.gov.

357 *According to the CPJ*: Committee to Protect Journalists website, http://cpj.org/ killed/, February 28, 2010.

357 *Reporters Without Borders counted*: "Reporters Without Borders' Letter to President Obama," July 1, 2009, Paris, at http://en.rsf.org/spip.php?page=article&id_ article=33702; Reporters Without Borders Predators page at www.rsf.org/ en-predateur13622-Dmitri_Medvedev_and_Vladimir_Putin.html. In the organization's 2010 list, Medvedev was dropped, but Putin remained.

357 *quoted in almost every article*: See, for instance, Luke Harding, "To Be a Journalist in Russia Is Suicide," *Guardian*, November 24, 2008, who quotes the CPJ's figures and states that "49 journalists have been murdered in Russia," since 1992— i.e. equating deaths in crossfire during war, etc., with murder. He then writes: "Underlying these attacks on Russian journalists is the nature of modern Russian society, and the sophisticated autocratic state created by Putin, in which the media play a key role."

357   *a close look at the numbers*: The reliability of these figures has been debated in Russia for some time. See, for example, Nabi Abdullaev, "Counting the Dead a Dicey Job," www.cjes.ru/media/?pid=2699, April 9, 2007.

358   *UNESCO publishes statistics*: See UNESCO Institute for Statistics, http://stats.uis.unesco.org/unesco/TableViewer/document.aspx?ReportId=136&IF_Language=eng&BR_Topic=0.

359   *five journalists died*: Yvan Scopan, Sergey Krasilnikov, Rory Peck, Igor Belozyorov, and Vladimir Drobyshev. See the Committee to Protect Journalists' writeup at http://cpj.org/deadly/1993.php.

360   *Another thirteen journalists were caught*: The CPJ database categorizes twelve of the deaths as due to crossfire; to these should be added the case of Viktor Pimenov, a photographer shot by a sniper in the Chechen war zone in 1996.

360   *Two more appeared to be robbery victims*: In these two cases, those of Vagif Kochetkov and Anatoly Levin-Utkin, the journalist was beaten with a heavy object and personal items were taken. In both cases, it is certainly possible that the real motive was to punish or intimidate the reporter for his reporting. But it is also quite possible that the motive was robbery. Police investigations failed to satisfactorily resolve the question. By contrast, I would classify the case of Natalya Skryl as murder confirmed to be related to her work because apparently nothing was stolen by her attackers.

360   *Just multiplying the number*: I use the average homicide and accidental death rates for 1995, 2000, and 2005—28 per 100,000 and 27 per 100,000 respectively, using the public health rather than the crime statistics (Goskomstat Rossii, *Demogra-fichesky yezhegodnik* [Moscow: Goskomstat Rossii, 2008]).

361   *the big-name cases familiar*: I do not include Anastasiya Baburova, a journalism student who was apparently not targeted, but was also killed by the assassin of the human rights lawyer, Stanislav Markelov, with whom she was walking. The two appear to have been murdered by a member of a neo-Nazi group, who was arrested in November 2009.

361   *only slightly greater than that for Brazil*: For Brazil, based on the CPJ's reports on the sixteen cases, eleven appear most likely linked to local government or the police, the other five to crime.

361   *The director-general of UNESCO*: UNESCO Press Release No. 2006–17, "UNESCO Director-General Condemns Murder of Russian Journalist Ilya Zimin," March 8, 2006.

361   *Freedom House mentioned the Zimin murder*: See www.freedomhouse.org/template.cfm?page=251&year=2007.

361   *killed in a drunken brawl*: The suspect denied having killed Zimin, although he admitted he had "pushed him hard twice" after Zimin "tried to embrace" him. He fled to Moldova, where he was eventually tried, but was acquitted by the jury. See "Moldavsky sud opravdal obvinyaemogo v ubiystve Ili Zimina," *Kommersant*, December 25, 2007.

361   *nothing to do with freedom of the press*: The CPJ seems to have got this one right, not including Zimin in its database of journalists confirmed killed because of

their profession. However, it continued to include him in its list of "uncon-firmed" cases (in which "it is possible that a journalist was killed because of his or her work") long after the details were established in the Moldovan courts (see http://cpj.org/deadly/2006.php).

361 *International Federation of Journalists*: International Federation of Journalists, *Partial Justice: An Inquiry into the Deaths of Journalists in Russia, 1993–2009* (Brussels: IFJ, 2009), 12. It adds that: "The overall numbers of killings are also on the decline."

361 *A milestone of sorts*: IFJ, *Partial Justice*, 11.

362 *In the last six years*: My arithmetic from the IFJ's database at http://journalists-in-russia.org/journalists/index/. Most of these were for homicides *not* related to work—but that is not surprising given that there were more homicides not con-nected to work than connected to work.

362 *one journalist was jailed in Russia*: See http://cpj.org/imprisoned/2009.php.
362 *"To kill, to kill, to kill!"*: Boris Stomakhin, "Smert Rossii!" and "Tushino, Budyonnovsk, 'Nord-Ost,' dalyee vezde . . . ," at http://rko.marsho.net/articl/mashadov.htm and http://rko.marsho.net/articl/tushino.htm.

362 *Opinion divided in the commentariat*: Maksim Sokolov, "Lovushka 282," *Izvestia*, November 23, 2006, http://www.izvestia.ru/sokolov/article3098675/.

362 *Even some of Russia's homegrown press freedom advocates*: The director of the Moscow-based Center for Journalism in Extreme Situations, Oleg Panfilov, accused the international press organizations of "publishing inflated numbers or unchecked accounts to create new heroes—'courageous journalists' who per-ished for freedom of expression in Russia." In his view, "this discredits journal-ism, as weak and immature as it is in Russia. In this light, every crime against a journalist is seen as a political assassination even if it is not linked to his or her job" (Oleg Panfilov, "Russia: Why Do Journalists Die?" *Transitions Online*, June 16, 2009, www.tol.cz/look/TOL/article.tpl?IdLanguage=1&IdPublication=4&Nr Issue=325&NrSection=2&NrArticle=20640).

363 *"Russia's future"*: Moisés Naím, "Russia's Oily Future: Overcoming Geology, Not Ideology, Will Become Moscow's Greatest Challenge," *Foreign Policy*, January–February 2004, 94–95.

363 *Tom Friedman*: Friedman, "The First Law of Petropolitics."

363 *Examining the world's oil producers*: Wacziarg, "The First Law of Petropolitics."

363 *Oil and gas income*: See Ross, "Oil and democracy revisited." There is also no evi-dence that minerals other than oil and gas impair democracy.

363 *among Latin American countries*: Thad Dunning, *Crude Democracy: Natural Resource Wealth and Political Regimes* (New York: Cambridge University Press, 2008).

363 *In Russia, the checks*: This assumes that all Russia's oil and gas were sold at world prices. In fact, much was sold for far less to domestic consumers. All data on the value of oil and gas income per capita at current world prices come from Michael Ross's database on oil and gas income. I am grateful to Ross for sharing these.

364 *Qatar's rulers*: Mehran Kemrava, "Royal Factionalism and Political Liberalization in Qatar," *The Middle East Journal* 63, no. 3 (2009); OECD, *Economic Surveys: Russian Federation* (Paris: OECD, 2009), 55.

364 *Russia's economic and social structure*: Treisman, "Is Russia Cursed." Value added in services may be somewhat overstated because of the use of transfer pricing to reclassify profits from oil production as profits from trade, reducing the tax liability.

364 *private oil companies were nationalized in*: Sergei Guriev, Anton Kolotilin, and Konstantin Sonin, "Determinants of Nationalization in the Oil Sector: A Theory and Evidence from Panel Data," *Journal of Law, Economics and Organization*, forthcoming.

365 *About three-quarters of oil drilled*: Charles McPherson, *National Oil Companies: Evolution, Issues, Outlook* (Washington, DC: World Bank, 2003), 3.

365 *estimated at from 37 to 43 percent*: Hanson, "The Resistible Rise," 15; OECD, *Economic Surveys: Russian Federation*, 2006, 38; Peter Rutland, "Oil and Politics in Russia" (Wesleyan University: manuscript, 2006).

365 *Steven Fish agrees*: Fish, *Democracy Derailed*, 134.

365 *A better way to assess the reality*: Daniel Treisman, "What Have We Learned About the Causes of Corruption from Ten Years of Cross-National Empirical Research?" *Annual Review of Political Science* 10 (June 2007), 211–44.

365 *World Business Environment Survey*: The World Business Environment Survey (WBES) 2000, The World Bank Group, http://info.worldbank.org/governance/wbes/.

367 *prices of commodities are more volatile*: David S. Jacks, Kevin H. O'Rourke, and Jeffrey G. Williamson, "Commodity Price Volatility and World Market Integration since 1700," NBER Working Paper No. 14748, February 2009.

367 *If it is moderate, it could*: If dependence is only moderate, however, the incumbents may be able to shield themselves from political instability by saving significant oil revenues in reserve funds—as Russia did—and using these funds to cushion price shocks. The effectiveness of such a strategy obviously depends on how great the price volatility is and how long the shocks last.

368 *"Russia's demography befits a country at war"*: "The Incredible Shrinking People," *Economist*, November 27, 2008.

368 *"The drop in population"*: Judy Dempsey, "Letter from Europe: Russia's Demographic Crisis," *New York Times*, September 6, 2007.

368 *Surveying the demographic challenges*: See Elizabeth Brainerd, "The Demographic Transformation of Post-Socialist Countries: Causes, Consequences, and Questions" (Brandeis University: manuscript, 2009), for an excellent review.

368 *Within Europe, only Iceland*: Eurostat, http://epeurostat.ec.europa.eu/portal/page/portal/population/data/main_tables.

368 *In almost all countries, more boys*: United Nations, *Demographic Yearbook 2007* (New York: UN Statistics Division, 2009), Table 7.

369 *In China and India, the high ratio*: Judith Banister, "Shortage of Girls in China Today," *Journal of Population Research* 21, no. 1 (2004): 19–45.

369 *there were respectively 1.15 and 1.11 boys*: Brainerd, "The Demographic Transformation," 6.

370 *In 2007 there were 14.6 deaths*: statistics from the UN's *Demographic Yearbook 2007*, Table 18, crude death rates. U.S. figure is for 2006, others for 2007.

370 *Infant mortality fell*: Goskomstat Rossii, *Rossiysky statistichesky yezhegodnik*, 2008.

370 *who, in Russia, tend to drink much more—than for women*: See A. V. Nemtsov, "Alcohol-Related Human Losses in Russia in the 1980s and 1990s," *Addiction* 97 (2002): 1413–25.

370 *58 percent of a sample of autopsies*: Nemtsov, "Alcohol-Related Human Losses," 1419.

370 *Another study of 25,000 autopsies*: David Zaridze et al., "Alcohol Poisoning Is a Main Determinant of Recent Mortality Trends in Russia: Evidence from a Detailed Analysis of Mortality Statistics and Autopsies," *International Journal of Epidemiology* 3 [2009]: 143–53.

371 *Between 1987 and 1994, the leading Russian expert*: Nemtsov, "Alcohol-Related Human Losses."

371 *fewer deaths on Tuesdays*: L. Chenet et al., "Alcohol and Cardiovascular Mortality in Moscow; New Evidence of a Causal Association," *Journal of Epidemiology and Community Health* 52 (1998): 772–74.

372 *the death rate fell in Uzbekistan*: Mezhgosudarstvenny Statistichesky Komitet Sodruzhestva Nezavisimykh Gosudarstv (MSKSNG), *15 let Sodruzhestva Nezavisimykh Gosudarstv* (Moscow: MSKSNG, 2006).

372 *death rate from lung cancer fell*: Elizabeth Brainerd and David M. Cutler, "Autopsy on an Empire: Understanding Mortality in Russia and the Former Soviet Union," *Journal of Economic Perspectives* 19, no. 1 (2005): 107–30.

372 *emission of pollutants*: Goskomstat Rossii, *Rossiysky statistichesky yezhegodnik*, 2006.

372 *more gained than lost weight*: V. Shkolnikov, M. McKee, D. Leon, "Changes in Life Expectancy in Russia in the Mid-1990s," *Lancet* 357, no. 9260 (2001): 917–21.

372 *quality of health care*: Brainerd and Cutler, "Autopsy on an Empire."

372 *effects of stress and despair*: One article even claimed to find a relationship between the rate of privatization and higher mortality in the postcommunist countries (David Stuckler, Lawrence King, and Martin McKee, "Mass Privatization and the Post-Communist Mortality Crisis: A Cross-national Analysis," *Lancet* 373, no. 9661 [2009]: 399–407). For a paper that questions the statistics used to support this claim, see John Earle and Scott Gehlbach, "Did Postcommunist Privatization Really Increase Mortality?" *Lancet* 375, no. 9712 (2010): 372.

372 *Nationwide, the degree of social tension*: Daniel Treisman, "Death and Prices: The Political Economy of Russia's Alcohol Crisis," *Economics of Transition* 18, no. 2 (2010): 281–331.

373 *it would buy forty-seven liters*: Treisman, "Death and Prices."

373 *schnapps was ubiquitous*: James S. Roberts, "Drink and Industrial Discipline in Nineteenth-Century Germany," in Lenard R. Berlanstein, ed., *The Industrial Rev-*

olution and Work in Nineteenth-Century Europe (New York: Routledge, 1992), 102–24, at 106–7.

373 *"There is no free lunch"*: Madelon Powers, "The Lore of the Brotherhood: Continuity and Change in Urban American Saloon Culture, 1870–1920," in Mack Holt, *Alcohol: A Social and Cultural History* (Oxford: Berg Publishers, 2006), 145–62, at 149.

373 *"a drunk is more frequently seen"*: Brodsky, *Less Than One*, 92.

373 *"resembled the cosmic rocket"*: Viktor Yerofeyev, "Vodka i intelligentsiya," July 2, 2009, www.erofeyev.ru/.

374 *In January 2007, 40 percent*: Fond Obshchestvennogo Mneniya, "Alkogolizm kak bolezn," January 11, 2007, http://bd.fom.ru/report/map/d0700125.

374 *Between 1990 and 2007, burglaries*: Goskomstat Rossii, *Rossiysky statistichesky yezhegodnik*, 2008. Of course, the likelihood that the published crime statistics in the Soviet period were massaged for propaganda purposes is high, and, in general, the reliability of such statistics is dubious, as discussed below.

374 *Russian police registered two crimes*: Goskomstat Rossii, *Rossiysky statistichesky yezhegodnik*, 2008.

374 *criminal paradises of New Zealand*: These statistics refer to 2000 or 1999 figures from the UN's 7th *Survey of Crime Trends and Operations of Criminal Justice Systems*, the latest to include data from Russia. This document compiles official statistics from all countries that respond to the UN's questionnaire. See www.unodc.org/unodc/en/data-and-analysis/Seventh-United-Nations-Survey-on-Crime-Trends-and-the-Operations-of-Criminal-Justice-Systems.html.

375 *repeated crime victims surveys*: Alvazzi del Frate and van Kesteren, "Some Preliminary Tables"; U. Zvekic, "Criminal Victimization in Countries in Transition" (Rome: UNICRI, 1998), Publication No. 61, Chapter 3, www.unicri.it/wwd/analysis/icvs/pdf_files/No61/n61.htm.

375 *Of the forty-six countries for which data*: I combined the data for European countries from Alvazzi del Frate and van Kesteren, "Some Preliminary Tables," with data from the same surveys for other developing countries in Anna Alvazzi del Frate, "Victims of Crime in the Developing Countries" (Rome: UNICRI, 1998), UNICRI Publication No. 57, Chapter 2, www.unicri.it/wwd/analysis/icvs/pdf_files/No57/n57.htm to get forty-six countries in total.

376 *Russia had the fourteenth highest rate of death*: World Health Organization, data for *Global Burden of Disease* project, 2004 update, at www.who.int/healthinfo/global_burden_disease/estimates_country/en/index.html.

376 *Tuva, an amazing 133 murders*: Goskomstat Rossii, *Yestestvennoe dvizhenie naseleniya Rossiyskoy Federatsii* (Moscow: Goskomstat Rossii, 2005). Figures derived from public health statistics, not registered crimes.

376 *46 in Detroit, 45 in Baltimore*: Data from the FBI's Uniform Crime Reporting Program at www.fbi.gov/ucr/cius2007/offenses/violent_crime/murder_homicide.html. Gavrilova and colleagues (Natalia S. Gavrilova et al., "Russian Mortality Cri-

sis and the Quality of Vital Statistics," *Population Research Policy Review* 27 (2008): 551–74) note that in Moscow an unusually high number of deaths are classified as "injuries of undetermined intent," and hypothesize that these may include a large number of misclassified homicides. V.G. Semenova and O.I. Antonova ("Dostovernost statistiki smertnosti [na primere smertnosti ot travm i otravleny v Moskve]," *Sotsialnye aspekty zdorovya naseleniya*, no. 2 [2007], http://vestnik.mednet.ru/content/category/5/29/30/) thoroughly reanalyzed the Moscow death certificates for 2003. If one accepts their recoding of murder cases and adds in all cases classified as "injuries resulting from contact with blunt or sharp instruments, and injuries from firearms with unclear intent," this would raise the murder total by 24 percent. If, in addition, one adds all cases of "injuries of an unclear nature, intention, etc."—only some of which are probably murders—this increases the total by 105 percent. In the first case, this would raise Moscow's murder rate to that of San Francisco; in the second, to in between the rates of Buffalo and Atlanta.

376 *had been drinking immediately before the crime*: Yuri Andrienko, "Crime and Violence," in Landis MacKellar, Elena Andriouchina, and David Horlacher, *Policy Pathways to Health in the Russian Federation* (Laxenburg, Austria: IIASA, 2004), 81–89, at 86.

376 *In regions where alcohol consumption increased*: William Pridemore, "Vodka and Violence: Alcohol Consumption and Homicide Rates in Russia," *American Journal of Public Health* 92, no. 12 (2002): 1921–30.

377 *Russia incarcerated 6.3 people per 1,000 inhabitants*: UN, 7th *Survey of Crime Trends*.

378 *"When asked to state a preference"*: Richard Rose, William Mishler, and Neil Munro, *Russia Transformed: Developing Popular Support for a New Regime* (New York: Cambridge University Press, 2006), 128.

378 *In recent years, from 55 to 67*: www.russiavotes.org/national_issues/national_issues_trends.php#514.

378 *two American journalists wrote*: Baker and Glasser, *Kremlin Rising*, 3.

378 *if the country needs a "strong leader"*: For example, the Pew Global Attitudes Survey asked Russians whether they thought Russia should rely on a democratic form of government or on a "leader with a strong hand" to solve the country's problems. Those who chose the strong leader were assumed to be antidemocratic. See Pew Global Attitudes Project, "Russia's Weakened Democratic Embrace," January 5, 2006, http://pewglobal.org/reports/display.php?ReportID=250.

379 *"worthy people in the country's leadership"*: Still, 59 percent said "laws" compared to 34 percent who said "worthy people" (Levada Center, *Obshchestvennoe mnenie 2008* [Moscow: Levada Center, 2008], 27).

379 *asked respondents in both Russia and Germany*: Levada Center, *Obshchestvennoe mnenie 2008*, 160.

379 *In a YouGov poll of British adults*: "Observer Terrorism Poll: Full Results," *Observer*, September 23, 2001; Robin Toner and Janet Elder, "A Nation Challenged: Attitudes; Public Is Wary but Supportive on Rights Curbs," *New York Times*, December 12, 2001.

380   *Henry Hale has now tied up*: Henry Hale, "The Myth of Mass Authoritarianism in Russia: Public Opinion Foundations of a Hybrid Regime" (George Washington University: manuscript, September 2009).

380   *the president should have more power*: See, for instance, www.russiavotes.org/national_issues/national_issues_trends.php#514.

381   *Timothy Colton and Michael McFaul asked*: Timothy J. Colton and Michael McFaul, "Putin and Democratization," in Dale Herspring, ed., *Putin's Russia: Past Imperfect, Future Uncertain* (Lanham, MD: Rowman and Littlefield, 2007), 13–38.

382   *60 percent thought there should be television*: Levada Center, *Obshchestvennoe mnenie 2008*, 99.

381   *Hale found that 59 percent*: Hale, "The Myth," 12–13. Interestingly, respondents had been more divided on this question when posed by Colton and McFaul in 1999. The Levada Center also found in mid-2008 that 61 percent thought that Russia needed a political opposition, against 21 percent who did not (Levada Center, *Obshchestvennoe mnenie 2008*, 85).

381   *Asked to rate this on a five-point scale*: Stephen Whitefield, "Russian Citizens and Russian Democracy: Perceptions of State Governance and Democratic Practice, 1993–2007," *Post-Soviet Affairs* 25, no. 2 (2009): 93–117, at 98–100.

381   *neither a pure democracy nor*: Rose, Mishler, and Munro, *Russia Transformed*; Hale, "The Myth."

381   *neither completely fair nor unfair*: Hale, "The Myth," 8–9.

381   *one-third said it was "mostly free"*: Levada Center, *Obshchestvennoe mnenie 2008*, 99.

381   *Russians tend to think their system has become more democratic*: See, for example, Whitefield, "Russian Citizens and Russian Democracy."

382   *Nine years later, only 9 percent*: See Levada Center, *Obshchestvennoe mnenie 2008*, 22, and www.russiavotes.org/national_issues/national_issues_trends.php#514. A year later, under the influence of the world financial crisis, those who saw development toward democracy had dropped to 36 percent and those who saw anarchy had risen to 21 percent.

382   *feel "a free person"*: Levada Center, *Obshchestvennoe mnenie 2008*, 86.

382   *"the possibility of expressing"*: Levada Center, *Russian Public Opinion 2007*, 135.

383   *decline in social solidarity, legality, and mutual trust*: On the last point, they are apparently correct. The World Values Survey asks respondents in different countries the question: "Generally speaking, would you say that most people can be trusted or that you need to be very careful in dealing with people?" In 1990, 35 percent of Russian respondents said that most people could be trusted; the average for all forty-three countries surveyed was 32 percent. In 2006, only 25 percent of Russians said that most people could be trusted; among the fifty-seven countries surveyed that year, the average was also 25 percent (data at www.worldvaluessurvey.org).

383   *"No dramatic revolution in Russia"*: Sarah E. Mendelson and Theodore Gerber, "Soviet Nostalgia: An Impediment to Russian Democratization," *Washington Quarterly*, Winter 2005–2006, 83–96, at 84.

384 *89 percent who said they did not want*: Mendelson and Gerber, "Soviet Nostalgia."

384 *Only 24 percent would like to return*: Levada Center poll of October 12–16, 2007; see www.russiavotes.org.

384 *protected by a generous welfare state*: This is demonstrated, for instance, by the results in Irina Denisova, Markus Eller, and Ekaterina Zhuravskaya, "What Russians Think about Transition: Evidence from RLMS Survey" (Moscow: CEFIR, 2007).

384 *65 percent of Russians think they are*: Denisova et al., "What Russians Think about Transition," 12, Figure 5.

384 *81.5 percent of Russians favor either renationalizing*: Irina Denisova, Markus Eller, Timothy Frye, and Ekaterina Zhuravskaya, "Who Wants to Revise Privatization and Why? Evidence from 28 Post-Communist Countries" (Moscow: CEFIR, 2007), 28.

385 *the United States comes second, chosen by 45 percent*: Levada Center poll, May 2009, www.russiavotes.org/security/security_russia_place.php#601.

385 *"good reason to fear Western countries in NATO"*: Levada Center poll, September 12–15, 2008, www.russiavotes.org/security/security_usa_nato.php.

385 *"The USA hypocritically tries"*: Levada Center, *Obshchestvennoe mnenie 2008*, 167.

385 *criticism of Russia's democracy*: Levada Center, *Obshchestvennoe mnenie 2008*, 147.

386 *Would they rather see Russia*: New Russia Barometer Poll, December 12–22, 2003, www.russiavotes.org/security/security_russia_place.php.

386 *"the same as other people"*: Levada Center poll, June 20–23, 2008, www.russiavotes.org/national_issues/racism.php.

386 *"Sooner or later, Russia will proceed"*: Levada Center, *Obshchestvennoe mnenie 2008*, 139.

386 *58 percent were more satisfied*: Sergei Guriev and Ekaterina Zhuravskaya ("(Un) Happiness in Transition," *Journal of Economic Perspectives* 23, no. 1 [2009]: 143–68) study the trajectory of life satisfaction across the postcommunist world, and show that there was a fall almost everywhere, followed by a recovery in most countries. The path of life satisfaction was closely related to the fall and rise in income. Other factors that may have made citizens of transition countries less satisfied include: the increase in economic insecurity, decreased government provision of public services, and—especially among the old—the lower value placed on the "human capital" of those educated under communism.

387 *strongly affected by age*: Guriev and Zhuravskaya ("[Un]Happiness in Transition,") show that this is true in general in postcommunist countries.

388 *"religious people"*: World Values Survey, www.worldvaluessurvey.org, percentages not excluding "don't knows."

ACKNOWLEDGMENTS

I have accumulated many debts in writing this book, more than can be acknowledged here. For stimulating discussions, I thank Yevgenia Albats, Blaise Antin, Anders Åslund, Maksim Boyko, Tim Colton, Marek Dabrowski, Steve Fish, Tim Frye, Andrew Healey, Andrei Illarionov, Mikhail Krasnov, Andrew Kuchins, Cliff Kupchan, Alena Ledeneva, Sergey Markov, Vladimir Mau, Rory McFarquhar, Michael McFaul, Valentin Mikhailov, Vladimir Milov, Thierry de Montbrial, Vyacheslav Nikonov, Nikolai Petrov, Anton Rushakov, Sergey Shpilkin, Olga Sidorovich, Georges Sokoloff, Josh Tucker, Mark Urnov, Natasha Volchkova, Andrei Yakovlev, Yevgeny Yasin, and Ekaterina Zhuravskaya. A number of colleagues, friends, and relatives read drafts of various parts of the manuscript, sometimes more than once, and have improved it by their comments. I am grateful for valuable suggestions to Mark Bond, Lev Freinkman, Scott Gehlbach, Martin Gilman, Vladimir Gimpelson, Sergei Guriev, David Laitin, Hans Landesmann, Tom Remington, Michael Ross, Richard Sakwa, Andrei Shleifer, Konstantin Sonin, Anne Treisman, Michel Treisman, and Igor Zevelev. Of course, all remaining errors are my own.

At The Free Press, Dominick Anfuso, Leah Miller, and Maura O'Brien showed great professionalism and patience, helping to shape an unwieldy manuscript into a more focused book. Deborah Treisman revealed yet another talent, standing in as agent for the project.

Susan Landesmann read the whole manuscript and was a source of continual encouragement. Alex and Lara put up with their father's preoccupation and absences and provided welcome distractions. It is to the three of them that this book is dedicated.

INDEX

493

CREDITS

Chapter 7 in *The Return* draws on some material from a chapter in *Russia After the Global Economic Crisis*: Copyright 2010, Peter G. Peterson Institute for International Economics and the Center for Strategic and International Studies, Washington, DC. Reprinted by permission.

Credits for Photo Insert

1. RIA Novosti
2. Courtesy Ronald Reagan Library
3. RIA Novosti
4. RIA Novosti
5. RIA Novosti
6. RIA Novosti
7. Eddie Op, Kommersant
8. RIA Novosti
9. RIA Novosti
10. Mikhail Evstafiev; Creative Commons Attribution ShareAlike 3.0 License, http://creativecommons.org/licenses/by-sa/3.0/
11. RIA Novosti
12. ITAR-TASS, www.kremlin.ru (by permission of Presidential Press and Information Office)
13. ITAR-TASS, www.kremlin.ru (by permission of Presidential Press and Information Office)
14. ITAR-TASS, www.kremlin.ru (by permission of Presidential Press and Information Office)
15. RIA Novosti
16. Dmitry Steshin; Creative Commons Attribution ShareAlike 3.0 License, http://creativecommons.org/licenses/by-sa/3.0/

ABOUT THE AUTHOR

DANIEL TREISMAN is a professor of political science at the University of California, Los Angeles and a leading specialist on the politics and economics of postcommunist Russia. He has written two books and numerous articles about the country's development since 1991, and was a consultant to the Russian government in 1997 on tax reform. Educated at Oxford and Harvard, where he received a Ph.D. in Political Science in 1995, he has been a Guggenheim Fellow and a National Fellow at the Hoover Institution (Stanford). He lives with his family in Malibu, California.